WORK AND ORGANIZATIONAL BEHAVIOUR

Message to students

Dear student,

Thank you for buying a copy of the popular and highly successful introductory organizational behaviour text *Work and Organizational Behaviour*. This book will provide you with an accessible but critical introduction to organizational behaviour. By 'critical' we mean that the book will help you reflect upon – and in your future professional life, perhaps act upon – how to make workplaces more effective given the challenges of global warming and resource depletion and, we would add, more equitable as well. That is a tall order to say the least. But remember, change does not happen on its own, and a better understanding of the workplace is a vital starting point.

We have made significant changes to this second edition, based upon extensive feedback from lecturers and students, to ensure that it contains all the material and latest literature you need to pass your course: in particular, the book now includes more international case studies and examples that you will find interesting and relevant to understanding work and management practices.

We have structured this second edition of *Work and Organizational Behaviour* into four parts, which are described in detail in the Preface. Each chapter follows a similar structure in order to help you navigate the text easily. The **Chapter outlines** and **Chapter objectives** summarise the key concepts that will be covered and the knowledge you will gain.

The main text includes **Stop and reflect** questions, which aim to encourage you to think critically about key issues and the effects of human action and processes on people at work. Other features, such as **OB in focus**, **OB and globalization** and **Work and society**, help to illustrate current practices in organizational behaviour in the global economy. **Critical insights** is intended to help you formulate questions about the subject, and organizational behaviour **Web links** will help you research topics further.

At the end of each chapter, you will find a **Summary** of the chapter content and a list of **Key concepts**. If you need to revisit any topics, page references are provided to enable you to find the relevant section. We also provide **Chapter review questions** to help you reinforce and check your learning, and details of **Further reading** to help you write an essay. The **Case studies** are designed to provide useful illustrations of the concepts and issues raised in the chapter. The **Web-based assignments** develop your research skills and provide further examples of organizational behaviour applied in the workplace, and the **OB in film** exercises offers entertaining insights into organizational behaviour.

Looking for a higher mark? The new **Research questions** at the end of each chapter are designed to help you find out about the subject in more depth, and the **companion website** to this book can also help you gain a better mark. It is loaded with multiple choice questions, a film guide, summary notes for each chapter, web links, a skill development guide to help you write essays, reports and presentations, and a searchable online glossary to check on definitions of key terms. You can access it at www.palgrave.com/business/brattonob2e.

If you are not a native speaker of English, we have several features to help you get the best out of this book. In the book itself, you will find a feature called **Vocab checklist for ESL students** at the end of each chapter. This is a list of key terms to learn and check; it is designed primarily for non-native speakers of English, but all students may find it a useful reference point. On the website, you will find definitions of all these terms, plus some useful tips on learning from an ESL expert.

We would welcome any feedback on the book and any suggestions on how we can improve the next edition; please contact us via our email addresses on the companion website. Good luck with your studies.

John Bratton
Peter Sawchuk
Carolyn Forshaw
Militza Callinan
Martin Corbett   January 2010

WORK and ORGANIZATIONAL BEHAVIOUR

2nd EDITION

John BRATTON

Peter SAWCHUK

Carolyn FORSHAW

Militza CALLINAN

Martin CORBETT

palgrave
macmillan

First published 2010 by
PALGRAVE MACMILLAN

Palgrave Macmillan in the UK is an imprint of Macmillan Publishers Limited,
registered in England, company number 785998, of Houndmills, Basingstoke,
Hampshire RG21 6XS.

Palgrave Macmillan in the US is a division of St Martin's Press LLC,
175 Fifth Avenue, New York, NY 10010.

Palgrave Macmillan is the global academic imprint of the above companies
and has companies and representatives throughout the world.

Palgrave® and Macmillan® are registered trademarks in the United States,
the United Kingdom, Europe and other countries.

ISBN: 978–0–230–23061–3

This book is printed on paper suitable for recycling and made from fully
managed and sustained forest sources. Logging, pulping and manufacturing
processes are expected to conform to the environmental regulations of the
country of origin.

A catalogue record for this book is available from the British Library.

A catalog record for this book is available from the Library of Congress.

10 9   8   7   6   5   4   3   2   1
19 18 17 16 15 14 13 12 11 10

Printed in China

Contents in brief

Contents

Figures

Plates

16 As children develop, they identify social roles, first within their family and later in the community. They also develop an understanding of status differences, and the ways in which roles interact with class, gender, ethnicity and race to create complex patterns of social behaviour.   116

17 It is estimated that 80 per cent of the information we perceive comes through our sense of sight. Even when someone is talking to us, we still rely heavily on a host of additional non-verbal, visual information when we attend to and interpret what is being said.   133

18 Some people would be surprised to learn that this woman is a firefighter. The stereotype is of men doing such hazardous work.   138

19 We know the fork is all in one piece, but our eyes deceive us.   140

20 Our emotional brain is impulsive and not well equipped to look into the future. This is why decision-making based on emotion and intuition is fraught with danger. What is your view on the safety or otherwise of tombstoning? To what extent is that view based on emotions, and to what extent on rationality?   152

21 Russian Ivan Pavlov is famous for his experiments with dogs, and is often referred to as the 'father of behaviourism'. Working with dogs as his experimental subjects, Pavlov trained them to salivate in response to a variety of stimuli, such as the sound of a bell.   167

22 Social-learning theory suggests that when an individual observes a 'model' performing a particular behaviour, this leads them to expect that if they perform the same behaviour, there will be a favourable result. For example, if a child observes their mother or father performing a task successfully, they will expect the same outcome when they perform the task.   170

23 Informal learning can occur – sometimes unconsciously – from an everyday situation or workplace experience.   173

24 Seeking to attract creative individuals, some organizations have sought to develop multifaceted centres designed to encourage innovation. This photo shows an interesting and innovative office space in Madrid, which is partially underground.   181

25 Will a person really focus on satisfying physiological needs before safety needs? Is this construction worker likely to stop to eat or drink before making sure the swinging girder is secured?   195

26 Expectancy theory can be used to better understand student motivation. It would predict that studying for an examination (effort) is conditioned by its resulting in answering questions in exams correctly.   205

27 The task of discovering what motivates different categories of employee in different work settings is of the same magnitude as finding the Holy Grail. For example, what factors motivate each of these men at work?   208

28 Women continue to be over-represented in the care-giving professions.   224

29 Gender inequality is in many ways felt most strongly by women workers who are stuck to the 'sticky floor', from Chinese garment workers in Canada and the United States, to women across the world who labour in sweatshops.   227

30 In male (main) stream organizational behaviour the interests and ideas of women, racial minorities and people with disability are largely neglected or marginalized.   233

31 A self-managed work team allows employees in the core work unit to have sufficient autonomy to manage the work process.   247

32 Organizations send their employees to outdoor corporate training centres where they learn to work as teams.   252

33 Team members can perceive a moral obligation to increase their level of effort on a job, and 'put in a full day' (or more) because of peer group pressure, or 'clan control', thereby unwittingly creating a control culture system.   267

34 In a small restaurant, the horizontal divisions might be divided into three main work activities: preparing the food, service and running the bar. A vertical division of labour would describe the coordinating and directing work of the head chef, the restaurant supervisor and the head bar tender, all of whom report to the restaurant manager.   280

35 Government organizations are typically bureaucratic. They have numerous rules and procedures that white-collar workers must follow, and concentrate decision making with high-ranking bureaucrats. This photo shows part of the parliament building in Wellington, New Zealand.   292

36 New technology can eliminate jobs. For instance workers can be replaced by industrial robots welding car bodies on a mass-production assembly line.   309

37 Technology has the capacity to either deskill or enskill.   319

Tables

John Bratton   *Peter H. Sawchuk*   *Carolyn Forshaw*   *Militza Callinan*   *Martin Corbett*

About the authors

John Bratton is Professor of Sociology at Thompson Rivers University, Kamloops, BC, Canada. He was the first Director of the Workplace Learning Research Unit at the University of Calgary, and has served on the faculties of several British universities. His research interests span work and employment issues, and he is a member of the editorial board of the *Journal of Workplace Learning*, the *Canadian Journal for the Study of Adult Education* and *Leadership*. In addition to co-authoring this book, he is co-author (with David Denham and Linda Deutschmann) of *Capitalism and Classical Sociological Theory* (2009); co-author (with Jeff Gold) of *Human Resource Management: Theory and Practice*, now in its fourth edition; co-author (with Peter Sawchuk, J. Helms-Mills and T. Pyrch) of *Workplace Learning: A Critical Introduction* (2004); co-author (with Keith Grint and Debra Nelson) of *Organizational Leadership* (2005); author of *Japanization of Work: Managerial Studies in the 1990s* (1992); and co-author (with Jeremy Waddington) of *New Technology and Employment* (1981).

Peter H. Sawchuk is a member of the Sociology and Equity Studies department at the University of Toronto. He teaches, researches and writes in the areas of technological design, learning, work and the labour movement. He is Director of the Centre for the Study of Education & Work (see www.learningwork.ca). His latest books include *Adult Learning and Technology in Working-class Life* (Cambridge, 2003), *Hidden Dimensions of Knowledge: Organized Labour in the Information Age* (co-authored with D. Livingstone; Rowman and Littlefield, 2004), and most recently *Critical Perspectives on Activity: Explorations of Education, Work and Everyday Life* (co-edited with N. Duarte and M. Elhammoumi; Cambridge, 2006) and *Challenging Transitions in Learning and Work* (Sense, 2009).

Carolyn Forshaw is a communications consultant. She lectured in professional writing at Thompson Rivers University until 2007. She has had over 25 years' experience in the field in Britain and Canada. Her professional interests include gender and language, post-colonial literary theory and Canadian and Caribbean literature.

Militza Callinan is a Chartered Psychologist and lectures in organizational behaviour and human resource management at Leeds University Business School, UK. Her main research interests are in the measurement and understanding of individual behaviour and characteristics such as personality, and how this knowledge about people is applied in the workplace for employee selection, assessment and development.

Martin Corbett is Associate Professor of Organisational Behaviour at the University of Warwick Business School where he teaches a range of organizational behaviour modules at undergraduate, specialist Master's and MBA level. His research interests include technophobia, the cultural history of the human sensorium, and non-unconscious influences on perception and decision making.

Karen Densky   Gretchen Fox   David MacLennan   Lori Rilkoff

About the contributors

Karen Densky lectures in English as a second language and ESL teacher training at Thompson Rivers University, Kamloops, BC, Canada. Her research and teaching interests include curriculum and methodology for the ESL classroom. She has worked in teacher-training programmes in Chile and Greenland. She is the author of *Creativity, Culture and Communicative Language Teaching* (2008).

Gretchen Fox completed Master's and PhD degrees in cultural anthropology at the University of North Carolina at Chapel Hill, USA. Her doctoral research focused on understanding cultural and economic approaches to natural resource use and management by Mi'kmaq First Nation people in Atlantic Canada. She is currently an Aboriginal Client Specialist and Project Manager at Timberline Natural Resource Group in Kamloops, BC, Canada.

David MacLennan teaches in the Department of Sociology and Anthropology at Thompson Rivers University, Canada. His main research interest is the sociology of learning. Current projects include research into the environmental factors that affect children's lives and how these operate over time; how teachers think about the knowledge that enables them to teach effectively; and 'place making' – the practices that confer value and meaning on particular places. His most recent publication (with D. Lawrence and W. Garrett-Petts) is 'Storymapping: Exploring the naturalists' sense of place' in C. Saper et al., *Imaging Place* (2009).

Lori Rilkoff holds the position of Human Resources Manager at the City of Kamloops, BC, Canada, and is a former lecturer in HRM at Thompson Rivers University in Kamloops. She acquired her MSc in Training and HRM from the University of Leicester, Centre for Labour Market Studies. Lori's research interest focuses on the practical application of HRM theory in the workplace.

Message to lecturers

Dear Lecturer,

Thank you for adopting the second edition of *Work and Organizational Behaviour*, which we have been preparing during the most serious economic crisis facing Europe since 1945. We have tried to make connections between the global crisis and organizational behaviour in a way that we hope your students will find interesting and relevant.

The book has been written specifically to fulfil the needs of students completing an introductory undergraduate organizational behaviour course, and as such it assumes no previous knowledge of the discipline by the student. Although the new edition has been informed by the recent economic recession and also by the extensive feedback we gathered from those using the book, it retains the unique approach of the first edition – in particular, its criticality and the emphasis given to organizational behaviour as a socially embedded discipline. A range of new features to support and enhance this approach have been introduced – including a **new chapter** on Organizational Culture, **new case studies** with more **global coverage** and additional material on key areas such as identity, emotion, innovation, ethics, corporate social responsibility, self-concept and organizational change, as well as a range of **new pedagogical features** and a **revised structure** designed to fit better to organizational behaviour courses. More detail on each of these new features is provided in the book's preface.

To add more value for your students using *Work and Organizational Behaviour* (2nd edition), we suggest that you make reference to the book during your lectures, for instance identifying relevant sections of the chapter, referring to the various pedagogical features, as well as asking students to attempt the end-of-chapter case study in preparation for your seminar or in-class discussion. There is also an extensive **companion website,** located at www.palgrave.com/business/brattonob2e, which provides supplementary materials for you and your students.

We would welcome any feedback on these features or any suggestions on how we can improve the next edition. Please contact us via our email addresses on the companion website.

John Bratton
Peter Sawchuk
Carolyn Forshaw
Militza Callinan
Martin Corbett   January 2010

Preface

Welcome to *Work and Organizational Behaviour: Understanding the Workplace*. This book has been written specifically to fulfil the needs of introductory undergraduate courses for an accessible analysis of behaviour in work organizations, which draws on the two major human sciences of psychology and sociology. It assumes no previous knowledge of psychology or sociology by the student, practitioner or general reader.

In the era of globalized capitalism, textbooks on organizational behaviour date quickly. It is only 3 years since we were writing the first edition of this book, but the synchronized global financial crisis and economic recession, as well as the suggestions from users for improving the book and our own thoughts, have already necessitated a revision. The founding principles of the book remain unchanged – yet the socioeconomic context in which we all find ourselves has fundamentally shifted.

Context

Since 1985, when the first edition of Huczynski and Buchanan's text *Organizational Behaviour* was published, the world of work and the way it is studied have changed. The major changes include the ascendancy of neo-liberalism, the implosion of Soviet and East European Communism and South African apartheid, the expansion of the European Union and North America Free Trade zone, the positioning of the People's Republic of China and India as major economic players, and the economic reverberations in the other Asian economies and beyond. The widespread application of microelectronics has seen the emergence of the Internet, the virtual knowledge-based organization, and the virtual or postmodern organization.

The earlier predictions of a 'leisure society' resulting from new technology have not materialized. Many managers and non-managers alike still work long hours, are electronically connected, through email, mobile phones and BlackBerries, and appear to be suffering increased levels of work-related stress. And in addition to movements of capital and goods, many people have migrated to Western Europe and North America, making the diverse workforce a reality. New management paradigms have come and gone: the ebb and flow of concepts associated with the 'Japanization' of work organization, the 're-engineered organization' and the learning organization to name just three major developments.

A major issue for academics and practitioners is the effect of globalization on aspects of organizational behaviour ranging from individual work motivation to organizational governance. As the globalization of world markets continues apace, there has been growing interest in studying whether managerial behaviour in work organizations outside North America is converging on the US way of doing things. Over the last decade, therefore, a major theme in the literature has been the convergence in managerial behaviour, affecting production, marketing, information technology, finance and employment policies and practices in different regions of the world.

The convergence debate has a solid and deep-rooted background in neoclassical economic theory. However, its detractors emphasize the existence of varieties of capitalism, and of divergence in organizational behaviour, which offers different ways to preserve the quality of life and effective ways to compete globally. The 'divergence' school tends to be sceptical of claims that convergence is occurring, believing that local cultures, social values and norms, and national business systems are strong forces against convergence. It would seem that the variations in the forms of capitalism that are found make it difficult, if not impossible, to extract management practices founded on organizational behaviour theory and research from one particular national setting and implant it into a different culture and matrix, and have them achieve the same results.

When it comes to organizational behaviour, there are no universal prescriptions. One size does not fit all. Additionally, the behaviour of corporate executives and corporate governance have come under close scrutiny following the exposure of fraudulent accounting practices, and the job and pension losses that occurred as a result, at Enron, WorldCom and other prominent US corporations in the early twenty-first century, and this has reduced the appeal of US-centred convergence.

The last 25 years have not only seen major changes in the global economy, society and the workplace. They have also seen some of the people who study the workplace – organizational theorists – abandoning the application of the rules of physical science to the study of social phenomena. The traditional approach to researching organizational behaviour can loosely be describe as 'positivism'. In the context of postmodernism, it has been challenged by 'constructivists'. The core argument of the constructivists is that organizational reality does not have an objective existence, but is constructed by people with power in the organizations, and by organizational behaviour theorists themselves. The constructivist view challenges researchers to re-examine their frame of reference, and their ideas about the research process itself and the production of knowledge.[1–4]

In some academic circles, postmodernism has fallen out of fashion in the analysis of organizational behaviour, in a similar manner to the Japanese management model that had been popular a few years earlier. The favoured theoretical foundation of today's discourse and research is the 'societal effects' approach, which argues that human behaviour in work organizations is socially embedded.[5,6] Scholars adopting this approach argue that work organizations are not 'free agents' able to design their own employment and governance practices, unfettered by social institutions and values. Rather, they argue, societal effects are central to the shaping of organizational practices. For example, the widespread demonstrations in France in spring 2006 against non-standard or precarious employment – with the slogan 'Non à la précarité!' – can be seen as confirmation of this.

Despite these global changes and rival intellectual traditions, which lead to competing research perspectives among those studying organizations, most organizational behaviour textbooks, at least for the undergraduate market, expose students only to the dominant orthodoxy in the subject, which is built on an extremely narrow set of theoretical assumptions. In general, they concentrate on the positivist-functionalist point of view: how to foster commitment, cooperation and integration, and ultimately improve organizational performance. Rival perspectives are rarely explored, and the textbooks have little, if anything, to say about gender, race, ethnicity, disability and social class, or about competing views of the workplace.[7–10]

Most of the popular textbooks are written from a managerial perspective, and largely ignore competing views of organizational behaviour presented by critical and feminist writers. They have a distinctly 'psychological' tone, and draw heavily on psychological studies of human behaviour. More pointedly, few encourage their readers to call into question the dominant assumptions underpinning US-centric management theory and practice. The first edition of *Work and Organizational Behaviour* was intended to counterbalance this bias in textbooks by providing a more critical approach and giving greater emphasis to sociological perspectives on the subject.

As we update the book for this second edition, most of the world's developed economies are in an economic abyss, and the economic slump is forecast to be by far the worst since 1945 – and this may appear to have far-reaching consequences for both work configurations and employment practices. The International Monetary Fund's twice-yearly *World Economic Outlook* projected a global decline in economic output (gross domestic product) of 1.3 per cent in 2009, its first fall in 60 years. In the Western economies, gross domestic product is expected to plummet by 3.8 per cent, and the contraction in the UK economy is projected to be 4.1 per cent, the fastest rate since 1979, when Margaret Thatcher became Prime Minister.

As in the Great Depression of 1929–33, the epicentre of this financial and economic earthquake, the biggest for generations, is the USA. Although there were early warnings about the US subprime mortgage crisis in September 2007, the financial bubbles on the stock markets of the USA and the UK began to burst in 2008, and the effects are still vibrating worldwide. The 1992–2007 cyclical boom was built on the speculative real-estate market that was itself lubricated by subprime mortgages, high levels of personal indebtedness and self-deluding optimism.

This worst cyclical economic recession will sooner or later come to an end, but it is apparent that this cataclysmic global economic downturn is deeper than policy makers and pundits feared. It is also evident that the seismic shocks to venerable financial institutions and the fall of economic indices (except unemployment) are worse in those Western economies that embraced the Anglo-Saxon economic model, that there are few sustainable 'green shoots' or signs that the worst is over, and that potentially, for the second time in the history of industrial capitalism, its interconnectedness and extremes seem to be system endangering.

For those men and women who, by definition have no control over corporate global strategies and decision making, the consequences of the global crisis are already clearly apparent: people are fearful for their jobs, their homes, their children's future and their pensions. Hence the traumatic effect of large-scale unemployment, home foreclosures and lost pensions on the politics of North America and the European Union.

Deep disillusionment in 2009 will not, however, be the death knell of capitalism as it was in 1989 for Communism. Capitalism is adaptable, and there exist far more varieties of capitalism from which lessons can be drawn. Whether the prevailing political mood will bring drastic reform or a return to 'business as usual' remains to be seen. In 2009, French President Nicolas Sarkozy's call for the 'moralization' of the capitalist system perhaps best captured the new political consensus. The moment was a powerful rhetorical symbol of the intellectual and political failure of the Anglo-Saxon market fundamentalism version of capitalism, characterized by far-reaching deregulation and privatization and the 'hollowing out' of government responsibilities and services.

As we argued in the first edition of this book, organizational behaviour is socially embedded and is profoundly influenced by contextual processes. As in the Great

Depression of 1929–33, and the recessions of 1973–75, 1980–83 and 1990–93, there is evidence that the current global economic meltdown is causing a psychological meltdown: people, whether employed or not, feel extremely vulnerable and afraid for their futures. In short, we live and work in an interconnected reality. Hence organizational behaviour in the early twenty-first century is incomprehensible without understanding the effects of the global economic recession and the response of nation-states to it.

The immediacy of the current events can easily distract us from more persistent trends and features of organizational life. Work configurations and employment practices cannot be uncoupled from national and global contexts. Thus, although the monumental failure of management in a deregulated system has put some aspects of organizational behaviour into a sharper relief and under scrutiny, the core attributes of work and how the employment relationship is managed remain unchanged. These attributes have been there since the era of globalization – the 1990s – and we examined them in the first edition of the book: the growth of non-standard or precarious employment, downsizing, the decline in trade union power and influence, inequity, deregulation, work intensification and consequential work-related stress.

We emphasized in 2006 that employers and managers operate within a wider institutional, cultural and social context, and that changing the way they behave requires a fundamental change in organizational context and culture. Following reports of white-collar crime and highly unethical behaviour, we wrote then that the solution did not lie in removing 'a few bad apples' but in 'changing the way organizations are regulated by government, changing the way managers are compensated, and by changing the values that ultimately prevail in society'.

We believe that the solution to the problems caused by the Anglo-Saxon economic model lies in fundamental changes to the system. This is not to underestimate the management roots of the global crisis. North American and UK business schools are partly to blame for the global crisis. For the most part, they have been uncritical advocates and 'cheerleaders' of the 'neo-liberal' Anglo-Saxon model, and ultimately they have a responsibility for educating a new cadre of managers who can help to change the system. The new features of this second edition are set out in the 'Message to Lecturers', but the broad aims remain the same as in the first: to encourage critical thinking and provide insight into and understanding of the sociology and psychology of work and the behaviour of people in work groups and organizations. We hope to make a modest contribution to developing the type of learning that will make workplaces more effective in a variety of ways – more productive, more ecologically sustainable, more satisfying, more equitable – and perhaps even help to forge more democratic workplaces through increased employee voice in the future.

Our approach

Our approach to explaining human behaviour in the workplace is rather different. We cover the three levels of analysis – individual, group and organizational – found in traditional organizational behaviour textbooks, and examine the concepts and issues that comprise the core of an introductory course in the subject. However, we depart from 'mainstream' texts on organizational behaviour in three important respects.

First, we attempt to take the student of organizational behaviour into realms rarely explored in most undergraduate courses in management. We try to offer an intellectual journey, which draws on familiar areas from workplace **psychology**,

but also takes readers to unfamiliar paradigms and res[...]
sociology. Our approach to studying organizational behavio[...]
that history and the interplay of people and society matter – that [...]
ation is embedded in the particularities of time and society, and in th[...]
the local and the global. Our intention is to draw upon both **mainst[...]
critical perspectives, as a requirement for generating a more eclectic inte[...]
plinary dialogue.

This is hardly an original orientation – but in adopting a more critical perspective, we believe this book embraces a more **educative** approach to studying organizational behaviour. It seeks to challenge students to question, to debate, to seek
multicausality and to develop their own understanding of organizational behaviour.
This is also an important element of our notion of a 'critical' approach, and is
enhanced by the book's many teaching features, discussed later in this Preface.

Second, this book emphasizes **six core themes**: competing standpoints, change
in the workplace, the relationship between the self and the social, diversity/equity,
power and globalization. In many ways, it is these core themes which constitute
and support what we understand as a 'critical' approach. That is, these core themes
encourage a pluralistic or multivoiced perspective on organizational behaviour,
leading to a more holistic and nuanced awareness of forces and processes shaping
the behaviour of people in the workplace and further differentiate *Work and
Organizational Behaviour* from the dominant managerially focused and psychologically based organizational behaviour texts.

Third, we have brought together an eclectic selection of academic material and
behaviour practices from the European Community, North America and parts of
Asia, offering a more **global** appreciation of behaviour at work. Thus, in an ever
more globalized world in which managers and the managed are increasingly
expected to be sensitive to cultural diversity, to be independent thinkers and to be
creative, *Work and Organizational Behaviour* offers students an accessible alternative to the more psychological, managerialist-oriented texts on the market.

New for this edition

As we have already mentioned, the new edition was prepared during the most
serious economic crisis facing Europe since 1945. Wherever possible, we have tried
to make connections between the global crisis and organizational behaviour in a
way that we hope will be interesting and relevant for students. This second edition
also includes new insights from current academic literature, and feedback from the
anonymous reviewers and users of the first edition.

Broadly speaking, the book retains the unique and successful approach of the
first edition outlined above – but this has been fine-tuned and supplemented with a
range of new features:

- A new **Chapter 12** on **Organizational culture** has been added. It follows two
  chapters on the more tangible aspects of organizational design and technology.
- Guided by reviewers' feedback, the functions and process of management have
  been incorporated into a reworked **Chapter 1, Capitalism and Organizational
  Behaviour**, and a new **Chapter 13, Leadership and Change**. The remaining
  chapters have also been **reordered** and formed into a new **four-part structure**
  designed to create a better fit with organizational behaviour courses.
- **Leadership** has been relocated and extended to cover leadership models of
  organizational change, and the chapter on **Human Resource Management,**
  which can be used to provide an introduction to a more specialized module on
  HRM, has been retained.

expanded or new sections on the following subjects have been added:
Work–Life Balance (Chapter 2), Identity (Chapter 4), Emotion in the
Workplace (Chapter 5), Innovation (Chapter 6), Self-concept (Chapter 7),
Organizational Change (Chapter 13) and a new case study covering
misbehaviour (Chapter 16).

There is a completely new section on **ethics** and **corporate social responsibility**
(in Chapter 15), which, given the nefarious behaviour of some corporate
executives, is of increasing concern to policy makers and the public.

- There are **15 new chapter case studies** that illustrate work and employment
  practices from different parts of the world.
- There are two completely new features called **OB and globalization** and **Work
  and society**, which are vignettes designed to give examples of work and
  employment practices in a global economy.
- The book has been reviewed by an ESL specialist, and the changes will make
  it **more accessible** to ESL students, while retaining the academic rigour of
  the text.
- New **Vocab checklists for ESL students** have been added to each chapter, to
  help non-native speakers of English get to grips with academic terminology and
  self-check their learning. Each term is linked to a definition on the book's
  companion website.
- Over 50 new **chapter research questions** have been added, designed to
  encourage students to think critically and to read around the subject. Each
  chapter includes three questions – the first with a group activity, the second
  referring to a chapter in a particular book and the third referring to an article.

Content

Work and Organizational Behaviour is divided into four major parts, based on the
traditional division of behavioural studies. These parts are of course interconnected, but we believe that the division provides a convenient heuristic (teaching)
device to guide the reader through the learning material. A brief outline of each
part is given below:

Part 1 examines the nature of organizational behaviour, gives a summary of the
historical dimensions of paid work, and present concepts and theories. This
provides a basis for evaluating the competing perspectives on what determines and
influences the behaviour of people in organizations.

Part 2 turns its attention to how various individual differences affect individual
behaviour in the workplace. Individuals have different personalities, perceptions
and learning styles. The chapters here emphasize that the work experiences of
women, visible minorities and the disabled may be different from those of white
male employees.

Part 3 examines some of the important social processes that take place in the
context of work groups.

Part 4 shifts the focus once again, this time to explore how organizational design,
technology, culture, leadership, communications power and politics and human
resource management practices influence social relations and the behaviour of
people in organizations.

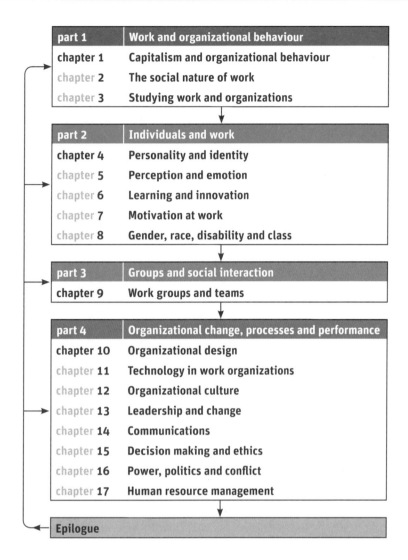

part 1	Work and organizational behaviour
chapter 1	Capitalism and organizational behaviour
chapter 2	The social nature of work
chapter 3	Studying work and organizations

part 2	Individuals and work
chapter 4	Personality and identity
chapter 5	Perception and emotion
chapter 6	Learning and innovation
chapter 7	Motivation at work
chapter 8	Gender, race, disability and class

part 3	Groups and social interaction
chapter 9	Work groups and teams

part 4	Organizational change, processes and performance
chapter 10	Organizational design
chapter 11	Technology in work organizations
chapter 12	Organizational culture
chapter 13	Leadership and change
chapter 14	Communications
chapter 15	Decision making and ethics
chapter 16	Power, politics and conflict
chapter 17	Human resource management

Epilogue

Teaching aspects of the book

Work and Organizational Behaviour includes a number of features that complement, supplement and reinforce the main text. In particular, they have been designed to promote critical thinking and to provide plentiful examples of organizational behaviour in practice in a diverse range of countries, prompting students to reflect on ideas, competing perspectives and implications of organizational behaviour. These features will help students learn the relevance of organizational behaviour to understanding life at work, and to promote self-awareness.

At the start of each chapter, you will find the:

- *Introduction*, beginning with a brief real-world example to show the immediate relevance of each organizational behaviour topic to readers
- *Chapter outline* and *chapter objectives* to give an overview of the chapter content and purpose.

Distributed throughout each chapter, you will find:

- *Graphic exhibits* including photographs, figures and tables to help explain organizational behaviour concepts
- *On-page glossary* to provide quick reference to key definitions
- *Stop and reflect* questions in the margins to encourage students to think critically, form their own opinions and consider how organizational behaviour relates to their own lives

- *Web links* in the margins providing links to relevant Internet resources
- *Critical insight* boxes to show what others have thought on the subject
- *OB in focus* boxes to illustrate or supplement the textual material
- *OB and globalization* vignettes to give an insight into organizational behaviour issues across the world
- *Work and society* vignettes to provide practical examples of the interconnection between organizational behaviour and its social context.

At the end of each chapter, you will find:

- *Chapter summary* to help check and revise learning
- *Key concepts* for quick reference and revision
- *Vocab checklist for ESL students* to help non-native speakers of English get to grips with unfamiliar terminology, which they can then look up on the book's companion website at www.palgrave.com/business/brattonob2e
- *Review questions* to promote discussion and debate
- *Research questions* to encourage group activities and further research and reading
- *Further reading*
- Full *case study* to illustrate major concepts of the chapter, plus references to relevant online case study material, identified with a 🌐 symbol
- *Web-based assignments* to bring organizational behaviour to life
- *OB in film* to provide an entertaining illustration and exploration of organizational behaviour concepts and issues
- *References* for all the texts cited in the chapter.

Finally, at the end of the book, you will find a *glossary*, together with three *indexes.*

Website

A variety of supporting materials are available for lecturers and students using *Work and Organizational Behaviour* via the companion website, at www.palgrave. com/business/brattonob2e.

For **lecturers,** the website will include:

- downloadable teaching supplements, including lecture notes and enhancement ideas
- PowerPoint slides that have been rewritten for the new edition
- a sample course outline
- a test-bank including multiple choice questions and a sample final exam paper
- a film guide exploring organizational behaviour through popular film
- guidance on using the book with non-native speakers of English.

For **students,** the website will include:

- additional case studies and OB in film features
- Web links and a research guide to aid further investigation
- a searchable glossary
- a test-bank to help check your progress and consolidate learning
- a skill development guide offering detailed guidance on completing assignments, including critical essays and oral presentations
- a film guide exploring organizational behaviour through popular film
- guidance on getting the best out of the book for non-native speakers of English.

We would welcome any feedback on these features or any suggestions on how we can improve the next edition. Please contact us via our email addresses on the companion website.

The authors

January 2010

 **References**

1 Clegg, S. and Hardy, C. (1999) *Studying Organization: Theory and Method,* Thousand Oaks, CA: Sage.

2 Charmaz, K. (2005) 'Grounded theory: objectivist and constructivist methods', pp. 509–35 in N. Denzin and Y. Lincoln (eds), *Handbook of Qualitative Research* (2nd edn), Thousand Oaks, CA: Sage.

3 Grey, C. (2005) *A Very Short, Fairly Interesting and Reasonably Cheap Book about Studying Organizations*, London: Sage.

4 Legge, K. (2005) *Human Resource Management: Rhetorics and Realities* (2nd edn), Basingstoke: Palgrave.

5 Jacoby, S. M. (2005) *The Embedded Corporation: Corporate Governance and Employment Relations in Japan and the United States*, Princeton, NJ: Princeton University Press.

6 Wright Mills, C. (1959/2000) *The Sociological Imagination* (40th anniv. edn), New York: Oxford University Press.

7 Burrell, G. and Morgan, G. (1979) *Sociological Paradigms and Organizational Analysis*, London: Heinemann.

8 Anderson, M. and Collins, P. (2004) *Race, Class and Gender* (5th edn), Thomson.

9 Wilson, F. M. (2003) *Organizational Behaviour and Gender*, Farnham, Surrey: Ashgate.

10 Mills, A., Simmons, A. and Helms Mills, J. (2005) *Reading Organizational Theory* (3rd edn), Toronto: Garamond.

Guided tour of the book

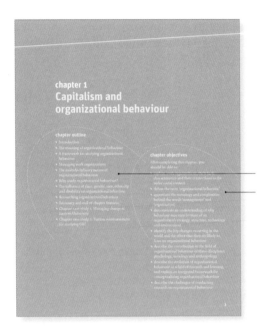

Chapter outline and chapter objectives to provide an overview of chapter content and aims

Introduction to show you the relevance of each organizational behaviour topic and how it links to the real world

OB in focus boxes to give extra insight into special issues

Critical insight boxes to show what others have thought

Web links for you to explore

OB and globalization vignettes to give an insight into organizational behaviour issues across the world

Work and society vignettes to provide practical examples of the interconnection between organizational behaviour and its social context

Stop and reflect questions for you to think about

Photos to help explain organizational behaviour concepts

Chapter summary to help check and revise learning

Key concepts for quick reference and revision

Vocab checklist for ESL students

Review questions to encourage discussion and debate

Research questions to help you read around the subject

Further reading

Case study illustrating some of the major concepts discussed

Web-based assignments to bring organizational behaviour to life

OB in film to provide an entertaining illustration and exploration of organizational behaviour concepts and issues

Acknowledgements

Writing a critical book on organizational behaviour is an audacious undertaking. The 4-year journey of creating the first edition of *Work and Organizational Behaviour* from an idea to a finished book had diversions and hold-ups, and at times it was also frustrating – and the second edition followed a similar trajectory. It has, however, also been exhilarating, and I have thoroughly enjoyed working with co-authors Peter Sawchuk, Carolyn Forshaw, Militza Callinan and Martin Corbett, as well as with the team of other experts who have contributed to the book, including in particular Justine Wheeler, Librarian at the University of Calgary, who produced the Instructor's guide for the first edition.

I am deeply indebted to Lori Rilkoff, Senior Human Resource Manager at the City of Kamloops, who contributed 11 chapter case studies to this new edition and edited, polished and doubled-checked several others. I would also like to extend sincere thanks to the lecturers and practitioners who have contributed cases and feature to the book, in particular, Jon Billsberry of the Open University Business School, UK, who contributed several new OB in film features; Karen Densky of Thompson Rivers University, BC, Canada, who devised and wrote the Vocab checklists for ESL students; Gretchen Fox of Timberline Natural Resource Group, Canada, who contributed the OB and globalization features; and David MacLennan of Thompson Rivers University, BC, Canada, who wrote the Work and society features. I am also very grateful to the following lecturers for contributing case studies to the previous edition of the book:

Dan Haley, School District No. 57, Prince George, BC, Canada
Len Hutt, Thompson Rivers University, BC, Canada
Gill Musson, University of Sheffield, UK
Ian Roper, University of Middlesex, UK
Susanne Tietze, University of Bradford, UK.

My research assistant, Kassia Trottier at Thompson Rivers University, retrieved 113 articles and data for updating this second edition. Palgrave Press subjected the manuscripts to an extensive and welcome peer review process, and we are very grateful to the many anonymous reviewers who made valuable suggestions for improving the content and style of this book. We are also grateful to the copyright holders who permitted us to reprint the extracts, diagrams and photographs.

I am also grateful to the talented and dedicated editorial team at Palgrave, Ursula Gavin, Catherine Travers and Lee Ann Tutton. Thanks, too, to those at Aardvark Editorial, who copy-edited, typeset and indexed the book, and to Jim Weaver who designed it.

My greatest debt is to my partner, Carolyn Forshaw, who for years has given me support and help. Finally, my thanks to my family – Amy, Andrew and Jennie – who continue to be an important part of my life.

John Bratton

Like John, I would like to thank my co-authors and Palgrave for their creativity, commitment and hard work. As always, my partner Jill deserves my acknowledgement and thanks for her generous sharing of our time with these pages.

Peter Sawchuk

Publishers' acknowledgements

The authors and publishers are grateful to the following for permission to reproduce copyright material:

CTVglobemedia Publishing Inc for *The Globe and Mail* articles used in the Chapter 14 OB in Focus, 'The $2-million comma' from Robertson, G. (2006) *The Globe and Mail*, 8 August, pp.Bi–2; and the Epilogue OB in Focus, 'A culture of overwork exacts an extreme price' from York, G. (2006) *The Globe and Mail*, 21 August, p. A2. [© CTVglobemedia Publishing Inc. All Rights Reserved.]

Cengage Learning for Figure 12.1, 'The influence of culture on human behaviour and behaviour on culture', adapted from Adler, N. J. and Gundersen, A. (2008), *International Dimensions of Organizational Behavior*, 5th edition, Mason, Ohio: Cengage Learning [Formerly Thomson South-Western], p. 19. [From ADLER. *International Dimensions of Organizational Behavior*, 5E. © 2008 South-Western, a part of Cengage Learning, Inc. Reproduced by permission. www.cengage.com/permissions]

Elsevier for Table 13.5, 'Substitutes for leadership', adapted from Kerr, S. and Jermier, J. M. (1978) 'Substitutes for leadership: Their meaning and measurement', *Organizational Behaviour and Human Performance*, December, pp. 375–403. [This article was published in *Organizational Behaviour and Human Performance*, Vol. 22, Kerr, S. and Jermier, J. M., 'Substitutes for leadership: Their meaning and measurement', pp. 375-403, Copyright Academic Press, Elsevier 1978.]

Emerald Group Publishing Limited for Figure 6.4, 'A model of work-related learning', from Hoeve, A. and Nieuwenhuis, L. (2006) 'Learning routines in innovation processes', *Journal of Workplace Learning*, **18** (3), Emerald, p. 175.

Grid International Inc for Figure 13.2, 'The Leadership Grid™', from Blake, R. R. and McCanse, A. A. (1991) *Leadership Dilemmas – Grid Solutions* (Formerly the Managerial Grid by Robert R. Blake and Jane S. Mouton), Houston: Gulf Publishing Company, p. 29. [Copyright 1991 by Scientific Methods, Inc. Reproduced by permission of the owners.]

The H. J. Eysenck Memorial Fund for Figure 4.3, 'Eysenck's major personality dimensions', from Eysenck, H. (1973) *The Inequality of Man*, London: Temple Smith. [With permission from the H. J. Eysenck Memorial Fund.]

Harvard Business School Publishing for Figure 1.4, 'The manager's ten roles', from Mintzberg, H. (1975) 'The manager's job: folklore and fact', *Harvard Business Review*, July–August; Figure 7.4, 'Herzberg's motivator-hygiene model', adapted from F. Herzberg (2003) 'One more time: How do you motivate employees?' *Harvard Business Review*, 81 (1): 87–96, p. 90; Figure 10.9, 'Divisional organizational structure based on strategic business units', from Hamel, G. and Prahalad, C. K. (1994) *Competing for the Future*, Boston, Mass.: Harvard Business School Press, p. 279; and Table 12.4, 'A Strategy for Cultural Change', from Kotter, J. (1996) *Leading Change*, p. 21.

The MIT Press for Table 7.1, 'McGregor's Theory X and Theory Y Motivation', from McGregor, Douglas (1957/1970) 'The Human Side of Enterprise', in Vroom, V. H. and Deci, E. (eds.) *Management and Motivation*, London: Penguin, pp. 306–319. [Originally from McGregor, Douglas; edited by Rob Roy McGregor, Martha McGregor and Gregory N. Colvard, *Leadership and Motivation: Essays of Douglas McGregor*; figure from essay, 'The Human Side of Enterprise', © 1966 Massachusetts Institute of Technology, by permission of The MIT Press.]

Dr Martin Clarke, Director of the Cranfield General Management Programme, for the extract used in the Chapter 17 OB in Focus, 'Raising the profile of the HR agenda' from *People Management*, 1 September 2005.

Professors Michael Beer and Bert Spector for Figure 17.2, 'The Harvard model of HRM', from Beer, M., Spector, B., Lawrence, P. R., Quin Mills, D. and Walton, R. E. (1984) *Managing Human Assets*, New York: Free Press.

The Michael G. Foster School of Business, University of Washington, for Figure 13.3, 'Representation of Fiedler's contingency model of leadership', adapted from Fiedler, F. E. (1974) 'The contingency model – new directions for leadership utilization', *Journal of Contemporary Business*, 3 (Autumn), p. 71.

Oxford University Press for Figure 12.3, 'Aristotle's model of rhetoric', from Grint, K. (2001) *Leadership*, Oxford: Oxford University Press. [By permission of Oxford University Press.]

Pearson Education Inc for Figure 9.8, 'Oldham and Hackman's job characteristics model', from Hackman, J. and Oldham, G. (1980) *Work Redesign*, Reading, Mass.: Addison-Wesley [Hackman/Oldham, WORK REDESIGN, Figure 11.5 p. 330 'Oldham and Hackman's Job Characteristics Model', © 1980 by Addison-Wesley Publishing Co., Inc. Reproduced by permission of Pearson Education, Inc.]

Penguin Books Ltd for Figure 7.8, 'Three poles for the measurement of well-being', adapted from Warr, P. (2002) *Psychology at Work*, 5th edition, London: Penguin Books.

People Management for the Chapter 9 OB in Focus, 'Few employees have a "good" job', adapted from Griffiths, J. (2005) 'Only 39 per cent of employees have a "good" job', People Management Online, 9 August.

The Policy Studies Institute for Figure 8.1, 'Proportion of people living in households in the UK with less than half the national average income, 1994', from Modood, T., Berthoud, R. et al (1997) *Ethnic Minorities in Britain: Diversity and disadvantage*, London: Policy Studies Institute.

SAGE Publications for Figure 9.4, 'Five phases of group development', from Tuckman, B. and Jensen, M. (1977) 'Stages of small group development revisited', *Group and Organization Management*, Vol. 2, No. 4, pp. 419–27. [Copyright © 1977 by SAGE Publications. Reprinted by Permission of SAGE Publications.] Also, for

Table 13.1, 'Distinguishing leadership from managership', adapted from Conger, J. A. and Kanungo, R. N. (1998), *Charismatic Leadership in Organizations*, Thousand Oaks, CA: Sage, p. 9. [Republished with permission of SAGE Publications, from *Charismatic Leadership in Organization*, Conger, J. A. and Kanungo, R. N., 1998; permission conveyed through Copyright Clearance Center, Inc.]

The Smithsonian Institution for Figure 2.2, 'A craft union response to Taylorism', from Kanigel, R. (1997): *The One Best Way*, New York: Viking Penguin.

Taylor & Francis Ltd for Figure 17.3, 'The Warwick model of HRM', from Hendry, C. and Pettigrew, A. (1990) 'Human resource management: an agenda for the 1990s',

International Journal of Human Resource Management, 1 (1), Routledge/Taylor & Francis Ltd, pp. 17–44, www.informaworld.com.

Thomson Reuters Canada Ltd for extracts from articles used for the Chapter 4 OB in Focus, 'Psychometric testing: ensuring the right fit', from Bakker, S. (2006) 'Psychometric testing: ensuring the right fit', *Canadian HR Reporter*, 27 March, p. 7, and for the Chapter 7 OB in Focus, 'Anxiety and stress in the workplace', from Kamkar, K. (2008) 'High cost of anxiety', *Canadian HR Reporter*, 15 December, p. 34.

University College London Special Collections for Figure 2.1, 'The panopticon building'.

John Wiley & Sons Inc for the extract used in the Chapter 3 OB in Focus, 'Developing organizational learning in the UK National Health Service', from Nutley, S. M. and Davies, H. T. O. (2001) 'Developing organizational learning in the NHS', *Medical Education*, 35 (1), Wiley-Blackwell, p. 35; Figure 16.2, 'Wrong on influence and power', from Wrong, D. H. (1979) *Power: Its Forms, Bases and Uses*, Wiley-Blackwell, p. 24; and Figure 17.1, 'The Fombrun, Tichy and Devanna model of HRM', from Fombrun, C. J., Tichy, N. M. and Devanna, M. A. (eds) (1984) *Strategic Human Resource Management*, New York and Chichester: Wiley. [Copyright © 1984 Wiley. Reproduced with permission of John Wiley & Sons, Inc.]

Every effort has been made to trace all copyright holders, but if any have been inadvertently overlooked, the publishers would be pleased to make the necessary arrangements at the first opportunity.

The authors and publishers are also very grateful to the following suppliers of the images in the book: Catherine Travers, Cheryl Dainty and Ben Harding, Digital Vision, EMPICS, Fotosearch, Getty Images, iStockphoto, Impactt Limited, Iwan Baan, John Bratton, London Fire Brigade, Marxists Internet Archive, Nick Hedges, Nick Tutton, SCORE*Golf*, Shutterstock and suburbanslice on Flickr.

WORK AND ORGANIZATIONAL BEHAVIOUR

In this part of the book, we examine the nature of organizational behaviour, give a summary of the historical dimensions of paid work, and present concepts and theories. This provides a basis for evaluating the competing perspectives on what determines and influences the behaviour of people in organizations.

In Chapter 1, we explain that organizational behaviour is a multidisciplinary field of study. We emphasize that globalized capitalism has a significant impact on the way people work and behave. We explore the process of management through a three-dimensional model. As an introduction to what follows, we discuss how the social dynamics of class, gender, disability, race and ethnicity underpin contemporary organizational behaviour.

In Chapter 2, we explore the continuities as well as the discontinuities in paid work over time. We highlight diversity and equity issues in the workplace in order to counterbalance the conventional preference for male history. We explore different types of paid and unpaid work, emotional labour and the work–life boundary. Our interpretation of the past leads us to conclude that employment is inherently and irreducibly constructed, interpreted and organized through social actions and social discourse.

In Chapter 3, we explain how the three founders of the sociology of work – Marx, Durkheim and Weber – all continue to have contemporary supporters and detractors. Organizational theorists have used different theoretical approaches to exploring work organizations – technical, human relations, neo-human relations, systems thinking, contingency, cultures, learning, control, feminist, social action, political and postmodern – and these are also examined.

chapter 1   **Capitalism and organizational behaviour**

chapter 2   **The social nature of work**

chapter 3   **Studying work and organizations**

chapter 1
Capitalism and organizational behaviour

chapter outline

- Introduction
- The meaning of organizational behaviour
- A framework for studying organizational behaviour
- Managing work organizations
- The multidisciplinary nature of organizational behaviour
- Why study organizational behaviour?
- The influence of class, gender, race, ethnicity and disability on organizational behaviour
- Researching organizational behaviour
- Summary and end-of-chapter features
- Chapter case study 1: Managing change at Eastern University
- Chapter case study 2: Tuition reimbursement for studying OB?

chapter objectives

After completing this chapter, you should be able to:

- explain work organizations, their basic characteristics and their connections to the wider social context
- define the term 'organizational behaviour'
- appreciate the meanings and complexities behind the words 'management' and 'organization'
- demonstrate an understanding of why behaviour may vary because of an organization's strategy, structure, technology and environment
- identify the key changes occurring in the world and the effect that they are likely to have on organizational behaviour
- describe the contribution to the field of organizational behaviour of three disciplines: psychology, sociology and anthropology
- describe the evolution of organizational behaviour as a field of research and learning, and explain an integrated framework for conceptualizing organizational behaviour
- describe the challenges of conducting research on organizational behaviour

Introduction

Most mornings, we turn the front
door handle of our home and set off to work in
formal organizations such as banks, insurance offices,
retail stores, garages, schools, universities, hospitals, sports
centres, police stations, hotels and factories. In work settings
like these, people engage in a host of work-related activities,
communicate and interact, and learn with and from each other. For
example, members of an organization may operate a computer, serve
customers, teach students, diagnose patients, coach athletes, apprehend and
arrest criminals, cook meals for guests or build cars. People's behaviour in their
workplaces – and indeed the way the workplaces and work processes themselves
have been set up – are the result of myriad factors. Partly, they reflect individual
preferences or psychologies among those in the workplace. But the full picture is
more complex: people are exposed to a multitude of organizational processes and
control systems that limit, influence or determine their behaviour in work
organizations.

capitalist modernity: a term
used to characterize the stages
in the history of social relations
dating roughly from the 1780s
that is characterized by the
constant revolutionizing of
production and culture

organizational behaviour: the
systematic study of formal
organizations and of what
people think, feel and do in
and around organizations

A 'work organization' is a physical and legal structure within which people undertake paid work, and it is the people rather than the organization of course who
undertake the relevant behaviours. The work organization is in fact the most
obvious symbol of **capitalist modernity**. Its presence affects our economic,
cultural, political and ecological environment, providing employment, producing
goods, delivering services, lobbying politicians and infecting the ecosystem.
Richard Scott observed, 'Ours is an organizational society' (ref. 1, p. 3). We sell our
mental or physical skills to organizations, and we buy the goods or services they
provide. Our 'experience' of organizations, as employees, customers or stakeholders, may be good, bad or indifferent, and standard approaches to **organizational behaviour** analyse and explain this using a variety of individual, group or
organizational processes. Theoretical accounts of organizational behaviour typically centre on how the behaviour of individuals evolves and adapts, how it is shaped
by group dynamics and how organizations are structured in different ways. It looks
at why organizational controls occur in the way they do, and how organizational
processes have an impact on societal and ecological stability or instability. The
emphasis is on how organizational behaviour theories underscore management
practices and organizational efficiency and effectiveness.

Organizational behaviour is not a subject that can be studied in isolation:
organizations and the people who work within them are socially embedded and
can be profoundly influenced by contextual processes, as the extraordinary global
economic recession that began in 2008–09 attests. Organizations are shedding
jobs, and those surviving are 'downsizing'; as people struggle to come to terms with
these events, they experience feelings of acute anxiety. As in previous economic

recessions, there is evidence that this global economic and financial meltdown has caused a psychological meltdown, an emotional state in which people, whether employed or not, feel extremely vulnerable and afraid for their futures.[2] The term '**psychological climate**' describes the psychological well-being of individuals, organizations and communities and how this may fluctuate over time.[3] We already know that the current downsizing and joblessness is – perhaps not surprisingly – having a damaging effect on the men and women, and their families, who experience it.[4] In concrete terms, it means redundancy, long-term unemployment, foreclosure and homelessness, immense upheaval and dislocation and poverty. In psychological terms, individuals may face feelings of guilt, shame and fear, as well as mental health-related problems. Writing about the 1980–81 economic recession in Britain, this writer characterized its social effects as the 'fear syndrome', which was succinctly expressed by a trade union leader this way: 'We've got three million on the dole, and another 23 million scared to death'.[5]

After 25 years of excess, when deregulation of the financial services industry spurred footloose capitalism, when the bonus culture inspired bankers and fund managers to engage in high-risk behaviour, and now this inequality has grown, there is evidence of a sea change in social attitudes that could lead to reform. Before the global economic recession that started in 2008–09, there was debate about the need for an alternative to so-called 'Anglo-American' capitalism,[6] but this debate has been highlighted by recent events. The Anglo-American model is characterized by low taxation, minimal regulation and a focus on exports. In the midst of the deepest recession for 70 years, prior to the G20 summit on the world financial and economic crisis in London, in 2009, French President Nicolas Sarkozy called for the 'moralization' of the capitalist system, arguing that 'Financial capitalism is a system of irresponsibility and … is amoral'.[7] German Chancellor Angela Merkel advocated the creation of an international 'architecture of institutions'.[8] In addition, British Prime Minister Gordon Brown urged the European Union to work with America to forge a new 'moral' global capitalism, saying, 'Just as globalization has been crossing national boundaries, we now know it has been crossing moral boundaries too.'[9]

As a result of their meeting in 2009, the G20 countries produced an official 'communiqué' outlining their interpretation of events and their plans to ensure a recovery. Potentially, this communiqué is of seminal importance, because it represents a serious intellectual and political challenge to the ideology of Anglo-Saxon neo-liberal capitalism, or market fundamentalism. Probably nothing demonstrates more both the universality and depth of this economic crisis and the profundity of its effects than the new consensus that government is the solution, not the problem, in regulating the financial sector and the economy. Such a seismic shift in both politics and public thinking is likely to change the nature of capitalism, and ultimately the way in which work and people are organized and managed in organizations.[10]

In this chapter, we look at organizational behaviour and explain in particular that it is a multidisciplinary field of study. We emphasize that globalized capitalism has a significant impact on the way in which people undertake paid work and behave in organizations. We explore the process of management through a three-dimensional model to help us understand that any social action by managers and other

psychological climate: the psychological well-being of individuals, organizations and communities and how this may fluctuate over time

plate 1 Graffiti outside the Bank of England sums up public anger about MPs' expenses and bankers' bonuses as job losses and home foreclosures hit unusually high levels in 2009. Responses to the recession and credit crunch may change the nature of capitalism, and ultimately the way work and people are organized and managed in organizations.

Photo: suburbanslice on Flickr

You can read the full text of the April 2009 G20 communiqué at www.g20. org/Documents/final-communique.pdf

weblink

employees is not isolated from the rest of society but is deeply embedded in it. So, as an introduction to what follows, we will discuss how the social dynamics of class, gender, disability, race and ethnicity underpin contemporary organizational behaviour, before examining the challenges of researching behaviour in workplaces.

The meaning of organizational behaviour

capitalism: an economic system characterized by private ownership of the **means of production**, from which personal profits can be derived through market competition and without government intervention

means of production: an analytical construct that contains the forces of production and the relations of production, which, when combined, define the socio-economic character of a society

This book is about how people in capitalist societies are organized and managed in organizations. **Capitalism** is a system for organizing economic activity. Although capitalist activities and institutions began to develop in Europe from the 1400s, modern capitalism has come to define the immense and largely unregulated expansion of commodity production, the related market and monetary networks and rule of law. The need to maximize profit from the 'rational' organization of work and exchange of goods or the delivery of services (see Chapter 3), rather than to satisfy the material needs of the producers, is the *leitmotiv* of capitalism. Capitalism creates a qualitatively distinct kind of work organization and society from any of those which preceded it.[11]

Theorizing about work organizations has deep historical roots. Well before the publication of any 'organizational behaviour' textbook, Adam Smith's (1776) *The Wealth of Nations* and Karl Marx's *Das Kapital* (1867) provided seminal accounts of how early factory owners organized and managed people. This current textbook has two broad aims. First, it aims to help the reader understand how people living in the era of mature global capitalism undertake paid work, how they interact with each other in organizations, and how the decisions made by managers affect others. Second, it aims to help the reader learn to influence the processes and shape events within organizations.

What are organizations?

work organization: a deliberately formed social group in which people, technology and resources are deliberately co-coordinated through formalized roles and relationships to achieve a division of labour designed to attain a specific set of objectives efficiently. It is also known as formal organization

society: a large social grouping that shares the same geographical territory and is subject to the same political authority and dominant cultural expectations

sociology: the systematic study of human society and social interaction

A **work organization** is a socially designed unit, or collectivity, that engages in activities to accomplish a goal or set of objectives, has an identifiable boundary and is linked to the external **society**. Work organizations can be distinguished from other social entities or collectivities – such as a family, a clan or tribe, or a complex society – by four common characteristics.

First, when we state that an organization is 'a socially designed unit or collectivity', we mean that one essential property is the presence of a group of people who have something in common, and who deliberately and consciously design a structure and processes. We use the term 'social structure' to refer to those activities, interactions and relationships that take on a regular pattern.

Some form of hierarchy exists in organizations. There are standard methods of doing things, norms, communications and control techniques that are coordinated and repeated every day. Organizations are made up of people, and they form relationships with each other and perform tasks that help attain the organization's goals. In **sociology**, we refer to this as the 'formal social structure'. Many aspects of the formal social structure are explicitly defined in organizational charts, job descriptions and appraisal documents. However, human activities, relationships and interactions emerge in the workplace that are not expressed in charts or written job descriptions. This covers an array of human behaviour including the communication of rumours – the 'grapevine' – destructive or misbehaviour such as the sabotaging of a computer or machine by a disgruntled employee, and trade union action. These activities are referred to as the 'informal social structure'. The formal and informal social structures are the basic building blocks of an organization.

plate 2 Today, our lives revolve around diverse work organizations, universities, banks, hospitals and factories. Work organizations are structures and groups of people organized to achieve goals efficiently. For-profit organizations have financial goals, normally profit maximization. Non-profit work organizations, such as Friends of the Earth, organize their activities around raising public awareness and lobbing politicians and governments to protect the environment and wildlife, and to reduce greenhouse gas emissions.

The second common characteristic of organizations is that human activity is directed towards accomplishing 'a goal or set of objectives'. For-profit organizations have financial goals – specific targets towards which human action is oriented, normally those of profit maximization. For Bakan, the modern for-profit organization is a 'pathological institution' that strives for profit and power and primarily exists 'to pursue, relentlessly and without exception, its self-interest, regardless of the often harmful consequences it might cause to others' (ref. 12, pp. 1–2). This means that making money is the first priority for for-profit businesses. They survive by minimizing their costs in any way they can within the law. As Stiglitz explains, the modern multinational corporation avoids paying taxes when possible, and many try to avoid spending on cleaning up the pollution they create, the cost being picked up by the governments in the countries where they operate.[13] Benevolent non-profit organizations have goals such as helping the destitute, educating students, caring for the sick or promoting the arts. In addition, most organizations have survival as a goal.

The third common characteristic is the existence of an 'identifiable boundary' that establishes common membership, distinguishing between the people who are inside and outside the organization. The fourth element of our definition connects the organization to the 'external society' and draws attention to the fact that organizational activities and action influence the environment or larger society. The impacts or 'outcomes' on society may include consumer satisfaction or dissatisfaction, political lobbying, pollution of the ecosystem and other by-products of the organization's activities. In Western capitalist economies, argues Stiglitz, big **corporations** have used their economic muscle to protect themselves from bearing the full social consequences of their actions.[13] Despite the rhetoric about organizations being 'socially responsible', the law 'compels executives to prioritize the interests of their companies and shareholders above all others and forbids them from being socially responsible – at least genuinely so' (ref. 12, p. 35).

Multiple types of work organization are possible. Organizations vary in their size, the product or services they offer and their purpose, ownership and management.

corporation: a large-scale organization that has legal powers (such as the ability to enter into contracts and buy and sell property) separate from its individual owner or owners

plate 3 Organizations vary in their size, the product or services they offer, their purpose, ownership and management. For example, we are all familiar with a small organization – such as a newsagent, grocery store or independent hotel – operating for profit. At the other end of the spectrum are large organizations, such as Ford Motor Company, and organizations not operating for profit, including charities such as Oxfam. Take a look at this typical English high street. How might a large chain such as Tesco measure its success or failure? And how would this be different from the small independent grocery store just two doors away?

Source: Nick Tutton

An organization's size is normally defined in terms of the number of people employed. We are all familiar with very small organizations such as independent newsagents, grocery stores and hotels. Larger organizations include the Ford Motor Company, Lloyds Bank, Google and governments. Organizations can be grouped into four major categories according to their products: *food production and extraction* (for example, farms, forestry and mining organizations), *manufacturing* (for example, apparel, cars and mobile phones), *services* (for example, hairstyling, and train and air transportation) and *information processing* (for example, market research). The growth in the number of people employed in the service and information categories defines the **post-industrial** society.

post-industrial economy:
an economy that is based on the provision of services rather than goods

Work organizations can also be categorized into those which operate for profit, and not-for-profit institutions. The purpose of for-profit organizations is to make money, and they are judged primarily by how much money is made or lost: the bottom line. Not-for-profit organizations, such as registered charities, art galleries and most hospitals, measure their success or failure not by profit but in some other way. A university, for example, might measure its success by the total number of students graduating or obtaining grants from research bodies.

The primary purpose of an organization is linked to who owns and manages the organization. Many are owned by one person, one family or a small group of people. An individual may own and manage a small business, employing a few other people. Not all businesses are incorporated (that is, are companies), but also many companies are owned by only a few individuals. It is estimated that one-third of US Fortune 500 companies (the top 500 companies in the USA) are family controlled. Privately owned organizations are a large part of the British and North American economy. Private companies may have corporate shares (that is, they are part-owned by other companies), but the shares are not traded publicly on a stock market.

Within capitalist countries, there are alternative ways of organizing and managing people in workplaces. The best known worker cooperative is probably the Mondragón Movement in Spain. For more information, go to www.iisd. org/50comm/commdb/desc/ d13.htm

weblink

In contrast, publicly held organizations issue shares that are traded freely on a stock market and are owned by a large number of people. These organizations normally pay dividends – a proportion of their profits – to their shareholders. The owners are its principals, and these individuals either manage the activities of the organization themselves or employ agents (the managers) to manage it on their behalf. Privately and publicly owned organizations have the rights, privileges and responsibilities of a 'person' in the eyes of the law. But because a company is not actually a 'person' as such, its director or directors are held responsible for its actions, and directors have been fined and even jailed for crimes committed by 'the organization'.

Now we have reviewed the basic characteristics and types of work organizations, we can look more directly at the meaning and scope of organizational behaviour.

What is organizational behaviour?

As a field of study, organizational behaviour is not easy to define because it is an extremely complex and wide-ranging area that draws upon numerous disciplines, theoretical frameworks and research traditions. Within the organizational behaviour academy, there is a collection of 'conversations' – from individuals with different standpoints on organizational **theories** – each offering a competing theory and interpretation of organizational behaviour.

Standard organizational behaviour textbooks begin with a single definition of the subject, and tend to emphasize the contentious relationship between organizational behaviour and management theory and practice. One popular North American text, for example, explains that organizational behaviour involves the systematic study of the attitudes and behaviours of individuals and groups in organizations, and provides insight about '*effectively managing* and changing them' (ref. 14, p. 8, emphasis added).

Organizations are arenas of situated social behaviour (that is, places in which particular kinds of social behaviour take place), which are both explicitly organized by management theory and practices, and fashioned consciously and unconsciously by values, beliefs, a community of practices, gender, ethnicity and national employment relations systems and practices.[15] Organizational behaviour is, in other words, embedded in the wider social, cultural and institutional fabric of society. It is best understood as a series of complex active processes in which people participate, formally and informally, at several levels including the micro, macro and global (Figure 1.1), in ways shaped by organizational roles and power.

A wider, more inclusive definition would recognize the importance of 'social embeddedness', and the external as well as internal forces that affect the behaviour of people in organizations. We can define organizational behaviour as *a multidisciplinary field of inquiry, concerned with the systematic study of formal organizations, the behaviour of people within organizations, and important features of the social context, that structures all the activities that occur inside the organization.* Workplace behaviour for this purpose includes face-to-face communicating, decision making, ethical practice, leadership style and cooperation over work processes, learning and innovation. Behaviour also includes cognitive behaviour, such as thinking, feeling or perceiving, and values. Furthermore, behaviour includes power struggles, alienation, absenteeism, bullying, racial, ethnic and gender discrimination, sabotage and other forms of misbehaviour, and **conflict** and resistance between managers, as well as between managers and workers.

The organization's **microstructures** and processes must be analysed and explained by reference to events and developments outside it. **Macrostructures**, composed of class relations, cultural, patriarchal, economic and political systems – the external environment – represent the 'macrocosm' or the immediate outer world that affects organizational life and behaviour. *Global structures* composed of international organizations, such as the World Bank, the International Monetary Fund and the International Labour Organization, and patterns of global communications, trade and travel also surround and permeate work organizations.

theory: a set of logically interrelated statements that attempts to describe, explain and (occasionally) predict social events. A general set of propositions that describes interrelationships among several concepts

conflict: the process in which one party perceives that its interests are being opposed or negatively affected by another party

microstructures: the patterns of relatively intimate social relations formed during face-to-face interaction

macrostructures: overarching patterns of social relations that lie outside and above a person's circle of intimates and acquaintances

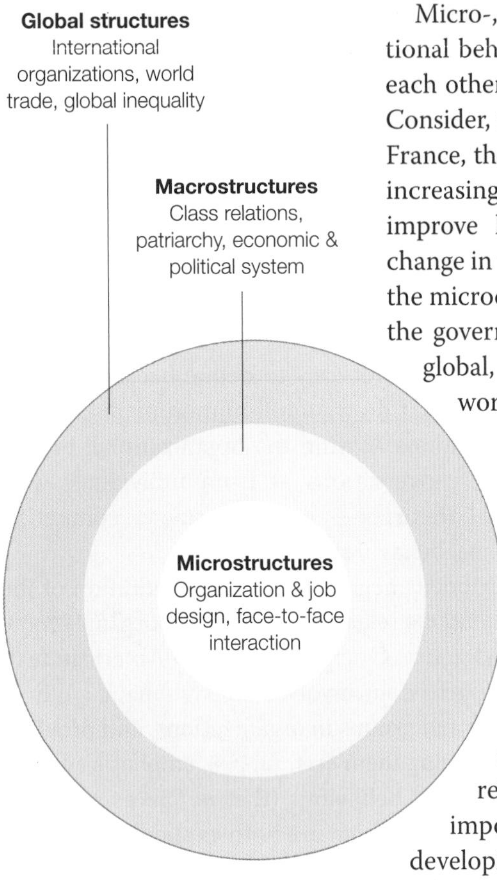

Global structures
International organizations, world trade, global inequality

Macrostructures
Class relations, patriarchy, economic & political system

Microstructures
Organization & job design, face-to-face interaction

figure 1.1 The three levels of social structure surrounding the organization

Micro-, macro- and global structures surround people and influence organizational behaviour. These social structures are also interrelated: they are shaped by each other, and action or change in one stimulates or affects action in the others. Consider, for example, a change in the patterns of global trade and investment. In France, the change might cause the government to amend 'macro' public policy by increasing the length of the working week, with politicians claiming that this will improve labour productivity and France's international competitiveness. The change in the macrostructure might in turn generate action inside the organization, the microcosm zone, as workers stop work and take to the streets to protest against the government policy. We can think of these three levels of social structures – global, macro and micro – as concentric circles radiating out from people in the workplace, as shown in Figure 1.1.

The leading American sociologist C. Wright Mills (1916–62) argued that we can only gain a full understanding of human experience when we look beyond individual experiences and locate those experiences within the larger economic, political and social context that structures them. Mills wrote in 1959 that the 'sociological imagination allows us to grasp the interplay of man [sic] and society, of biography and history, of self and world' (ref. 16, p. 4). We agree with Mills here, and suggest that the behaviour of managers, and the agency of individuals and work groups, cannot fully be understood without reference to the outer organizational context. While we focus here primarily on issues related to workplace behaviour in advanced capitalist economies, it is important to remind ourselves that 73 per cent of the world's workers live in developing economies.[17]

The workplaces employing the other 27 per cent of workers are arenas of competing social forces that mirror and generate paradox, tension, misbehaviour, conflict and change. This characterization of the organization as an 'arena' provides a theoretical framework for examining the behaviour of managers and other employees in relation to politics, gender, power and ideology (for early literature on this, see refs 18–20). There are many valid ways of studying organizational behaviour, but by recognizing the interplay between the global, macro and micro social dimensions, we are led to acknowledge the dynamic linkages between external forces on the one hand, and internal management processes and individual and group agency on the other. At the risk of simplification, we illustrate the multifaceted and interdisciplinary nature of organizational behaviour in Figure 1.2.

A framework for studying organizational behaviour

The manifestations of human behaviour provide parameters within which a number of interrelated dimensions can be identified. These collectively control and shape how people and work are organized and managed. In Figure 1.2, we offer a simple integrative or 'open' model for studying organizational behaviour. It is divided into four components.[21] These are:

- environmental forces as external context inputs
- processes for converting the inputs into outputs in a managerial context
- the evaluation of outputs
- a feedback loop that links the processes and external forces with the feedback flowing into the organization, and from the organization into the external context.

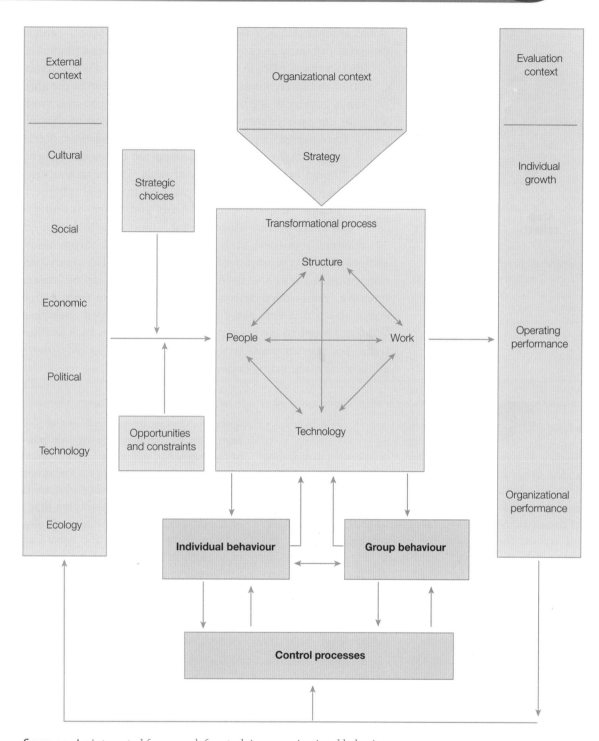

figure 1.2 An integrated framework for studying organizational behaviour

The external context: global capitalism

In examining the external context, we shall highlight a few of the 'inputs' that are most crucial for the study of organizational behaviour. This discussion is meant to be illustrative – rather than exhaustive – of how the external context affects organizational processes through, for example, global economic activity, government regulations, technological change, cultural influences and ecological pressures. Globalization underscores the need to examine the organization within its totality, the embedded nature of organizational behaviour and the processes by which those with most power respond to the demands of the external context.[22-25] However, globalization itself is a thoroughly contested concept, depending whether it is viewed as primarily an economic, a political or a social phenomenon.

The fact that we live in a globally interconnected world has become a cliché. As part of this interconnected world, the acceleration of the **globalization** of economic activity is one of the defining political economic paradigms of our time. In the early twenty-first century, globalization is arguably about the unfettered pursuit of profit.[26] International management literature gives accounts of how higher profits can be realized by relocating production operations abroad and by economies of scale. Organizations are embedded within their own economic, political, legal and social spheres. Levels of corporate taxation, employment standards and other 'business-friendly' incentives can affect profits. Since capital is portable (that is, it can be employed in different countries), it is possible for global corporations to indulge in an endlessly variable geometry of profit searching.[27] The logic of unfettered globalization, propelled over the twentieth century by cheap oil, means that any labour-intensive, value-added activity is likely to migrate from high-wage to low-wage economies – that is to say, from the rich, developed countries like the USA and Western Europe to the poorer developing countries such as China, Bangladesh and India. For our purpose, as the global recession unfolds, the main issue is how globalization is affecting organizational behaviour.

stop reflect

How have external environment factors impacted on work organizations that you, or members of your family or your friends, have worked for? How did these external factors influence the behaviour of people in the organization?

globalization: when an organization extends its activities to other parts of the world, actively participates in other markets, and competes against organizations located in other countries

Critical insight

By its very nature, globalization implies both a broadening and a deepening. Economic and social phenomena that once affected a particular nation-state or region in the European Union now have broader implications and must of necessity include a greater number of states and powerful actors. The globalization of economic activities has given rise to renewed interest in the actions of 'big business', and more specifically in the managerial behaviour of large work organizations that operate in the global marketplace.

One part of the debate involves assessing the extent to which managerial behaviour is 'disembedded' from the domestic institutional and social contexts that affect management actions. It is argued that any understanding of the impact of globalization on organizational behaviour must recognize that managers and other actors are exposed to multiple and conflicting systematic constraints and opportunities, with no guarantee that the societal effects of the organization's home base will always prevail.

As an introduction to the debate about the effects of organizations being 'embedded' in society, obtain a copy of a book edited by Marc Maurice and Arndt Sorge, *Embedding Organizations*.[28] Consider its arguments, and ask yourself, does globalization mean that managerial behaviour will be universal? What are the counteracting forces to the implied 'convergence' of work and employment practices?

The organizational context

strategy: the long-term planning and decision-making activities undertaken by managers that are related to meeting organizational goals

organizational structure: the formal reporting relationships, groups, departments and systems of the organization

bureaucracy: an organizational model characterized by a hierarchy of authority, a clear division of labour, explicit rules and procedures, and impersonality in personnel matters

The structure of the organization is formed from the interaction between individuals, groups and organizational controls. Organizational context describes the regular, patterned nature of work-related activities, technology and processes that is repeated day in and day out. There are at least six identifiable variables that impact on the active interplay of people within the structure of the organization: strategy, structure, work, technology, people and control processes.

In an organizational context, **strategy** refers to what senior managers do over time to accomplish an organization's goals. **Structure** is defined as the manner in which an organization divides up its specific work activities and achieves the coordination and control of these activities. The structure of organizations can take many forms. Much debate on changing organizational forms has centred on the argument of whether organizations have shifted from **bureaucratic** forms with highly specialized tasks and a hierarchical authority to post-bureaucratic forms with low specialization and 'flat' authority. Empirical studies suggest that in spite of 'virtual' and 'lean' organizational forms, the majority of organizations still rely on a fundamental division of labour and are rule-bound. Chapter 10 examines developments in organizational design.

The way people interact within the organization will be strongly influenced by the way the work is designed, for example how tasks are divided into various jobs and the degree of autonomy employees have over their work. Chapter 2 examines how paid work is designed. **Technology** affects the behaviour of individuals, groups and operating processes. Here we would just note that technology is a multidimensional concept. Chapter 11 examines the technology–behaviour relationship.

By now, it should be obvious that organizational behaviour is concerned with *people*. The study of people's values and behaviours in the workplace, of work organizations, necessitates that we make an important distinction between employees or workers, and employers or their agents, that is, managers. The social relations between these two groups constitute the *employment relationship*. The nature of the employment relationship is an issue of central importance to organizational behaviour. In some workplaces, these relations are supportive, fostering a sense of autonomy and human development. In other workplaces, these relationships are toxic, discouraging learning and putting health-damaging stress on individuals. The differences in work activities, motivation and rewards associated with being either a worker or a manager mean that the individual actors in these two groups more likely perceive and respond to events and social actions in the workplace rather differently (see Chapter 5). Analyses of workers' and managers' behaviours imply, even if they do not explicitly state, a perspective of the employment relationship.[29]

Within the notion of 'behaviour', we include individual action and *emotion*, whether expressed in an individual capacity or as a member of a work team, and whether it is prompted by global forces or by organizational processes of control. It is *people*, not inanimate organizations or technology, who make organizational processes happen, who produce goods and deliver services through human labour, creativity, learning and effort. People differ on a number of dimensions that are relevant to organizational behaviour. Demographics such as age, education, experience, skills, abilities and learning styles are just a few of the variables that can affect how individuals and groups behave and relate to each other in the workplace.

Understanding the dynamics of the employment relationship and individual behaviour is both complex and fascinating, and requires us to examine the concepts of personality and identity (see Chapter 4). The dynamics of both are shaped by the psychological contract (see Chapter 5), that is, what an employee can expect of the organization beyond the formal employment contract (for example, wage or salary, job security or job satisfaction). Employee *misbehaviour* – such things as arson, fraud, lying, pilferage and sabotage – tends to be under-reported, but these 'warts' constitute part of organizational reality.[30] Studies emphasize that gender, class, race, ethnicity and disability make an overwhelming difference to the organizational reality too.[31–35] Thus, the 'people' aspects of our model cannot be examined in isolation. As others have also emphasized, we need to adopt a multidimensional approach to studying organizational behaviour:

> The time-honoured distinctions between three levels of analysis – the individual, the organization, and the environment – are clearly breaking down. The previous certainty of discrete, self-contained individuals, fully informed by their roles in organizations, has been shattered. (ref. 36, p. 9)

Given the general nature of the divergent interests between managers and the managed, our reciprocal model contains *control* processes. Control systems enable

technology: the means by which organizations transform inputs into outputs, or rather the mediation of human action. This includes mediation by tools and machines as well as rules, social convention, ideologies and discourses

Visit www.fastcompany. com for some short articles on management strategy. You will also find articles that analyse the strategies of various organizations

weblink

managers to accomplish the organization's objectives and to deal with recalcitrant subordinates. Numerous studies suggest that formal organizations are in essence 'structures of control'.[19,37,38] If we accept this premise, the question is, how exactly is this control exercised and by whom, and why is control necessary? Control may be exercised directly by technology or indirectly by peer pressure within groups, or by **organizational culture**, or by an array of human resource management techniques designed to make people's behaviour more predictable and controllable (see Chapter 17).

organizational culture: the basic pattern of shared assumptions, values and beliefs governing the way employees in an organization think about and act on problems and opportunities

The evaluative context

Organizational processes are not an end in themselves, but are explicitly related to the goals of the over-arching organization. The evaluative context addresses the much-researched question, 'Do certain behaviours actually lead to high-performance organizations?' Issues of individual, operating and financial performance are all involved. But although there is well-documented evidence that a combination of determinate organizational behaviour variables is associated with positive performance outcomes, the association is by no means uncontested. Any serious analysis of the goals of management brings into focus the build-up of internal contradictions and the control of 'strategic tensions'.[39] Among the most challenging are the tensions between maximizing profit or shareholder return and employee security, between organizational control and employee motivation, and between managerial autonomy and social responsibility. The more critical accounts of organizational behaviour expose internal tensions and paradoxes.

Managing work organizations

How work is designed and how people behave inside organizations is strongly influenced by management decisions, as well as by what happens outside the boundaries of the organization. The term 'manager' refers to an occupational group that organizes and coordinates, and makes decisions about what work is done, how it is done and by whom. Management is distinguished from 'leadership' by a greater emphasis upon directing others through control systems and a reliance upon hierarchical position, rather than through inspiration, and upon the mobilization of higher employee commitment (see Chapter 13).

It is important to understand that there is a relationship between economic stability or instability outside, and decision making and behaviour inside, the organization. The external context, the business strategy, structural design and control processes, and the abilities and attitudes of employees, all affect the way the manager performs managerial activities. The manager can adopt a wide array of means to accomplish his or her ends. These may range from common processes such as communicating, motivating and coercing, to complex technologies. Combined, these constitute the manager's repertoire for 'getting things done through people', and each individual manager may be more or less skilled in or disposed towards using a particular process. This section aims to provide a short overview of the nature of management, and to consider how managerial behaviour affects the behaviour of other employees.

The meaning of management

The words 'manage' and 'manager' are derived from the Italian word *maneggiare* – to handle or train horses.[40] Henri Fayol (1841–1925), regarded as the 'father of modern management', provided the classic definition of management as a series of four key activities that managers must continually perform: planning, organizing, directing and controlling (Figure 1.3).

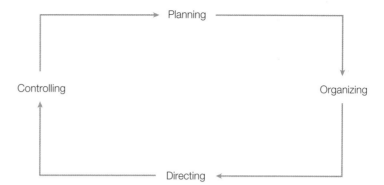

figure 1.3 The classic Fayolian management cycle

The management cycle presents the job of the manager in a positive way, and to this day all mainstream management textbooks present management as having four central functions: to plan, organize, direct and control – the PODC tradition. For Fayol, *planning* meant to study the future and draw up a plan of action. *Organizing* meant coordinating both the material and the people aspects of the organization. *Directing* refers to ensuring that all efforts focus on a common goal, and *controlling* means that all workplace activities are to be carried out according to specific rules and orders. In Peter Drucker's canonic text, *The Practice of Management*, management is seen as both a function and a social group. The emergence of management as a social group is seen as one of the most significant events in modern history: 'Management expresses basic beliefs of modern Western society' (ref. 41, p. 4).

The process of management

To study behaviour in workplaces, we need to address two related questions: 'What do managers do?' and 'Why do managers do what they do?' The nature of managerial work is an amorphous topic in the literature. Since the mid-twentieth century, studies have offered a comprehensive picture of what managers do. Many are in the Fayolian genre: that is, managerial behaviour is represented as a rational and politically neutral activity. Other studies offer a more complex account, emphasizing the time spent building a reciprocal network of social relationships. Managers' work is typically characterized by brevity, fragmentation and variety.[42,43]

Henry Mintzberg offers a multifaceted concept of managers' work consisting of three sets of behaviours: *interpersonal*, *informational* and *decisional* (Figure 1.4).[43,44] 'Role' here refers to a set of behaviours that individuals are expected to perform because of the position they hold within the organization. Mintzberg usefully distinguished three different interpersonal roles – figurehead, leader and liaison – which arise directly from the manager's formal authority.

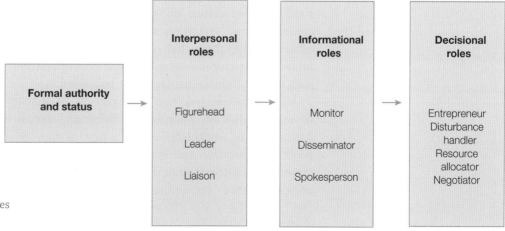

figure 1.4 The manager's 10 roles

Source: adapted from Mintzberg (1989/1975)[44]

By virtue of these interpersonal encounters, with both other managers and non-managers, the manager acts as a 'nerve centre' for the dissemination of information. The manager's three informational roles – monitor of information, disseminator of information and spokesperson – flow from the interpersonal roles. Finally, the interpersonal and informational roles enable the manager to perform four decision-making roles: entrepreneur, disturbance handler, resource allocator and negotiator. The extent to which managers perform these functions will depend upon their position in the organization's hierarchy and their specific functional responsibilities. For example, we would expect human resource managers to give relatively more attention to the disturbance-handling and negotiating roles, given the nature of their work.

Unsurprisingly perhaps, studies have found that the relative importance of managerial work varies not only with the respondent's position in the management hierarchy, but also with the level of education of the co-workers. Interestingly too, managerial work in 'creative milieus' may not follow the conventional activities. Evidence shows that, in research-intensive organizations, managers not only coordinate day-to-day work, but, as scientists, play a major role in scaffolding the research project, and 'conventional management practices and managerial concerns come, at best, second'.[45] Despite claims to the contrary, surveys of managerial work exhibit striking parallels with the classic Fayolian management cycle (Table 1.1).[46]

table 1.1 Summary of managerial work

Acting as a figurehead or leader of an organizational unit
Liaising with other managers
Monitoring, filtering and disseminating information
Allocating resources
Handling conflicts and maintaining workflows
Negotiating with other managers or representatives
Creative and innovative
Planning
Controlling and directing subordinates

Source: adapted from Hales (1986)[46]

Much of the earlier research reflects an Anglo-American bias. Some more recent studies have challenged the universality of managerial behaviour, and have emphasized the importance of factoring into the analysis gender and cross-cultural considerations.[47–51] Others suggest that managerial behaviour is 'gendered', while others counter-argue that male and female managers' behaviour is largely determined by structural, control and market imperatives – in other words, there is no such thing as 'female' management behaviour.[35]

An alternative, less flattering picture of managerial behaviour is indicated through studies on workplace bullying and sexual harassment.[52,53] Bullying and harassment in workplaces is not a new phenomenon. Indeed, in the context of profit maximization and managerial control, bullying is part of the management repertoire of getting things done through people, and reflects the significance of the unequal balance of power in workplaces.

An integrated model of management

The different dimensions of manager's work are brought together in the three-dimensional model shown in Figure 1.5. The vertical axis lists activities that answer the first question, 'What do managers do?' The horizontal axis shows the contingencies, and relates to the second question, addressed later in this chapter, 'Why do managers do what they do?' The diagonal axis relates to the third question, 'How do managers do what they do?', topics that are examined throughout this book.

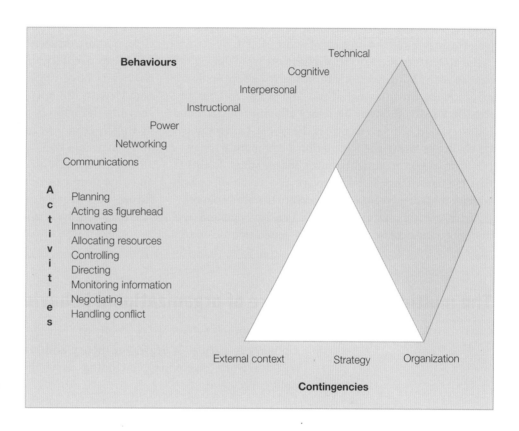

figure 1.5 An integrated model of management

The set of managerial activities is strikingly similar to those found in the classic Fayolian management cycle.[26] The contingencies are those forces and events, both outside and inside the organization, that affect management behaviour, as shown in Figure 1.2, above. The third dimension, managerial behaviours, lists various means by which managers communicate ideas, gain acceptance of them and motivate others to change in order to implement the ideas. Managers use technical, cognitive and interpersonal processes and skills to accomplish their work. Power is included in the list because it is part of the influence process. Management involves a blend of processes, and individuals will vary in terms of their capacity or inclination to use them, but these processes are ultimately about human interaction and relationships.

The model suggests that management is a multidimensional integrating and controlling activity, which permeates every facet of paid work experience and profoundly shapes the employment relationship and human behaviour. It does not assign values to the relationships and does not claim to be predictive. The model is, however, a useful heuristic device that helps us explore how management functions are translated into means, such as leadership processes, and equally how various contingencies influence behaviour in workplaces.

OB in focus   Climate change – a challenge for us all

Mount Kilimanjaro – the tallest mountain in Africa – has been topped with snow for millennia. But scientists are predicting that its ice cap may have less than a decade left, with ice quantities falling by over 80 per cent in the past 100 years. As our planet warms up, Kilimanjaro's disappearing snow cap aptly illustrates both the climate challenge facing us and the urgency of addressing it.

The 10 hottest years on record have occurred during the past 15 years. Margaret Beckett, formerly British Secretary of State for Environment, Food and Rural Affairs, and Patricia Hewitt, formerly Secretary of State for Trade and Industry, said, 'Climate change is the greatest environmental challenge facing the international community today … It's now widely accepted by most independent scientists that climate change is taking place as a result of human activity releasing greenhouse gases into the atmosphere.'

As the world's economy grows, energy demand will undoubtedly increase. In 2002, the generation of energy and heat accounted for 40 per cent of worldwide carbon dioxide emissions. In China, 80 per cent of the power plants that will be used by 2020 have yet to be built. Climate change is not just an environmental challenge; it is an economic challenge too. It has been estimated that the economic cost of global warming could double to US$150 billion each year in the next 10 years, hitting insurance companies with US$30–40 billion in annual claims.

'We must achieve increased awareness of the need for cleaner, more efficient technology in the short term, and R&D into new technologies in the longer term, but this doesn't remove the need for action now,' said Beckett and Hewitt. G8 members are reported to be already showing leadership, particularly on work towards a hydrogen economy, carbon dioxide capture and storage and renewable technologies. Climate change affects us all today, and will increasingly affect future generations and therefore can not be viewed as a far-off, abstract, future inconvenience. The international community must act decisively now.

The multidisciplinary nature of organizational behaviour

Organizational behaviour as a body of knowledge and field of inquiry is multidisciplinary in nature. It draws on theory and research findings from a number of social science disciplines, including psychology, sociology, anthropology and political science.

Psychology

The word 'psychology' literally means 'the science of the mind'. Psychology can be defined as the systematic study of human behaviours and mental processes. (For more information on the development, definition and scope of psychology, see, for example, refs 54 and 55.) Although we cannot directly observe mental processes (at least in the sense that we cannot readily tie what we can see of brain activity to behaviour of complex kinds), we have concepts for a wide range of them, for instance thinking, imaging and learning. Psychologists concern themselves with studying and attempting to address one key question: 'Why did this individual behave in this way?' The branch of psychology that deals with people in work organizations has been labelled as 'occupational' and 'organizational' psychology. Whichever label is used, 'work' psychology is primarily concerned with developing generalizable models about human behaviour in the workplace, with an emphasis on **social interaction** at the level of the individual, groups or entire organizations, and with testing theoretical predictions against observable facts.

Sociology

Sociology is the systematic study of the pattern of social relationships that develop between human beings, with a particular focus on the analysis of industrialized societies. Sociologists have made their greatest contribution to organizational

Go to the following sites for information and a list of resources on industrial-organizational psychology and social psychology: www.socialpsychology.org/io.htm; www.socialpsychology.org/

weblink

social interaction: the process by which people act toward or respond to other people

behaviour through their study of formal organizations. They have explored the relationship between organizational actions and culture, and analysed the effects of macrostructures and global structures in buttressing or undermining organizational structures and processes. Sociology addresses such questions as: 'What is society?' 'Is society made up only of individual people in different types of relationship, or are social groups, such as social classes, more important than individuals?' 'Or is society something which exists over and above individuals?' 'Who exercises power in society, and how does power impact on relations in the workplace?'

Anthropology

Anthropology is the scientific study of humanity. Cultural anthropology, or ethnology, a subdiscipline of the field, is the study of contemporary and historically recent human societies and cultures. Ethnologists are especially enthralled by the great variety of the world's cultures. Multiculturalism as a European and North American phenomenon can be examined and understood from an anthropological perspective, focusing, for example, on concepts of ethnocentrism, cultural relativism and culture shock. **Ethnocentrism** is the tendency for people to view their own culture as superior to all others. In contrast, **cultural relativism** is the appreciation that all cultures have intrinsic worth and should be judged and understood on their own terms. It is an ethical positive which assumes that people should not evaluate other people's customs and mores without understanding them. When workers migrate and encounter cultures that are very different from their own, they may experience a feeling of disorientation, isolation, loneliness and depression. This is called *culture shock*. In terms of organizational behaviour, being aware of ethnocentrism, cultural relativism and culture shock helps you to become a more informed and critical thinker, and a better manager.

Political science

Political science is the study of individual and group behaviour within a political system. The essence of politics involves not only making and executing decisions for society, but also choosing between competing demands in the midst of social conflict. Politics, therefore, might be defined as the struggle for power and the management of conflict. It is often viewed as a junior discipline in terms of its influence on organizational behaviour, but in recent years it has made a significant contribution to the understanding of managerial behaviour, in particular towards the understanding of power and how individuals and groups manipulate power for self-interest. Recognizing the relevant work of psychologists, sociologists, anthropologists and political scientists aids our ability to accurately explain and predict the behaviour of people in organizations. This multidisciplinary framework and the major contributions to the study of organizational behaviour are shown in Table 1.2.

Go to the following site for further information and resources related to the sociology of work: www.intute.ac.uk/socialsciences/sociology

weblink

ethnocentrism: the tendency to regard one's own culture and group as the standard, and thus superior, whereas all other groups are seen as inferior

cultural relativism: the appreciation that all cultures have intrinsic worth and should be judged and understood on their own terms

table 1.2 Towards a multidisciplinary approach to organizational behaviour

Social science	Contribution		Levels of analysis
Psychology	Personality	Communication	Individual
	Perception	Leadership	
	Learning	Group processes	
	Motivation		
Sociology	Class relations	Control processes	Group organization
	Power	Gendering of work	
	Bureaucracy	Technology processes	
	Conflict		
	Group interaction		
Anthropology	Comparative attitudes	Organizational environment	Group organization
	Comparative beliefs & values	Cross-cultural analysis	
	Organizational culture		
Political science	Conflict	Decision making	Organization
	Power		

Why study organizational behaviour?

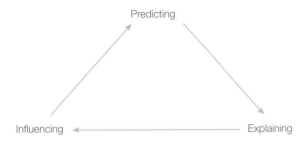

figure 1.6 Reasons for studying organizational behaviour

At this point, the sceptical reader may be thinking 'I cannot see the practical use of organizational behaviour. I don't see how it helps the manager.' Organizational behaviour is more than just an intellectual exercise – it is an applied social science with practical, everyday management uses. The practical use of organizational behaviour is to make the student and manager more attentive to unexamined common assumptions that may be influencing their decision making. It is best understood as a set of intellectual tools designed to help people predict, explain and influence organizational activities (Figure 1.6).

Both outside and inside the organization, predicting the behaviour of other people is an inherent requirement of everyday life. In other words, we want to be able to say that if X happens, then Y will occur. Our lives are made easier by our ability to predict when people will respond favourably to a request or when workers will respond favourably to a new reward system. So-called 'common-sense' predictions of human behaviour are often unreliable. The discipline of organizational behaviour makes generalizations and predictions about behaviour as systematically as possible in the light of available research and theory. Studying organizational behaviour will help you further develop your knowledge of human behaviour, and so help you more accurately predict human behaviour within work organizations.

Although it is important to predict human behaviour, it is also vital to understand and *explain* the behaviour of people in complex organizations. Prediction and explanation are not the same. Accurate prediction usually precedes understanding and explanation. Through observation and experience, we are all capable of predicting the downward direction of an apple when it falls off a tree, but unless we have knowledge of the theory of gravity developed by Isaac Newton (1642–1727), we cannot fully explain *why* the apple falls to the ground. In the work context, organizational behaviour will help us explain (for instance) why individuals are less or more motivated when certain aspects of their job are redesigned, why various aspects of team processes cause misbehaviour and why networks and new forms of organization can have negative effects on performance.

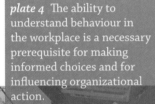

plate 4 The ability to understand behaviour in the workplace is a necessary prerequisite for making informed choices and for influencing organizational action.

Source: Getty Images

The ability to understand human behaviour is a necessary prerequisite for making informed choices and for influencing organizational actions. According to Chris Grey, 'Theory is a weapon used to bludgeon others into accepting practice' (ref. 56, p. 14). The key question is 'What is *really* happening in workplaces?' There is well-documented evidence demonstrating a positive relationship between certain 'clusters' of organizational practices and behaviours and superior performance. For Jeffrey Pfeffer, for example, the real source of sustainable competitive advantage, he persuasively argues, is derived from 'the culture and capabilities of your organization that derive from how you manage your people' (ref. 57, p. 5). In other words, sustainable development increasingly comes from understanding and managing organizational behaviour.

Can you think of other reasons for studying organizational behaviour?

**stop
reflect**

As we have explained already, work organizations are social structures, designed and created by people who have the capacity to shape and change them. Learning organizational behaviour theory is indispensable because it provides a conceptual 'toolbox' to at best understand and at worst justify social action: it can be characterized as a journey of self-enlightenment. We suggest that studying organizational behaviour is a requirement for active citizenship in advanced capitalist societies that are subject to periodic turbulence and change. We need to go to the root of the nature and tendencies of work organizations, and to exercise our sociological imaginations by presenting options for changing the way they function in society.

The influence of class, gender, race, ethnicity and disability on organizational behaviour

Anyone who takes even a cursory look inside a contemporary organization will most likely see a diverse workforce. Although different groups will be segregated into specific jobs, the presence of women and visible minorities will be evident. Together, people of Afro-Caribbean, Bangladeshi, Pakistani, Asian, Chinese and East European origin account for an increasing proportion of the British workforce, and the same is true in many other European Union states and other countries that have expanded their populations through immigration, such as Australia and Canada. Studying diversity is not simply a matter of learning about other people's cultures: it involves discovering how social class, gender, disability, race and ethnicity frame people's life chances and work experience. It may come as a surprise, therefore, to learn that academic journals and most mainstream textbooks in the organizational behaviour field show little interest in social class, gender, disability, race and ethnicity. Why is this? We address this serious question more fully in Chapter 8, but to frame our discussion at the outset, we suggest that class relationships, for example, are so deeply embedded in capitalist employment relations as to become all but invisible.

We focus on diversity and equity here not because they are an interesting yet benign fact of the modern workplace, but because we consider that the social dynamics of class, gender, race, ethnicity and disability underpin contemporary organizational behaviour. To understand the significance of class, gender, race, ethnicity and disability is to give emphasis to power imbalances, and to put the behaviour of individuals and groups in the organization into a wider social context. However, no book can contain everything: the material we have chosen inevitably not only reflects our personal bias, but is also highly selective. Although we draw mainly from the narrow field of workplace psychology and sociology, we cannot cover everything, even in a cursory fashion.

In every society, inequalities exist between individuals and groups, with some people having more money, wealth, schooling and power than others. Sociologists use the term 'social stratification' to refer to a system by which each society ranks people in a hierarchy. One type of stratification is the class system. A social **class** is defined as a large group of people in a given society who have a similar degree of access to a material resource such as income, wealth or property. The sociological analysis of class has been strongly influenced by the work of Karl Marx (1818–83) and Max Weber (1864–1920). In Marx's view, class is rooted in people's relationship to the means of production – the means by which they gain an economic livelihood. Under industrial capitalism, capitalists exploit workers who sell their productive labour for wages. Marx believed that the relationship generates perpetual social conflict.

class: the relative location of a person or group within a larger society, based on wealth, power, prestige or other valued resources

OB and globalization

Hijab on the job: religion in organizational culture

With the acceleration of the global movement of both workers and organizations, questions have arisen about the sometimes uneasy relationship between religion and the workplace. How can an organization accommodate workers' rights to free expression without violating the rights of other workers? What constitutes a reasonable accommodation of religious beliefs, practices and symbols in the workplace? Does the banning of religious symbols from the workplace constitute discrimination? These questions, and organizations' work to address them, have garnered much attention in the media and in legal arenas in recent years.

One of the most public and vigorous debates has been around the right of workers to wear the hijab, a traditional head scarf worn by Muslim women, while at work. This debate garnered international attention in 2004 when France banned the wearing of religious symbols including the hijab, Christian crosses, Sikh turbans and Jewish skullcaps in state schools.

Other countries, such as Britain, have taken different approaches to the incorporation of religious symbols and practices into public and work life. In 2001, for instance, the London Metropolitan Police, 'the Met', determined that female officers would be able to wear the hijab as part of their police uniform. Incorporating the hijab as an optional component of the office police uniform was expected to increase the number of Muslim women interested in joining the force. An article from the *Daily Telegraph* (McIlroy, 2001) hints at other moves towards the accommodation of religion within workplace culture being considered by the Met:

> Sikh officers are allowed to wear turbans and the Met is also considering whether to let potential recruits from London's 10,000 Rastafarians have dreadlocks. Other changes being discussed include the provision of prayer rooms in police stations, halal food in staff canteens and special washing facilities for Muslim officers.

Although the hijab has been endorsed by London's Met, other countries and organizations have banned the traditional garment in the workplace. For instance, the Philadelphia Police Department in the USA has banned female officers from wearing the hijab on the job, citing the city's policy of religious neutrality (Duffy, 2007). Some organizations, scholars and members of the public have argued that, as a religious symbol, the hijab has no place in secular public organizations. Others point out that religious and cultural symbols and practices, like bank holidays that coincide with Judeo-Christian religious celebrations, are already ingrained in the organizational culture of many public and private workplaces in Western countries. Accommodating workers who wish to wear the hijab, they argue, signals a welcome move toward what religious scholar Douglas Hicks (2003) calls 'respectful pluralism' in workplace culture.

Respectful pluralism is a 'set of ideas for creating a culture that models ... mutual respect amidst diversity' (Hicks, 2003, p. 37). Hicks asserts that religion forms an integral part of many workers' identities, and that the suppression of worker's identities may violate their basic human right to dignity. Under the framework of respectful pluralism, workers should be permitted to incorporate aspects of their religious beliefs in their work life, as long as they do not degrade or coerce others in the organization, or interfere with the productivity of the organization.

The move by the Met to permit officers to wear the hijab as part of their uniform indicates that ideas like respectful pluralism are gaining a foothold, as organizations and their workers exist in an increasingly globalized world.

stop! What do you think about the place of religious and cultural symbols and practices in the workplace? Can you think of any ways in which organizations may unwittingly promote particular religious and cultural beliefs or practices? What is your opinion about the concept of respectful pluralism in the workplace?

Sources and further information

Barrett, D. (2009) 'Christian health workers faces sack over crucifix necklace', *Daily Telegraph*, May 23, 2009. Available at: www.telegraph.co.uk/news/newstopics/religion/5374277/Christian-health-worker-faces-sack-over-crucifix-necklace.html.

BBC News (2006) 'Woman to sue BA over necklace row', October 15, 2006. Available at: http://news.bbc.co.uk/2/hi/uk_news/england/london/6052608.stm.

Duffy, S. (2007) 'Muslim police officer loses suit over headscarf', *Legal Intelligencer*. Available at: www.law.com/jsp/article.jsp?id=900005555748#.

Hicks, D. A. (2003) 'Religion and respectful pluralism in the workplace: a constructive framework', *Journal of Religious Leadership*, **2**(1), pp. 23–51.

Knox, K. (2004) 'World: Head scarves in the headlines, but countries take different approaches', Radio Free Europe/Radio Liberty, April 8, 2004. Available at: www.rferl.org/Content/Article/1052223.html.

McIlroy, A. J. (2001) 'Met will let Muslim WPcs wear traditional headscarf', *Daily Telegraph*, June 15, 2001. Available at: www.telegraph.co.uk/search/?queryText=Met+will+let+Muslim+WPcs+wear+traditional+headscarf%92&Search=Search.

National Film Board of Canada (1999) *Under One Sky: Arab Women in North America Talk About the Hijab*. Directed by Jennifer Kawaja.

Note: This feature was written by Gretchen Fox, PhD, Anthropologist, Timberline Natural Resource Group, Canada.

Weber expanded upon Marx's theory of class by arguing that there are internal divisions within each group, based on status, social prestige and power. For Weber, people's position in the class hierarchy derives not from only their ability (or inability) to control the means of production, but also from their 'market position', which is determined by the possession of skills and qualifications. Weber's more complex, multidimensional view of class also led him to believe that a person's market position strongly influences her or his overall '**life chances**'. In the contemporary workplace, class translates into the employment relationship between the employer or agent (manager) and workers. The analysis of this relationship in class terms has been important in allowing us to predict, explain and manage work-based conflict.

Traditionally, studies of organizational behaviour have devoted little attention to the question of gender. **Gender** refers to the attitudes, feelings and behaviours members of a society typically associated with being male or female. Gender is a dimension of social organization, affecting how we interact with others, how we think about our identity, and what social behaviours and roles are expected of men and women in society in general, and the workplace in particular. Gender involves hierarchy, because men and women tend to be found in different social positions, as judged by their access to resources and power.

The feminist movement has produced a body of literature that offers various explanations for gender inequality. Radical feminism, for example, looks for explanations of gender inequality through the analysis of patriarchy: the systematic domination of women by men. From this perspective, men's power characterizes all relationships between the sexes, including those in the public world of organizational activity, and is sustained by the whole of our culture.[34,58,59]

Gender is embedded in the modern workplace. Organizational structures and hierarchies are characterized by gender segregation, in which women predominantly occupy jobs that are part time, low skilled and low paid, whereas men occupy full-time, high-skilled, high-pay positions and are allowed to climb the corporate ladder to senior management. A career in management is typically viewed as a 'male career'. Some feminists emphasize that patriarchal society confuses sex and gender, deeming appropriate for women only those occupations associated with the feminine personality. So in Western societies, for example, young women are encouraged to enter child care, nursing and elementary school teaching, and discouraged, or even barred, from entering such 'masculine' jobs as mining or working on oil rigs.

The gendering of work and organizations in 'malestream' organizational behaviour textbooks is normally discussed – if at all – in the context of the benefits to the organization (in economic terms) of a 'diverse' workforce. As Fiona Wilson correctly argues, 'women and issues about their work have been considered by many as less important than that of men' (ref. 34, p. 3). In our view, one of the most important consequences of acknowledging the crucial role of gender analysis in organizational behaviour studies is its power to question organizational behaviour research findings and analysis that segregates studies of work behaviour from occupational gender segregation, 'dual-role' work–family issues, the consideration of patriarchal power and issues of gender inequality.

Race and ethnicity are complex sociological concepts to introduce in organizational behaviour. Race can be understood as a socially constructed community composed of people who share biological characteristics that members of a given society consider important. Typically, people in Britain attach more meaning to skin colour and hair texture than, for instance, people in Cuba do. The variety of racial traits found in Britain and the European Union today is the product of

---

life chances: Weber's term for the extent to which persons have access to important scarce resources such as food, clothing, shelter, education and employment

gender: the culturally and socially constructed differences between females and males found in the meanings, beliefs and practices associated with 'femininity' and 'masculinity'

Go to the following sites for more information and resources on race, ethnicity and human rights in the workplace: www.ethnos. co.uk is the site of a consulting company that researches ethnic minorities in the UK; www.coe.int/t/E/human_rights/ecri/ is the Council of Europe's site on human rights; www.businessweek.com/magazine/ content/01_31/b3743084.htm gives an article on the subject

weblink

European colonialism and subsequent migration, so that genetic traits once common to a single place are now found in all European Union member states.

Whereas the concept of 'race' implies something biological and permanent, 'ethnicity' is purely social in meaning.[60,61] It refers to the shared cultural practices and heritage of a given category of people that set them apart from other members of society. Britain is a multiethnic society in which English is the official language, yet many people speak other languages at home, including Hindi, Punjabi and Mandarin. Ethnic differences are learned, and for many people ethnicity is central to individual identity.

The concepts of race and ethnicity are fundamental to an awareness of racism and discrimination in society and the workplace. Prejudice is an attitude that judges a person on her or his group's real or imagined characteristics. Racism refers to the prejudices held by members of one group towards another based on socially important traits. In Weberian sociology, race appears to have a major influence on life chances. **Discrimination** is a behaviour affecting all minorities in work organizations. Discrimination can be direct or indirect, and takes many forms. Direct discrimination at work involves, but is not limited to, cases whereby individuals of a particular race, ethnic group or sex are treated less favourably than other members of the organization. In the UK, such behaviour is disallowed and is unlawful under the Race Relations Act 1976 (amended in 2000) and the Sex Discrimination Act 1975 (amended in 1986).

discrimination: the actions or practices of dominant group members (or their representatives) that have a harmful impact on the members of a subordinate group

Although it is important to assess class, gender and ethno-racial issues in the workplace in order to generate a broad and critical view of organizational behaviour, here we wish to introduce another important under-researched area of inequality and disadvantage in the workplace: disability. Theoretical and empirical organizational behaviour or sociological research on disability has been extremely limited, as disability has tended to be analysed primarily within a 'medical model'. Disability is viewed as a specialized medical condition requiring the intervention of qualified medical professionals. Disabled people and their families are viewed as passive recipients of care who have no informed opinion and therefore need not be consulted about matters that directly concern them; disabled people's needs are seen as special and different from everyone else's.[62] The common assumptions about disability focus on disabled people's lack of abilities. In the UK, for example, more than 2.4 million people are disabled, and those who are disabled are three times more likely to be unemployed than others. A critical perspective on disability draws to our attention how the capitalist mode of production is itself disabling for some people, and calls for the 'normalization' of disabled individuals as socially valued members of society, and for an end to inequitable treatment in the workplace.[63]

Have you experienced or observed discrimination in the workplace based on class, gender, race or ethnicity, or disability? What form did it take? How did management handle the discrimination?

stop reflect

In our view, the various permutations of relationships at work stemming from the variables of class, gender, race, ethnicity and disability are necessary factors in explaining the social world of work and contemporary organizational behaviour. We do not suggest that this book single-handedly redresses the imbalance in research and writing on these topics, and here we can do little more than skim the surface, but we hope that by adding class, gender, race and ethnicity, and disability to the work behaviour equation, we can encourage more lecturers in organizational behaviour to give major coverage to these important issues, and support more students in asking serious questions about diversity/equity issues.

Researching organizational behaviour

It has been said that what you see depends on where you stand, especially when studying organizational life. How researchers approach their study of work and

Work and Society: Knowledge, evidence and propaganda

How do we produce knowledge about a phenomenon as complex as organizational behaviour? How do we find out what is true and what works in this particular area of human endeavour?

Philosopher Paul Boghossian (2006) offers us one way to think about these difficult questions. Using the subject of the first inhabitants of North America as an example, he offers the following perspective on how we arrive at rational beliefs:

> We may not know the facts [about North American's first inhabitants] ... but, having formed an interest in the question, we seek to know. And we have a variety of techniques and methods – observation, logic, inference to the best explanation and so forth, but not tea-leaf reading or crystal ball gazing – that we take to be the only legitimate ways of forming rational beliefs about the subject. These methods – the methods characteristic of what we call 'science' but which also characterize ordinary modes of knowledge-seeking – have led us to the view that the first Americans came from Asia across the Bering Strait. This view may be false, of course, but it is the most reasonable one, given the evidence. (p. 4)

This perspective on knowledge is one version of what Boghossian calls the classical view of knowledge. This classical view typically includes the following set of assumptions:

- We should have evidence for believing something is true.
- We should look impartially at all the evidence, not just the evidence that confirms what we already believe to be true.
- We should acknowledge that our beliefs are fallible.
- When confronted by new evidence, we should be willing to revise our beliefs about what is true or what works.

The classical view of knowledge offers a powerful way to think about how knowledge about any given thing or process ought to be produced. It serves as an invaluable reference point for those who seek to understand how organizations work, and why people in organizations behave the way they do. So, for example, we could ask whether an organization is attaining its goals and, if it is not, what course of action might enable it to attain its goals. Evidence enters into this investigation at two key points: evidence that supports a claim that the organization's goals are not being met, and evidence that supports the claim that a particular course of action would enable it to attain its goals.

Obviously, the classical model of knowledge, with its emphasis on evidence, is relevant here. But does it follow that the study of organizational behaviour is 'value-free'

and is somehow insulated from politics and power? Not necessarily. Researchers need to recognize that an organization's goals may be contested and that the most obvious, official, versions of the organization's goals may not tell the whole story. Moreover, researchers have long recognized the existence of bureaucratic propaganda. Organizations may manipulate evidence to make it appear that official goals are being met.

So it makes sense for students of organizational behaviour to be aware of classical views of truth and evidence. The idea that we should use evidence to determine what is true and what works in the world of organizations is a useful starting point. But politics has a way of infiltrating the world of organizations and the knowledge we produce about organizations. Students should therefore be open to critical views of truth and should recognize that goal conflict, misinformation and manipulation of evidence are not uncommon in the world of organizations.

 stop! Debates over the role of Wal-Mart in society offer an interesting perspective on the issues of propaganda and counter-propaganda. Critics charge that Wal-Mart is guilty of discrimination and, more generally, that it contributes to 'reproletarianization' (a process that turns back the clock on the rights and protections that workers have won over the last century). Wal-Mart has fought back, pointing to the various benefits it has brought to the communities where it is located.

- Take a moment to assess critically the various positions in this debate, starting with the following resources:
  - www.walmartwatch.com (for a critique of Wal-Mart)
  - www.walmartfacts.com (for a defence of Wal-Mart).
- If you were researching organizational behaviour in Wal-Mart, what biases might you yourself bring to the subject, and why?

Sources and further information

Boghossian, P. (2006) *Fear of Knowledge: Against Relativism and Constructivism*, Oxford: Oxford University Press.
Gereffi, G. and Christian, M. (2009) 'The impacts of Wal-Mart: the rise and consequences of the world's dominant retailer', *Annual Review of Sociology*, **35**, pp. 573–91.

Note: This feature was written by David MacLennan, Assistant Professor at Thompson Rivers University, BC, Canada.

organizations depends on their life experiences and a whole series of assumptions they make about people and society. Although this is acknowledged in most standard textbooks, accounts of organizational behaviour tend to be presented in a sanitized, matter-of-fact-way; as an uncontested field of study devoid of controversy. Yet there are profound differences of opinion among academics about how work and organizations are designed, how people are managed and how they should be studied. Much of the controversy stems from competing theoretical perspectives, which we can define for our purposes as frameworks of interconnected beliefs, values and assumptions that guide thinking and research on the nature of the social world. In organizational behaviour, these rival perspectives or ideologies tend to be reflected in different schools of thought, each of which disseminates its research findings through particular academic journals.[64,65]

When people ask, 'What's your perspective on this?', they might just as well be asking, 'What is your bias on this?' because each **perspective** reflects a particular bias, based on our life experience, how we see an issue and our vested interests. Thus, perspectives are theoretical 'lenses' or 'road maps' we use to view the social world. When we refer to a perspective on organizational behaviour, we are therefore speaking of an interconnected set of beliefs, values and intentions that legitimize academic and organizational behaviours. Before we continue further with our educational journey in organizational behaviour, it is worth considering two fundamental questions: 'What major perspectives do academics adopt when studying behaviour in work organizations?', and 'To what extent can researchers construct a truly objective account of behaviour in work organizations?'

Major theoretical perspectives on organizational behaviour

Organizational behaviour theorists using one or more theoretical perspectives or 'lenses' offer many different explanations to the question, 'Why do people in organizations do what they do?' At the risk of glossing over a multiplicity of theoretical perspectives that academics identify with and defend with passion, it is possible to identify four competing ideological camps into which many, or most, academics fall. They are the managerialist, the **conflict**, the symbolic-interactionist and the feminist camps. These perspectives or **paradigms** will serve as useful points of reference for understanding the competing views discussed throughout the remainder of the book.

The managerialist perspective

The managerialist perspective is also referred to as the structural-functionalist perspective in sociology, and is adhered to by most studying organizations. Managerialists view organizations as complex systems whose parts work together to promote consensus and stability. They are interested in order, employee commitment and performance issues, with a partisan preference for managers rather than the managed. Although there are variations and tensions, functionalists make a number of core assumptions about the nature of organizational behaviour.

In their view, the question, 'Why do managers do what they do?' is largely explained by the fact that managers serve as 'agents' of owners and investors, and that, as agents, they strive to maximize the efficiency and profits or meet set targets by minimizing the costs of (people or materials or machines) inputs. Managers strive to be rational. That is, they systematically apply various techniques to accomplish some given goal. The organization itself is characterized as a paragon of rational decision making. Managers do what they do because the imperatives of markets or government require that it is done. Those who do not manage in this way are deemed to be 'unsuccessful'. The managerialist perspective, therefore,

perspective: an overall approach to or viewpoint on some subject

conflict perspective: the sociological approach that views groups in society as engaged in a continuous power struggle for the control of scarce resources

paradigm: a term used to describe a cluster of beliefs that dictates for researchers in a particular discipline what should be studied, how research should be conducted and how the results should be interpreted becomes inseparable from the notion of efficiency and effectiveness. Most functionalist thinking also assumes that work organizations are harmonious bodies, tending towards a state of equilibrium and order. The focus of much of the research endeavour is about finding the 'winning formula' so that more managers can become 'successful' in achieving prescribed goals by successfully shaping the behaviour of other employees.

Within the mainstream functionalist school, there are differences of view. The **contingency** literature focuses largely on the internal authority structure of the organization, and acknowledges that different technologies, depending upon their complexity, strongly explain managerial behaviour and impose different kinds of demands on people and organizations.[66] Contingency theory is helpful for understanding variations in organizational structures and, ultimately, managerial behaviour in the workplace. The *political* perspective focuses upon pressures, constraints and power relationships as causal explanations of managerial behaviour. Rather than presenting an image of managers as simple agents of owners, managers are viewed as having to respond to pressures from various stakeholder groups such as shareholders, suppliers, consumers and employees. The organization is viewed as a coalition of stakeholder groups.[67] The **strategic choice** literature (see Figure 1.2, above) stresses that management is a social process. Accordingly, managerial behaviour is 'bounded' by such factors as cognitive capacity, imperfect information, organizational politics, strategic business decisions, worker resistance and misbehaviour, and managerial beliefs, values and philosophies. Common to most variations of the managerialist paradigm is a failure to connect organizational behaviour to the larger dominant political economic paradigm of neo-liberalism.

contingency approach: the idea that a particular action may have different consequences in different situations

strategic choice: the idea that an organization interacts with its environment rather being totally determined by it

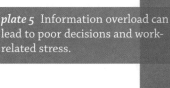
plate 5 Information overload can lead to poor decisions and work-related stress.

Source: Getty Images

The critical perspective

The critical perspective views capitalism and work organizations as a system that is both economically exploitative and socially alienating. The workplace here is understood as an arena of inequality, exploitation and structured antagonism that generates conflict. Accordingly, understanding managerial behaviour is related to action to reduce the indeterminacy resulting from the unspecified nature of the employment relationship by exerting control over others. In turn, employee misbehavior and open conflict between employer and employee reflects some level of individual or collective discontent with the employment relationship. Critical analysts argue that managers' attempt to extract the maximum of effort from workers for minimum reward is the primary cause of conflict and employee misbehaviour. As such, critical theorists are interested in power, control, the degradation of work, inequality and conflict, with a partisan preference for the less powerful, the managed rather than the managers. They attempt to discover the ways in which asymmetrical power relations affect the social relations between employers and workers. They also believe, to varying degrees, in a positive role for government in the economy and in the rights of workers to organize into trade unions.

As is the case with the mainstream managerialist perspective, the critical perspective is based on numerous theoretical ideas. Obviously, the starting point is criticism itself, that is, an identification of the limitations, paradoxes, contradictions and ideological functions of the orthodox standpoint.[38] Consequently, organizational behaviour theory and practice can only be understood as something in process and located within a structural setting.

The symbolic-interactionist perspective

The behaviours of managers and other employees interacting in the workplace are the typical social behaviours that catch the attention of symbolic interactionists. Whereas managerialist and conflict theorists both analyse macro-level patterns of behaviour, the symbolic-interactionist perspective generalizes about everyday forms of individual-level social interaction in order to understand social behaviour.

The European philosopher Georg Simmel (1858–1918) is credited with the development of symbolic interactionism. He was interested in how individuals interact with one another in small groups, and wrote about the 'web of group affiliations' – aspects of social reality that are invisible in macro-sociological analysis. George Herbert Mead (1863–1931) and Charles Cooley (1864–1929) developed Simmel's ideas. Charles Cooley introduced the notion of the 'looking-glass self' that we form by looking into the reactions of people around us. If everyone treats us as intelligent, for instance, we conclude that we are.

Mead focused on the role of communications in human behaviour. He argued that most social interactions revolve around individuals reaching a shared understanding through the use of symbols such as language, non-verbal cues and gestures. The symbolic-interactionist paradigm is captured in Karl Weick's notions of 'enactment' and 'sense-making'.[68] It is argued that a sense of mission, goals and a language are constructed and communicated (or 'enacted') so that employees can make sense of what it is they do, and explain what it is they have accomplished. Employees are embedded in a symbolic context.

The feminist perspective

feminism: the belief that all people – both women and men – are equal and that they should be valued equally and have equal rights

The **feminist** perspective emerged out of criticisms of traditional research, which feminist scholars argued has been mainly concerned with research *on* men *by* men. The feminist perspective involves more than criticizing the use of masculine pronouns and nouns (see Chapter 14). It is rooted in a critical analysis of society, and draws attention to aspects of organizational life that other perspectives neglect. In part, feminist research has focused on gender differences and how they relate to leadership styles, interpersonal communications, discrimination and inequality of opportunities in paid work. Feminist scholars not only reveal sexual discrimination or the experience of oppression, but often also point to limitations in how other aspects of organizational behaviour are examined and understood.

Which of the four perspectives should a student use when studying workplaces? Each offers unique insights into behaviour in organizations (Table 1.3). We do not aim to privilege a singular perspective, but rather to provide a frame of reference against which readers can learn and develop their own understanding of organizational behaviour. Our view is that organizational behaviour cannot be understood without appreciating that organizations are places where those with power determine what work is done, how it is done and the effects on people by getting work done in a certain way. We think these are really important issues that should be examined and debated in any study of organizational behaviour.

table 1.3 Comparing major perspectives on organizational behaviour

Topic	Managerialist	Conflict	Symbolic-interactionist	Feminist
View of society	Stable Well integrated	Unstable Tension	Dynamic	Inequality
Key concepts	Functions Dysfunctions	Capitalism Power	Symbols Communications	Patriarchy
Primary focus	Management practices Performance	Conflict Control	Sense-making	Gender equality
Prescriptions	Better practices Greater cooperation	Employee ownership and control	Create space Dialogue	Law reforms
Proponents	Emile Durkheim Talcott Parsons	Karl Marx Richard Hyman	George Mead Karl Weick	Mary Wollstonecraft Kate Millett

Organizational theorists as researchers

Organizational behaviour theorists do not merely approach their subject from different paradigms; they also make different assumptions about the way in which organizations should be investigated. In addition, they employ varied research methods to build and test organizational behaviour theory. The second question we asked – 'To what extent can academics construct a truly objective account of behaviour in work organizations?' – brings up issues of social ontology (which deals with the nature of being), **epistemology** (the theory of knowledge) and research methodology, which all affect the conduct of organizational behaviour research. We have no wish to re-route our intellectual journey into an academic quagmire, but you need some sense of these issues in order to appreciate some rather different aspects of the debate about organizational behaviour.

Social **ontology** issues are concerned with whether social entities, such as formal organizations, can and should be considered as objective entities with a reality external to individuals, or whether they can and should be considered as no more than social constructions built up from the perceptions and actions of individuals. These positions are referred to respectively as **objectivism** and **constructionism**. One simple way to think about this distinction is to look at the working of a hospital. In any hospital, there is a hierarchy of authority, a mission statement, a division of labour that assigns people to different jobs, and rules and regulations for doing those jobs. People learn the rules and follow the standardized procedures. The organization represents a social order in that it exerts pressure on members to conform to the rules and regulations.

epistemology: a theory of knowledge particularly used to refer to a standpoint on what should pass as acceptable knowledge

ontology: a theory of whether social entities such as organizations can and should be considered as objective entities with a reality external to the specific social actors, or as social constructions built up from the perceptions and behaviour of these actors

objectivism: an *ontological* position which asserts that the meaning of social phenomena has an existence independent of individuals; compare this with *constructionism*

constructionism: the view that researchers actively construct reality on the basis of their understandings, which are mainly culturally fashioned and shared. It contrasts with **realism** (see below)

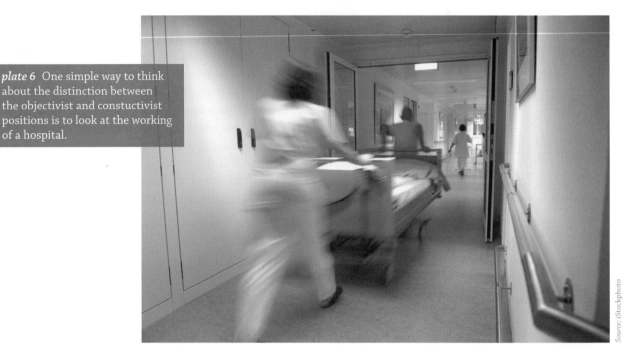

Source: iStockphoto

plate 6 One simple way to think about the distinction between the objectivist and constuctivist positions is to look at the working of a hospital.

The 'objectivist' view is that the hospital (as an organization, not as a building) possesses a reality that is external to any individual who occupies it. Individuals come and go, but the organization persists, so it is something that is 'out there' in the social world, and not just something that exists in people's minds.

Constructionism is an ontological position which asserts that social entities such as work organizations are produced or constructed by individuals through their social interaction. The core of the 'constructivist' discourse is that organizational reality does not have an objective existence, but is constructed in the accounts of organizational researchers and others. The constructivist concept of a hospital, for example, is one of a 'social order'. The hospital does not just encompass the formal rules; it is concerned with informal rules and activities as well. For instance, the official rules may state that only a doctor can increase a patient's medication but, unofficially, nurses are routinely given the power to do this. Both these understandings become part of the researcher's construction of the hospital.

The social order of any work organization is characterized as an outcome of agreed-upon patterns of actions among the different social actors involved, and the social order is in a constant state of change because the informal agreements are being constantly established, revoked or revised.[69–71] The notion that knowledge and truth are created, rather than objectively discovered by researchers, means that constructionists are more inclined to challenge researchers to re-examine their perspectives, the research process itself and the whole process of the production of knowledge.

An epistemological issue concerns the question of what is (or should be) regarded as acceptable knowledge in the social sciences, for example what forms of knowledge can be collected, and what is to be regarded as 'true' or 'false'. An important issue in this context is whether organizational behaviour can and should be investigated according to the same principles and methods as the physical sciences. The doctrine of **positivism** affirms the importance of modelling social science research on the physical sciences.

The French social theorists Auguste Comte (1798–1857) and Emile Durkheim (1858–1917) were early leaders in embracing positivist approaches to understanding human behaviour. There are five working assumptions that 'positivists' make in approaching their research. First, knowledge is arrived at through the gathering of

positivism: a view held in quantitative research in which reality exists independently of the perceptions and interpretations of people; a belief that the world can best be understood through scientific inquiry social facts, which provide the basis for generalizations or laws by which human behaviour operates. Second, the purpose of theory is to generate hypotheses that can be tested, and this allows explanations of laws to be assessed. Third, only phenomena and regularities confirmed by the senses (that is, by, for example, sight or hearing) can genuinely be warranted as knowledge. Fourth, research can and must be conducted in a way that is value-free. And finally, social science must distinguish between 'scientific' statements and normative statements.[72] This means the social science deals with 'what is', not with what 'should be'.

It is a common mistake to equate positivism with the 'scientific'. Many social scientists differ fundamentally over how best to characterize scientific practice. An alternative term to describe the nature of social 'science' practice is **realism**.[73,74] This epistemological position shares two features with positivism: a belief that the social sciences can and should use the same approach to the collection of data and to its analysis, and a commitment to an external reality.

Two forms of realism can be identified. Empirical realism simply asserts that, using appropriate methods, social reality can be understood. **Critical realism** is a philosophy of and for the social sciences. It distinguishes between the social world and people's experience of it, as well as between the real, the actual and the empirical. It maintains that deeper social structures and generative processes lie beneath the surface of observable social structures and patterns. For empirical realists, a social scientist is only able to understand the social world – and so change it – if the structures at work that generate human activity are identified.

An example of the application of both symbolic interactionism and critical realism is the work of Yrjö Engeström on informal workplace learning (discussed in Chapter 6). Individual and small group learning is understood as an observable social process – the 'tip of the iceberg' – but learning is also embedded in an interlocking human activity system – the 'submerged part of the iceberg' – consisting of a community of practice, rules and division of labour.

The doctrine of **interpretivism** is a contrasting epistemology to positivism. The interpretivists' preference is for an empathetic 'understanding' and interpretation of human behaviour. For them, it is important to examine how people define their situation, how they make sense of their lives, and how their sense of self develops in interaction with other people. The interpretive approach has its intellectual roots in Max Weber's concept of understanding, or *Verstehen* (*Verstehen* being a German word that can be translated as 'human understanding'). In Weber's view, the social scientist should try to imagine how a particular individual perceives social actions, and understand the meaning an individual attaches to a particular event. The symbolic-interactionist perspective attempts to provide an empathetic understanding of how individuals see and interpret the events of their everyday work experiences.

The purpose of this brief discussion of epistemological issues in social research is to point out that, over the last 25 years or so, some organizational theorists have abandoned the application of the canons of physical science – positivism – to the study of human inquiry. The ontological and epistemological issues we outlined above have direct implications for research methodology.

Research methodologies can be broadly classified as either **quantitative** or **qualitative**. Each strategy reflects differences in ontological and epistemological considerations: differences in the types of question asked, the kinds of evidence considered appropriate for answering a question, the degree to which the analysis is done by converting observations to numerical or non-numerical data, and the methods used to process the data.

Quantitative research can be defined as a research strategy that emphasizes numerical data and statistical analyses, and that entails **deductive theorizing**. It incorporates the practices and norms of positivism, is oriented towards aggregated

realism: the idea that a reality exists out there independently of what and how researchers think about it. It contrasts with constructionism

critical realism: a realist epistemology which asserts that the study of human behaviour should be concerned with the identification of the structures that generate that behaviour in order to change it

interpretivism: the view held in many qualitative studies that reality comes from shared meaning among people in that environment

qualitative research: refers to the gathering and sorting of information through a variety of techniques, including interviews, focus groups and observations, and inductive theorizing

quantitative research: refers to research methods that emphasize numerical precision and deductive theorizing

deductive approach: research in which the investigator begins with a theory and then collects information and data to test the theory

data that compile responses from many respondents so that general patterns are visible (a process called nomothetic analysis), and embodies a view of social reality as a relatively constant, objective reality.

Qualitative research, on the other hand, can be defined as a research strategy that emphasizes non-numerical data, entails inductive theorizing, rejects positivism, is oriented towards case studies (a process called ideographic analysis), and embodies a view of social reality as the product of individual thought.

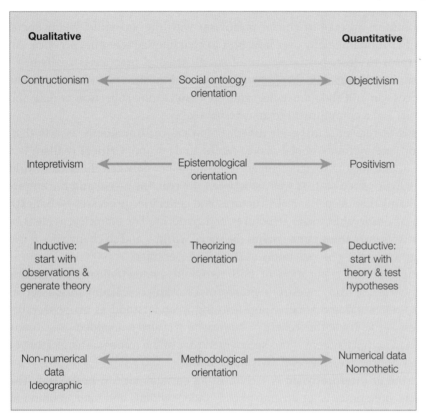

Qualitative		Quantitative
Contructionism	⟵ Social ontology orientation ⟶	Objectivism
Intepretivism	⟵ Epistemological orientation ⟶	Positivism
Inductive: start with observations & generate theory	⟵ Theorizing orientation ⟶	Deductive: start with theory & test hypotheses
Non-numerical data Ideographic	⟵ Methodological orientation ⟶	Numerical data Nomothetic

figure 1.7 A scheme for comparing quantitative and qualitative research strategies

Source: Burrell and Morgan (1979)[64]

Figure 1.7 compares the differences between quantitative and qualitative, at least as they have historically been associated with different assumptions. At first glance, the quantitative/qualitative distinction seems to be about whether quantitative researchers employ more 'hard' measurements than qualitative researchers do, but there is in fact much more to it than that. These two approaches affect how social scientists do research, and are fundamental to understanding any inquiry into organizational behaviour.

Drawing on the elements in Figure 1.1 above, you should now be better able to account for the misrepresentation of social reality by researchers. First, researchers make different ontological assumptions that affect how they attempt to investigate and obtain 'knowledge' about organizational behaviour. For example, if a researcher subscribes to the view that organizations are objective social entities that shape individual behaviour, the research endeavour is likely to focus upon an analysis of the formal properties and regularities between the various elements of the organization. Alternatively, if the researcher subscribes to a view that emphasizes the dynamic nature of organizational life, the researcher will focus on the active participation of individuals in reality construction.

Second, the epistemological assumptions that researchers make about the social world affect how they attempt to investigate and obtain 'knowledge' about organizational behaviour. As we have discussed, at the heart of epistemology lie questions such as 'What is the relation between seeing and knowing?' and 'Whose knowledge is produced in surveys and interviews?' For the positivists, the challenge is to discover the laws of human behaviour, and perhaps then predict future social action. The constructivists reject the notion that we can ever have an objective account of the phenomenon under investigation, because all such accounts are 'linguistic reconstructions'.

As we have seen, the constructivist approach recognizes that the researcher and those being researched create the data. Researchers' data do not discover social reality; rather, the 'discovery' arises from the interactive process (between the researcher and the organization) and the political, cultural and structural contexts. Traditionally, the interview, for example, is viewed as an opportunity for knowledge to be transmitted between, for instance, a manager and a researcher. Yet, through the interactional process, the viewed and the viewer are active *makers of meaning*, assembling and modifying their questions and answers in response to the dynamics of the interview. The researcher is not simply a conduit for information, but is in fact deeply implicated in the production of knowledge.[75]

The constructivist approach suggests that what the manager and the situation actually are is a consequence of various accounts and interpretations. From this perspective, managers act as the 'practical authors' of their own identities. Furthermore, some interpretations are more equal than others. For example, one account of British Prime Minister Tony Blair's leadership performance following the September 11, 2001 attack on the World Trade Center in New York might describe it as 'Churchillian eloquence'. Others could interpret his speeches as populist rhetoric. The point here is that if more powerful 'voices' (including the popular press and television news channels) support Blair, 'the Churchillian' view will prevail, and the negative voice will carry little weight. The constructivist conclusion in this case is that what is important is not what the leader (or the organization) is 'really' like, but the processes by which he or she (or it) is perceived and defined as a success or failure. In terms of managerial behaviour, what constitutes a 'good' manager does not rest on an objective evaluation but on criteria generated by the social setting.[76,77]

This does not mean that knowledge is impossible. Rather, it means that the knowledge that is produced on what people in organizations allegedly do cannot be an objective narrative about their workplace activities. We must maintain a healthy scepticism as we read what researchers have to say about organizational behaviour.

Third, there are different research strategies, or general orientations to the conduct of the inquiry. The different research designs – such as questionnaire surveys, interviews and observational studies – may capture distortions of reality. For example, the mail survey (a questionnaire sent out to employees or customers) is favoured by quantitative researchers, but it can at best only provide a 'snapshot' of managerial and employee workplace activities. It cannot hope to provide an accurate picture of the subtleties and dynamics of employment relations, or of how individuals perceive social actions. The sample size may vary considerably, and if small samples of organizational members are surveyed, one or more atypical participants could unduly influence the findings. Case studies and direct observational techniques, favoured by qualitative researchers, often provide 'rich' data on workplace activities but may not capture cognitive processes. For example, a manager or group leader who is captured sitting in his or her office staring through the window could be either reflecting on a long-term plan or simply admiring the spring blossom.

Finally, we should be aware that management is embedded in the social structure and is highly political. This means that it involves power relationships between managers and non-managers, and between managers and other managers. As a result, political issues will rarely be far removed from the research process.[78] Consequently, the data gathered by researchers might not provide a 'reality report' on what managers do inside the organization, but rather reflect the diversity of managers and their need for self-justification, perhaps in connection with complex internal power struggles.

To extend our discussion of the limitations of research methodology a little further, managerial behaviour is most often analysed using 'scientific' or positivist methods, but organizational behaviour theorists sometimes quote managers' opinions to the exclusion of other people who are affected by the managers' actions (not least, their subordinates). Interviewing people from a cross-selection of the organization, including lower-level workers and trade union representatives in unionized establishments, is always likely to provide 'nuggets' of information that rarely surface in positivist research, and to suggest different lines of interpretation of human behaviour in the workplace.[79]

stop reflect

According to the constructivist approach to knowledge making, language does not transmit truth; instead, it produces what we come to regard as truth. What are your views of the constructivist model? What are the implications of this view for understanding behavioural studies?

Chapter summary

- In this introductory chapter, we have attempted to cover a wide range of complex issues. We have emphasized that external contexts have a significant impact on the way in which individuals and groups work and behave. The external context influences the structure and behaviour of work organizations and, in turn, organizations influence the wider society. The linkage between the external contexts and the search for competitive advantage through employee behaviour is complex. Globalization means that there is a need for a multidimensional approach to the study of behaviour in organizations.

- We have reviewed orthodox treatments of management – as a set of technical competencies, functionally necessary tasks, and universal roles and processes found in any work organization.[41,43,80–82] For the traditionalist, managerial work is regarded as rational, morally and politically neutral, and its history and legitimacy are taken for granted. Alternative accounts of management emphasize that managerial work is embedded in a politically charged arena of structured and contested power relationships.

- To help us deconstruct the many facets of organizational complexity, we have used a three-dimensional management model. This encourages us to go beyond simply describing managerial behaviour, to provide an understanding of the contingencies that explain why managerial policies and behaviour vary in time and space. Managers' behaviour does not follow the famous Fayolian management cycle. They are typically engaged in an assortment of frenetic, habitual, reactive, fragmented activities.

- Organizational behaviour is a complex field of study with no agreed boundaries, and draws from a variety of disciplines including industrial psychology, sociology, anthropology and political science. We have defined it as a multidisciplinary field of inquiry, concerned with the systematic study of formal organizations, the behaviour of people within organizations, and important features of their social context that structure all the activities that occur inside the organization. To draw on the work of American sociologist C. Wright Mills, an 'organizational behaviour imagination' allows us to grasp the interplay of people in organizations and the larger economic, political and social context that structures the behaviour.

- Studying organizational behaviour can help put people in a stronger position to influence and shape the workplace and their own future. Organizational behaviour is very much an applied social science, which provides a conceptual 'toolbox' to help people predict, explain and influence organizational actions.

- We also focused on diversity because we consider the social dynamics of class, gender, race and ethnicity to underpin contemporary organizational behaviour. Understanding the significance of class, gender, race and ethnicity, and disability puts the behaviour of individuals and groups in the organization into a wider social context.

- We identified four major theoretical frameworks or paradigms used by organizational behaviour theorists for the study of behaviour in organizations: the structural-functionalist perspective, the symbolic-interactionist perspective, the conflict perspective and the feminist perspective. The managerialist or structural-functionalist perspective represents 'mainstream' organizational behaviour analysis. It assumes that work behaviour takes place in rationally designed organizations, and is inseparable from the notion of efficiency. The symbolic-interactionist perspective focuses on the microanalysis of small workgroups, and interpersonal interaction in the organization. The critical and feminist perspectives set out to discover the ways in which power, control, gender and legitimacy affect relations between managers, and between managers and non-managers.

- Finally, we discussed two ontological orientations – objectivism and constructionism – and two epistemological orientations – positivism and interpretivism – and outlined how these influence decisions on research methodology. Depending on the researcher's perspective, which reflects a whole series of assumptions about the nature of the social world, organizational behaviour researchers will tend to lean towards either quantitative or qualitative research strategies.

Key concepts

class	21
constructivist approach	29
employee misbehaviour	13
employment relationship	13
gender	23
management	14
managerial behaviour	15
positivist approach	30
qualitative research	31
quantitative research	31
strategic choice	27
Verstehen	31

Vocab checklist for ESL students

- ☐ Anthropology, anthropological, anthropologist
- ☐ Bureaucracy, bureaucratic, bureaucrat, bureaucratization
- ☐ Capitalist, capitalism, capitalize
- ☐ Conflict
- ☐ Conflict perspective
- ☐ Constructivism
- ☐ Critic, critical, criticize
- ☐ Critical realism
- ☐ Deductive
- ☐ Dialectical
- ☐ Discrimination, discriminate
- ☐ Economy, economics, economical, economic, economist
- ☐ Epistemology
- ☐ Ethics, ethical
- ☐ Evaluation, evaluative
- ☐ External

- ☐ Feminist
- ☐ Gender
- ☐ Global
- ☐ Interactionist
- ☐ Interpretivism
- ☐ Life chance
- ☐ Macro
- ☐ Manager, management, managerial, manage
- ☐ Means of production
- ☐ Micro
- ☐ Multidisciplinary
- ☐ Objective
- ☐ Ontology
- ☐ Organization, organize, organizational
- ☐ Organizational behaviour
- ☐ Organizational culture
- ☐ Organizational structure
- ☐ Paradigm
- ☐ Perspective
- ☐ Political science
- ☐ Positivism, positivist
- ☐ Post-industrial
- ☐ Proletariat
- ☐ Psychology, psychological, psychologist
- ☐ Qualitative
- ☐ Quantitative
- ☐ Realism
- ☐ Social class
- ☐ Social interaction
- ☐ Society, social
- ☐ Sociology, sociologist
- ☐ Strategy, strategic, strategist
- ☐ Symbolic, symbolism, symbolize
- ☐ Technology, technological, technologist
- ☐ Theory, theoretical, theorist

Chapter review questions

1. What is meant by 'organizations' and 'organizational behaviour'?
2. What are capitalism, management and globalization?
3. Self-regulation and laissez-faire are finished, declared France's President Nicolas Sarkozy in 2009. Is this true? Why? If it is true, what are the implications for organizing and managing people at work?
4. Give three reasons for studying organizational behaviour.
5. Some authors state that organizational behaviour relates to the process of a manager's job. What does this mean?
6. Which of the four sociological perspectives do you think best fits your own ideas about human behaviour in work organizations?
7. Why is it important to include gender, race and disability in the study of behaviour at work?
8. If you were asked to conduct research in organizational behaviour, which research approach would you use? Explain your preference.

Chapter research questions

1. Form a study group of three to five people. Each member is to share with the group the number of organizations she or he has a connection with, for example, credit card (bank), driving licence (government agency), student ID card (university) and so forth. Using the Internet and/or newspaper sources, collect examples of the effects of the global economic and financial recession that started in 2008 on the functioning of at least two known organizations. What are the implications of restructuring for organizational behaviour in the next 5 years?
2. Obtain a copy of Stephen Ackroyd's and others (2006) *The Oxford Handbook of Work and Organization*. Read Chapter 3, 'Gender, race, and the restructuring of work' (pp. 74–94). What have been the implications of Anglo-Saxon capitalism for existing configurations of gender and racial inequality?
3. Retrieve and read Ulrich Beck's (2008) article, 'Reframing power in the globalized world', *Organization Studies*, **29**(5), pp. 793–804. Why does the author argue that, in an age of global crisis, the creation of a dense network of transnational interdependencies is what is needed to regain national autonomy? What implications does this have for the development of organizational management?

Further reading

Anonymous (2009) The jobs crisis. *Economist*, March 14, p. 11.

Atkinson, C. (2008) 'An exploration of small firm psychological contracts', *Work, Employment and Society*, **22**(3): 447–65.

Bakan, J. (2004) *The Corporation*, London: Penguin.

Beck, U. (2008) 'Reframing power in the globalized world', *Organization Studies*, **29**(5), pp. 793–804.

Challiol, H. and Mignonac, K. (2005) Relocation decision-making and couple relationships: a quantitative and qualitative study of dual-earner couples. *Journal of Organizational Behaviour*, **26**, 247–74.

Collin, K. (2009) Work-related identity in individual and social learning at work. *Journal of Workplace Learning*, **21**(1/2), pp. 23–35.

Jacoby, S. (2005) *The Embedded Corporation*. Princeton, NJ: Princeton University Press.

Sklair, L. (2002) *Globalization: Capitalism and its Alternatives*. Oxford: Oxford University Press.

Sorge, A. (1997) 'Organization behaviour', pp. 3–21 in A. Sorge and M. Warner (eds), *The IEBM Handbook of Organizational Behavior*, Boston, MA: International Thomson Business Press.

Stiglitz, J. E. (2006) *Making Globalization Work*, New York: Norton.

Thompson, P. and McHugh, D. (2009) 'Studying organizations: an introduction', pp. 3–19 in *Work Organizations* (4th edn), Basingstoke: Palgrave.

Tyler, M. and Wilkinson, A. (2007) 'The tyranny of corporate slenderness: "corporate anorexia" as a metaphor for our age', *Work, Employment and Society*, **21**(3), pp. 537–49.

Weick, K. (2006) 'Faith, evidence, and action: better guesses in an unknowable world', *Organization Studies*, **27**(11), pp. 1723–36.

Wilson, F. M. (2003) *Organizational Behaviour and Gender*, Aldershot: Ashgate.

Wright Mills, C. (1959/2000) *The Sociological Imagination* (40th anniversary edn), New York: Oxford University Press.

Chapter case study 1

Managing change at Eastern University

Setting

In Canadian universities, it is evident that there is a need for positive change, including in how they manage and lead their employees. Various reports emphasize that they compete not only for government and sponsorship funding, but also for the market share of potential students in the increasingly competitive local, provincial and international arenas. In a university setting, key factors in facing these challenges successfully are cooperative and collaborative relationships between administration and the unions representing the university's workers, including support and faculty employees. Publicly funded universities are under increasing pressure to thrive in an atmosphere of reduced funding and increased competition. Working collaboratively in the same direction can produce a viable enduring future.

Background to the case study

Eastern University College is located in Ontario, Canada, and has approximately 14,000 full-time and part-time students. It was recently granted full university status, enabling the institution to grant its own degrees. In addition, it was expanded to include a comprehensive distance learning programme as an alternative to traditional classroom learning. Resources for new research and developing postgraduate programmes are also planned for the near future. With these fresh opportunities, it was recognized that changes were needed in the institution's strategic direction, including in its management policies and practices.

The university's labour relations were a particular area of focus. Over the years, the university had developed an adversarial and confrontational relationship with the union representing the institution's 300 support workers. In a study undertaken by the administration to identify the drivers or resistors in creating a more positive alliance with the union, it was found that the university's hierarchical and bureaucratic organizational structure was one possible reason for the dysfunctional relationship. Agreements on issues became stalled as administrators were required to take items back to senior managers for their perusal. The union contributed to the delay of reaching resolutions as it referred back to its members for approval on any decisions to be made. In the process, each group sought to protect its own interests. The net result was loyalty to factions, departments, leaders and unions, rather than to the organization as a whole.

Management meeting: preparing for change

Lisa Chang, 28, was the new Assistant Human Resource Manager for Eastern University. Improving student services at the university was a high priority for Chang. Based on feedback from the students' union, one idea she had was to extend access to the computer labs so they would be available for student use 24 hours a day, 7 days a week, except when they were being used by lecturers for teaching.

Chang visited the websites of several universities and downloaded details of their student computer services. She met with the Manager of Facilities, Doug Brown, the Vice-president of Student Services, Dr Susan Allen, and the Head of Campus Security, Paul McGivern. Chang presented her proposal, which included the estimated cost, and was able to resolve the few questions the others had with examples and information acquired from other comparable universities. It was agreed that Chang would present her proposal to the next meeting of the Council of Deans.

The presentation to the deans went flawlessly. Chang was confident that the deans would agree to her proposal. But just as the meeting was to wrap up, the Dean of Arts said, 'Have the union agreed to this?' Alarm bells went off in Chang's head. 'Union?', she thought. 'Why wouldn't they agree to the new service?' She told the Dean she would discuss it with her boss Peter Webster, Director of Human Resources.

At the next human resources management meeting to discuss the labour relations situation, administrators were reviewing the most recent grievances and potential arbitrations, and the generally poor relationship with the union representing the support staff. Peter Webster, a manager who had several years' experience in dealings with the union, sighed in frustration as he echoed a sentiment of many in the room. 'It seems to be impossible to work together collaboratively with this union. I think we may as well accept it.'

'It doesn't have to be this way,' said Chang, as she handed out copies of her proposed new student service. 'When I talked to one of the stewards last week, he actually expressed the same desire for a more cooperative relationship. That is a sign of positive change already.'

After some discussion on what could be done to build upon this progress, the group asked Lisa Chang to prepare a detailed report for the next meeting outlining the next steps.

Tasks

Working either alone or in a small group, prepare a report drawing on the material from this chapter addressing the following:

1. Thinking about the situation at Eastern University, how effective are Lisa Chang's and Peter Webster's performances in each of Mintzberg's managerial roles?
2. What recommendations would you make to the university's senior management? How would this help?

Sources of additional information

Mintzberg, H. (1990) 'The manager's job: folklore and fact', *Harvard Business Review*, March–April, pp. 163–76.
Kersley, B., Alpin, C., Forth, J. et al. (2006) 'The management of employment relations', pp. 36–70 in *Inside the Workplace: First Findings from the 2004 Workplace Employment Relations Survey (WERS2004)*, London: Routledge.
Visit www.change-management.com for information on change management.

Note

This case study was written by Dan Haley, Director of Human Resources, School District No. 57, Prince George, BC, Canada.

Chapter case study 2

Tuition reimbursement for studying OB?

Visit www.palgrave.com/business/brattonob2e to view this case study

Web-based assignment

To help you develop your understanding of the subject, we have developed an activity that requires you to maintain a learning journal or log. A learning journal is a simple and straightforward way to help you integrate content, process, personal thoughts and personal work experience of organizational behaviour. Learning logs operate from the stance that people learn from reflection and through writing.

We suggest you make an entry in your log after each completed week of class time. Properly understood and used, learning journals assist the learning process by becoming a vehicle for understanding the complex nature of human behaviour in the workplace. Visit the website http://olc.spsd.sk. ca/DE/PD/instr/strats/logs for information on the value of learning journals.

Learning journals are concise, objective, factual and impersonal in tone. The following questions could be used to guide you in making thoughtful entries in your learning journal about organizational behaviour:

* What did I learn in class this week?
* What did I find interesting?
* How well does the material connect with my work experience?
* How well does the organizational behaviour material connect with my other management courses?
* What questions do I have for the instructor about what I learned?

Later in the book, we shall be asking you to use your completed learning journal to help evaluate your studies of organizational behaviour.

OB in film

In the film *Working Girl* (1988), Tess McGill (played by Melanie Griffith) is employed as a secretary to Katharine Parker (played by Sigourney Weaver). When her boss breaks her leg in a skiing accident, Tess has an opportunity to implement some of her own ideas for new business ventures. An investment banker, Jack Trainer (played by Harrison Ford), helps Tess to present her proposal to a group of senior business executives. The film humorously illustrates the meaning of gender harassment and organizational politics.

Watch the early scenes in the film. How is Tess treated by her male co-workers? What does the film tell us about the gendering of organizations? When Tess is presenting her proposal, what is her power base, and does this shift in the scenes near the end of the film?

References

1 Scott, R. W. (2003) *Organizations: Rational, Natural, and Open Systems*, Upper Saddle River, NJ: Prentice-Hall.

2 Furness, V. (2008) 'Impact of economic downturn on the psychological contract between employer and employee'. Available at: www.employeebenefits.co.uk/item/7912/23/307/3 (accessed February 27, 2009).

3 Williams, D. (2001) 'Power or peace? Trauma, change and psychological climate in national and international affairs'. Available at: www.eoslifework.co.uk/pop1.htm (accessed February 27, 2009).

4 Anderssen, E. (2009) 'Men open up like never before as recession takes its toll', *Globe and Mail*, April 1, p. A1.

5 Todd, R. Quoted in Bratton, J. (1992), *Japanization at Work*, London: Macmillan, p. 70.

6 Sklair, L. (2002) *Globalization: Capitalism and its Alternatives*, Oxford: Oxford University Press.

7 'New world order to save earth'. Available at: http://timescorrespondence (accessed March 25, 2009).

8 Thaiindian News. Available at: www.thaiindian.com/newsportal/business/ (accessed March 25, 2009).

9 'PM urges 'moral' global capitalism'. Available at: www.onenewspage.com/news/UK/ (accessed 26 March, 2009).

10 'Global heroes: a special report on entrepreneurship', *Economist*, March 14, 2009, p. 11.

11 Sayer, D. (1991) *Capitalism and Modernity*, London: Routledge.

12 Bakan, J. (2004) *The Corporation*, London: Penguin.

13 Stiglitz, J. E. (2006) *Making Globalization Work*, New York: Norton.

14 Johns, G. and Saks, A. (2001) *Organizational Behaviour* (5th edn), Toronto: Addison-Wesley.

15 Clegg, S. and Hardy, C. (1999) *Studying Organization: Theory and Method*, Thousand Oaks, CA: Sage.

16 Wright Mills, C. (1959/2000) *The Sociological Imagination* (40th anniv. edn). New York: Oxford University Press.

17 Ghose, A. K., Majid, N. and Ernst, C. (2008) *The Global Employment Challenge*, Geneva: International Labour Organization.

18 Giddens, A. (1979) *Central Problems in Social Theory*, London: Macmillan.

19 Clegg, S. and Dunkerley, D. (1980) *Organization, Class and Control*, London: Routledge & Kegan Paul.

20 Esland, G. and Salaman, G. (1980) *The Politics of Work and Occupations*, Milton Keynes: Open University Press.

21 Nadler, D. A. and Tushman, M. L. (1997) *Competing by Design: The Power of Organizational Architecture*, New York: Oxford University Press.

22 Scholte, J. A. (2005) *Globalization: A Critical Introduction*, Basingstoke: Palgrave Macmillan.

23 Hoogvelt, A. (2001) *Globalization and the Postcolonial World* (2nd edn), Basingstoke: Palgrave.

24 Stiglitz, J. E. (2002) *Globalization and its Discontents*, New York: Norton.

25 Saul, J. R. (2005) *The Collapse of Globalism*, Toronto: Viking.

26 Hertz, N. (2002) *The Silent Takeover: Global Capitalism and the Death of Democracy*, London: Arrow.

27 Castells, M. (2000) 'Information technology and global capitalism', pp. 52–74 in W. Hutton and A. Giddens (eds), *On the Edge: Living with Global Capitalism*, London: Cape.

28 Maurice, M. and Sorge, A. (2000) *Embedding Organizations*, Amsterdam: John Benjamins.

29 Brown, R. K. (1988) 'The employment relationship in sociological theory', pp. 33–66 in D. Gallie (ed.), *Employment in Britain*, Oxford: Blackwell.

30 Ackroyd, S. and Thompson, P. (1999) *Organizational Misbehaviour*, London: Sage.

31 Alvesson, M. and Due Billing, Y. (1997) *Understanding Gender in Organizations*, London: Sage.

32 Mills, A. and Tancred, P. (eds) (1992) *Gendering Organizational Analysis*, Newbury Park, CA: Sage.

33 Hearn, J., Sheppard, D., Tancred-Sheriff, P. and Rand Burrell, G. (eds) (1989) *The Sexuality of Organization,* London: Sage.

34 Wilson, F. M. (2003) *Organizational Behaviour and Gender*, Farnham: Ashgate.

35 Wajcman, J. (1998) *Managing Like a Man: Women and Men in Corporate Management*, Cambridge: Polity Press/Penn State University Press.

36 Clegg, S., Hardy, C. and Nord, W. (eds) (1999) *Managing Organizations: Current Issues*, Thousand Oaks, CA: Sage.

37 Salaman, G. (1979) *Work Organizations: Resistance and Control*, London: Longman.

38 Thompson, P. and McHugh, D. (2009) *Work Organizations: A Critical Approach* (4th edn), Basingstoke: Palgrave.

39 Boxall, P., Purcell, J. and Wright, P. (eds) (2008) *The Oxford Handbook of Human Resource Management*, Oxford: Oxford University Press.

40 Williams, R. (1983) *Keywords*, New York: Oxford University Press.

41 Drucker, P. (1954/1993) *The Practice of Management*, New York: Harper Collins.

42 Carlson, S. (1951) *Executive Behaviour: A Study of the Workload and Working Methods of Managing Directors*, Stockholm: Stromberg.

43 Mintzberg, H. (1973) *The Nature of Managerial Work*, New York: Harper & Row.

44 Mintzberg, H. (1989) *Mintzberg on Management*, New York: Free Press, p. 16. (Originally sourced from Mintzberg, H. (1975) 'The manager's job: folklore and fact', *Harvard Business Review*, July/August.)

45 Sundgren, M. and Styhre, A. (2006) 'Leadership as de-paradoxification: leading new drug development work at three pharmaceutical companies', *Leadership*, **2**(1), pp. 31–51.

46 Hales, C. (1986) 'What do managers do? A critical review of the evidence', *Journal of Management Studies*, **23**, pp. 88–115.

47 Willmott, H. (1989) 'Images and ideals of managerial work', *Journal of Management Studies*, **21**(3), pp. 349–68.

48 Knights, D. and Willmott, H. (eds) (1986) *Gender and the Labour Process*, Aldershot: Gower.

49 Alvesson, M. and Willmott, H. (1996) *Making Sense of Management: A Critical Introduction*, London: Sage.

50 Stewart, R., Barsoux, J.-L., Kieser, A., Ganter, H. and Walgenbach, P. (1994) *Managing in Britain and Germany*, Basingstoke: Macmillan.

51 Helgesen, S. (1995) *The Female Advantage: Women's Ways of Leadership*, New York: Doubleday.

52 Hoel, H. and Beale, D. (2006) 'Workplace bullying, psychological perspectives and industrial relations: towards a contextualized and interdisciplinary approach', *British Journal of Industrial Relations*, **44**(2), pp. 239–62.

53 Bolton, S. (2005) *Emotion Management in the Workplace*, Basingstoke: Palgrave.

54 Plotnik, R. (2005) *Introduction to Psychology* (7th edn), Belmont, CA.: Thomson/Wadsworth.

55 Carlson, N., Buskist, W., Enzle, M. and Heth, C. (2005) *Psychology* (3rd edn), Toronto: Pearson Education.

56 Grey, C. (2005) *A Very Short, Fairly Interesting and Reasonably Cheap Book about Studying Organizations*, London: Sage.

57 Pfeffer, J. (1998) *The Human Equation: Building Profits by Putting People First*, Boston, MA: Harvard Business School Press.

58 Millett, K. (1985) *Sexual Politics*, London: Virago.

59 Bryson, V. (2003) *Feminist Political Theory* (2nd edn), Basingstoke: Palgrave.

60 Tong, R. P. (1998) *Feminist Thought* (2nd edn), Boulder, CO: Westview Press.

61 Giddens, A. (2001) *Sociology* (4th edn), Cambridge: Polity Press.

62 Camilleri, J. M. (1999) 'Disability: a personal odyssey', *Disability and Society*, **14**(4), pp. 79–93.

63 Oliver, M. (1996) *Understanding Disability*, Basingstoke: Palgrave.

64 Burrell, G. and Morgan, G. (1979) *Sociological Paradigms and Organizational Analysis*, London: Heinemann.

65 Mills, A., Simmons, A. and Helms Mills, J. (2005) *Reading Organizational Theory* (3rd edn), Toronto: Garamond.

66 Woodward, J. (1965) *Industrial Organizations: Theory and Practice*, London: Oxford University Press.

67 Cyert, R. M. and March, J. G. (1963) 'A behaviour theory of organizational objectives', in M. Haire (ed.), *Modern Organizational Theory*, New York: Wiley.

68 Weick, K. E. (1995) *Sensemaking in Organizations*, London: Sage.

69 Palys, T. (2003) *Research Decisions: Quantitative and Qualitative Perspectives* (3rd edn), Scarborough, Ontario: Thompson-Nelson.

70 Neuman, W. L. (2007) *Basics of Social Research* (2nd edn), London: Pearson.

71 Schwandt, T. A. (1994) 'Constructivist, interpretivist approaches to human inquiry', pp. 118–37 in N. K. Denzin and Y. Lincoln (eds), *Handbook of Qualitative Research*, Thousand Oaks, CA: Sage.

72 Bryman, A. and Teevan, J. (2005) *Social Research Methods*, Oxford: Oxford University Press.

73 Bhaskar, R. (1989) *Reclaiming Reality*, London: Verso.

74 Sayer, A. (2000) *Realism and Social Science*, London: Sage.

75 Charmaz, K. (2005) 'Grounded theory: objectivist and constructivist methods', pp. 509–35 in N. Denzin and Y. Lincoln (eds) *Handbook of Qualitative Research* (2nd edn), Thousand Oaks, CA: Sage.

76 Grint, K. (1995) 'The culture of management and the management of culture', pp. 162–88 in *Management: A Sociological Introduction*, Cambridge: Polity Press.

77 Bratton, J., Grint, K. and Nelson, D. (2005) *Organizational Leadership*, Mason, OH: Thomson-South-Western.

78 Easterby-Smith, M., Thorpe, R. and Lowe, A. (1991) *Management Research: An Introduction*, London: Sage.

79 Nichols, quoted in Bratton, J. (1992) *Japanization at Work*, Basingstoke: Macmillan, p. 14.

80 Taylor, F. W. (1911) *The Principles of Scientific Management*, New York: Harper.

81 Fayol, H. (1949) *General and Industrial Management*, London: Pitman.

82 Kotter, J. P. (1982) *The General Managers*, New York: Free Press.

chapter 2
The social nature of work

chapter outline

- Introduction
- Work and non-work
- The development of work
- Work in organizations: an integration of ideas
- Gender and the sexual division of work
- Work less, live better? Managing the work–life balance
- Summary and end-of-chapter features
- Chapter case study 1: Service with a smile: McJobs in China
- Chapter case study 2: Home-working at Matherdom City Council

chapter objectives

After completing this chapter, you should be able to:

- explain the function and meaning of work
- explain the relationship between work and an individual's personal and social identity
- summarise the historical dimensions of work, pre-industry, the factory system, occupational changes, and the emergence of knowledge work in the virtual worksite
- identify some key strategic issues involved in designing work
- discuss the debates around issues of emotional work and work–life balance

Introduction

It is a paradox of life that its recognizable features are often the most difficult to understand. This observation is highly relevant to the topic of this chapter: work. Benjamin Franklin said that 'in this world nothing can be said to be certain, except death and taxes'. He was wrong. There is another certainty for most of us, and that is work. Whether defined in conventional economic terms as 'paid work' or defined more inclusively as a broad range of activities beyond the boundaries of paid employment, work is an almost inescapable feature of industrialized societies. Decisions about how paid work is organized and performed have created many different and contrasting types of work and employment relationships.

deindustrialization: a term to describe the decline of the manufacturing sector of the economy

occupation: a category of jobs that involve similar activities at different work sites

Since the Industrial Revolution, as factories have become more capital intensive, manual labour has undergone a transformation. Most traditional 'trade' or 'craft' jobs based on tacit knowledge have disappeared or have been 'deskilled', lessening control by craft workers. Factory work has increasingly been influenced by the 'scientific management' principle of 'one best way' of organizing particular work tasks. As employment shifted from manufacturing to the service sector, the process of **deindustrialization**, the principles of scientific management became incorporated into clerical labour and professional work. A trend throughout the twentieth century has been the growing presence of women in virtually all **occupations**. Another noticeable trend, especially since the 1990s, has been the global growth of flexible labour, a plethora of employment contracts that are part time, fixed term, short term or seasonal and create what has become known as 'precarious' employment.

The essence of being human is to engage in waged labour, but most people have little influence over how their labour is designed and performed. Organizations can be regarded as the architects of waged work, as it is within organizations that work is structured, jobs are designed and the employment relationship is formed.[1] Paid work for most individuals and families is the primary source of income that determines their standard of living. But it is important for more than economic reasons. Bolton and Houlihan's latest book, *Work Matters*,[2] juxtaposes both the bad and the good aspects of work. Waged work can be arduous, tedious, dirty, unhealthy and at times dangerous, but it can also bring connections and friendship, be a principal source of individuals' self-fulfilment and form part of their social identity. At the society level, how and where work is performed has consequences not only for the individuals who do it, but also for families and for the communities they live in.

Writing about the 'transformation of work' might be described as a cottage industry. Since the late 1970s, many books and research articles have been published, offering optimistic and pessimistic accounts of the effects of globalization and technological change on the nature of work. The optimistic scenario focuses on the liberating effect of information technology. Andre Gorz in 1982 predicted 'the liberation of time and the abolition of work' (ref. 3, p. 1). For more than a decade, Gorz set the trend for polemical 'future of work' books.[5–12] More recently, Jeremy Rifkin has argued that sophisticated 'Information Age' technologies are 'freeing up' the talent of men and women to create social capital in local communities.[4] Similarly, Microsoft's Bill Gates has argued that computers allow us to increase leisure time.[6] Both Rifkin and Gates write very persuasively, and their material has reached a wide audience.

Critical scholarship offers strikingly different accounts of work found in the Information Age rhetoric and captures the realities of lower-skilled work. Such accounts argue that the latest idiom of **flexibility** creates regimes that lead to the intensification of work, deskilling, tighter managerial control over work activities, and work-based inequalities.[7–12] With a particular eye to the gendering of work, it is argued that 'Where the goal of most employers throughout the world is to get the work of one full-time male done for one part-time female at a fraction of the cost, talk of the new liberation from toil can sound offensive' (ref. 5, p. 752). There is a growing consensus that there is currently a shortage of 'decent' work, with 'good' work being the preserve of a privileged minority in the new 'labour aristocracy' found in the professional, high-tech and creative industries loosely defined as 'knowledge workers'.[2]

This chapter has a very bold objective: to explain the nature of work in advanced capitalist societies, and why the design of work is important to understanding behaviour in organizations. This requires us to trace the evolution of work from early capitalism to late modernity. We look at the historical dimension of work in the belief that present problems associated with work are an outcome of the past, and that the problems of the future are embedded in the social relations of work designed in the present. The broader context of work provides an essential background for understanding the connection between work, identity, work and private life, and behavioural decisions in the workplace, and the implications for managing the employment relationship.

Work and non-work

'What kind of work do you do?' is such a classic question that it is repeatedly asked in social conversation. This question is significant because it underscores the fact that paid work – employment – is generally considered to be a central defining feature of our identity. It is also one important means by which we judge others. Adults with paid jobs usually name their occupation by way of an answer, but we can see this question in a wider sense too. It invites us to explore the nature of work in relation to time, space and **social structure**.

Consider this everyday scene in any Western town or city. It is 2 o'clock in the afternoon, and a neighbourhood park is busy with adults and children enjoying themselves. Some are walking quickly through the park, perhaps going back to their office or store after their lunch break. A city employee is pruning roses in one of the flower beds. Near the bandstand, three musicians are playing a saxophone, a clarinet and a violin. Two people are playing tennis. Others are watching young children play. A man sitting on a bench is reading a book, a woman is using a mobile

---

Many predictions have been made about 'new' technology deskilling workers but, on the other hand, liberating people from mundane work, and some even suggest that technology can create a 'leisure' society. What is your own view of the effects of information technology on work? Is it liberating or a curse?

stop reflect

flexibility: action in response to global competition, including employees performing a number of tasks (functional flexibility), the employment of part-time and contract workers (numerical flexibility), and performance-related pay (reward flexibility)

social structure: the stable pattern of social relationships that exist within a particular group or society

phone, and a teenager is completing a printed form. This scene draws attention to the blurred boundary between work and non-work activity. It gives us an entry point for answering the question, 'What is work?'

If we try to define some of these individual activities as work, the confusion and ambiguity about the meaning of work will become apparent. For example, the people walking back to their offices or to the shops might prune the roses in their gardens at the weekend, but they are unlikely to see the task in the same way as the gardener who is employed to do tasks such as pruning. The three musicians might be playing for amusement, or they might be rehearsing for an evening performance for which they will be paid. An amateur who plays tennis for fun and fitness does not experience or think of the game in the same way as a professional tennis player. Similarly, a parent keeping an eye on a child playing does not experience child-minding in the same way as a professional nanny. The person using the mobile phone might be talking to a friend, but she could be, say, a financial adviser phoning a client. The person filling in the form might be applying for a student grant, or a clerical worker catching up with an overdue job during his lunch hour. We can see from these examples that work cannot be defined simply by the activities that are carried out.

So what is work, exactly? 'Work' can be contrasted with 'labour'. According to Williams, labour has a 'strong medieval sense of pain and toil' (ref. 13, p. 335), and 'work' can be distinguished from 'occupation', which is derived from a Latin word meaning 'to occupy or to seize' (ref. 14, p. 2). The terms 'work', 'occupation' and 'job' have become interchangeable: work is not just an activity, something one *does*, but something a person *has*.[3] Conventionally, to 'have worked' or to 'have a job' is to use a place (or space) and sell time.

A substantial number of people have an *instrumental* orientation to work. They work for economic rewards in order to do non-work or leisure activity that they 'really enjoy'. For these people, life begins when work ends. Different occupations provide different levels of pay, so those doing them have different life chances and opportunities in terms of health, education, leisure pursuits and quality of life. Among people who 'have work', it is not simply the case that people need to work in order to have enough money to live on. People do paid work to earn money to acquire 'consumer power'. Thus, paid work for many is a means to an end – commodity consumption (buying designer clothes, fast cars, mobile phones and so on) or social consumption (such as drinking, dining out and holidaying). The central differentiating feature between people 'out of work' and those 'in work' is that the latter have much higher levels of consumer power and more choice about their lifestyle.

However, pay is only part of the equation. Research suggests that many people do paid work not primarily for extrinsic rewards (such as pay), but for the intrinsic rewards that work can bring, such as self-esteem, friendship, enjoyment and the social purpose of work. Traditionally, people occupying higher positions in an organization's hierarchy obtain more prestige and self-esteem than those in lower positions, and most people get satisfaction from participating in activities that demonstrably contribute to human well-being.[15,16]

We can begin to understand the complexity of work and its social ramifications by exploring the following definition:

> Work refers to physical and mental activity that is carried out to produce or achieve something of value at a particular place and time; it involves a degree of obligation and explicit or implicit instructions, in return for pay or reward.

This definition draws attention to some central features of work.[17] First, the most obvious purpose of work is an economic one. The notion of 'physical and mental'

**stop
reflect**

Write down your own definition of 'work'. To help you, consider a chef preparing a meal at a five-star hotel, and the same chef going home and preparing the family meal. Are both activities 'work'?

plate 7 Work in the service sector often requires workers to provide more than physical labour. Jobs such as flight attendants, shop assistants and waiting at tables require workers to manage their feelings in order to create a publicly observable facial display: what Hochschild calls 'emotional labour'.

Source: Getty Images

and 'value' suggests that the activities of both a construction worker and a computer systems analyst can be considered as work. The 'mental activity' also includes the commercialization of human feeling, or what is called 'emotional labour'.

Second, work is structured spatiality – how social life is organized geographically – and by time, and people's spatial embedding shapes work and management practices.[18] Throughout most of the twentieth century, work was typically carried out away from home and at set periods of the day or night. Thus 'place and time' locates work within a social context. However, in advanced capitalist economies, there are new expectations of spatial mobility and temporal flexibility.[19,20] The mass timetable of the '8 to 5' factory world, of the '9 to 5' office world and of recreational Sundays has given way to a flexi-place, flexi-time world. The Internet means that the timing of the working day may be shaped by working times in a number of time zones.

Third, work always involves social relations between people: between employer and employee, between co-workers, between management and trade unions, and between suppliers and customers. Social relations in the workplace can be cooperative or conflictual, hierarchical or egalitarian. When a parent cooks dinner for the family, he or she does tasks similar to those performed by a cook employed by a hospital to prepare meals for patients. However, the social relations involved are quite different. Hospital cooks have more in common (in this sense) with factory or office workers than with parents, because their activities are governed by rules and regulations. They accept 'instructions' from the employer or the employer's agent, a manager. Obviously, then, it is not the nature of the activity that determines whether it is considered 'work', but rather the nature of the social relations in which the activity is embedded. Thus, to be 'in work' is to have a definite relationship with some other who has control of the time, place and activity.

Finally, work is remunerated (that is, there is a reward for it). There are two types of reward, **extrinsic** and **intrinsic**. The worker provides physical effort and/or mental application, and accepts fatigue and the loss of control over his or her time. In return, the extrinsic work rewards that he or she usually receives consist (primarily) of wages and bonuses. The intrinsic rewards he or she might get from the job include status and recognition from his or her peers.

extrinsic reward: a wide range of external outcomes or rewards to motivate employees

intrinsic reward: inner satisfaction following some action (such as recognition by an employer or co-workers) or intrinsic pleasures derived from an activity (such as playing a musical instrument for pleasure)

Go to the following websites for more information on employment trends: in Britain (www.statistics.gov.uk), Canada (www.statcan.ca/start.html and the Canadian Labour Force Development Board www.hrmguide.net/canada/), the European Union (www.eurofound.europa.eu/eiro), the USA (www.bls.gov and www.hronline.com, South Africa (www.statssa.gov.za) and Brazil (www.ibge.gov.br/english/)

weblink

Although our definition helps us to identify key features of work, it is too narrow and restrictive. First, not all work, either physical or mental, is remunerated. We cannot assume that there is a simple relationship in which 'work' means a paid employment or occupation, 'real' work that is remunerated. Our definition obscures as much as it reveals. Most people would agree that some activities that are unpaid count as work. This work can be exhilarating or exhausting. Some of it is household-based work – cooking, child rearing, cleaning and so on – and some of it is done voluntarily, for the good of society – for instance, working for the Citizen's Advice Bureau. The activities that are done in the course of this unpaid or 'hidden' work are identical to those in some paid jobs, such as working in a nursery or advising people on their legal rights. Is it fair to exclude it simply because it is not paid?

Furthermore, whether an activity is experienced as work or non-work or leisure is dependent on social relations, cultural conditions, social attitudes and how various activities are perceived by others. So, for example, 'an active woman, running a house and bringing up children, is distinguished from a woman who works: that is to say, takes paid employment' (ref. 13, p. 335). Historically, unpaid work is undertaken disproportionately by one-half of the population: women. This book concentrates on paid work, and as a consequence we largely omit the critically important area of women's unpaid work in the household, but that is not to suggest that we see it as unimportant.

Second, our definition of paid work says little about how employment opportunities are shaped by gender, ethnicity, age and abilities or disabilities. For example, when women do have access to paid work, they tend to receive less pay than men doing similar work. Women are disproportionately represented in paid work that involves tasks similar to those they carry out in their domestic life – catering, nursing, teaching, clerical and retail employment. Ethnic and racially defined minorities experience chronic disadvantage in paid work because of racism in organizations and in recruitment. The likelihood of participating in paid work varies with age and certain types of work. For example, young people are disproportionately represented in more physically demanding paid work. Disabled adults, especially disabled young adults, experience higher levels of unemployment and under-employment than do those who are able bodied.[21]

Third, paid work can be dangerous and unhealthy, but the hazards are not distributed evenly. Manual workers face more work-related hazards, and have more accidents at work, than do (for example) office workers. It has been argued that this unequal distribution of work-related accidents is not only related to the risks the individuals face, but is also influenced by **values** and economic pressures.

value: a collective idea about what is right or wrong, good or bad, and desirable or undesirable in a particular culture

values: stable, long-lasting beliefs about what is important in a variety of situations

Our approach to understanding the issue of inequality surrounding work involves an analysis of the differential treatment of people based on class, gender and race. We need to look at who does what job, analysing the social and sexual division of labour. We need to consider what sort of occupations there are, and who exercises power or control over the social institutions.

Fourth, our definition obscures an important element of the employment relationship: the *psychological contract*.[22–25] The 'psychological contract' is a metaphor that captures a wide variety of largely unwritten expectations and understandings of the two parties (employer and employee) about their mutual obligations. Denise Rousseau defines it as 'individual beliefs, shaped by the organization, regarding terms of an exchange agreement between individuals and their organization' (ref. 25, p. 9). Most commentators view the concept as a two-way exchange of perceived promises and obligations. The concept has been around since the early 1960s, but in recent years it has become a 'fashionable' framework to support the development of more nuanced understandings of large and small organization employment relationships.[26] In Chapter 5, we examine this contemporary concept more fully. As we discuss more fully below and throughout the book, work shapes the employment relationship, the behaviour of all employees, and the relations between men and women inside and outside the workplace, and it has a significant bearing upon personal identity, fulfilment and social life.[27,28]

The development of work

Do you think that managers need to manage the employment relationship differently for knowledge workers and for manual industrial workers? Why and how?

stop reflect

Industrial Revolution: the relatively rapid economic transformation that began in Britain in the 1780s. It involved a factory- and technology-driven shift from agriculture and small cottage-based manufacturing to manufacturing industries, and the consequences of that shift for virtually all human activities

the economy: the social institution that ensures the maintenance of society through the production, distribution and consumption of goods and services

To what extent does a 'good' or 'bad' work design depend on which approach we use and which theorist we believe?

stop reflect

The structure of the labour market and paid work is not static: it reflects patterns of substantial change in the ways in which work is organized in specific industrial sectors. This is the essence of industrialization and a new emerging form of life – modernity. In this section, we trace the emergence of new work forms, starting with the **Industrial Revolution** (around 1780–1830) in Britain and finishing with a look at employment in what has been called 'post-industrial' work.

We provide this brief historical overview of work because, in our view, it provides a perspective on contemporary work issues and problems, which often result from decisions made in the past. Additionally, when we look at how work forms have developed, it becomes apparent that most 'new' work forms have deep historical roots. Contemporary management gurus might claim to have 'discovered' the importance of informal work-related learning, but such a mode of learning was important in the apprenticeship system of pre-industrial Europe. Similarly, that 'virtual' home-based work reduces the need for office space and costs was well understood by employers in the eighteenth century who operated the 'putting-out' system of home-working discussed below. In effect, these claims of 'new' or 'innovative', when viewed through a historical lens, might be a rediscovery of past practices that had been forgotten or abandoned.

Before we retrace the organization of work in **the economy**, we need to take a moment to make some general observations and highlight some challenges that this task presents. The history of work emphasizes that work is a social activity, not an individual one. Even those who work alone do so within a socially constructed network of relations among people associated with the pursuit of economic activity. History tends to contradict the suggestion that divisions on the basis of class, gender and race are systematic features created by, and found solely in, industrial capitalism. The social inequality of work, however, long predates the rise of capitalism. The history of industrial capitalism fosters the image of work as a predominantly male activity, separate from, and unrelated to, the home. Again, this is historically atypical: 'home and the place of work have always been, and still are, intimately connected by a seamless web of social inter-dependence' (ref. 29, p. 46).

Studying work and organizational forms from a historical perspective is a challenge for a number of reasons. By its very nature, such an exercise involves a compression of time periods and of different ways of organizing work. As Eric Hobsbawm wrote, 'The past is a permanent dimension of the human consciousness, an inevitable component of institutions, values and other patterns of human society (ref. 30, p. 10). The problem for social theorists is to avoid presenting the emergence of new work forms as a coherent, orderly and inevitable process of change.

Looking back from the vantage point of the early twenty-first century, it might seem reasonable to talk of the emergence of the factory, or of new forms of management control. But, as others have pointed out, the development of new work forms and social relations took place piecemeal, sporadically and slowly – and frequently they were resisted. Many features of work in the pre-industrial economy (the period before 1780) survived until late into the nineteenth and twentieth centuries, and similarly many twentieth work forms survive in the early twenty-first century. When we outline general trends, this not only compresses wide variations and collapses time periods, but also attaches a coherent pattern to these changes, which they did not show in reality.[31,32]

With this caveat, the rest of this section examines pre-industrial work, the transition to factory forms of work, the significance of concentrated production, the rise of trade unions and the interventions of the state.[30]

Pre-industrial work

In the middle of the eighteenth century, the most striking feature of the economy in Europe was the importance of agriculture as a basic human activity. Manufacturing operated on a small scale, employed labour-intensive methods and used little fixed capital. Agricultural and industrial work was characterized by low productivity. Population growth created an ever-growing class of landless labourers who were compelled to relocate to towns and sell their **labour power** to survive. The human movement to the new cities was critical for industrial capitalism to develop. As Max Weber explained, 'only where … workers under the compulsion of the whip of hunger, offer themselves' to employers does capitalism develop.[33]

Before 1780, the English economy was characterized by regulation. The central government intervened in the economy. The Statute of Artificers of 1563, for example, set the level of wages and conditions of employment, regulated the mobility of labour (as the government did during the Second World War, 1939–45), and protected and promoted, by force if necessary, domestic manufacturing and trade. In the towns, craft guilds regulated all activities related to their trade, including apprenticeship training, wages and prices, and standards of work.

Away from the town-based guilds, the rural-based **putting-out system** was a feature of the pre-Industrial Revolution manufacturing of woollen garments and many branches of metal working. The putting-out system was a decentralized method of manufacturing that, in the case of producing woollen cloth for example, involved the various processes of combing, spinning and weaving the wool usually being performed by different workers in their cottages. Such a form of work organization had profound consequences for the social organization of work and the nature of workers' reactions to the Industrial Revolution:

> It could not be used in industries requiring bulky plant and power-driven machinery. Neither was it suitable for crafts demanding a high degree of skill or which needed close supervision … Even when technical conditions were favourable to the use of out-workers, high costs of distribution and losses arising from pilfering and fraud by the workers were serious weaknesses. (ref. 34, p. 102)

Thus, the putting-out system, a pre-modern variant of home-working, contained considerable rigidities and inefficiencies, which were apparent when markets expanded and there was a need for large-scale manufacturing.

Gender-based patterns of work predate industrial capitalism. In the pre-industrial European family, both men and women produced goods for the household and were also engaged in paid work as part of the putting-out system, but depending on local norms and customs, there were 'rather strict ideas about women's work and men's work within the specific community' (ref. 35, p. 55). Moreover, work was 'a social activity circumscribed by custom and traditions that went deeper than the cash nexus' (ref. 29, p. 52), and work and family life were not regarded as separate spheres.

Factory-based work

The traditional work rhythms and practices of pre-industrial society gave way to the specialization and discipline of the **factory system**. We can describe the Industrial Revolution as a fundamental change in the structure of the economy,

labour power: the potential gap between a worker's capacity or potential to work and its exercise

putting-out system: a pre-industrial, home-based form of production in which the dispersed productive functions were coordinated by an entrepreneur

factory system: a relatively large work unit that concentrated people and machines in one building, enabling the specialization of productive functions and, at the same time, a closer supervision of employees than did the pre-industrial putting-out system. Importantly, the factory system gave rise to the need for a new conception of time and organizational behaviour

Work and Society: Were socialist firms inefficient?

In a study published over two decades ago, Michael Burawoy asked a provocative question: 'Can state socialist firms be as efficient as capitalist firms?' To answer this question, he and a colleague, Janos Lukacs, studied two machine shops – one in the USA (which they called Allied) and one in Hungary (which they called Banki). Their answer may surprise some readers. In the conclusion to their analysis of the two firms, Burawoy and his co-investigator offered the following summary of their key ideas:

> We have argued that the technical efficiency at Banki's machine shop was greater than at Allied's. In comparison to Allied, Banki operators work as hard if not harder and produce higher quality work, norms are better adjusted to jobs, pressure for innovation is more continuous, planning on the shop floor is more effective, the external labor market is better able to tie rewards to skills and experience, and bureaucratic rules that interfere with production are more limited. (p. 734)

Among the rationales for this study was a belief that existing views of work in socialist societies were dominated by stereotypes. Burawoy and Lukacs hoped that their research would help readers move beyond these stereotypes towards a more accurate picture of work in the two kinds of society. Their article succeeds in unmasking some of the myths that have led to false or superficial accounts of the differences between capitalist and socialist ways of organizing work.

This is no small achievement. In the period after the Second World War, the war of ideology (the Cold War) between the West and the USSR made it difficult to engage in objective comparative analysis of different aspects of life in capitalist and socialist societies. Burawoy and Lukacs broke new ground in their efforts to demonstrate how such research ought to be conducted.

Two features of their research stand out as particularly noteworthy. Both Burawoy and Lukacs spent time working at the machine shops they studied. As a result, they offer detailed accounts of what was actually happening on the shop floor. An accurate description of what is happening in two different contexts is a necessary element of high-quality comparative research.

But an accurate and detailed description of social reality is not the only strength of this particular research study. Burawoy and Lukacs also devote considerable attention to the question of causal mechanisms. Put differently: not only do they describe *how* the two patterns of work organization vary, but they also develop an explanation of *why* the two patterns of work organization vary. For example, a key difference between the two firms was the willingness of workers and local management to innovate. In the socialist firm levels of innovation were relatively high, while in the capitalist firm levels of innovation were relatively low. How do Burawoy and Lukacs explain this counter-intuitive finding?

They argue that, as a division of a large multinational company, the capitalist firm was forced to adhere to strict rules for organizing production imposed by its corporate headquarters. The capitalist firm had to produce a predetermined number of engines of a specified type, and there was no incentive to innovate. For the socialist firm, however, there was an incentive to innovate. There was some pressure to reduce over time the amount workers would be paid for a specified output (to 'tighten' production norms). However, production norms would be relaxed if management introduced 'New machines or new products' (p. 729). The prospect of looser production norms appealed to both management and workers. As a result, there were higher levels of innovation in the socialist firm. This incentive for innovation is evident in other socialist firms as well: 'in the Hungarian steel industry,' Burawoy and Lukacs note, 'managers [could] more than double their income through sponsoring innovations' (p. 729).

One may question the causal analysis offered by Burawoy and Lukacs, and suggest other possible causes of the innovations they observed in the socialist firm. Perhaps, for example, this willingness to innovate reflected local craft traditions that existed before the industrial revolution and before the socialist takeover of Hungary. It would also be instructive to look at one of Toyota's machine shops to understand how the Japanese system supports or fails to support innovation.

stop! This article encourages you to examine your assumptions about the superiority of particular ways of organizing work. Many successful businesses assumed that their success would last for ever. They assumed further that their approach to organizing work was superior to all others. Can you think of once-successful companies whose current difficulties stem in part from complacency with regard to the organization of work? How might successful companies avoid the trap of complacency?

Sources and further information

Burawoy, M. and Lukacs, J. (1985) 'Mythologies of work: a comparison of firms in state socialism and advanced capitalism', *American Sociological Review*, **50**(6), pp. 723–37.

Harvard Business Review on Manufacturing Excellence at Toyota, Boston, MA: Harvard Business School Press, 2008.

Ragin, C. (1994) *Constructing Social Research*, Thousand Oaks, CA: Pine Forge Press.

Note: This feature was written by David MacLennan, Assistant Professor at Thompson Rivers University, BC, Canada.

in which the capitalists' pursuit and accumulation of profit guided the mode of organizing work, harnessing technology and determining the social relations of work. The change was characterized by the rise of the factory, a combination of power technology and specialized machines with specialized occupations. The significance of the concentration of workers lay in the potential for extending the division of labour, installing machines, regulating the flow of raw materials, and controlling and moulding workers' behaviour to meet the specific needs of large-scale production.

division of labour: the allocation of work tasks to various groups or categories of employee

Here, the focus is on the **division of labour** within the factory organized by the owner. The factory offered the opportunity to improve each specialized task through the use of innovative technology, more than was possible with the decentralized putting-out system: 'The very division of labour … prepared the ground from which mechanical invention could eventually spring,' wrote one historian (ref. 36, p. 145). The factory also enabled a tighter control of the work in process than was possible with the domestic system. With the putting-out system, it was difficult to control the behaviour of cottage-based workers because the employer had 'no way of compelling his [sic] workers to do a given number of hours of labour; the domestic weaver or craftsman was master of his time, starting and stopping when he [sic] desired' (ref. 37, p. 59). The factory system offered new opportunities for controlling the pace and quality of work by the 'discipline of mechanization' – the actual speed of the machine – and by a hierarchy of control over the work in process.

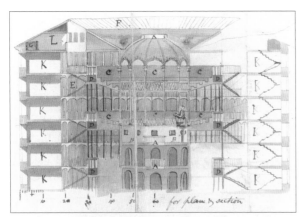

figure 2.1 The panopticon building

Historians have debated the role of technology in factory work organization. For example, it is argued that the origins of management within capitalist production lie not in the extended division of labour created by technical developments, but in the desire for social control on the part of capitalists, so that levels of exploitation could be increased.[38] Factories were not the inevitable results of technical change, nor were they the inexorable results of the search for simple efficiency. The architecture of the new factories had much in common with prisons. Jeremy Bentham coined the term 'panopticon' in 1816 to describe a circular building that could provide 'hierarchical observation' and 'normalizing judgement' (Figure 2.1). Observing Victorian architecture and Bentham's idea of a panopticon, the twentieth-century philosopher Michel Foucault asked, 'Is it surprising that prison resembles factories, schools, barracks, hospitals, which all resemble prisons?' (ref. 33, p. 30). The suggestion is that the factory, with its specialization and logical flows of processes, provided capitalists with a formal role as managers or coordinators. An alternative interpretation for the new forms of organizing work emphasizes the inadequacy of the family-based putting-out system in the face of expanding markets.[39]

The new factory system transformed the social organization of work. Factories needed a disciplined workforce. In this lay another key development associated with factory-based work – the shaping of workers' behaviour based on new concepts of commitment and time. In the early period of industrialization, changing workers' behaviour had a number of aspects: both entering the factory itself, and the **work ethic**. Workers, particularly men, were reluctant to enter the factories, with their unaccustomed rules and discipline, because they 'lost their birthright,

work ethic: a set of values that stresses the importance of work to the identity and sense of worth of the individual and encourages an attitude of diligence in the mind of the people

These days, people increasingly expect businesses to be open all hours – yet many companies are having to lay off workers as a result of a downturn in the global economy. As a result, staff are under increasing pressure to deliver more and work harder. Does the law need to intervene?

The European Union Working Time Directive states that working hours should not exceed 48 hours per week, which is causing problems in the UK, as the National Health Service struggles to comply with this rule and reduce doctors' working hours without compromising on care (1). Across the Channel in France, the much-vaunted 35 hour working week,

introduced in 2000, has effectively been abolished under a new law passed in 2008 allowing companies to 'strike individual deals with unions on working hours and overtime'(2). Canada is grappling with similar issues as it considers whether middle managers (who are currently 'not covered by labour standards legislation'(3)) should be offered protection.

What do *you* think? What role should the law, and trade unions, play in determining working conditions? Should these laws apply equally to all job types? Are there any cases where 'long hours come with the territory?'(3).

Sources: (1) 'Doctors warn over working rules', BBC news online, May 27, 2009. (2) 'MPs scrap France's 35-hour week', BBC news online, July 24, 2008. (3) Gate, V. (2005) 'Worn-out middle managers may get protection: Labour Code review could expand reach', *Globe and Mail*, January 3, p. B1.

independence' (ref. 40, p. 51). The majority of workers were women and children, who were more pliant and easier to manage.

Once in the factory, the employers had to develop 'appropriate' and 'responsible' behaviour that met the needs of the new work regime. This involved the management instilling in workers attitudes of obedience to factory regulations and punctuality. What the employers required was a 'new breed of worker' whose behaviour reacted favourably to the inexorable demands of the pace-setting machine, factory rationality and the 'tyranny of the clock'. The process took several generations: 'by the division of labour; the supervision of labour; fines; bells and clocks; money incentives; preaching and schooling; the suppression of fairs and sports – new labour habits were formed, and a new time-discipline was imposed' (ref. 41, p. 90). From the preoccupation with workers' work motivation and behaviour, there eventually emerged a specialized branch of management: personnel, or human resource management.

Taylorism and Fordism

In this section, we turn to what others call 'classical' work organization – Taylorism and Fordism. They are considered classical partly because they represent the earliest contributions to modern management theory, but they are also classical because they identify ideas and issues that keep occurring in contemporary organizational behaviour and management literature, although writers now tend to use a different vocabulary.[42] We will now consider each of these influential classical approaches to work organization.

Taylorism

The American Frederick W. Taylor (1856–1915) pioneered the scientific management approach to work organization, hence the term **Taylorism**. Taylor developed his ideas on work organization while working as superintendent at the Midvale Steel Company in Pennsylvania, USA. Taylorism represents both a set of management practices and a system of ideological assumptions.[27] The autonomy (freedom from control) of craft workers was potentially a threat to managerial control. For the craft worker, the exercise of control over work practices was closely linked to his personality, as this description of 'craft pride', taken from the trade journal *Machinery* in 1915, suggests:

plate 8 The First World War (1914-18) saw large numbers of women finding employment in the munitions and engineering factories.

Source: Nick Hedges

Taylorism: a process of determining the division of work into its smallest possible skill elements, and how the process of completing each task can be standardized to achieve maximum efficiency. Also referred to as scientific management

[The craftsman] is engaged in tasks where the capacity for original thought is exercised: he has refined and critical perceptions of the things pertaining to his craft. His work creates a feeling of self-reliance ... he lives a full and satisfying life. (ref. 43, p. 97)

As a first-line manager, Taylor not surprisingly viewed the position of skilled shop-floor workers differently. He was appalled by what he regarded as inefficient working practices and the tendency of his subordinates not to put in a full day's work, what Taylor called 'natural soldiering'. He believed that workers who did manual work were motivated solely by money – the image of the 'greedy robot' – and were too stupid to develop the most efficient way of performing a task – the 'one best way'. The role of management was to analyse 'scientifically' all the tasks to be undertaken, and then to design jobs to eliminate time and motion waste.

Taylor's approach to work organization and employment relations was based on the following five principles:

- maximum job fragmentation
- separate planning and doing
- separate 'direct' and 'indirect' labour
- a minimization of skill requirements
- a minimization of handling component parts and material.

The centrepiece of scientific management is the separation of tasks into their simplest constituent elements – 'routinization of work' (the first principle). Most manual workers were viewed as sinful and stupid, and therefore all decision-making functions had to be removed from their hands (the second principle). All preparation and servicing tasks should be taken away from the skilled worker (direct labour), and, drawing on Charles Babbage's principle, performed by unskilled and cheaper labour (indirect labour, in the third principle). Minimizing the skill requirements to perform a task would reduce the worker's control over work activities or the labour process (the fourth principle). Finally, management should ensure that the layout of the machines on the factory floor minimized the movement of people and materials to shorten the time taken (the fifth principle).

While the logic of work fragmentation and routinization is simple and compelling, the principles of Taylorism reflect the class antagonism that is found in employment relations. When Taylor's principles were applied to work organization, they led to the intensification of work: to 'speeding up', 'deskilling' and new techniques to control workers, as shown in Figure 2.2. And since gender, as we have discussed, is both a system of classification and a structure of power relations, it should not surprise us that Taylorism contributed to the shift in the gender composition of engineering firms. As millions of men were recruited into the armed forces for the First World War (1914–18), job fragmentation and the production of standardized items such as rifles, guns and munitions enabled women 'dilutees' to be employed in what had previously been skilled jobs reserved exclusively for men.[43]

> Can you think of jobs in the retail and service sector that would support the charge that work systems in the modern workplace continue to be affected by neo-Taylorism?
>
> **stop reflect**

Some writers argue that Taylorism was a relatively short-lived phenomenon, which died in the economic depression of the 1930s.[44] However, others have argued that this view underestimates the spread and influence of Taylor's principles: 'the popular notion that Taylorism has been "superseded" by later schools of "human relations", that it "failed" ... represents a woeful misreading of the actual dynamics of the development of management' (ref. 45, p. 56). Similarly, others have made a persuasive case that, 'In general the direct and indirect influence of Taylorism on factory jobs has been extensive, so that in Britain job design and technology design have become imbued with neo-Taylorism' (ref. 10, p. 73).

A TAYLOR SYSTEM MACHINIST "UP-TO-DATE"

figure 2.2 A craft union response to Taylorism

Fordism

Henry Ford (1863–1947) applied the major principles of scientific management in his car plant, as well as installing specialized machines and adding a crucial innovation to Taylorism: the flow-line principle of assembly work. This kind of work organization has come to be called **Fordism**. The moving assembly line had a major impact on employment relations. It exerted greater control over how workers performed their tasks, and it involved the intensification of work and labour productivity through ever-greater job fragmentation and short task-cycle times. In 1922, Henry Ford stated his approach to managing shop-floor workers: 'The idea is that man … must have every second necessary but not a single unnecessary second' (ref. 46, p. 33).

The speed of work on the assembly line is determined by the technology itself rather than by a series of written instructions. Management's control of the work process was also enhanced by a detailed time and motion study inaugurated by Taylor. Work study engineers attempted to discover the shortest possible task-cycle time. Recording job times meant that managers could monitor more closely their subordinates' effort levels and performance. Task measurement therefore acted as the basis of a new structure of control.

Fordism is also characterized by two other essential features. The first was the introduction of an interlinking system of conveyor lines that fed components to different work stations to be worked on, and the second was the standardization of commodities to gain economies of scale. Thus, Fordism established the long-term principle of the mass production of standardized commodities at a reduced cost.

Ford's production system was, however, not without its problems. Workers found the repetitive work boring and unchallenging, and their job dissatisfaction was expressed in high rates of absenteeism and turnover. In 1913, for example, the turnover of Ford workers was more than 50,000. The management techniques developed by Ford in response to these employment problems serve further to differentiate Fordism from Taylorism. Henry Ford introduced the 'five dollar day' – double the pay and shorter hours for those who qualified. Benefits depended on a factory worker's lifestyle being deemed satisfactory, which included abstaining from alcohol. Ford's style of paternalism attempted to inculcate new social habits, as well as new labour habits, that would facilitate job performance.

Fordism: a term used to describe mass production using assembly-line technology that allowed for greater division of labour and time and motion management, techniques pioneered by the American car manufacturer Henry Ford in the early twentieth century

Taylorism and Fordism became the predominant approaches to job design in vehicle and electrical engineering – the large-batch production industries – in the USA and Britain.[10,46]

Post-Fordism

As a strategy of organizing work and people, Taylorism and Fordism had their limitations. First, work simplification led to boredom and dissatisfaction, and tended to encourage adversarial relations and conflict, including frequent work stoppages. Second, Taylor-style work involves control and coordination costs. As specialization increases, so do indirect labour costs as more production planners, supervisors and quality control inspectors are employed. The economies associated with the division of labour tend to be offset by the diseconomies of management control costs.

Third, Taylorism and Fordism affect what might be called 'cooperation costs'. As management's control over the quantity and quality of workers' performance increases, workers experience increased frustration and dissatisfaction, which leads to a withdrawal of their commitment to the organization. The relationship between controller and controlled can deteriorate so much that it results in a further increase in management control. The principles of Taylorism and Fordism thus reveal a basic paradox, 'that the tighter the control of labour power, the more control is needed' (ref. 10, pp. 36–7). The adverse reactions to the extreme division of labour led to the development of new approaches to work organization that attempted to address these problems.

The 'human relations' movement attempted to address the limitations of Taylorism and Fordism by shifting attention to the perceived psychological and social needs of workers. The movement grew out of the Hawthorne experiments conducted by Elton Mayo in the 1920s. Mayo set up an experiment in the relay assembly room at the Hawthorne Works in Chicago, USA, which was designed to test the effects on productivity of variations in working conditions (lighting, temperature and ventilation). The Hawthorne research team found no clear relationship between any of these factors and productivity. However, the study led the researchers to develop concepts that might explain the factors affecting worker motivation. They concluded that more than just economic incentives and the work environment motivated workers: recognition and social cohesion were important too.

The message for management was also quite clear: rather than depending on management controls and financial incentives, it needed to influence the work group by cultivating a culture that met the social needs of workers. The human relations movement advocated various techniques such as worker participation and non-authoritarian supervisors, which would, it was thought, promote a climate of good (neo)-human relations in which the quantity and quality needs of management could be met. This largely forgotten history, which examined concepts such as atmosphere, informal structures and organizational climate, reminds us that twenty-first-century culturalist scholarship (see Chapter 12) is not a completely new development in the thinking about organizations.[47]

Criticisms of the human relations approach charged managerial bias and the fact that its advocates tended to play down the basic economic conflict of interest between the employer and employee. Critics pointed out that when the techniques were tested, it became apparent that workers did not inevitably respond as predicted. The human relations approach also neglects wider socioeconomic factors (see ref. 12 for an excellent critical analysis of this approach to work). Despite these criticisms, however, the human relations approach to job design began to have some impact on management practices in the post-Second World War environment of full employment.

In the 1970s, new approaches to work design stressed the principles of closure, whereby the scope of the job is such that it includes all the tasks to complete a product or process, and task variety, whereby the worker acquires a range of different skills so that job flexibility is possible and the worker can personally monitor the quantity and quality of the work. This thinking spawned new techniques such as 'job enrichment', which gave the worker a wider range of tasks to perform and some discretion over how those tasks were done. For example, in the context of a fast-food outlet, an employee's job would, instead of being limited to grilling burgers, be enlarged to grilling the burgers, preparing the salad, ordering the produce from the wholesaler and inspecting the quality of the food on delivery.

Some theorists have been critical of these new work designs. An influential study argues that although job enrichment techniques may increase job satisfaction and commitment, the key focus remains managerial control. Although post-Fordism work design strategies gave individuals or work groups a wider measure of discretion over their work, or 'responsible autonomy', the strategy is a 'tool of self-discipline' and a means of maintaining or even intensifying managerial control.

With the growth of call centres over the past decade, critical research has drawn attention to 'new' forms of Taylorism. It is alleged that sophisticated electronic eavesdropping on salesperson–client conversations, and peer group scrutiny, have created 'electronic sweatshops' or a form of 'electronic Taylorism'.[12,48–50]

Work teams and high-performance workplaces

The favoured work configuration over the last two decades has been team working. The focus on work teams has grown out of, drawn upon and sometimes reacted against Taylorism and Fordism.[42] The centrepiece of team working is functional flexibility, with members undertaking a wide range of tasks with a high degree of autonomy.

In the 1980s, Japanese work and employment practices were held up as a model for the struggling UK and North American manufacturing sectors.[51–55] The Japanese model has been a 'contested concept' in its description, interpretation and explanation.[56] Pioneering interpretations of the model identify three notable elements: flexibility, quality control and minimum waste.

Flexibility is achieved by arranging machinery in a group – what is known as 'cellular technology' – and by employing a multiskilled workforce. Thus, the work organization is the opposite of that of 'Taylorism': a generalized, skilled machinist with flexible job boundaries is a substitute for the specialized machinist operating one machine in one particular workstation. Higher-quality standards are achieved by making quality every worker's responsibility. Minimum waste, the third element of the Japanese model, is achieved by just-in-time techniques. As the name suggests, this is a hand-to-mouth mode of manufacture that aims to produce no more than the necessary components, in the necessary quantities, of the necessary quality and at the necessary time. Team working has a cultural and social dimension. The practices aim to generate social cohesion and a 'moral commitment' to common organizational goals. We examine work teams in more detail in Chapter 9.

The managerial mantra of the 1990s was flexibility, although various terms were used to describe these fashions in work organization: flexible specialization or 'flex-spec', 'lean production', 're-engineering' and 'high-performance work systems' are well established in the literature. In the late 1990s, Japan experienced slow economic growth, and thereafter the US model of work organization was again held up as the exemplar. The new debate focused on whether the high-performance workplace, comprising a combination of work and employment variables or 'bundles' of 'best' practices, can deliver comparative advantage.

Go to the 2004 Workplace Employee Relations Survey website www.berr.gov.uk for more information on trends in work organization

weblink

Post-industrial work

The 'Information Revolution', which we date from 1980 with the development of the silicon chip, marks, as does the Industrial Revolution 200 years earlier, a fundamental transformation of human activity. One theme running through this chapter has been the continuities as well as the discontinuities across time. There is no doubt that, for many people, paid work has changed profoundly during the Information Age, but these changes must be set in a historical context if we are to appreciate their significance and relevance.

Critical insight

As you study organizational behaviour, you should look at less orthodox material – expanding voices – as well as the established experts in the field. Leslie Salzinger's book *Genders in Production* is an example of the kinds of other voice it is useful to consider.[57] Through case studies of employment and management in four different transnational factories, the author provides a sophisticated analysis of gender relations in the workplace. She explains the variability and flexibility of concepts of femininity and masculinity, and the fact that they are context-dependent behaviours.

As Salzinger asserts, in a globalized world the creation of 'cheap labour' is central to the economic process. However, although the young women at the factories she studied are generally perceived to be intrinsically 'cheap, docile, and dextrous', she comments that 'Panoptimex, like all effective arenas of production, makes not only TVs but workers.'

Obtain a copy of Salzinger's book and read Chapter 2, 'Producing women – femininity on the line'. What does Salzinger mean when she states that Panoptimex makes not only TVs but also workers?

Knowledge work

knowledge work: paid work that is of an intellectual nature, non-repetitive and result-oriented, engages scientific and/or artistic knowledge, and demands continuous learning and creativity

The emergence of **knowledge work** – intellectual capital – and the 'knowledge worker' – employees who carry knowledge as a powerful resource which they, rather than the organization, own – is closely associated with the contemporary, sophisticated, Internet-based information technologies. Defining the notion of knowledge work and knowledge worker has proven problematic. Following Horwitz et al., however, we can say that knowledge work is characterized as 'ambiguity intensive', and a knowledge worker is an individual with the ability to communicate and apply professional knowledge, as well as manage other employees (see ref. 58, p. 31).

The nature of knowledge work is said to be fundamentally different from what we have traditionally associated with the 'machine age' and mass production, and hence it requires a different order of employment relations. It should not be confused with routine clerical work. It requires knowledge workers to learn a broad range of skills and knowledge, often with a focus around problems or customers, and to work in small groups or project teams to co-create new insights. It is also said to require a different employment relationship, with a psychological contract that has implications for employee commitment and career trajectory.

These differences in the nature of traditional work and knowledge work are spelled out in Table 2.1. In the Information Age, when an organization's wealth and ability to compete may exist 'principally in the heads of its employees' and human competitiveness can effectively 'walk out the gates' every day, it is not surprising that organizations are concerned with 'better' human resource practices and 'knowledge management' (ref. 59, p. 48). Information technology, new employment contracts and knowledge work have changed the 'spatiality' of work: some people do paid work at home, and others undertake more short-term work assignments as organizations reduce their 'core' employees and contract work out.[19] Critical accounts of contemporary work in advanced capitalist economies offer a counter-weight to the bullish management perspectives on the knowledge economy and provide data showing that the International Labour Organization's definition of 'decent work' remains elusive only for the privileged minority.[60,61] As European studies attest, there are too many businesses taking the 'low road' and striving for competitive advantage on the basis of a low-skill and low-pay workplace.[2]

table 2.1 The nature of traditional work and knowledge work

	Traditional work	**Knowledge work**
Skill/knowledge sets	Narrow and often functional	Specialized and deep, but often with diffuse peripheral focuses
Locus of work	Around individuals	In groups and projects
Focus of work	Tasks, objectives, performance	Customers, problems, issues
Skill obsolescence	Gradual	Rapid
Activity/feedback cycles	Primary and of an immediate nature	Lengthy from a business perspective
Performance measures	Task deliverables Little (as planned), but regular and dependable	Process effectiveness Potentially great, but often erratic
Career formation	Internal to the organization through training, development, rules and prescriptive career schemes	External to the organization, through years of education and socialization
Employee's loyalty	To organization and his or her career systems	To professions, networks and peers
Impact on company success	Many small contributions that support the master plan	A few major contributions of strategic and long-term importance

Source: adapted from Despres and Hiltrop (1995)[102] and Boud and Garrick (1999)[59]

Emotional work

With the growth of routinized service work, with its demands of customer sovereignty – such as fast food, tourism, hotels and call centres – new kinds of social relationship and aspects of the self have developed and come under scrutiny. As the service sector has grown in importance, there has, not surprisingly, been a growing interest in the embodied attributes and dispositions that are stereotypically feminine, such as patience, deference to the customer and a pleasant demeanour, associated with what sociologists call 'emotional labour'. Much has been written in recent years on how emotion is an important part of the effort–wage exchange, that workplaces in general have 'emotions',[62,63] and that 'strong' cultures strive to engender emotional energy, affection and even love for the organization (see Chapter 12).

Although the sociological analysis of workplace emotions is an expanding field of research, the classical sociological canons of Marx, Durkheim and Weber do contain important ideas about emotions. For instance, alienation engendered feelings of anger, and sentimentality was eliminated in bureaucracies gripped in the 'iron cage' of rationality (see Chapter 3). Modern critical scholarship emphasizes the servility of routine interactive workers within the service interface.[64]

It was the pioneering work of Arlie Hochschild that drew attention to the significance of social interaction as a crucial element of service provision. She considered emotional labour as part of the employment contract when 'the emotional style of offering the service is part of the service itself'.[65] Although servers in restaurants have always been trained to 'serve with a smile', there has been growing recognition that emotional labour is far more significant for a larger proportion than this of service employees, as management theorists emphasize 'customer service' as a vital aspect of business competitiveness. Emotional labour exists when workers are required, as part of the wage–effort bargain, to show emotions with the specific aim of causing customers or clients to feel and respond in a particular way. They might do this by verbal means – 'Good morning, sir/madam' – or non-verbal means, for example by smiling. Thus, the recent interest in emotional labour is focused on mobilizing emotions into the 'service' of the organization as an added dimension of the 'self' (see Chapter 4) that the organization can appropriate, as has traditionally occurred with physical and mental labour.[66]

It is important to understand that emotional labour, like physical and intellectual labour, is bought by the employer for a wage. It requires a specific set of attributes and behaviours, and it can be a potential source of stress and alienation. Emotional labour 'carries the potential for individuals to become self-estranged – detached from their own "real" feelings – which in turn might threaten their sense of their own identity' (ref. 15, p. 193). The embodied attributes and skills associated with emotional labour compromise a particular type of working-class masculine identity. Manual labour has traditionally been a key source of identity, self-esteem and power for many working-class men. Emotional labour, however, is antithetical to muscular masculine identity. A study by Nixon in 2009 suggests that unskilled unemployed male workers were psychologically mismatched to the demands of customer sovereignty.[67] He found that those men who had been employed in service jobs did not last long: 'I've got no patience with people basically. I can't put a smiley face on, that's not my sort of thing,' said one 24-year-old unskilled manual worker. Others said they disliked the pressure to 'chase customers', and found work at call centres involved 'Too much talking' (ref. 67, pp. 314–15). The seismic shifts associated with the 'new economy' appear to have eliminated not only particular types of jobs, but also a type of masculine identity.

Our brief history of work organization suggests that when an economy enjoys economic success, its work and management practices will often be regarded as a model by slower-growing economies.[68] Consistent with this prediction, European organizations adopted US management ideas for most of the twentieth century, and adopted the 'Japanese model' in the 1980s, including team working. The 2004 Workplace and Employee Relations Survey (WERS) provides data on how these work practices are applied in UK workplaces.

Much of the literature on 'new' forms of work simplifies the analysis to a polar comparison between 'traditional' Fordism and new 'post-Fordism' work team characteristics. But although it looks elegant to draw up lists of opposite characteristics, this is not a good reflection of reality.[69,70] We can today still witness old 'boring' work forms existing alongside new 'decent' work configurations. Work in post-industrial capitalism is still routinized in both the manufacturing and the service sectors. In this brave new world of work, task variety is low, skill requirements are low, security and dignity are low, and managerial control, reminiscent of Frederick Taylor's philosophy of a century ago, remains rule bound. All this suggests that the nature of work remains largely unchanged for millions of workers, that the design of work is not a smooth transition from one model to another, and that contemporary work regimes are most likely to resemble a hybrid configuration, with elements from the old work design and parts of the new.

stop reflect

A major theme of this section has been the continuities as well as the discontinuities across time in paid work. Can you see any similarities between knowledge work in home-based distributed environments and the putting-out system? Look at Plate 7 (page 43), showing a scene of customers and a server. What does the picture reveal about emotional labour? Have you ever been in a situation at work where you had to manage your feelings before customers? If so, what did it do to your sense of self?

weblink

Go to the following websites for more information and statistics on economic trends and gender relations in the workplace: www.statistics.gov.uk; www.eiro.eurofound.ie; www.un.org/womenwatch; www.isreview.org (search for Eleanor Burke Leacock)

Work in organizations: an integration of ideas

In discussing post-Fordism, we emphasized competing claims over whether new forms of work lead to an enrichment of work or the degradation of work. Managerial optimists argue that new work structures empower employees, and celebrate the claim that managerial behaviour has shifted its focus from 'control' to 'commitment'.[71] Critical analysts contend that some new work regimes are 'electronic sweatshops', and are basically a euphemism for work intensification. To capture the new realities of the modern workplace, critics often use the term 'McWorld' or '**McDonaldization**', meaning that a vast amount of work experience, especially for young people, women and workers of colour, involves menial tasks, part-time contracts, close monitoring of performance and entrenched job insecurity (for a good critical review of this trend, see refs 50 and 72–75).

In Figure 2.3, we draw together the developments in work and employment practices over the last 200 years, by highlighting four paradigms or distinctive approaches: craft/artisan, Taylorism/Fordism, neo-Fordism and post-Fordism. Work is shown to vary along two dimensions: the *variety of work* – the extent to which employees have an opportunity to do a range of tasks using their various skills and knowledge – and the *autonomy in work* – the degree of initiative that employees can exercise over how their immediate work is performed.

McDonaldization (also known as 'McWork' or 'McJobs'): a term used to symbolize the new realities of corporate-driven globalization that engulf young people in the twenty-first century, including simple work patterns, electronic controls, low pay and part-time and temporary employment

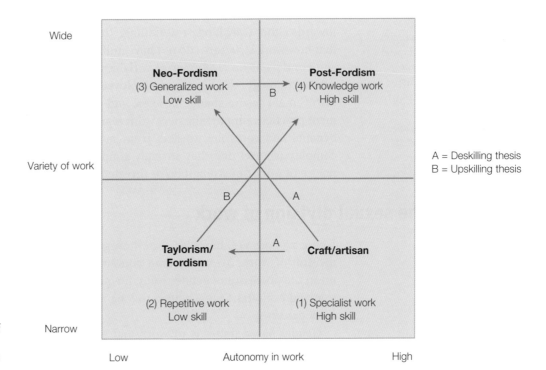

figure 2.3 Development of work organization and employment relationships

Here, *craft/artisan* means the types of work organization that are based on craft-based skills and often associated with a narrow range of specialized tasks, a high level of skill and a high degree of autonomy. Taylorism/Fordism means the adoption of basic scientific management principles and the assembly-line methods pioneered by Henry Ford, and **neo-Fordism** refers to a work configuration that has modified the core principles of Fordism through flexible working practices to fit contemporary operations. In contrast to the craft/artisan paradigm, the Taylorism/Fordism and neo-Fordism paradigms are often associated with a narrow variety of tasks, a low level of skill and a low degree of autonomy in work. **Post-Fordism**

neo-Fordism/post-Fordism: the development from mass production assembly lines to more flexible manufacturing processes refers to organizations that do not rely on the principles of Taylorism or Fordism, and is often associated with 'high-performance work systems', with self-management and with a high degree of autonomy in work.

As others have mentioned, the strength of this conceptual model is as a heuristic device – a teaching aid – to help us summarise the complex development of work organization and employment relations. The research on the trends in work design suggests that Taylorism and Fordism have dominated the managerial approaches to work organization.

In addition to the four broad classifications of work organization, the model shows two trends proposed by the proponents of the 'deskilling' and 'upskilling' theses. The deskilling thesis maintains that, in Western capitalist economies, there is a general trend in paid work towards a narrow variety of tasks and low autonomy; the arrows marked 'A' represent this trend in the diagram. The upskilling thesis suggests an opposite trend towards a wide variety of tasks and high autonomy in work; the arrows marked 'B' represents this trend. It is important to understand that different regimes of work organization affect the nature of the employment relationship, whether or not this is explicitly acknowledged in the writings of organizational theorists. For example, if work is reorganized to deskill or upskill employees, this will change the degree of interdependency, and typically the power dynamics, between the employer and employee.

To sum up, some of the more recent empirically based literature offers a context-sensitive understanding of the development of work, and rejects a general tendency towards either deskilling or upskilling. The 'context-sensitive' view makes the point that new work structures do not have uniform outcomes, but are likely to be 'mixed' and contingent on a number of variables, such as business strategy, the nature of new technology, the degree of employee involvement in decision making, union involvement in the change process, and the extent to which 'bundles' of employment practices support the new work regime. In sum, the identification of potential benefits and costs for workers from new work configurations provides a more complex picture, one that strongly supports the **hypothesis** that changes in the nature of work can strengthen or threaten the 'psychological contract'.

hypotheses: statements making empirically testable declarations that certain variables and their corresponding measure are related in a specific way proposed by theory

hypothesis: in search studies, a tentative statement of the relationship between two or more concepts or variables

Gender and the sexual division of work

Figure 2.3 does not, however, show how gender ideologies shape work or the sexual division of work. To understand contemporary issues of gender – by which we mean the processes of gender roles, inequalities in society and women's subordination and exploitation – we need to look at the historical developments of gender–work patterns.

Gender-based patterns of work and gender inequality were universal in early industrial capitalism. In 1838, over 70 per cent of factory textile workers were adult women and children. Family labour, with women and their children working together, was a feature of employment relations in the new factory system. The factory owner did not accept direct responsibility for the conditions of employment or supervision of the workforce, but subcontracted these people-management functions to an intermediary. Factory owners negotiated with the heads of families for the whole family unit. There is evidence that the worst conditions of employment under industrial capitalism existed in these circumstances. Child labour began at the age of 4 in some cases in order to oblige parents, but most child workers started between the ages of 7 and 10. An adult man entered the new textile factories with his family, and the 'fact that discipline was imposed on the children largely by their own parents made the harshness of the new disciplines socially tolerable' (ref. 76, p. 202).

After 1850, with the exception of waged work in domestic service and textiles, industrial capitalism tended to create a clear distinction between the paid work opportunities of women (particularly married women) and of men. With the spread of the factory system, the need for cheap labour power provided opportunities for working-class women to do wage work in areas unrelated to their former work in the home. Large-scale food-processing factories – for example, bakeries – were female dominated in the late nineteenth century. In working-class families, women often remained in the labour market to support the family income. When middle-class women married, they were primarily expected to withdraw from paid employment to take care of the house and children. Reinforcing the belief that work and family life were two separate spheres – the stereotypes of men as strong and competitive and women as frail and nurturing – began to emerge: 'images that depicted men as naturally suited to the highly competitive nineteenth-century workplace and women as too delicate for the world of commerce' (ref. 77, p. 21).

Gender-based patterns of work changed when war broke out in Europe in 1914. The First World War was the first 'mass' war in the sense that it required the mobilization of massive quantities of products and people. Whereas Napoleon waged war against Prussia in 1806 using no more than 1500 rounds of artillery shells, in 1917 the French munitions industry had to produce 200,000 shells a day: 'Mass war required mass production' (ref. 78, p. 45). It also made it necessary to rethink the social organization of work. As Britain mobilized 12.5 per cent of its able-bodied men for the armed forces, the government encouraged women to enter the munitions and engineering factories, and this led to a revolution in waged work for women outside the household. It resulted in several occupations turning permanently into female preserves, including offices, hotels, shops, cinemas and to a lesser extent transport. In other occupations, such as engineering, men were reabsorbed in 1919 and women went back to pre-war patterns of paid or unpaid work.

Did industrial capitalism segregate the home from work, and allocate women to the former and men to the latter? Gender-based patterns of work and family-located sites of work are forms that predate capitalism: they are not the results of social changes induced by capitalism. Women's work tended to be concentrated around six human activities that predate capitalism: to bear children, to feed them and other members of the family, to clothe the family, to care for the young and old when sick, to educate children, and to take care of the home.[35,79] Explanations for why some work was men's and some was women's are almost as various as the patterns of wages that have existed. In the pre-Industrial Revolution period, there is some evidence that women did a much greater variety of jobs, but even then gender influenced the allocation and reward of work. A disproportionate number of women undertook the most menial, poorly paid and domestically related jobs.

Evidence about work-related gender relations before the nineteenth century is sparse. Contemporary accounts emphasize that the gender division of work is socially constructed, and that work tended to be labelled female or male on the basis of socially changeable expectations about how to view, judge and treat the two sexes. Part of the long historical process of gender inequality at work can be explained by the activities of the pre-industrial craft guilds and the **trade unions**. The town-based craft guilds, the forerunners of trade unions, tended to

trade union: an organization whose purpose is to represent the collective interest of workers

Go to the following websites for more information on the history of trade unions and current statistics on trade union organization: www.tuc.org.uk; www.icftu.org; www.cosatu.org.za

weblink

be exclusively male oriented, with severe restrictions on women's membership. In the context of competitive pressure to reduce labour costs and the economic effect of female workers in terms of depressing wages, male-dominated trade unions worked hard to maintain or restore wage levels and traditional employment privileges.[80]

Trade union bargaining strategies developed gender-based occupational segregation. One function of trade unionism, according to one union leader, was 'to bring about a condition … where wives and daughters would be in their proper sphere at home, instead of being dragged into competition for livelihood against the great and strong men of the world' (ref. 81, p. 185). Prior to 1858, women participated in medicine quite widely, but thereafter, as in other traditional professions, the work became a male preserve. With the exception of midwifery and nursing, a combination of government legislation and male tactics excluded middle-class women from all medical practices.[82] Feminist critiques of the sociology of work have demonstrated in important ways the manner in which both the theory and practice of work and work behaviour have excluded women as subjects, as well as their experiences and voices.[83]

Married women were systematically removed from waged work after the initial phase of the Industrial Revolution. The new factory system proved beneficial to working-class women, particularly unmarried women, providing waged work outside the grossly exploitative decentralized putting-out system. Throughout the nineteenth century and well into the twentieth century, men managed to effectively exclude working-class and middle-class women from participating in many trade and professional occupations, by retaining old 'skills' or monopolizing new ones, using their professional privilege and power, using strategies of closure and demarcation, and encouraging the concepts of 'skill' and 'profession' to be seen as male property.[84]

In the twenty-first century, although the realities of workplaces have changed, ideas about them have lagged far behind.[85] Many Europeans and North Americans still believe in the 'traditional' male breadwinner/female home-keeper model, even though household lives and financial imperatives no longer reflect it. In Germany, for example, the traditional sense of family roles remains strong, and women who do paid work can be called *Rabenmutter*, meaning a raven mother. Commenting on German social values in 2006, Reiner Klingholz, head of the Berlin Institute for Population and Development, said, 'These old-fashioned ideas about the sexes aren't really part of mainstream German thought any more, but it's still embedded in the neurons of our brains that women have to stay home and take care of the children' (quoted in ref. 86).

Go to the following websites for more information and statistics on women employed in advanced capitalist societies: http://europa.eu/index_en.htm; www.statistics.gov.uk; www.iegd.org

weblink

Work less, live better? Managing the work–life balance

work–life balance: the interplay between working life, the family and the community, in terms of both time and space

discourse: a way of talking about and conceptualizing an issue, presented through concepts, ideas and vocabulary that recur in texts

The interplay between working life, the family and the community, often expressed as '**work–life balance**', is a 'hot' topic of debate and research that is receiving increasing attention from policy makers and managers.[87–89] The main message of the debate is that a balance between work and life is desirable, and that too much work has negative effects on private life – in effect, a more sophisticated version of the popular proverb 'All work and no play makes Jack a dull boy.' In spite of the spate of literature, for Warhurst and his colleagues, the current debate on work–life balance remains problematic both empirically and conceptually.[90] Empirical research does indeed reveal a significant degree of interest in many organizations, but data show a mismatch between the work–life balance **discourse** and the reality in most workplaces.

This gap is illustrated by the findings from WERS 2006. The European Union Social Charter of 1961 obliged Member States to ensure 'reasonable and weekly working hours', yet research indicates that British workers work the longest hours in the EU-15 Member States.[91] Not surprising, therefore, the UK labour market has been characterized as the 'long hours culture'.[92] Setting a limit on the number of hours an employee must work in a working day and week most directly affects the work–life balance.

Paid work	Life
Tasks	Child care
Projects	Housework
Deadlines	Elder care
Travel	Community activities
Meetings	Hobbies
Client demands	Holidays

figure 2.4 The notion of the work–life balance

plate 9 The interpenetration between work and life is most obvious in contemporary home-working, which allows professionals to engage in paid work and domestic activities in the same physical space, and perhaps even on occasion at the same time.

Source: Getty Images

The boundary between work and private life is influenced by flexible working arrangements, such as 'home-working'. UK survey data show that the incidence of 'home-working' increased 12 per cent between 1998 and 2004. Women were more likely than men to have access to home-working arrangements, yet home-working was slightly more prevalent in workplaces where women were not in the majority.[93] There are a number of possible causes for this, including inadequate child care provision, non-standard or precarious employment and perhaps, in more recent years, a 'flight to work' in a period of economic uncertainty.

The concept at the centre of the work–life balance debate is problematic. The notion of work–life balance has been defined as 'the relationship between the institutional and cultural times and spaces of work and non-work in societies where income is predominantly generated and distributed through labour markets' (ref. 94, p. 56). Warhurst et al. argue that the concept of work–life *balance* is based on a traditional, large-scale workplace model which presumes that paid work and life constitute two distinct spheres, separated by time and space (Figure 2.4).[90] This orthodox binary interpretation adopts a particular interpretation of labour under capitalism, viewing paid work as an encroachment on people's 'real' private life, particularly family life, and seeing it as something that therefore has to be contained. As the examples and case studies included throughout this book suggest, work can be boring and alienating – a 'blank patch' between morning and evening – unhealthy and at times dangerous. Yet work brings fulfilment and friendship, and people can potentially derive joy from it.[2] Work brings structure to people's lives, dignity and satisfaction, and is an important source of identity.

Warhurst's et al. premise is that the work–life interface is not best articulated as one of 'balance' because 'interpenetration' occurs between the two spheres.[90] This interpenetration between work and life is most obvious in contemporary home-working, which, through information and communication technology, allows professionals to engage in paid work and domestic activities in the same physical space and maybe at the same time. Thus, the concept of work–life balance, with its suggestions of a binary opposition between 'work' and 'life', does not indicate how the complex interplay of personal choice and constraints, competing interests and power relations, shapes the relationship between work and life.

People are what Anthony Giddens[95] has called 'knowledgeable agents' – that is, they construct perceptions of work and life – and through their agency they produce social practices, which can be translated into what Warhurst et al.[90] call 'work–life patterns'. These social patterns and practices that human beings construct relate to work, family activities, maintaining friendships and the pursuit of leisure activities. Naturally, depending on the individual's context, the way in which work–life patterns are experienced can vary markedly between individuals. The advocates of the work–life pattern approach identify four implications for researchers and discerning managers:

1. The focus of praxis proposes an analysis of actual work practices and the impact these have on work–life patterns. For example, if work is takes place in a fixed and unmovable location (for example, assembly-line work), work–life patterns are likely to exhibit a clear delineation between work and life.

2. Employment analysts and practitioners need to understand the structural constraints (economic, social and cultural resources) that fashion work–life patterns. For example, economic capital can buy additional time for work (for example, hiring a nanny) or life (for example, only part-time paid work); cultural (for example, education) and social (for example, extended family) resources also affect job opportunities and work–life choices and opportunities.

3. Lifestyles – values, beliefs and work-related perceptions – influence individual practices and work–life patterns. Max Weber first proposed a connection between lifestyle (religion and asceticism) and work–life patterns.[96] The lifestyle of artists, musicians or theatre actors, for example, might promote a fusing or 'amalgamation' of a work–life pattern. Thus, creative artists are more likely to regard 'work as life, and life as work' (ref. 90, p. 14). Neither is the notion of a fusing of a work–life pattern restricted to artistic labour. As Michelle Gillies, a recently unemployed professional who had been a promotion manager and producer in the Canadian broadcasting sector, said, 'My job was me. I spent 10 years so closely linked to what I did there that there were no lines separating the two' (quoted in ref. 97). Examples of work–life amalgamation illustrate that experience of work and life cannot be understood using a simple model that separates the two spheres and sets them into opposition.

4. Work–life patterns are constructed following a range of logics, depending on the context. Whereas work centres on exchanges between effort and pay, life embraces a multitude of logics, such as unconditional love for family, the reciprocity of friendships and self-gratification through conspicuous consumption. These logics of work and life coexist, allowing individuals 'a fairly frictionless *alternation* between the two distinct spheres' (ref. 90, p. 15).

Work–life patterns are continually (re)constructed as employees' work and life cycles change. Examples of such changes might include:

- the shift from independent single person to mid-life with family dependants and so on
- a change in perceived economic insecurity
- government incentives and regulations to help individuals achieve work–life goals.[98]

Complex and problematic though the idea of work–life 'balance' may be, employers' strategies in this area can have important benefits for the organization. For example, work–life policies and practices might be important for attracting and motivating professionals and innovative behaviours[99,100] – and conversely, failure to introduce such policies and practices can have a detrimental effect. Many law firms in North America, for example, retain 'a dominant male hierarchy and a suspicion of women who crave a balance between work and family', and the industry is losing talented professionals as a result. As one anonymous lawyer attests, 'A lot of male lawyers ... were extremely unhappy about losing these really high-calibre people'.[101]

However, the idea of achieving a work–life 'balance' still seems remote for millions of low-income families. As we have seen, the work–life pattern approach is more complex than the notion of 'balance' between two separable spheres, and it is a perspective that has important implications for how work and people are managed in the workplace. In the next chapter, we move on to examine how developments in work have been conceptualized and theorized.

Go to the following website for more information on the European Union Working Time Developments: www.eurofound.europa.eu/eiro/studies/tn0804029s/tn0804029s.htm. Information is also available for preceding years, and can be accessed at www.eurofound.europa.eu/eiro/comparative_index.htm

weblink

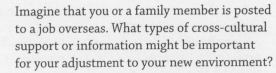

OB and globalization

A family affair – cross-cultural adjustment to overseas work

The rapid growth of multinational organizations has been accompanied by an increase in the number of expatriate workers – people who work for a foreign branch of a parent company based in their home country. Sometimes, expatriate workers leave their families in the home country while they travel abroad for work. At other times, the parent company encourages workers' families to accompany them overseas.

Studies have shown that the rate of failure for overseas placements is high, with many workers returning home before the end of their overseas assignment. One of the top reasons given for this failure is the inability of workers' families to adjust to life in the host country. The failure of overseas work assignments can be personally stressful and defeating for the workers, can cost the parent company money, and can result in damage to business relationships with the host country. A 2008 *New York Times* article (Mohn, 2008) describes the interconnected challenges to work and family life that can accompany overseas work assignments:

> The initial excitement of an exotic new posting can turn to culture shock, loneliness, identity loss and depression, and it is often the employee's spouse and children – without the familiar routine of work – who are most affected.

When an employee's family does not adapt well to an overseas work assignment, familial happiness is not the only thing at stake. According to workforce mobility expert Brenda Fender, overseas postings can fail when employees' families are unhappy, resulting in substantial financial losses to companies (Mohn, 2008). This outcome is far from inevitable. Increasingly, organizations relying on expatriate workers to manage overseas operations are recognizing the relationship between organizational success and the ability of workers' families to adjust to life abroad, and they are developing strategies to support both business success and family happiness.

Caligiuri et al. (1998) emphasize the importance of organizations providing cross-cultural support, such as language training, to help expatriate workers and their families achieve social and cultural adjustment in the host country. When expatriate families felt that their cultural and social adjustment was supported by the organization, they were more likely to support the family member working for the organization, which in turn resulted in success for the worker and for the organization.

stop! Imagine that you or a family member is posted to a job overseas. What types of cross-cultural support or information might be important for your adjustment to your new environment?

As an employee posted overseas, how might your sense of 'work–life balance' be affected by the experiences of other members of your family? What is the role of workers' families in organizational culture?

Sources and further information

Caligiuri, P. M., Hyland M. M., Bross A. S. and Joshi, A. (1998) 'Testing a theoretical model for examining the relationship between family adjustment and expatriates' work adjustment', *Journal of Applied Psychology*, 83(4), pp. 598–614.

Expat Finder Blog. Available at: www.expatfinder.com/blog.

Mohn, T. (2008) 'The dislocated Americans', *New York Times*, December 1, 2008. Available at: www.nytimes.com/2008/12/02/business/worldbusiness/02expat.html.

Sharples, J. (2005) 'Regrets and resentment over relocation', *Daily Telegraph*, January 19, 2005. Available at: http://www.telegraph.co.uk/expat/4194833/Regrets-and-resentment-over-relocation.html.

Note: This feature was written by Gretchen Fox, PhD, Anthropologist, Timberline Natural Resource Group, Canada.

Chapter summary

- One of the major themes running through the study of paid work has been the continuities as well as the discontinuities across time. There is no doubt that changes occur all the time, but these must be adequately contextualized if we are to appreciate their relevance. Thus, we can only really talk about a rise in instrumental orientations to work if we know what previously existed.

- Trying to summarise the experience of work over several millennia is a difficult task. There is so much material to cover that no text of conventional size would be able to deal adequately with the complexities. However, this chapter has been written on the assumption that some knowledge is preferable to complete ignorance, especially if, to understand the present, we have to situate it against the past. The chapter has tended to highlight gender issues in the workplace to balance out the conventional preference for male history.

- The complexity of the experience of work defies any simple assumptions about the significance of work. However, we can perhaps salvage from the past a conclusion that illuminates the significance of the social. Work, like other institutions, is inherently and irreducibly constructed, interpreted and organized through social actions and social discourse.

- We explained how, with the growth of routinized service work, new kinds of social relations and aspects of the self have developed and come under scrutiny. As the service workforce has grown in importance, we noted the growing interest in 'emotional work', pioneered by Arlie Hochschild.

- The persistence of gender ideologies on work, discrimination and the sexual division of paid work have been discussed, as has the persistent belief in the 'traditional' male breadwinner/female home-keeper model, particularly in periods of economic recession.

- We have explored the concept of work–life balance and why this orthodox binary view is based on traditional large-scale work and life patterns separated by time and space. As such, paid work is regarded as an activity that is an encroachment on people's private life. A more complex approach is represented by the notion of work–life patterns, which sees the activity of labour itself as an important source of identity and satisfaction.

Key concepts

Vocab checklist for ESL students

- ☐ Artisan
- ☐ Control
- ☐ Corporation, corporate
- ☐ Deindustrialization
- ☐ Deskilling
- ☐ Discourse
- ☐ Division of labour
- ☐ Emotional work
- ☐ Extrinsic reward
- ☐ Factory system
- ☐ Flexibility, flexible
- ☐ Fordism
- ☐ Hypotheses
- ☐ Hypothesis
- ☐ Industrial Revolution
- ☐ Intrinsic reward
- ☐ Knowledge work
- ☐ Labour power
- ☐ Neo-Fordism
- ☐ Occupation, occupy
- ☐ Post-Fordism
- ☐ Post-industrial
- ☐ Pre-industrial
- ☐ Putting-out system
- ☐ Quality of working life
- ☐ Social structure
- ☐ Taylorism
- ☐ Trade union
- ☐ Upskilling
- ☐ Values, valuable
- ☐ Work ethic

Chapter review questions

1. What is work?
2. What were the advantages and disadvantages of the putting-out system?
3. Why were men reluctant to enter the new factories during the Industrial Revolution?
4. Why were male trade unionists so hostile to women entering traditional occupations?
5. Explain the importance of 'control' in a factory system.
6. How does knowledge work different from traditional work?
7. How does emotional labour differ from traditional paid work?

8. What is the difference between work–life balance and work–life patterns? Why is it considered important for managers to understand these concepts?

❓ Chapter research questions

1. Form a study group of three to five people. Look at Figure 2.3, which draws together the development of paid work and employment relations. As a group, discuss how each major job/organization design influences the job of a manager. What intrinsic rewards do employees obtain when working under (a) craft, and (b) post-Fordism? What are the advantages/disadvantages of home-working for (a) the employer, and (b) the employee? Why, if at all, is it important to manage work–life patterns?

2. Obtain a copy of Chris Warhurst's et al.'s (2008) *Work Less, Live More?*[90] Read Chapter 5, 'On the edge of the time bind: time and market culture'. How does the 'market culture' affect the modern family? How can the 'logic of work' crowd out 'life logics', and why is this important in understanding the debate on work–life patterns?

3. Retrieve and read Carol Emslie and Kate Hunt's (2009) article, '"Live to work" or "work to Live"? A qualitative study of gender and work–life balance among men and women in mid-life' (see Further Reading, below). Why should managers understand the work–life interface through a gender lens? How does the author explain how individual choices about work–life patterns are constrained by their socioeconomic resources and cultural norms?

📑 Further reading

Bolton, S. and Boyd, C. (2003) 'Trolley dolly or skilled emotion manager? Moving on from Hochschild's managed heart', *Work, Employment and Society*, **17**(2), pp. 289–308.

Bolton, S. C. and Houlihan M. (2009) *Work Matters*, Basingstoke: Palgrave Macmillan.

Edgell, S. (2006) *The Sociology of Work*, London: Sage.

Emslie, C. and Hunt, K. (2009) '"Live to work" or "work to live"? A qualitative study of gender and work–life balance among men and women in mid-life', *Gender, Work and Organization*, **16**(1), pp. 151–72.

Frenkel, S. J. (2006) 'Service workers in search of decent work', pp. 356–75 in S. Ackroyd, R. Batt, P. Thompson and P. Tolbert (eds), *The Oxford Handbook of Work and Organization*, New York: Oxford University Press.

Hardill, L. and Green, A. (2003) 'Remote working – altering the spatial contours of work and home in the new economy', *New Technology Work and Employment*, **18**(3), pp. 212–22.

Kelan, E. (2008) 'Gender, risk and employment insecurity: the masculine breadwinner subtext', *Human Relations*, **61**(9), pp. 1171–202.

Kvande, E. (2009) 'Work–life balance for fathers in globalized knowledge work. Some insights from the Norwegian context', *Gender, Work and Organization*, **16**(1), pp. 58–72.

Lewchuk, W., Clarke, M. and de Wolff, A. (2008) 'Working without commitments: precarious employment and health', *Work, Employment and Society*, **22**(3), pp. 387–406.

McCormick, K. (2007) 'Sociologists and "the Japanese model": a passing enthusiasm?', *Work, Employment and Society*, **21**(4), pp. 751–71.

McIvor, A. (2001) *A History of Work in Britain, 1880–1950*, Basingstoke: Palgrave Macmillan.

McKinlay, A. and Smith, C. (2009) *Creative Labour*, Basingstoke: Palgrave Macmillan.

Noon, M. and Blyton, P. (2009) *The Realities of Work*, Basingstoke: Palgrave Macmillan.

Salzinger, L. (2003) *Genders in Production*, Berkley, CA: University of California Press.

Warhurst, C., Eikhof, D. R. and Haunschild, A. (2008) *Work Less, Live More?*, Basingstoke: Palgrave.

Chapter case study 1

Service with a smile: McJobs in China

Setting

Although McDonald's is well known for its Fordist method of food production, China has had experience using an assembly-line approach to feed many people for over two centuries. As early as the nineteenth century, Chinese public dining halls had perfected breaking down the cooking process into basic procedures performed by a separate team of workers.

McDonald's brought its own brand of food production and management to China in 1990 when it opened its first restaurant in a city called Shenzhen. In 1992, the world's largest McDonald's was opened in Beijing, serving 40,000 customers on that first day. McDonald's now operates 1000 restaurants in more than 190 Chinese cities, with further expansion plans well underway.

More than 70 per cent of McDonald's restaurants worldwide are owned and operated independently by local men and women. In recent years, McDonald's future growth strategy has focused on China's smaller urban areas, known as second- and third-tier cities. McDonald's is not alone as many multinational and domestic companies are now looking to expand outside the traditional economic bases in the larger Chinese centres. McDonald's faces particularly stiff competition from KFC, a fellow American fast-food restaurant chain, which dominates the Chinese market.

While Chinese fast food operators do not deal with the high turnover rates seen in American cities (sometimes as high as 300 per cent for non-managerial employees), the rapid expansion by multiple companies has resulted in competition for quality workers and rising wage costs in the new tighter labour markets.

Problem

Hai Yan is one of the new owners of a McDonald's franchise in an area several hours outside Beijing. As with other franchisees, Hai relied on the McDonald's corporation to assist him with recruiting and training his new employees to bring them in line with the company's expectations.

Peter Bepple, a new Human Resources Manager assigned to the region, flew in from New York to help. Peter had never worked in China before and was looking forward to getting the new franchises up and running. He had been briefed on the recruiting issues and was told that although the Chinese were hard workers who respected management authority and leadership, they also expected their managers to build supportive relationships with them.

Upon his arrival in Hai's area, Peter immediately set up recruitment advertising on the company website, interviewed applicants on the phone, and made arrangements for selected candidates to come into Hai's restaurant for 3 days of work. Accompanied by a McDonald's employee, each candidate tried various roles from waiter to assistant manager in the restaurant. To Hai's dismay, 80 per cent of the candidates were not offered permanent employment. He became concerned that he would not find enough suitable workers to serve customers on his restaurant's opening day. Hai decided to approach Peter to find out why so many of the candidates had not been successful during the recruitment process.

Peter was sympathetic but explained to Hai that he had observed each failed candidate's reactions to the customers and was not impressed. 'The main challenge is to maintain a positive attitude and provide good service,' Peter told Hai. 'The most important characteristic is the willingness to communicate with others and that is best reflected with a smile. Those candidates simply did not smile enough.'

Hai was taken aback by the comment. 'Here in China customers are suspicious of workers who smile on the job,' he said to Peter.

Peter was surprised by this, but decided to check with his counterparts in other McDonald's locations in China to see if this was actually the case. They confirmed what Hai had said. 'Customers in China expect employees to be serious about their work,' he was told. 'The customers are more concerned about the efficiency, reliability and cleanliness of the restaurant than if the worker smiles at them.'

Before returning to New York, Peter's head office called and asked him to prepare a report on what he had learned on his first overseas assignment.

Tasks

Prepare a short report, incorporating answers to the following questions:

1. How important is it for the McDonald's customer service strategy to insist on having its employees provide 'service with a smile'?
2. What possible effects will forcing smiles have on the Chinese workers?
3. How could Peter have better prepared himself for working in China?
4. To what extent do you think the success of the US-based McDonald's corporation influences local Chinese companies to adopt its management practices, despite the cultural differences?

Essential reading

Deery, S. (2005) 'Customer service work, emotional labour and performance', Chapter 13 in S. Bach (ed.), *Managing Human Resources: Personnel Management in Transition*, Oxford: Blackwell.

Earnhardt, M. (2009) 'The successful expatriate leader in China', *Graziado Business Report*, **12**(1). Available at: http://gbr.pepperdine.edu/091/expatriatesinchina.html.

Mujtaba, B. and Patel, B. (2007) 'McDonald's success strategy and global expansion through customer and brand loyalty', *Journal of Business Case Studies*, **3**(3), pp. 55–66.

Watson, J. (2006) *Golden Arches East: McDonald's in East Asia*, Stanford: Stanford University Press.

Note

This case study was written by Lori Rilkoff, MSc, CHRP, Senior Human Resources Manager at the City of Kamloops, and lecturer in HRM at Thompson Rivers University, BC, Canada.

Chapter case study 2

Home-working in Matherdom City Council

 Visit www.palgrave.com/business/brattonob2e to view this case study.

▶ Web-based assignment

Central to the advance of organizational behaviour as a field of critical inquiry is an openness to expanding our understanding of both work and the 'workplace'. We believe it is important to understand that work expands beyond the boundaries of 'paid work', and importantly, the place where work is performed extends beyond the formal organization. The notion of work–life pattern has increasing relevance to workers, particularly to women, in the early twenty-first century.

On an individual basis, or working in a small group, visit the following websites and write a brief report of the research and practical issues associated with (a) home-working, and (b) work–life balance: www.berr.gov.uk; www.tca.org.uk; www.theworkfoundation.com/difference/e4wlb.aspx.

OB in film

The film *Modern Times* (1936) features Charlie Chaplin in a scathing portrayal of North American assembly-line work. The first 15 minutes of the film humorously illustrate the meaning of Taylorism and the stress associated with working on an assembly line. The film led Charlie Chaplin to be banned from the USA and some of the actors to be investigated by the Federal Bureau of Investigation.

Watch the first 15 minutes of the film. What does the film tell us about Taylorism? How would you rate Chaplin's job in terms of 'job enrichment' techniques?

References

1   Rubery, J. (2006) 'Labour markets and flexibility', pp. 31–51 in S. Ackroyd, R. Batt, P. Thompson and P. Tolbert (eds), *The Oxford Handbook of Work and Organization*, New York: Oxford University Press.

2   Bolton, S. C. and Houlihan, M. (eds) *Work Matters*, Basingstoke: Palgrave.

3 Gorz, A. (1982) *Farewell to the Working Class*, London: Pluto.

4 Rifkin, J. (1996) *The End of Work*, New York: Tarcher/Putnam.

5 Pahl, R. E. (ed.) (1988) *On Work*, Oxford: Blackwell.

6 Gates, W., with Myhrvold, N. and Rinearson, P. (1996) *The Road Ahead*, New York: Penguin.

7 Wood, S. (ed.) (1982) *The Transformation of Work?*, London: Unwin Hyman.

8 Zuboff, S. (1988) *In the Age of the Smart Machine*, New York: Basic Books.

9 Hearn, J., Sheppard, D., Tancred-Sheriff, P. and Rand Burrell, G. (eds) (1989) *The Sexuality of Organization*, London: Sage.

10 Littler, C. R. and Salaman, G. (1984) *Class at Work: The Design, Allocation and Control of Jobs*, London: Batsford.

11 Mills, A. and Tancred, P. (eds) (1992) *Gendering Organizational Analysis*, Newbury Park, CA: Sage.

12 Thompson, P. (1989) *The Nature of Work* (2nd edn), London: Macmillan.

13 Williams, R. (1983) *Keywords*, New York: Oxford University Press.

14 Christiansen, C. H. and Townsend, E. A. (2004) *Introduction to Occupation: The Art and Science of Living*, Upper Saddle River, NJ: Prentice Hall.

15 Noon, M. and Blyton, P. (2002) *The Realities of Work*, Basingstoke: Palgrave Macmillan.

16 Rinehart, J. W. (2006) *The Tyranny of Work: Alienation and the Labour Process* (4th edn), Scarborough, ON: Nelson Thomson.

17 Thomas, K. (1999) 'Introduction', pp. xiii–xxiii in K. Thomas (ed.), *The Oxford Book of Work*, Oxford: Oxford University Press.

18 Herod, A., Rainnie, A. and McGrath-Champ, S. (2007) 'Working space: why incorporating the geographical is central to theorizing work and employment practices', *Work, Employment and Society*, **21**(2), pp. 247–64.

19 Hardill, L. and Green, A. (2003) 'Remote working – altering the spatial contours of work and home in the new economy', *New Technology, Work and Employment*, **18**(3), pp. 212–22.

20 Coyle-Shapiro, J. A.-M., Shore, L., Taylor, M. S. and Tetrick, L. (2005) *The Employment Relationship*, Oxford: Oxford University Press.

21 Barnes, C. (1996) 'What next? Disability, the 1995 Disability Discrimination Act and the Campaign for Disabled Peoples' Rights', National Bureau for Disabled Students Annual Conference, March 2, Leeds, UK.

22 Guest, D. E. and Conway, N. (2002) 'Communicating the psychological contract: an employer perspective', *Human Resource Management Journal*, **12**(2), pp. 22–38.

23 Herriot, P. (1998) 'The role of human resource management in building a new proposition', pp. 106–16 in P. Sparrow and M. Marchington (eds), *Human Resource Management: A New Agenda*, London: Financial Times Management.

24 Kramer, R. M. and Tyler, T. R. (1996) *Trust in Organizations: Frontiers of Theory and Research*, Newbury Park, CA: Sage.

25 Rousseau, D. M. (1995) *Psychological Contracts in Organisations: Understanding Written and Unwritten Agreements*, Thousand Oaks, CA: Sage.

26 Atkinson, C. (2008) 'An exploration of small firm psychological contracts', *Work, Employment and Society*, **22**(3), pp. 447–65.

27 Sveiby, K. E. (1997) *The New Organizational Wealth: Managing and Measuring Organizational Wealth*, San Francisco, CA: Berrett-Koehler.

28 Hodson, R. and Sullivan, T. A. (2002) *The Social Organization of Work* (3rd edn), Belmont, CA: Wadsworth/Thomson Learning.

29 Grint, K. (1998) *The Sociology of Work* (2nd edn), Cambridge: Polity Press.

30 Hobsbawm, E. (1997) *On History*, London: Weidenfeld & Nicolson.

31 Littler, C. R. (1982) *The Development of the Labour Process in Capitalist Societies*, London: Heinemann.

32 Salaman, G. (1981) *Class and the Corporation*, London: Fontana.

33 Weber, M. (1927/2003) *General Economic History*, New York: Dover Publications.

34 Clarkson, L. A. (1971) *The Pre-Industrial Economy of England, 1500–1750*, London: Batsford.

35 Alvesson, M. and Due Billing, Y (1997) *Understanding Gender in Organizations*, London: Sage.

36 Dobb, M. (1963) *Studies in the Development of Capitalism*, London: Routledge.

37 Landes, D. S. (1969) *The Unbound Prometheus*, Cambridge: Cambridge University Press.

38 Marglin, S. (1982) 'What do bosses do?: the origins and functions of hierarchy in capitalist production', in A. Giddens and D. Held (eds), *Classes, Power and Conflict*, Basingstoke: Macmillan.

39 Kelly, J. (1985) 'Management's redesign of work: labour process, labour markets and product markets', in D. Knights, H. Willmott and D. Collinson (eds), *Job Redesign: Critical Perspectives on the Labour Process*, Aldershot: Gower.

40 Hobsbawm, E. (1968) *Industry and Empire*, London: Weidenfeld & Nicolson.

41 Thompson, E. P. (1967) 'Time, work and discipline, and industrial capitalism', *Past and Present*, **38**, pp. 56–97.

42 Grey, C. (2005) *A Very Short, Fairly Interesting and Reasonably Cheap Book about Studying Organizations*, London: Sage.

43 Hinton, J. (1973) *The First Shop Stewards Movement*, London: Allen & Unwin.

44 Rose, M. (1988) *Industrial Behaviour*, London: Penguin.

45 Braverman, H. (1974) *Labor and Monopoly Capitalism: The Degradation of Work in the Twentieth Century*, New York: Monthly Review Press.

46 Beynon, H. (1984) *Working for Ford*, Harmondsworth: Penguin.

47 Parker, M. (2000) *Organizational Culture and Identity*, London: Sage.

48 Friedman, A. (1977) *Industry and Labour: Class Struggle at Work and Monopoly Capitalism*, London: Macmillan.

49 Callaghan, G. and Thompson, P. (2001) 'Edwards revisited: technical control and worker agency in callcentres', *Economic and Industrial Democracy*, **22**, pp. 13–37.

50 Sewell, G. (1998) 'The discipline of teams: the control of team-based industrial work through electronic and peer surveillance', *Administrative Science Quarterly*, **43**, pp. 406–69.

51 Bratton, J. (1992) *Japanization at Work*, Basingstoke: Macmillan.

52 Elger, T. and Smith, C. (eds) (1994) *Global Japanization?*, London: Routledge.

53 Thompson, P. and McHugh, D. (2006) *Work Organizations: A Critical Introduction* (4th edn), Basingstoke: Palgrave.

54 Womack, J., Jones, D. and Roos, D. (1990) *The Machine that Changed the World*, New York: Rawson Associates.

55 Oliver, N. and Wilkinson, B. (1992) *The Japanization of British Industry*, Oxford: Blackwell.

56 McCormick, K. (2007) 'Sociologists and "the Japanese model": a passing enthusiasm?', *Work, Employment and Society*, **21**(4), pp. 751–71.

57 Salzinger, L. (2003) *Genders in Production*, Berkeley: University of California Press.

58 Horwitz, F. M., Chan Feng Heng and Quazi, H. A. (2003) 'Finders, keepers? Attracting, motivating and retaining knowledge workers', *Human Resource Management Journal*, **13**(4), pp. 23–44.

59 Boud, D. and Garrick, J. (eds) (1999) *Understanding Learning at Work*, London: Routledge.

60 Ackroyd, S., Batt, R., Thompson, P. and Tolbert, P. (2005) *The Oxford Handbook of Work and Organization*, Oxford: Oxford University Press.

61 Baldry, C., Bain, P., Taylor, P. et al. (2007) *The Meaning of Work in the New Economy*, Basingstoke: Palgrave.

62 Bolton, S. C. (2005) *Emotion Management in the Workplace*, Basingstoke: Palgrave.

63 Fineman, S. (2003) *Understanding Emotion at Work*, London: Sage.

64 Warhurst, C. and Nickson, D. (2007), 'A new labour aristocracy? Aesthetic labour and routine interactive service', *Work, Employment and Society*, **21**(4), pp. 785–98.

65 Hochschild, A. (2003) *The Second Shift*, New York: Penguin.

66 Linstead, S., Fulop, L. and Lilley, S. (2009) *Management and Organization: A Critical Text* (2nd edn), Basingstoke: Palgrave.

67 Nixon, D. (2009) '"I can't put a smiley face on": working-class masculinity, emotional labour and service work in the "new economy"', *Gender, Work and Organization*, **16**(3), pp. 300–22.

68 Jacoby, S. M. (2005) *The Embedded Corporation: Corporate Governance and Employment Relations in Japan and the United States*, Princeton, NJ: Princeton University Press.

69 Jaffee, D. (2001) *Organization Theory: Tension and Change*, Boston, MA: McGraw-Hill.

70 Vallas, S. (1999) 'Re-thinking post-Fordism: the meaning of workplace flexibility', *Sociological Theory*, **17**(1), pp. 68–85.

71 Walton, R. (1985) 'From control to commitment in the workplace', *Harvard Business Review*, March/April, pp. 77–84.

72 Hyman, R. and Mason, B. (1995) *Managing Employee Involvement and Participation*, London: Sage.

73 Reiter, E. (1992) *Making Fast Food: From the Frying Pan into the Fryer*, Montreal: McGill-Queen's University Press.

74 Ritzer, G. (2000) *The McDonaldization of Society*, Thousand Oaks, CA: Pine Forge Press.

75 Leidner, R. (1993) *Fast Food, Fast Talk: Service Work and the Routinization of Everyday Life*, Berkeley, CA: University of California Press.

76 Mathias, P. (1969) *The First Industrial Nation*, London: Methuen.

77 Reskin, B. and Padavic, I. (1994) *Women and Men at Work*, Thousand Oaks, CA: Sage.

78 Hobsbawm, E. (1994) *Age of Extremes*, London: Abacus.

79 Berg, M. (1988) 'Women's work, mechanization and early industrialization', in R. E. Pahl (ed.), *On Work*, Oxford: Blackwell.

80 Bradley, H. (1986) 'Technological change, management strategies, and the development of gender-based job segregation in the labour process', pp. 54–73 in D. Knights and H. Willmott (eds), *Gender and the Labour Process*, Aldershot: Gower.

81 Turner, H. A. (1962) *Trade Union Growth, Structure and Policy: A Comparative Study of the Cotton Unions*, London: Allen & Unwin.

82 Witz, A. (1986) 'Patriarchy and the labour market: occupational control strategies and the medical division of labour', in D. Knights and H. Willmott (eds), *Gender and the Labour Process*, Aldershot: Gower.

83 Sydie, R. A. (1994) *Natural Women, Cultured Men*, Vancouver: UBC Press.

84 Knights, D. and Willmott, H. (eds) (1986) *Gender and the Labour Process*, Aldershot: Gower.

85 Kimmel, M. (2004) *The Gendered Society* (2nd edn), New York: Oxford University Press.

86 Saunders, D. (2006) 'Politician-mom seeks to change dated German social values', *Globe and Mail*, June 22, p. A3.

87 Greenhaus, J. H. (2008), 'Innovations in the study of the work–family interface: introduction to the Special Section', *Journal of Occupational and Organizational Psychology*, **81**, pp. 343–8.

88 Purcell, J., Purcell, K., and Tailby, S. (2004) 'Temporary work agencies: here today, gone tomorrow?', *British Journal of Industrial Relations*, **42**(4), pp. 705–25.

89 Sturges, J. and Guest, D. (2004) 'Working to live or living to work: work/life balance and organizational commitment amongst graduates', *Human Resources Management Journal*, **14**(4), pp. 5–20.

90 Warhurst, C., Eikhof, D. R. and Haunschild, A. (2008) *Work Less, Live More?*, Basingstoke: Palgrave.

91 European Trade Union Confederation. 'Factsheet: Working Time Directive'. Available at: http://www.etuc.org/a/504 (accessed November 2, 2009).

92 Bonney, N. (2005) 'Overworked Britains?: part-time work and work–life balance', *Work, Employment and Society*, **19**(2), pp. 391–401.

93 Kersley, B., Alpin, C., Forth, J. et al. (2006) *Inside the Workplace: Findings from the 2004 Workplace Employment Relations Survey*, London: Routledge.

94 Felstead, A., Gallie, D. and Green, F. (2002) *Work Skills in Britain: 1986–2001*, London: HMSO.

95 Giddens, A. (1984) *The Constitution of Society*, Cambridge: Polity Press.

96 Weber, M. (1905/2002) *The Protestant Ethic and the 'Spirit' of Capitalism*, London: Penguin.

97 *Globe and Mail*, April 22, 2009, p. C1.

98 Kvande, E. (2009) 'Work–life balance for fathers in globalized knowledge work. Some insights from the Norwegian context', *Gender, Work and Organization*, **16**(1), pp. 58–72.

99 Scholarios, D. and Marks, A. (2004) 'Work–life balance and the software worker', *Human Resource Management Journal*, **14**(2), pp. 54–74.

100 De Cieri, H., Holmes, B., Abbot, J. and Pettit, T. (2002) *Work/Life Balance Strategies: Progress and Problems in Australian Organizations*. Working Paper 58/02. Melbourne: Department of Management, Monash University.

101 Makin, K.(2009) 'Lawyer-moms aim to change law firms' punishing work culture', *Globe and Mail*, April 11, p. 4.

102 Despres, C. and Hiltrop, J-M. (1995) 'Human resource management in the knowledge age: current practice and perspectives on the future', *Employee Relations*, **17**(1), pp. 9–23.

chapter 3
Studying work and organizations

chapter objectives

After completing this chapter, you should be able to:

- explain the classical approaches to studying work through the ideas of Marx, Durkheim and Weber
- explain contemporary theories of work organizations and the importance of theory to understanding work and behaviour in the workplace

Introduction

This chapter examines classical and contemporary approaches to studying work and work organizations. We begin by considering the classical social theories about paid work through the ideas of Marx, Weber and Durkheim. These can be described as classical partly because they had their roots in European industrialization and culture – from about 1800 through to the early 1900s – and also because, in their response to industrial capitalism, the early social theorists set out a series of themes, concepts, assumptions, problems and ideas that continue to exercise an enormous influence over contemporary organizational theory. As others have pointed out, both the perspectives of analysis that are clearly set out in the works of the classical theorists, and the characteristic focuses of those traditions, continue to dominate study of the sociology of work.[1–3]

As we discussed in Chapter 1, over the last three decades not only have organizations fundamentally changed how they organize work, but new approaches and concepts have also been developed for studying work organizations. In the 1970s, the orthodox consensus on organization theory focused on 'functionalism', which emphasized consensus and coherence rather than asymmetrical power relations and conflict.[4] The key concept is that of the organization as a 'system' that functions effectively if it achieves explicit goals, which are formally defined through 'rational' decision making. Alternative theoretical approaches have since challenged the supremacy of functionalism.

A multitude of contemporary theories of formal organizations exist, so we cannot hope to do justice to the complexities of such a wide-ranging debate. We therefore seek here to highlight the major distinguishing themes related to work and organizations. Drawing on the work of Keith Grint,[5] we review 12 competing theoretical perspectives or 'conversations' in organization theory: the technical, human relations, neo-human relations, systems thinking, contingency, cultures, learning, control, feminist, social action, political and postmodernist perspectives.

Classical approaches to studying work

Marx, Durkheim and Weber each analysed the new work forms, but also placed their analysis within a wider discourse on modern society and social change. While Karl Marx focused on social fragmentation, conflict and social change, Emile Durkheim concerned himself with social fragmentation and the nature of order, and Max Weber developed his theory of rationality and bureaucracy.

Karl Marx (1818–83)

Do contemporary organizational behaviour theorists have anything to learn from the classical sociologists such as Marx, Durkheim and Weber?

stop reflect

plate 10 Karl Marx.

Source: Marxists Internet Archive

objectification: Karl Marx's term to describe the action of human labour on resources to produce a commodity, which under the control of the capitalist remains divorced from and opposed to the direct producer

surplus value: the portion of the working day during which workers produce value that is appropriated by the capitalist

Marx believed that industrialization was a necessary stage for the eventual triumph of human potential, but that the mainspring of this social formation was capitalism, and not industrialism as such. It is only capitalism that carries within it the seeds of its own destruction. For Marx, the human species is different from all other animal species, not because of its consciousness, but because it alone produces its own means of subsistence.

Marx's argument is that what distinguishes humans from other animals is that our labour creates something in reality that previously existed only in our imagination:

> We presuppose labour in a form that stamps it as exclusively human … But what distinguishes the worst architect from the best bees is this, that the architect raises his structure in imagination before he erects it in reality. At the end of every labour process we get a result that existed in the *imagination* of the labourer at its commencement. He not only effects a change of form in the material on which he works, but he also realizes a purpose. (ref 6, p. 178, emphasis added)

Marx calls this process whereby humans create external objects from their internal thoughts **objectification**. This labour does not just transform raw materials or nature; it also transforms humans, including human nature, people's needs and their consciousness. We can begin to understand Marx's concept of objectification by thinking of the creative activity of an artist. The artist's labour is a representation of the imagination of the artist: 'the art work is an objectification of the artist'.[7] In addition, through the labour process, the artist's ideas of the object change, or the experience, may prompt a new vision or creativity that needs objectification. Labour, for Marx, provides the means through which humans can realize their true human powers and potential. By transforming raw materials, we transform ourselves, and we also transform society. Thus, according to Marx, the transformation of the individual through work and the transformation of society are inseparable.

Marx's discussion of work under capitalism focuses on the nature of employment relationships. Under capitalism, the aim is to buy labour at sufficiently low rates to make a profit. Marx is careful to distinguish between 'labour' and 'labour power'. Human labour is the actual physical or mental activity incorporated in the body of the worker. Labour power, on the other hand, refers to the *potential* of labour to add use value to raw materials or commodities. This labour power is bought by the capitalist at a value less than the value it creates. In purchasing the worker's potential or capacity to labour and add use values to materials, at a wage level less than the value created by the worker's labour, the capitalist is able to make a profit.

We can begin to appreciate the significance of Marx's use of the term 'labour power' when we think of it as a promise: it is therefore indeterminate, and there may be a gap between the potential or promise of labour and the actual labour. This distinction between 'labour' and 'labour power' allowed Marx to locate the precise mechanism that creates profit in capitalist societies. It also gives rise to the creation of two classes that are potentially, if not always in practice, in conflict with each other.

Capitalism involves the work relationship between the buyers and sellers of labour power. Marx's concept of **surplus value** is rooted in this social relationship. Surplus value is the value remaining when the worker's daily costs of subsistence have been subtracted from the value that she or he produces for the capitalist. As such, it is unpaid and 'goes to the heart of the exploitation of the worker'.[8]

In the workplace, the primacy of profit and conflict relationships gives rise to three broad necessary features of activity and change. Each of these involves substantial shifts in the work performed. Most significant is the need for the capitalist to centralize the labour power that is purchased, and to discipline the interior of the factory, by organizing space, time and the behaviour of workers whose commitment is unreliable. The aim is to close or minimize the gap between potential labour power and actual labour power. For Marx, the accumulation of profit is inevitably and irrevocably mediated by managerial control strategies. It is the inevitable outcome of capitalism: 'The directing motive, the end and aim of capitalist production, is to extract the greatest possible amount of surplus-value, and consequently to exploit labour-power to the fullest possible extent' (ref. 6, p. 331).

The second broad plane of activity changing the nature of work is the **division of labour**. To increase control and surplus value for the capitalist, extensive division of labour takes place within the factory. According to Marx, 'Division of labour within the workshop implies the undisputed authority of the capitalist over men that are but parts of a mechanism that belong to him' (ref. 6, p. 356). As an example, Marx described the manufacture of horse carriages. In pre-capitalist production, the manufacture of carriages involved the simple cooperation of various trades: coach construction, ironwork, upholstery and wheelwright work. Each of these trades was regulated by guilds in order to maintain their specialization and control over these operations. In capitalist production, simple cooperation gives way to what Marx described as 'complex cooperation', as individual trades lose their specialized skills, and workers perform operations that are disconnected and isolated from one another, and carried out alongside each other. According to Marx and his colleague Engels, this mode of production also creates a hierarchy of managers and supervisors:

> Modern industry has converted the little workshop of the patriarchal master into the great factory of the industrial capitalist. Masses of labourers, crowded into the factory, are organized like soldiers. As privates of the industrial army they are placed under the command of a perfect hierarchy of officers [managers] and sergeants [supervisors]. (ref. 9, p. 227)

Marx examined the impact of technological change on employment relationships. He argued that machinery is used by the capitalist to increase surplus labour by cheapening labour, to deskill workers and thus make it easier to recruit, control and discipline workers. Machinery, he argued, led to the progressive reduction of skills:

> On the automatic plan skilled labour gets progressively superseded. The effect of improvements in machinery [results] in substituting one description of human labour for another, the less skilled for the more skilled, juvenile for adult, female for male, [and] causes a fresh disturbance in the rate of wages. (ref. 6, p. 433)

Machinery allows the capitalist to transfer the knowledge and skill in production from the worker to reliable agents of capital – that is, managers. Marx described the process like this: 'Intelligence in production expands in one direction, because it vanishes in many others. What is lost by the detail labourers, is concentrated in the capital that employs them' (ref. 6, p. 361). Machinery also increases the capitalist's control over workers' work activities. In what Marx referred to as the despotism of the factory, machinery sets the pace of work and embodies powerful mechanisms of control: 'the technical subordination of the workman to the uniform motion of the instruments of labour [machinery] … gave rise to a barrack discipline'. He continued: 'To devise and administer a successful code of factory discipline, suited to the necessities of factory diligence, was the Herculean enterprise, the noble achievement of Arkwright!' (ref. 6, pp. 423–4).

These characteristics of work in industrial capitalism have two major consequences: the **alienation** of the workers, and conflict resulting ultimately in social change. Whereas objectification embodies the worker's creativity, work under capitalism is devoid of the producer's own potential creativity and sensuousness.

division of labour: the allocation of work tasks to various groups or categories of employee

alienation: a feeling of powerlessness and estrangement from other people and from oneself

Because workers' labour is not their own, it no longer transforms them. Hence, the unique quality of human beings – their ability to control the forces of nature and produce their own means of existence, to realize their full creative capacity through work – is stultified by capitalism.

Drawing on the 1807 work by Georg Hegel, *The Phenomenology of Mind*, Marx developed the theory of alienation. In essence, alienation ruptures the fundamental connection that human beings have to the self-defining aspect of their labouring activity.[8] Marx broke down the formulation of alienation into four conceptually discrete but related spheres. First, workers are alienated (or separated) from the product of their labour. The product – its design, quality, quantity and how it is marketed and disposed of – is not determined by those whose labour is responsible for its manufacture.

Second, workers are alienated from productive activity. Marx emphasized the tendency for machinery to deskill work:

> Owing to the extensive use of machinery and to division of labour, the work of the proletarians has lost all individual character, and, consequently, all charm for the workman. He becomes an appendage of the machine, and it is only the most simple, most monotonous, and most easily acquired knack, that is required of him. (ref. 9, p. 227)

Thus, work offers no intrinsic satisfaction. Workers only work for the money; workers only work because they have to. Marx called this the 'cash nexus'. Accordingly, work takes on an instrumental meaning: it is regarded simply as a means to an end.

The third type of alienation discussed by Marx is alienation from the human species. Marx contended that self-estrangement develops because of the 'cash nexus'. In order to be clear on Marx's meaning, we need to know that Marx believed that people were essentially creative and that individuals expressed creativity through their work. Work, according to Marx, is the medium for self-expression and self-development. It is through work that people should be able to shape themselves and their communities in accordance with their own needs, interests and values. Under alienating conditions, however, work becomes not a social activity that personifies life, but simply a means for physical survival: people become detached from their true selves.

The fourth type of alienation discussed by Marx is alienation from fellow human beings and from the community. This results when the sole purpose of life is competition and all social relations are transformed into economic relations. Workers and managers are alienated from each other. This economic relationship – between those who are controlled and the controllers – is an antagonistic one. And this asymmetry of social relationships in the workplace creates the foundation for a class structure that necessitates sharp differences in power, income and life chances.

Marx's analysis of the social organization of work underscores the fact that people express themselves through their work, and in so far as their labour is merely a commodity to be paid for with a wage, they are alienated. Although Marx did not explicitly focus on the analysis of emotion in the workplace, he did acknowledge that the way in which industrial work was organized and managed did provoke in workers feelings of numbness, anger and resentment. Alienation is characteristic of a certain kind of organization of work – industrial capitalism – that is predicated on a set of socioeconomic conditions. In short, then, capitalism destroys the pleasure associated with labour, the distinctively human capacity to shape and reshape the world.

The second major consequence of work in capitalism, that relations between capitalists and workers are in constant conflict, is the engine of social change. Impelled

contradictions: contradictions are said to occur within social systems when the various principles that underlie these social arrangements conflict with each other

class consciousness: Karl Marx's term for awareness of a common identity based on a person's position in the means of production

class conflict: a term for the struggle between the capitalist class and the working class

bourgeoisie (or capitalist class): Karl Marx's term for the class comprising those who own and control the means of production

proletariat (or working class): Karl Marx's term for those who must sell their labour because they have no other means of earning a livelihood

by its internal **contradictions**, the reverberation of work under capitalism helps the development of **class consciousness** among the workers or proletariat. The defining features of work – deskilling, intensification of work, constant pressure to lower the wages allocated to labour – encourage the development of **class conflict**. Marx and Engels explain the logic whereby capitalism develops and then destroys itself. In their search for profits, capitalists closely control and discipline workers.[9]

Capitalism creates new contradictions, such as the concentration of workers into factories. As workers are concentrated under one roof, they become aware of their common exploitation and circumstances. As a result, over time, workers begin to resist capitalist controls, initially as individuals, and then collectively as groups. Gradually, the workers become organized, through trade unions, and increasingly they become more combative and engage the ruling class in wider social struggles, which Marx believed would culminate in replacing the rule of the **bourgeoisie** and ridding society of capitalism: 'What the bourgeoisie therefore produces above all, is its own gravediggers. Its fall and the victory of the **proletariat** are equally inevitable.'[9] Thus, those selling their labour power, the workers, are exposed to such exploitation and degradation that they begin to oppose capitalists, in order to replace the system.

Marx provides a sophisticated theory of capitalism, with the working class as the embodiment of good, but his concentration on the extraction of surplus value in the labour process inhibits him from considering managerial and government strategies that serve to develop consent and cooperation. The capitalist mode of production is not characterized solely by the conflict between employer and labour: it is also marked by competition between organizations and economies. To put it another way, profits are realized by gaining a competitive advantage, and the need to gain workers' cooperation undermines the contradictory laws that promote constant conflict and crises. Thus, Marx systematically underestimates the possibility that management may need to organize on the basis of consent as well as coercion.

The reconceptualization of management as necessarily engaged in consent building also suggests that Marx's zero-sum theory of power is insufficient. Critics argue that although the interests of labour and capital do not coincide, the assumption that they are irreconcilably and utterly antagonistic is misleading. Therefore, the inadequacy of Marx's account lies at the level of analysis. Marx emphasized the irreconcilable interests of social classes at the societal level, and this obscures the very real way in which, in the workplace, the interests of employers and employees may be very closely intertwined.

Despite the strong criticisms of Marx's analysis of work on capitalism, his impact on the sociology of work is immense. His illumination of the politics of work and organizations – the relationship between work and the distribution of interests and power in the society outside the workplace, and the relationships of power and managerial strategies inside the workplace – still informs contemporary analyses of work and employment relations, as we shall see later in this chapter.

Go to the following websites for more information on Marx: http://plato.stanford.edu/entries/marx; www.anu.edu.au/polsci/marx/classics/manifesto.html; www.marxists.org

weblink

Emile Durkheim (1858–1917)

social solidarity: the state of having shared beliefs and values among members of a social group, along with intense and frequent interaction among group members

urbanization: the process by which an increasing proportion of a population lives in cities rather than in rural areas

Emile Durkheim's contribution to our understanding of work is essentially derived from his book *The Division of Labor in Society*,[10] and its discussion of the relationship between individuals and society, and the conditions for social cohesion. Durkheim was preoccupied with the issue of **social solidarity** and unity during a time when France was subject to the profound revolutionary changes that created modern society. The popular belief of the time was that the collapse of social life was imminent, in response to the expansion of the division of labour, ever-increasing industrialization and **urbanization**, and the declining significance of

plate 11 Emile Durkheim.

mechanical solidarity: a term to describe the social cohesion that exists in pre-industrial societies, in which there is a minimal division of labour and people feel united by shared values and common social bonds

organic solidarity: a term for the social cohesion that exists in industrial (and perhaps post-industrial) societies, in which people perform very specialized tasks and feel united by their mutual dependence

anomie: a state condition in which social control becomes ineffective as a result of the loss of shared values and a sense of purpose in society

traditional moral beliefs. This was described as the transition from *Gemeinschaft* or 'community' forms of society, to *Gesellschaft* or 'social' forms, representing mere 'associations' where social solidarity was disintegrating. Durkheim suggested that such fears were not just exaggerated, but actually wrong. His thesis held that heightened feelings of group solidarity and order were being reconstructed in a different form. Durkheim's position was that the interdependence resulting from the progressive differentiation and specialization of labour gave rise to a new form of social solidarity, which is the bond that unites individuals when there is no normative consensus.

Durkheim's prime question was, if pre-industrial societies were held together by shared understandings, ideas, norms and values, what holds a complex industrial society together? He believed that the increasing division of labour has enormous implications for the structure of society. In pre-industrial society, social solidarity is derived from people's similarities and the rather suffocating effects of uniformity of experience and thought. Such societies are held together through the collective consciousness at the direct expense of individuality: 'individual personality is absorbed into the collective personality', as Durkheim put it (ref. 10, p. 85). He called this form of social unity **mechanical solidarity**. In contrast, the increasing division of labour causes a diminution of collective consciousness, and 'this leaves much more room for the free play of our imitative' (ref. 10, p. 85).

Complex industrial societies, with new work forms based on functional specialization, are held together by relations of exchange and people's reciprocal need for the services of many others. This symmetry of life Durkheim called **organic solidarity**. He believed that in societies whose solidarity is organic, individuals are linked increasingly to each other rather than to society as a whole. The totality of the nature of these social links compels individuals to remain in contact with one another, which in turn binds them to one another and to society. Thus, each of us becomes aware of our dependence on others and of the new cultural norms that shape and restrain our actions.

For Durkheim, only the division of labour could furnish social solidarity and ethical individualism: 'Since the division of labour becomes the source of social solidarity, it becomes, at the same time, the foundation of moral order' (ref. 10, p. 333). In summary, he argued that there was no necessary correlation between increased division of labour and decreasing solidarity. On the contrary, it was a source not of disorder and conflict, but of order and social solidarity. The nature of moral solidarity in industrial society has not disappeared, but changed.

Of course, Durkheim was not oblivious to the reality of industrialization in Western Europe, which might have been argued to show the opposite. Not least, there were intense class conflicts and widespread labour strikes in France, often led by radical workers known as revolutionary syndicalists, in unions organized in the *Confédération Générale du Travail*. Durkheim explained the existence of instability and social fragmentation by analysing what he called 'abnormal' forms of the division of labour. These abnormal forms occur when the development of the division of labour is obstructed and distorted by various factors. He identified these as the anomie division of labour, the forced division of labour and the mismanagement of operations.

The first abnormal effects can arise because of the 'anomie' condition of the division of labour. The word **anomie** comes from the Greek *anomia*, meaning 'without law'. For Durkheim, anomie results from a condition in which social norms and/or moral norms are confused or simply absent. Generally, Durkheim believed that anomie results from widespread business failure, or when there is rapid and uneven economic development that has expanded ahead of the necessary developments in social regulation. In such circumstances, he suggests, breaches occur in the social solidarity existing between specialized occupations, causing tensions in social relationships and eroding social cohesion.

Durkheim also considered anomie as another 'pathology' of industrialization, but believed that such deviant behaviour could be 'cured' through the proper level of regulation. He argued that occupational associations centred within civil society are the most effective means of regulating anomie in modern society. Such collective institutions provide moral authority, which dominates the life of their members. They are also a method by which individualistic egotism can be subordinated harmoniously to the general interest.

Durkheim explained the importance of occupational groups like this: 'wherever a group is formed, a moral discipline is also formed.' He continued:

> A group is not only a moral authority regulating the life of its members, but also a source of life *sui generis*. From it there arises warmth that quickens or gives fresh life to each individual, which makes him disposed to empathise, causing selfishness to melt away. (ref. 10, p. 111)

Durkheim also warned that the mere construction of consensually grounded goals without any associated provision of opportunities to achieve such goals would extend the form of social 'pathology' under which anomie prevailed.

The second factor causing abnormal development, according to Durkheim, is the 'forced division of labour' (ref. 10, p. 310). He emphasized that the division of labour is frequently not 'spontaneous' because of class and inherited privilege that operate to limit life chances. Durkheim, then, is considered to be a supporter of meritocracy. The normal division of labour would occur if social inequalities mirrored what Durkheim took to be personal inequalities:

> The division of labour only produces solidarity if it is spontaneous, and to the degree that it is spontaneous. But spontaneity must mean not simply the absence of any deliberate, formal type of violence, but of anything that may hamper, even indirectly, the free unfolding of the social force each individual contains within himself … In short, labour only divides up spontaneously if society is constituted in such a way that social inequalities express precisely natural inequalities. (ref. 10, pp. 313–14)

Thus, Durkheim's 'normal' division of labour is a 'perfect meritocracy' produced by the eradication of personal inheritance.[1,5] For the division of labour to engender solidarity, society must allocate functions based on ability, not class or hereditary tendencies, so that 'The sole cause then determining how labour is divided up is the diversity of abilities' (ref. 10, p. 313).

The third factor responsible for an 'abnormal' development of the division of labour is mismanagement of functions in society. Durkheim believed that when functions are faltering or are badly coordinated with one another, individuals are unaware of their mutual dependence, and this lessens social solidarity. Thus, if work is insufficient, as a result of mismanagement and organization, Durkheim argues that solidarity 'is itself naturally not only less than perfect, but may even be more or less completely missing' (ref. 10, p. 326).

In addition, if class-based social inequalities are imposed on groups, this not only forces the division of labour, but also undermines social linkages. It means that individuals are mismatched to their functions, and that linkages between individuals are disrupted, and this creates inequitable forms of exchange. In the absence of restraint from a centralized authority (either the state or the government), there is disequilibrium, which leads to instability and conflict. For Durkheim, most of the pathologies of the new industrial order were attributed to the prevalence of anomie.

In sum, while Marx's critique was directed at capitalism, Durkheim's critique was aimed not at the essence of capitalism, but at industrialism. Whereas Marx is against the fragmentation of work and for the reintegration of skills, Durkheim is for the expansion of specialization in line with individuals' 'natural' abilities. Although the concepts of alienation and anomie lead to significantly different analysis and political results, and are different too in their assumptions about human nature, the two concepts have been compared by sociologists. For Marx, alienation results from certain kinds of social control; on the other hand, according to Durkheim, anomie results from the absence of social control. While Marx's solution to the crisis of capitalism is dependent on the state or government, Durkheim argued that central-ized government was too far removed from the everyday experience of people to play this role. He believed that mediating organizations would form the primary mode of social organization. For Durkheim, the crisis of modern society is a moral one, caused by a lack of social unity. The solution is therefore achieved by socially regulated institutions coupled with an ever-widening division of labour. He believed this would facilitate the development of individual potential and create a future Utopia. The process of social change was to be evolutionary, not revolutionary.

In this chapter, we cannot provide a thorough critique of Durkheim's theory of the relationship between the increasing differentiation and specialization of labour, and transformative social change. However, we must critically assess some of his assumptions, for example those about 'natural' inequalities. He regarded men as more intelligent than women, and industrial workers as more intelligent than farmers. Durkheim also assumed that the gender-based domestic division of labour was a good example of the social harmony generated when social inequalities were allowed to mirror 'natural' inequalities. His assumptions about gender relations provoked the beginnings of a critique of patriarchy.[5]

Go to the following website for more information on Durkheim: www.epistemelinks. com/Main/Philosophers. aspx?PhilCode=Durk

weblink

Max Weber (1864–1920)

Max Weber's work is broad and wide-ranging, and has been much misrepresented. It is often assumed to be a dialogue with the ghost of Marx, but that does not do justice to it. Weber wrote on a wide range of topics including art, architecture and music; he examined the role of ideology in social change; and he explored the emer-gence and nature of modernity. His contribution to the study of work and work organizations has been extensive. The main contributions he made are: first, his theory concerning the rise of capitalism; second, his arguments concerning ration-ality, the nature of bureaucracy and authority; third, his theory of social class and inequality; and fourth, his methodology and theory of knowledge.

The rise of capitalism and rationalization

Weber's interpretation of the rise of capitalism in the West is presented in his best-known work, *The Protestant Ethic and the 'Spirit' of Capitalism* (written in 1905),[11] which links the rise of modern capitalism to Protestant (or, more precisely, Calvinist) religious beliefs and practices. Briefly, he argued that a new attitude to work and the pursuit of wealth was linked to the rise of Calvinism. In this attitude, work became a means of demonstrating godliness, and Weber saw this cultural shift as being associated with the rise of 'rational' capitalism itself.

According to Weber, while Catholics believed they could secure their place in heaven through (among other things) 'good works' on behalf of the poor or by performing acts of faith on earth, Calvinism developed a set of beliefs around the concept of predestination, which broke the hold of tradition. It was believed by followers of Calvin that it was already decided by God ('predestined') whether they would go to heaven (as one of the 'elect') or hell after their death. They had no means

Source: Wikipedia

plate 12 Max Weber.

of knowing their ultimate destination, and also no means of altering it. This uncertainty led Calvinists to search for signs from God, since naturally they were anxious to be among the elect. Wealth was taken as a manifestation that they were one of God's elect, and this encouraged followers of Calvin to apply themselves rationally to acquiring wealth. They did this through their ascetic lifestyles and hard work.

The distinctive features of 'rational capitalism' that Weber identified – limits on consumption, especially luxury consumption, and a tendency to reinvest profits in order to systematically accumulate more wealth – had a clear similarity to the Calvinist lifestyle. Although Weber did not believe that Calvinism was the cause of the rise of industrial capitalism, he did believe that capitalism in part grew from Calvinism. Contrary to Marx, Weber argued that the development of rational capitalism could not be explained through wholly material and structural forces; the rise of modern Western society was embedded in the process of rationalization.

Rationalization

Central to Weber's analysis of the rise of capitalism and new organizational forms is this concept of rationalization. But what did he mean by this term? Weber's use of **rationality** is complex and multifaceted. He used the term to describe the overall historical process 'by which nature, society and individual action are increasingly mastered by an orientation to planning, technical procedure and rational action' (ref. 8, p. 218). For Weber, all societies exhibit rationality, in that all people can explain the basis of their behaviour, but only in the West does a particular type of rationality, based on capitalization, bureaucracy and calculation, become dominant. The essence of the concept consisted of three facets: secularization, calculability and rational action.

Rationality means the decline of magical interpretations and explanations of the world. Scientific models of nature and human behaviour are good examples of this type of rationalization, which involves calculating maximum results at minimum cost. It means the replacement of 'traditional' action by 'rational' action. Rationalization depends on two types of activity: strategies of human action, and modification of the means and ends of action in the pursuit of goals. Rather than doing things for emotional reasons, people do things because they calculate that the benefits will outweigh the cost, or because they assess the action as being the most efficient way to achieve their goals. Human actions are also guided by the use of rational decision making in pursuit of unlimited profit. Rules are obeyed because they appear to be built upon rational principles and common sense. In the business sphere, for example, technical and managerial rules are obeyed because they result in efficiency and profits.

Rationalization is different from rationality. Rationalization, the principal process of modernity, refers to the overall process by which reality is increasingly mastered by calculation and rational action, while rationality refers to the capacity of human action to be subject to calculation about means and ends.

Four types of rationality have been identified in Weber's work: practical, theoretical, formal and substantive:

- *Practical rationality* assumes that there are no external mystical causes affecting the outcome of human actions, and sees reality in terms of what is given.
- *Theoretical or technical rationality* involves a cognitive effort to master the world through causality, logical deduction and induction. This type of rationality allows individuals to understand the 'meaning of life' by means of abstract concepts and conceptual reasoning.
- *Formal rationality* refers to the accurate calculation procedures that go into decisions, to ensure consistency of outcome and efficiency in attaining goals.

rationality: the process by which traditional methods of social organization, characterized by informality and spontaneity, are gradually replaced by efficiently administered formal rules and procedures – bureaucracy

- *Substantive rationality* refers to the degree to which human action is guided or shaped by a value system, regardless of the outcome of the action. Accordingly, 'Where formal rationality involves a practical orientation of action regarding outcomes, substantive rationality involves an orientation to values' (ref. 8, p. 222).

Although these four different rationalization processes can complement each other, they can also conflict. For example, the pursuit of efficiency and productivity by calculating the 'best' means to achieve a given end (formal rationality) sometimes conflicts with ethical behaviour (substantive rationality). When examined through a substantive lens, formal rationality is often irrational. In his book, *The McDonaldization of Society*,[12] George Ritzer makes a strong case that formal rationality, embodied in standardized fast-food products, undermines values of social responsibility and individualism in the pursuit of efficiency. In the early twenty-first century, rationalization shapes the subjective experiences of peoples as they understand and evaluate climate change and global warming in terms of non-sustainable growth, profit maximization and **corporate social responsibility**.

Bureaucracy

According to Weber, **bureaucratization** is an inescapable development of modern society. Weber's analysis of the development of capitalism was similar to that of Marx, in that he believed that the rise of capitalism had been marked by the centralization of production, by increased specialization and mechanization, by the progressive loss by workers of the means of production, and by an increase in the function and growth of management. With centralized production, all human activity gives way to a more systematic, rational and extensive use of resources, including labour, which is facilitated by calculable techniques such as accounting. Weber's contention was that 'Where capitalist acquisition is rationally pursued, the corresponding action is oriented towards the calculation of capital. In other words, such action takes place within a planned utilization of material or personal output' (ref. 11, p. 359).

According to Weber, bureaucracies are goal-oriented organizations, administered by qualified specialists, and designed according to rational principles in order to efficiently attain the stated goals. He saw the development of bureaucracy as involving the exorcism of emotional or 'irrational' personal elements such as hate, love or sentiment. In his *Economy and Society*, written in 1921, Weber explained that 'Bureaucracy ... is fully developed in the private economy only in the most advanced institutions of capitalism' (ref. 13, p. 956). He also noted that as the complexity of modern society increases, bureaucracies grow. He defined the bureaucratic 'ideal type' by these characteristics: business is continually conducted, there are stipulated rules, individual spheres of competence are structured in a hierarchy, offices (that is, positions at work) are not owned, selection and promotion is through proven ability, and rewards are commensurate with people's qualifications, ability and performance.

Two core ideas underscore Weber's concept of bureaucracy: formal rationality and **formalized** decision making. Formal rationality operates on the principles of expert knowledge and calculability, whereas formalized decision making operates on the basis of set procedures. This means that decisions can be judged as correct or otherwise by reference to a body of rules.

It would, however, be a misrepresentation of Weber to assume that he was an avid supporter of bureaucracy. Weber was not unaware of the dysfunctions of any over-formalized work form. Bureaucracy removes workers from the decision-making process. It consists of rational and established rules, and restricts individual activity. As a result, it can resemble an 'iron cage and it can mean that

corporate social responsibility: an organization's moral obligation to its stakeholders

bureaucratization: a tendency towards a formal organization with a hierarchy of authority, a clear division of labour and an emphasis on written rules

formalization: the degree to which organizations standardize behaviour through rules, procedures, formal training and related mechanisms organizational behaviour becomes less and less regulated by ethical principles, as these are replaced by technical means and ends' (ref. 8, p. 297). Weber's argument is that because bureaucratic work forms remove workers, including white-collar and managerial staff, from ownership of the means of production, there is a loss of democracy in the workplace, and a panoply of managerial control measures are then necessary to keep the workers in line.[13]

Types of authority

All systems of work require a minimum of 'voluntary compliance' and some mechanism of coordination and control over the activity. This compliance, which is defined as 'an interest in obedience' (ref. 13, p. 212) of the subordinate controlled (such as a worker) to the dominant controller (such as a manager), is based on the ulterior motives of the subordinate, which are governed by custom and a material calculation of advantage, as well as her or his perception of the employment relationship.

Weber's analysis of authority relations provides another insight into the changing structure of work systems. Weber used the terms 'domination' and 'authority' interchangeably in *Economy and Society.* Both derive from the German term *Herrschaft*, which points to leadership, and his theory of domination does have direct relevance to theories of organizational leadership (see Chapter 13). However, Weber did make a distinction between power and domination. He defined **power** as the ability to impose one's will on others in a given situation, even when the others resist. Domination, or authority, is the right of a controller to issue commands to others and expect them to be obeyed. Underscoring Weber's study of authority is his concern for 'legitimacy'. Essentially, he was interested in knowing on what basis subordinates actively acknowledge the validity of authority figures in an established order, and give obedience to them, and on what basis men and women claim authority over others.

Subordinates and the controlled obey dominant controllers by custom and for material advantage and reward, but a belief in legitimacy is also a prerequisite. Weber pointed out that each authority system varies 'According to the kind of legitimacy which is claimed, the type of obedience, the kind of administrative staff developed to guarantee it, and the mode of exercising authority' (ref. 13, p. 213). He then went on to propose three types of legitimate authority: traditional, rational-legal and charismatic. All types of authority, however, require a managerial system characterized by efficiency and continuity.

power: a term defined in multiple ways, involving cultural values, authority, influence and coercion as well as control over the distribution of symbolic and material resources. At its broadest, power is defined as a social system that imparts patterned meaning

plate 13 Rational-legal authority is derived from the rationality of the authority. For example, car drivers usually obey police officers imposing traffic laws (like this one in Paris) because their actions appear to make sense, not because police officers have some inherited authority or are charismatic.

Source: Nick Tutton

Traditional authority is based on the sanctity of tradition and the legitimacy of those exercising authority under such regimes. It is usually acquired through inheritance: this, for example, is the kind of authority held by kings and queens in monarchies. Compliance rests on a framework of obligations that binds followers to leaders by personal loyalties.

Rational-legal authority is derived from the rationality of the authority. For example, car drivers usually obey traffic laws because they appear to make sense, and not because police officers have some inherited authority or are charismatic.

Charismatic authority refers to an attribute or exceptional quality possessed by an individual. In charismatic domination, the leader's claim to legitimacy originates from his or her followers' belief that the leader is to be obeyed because of his or her extraordinary attributes or powers of inspiration and communication.

Weber's typology of authority is important in understanding why individuals behave as they do in the workplace. He was one of the earliest social theorists who saw domination as being characteristic of the relationship between leaders and followers, rather than an attribute of the leader alone.

Social class, inequality and types of class struggle

Authority is equated to possessing power, and difference in the degree of power is one factor that gives rise to differentiated social classes. Weber's description of social class was similar to Marx's, in that he defined a social class by property ownership and by market relations. He stated that:

> a class is a number of people having in common a specific causal component of their life chances. This component is represented exclusively by economic interests in the possession of goods and opportunities for income, under the conditions of the commodity or labour markets. (ref. 13, p. 927)

However, whereas Marx had proposed that individuals carry forward their class interests by virtue of dominant economic forces, Weber argued that the 'mere differentiation of property classes is not "dynamic", that is, it need not result in class struggles and revolutions' (ref. 13, p. 303). He argued instead that the complex and multidimensional nature of social stratification in modern society necessarily inhibits the acquisition of the degree of class consciousness that is necessary for a revolution to occur.

In this argument, people who experience inequality and who have a degree of political consciousness are much more likely to form into rational associations (such as trade unions and social democratic political parties) that would thrust them to the forefront of political activity, than they are to start a revolution. Under these conditions, there are no class interests as such, only the 'average interests' of individuals in similar economic situations, and therefore the class struggle and revolution predicted by Marx are extremely unlikely to happen. Instead, the nature of class conflict changes in a modern society in two fundamental ways. First, there is a shift from direct confrontation between the owners of capital and workers to mediated pay disputes, and second, conflicts between social classes are resolved through the courts and legal means.

Weber's methodology

Between 1902 and 1903, Weber wrote two papers that were central to shaping his views about the nature of doing research in the social sciences, and which continue to influence contemporary inquiry into work and behaviour in the workplace. Let us look at two concepts he developed: ideal types and *Verstehen*.

The **ideal type** is one of Weber's best-known contributions to contemporary organizational theory. At its most basic level, an ideal type is a theoretical abstraction constructed by a social scientist, who draws out important characteristics and simultaneously suppresses less important characteristics. It can be viewed as a measuring rod or yardstick whose function is to compare **empirical** reality with preconceived notions of a reality. Weber put it like this: 'It functions in formulating terminology, classifications, and hypotheses, in working out concrete causal explanation of individual events' (ref. 13, p. 21). As a methodological construction, ideal types are neither ideal nor typical. That is, they are not ideal in any evaluative sense, nor are they typical because they do not represent any norm. They merely

ideal type: an abstract model that describes the recurring characteristics of some phenomenon

empiricism: an approach to the study of social reality that suggests that only knowledge gained through experience and the senses is acceptable

approximate reality. To put it differently, ideal types are heuristic devices (teaching aids) that are used to study slices of reality and enable us to compare empirical forms. Organizational theorists refer for example to an 'ideal type of bureaucracy' or 'ideal flexibility'.

Verstehen: a method of understanding human behaviour by situating it in the context of an individual's or actor's meaning

The second concept, *Verstehen*, we introduced when we discussed research methods in Chapter 1. Weber believed that social scientists must look at the actions of individuals and examine the meanings attached to these behaviours. His approach to understanding human behaviour suggests that observational language is never theoretically independent of the way in which the observer sees a phenomenon and the questions he or she asks about the action. As a consequence, an individual researcher's interpretation of human activity is an inherent aspect of knowledge about organizational behaviour. Weber's 'interpretative' methodology is based on *Verstehen*, meaning 'human understanding'. Human subjects, in contrast to the objects studied in the natural sciences, always rely on their 'understanding' of each other's behaviour and on the 'meanings' they assign to what they and others do.

Go to this website for more information on Weber: www.marxists.org/reference/archive/weber

weblink

This interpretive approach to studying reality is best illustrated by distinguishing between someone walking in a park as a pleasurable leisure experience, and someone walking in a park in an aimless way to kill time because he or she is unemployed and bored. The outer behaviour is exactly the same, but the inner state of the two people is different. It is difficult for a researcher to understand and explain the fundamental distinction between the inner states of the employed and unemployed (in this case) just by observing their outer states, or behaviour. We need an interpretive understanding in order to give a convincing analysis of what is seen.

Can you think of any workplace studies that have based their findings on data gathered through observing people in the workplace? How should the interpretative method affect your evaluation of the studies?

stop reflect

Weber's theories have been challenged. For instance, it is argued that the earliest examples of rational capitalism are not restricted to Calvinist or even Protestant nations. Some Calvinist countries, such as Scotland, failed to 'take off' as capitalist industrialized nations, and some Catholic nations, such as Belgium, were among the market leaders.

As our review of the theories of work moves from the classical sociological theories of the 'big three' – Marx, Durkheim and Weber – to contemporary perspectives on work organizations, we will be better equipped to see how these classical theories continue to inform contemporary theories of work, organizational design and managerial behaviour.

Contemporary theories of work organizations

Organizational studies constitute a discipline in itself, with a plethora of alternative theoretical perspectives. In recent years, different theoretical approaches to studying work and organizations have forced organizational theorists to re-examine and be more reflexive about organizational 'knowledge'. With these changes, as Clegg and Hardy put it, 'Gone is the certainty about what organizations are; gone, too, is the certainty about how they should be studied' (ref. 4, p. 3). In this chapter, we cannot hope to do justice to the complexities of the bewildering variety of perspectives, and we shall therefore seek to highlight what Clegg and Hardy call the major 'conversations' in organizational studies.

How we represent these conversations always involves a choice concerning what theories we wish to represent and how we represent them. To help, we have drawn a schema of organizational theories. The competing theories are plotted along two interlocking axes: the horizontal critical–managerial axis, and the vertical positivist–interpretivist axis (Figure 3.1).

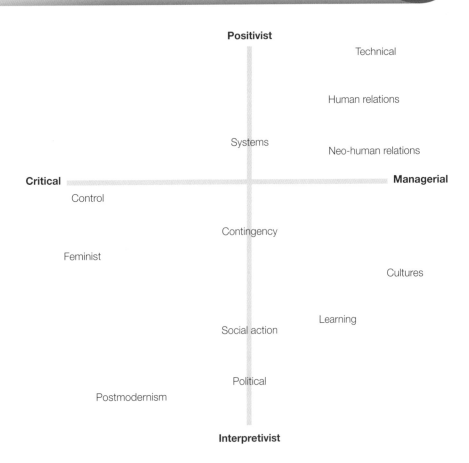

figure 3.1 Contemporary theories of work organizations

The *critical–managerial axis* represents the political left–right continuum (see Chapter 1). At one extreme, the managerial pole positions those perspectives which are essentially concerned with issues of organizational efficiency and performance. Thus, researchers adopting this approach have tended to develop theoretical frameworks and generate empirical data aimed at understanding organizational structures, work arrangements and social processes that can improve labour productivity and organizational effectiveness, or can help solve people-related 'problems' in the workplace. As we explained in Chapter 1, this particular framework is often viewed as mainstream thinking in organizational behaviour texts. At the other extreme, the critical pole, lie critical explanations of work and organizational behaviour that have traditionally been concerned with issues of exploitation and the alienating effects of dividing and routinizing paid work. Researchers adopting this perspective tend to conceptualize organizational structures and management behaviour as control mechanisms that function to fulfil economic imperatives.

The *positivist–interpretivist axis* affirms the importance of epistemological considerations when conducting research: what is (or should be) regarded as acceptable knowledge in organizational behaviour theory. The axis distinguishes between the doctrines of 'positivism' and 'interpretivism'. The positivist epistemological position is generally taken to involve the application of natural science research methods to the study of work organizations, as we saw in Chapter 1. It puts emphasis on the scientific and technical way in which organizational activities can be studied and assessed (using goals, efficiency ratios, rational decision making, productivity measures and so on). In contrast, the interpretivist position maintains that human behaviour is not fully controllable, and therefore a research strategy for organizational behaviour must respect the differences between people and inanimate objects. For interpretivists, the role of the social scientist is to grasp the subjective meaning of behaviour or social action. Researchers focus on the indeterminate and contingent nature of social reality, the unintended consequences of human action and the influence of interpretation.

Where these 12 conversations or theories are plotted on the 'map' is clearly a matter of interpretation and subject to dispute; here the map's function is to act as a heuristic device.

Technical

The 'technical' approach to studying work organizations is most closely associated with the work of Frederick Winslow Taylor (1865–1915). Taylor, an engineer at an American steel mill, experimented with work arrangements to improve labour productivity. Taylor's work configuration rests upon the principle of the technical and social divisions of mental and manual labour. The technical division of labour generally refers to how a complex task is broken down into component parts. Adam Smith's classic observations on pin manufacturing[14] give us one of the first discussions of this in relation to potential increases in labour productivity.

The social division of labour refers to issues of which individuals occupy specific positions in the technical division of labour, how, why and for how long. In addition, **scientific management**, or Taylorism (as it became known), involved the following five principles: maximum job fragmentation, the separation of planning and doing, the separation of direct and indirect labour, minimum skill requirements and minimum material handling (see Chapter 2). These five job design principles gave to management 'the collective concept of control' (ref. 15, p. 97).

Other important theorists contributing to this organization studies genre were Henry Gantt (1861–1919), a protégé of Taylor, who designed the Gantt chart, a straight-line chart to display and measure planned and completed work as time elapsed, Frank Gilbreth (1868–1924), who helped to improve labour productivity through the pioneering use of time and motion techniques, and Henry Ford (1863–1947), who perfected the application of the principles of scientific management to assembly-line production, an approach others would later call 'Fordism'. For most of the twentieth century, the essential principles of Taylorism and Fordism represented a 'common-sense' management strategy in North America and Western Europe.[16–18]

scientific management: this involves systematically partitioning work into its smallest elements and standardizing tasks to achieve maximum efficiency

Go to the following websites for more information on Taylorism and Fordism: http://kapitalism101.wordpress.com/frederick-taylor-the-biggest-bastard-ever; www.nationmaster.com/encyclopedia/Taylorism; www.nosweat.org.uk; www.nationmaster.com/encyclopedia/Fordism

weblink

Human relations

Disenchantment with the technical approach to work and organizational design led to the development of the **human relations** school of thought. Data gathered at the Hawthorne plant of the Western Electric Companies – subsequently known as the Hawthorne studies – suggested a positive association between labour productivity and management style. The phenomenon can be explained like this: 'The determinants of working behaviour are sought in the structure and culture of the group, which is spontaneously formed by the interaction of individuals working together' (ref. 19, p. 99).

human relations: a school of management thought that emphasizes the importance of social processes in the organization

Elton Mayo is most closely associated with the Hawthorne studies. Another pioneering management theorist, Mary Parker Follett, is associated with the early human relations management movement. She contended that traditional authority as an act of subordination was offensive to an individual's emotions, and therefore could not serve as a good foundation for cooperative relations in the workplace. Instead, Follett proposed an authority function, whereby the individual has authority over her or his own job area.[15]

The Hawthorne studies have been criticized at both the technical and the political level. Technically, it has been contended that the researchers used a 'rudimentary' research design and that their analysis of the data was faulty. At a political level, charges of managerial bias, insularity from wider socioeconomic factors, a neglect of workers' organization (that is, trade unions) and organizational conflict were effectively levelled against the researchers. The critique included the charge that human relations theorists conceptualized the 'normal' state of the work organization in 'romantic' and harmonious terms, and neglected workplace conflict because of their pro-management bias.[20,21]

Despite the criticisms, the Hawthorne studies provided the impetus for a new 'common-sense' management strategy sometimes known as 'neo-human relations', which revisited Mayo's work. The human relations school focused on a paternalistic style of management, emphasizing workers' social needs as the key to harmonious relations and better performance, albeit narrowly conceived. Prominent contributors to human relations theory were Abraham Maslow (1908–70), with his idea of 'self-actualization' needs, and Douglas McGregor (1906–64), with his Theory X and Theory Y approach to work motivation (see Chapter 7). These contributions to organizational studies promoted five principles of 'good' work design: closure, whereby the scope of the job includes all the tasks to complete a product or process; task variety, whereby the worker learns a wider range of skills to increase job flexibility; self-regulation, allowing workers to assume responsibility for scheduling their work and quality control; social interaction to allow cooperation and reflectivity; and continuous work-based learning.[22]

Systems theory

Systems theory has played, and continues to play, an influential part in attempts to analyse and explain work organizations. Systems theory involves providing holistic explanations for social phenomena, with a tendency to 'treat societies or social wholes as having characteristics similar to those of organic matter or organisms'.[23] It shows the relationships and interactions between elements, and these in turn are claimed to explain the behaviour of the whole. The notion of 'system' is associated with 'functionalism' and the work of Talcott Parsons (1902–79). Parsons used a systems model that was designed to demonstrate how formal organizations carry out a necessary set of functions to ensure survival.[24] The Parsonian model was also adopted by Dunlop to explain rule-bound behaviour among all major actors within the industrial relations system: unions, management and government.[25] Peter Senge's elaboration of systems thinking provides insight into 'personal mastery', team learning and 'shared vision'.[26] A systems perspective is also used to examine the multidimensional and changing nature of the work context.[27]

Figure 3.2 shows a systems model, with a set of interrelated and interdependent parts configured in a manner that produces a unified whole. That is, any working system takes inputs, transforms them and produces some output. Systems may be classified as either 'closed' or 'open' to their environment. Work organizations are said to be **open systems** in that they acquire inputs from the environment (such as materials, energy, people and finance), transform them into services or products, and discharge outputs in the form of services, products and sometimes pollutants to the external environment.

The open-system model emphasizes that management action is not separate from the world but is connected to the wider context. That is, 'The existing internal structure, strategy, and success of an organization is heavily influenced by environmental forces in which it operates and with which it interacts and competes' (ref. 28, p. 209). However, it is too simple to regard the influence of context as only a one-way flow. Systems thinking is closely linked to the Weberian notion of the paradox of consequences in organizational life. A systems approach can illustrate how managerial behaviour and actions designed to advance a goal or solve a problem have unintended consequences that undermine or exacerbate the problem.[5]

What contemporary jobs tend to incorporate neo-human relations principles into job design, and what kind of jobs seem to be imbued with neo-Taylorism?

stop reflect

---

open systems: organizations that take their sustenance from the environment, and in turn affect that environment through their output

---

Can you think of an example from your own work experience of the paradox of consequences? What did management do, and what was the unintended outcome(s)?

stop reflect

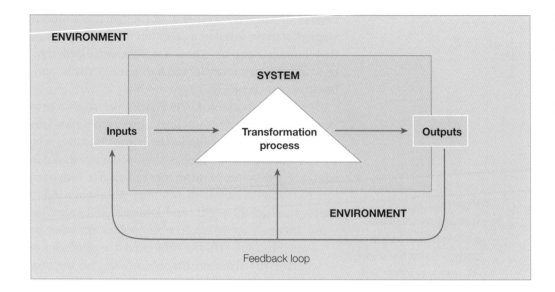

figure 3.2
An open system

This kind of systems or functionalist thinking highlights the apparent functions of different work organizations. But the system has its critics. Detractors emphasize that systems analysis reifies organizations: in other words, it treats a concept as if it were a real thing. To assert that organizations make decisions implies that organizations have an existence beyond their human members, but it can be argued that this is not so: organizations are merely legal constructs. So when we talk of organizations 'making decisions', we really mean that some or all of the dominant controllers of an organization make the decisions.

Second, systems theory suggests a greater degree of stability and order in organizations than might actually exist across time. Third, systems theories tend to downplay the significance of historical developments to explain contemporary organizational phenomena. And finally, the essential thrust of functionalism or systems analysis is towards consensus. It is inherently deterministic: it 'is not only technocratic in its denial of conflicting ideologies and material interests but also deterministic in its pursuit of the correct prediction of behaviour through an analysis of organizational rules' (ref. 5, pp. 132–3).

Contingency theory

Contingency theory focuses on the three-way relationship between structure, contingency and outcomes, and has proved to be one of the most influential of all organizational theories. Contingency, as it applies to work organizations, means that the effectiveness of a particular strategy, structure or managerial style depends on the presence or absence of other factors or forces. Accordingly, there are no absolutely 'one best' strategies, structures or styles. Instead, whether an action is 'best' must be gauged relative to the context, the circumstances or the other factors.

The most noted contingency research was conducted over 40 years ago.[29–32] Joan Woodward, for example, found that there was no best way of organizing production, but that a particular organizational design and managerial style of behaviour was most appropriate for each technological situation (for example, worker-oriented production as found in car assembly compared with process production as found in a chemical plant). She reported that organizations differed not only in the general character of their structure and technology, but also in such detailed respects as managerial behaviour, methods of intermanagement communication, and interactions. In some organizations studied, 'it was not always easy to distinguish between those who gave and those who took orders' (ref. 30, p. 27).

The British writers Burns and Stalker suggested that organizational structures and managerial behaviours differed according to a range of environments differentiated by their degree of predictability and stability. Management styles would tend to be different in what they called 'mechanistic' or 'organic' systems. The American researchers Lawrence and Lorsch developed contingency analysis, by showing the importance of establishing integrative mechanisms to counter the centrifugal forces that differentiate and fragment managers and non-managers alike.

For dominant controllers of work organizations, the appeal of a contingency perspective is in part because the 'if–then' formula represents an explicit fracture with the simpler 'one best way' approach, while offering persuasive normative guidelines for what organizational leaders should do to sustain organizational performance. Where the contingency approach is most vulnerable to criticism is in its construction of independent variables, and this is why it is positioned close to the determinist line. The various studies argue that although some degree of contingency exists, in so far as controllers can choose between different forms of organizational structure, only those who choose the most 'appropriate' structure are likely to be successful. Others have noted the role of 'environmental determinism', and the removal of contingency by specifying the external conditions under which success can be determined: 'environments are not only given determinate power ... but they are literally reified through the language of environments acting on passive organizations' (ref. 33, p. 63).

Culture theory

The notion of applying 'cultural' thinking to organizational studies is derived from Durkheimian concerns for organizational solidarity through ideological consensus, and from Max Weber's pronouncements in *The Protestant Ethic* on the connections between a distinctive 'cultural phenomenon' and Western capitalist modernity. Organizational culture refers to artefacts, the shared beliefs and values and core assumptions that exist in an organization. Typically, the approach tends to be normative: that is, it is intended to explain not so much what the contemporary culture of an organization is, but what it should be. Thus, it may well persuade managers to act as if the preferred cultural attributes already existed, so the acting out of a cultural myth becomes the organizational reality.[34] A less manipulative approach to the significance of organizational cultures is provided by Gareth Morgan.[35] According to Morgan, culture is shared property and has a language and symbolism that can be decoded.

Morgan believes that how we define, understand and conceptualize organizations depends on our images or mental models of the essential shape, artefacts and features of organizations. He has argued that most definitions and theories of work organizations can be associated with a particular organizational metaphor. The most common metaphors view organizations as cultures, organisms, an iron cage, machines, networks or learning systems. These metaphors are embedded in various theories of organizational behaviour.

Charles Handy has suggested that 'role cultures', which are typically found in large bureaucracies, exude rationality, specialization, routines and rule following.[36] Generally speaking, he suggests that the larger an organization, the more expensive its technology, and the more routine its environment, the more likely it will be to adopt a role culture.

The cultural perspective converges with popular human resource management models, which highlight the importance of 'contextual relations' and organizational 'climate' to generate employee commitment.[37,38] Although the use of metaphor has entered popular culture, we need to be aware of the common error of treating metaphors as literal descriptions of social reality (for early literature on this, see ref. 39). See Chapter 12 for more discussion on organizational culture, and Chapter 14 on the use of metaphors in organization communications.

Learning theories

Go to the following website for more information on **organizational learning**: www. fieldbook.com

weblink

organizational learning: the knowledge management process in which organizations acquire, share and use knowledge to succeed

The learning organization and 'workplace learning' are two popular, and relatively new, metaphors in organizational studies. A learning organization is one that 'facilitates the learning of all its members and continually transforms itself'.[34] Proponents of management and workplace learning equate the learning organization with organizational economic success.[40] Typically, the learning organization approach is interpretive, because it is more closely related to the concept of organizational culture than to something tangible. The focus in a learning organization is on creating an environment that fosters learning through strategies that promote a 'growth-oriented workplace'.[22,41,42] A learning organization is normally understood as one that is 'good' at learning because of the types of activity it employs. Learning organizations are understood as places where individuals can be 'creative' and where people 'learn how to learn together'. We discuss workplace learning further in Chapter 6.

Critical insight

Learning organizations and organizational learning

For a critical review and evaluation of the literature on learning organizations and organizational learning, see

Chapter 4 of *Workplace Learning: A Critical Introduction*, by John Bratton, Jean Helms Mills and Peter Sawchuk.[22] A review of this literature is also given by Thomas Garavan in his article 'The learning organization: a review and evaluation'.[42]

Social action theory

The most influential contributions to social action theory were those of Silverman.[43] He provided a powerful critique of the reification embodied in systems thinking, and advocated a view of organizations as the product of individuals pursuing their own ends with the available means. He argued that social reality did not just happen, but had to be made to happen. The implication of this was that, through social interaction, people could modify and possibly even transform social meanings, and therefore any explanation of human activity had to take into account the meanings that those involved assigned to their actions. For example, whether a failure to obey a manager's instruction is a sign of worker insubordination or militancy, or caused by the beginnings of deafness, depends not on what managers or researchers observe to happen, but on what the worker involved means by her or his behaviour. This approach drew from Weber's work on the methodology and theory of knowledge action.

The social action approach involves examining six interrelated areas:

- the nature of the role system and pattern of interaction that has developed in the organization
- the nature of involvement of 'ideal-typical' actors and the characteristic hierarchy of ends they pursue
- the actors' present definitions of their situation within the organization, and their expectations of the likely behaviour of others
- the typical actions of different actors, and the meaning they attach to their actions

- the nature and source of the intended and unintended consequences of action
- any changes in the involvement and ends of the actors and in the role system.[44]

This method of analysing workplace behaviour is influenced by the work of George Herbert Mead (1863–1931) and symbolic interactionism (see Chapter 1). The approach assumes that human beings act towards things on the basis of subject meanings, and these meanings are the product of social interaction in human society. Organizational study, therefore, involves notions of 'symbolic meaning' and 'sense making' so that individuals can make sense of what they do. Critics have stressed that the micro-level approach of symbolic interactionism does not give sufficient attention to the 'big picture' and the inherent conflict of interest between the key actors representing capital and labour.

Political theory

The political approach to understanding work organizations characterizes the workplace as a purposive miniature society, with politics pervading all managerial work. By politics we mean the power relationships between managers and relevant others, and in turn the capacity of an individual manager to influence others who are in a state of dependence. It refers to those social processes which are not part of a manager's formal role, but which influence (perhaps not directly) the distribution of resources for the purpose of promoting personal objectives.

OB in focus   Developing organizational learning in the UK National Health Service

Learning has been identified as a central concern for a modernized British National Health Service (NHS). Continuing professional development has an important role to play in improving learning, but there is also a need to pay more attention to collective (organizational) learning. Such learning is concerned with the way organizations build and organize knowledge.

The recent emphasis within the NHS has been on the codification of individual and collective knowledge – for example, in guidelines and National Service Frameworks. This needs to be balanced by more personalized knowledge management strategies, especially when dealing with innovative services that rely on tacit knowledge to solve problems. Having robust systems for storing and communicating knowledge is only one part of the challenge. It is also important to consider how such knowledge gets used, and how routines become established in organizations to structure the way in which knowledge is deployed.

In many organizations, these routines favour the adaptive use of knowledge, which helps organizations to achieve incremental improvements in existing practice. However, the development of organizational learning in the NHS needs to move beyond adaptive (single-loop) learning, to foster skills in generative (double-loop) learning and meta-learning. Such learning leads to a redefinition of the organization's goals, norms, policies, procedures or even structures. However, moving the NHS in this direction will require attention to the cultural values and structural mechanisms that facilitate organizational learning.

Source: Sandra M. Nutley and Huw T. O. Davies (ref. 45, p. 35).

Politics in organizations is simply a fact of life. However, as others have observed, the political quality of the management practice is 'denied' or 'trivialized' in many studies of work organizations. And although individual managers might privately question the moral value and integrity of their actions, 'Caught in the maelstrom of capitalist organization, managers are pressured to emulate and reward all kinds of manipulative and destructive behaviours' (ref. 46, p. 39). This perspective on studying organizations offers an approach that examines individual managers as 'knowledgeable human agents' functioning within a dynamic arena where both organizational resources and outcomes can be substantially shaped by their actions. It also reinforces the theoretical and practical importance attached to building alliances and networks of cooperative relationships among organizational members.

These negotiating processes shape, and in turn are shaped by, organizational dynamics (see Chapter 16).

An early study of management adopting a political perspective was undertaken by Dalton in 1959.[47] Building on work by Fox,[48] Graeme Salaman pronounced the political approach most clearly. Power relations that reflect the social inequality prevailing in the wider society determine the structure of work organizations. Organizations are not independent bodies but are embedded into a wider (again political) environment. Furthermore, notions of identity and the part played by organizational life in the construction of both individual and group identity are important.

The political perspective has also drawn attention to the role of strategic choice in shaping organizational structures and management behaviour.[49-52] The strategic choice approach emphasizes the importance of the political power of dominant coalitions and ideological commitments in explaining variations in managerial policies and behaviour, and ultimately explaining variations in managerial effectiveness and organizational outcomes. The political perspective has been criticized for failing to offer little or no explanation of the asymmetrical nature of power, which is the essence of the 'radical' control perspective on management.

Control theories

At the critical pole of the managerial–critical continuum lie the 'control' theories. Much of this work has its roots in Marx's analysis of capitalism. This approach to work and management has come to be associated with the seminal work of Harry Braverman.[16] Organizational theorists approaching the study of work and organizations from this perspective stress the inherent source of tension in organizations arising from technological rationality.[20,53-58] A related focus is the **labour process** approach, which conceptualizes organizational managers as controlling agents who serve the economic imperatives imposed by capitalist market relations. Managerial control is thus *the* central focus of management activity. According to this perspective, organizational structures and employment strategies are instruments and techniques to control the labour process in order to secure high levels of labour productivity and corresponding levels of profitability.

The control perspective views work organizations as hierarchical structures in which workers are deskilled by scientific management techniques and new technology. Managerial behaviour is characterized primarily as control relations: 'organizations are structures of inequality and control'.[17] Such an approach recognizes the existence of inconsistent organizational designs and management practices, and these paradoxical tendencies provide the source of further management strategies that attempt to eradicate the tensions caused by them. The most important of these paradoxes is considered to be the simultaneous desire for control over workers, and cooperation and commitment from them.

The control perspective has also attracted much criticism from both critical and mainstream management theorists. For example, critiques of the deskilling and control thesis draw attention to moderating factors such as markets, worker resistance and batch size.[59-61]

Feminist theory

Until relatively recently, studying the workplace using a 'feminist' approach had not been a major topic of inquiry. The organizational discourse is still, in the main, a masculine endeavour to illuminate organizational behaviour. For radical feminists, science is not sexless: on the contrary, 'the attributes of science are the attributes of males' (ref. 62, p. 207). Research about work organizations tends to

labour process: the process whereby labour is applied to materials and technology to produce goods and services that can be sold in the market as commodities. The term is typically applied to the distinctive labour processes of capitalism in which owners/managers design, control and monitor work tasks so as to maximize the extraction of surplus value from the labour activity of workers

Work and Society: Benign control and precarious work

Sociologist Derek Layder argues that interpersonal control in its many forms is the 'bedrock' on which all social institutions (including work organizations) rest. Central to his argument is a distinction between benign and more problematic and exploitative forms of control. Layder (2004) suggests that we are accustomed to thinking about control in negative ways. The typical image of control portrays a stronger person dominating a weaker person. In Layder's view, this negative image of control is only part of the larger domain of control – and we have failed to conceptualize fully the more benign forms of control that lie at the heart of everyday interactions. As he puts it:

> The common thread in all control is that it is aimed at securing the compliance of the target ... Benignity in control is reflected in its attempt to take the interests of others at least partly into account. By contrast, in domination the interests of the more powerful person are overriding. Also benign control is inherently partial and open-ended ... the control remains benign only as long as a broadly equal reciprocity is maintained, where each party has an opportunity to 'have their say' and 'get their way'. (p. 60)

Layder's comments on the informal face-to-face interactions that form the basis of all social life offer us a useful vantage point on the social nature of work. In fact, we could use his continuum (benign control at one end and domination at the other end) to think about and describe the nature of control in any given work organization. Especially worthwhile would be exercises that enabled managers and employees to participate in discussions about the qualities that distinguish benign informal social control from domination. Such exercises are valuable not just for their contribution to team building, trust and a sense of security among workers, but also because they prepare employees to participate in the processes of collaborative problem solving that are essential to effective organizations.

It is important, however, to place the idea of benign control in a larger context. Layder is right to stress that academic interpretations of control have focused on its negative forms and features and that, consequently, a theoretical account of benign control has not received sufficient attention. But there is perhaps good reason for this: if we look at work from a historical and comparative perspective, we find no shortage of examples of workers whose working lives have been characterized by coercion and domination.

The history of the employment contract is itself very telling. Mac Neil (2002) notes that the employment contract has roots in the master–servant relationship. Although there is evidence that, throughout the twentieth century, Western industrialized nations have moved away from the idea of a master–servant relationship towards a workplace

where benign control has triumphed over coercion and domination, there is also, sadly, evidence of the opposite. Kalleberg (2009) reminds us of the immense variability of employment relations, even in the developed world. Some employment relations are characterized by respect, security reasonable pay and other indications of quality. Yet among large segments of the workforce, there is a trend towards 'precarious work' and an overall reduction in the quality of working life. (Kalleberg cites as a cause of this trend employer efforts to 'obtain greater flexibility to meet growing competition' (p. 12).)

What are the implications of the trend towards precarious work for the forms of social control identified by Layder? As work becomes more precarious, will the balance between benign and more problematic forms of control be tilted towards the problematic end of the continuum? Will historical forms of employment relations reappear, causing workers to once again occupy 'the subservient status of the servant' (Mac Neil, 2002, p. 174)? These questions are best answered by focusing on particular cases.

 stop! Consider the following definition: '"precarious work" ... [is] employment that is uncertain, unpredictable, and risky from the point of view of the worker' (Kalleberg, p. 2). Now, reflect on the following questions:

- What kinds of organization are likely to generate precarious work for their employees?
- Are some workers more likely than others to experience the negative effects of precarious work?
- Will the workers subjected to precarious work inevitably experience problematic forms of social control?
- What can be done to reduce the likelihood that problematic control will trump benign control in organizations employing large numbers of precarious workers?

Sources and further information:

Kalleberg, A. (2009) 'Precarious work, insecure workers: employment relations in transition', *American Sociological Review*, **74**, pp. 1–22.
Layder, D. (2004) *Emotion in Social Life: The Lost Heart of Society*, London: Sage.
Mac Neil, M. (2002). 'Governing employment', pp. 171–87 in M. Mac Neil, N. Sargent and P. Swan (eds), *Law, Regulation and Governance*, Dons Mills, ON: Oxford University Press.

Note: This feature was written by David MacLennan, Assistant Professor at Thompson Rivers University, BC, Canada.

be both androcentric (focused on males) and ethnocentric (focused on the white Anglo-Saxon culture). One interpretation is that it has focused on the management agenda, and up to now this has consisted largely of 'important' white men in one field (academia) talking to, reflecting on and writing about 'important' white men in another field (organizations).[63]

Theoretically, one of the most important consequences of gender analysis in organizational studies is its power to question research findings that segregate organizational behaviour from the larger structure of social and historical life. Accordingly, much of the recent work most directly related to the feminist approach requires us to look at the interface between social context and work. It is argued that this shapes and reshapes the employment relationship. We need to look at gender divisions in the labour market, patriarchal power, issues of sexuality and inequality in society and at work, and the interface between home and work (the 'dual-role' syndrome). More importantly, however, incorporating gender development into the study of organizational studies will represent the life experience of both men and women in a more comprehensive and inclusive way.

Postmodernism

postmodernism: the sociological approach that attempts to explain social life in modern societies that are characterized by post-industrialization, consumerism and global communications

A new focus for organization theory is **postmodernism**. While traditional writings on organization theory tend to view work organizations as fine examples of human rationality, postmodernists such as Michel Foucault regard organizations as more akin to defensive reactions against inherently destabilizing forces.[5,64] The postmodernist perspective has its roots in the French intellectual tradition of post-structuralism, an approach to knowledge that puts the consideration of 'reflexivity' and how language is used at the centre of the study of all aspects of human activity. Thus, postmodern perspectives question attempts to 'know' or 'discover' the genuine order of things (what is known as representation). Researchers must possess the ability to be critical of their own intellectual assumptions (that is, exercise reflexivity).

This approach plays down the notion of a disinterested observer, and instead stresses the way in which people's notion of who and what they are – their agency, in other words – is shaped by the discourses that surround them. This is known as decentering the subject. Postmodernists also believe that researchers are materially involved in constructing the world they observe through language (by writing about it). Thus, where modernists perceive history as a grand narrative of human activity, rationality and progress, postmodernists reject the grand narrative and the notion of progressive intent. Clegg and Hardy frame the postmodern approach this way: 'They are histories, not history. Any pattern that is constituted can only be a series of assumptions framed in and by a historical context' (ref. 4, p. 2).

Michel Foucault's relevance to organizational theory lies in several related spheres.[65,66] First, he argues that contemporary management controls human behaviour neither by consensus nor by coercion, but rather by systems of surveillance and human relations management techniques. Second, he suggests that although an organization is 'constructed by power', its members do not 'have' power. Power is not the property of any individual or group. While modernists see the direction of power flowing downwards against subordinates, and its essence as negative, Foucault argues that power should be configured as a relationship between subjects. It has 'capillary' qualities that enable it to be exercised *within* the social body, rather than *above* it' (ref. 67, p. 39). Third, with the ever-increasing expansion of electronic surveillance in the workplace, Foucault offers his own image of an 'iron cage' in the form of the extended panopticon – hidden surveillance.

Postmodernism is a useful way to study work organizations. In particular, the notion of power as a 'web' within which managers and non-managers are held has much to offer. However, some critics, for example Martin Parker, have described postmodern epistemology as a reactionary intellectual trend, which amounts to a 'fatal distraction' from engagement in a rigorous analysis of organizational changes located within late modernity.[68]

The value of theory about contemporary organizational behaviour

In this chapter, we have reviewed the main themes and arguments of both classical and contemporary theories of work. As we explained, the classical theories are derived from the works of Karl Marx, Emile Durkheim and Max Weber, and are an intellectual response to the transformation of society caused by industrial capitalism. A legitimate question for students of organizational behaviour is, 'Why bother studying sociological classics – three "dead white men"?' We believe that an understanding of the classical accounts of work is important because, as others have also argued, the epistemological, theoretical and methodological difficulties that were identified and debated by Marx, Durkheim and Weber remain central to the conduct of contemporary research on organizational behaviour.[2,69–73] Those of us who study contemporary work organizations are informed by the 'canonical' writers and constantly return to them for ideas and inspiration.

In terms of understanding what goes on in the workplace, theory cannot be separated from management practice. It is used both to defend existing management practices and to validate new ways of organizing work, or *doing*. The nature of the employment relationship is clearly an issue of central importance to understanding human behaviour in work organizations. The classical sociologists developed a body of work that, directly or by inference, provides an account of the relations between employers and employees.

For Marx, conflict is structured into the employment relationship and is, for most of the time, asymmetrical. That is, the power of the employer or agent (manager) typically exceeds that of the workers. Durkheim's work influenced how theorists have studied organizations, and he reminds us that there are multiple ways in which society imposes itself upon us and shapes our behaviour.

A number of Weber's concepts also continue to have much relevance in the early twenty-first century. For example, his concept of charismatic domination is prominent in contemporary leadership theories. In addition, Weber's concepts of bureaucracy and rationalization have been applied to the fast-food sector, and have exposed the irrationality associated with the paradigm of McDonaldization. Weber's interpretive method, and in particular the researcher's capacity to assign different meanings to shared reality, gives a postmodern ring to his theory.

Finally, classical theories enter the contemporary debates on work organization and management practices by reinforcing the message that understanding the nature of the employment relationship necessarily involves considering organizational culture, societal values and norms as well as national institutions. It is through these that individuals acquire a self-identity and the mental, physical and social skills that shape their behaviour both outside and inside the work organization.

Summary

- The three founders of the sociology of work all continue to have their contemporary adherents and detractors.

- Marx's fascination with class, conflict and the labour process formed the basis for the most popular new approach throughout much of industrial sociology, from the late 1960s to the 1980s. It spawned a complete school of thought in the labour process tradition, but its limitations became more evident as the approach attempted to explain all manner of social phenomena directly through the prism of class.

- Durkheim's moral concerns continue to pervade the market economy, and make predictions about human actions that are based on amoral, economically rational behaviour less than convincing. Perhaps where Durkheim has been most vigorously criticized has been in relation to the allegedly cohering effects of an extended division of labour. The mainstream of managerial theories does not support Durkheim on this point: dependency does not generate mutual solidarity.

- Weber's theories of rationalization and bureaucracy have never been far from the minds of those analysing the trend towards larger and larger organizations, and the recent movement towards more flexible work organization patterns. Again, however, Weber's over-rationalized approach underestimated the significance of destabilizing and sectional forces within work organizations.

- This chapter has reviewed 12 theoretical approaches or conversations on organizational studies: the technical, human relations, neo-human relations, systems thinking, contingency, cultures, learning, control, feminist, social action, political and postmodernist approaches. It has adopted a particular form of differentiating between the various theories through an organizational grid based on two axes: managerial–critical and determinist–interpretative. This is a heuristic way of structuring the various possibilities.

Key concepts

alienation 72
androcentrism 92
anomie 75
ideal type 81
labour power 71
paradox of consequences 85
rationality 78–9
strategic choice 90

Key vocab checklist for ESL students

- [ ] Alienation
- [ ] Anomie
- [ ] Bourgeoisie
- [ ] Class conflict
- [ ] Class consciousness
- [ ] Contingency theory
- [ ] Contradiction, contradict
- [ ] Corporate social responsibility
- [ ] Division of labour
- [ ] Empiricism, empirical
- [ ] Formalization, formal, formalize
- [ ] Human relations
- [ ] Ideal type
- [ ] Input
- [ ] Labour process
- [ ] Mechanical solidarity
- [ ] Objectification, objectify
- [ ] Open systems
- [ ] Organic solidarity
- [ ] Organizational learning
- [ ] Output
- [ ] Postmodernism
- [ ] Power
- [ ] Proletariat
- [ ] Rationalization, rationality, rational, rationalize
- [ ] Scientific management
- [ ] Social solidarity
- [ ] Surplus value
- [ ] Survey
- [ ] Urbanization
- [ ] *Verstehen*

Review questions

1. To what extent has the decline of Communism undermined the utility of Marx's ideas?
2. Why was Weber so pessimistic about work when Durkheim and Marx were so optimistic?
3. Do we need theory to explain the way organizations work?
4. What is the relevance of Weber's concept of *Verstehen* for organizational behaviour researchers?
5. What is meant by open systems, contingency theory and social action theory? Why is it important to understand each of them?
6. What is meant by the suggestion that theory cannot be separated from management practice?

Research questions

1. Form a study group of three to five people. Having read a review of the classical sociological theorists and contemporary approaches to studying work and organizations, is the role of the academics in organizational behaviour to unmask inequality in organizational life or to be detached? Is it possible for organizational behaviour researchers to be value-free and objective in their research? If a researcher adopted a feminist perspective, how would this guide his or her research?
2. Obtain a copy of Stephen Ackroyd and others' (2006) *The Oxford Handbook of Work and Organization* and read pages 2–8. To what extent are this textbook – *Work and Organizational Behaviour* – and the topics selected for study a product of its times? If you had to do some organizational

behaviour research, what would your topic be and what factors would influence your choice?

3. Retrieve and read Christine Coupland and others' (2008) article, 'Saying it with feeling: analyzing speakable emotions' (see Further reading, below). What does the term 'constructionism' mean? How does Marx's analysis of capitalist employer–employee relations help us to understand that how people talk about emotional experiences in the workplace is bound up in relations of power?

Further reading

Bratton, J., Denham, D. and Deutschmann, L. (2009) *Capitalism and Classical Sociological Theory*, Toronto: University of Toronto Press.

Coupland, C., Brown, A. D., Daniels, K. and Humphreys, M. (2008) 'Saying it with feeling: analyzing speakable emotions', *Human Relations*, **61**(3), pp. 327–53.

Heracleous, L. and Jacob, C. D. (2008) 'Understanding organizations through embodied metaphors', *Organization Studies*, **29**(1), pp. 45–78.

Jaffee, D. (2001) *Organization Theory: Tension and Change*, Boston, MA: McGraw-Hill, Chapters 1 and 2.

Manning, P. K. (2008) 'Goffman on organizations', *Organization Studies*, **29**(5), pp. 677–99.

Parker, M. (2000) 'The sociology of organizations and the organization of sociology: some reflections on the making of a division of labour', *Sociological Review*, **4**(1), pp. 124–46.

Reed, M. (1999) 'Organizational theorizing: a historically contested terrain', pp. 25–50 in S. R. Clegg and C. Hardy (eds), *Studying Organization: Theory and Method*, London: Sage.

Rowlinson, M. (2004) 'Challenging the foundations of organization theory', *Work, Employment and Society*, **18**(3), pp. 607–20.

Swingewood, A. (2000) *A Short History of Sociological Thought*, New York: St Martin's Press, Chapters 2, 3 and 4.

Tsoukas, H. (1992) 'Postmodernism, reflexive rationalism and organizational studies: a reply to Martin Parker', *Organizational Studies*, **13**(4), pp. 643–9.

Chapter case study 1

Butting out smoking in Russia

Setting

With the collapse of the Soviet Union, the privatization of Russia's tobacco industry began. In the new Russia, tobacco advertising is unavoidable. Smoking is promoted on half of all billboards in Moscow and on three-quarters of the plastic bags in the country. As a result of tobacco companies promoting smoking as part of a 'Western lifestyle' and striving to capitalize on the public's new disposable income, smoking rates have doubled. Russia is now the fourth heaviest smoking country in the world, with one in four boys under the age of 10 and 60 per cent of men over the age of 15 classified as smokers. While most of the Western world is experiencing a decrease in smoking rates, the number of Russian smokers continues to climb.

The government has proposed legislation banning smoking in workplaces and other public places, such as on aircraft, trains and municipal transport as well as in schools, hospitals, cultural institutions and government buildings. The legislation also requires specially designated smoking areas to be set up, and for restaurants and cafes to set up no-smoking areas. The changes will affect not only Russian companies, but also international firms looking to invest in the expanding privatization of the economy. The emerging middle class has produced a potential market of 150 million consumers that lures companies from all over the world hoping to tap into the vast natural resources, advanced technology and skilled workers that Russia has to offer.

The problem

Kendles & Smith is a global British pharmaceutical, medical devices and consumer packaged goods manufacturer, with 150 subsidiary companies operating in over 32 countries. It recently opened a new operation in Moscow as part of a strategy to make its mark on the new prosperous Russian economy.

The management at Kendles & Smith were versed in Russian history and understood that worker attitudes and behaviours had been shaped by 70 years of Communist dictatorship, a centrally planned economic system, and government bureaucracy that had ruled the people's lives. Like most international firms, management at Kendles & Smith found Russian workers to be cooperative and compliant, but not risk takers. Many of the supervisors hired from the local labour pool lacked confidence and drive. Although they followed corporate policies strictly, the employees in turn expected the new company to take care of them and their families.

With the UK having one of the lowest smoking rates in Europe, the management at Kendles & Smith were surprised at the number of the employees who were smokers – almost 65 per cent. As a company with a focus on health products, one of its first goals was to develop a voluntary tobacco reduction programme, including counselling and nicotine cessation aids, to improve the health of its new staff. Unfortunately, only a small group of workers took advantage of the programme in its first year, and the majority of these were supervisors.

The next step was to implement a smoking ban in the Russian operations. Although it was made clear to all employees that the company president wanted to see the worksites smoke-free, regardless of the government's legislation, only the supervisors were to be given an opportunity to express their positions on the matter. Jonathan Williams, one of the UK managers assigned to the Moscow operation, was given the task of doing the research. There were over 100 supervisors, and Jonathan was given only a short time-frame within which to present his findings. Although Jonathan was free to speak to the supervisors, the company president stressed that he really just wanted to know whether or not the majority of the supervisors favoured the ban.

As Jonathan had not conducted workplace research before, he felt overwhelmed when he began reading about the various methods that could be used. He wanted the rich qualitative information that in-person interviews could give, but he thought that taking a more quantitative approach, such as using a questionnaire, would provide the anonymity that the supervisors might need to be honest with their answers.

Tasks

As Jonathan, ask yourself the following questions:

1. What would be the disadvantages of using a questionnaire in this case?
2. What might be missed by gathering only the supervisors' opinions?
3. What qualities do the Russian workers exhibit that could influence the research results? Why?

Further reading

Allan, G. and Skinner, C. (eds) (1991) *Handbook for Research Students in the Social Sciences*, London: Falmer Press.

Bryman, J. (ed.) (1988) *Doing Research in Organizations*, London: Routledge.

Elenkov, D. (1998) 'Can American management concepts work in Russia?', *California Management Review*, 40(4), pp. 133–56.

Oppenheim, A. N. (1992) *Questionnaire Design, Interviewing and Attitude Measurement*, London: Pinter.

Visit http://pre.ethics.gc.ca/eng/policy-politique/tcps-eptc/readtcps-lireeptc for an example of a research ethics policy.

Note

This case study was written by Lori Rilkoff, MSc, CHRP, Senior Human Resources Manager at the City of Kamloops, and lecturer in HRM at Thompson Rivers University, BC, Canada. Data on smoking in Russia were taken from http://news.bbc.co.uk/2/hi/health/7209551.stm; www.scientificblogging.com/news_releases/russian_women_exercise_post_soviet_free_will_by_smoking_a_lot_more

Chapter case study 2

Research at Aeroprecision AB

Visit www.palgrave.com/business/brattinob2e to view this case study

Web-based assignment

How are we to make sense of the competing assortment of theoretical approaches to organizational behaviour? We address this question here with reference to the classical accounts of sociology and contemporary approaches to studying formal organizations. Our collective experience in teaching and researching aspects of organizational behaviour has made it clear that the contemporary student of organizational behaviour cannot understand the discipline without an appreciation of the works of Marx, Weber and Durkheim. In their own way, each addressed the following two fundamental questions:

*   What is the source of societal and organizational conflict?
*   What is the relationship between consciousness (the 'self' or 'inside') and society or social structure (the 'outside')?

On an individual basis, or working in a small group, visit the following websites and write a brief summary of how Marx,

Weber and Durkheim have fundamentally shaped the modern debate about work and organizations:

*   http://plato.stanford.edu/entries/marx
*   www.epistemelinks.com/Main/Philosophers.aspx?PhilCode=Durk
*   www.marxists.org/reference/archive/weber

OB in film

The film *Roger & Me* (1989), directed by Michael Moore, is a documentary about the closure of General Motors' car plant at Flint, Michigan, which resulted in the loss of 30,000 jobs. The film provides insight into corporate restructuring and US deindustrialization, and details the attempts of the film maker to conduct a face-to-face interview with General Motors Chief Executive Officer Roger Smith. The film also raises questions about values, politics and the practical considerations of doing organizational behaviour research.

Values reflect the personal beliefs of a researcher. Gaining access to organizations, particularly to top managers, is a political process. Access is usually mediated by gatekeepers concerned not only about what the organization can gain from the research, but also about the researcher's motives.

Watch the documentary, and consider these questions:

*   Can organizational behaviour researchers be value-free and objective in their research?
*   Who are the gatekeepers in *Roger & Me*? How can gatekeepers influence how the inquiry will take place?

Practical considerations refer to issues about how to carry out organizational behaviour research: for example, choices of research design or method need to be dovetailed with specific research questions.

*   What alternative methods could a researcher use to investigate the closure of General Motors' factory at Flint?

References

1   Salaman, G. (1981) *Class and the Corporation*, London: Fontana.
2   Turner, B. S. (1999) *Classical Sociology*, London: Sage.
3   Hurst, C. (2005) *Living Theory*, Boston, MA: Pearson.
4   Clegg, S. and Hardy, C. (1999) *Studying Organization: Theory and Method*, Thousand Oaks, CA: Sage.
5   Grint, K. (1998) *The Sociology of Work* (2nd edn), Cambridge: Polity Press.
6   Marx, K. (1867/1970) *Capital: A Critique of Political Economy*, Volume 1, London: Lawrence & Wishart.
7   Ritzer, G. and Goodman, D. J. (2004) *Classical Social Theory* (4th edn), New York: McGraw-Hill.
8   Morrison, K. (1995) *Marx, Durkheim, Weber*, London: Sage.
9   Marx, K. and Engels, F. (1848/1967) *The Communist Manifesto*, London: Penguin.
10 Durkheim, E. (1893/1997) *The Division of Labor in Society*, New York: Free Press.
11 Weber, M. (1905/2002) *The Protestant Ethic and the 'Spirit' of Capitalism*, London: Penguin.
12 Ritzer, G. (2000) *The McDonaldization of Society*, Thousand Oaks, CA: Pine Forge Press.
13 Weber, M. (1922/1968) *Economy and Society*, New York: Bedminster.

14 Smith, A. (1776/1982) *The Wealth of Nations*, Harmondsworth: Penguin.

15 George, C. S. (1972) *The History of Management Thought* (2nd edn), Englewood Cliffs, NJ: Prentice-Hall.

16 Braverman, H. (1974) *Labor and Monopoly Capitalism: The Degradation of Work in the Twentieth Century*, New York: Monthly Review Press.

17 Littler, C. R. and Salaman, G. (1984) *Class at Work: The Design, Allocation and Control of Jobs*, London: Batsford.

18 Thompson, P. and McHugh, D. (2006) *Work Organizations: A Critical Introduction* (4th edn), Basingstoke: Palgrave.

19 Mouzelis, N. (1967) *Organization and Bureaucracy*, London: Routledge & Kegan Paul.

20 Clegg, S. and Dunkerley, D. (1980) *Organization, Class and Control*, London: Routledge & Kegan Paul.

21 Thompson, P. (1989) *The Nature of Work* (2nd edn), London: Macmillan.

22 Bratton, J., Helms Mills, J. and Sawchuk, P. (2004) *Workplace Learning: A Critical Introduction*, Toronto: Garamond.

23 Cohen, P. S. (1968) *Modern Social Theory*, London: Heinemann.

24 Parsons, T. (1960) *Structure and Process in Modern Societies*, Chicago: Free Press.

25 Dunlop, J. T. (1958) *Industrial Relations System*, New York: Holt.

26 Senge, P. (1990) *The Fifth Discipline*, New York: Doubleday.

27 Scott, R. W. (2003) *Organizations: Rational, Natural, and Open Systems*, Upper Saddle River, NJ: Prentice-Hall.

28 Jaffee, D. (2001) *Organization Theory: Tension and Change*, Boston, MA: McGraw-Hill.

29 Woodward, J. (1958) *Management and Technology*. Problems of Progress in Industry No. 5, London: HMSO.

30 Woodward, J. (1965) *Industrial Organizations: Theory and Practice*, London: Oxford University Press.

31 Burns, T. and Stalker, G. M. (1961) *The Management of Innovation*, London: Tavistock.

32 Lawrence, P. R. and Lorsch, J. W. (1967) *Organisation and Environment: Managing Differentiation and Integration*, Cambridge, MA: Harvard University Press.

33 Thompson, P. and McHugh, D. (2009) *Work Organizations: A Critical Introduction* (4th edn), Basingstoke: Palgrave.

34 Lopez, J. (2003) *Society and its Metaphors: Language, Social Theory and Social Structure*, London: Continuum.

35 Morgan, G. (1997) *Images of Organization* (2nd edn), Thousand Oaks, CA: Sage.

36 Handy, C. (1985) *Understanding Organizations*, London: Penguin.

37 Rigney, F. (2001) *The Metaphorical Society: An Invitation to Social Theory*, Lanham, MD: Rowman & Littlefield.

38 Crow, G. (2005) *The Art of Sociological Argument*, Basingstoke: Palgrave.

39 Etzioni, A. (1988) *The Moral Dimension*, New York: Free Press.

40 Pedler, M., Boydell, T. and Burgoyne, J. (1988) *The Learning Company Project Report*, Sheffield: Employment Department.

41 Fenwick, T. (1998) 'Questioning the concept of the learning organization', pp. 140–52 in S. Scott, B. Spencer and A. Thomas (eds), *Learning for Life*, Toronto: Thompson Educational.

42 Garavan, T. (1997) 'The learning organization: a review and evaluation', *Learning Organization*, **4**(1), pp. 18–29.

43 Silverman, D. (1970) *The Theory of Organizations*, London: Heinemann.

44 Brown, R. K. (1992) *Understanding Industrial Organizations*, London: Routledge.

45 Nutley, S. M. and Davies, H. T. O. (2001) 'Developing organizational learning in the NHS', *Medical Education*, **35**(1), Wiley-Blackwell, p. 35.

46 Alvesson, M. and Willmott, H. (1996) *Making Sense of Management: A Critical Introduction*, London: Sage.

47 Dalton, M. (1959) *Men Who Manage*, New York: McGraw-Hill.

48 Fox, A. (1971) *The Sociology of Work in Industry*, London: Collier Macmillan.

49 Child, J. (1972) 'Organizational structure, environment and performance: the role of strategic choice', *Sociology*, **6**(1), pp. 331–50.

50 Pettigrew, A. (1973) *The Politics of Organizational Decision-Making*, London: Tavistock.

51 Kotter, J. P. (1979) *Power in Management*, New York: Amocom.

52 Kochan, T. E., Katz, H. and McKersie, R. (1986) *The Transformation of American Industrial Relations*, New York: Basic Books.

53 Alvesson, M. (1987) *Organization Theory: Technocratic Consciousness*, Berlin: De Gruyter.

54 Alvesson, M. and Willmott, H. (eds) (1992) *Critical Management Studies*, London: Sage.

55 Habermas, J. (1970) *Towards a Rational Society*, London: Heinemann.

56 Habermas, J. (1971) *Knowledge and Human Interests*, London: Heinemann

57 Marcuse, H. (1964) *One Dimensional Man*, Boston, MA: Beacon.

58 Marcuse, H. (1969) *An Essay on Liberation*, Boston, MA: Beacon.

59 Kelly, J. (1985) 'Management's redesign of work: labour process, labour markets and product markets', in D. Knights, H. Willmott and D. Collinson (eds), *Job Redesign: Critical Perspectives on the Labour Process*, Aldershot: Gower.

60 Wood, S. (ed.) (1982) *The Transformation of Work?*, London: Unwin Hyman.

61 Bratton, J. (1992) *Japanization at Work*, Basingstoke: Macmillan.

62 Sydie, R. A. (1994) *Natural Women, Cultured Men*, Vancouver: UBC Press.

63 Townley, B. (1994) *Reframing Human Resource Management: Power, Ethics and the Subject of Work*, London: Sage.

64 Hassard, J. and Parker, M. (eds) (1993) *Postmodernism and Organizations*, London: Sage.

65 Foucault, M. (1977) *Discipline and Punish: The Birth of the Prison*, New York: Pantheon.

66 Foucault, M. (1979) *The History of Sexuality*, Harmondsworth: Penguin.

67 Sheridan, A. (1980) *Michel Foucault: The Will to Power*, London: Tavistock.

68 Parker, M. (1993) 'Life after Jean-Francois', pp. 204–12 in J. Hassard and M. Parker (eds), *Postmodernism and Organizations*, London: Sage.

69 Ray, L. J. (1999) *Theorizing Classical Sociology*, Buckingham: Open University Press.

70 Craib, I. (1997) *Classical Social Theory*, Oxford: Oxford University Press.

71 Delaney, T. (2004) *Classical Social Theory: Investigation and Application*, Upper Saddle River, NJ: Pearson/Prentice-Hall.

72 Smart, B. (2003) *Economy, Culture and Society*, Buckingham: Open University Press.

73 Goodwin, G. A. and Scimecca, J. A. (2006) *Classical Social Theory*, Belmont, CA: Thomson.

INDIVIDUALS
AND WORK

**In this part of the book,
we turn our attention to how various
individual differences affect individual behaviour
in the workplace. Individuals have different personalities,
perceptions and learning styles. The chapters here emphasize
that the work experiences of women, visible minorities and the
disabled may be different from those of white male employees.**

Chapter 4 examines personality, which we define as the distinctive and relatively enduring pattern of thinking, feeling and acting that characterizes a person's response to her or his environment, and identity, defined as the ongoing process of self-development through which we construct a unique sense of ourselves and our relationship to the world around us.

In Chapter 5, we learn that perception, like personality, is interdependent with socialization, and impacts on people's behaviour in the workplace in complex ways. Understanding perception is important because the fundamental nature of perceptual processes means that individuals usually interpret other people and situations differently and so routinely hold different views of reality, which in turn strongly influence their attitudes and actions.

In Chapter 6, we explore learning and innovation in the workplace. Here, we explain the growing interest in workplace learning, and how the learning experience and innovation may depend upon how the organization is structured, how work is designed and how individuals engage, interact and construct knowledge from their work situations.

In Chapter 7, we explain
that motivation is the driving force in
individuals that affects their direction, intensity and
persistence of work behaviour in the interest of achieving
organizational goals. We go on to explore two competing
approaches to understanding motivation: the needs-based and process
theories of motivation.

We begin Chapter 8 with the claim that understanding issues of equity across
the major social divisions of society is vital for a full understanding of
organizational behaviour. We explore the general and specific tensions in organizations
that make the issues of equity, inequity and justice relevant topics for learning and
research. We also ask the following question: 'If the vast majority of people in our society
experience systematic inequities in relation to work, why is it so difficult to realize significant,
positive change?'

chapter 7   **Motivation at work**

chapter 8   **Gender, race, disability and class**

chapter 4
Personality and identity

chapter objectives

After completing this chapter, you should be able to:

- define personality and identity and understand their importance in the workplace
- distinguish between the trait and psychodynamic theories of personality
- understand how cultural and life-long social experience shapes personality
- critically assess how individual identity affects and is affected by the organization
- understand more of the main characteristics of your own personality and identity
- apply the key findings of personality research to the workplace

Introduction

At the morning coffee break, three nurses sat around a table in the hospital's cafeteria. Elizabeth spoke first. 'I'm really disappointed in Alan's behaviour. He became really excitable and loud again during the night shift when I asked him to assist in the emergency ward. He seems to be emotional and excitable whenever we have more than two or three critical cases in the ER. At the interview he came over as so confident and experienced.' And he had a wonderful CV,' Eleanor added.

'Interviews and good reference letters can't tell you about a person's personality and how they will perform under stress,' said charge nurse Judy Finnigan. 'He's not easy to get along with either, especially in the mornings. You ask a question and he jumps down your throat.'

'Yet, you know, he can be totally different outside the ER. He's sociable and pleasant when we go to the pub or when things are quiet on the ward,' replied Elizabeth.

How is Alan able to be such a different person in different situations? Are certain personality types better adapted for certain job types? Should managers try to recruit all employees with similar personalities? How does the personality characteristic influence motivation at work? Why do some people find it difficult to work in a team, while others excel as 'team players'? What personality types make for a 'good' team player?

Behaviour analysts have long been interested in relationships between personality traits and job performance, and whether personality homogeneity (people having similar personalities) facilitates a high-performance workplace. As we shall see in this chapter, many researchers have attempted to understand how both personality and identity are important factors shaping behaviour in the workplace.

In this chapter, we present psychological and sociological theories that have made significant contributions to our understanding of personality and identity, and some of the ways in which these theories are being applied in the workplace. There are at least 24 academics or groups of researchers who have contributed to theories of personality. Therefore our coverage in this chapter is highly selective, and we can hope to provide only

Go to www.queendom.com/tests.html and www.apa.org/science/testing.html for more information on personality testing instruments. In the UK, the British Psychological Society (www.bps.org.uk) assesses employment selection tests

weblink

a glimpse of the complexity and scope of the theories. We conclude the chapter with a discussion of the connections between personality and job performance, and personality and social integration, along with a critique of how personality tests are used in the workplace.

What is personality?

The notion of personality permeates popular culture and discussion in the workplace. In Western cultures, the mass media – print, radio, television, films and other communication technologies – endlessly discuss 'cool' or 'nice' personalities. And like Alan in our opening vignette, we sometimes meet people at work who seem to have a personality that does not 'fit' with the job requirements or work group. We all use the term 'personality' quite often, and most people feel they understand it intuitively. But what exactly is personality? Although there is no universally accepted definition, we define personality here as a relatively enduring pattern of thinking, feeling and acting that characterizes a person's response to her or his environment.

There are several aspects of this definition that need further explanation:

- The concept of personality refers to notions of individuality; people differ significantly in the ways in which they routinely think, feel and act.
- Personality refers to an enduring set of characteristics and tendencies of a person. An individual's personality encapsulates her or his way of responding to their world. Personality rests on the observation that people seem to behave somewhat consistently over time and across different life situations. Thus, we would not characterize a person as having a shy personality if that individual tended to be dominantly shy and retiring only some of the time, and on other occasions was frequently observed to be very sociable and outgoing.
- Similarly, we need to be aware that individual behaviour is influenced by social context. Individuals may be shy and retiring in a situation where they perceive the context to be unfavourable (such as meeting new people on the first day of employment), but outgoing when the situation is perceived as favourable. From this perceived consistency comes the notion of 'personality traits' that characterize individuals' customary ways of responding to their environment. Research suggests that stability or consistency becomes greater as we enter adulthood, but even in adulthood, there remains a capacity for meaningful personality change.[1]
- Finally, our definition of personality draws attention to the fact that, in studying personality, we are interested in factors within people that cause them to behave consistently as they do.

The patterns of thinking, feeling and actions that are viewed as reflecting a person's personality typically have three characteristics. First, they are seen as elements of identity that distinguish that individual from other people. Second, the individual's behaviours seem to 'interconnect' in a meaningful fashion, suggesting an inner element that shapes and directs behaviour. Third, the behaviours are viewed as being caused primarily by 'internal' rather than contextual factors.

In studying personality, we need also to look at how social experience structures or shapes personality. People develop a personality by internalizing – or taking in – their social experiences or surroundings. Without social experience, personality cannot develop. Sociological research on the effects of social isolation on feral (meaning 'wild') children points to the crucial role of social experience in forming personality.[2–4] Sociologists suggest that, in the process of interacting with parents, siblings, relatives, teachers and others, people develop an individual identity. We shall examine identity later in this chapter, but we define it here as the core

What do you think of these typical observations of people that give rise to the concept of personality? Do they accurately reflect how you form an opinion of a person's 'personality'?

stop reflect

understandings human beings hold about who they are and what is meaningful to them. Figure 4.1 illustrates some perceived characteristics of behaviours that are seen as reflecting an individual's personality.

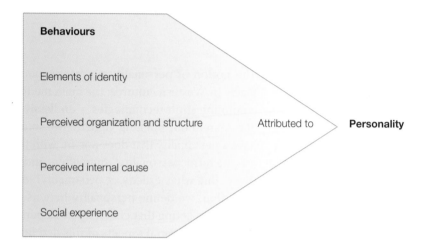

figure 4.1 Perceived characteristics of behaviours that are seen as reflecting an individual's personality

The trait, psychodynamic and sociocultural perspectives have guided the study of personality. These approaches provide very different conceptions of what personality is and how it functions. No doubt, as in other chapters of this book, you will find some of the theories more in accord than others with your own life views. Before we describe and evaluate each of the theories, we need to offer a few words of warning about personality in the workplace:

- As we have already said, there is no 'one best' personality type. Some personality characteristics are useful in certain situations, and organizations need to appreciate the value of diversity. When all employees hold similar personality traits and have similar values, studies suggest that fewer rules are needed to get things done. For many managers, this may seem like a good thing, but in some circumstances this same homogeneity could hinder the organization's ability to adapt to change.[5]
- Although many organizations consider personality to be an important criterion for employment, personality tests are still considered to be a relatively poor instrument for selecting people for key positions, such as management roles.
- The excessive 'classification' of personality types may prevent others from appreciating a person's potential to contribute to an organization.
- If we draw attention to context and social experience, there is less likelihood of exaggerating the effect of personality on individual work-related behaviour. In highly structured situations – such as the armed forces – with clearly defined rules, roles and punishment contingencies, personality will have the least effect on work-related behaviour. In less structured situations – such as a volunteer community organization – personality will have the most effect on organizational behaviour.[6]

In what follows, we examine three approaches to the study of personality: the trait, psychodynamic and sociocultural approaches.

Trait theories of personality

Almost two thousand years ago, the ancient Greeks used the humoral theory to explain individual differences in personality.[7] The body was thought to contain four humours or fluids: black bile, blood, phlegm and yellow bile. The personality of individuals was classified according to the disposition supposedly produced by the

plate 14 Observable traits, such as friendliness, are those traits that are obvious to others.

Source: Getty Images

predominance of one of these humours in their bodies. Optimistic or sanguine people, who had a preponderance of blood (*sanguis*), were cheerful and passionate. Melancholic people, who had an excess of black bile, had a pessimistic temperament. Phlegmatic individuals, whose body systems contained an excessive proportion of phlegm, were calm and unexcitable. Choleric individuals, on the other hand, had an excess of yellow bile and were bad-tempered and irritable. Although subsequent research discredited the humoral theory, the notion that people can be classified into different personality types has persisted to this day.

If you were to describe the personality of a close friend or relative, you would probably make a number of descriptive statements, for example, 'He is a real extrovert. He likes to be the focus of attention, is abrasive in debate, but is also brilliant and charming. He works hard but he is generous with his time, and he is a truly caring person. He will always try to help if he can.' In other words, you would describe others by referring to the kind of people they are ('extrovert') and to their thoughts ('caring' and 'brilliant'), feelings ('attention'), and actions ('works hard'). Together, these statements describe personality traits, enduring personal characteristics that reveal themselves in a particular pattern of human behaviour in different situations.

The English dictionary contains approximately 18,000 words that could be used to describe personal traits, and obviously it would be impractical, even if it were possible, to describe people in terms of where they fell on some vast scale. Trait theorists therefore attempt to condense various descriptors into a manageable number of core personality traits that people display consistently over time, in order to understand and predict human behaviour.

Gordon Allport (1897–1967) pioneered research on personality traits. He believed that the set of words chosen to describe an individual reflect that person's central traits, personal characteristics that are apparent to others and that shape behaviour in a variety of environments. A central trait is equivalent to the descriptive terms used in a letter of reference (such as 'conscientious' or 'reliable'). Another aspect of what Allport called the 'building blocks' of personality is secondary traits, those which are more specific to certain situations and have less impact on behaviour. An example of a secondary trait is 'dislikes crowds.'[8]

factor analysis: a statistical technique used for a large number of variables to explain the pattern of relationships in the data

Psychologists have used the statistical tool of **factor analysis** to identify clusters of specific behaviours that are correlated with one another so highly that they can be viewed as reflecting basic personality traits. Different people fall into these different clusters. For example, you might find that most people who are shy and socially reserved stay away from parties and enjoy solitary activities such as reading. At the other end of the spectrum are people who are talkative and outward-going, like parties and dislike solitary activities such as reading. These behavioural patterns define a dimension that we might label introversion–extroversion. At one end of the dimension are highly introverted behaviours, and at the other end are highly extroverted behaviours. As we describe below, studies have found introversion–extroversion to be a major dimension of personality.

In 1965, Raymond Cattell, a British psychologist, built upon Allport's investigations to develop his theory of personality. Cattell used a process of factor analysis to identify clusters of traits that he believed represented a person's central traits. He analysed questionnaire responses from thousands of people, and also obtained ratings from people who knew the participants well, eventually identifying 16 basic behaviour clusters, or factors. These 16 traits he called 'source traits' because they were, in his view, the building blocks upon which personality is built. From his data, Cattell developed a personality test called the 16 Personality Factor Questionnaire (16PF) to measure individual differences on each of the dimensions, and provide personality profiles for individuals and for groups of people. Figure 4.2 compares the personality profiles of a hypothetical individual rated on Cattell's 16PF test.

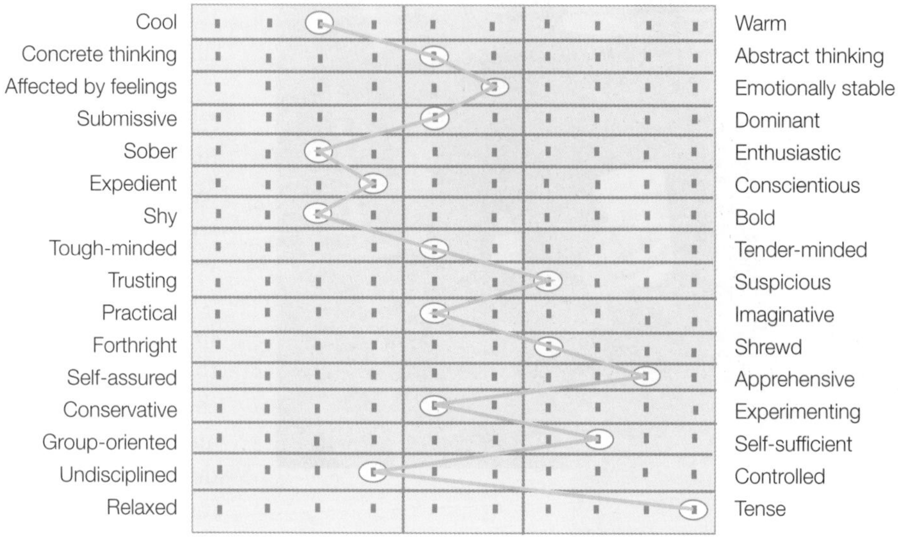

figure 4.2 Two hypothetical personality profiles using Cattell's 16PF test

Eysenck's three-factor model of personality

Hans J. Eysenck (1916–1997), another well-known British psychologist, also used factor analysis to devise his theory of personality. From his research, Eysenck concluded that normal personality can be understood in terms of three basic factors or dimensions: introversion–extroversion, stability–instability and psychoticism.[9] These factors are bipolar dimensions. Introversion is the opposite of extroversion, stability is the opposite of instability (sometimes called neuroticism), and psychoticism is the opposite of self-control.

Introversion refers to a reserved nature and the pursuit of solitary activities. Introverts tend to be shy, thoughtful, risk avoiders, and shun social engagements.

Extroversion refers to the opposites of these human characteristics. Extroverts tend to be sociable and spontaneous, thrive on change and be willing to take risks. *Psychoticism* refers to an aggressive, egocentric and antisocial nature. People high on psychoticism display such attributes as aggression, coldness and moodiness, are fraught with guilt and are unstable. People who score low on psychoticism do not show these attributes. Such people tend to be even-tempered and are characterized by emotional stability. Eysenck believed that the most important aspects of a person's personality can be captured by a two-dimensional model (Figure 4.3).

Figure 4.3 illustrates the effects of various combinations of the three dimensions of introversion–extroversion, stability–instability and psychoticism, and relates them to the four personality types described by the Greek physician Galen in the second century AD. We should note that the two basic dimensions intersect at right angles (meaning that they are statistically uncorrelated or independent). Therefore, knowing how extrovert an individual is reveals little about a person's level of emotional stability – she or he could fall anywhere along the stability dimension.

introversion: a personality dimension that characterizes people who are territorial and solitary

extroversion: a personality dimension that characterizes people who are outgoing, talkative, sociable and assertive

The secondary traits shown in the diagram reflect varying combinations of these two primary dimensions. Thus, we can see that the emotionally unstable (neurotic) extrovert is touchy, restless and aggressive. In contrast, the stable extrovert is a carefree, lively individual who tends to seek out leadership roles. The unstable introvert is moody, anxious and rigid, but the stable introvert tends to be calm, even-tempered and reliable.

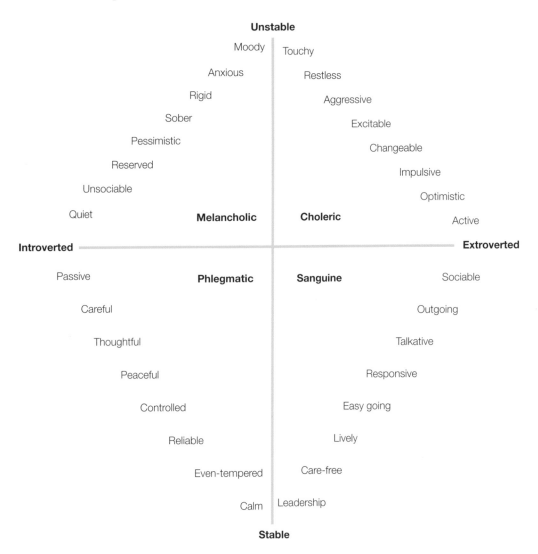

figure 4.3 Eysensk's major personality dimensions

Source: Eysenck (1973)[54]

Eysenck's research produced data to show that test scores measuring these two basic personality dimensions can predict people's key personality patterns, including specific behaviour tendencies or disorders. Leaders, for example, are likely to be in the 'sanguine' quadrant and tend to display outgoing, sociable behaviour. Criminals, on the other hand, are likely to be in the 'choleric' quadrant and tend to display aggressive and impulsive behaviour. Eysenck's trait theory of personality has received considerable support because the three dimensions have been replicated in factor analyses performed by many different researchers.[7]

The five-factor model of personality

As we have seen, trait theorists tend to divide into those who suggest that personality is best captured by measuring a large number of basic traits, such as Gordon Allport and Raymond Cattell, and those who suggest that the basic structure of personality can be captured by grouping 'high-order' dimensions, such as Hans

Eysenck. The 'Big Five' model of personality trait structure proposes that personality is organized around only five core dimensions: openness, conscientiousness, extroversion, agreeableness and neuroticism.[10,11] These Big Five personality dimensions, represented by the handy acronym 'OCEAN' (or 'CANOE' if the words are reconfigured), are shown in Table 4.1.

table 4.1 The Big Five model of personality trait structure and the associated lower-order traits

Dimensions	Lower-order traits
Openness	Artistically sensitive, intellectual interests, reflective, insightful, curious, imaginative
Conscientiousness	Efficient, reliable, responsible, scrupulous, ethical, persevering, organized, self-disciplined
Extroversion	Talkative, outgoing, candid, adventurous, sociable, assertive, gregarious, energetic
Agreeableness	Good-natured, forgiving, generous, non-critical, warm, gentle, cooperative, trusting, compassionate
Neuroticism	Anxious, self-pitying, nervous, tense, hostile, excitable, emotionally unstable, impulsive

Source: Adapted from Bernstein et al. (2000)[8]

Researchers using the Big Five model hold that when a person is placed at a specific point on each of these five core personality dimensions by means of a test or direct observations of behaviour, the essence of that person's personality is captured. These Big Five personality dimensions may be universal, since they were found to be consistent in a study of women and men in diverse Asian, European and North American cultures.[11–13]

The research also shows evidence that some personality dimensions tend to be more stable than others over time. For example, introversion–extroversion tends to be quite stable from childhood into adulthood and across the adult years. When it comes to stability of behaviour across situations, personality again shows both a degree of stability and some capacity for change. For example, regarding the higher-order trait of 'conscientiousness', an employee might be highly conscientious in one situation (such as handing in class assignments on time to complete a college programme of studies) without being conscientious in another (such as coming to work on time).

Trait theorists have made an important contribution by focusing attention on the value of identifying, classifying and measuring stable and enduring personality characteristics. But this so-called nomothetic approach to understanding personality has severe limitations. It is argued elsewhere, for example, that researchers need to pay more attention to how traits interact with one another to affect various behaviours if we are to capture the true personality. There is a tendency for researchers to make predictions on the basis of a single measured personality trait without taking into account other personality factors that also might influence the action in question.[1]

> Where would you place yourself on the personality scales? What is your reaction to the models? Are personality traits inherited or do they arise from social experience? What are the predictive advantages of the broad general traits and the narrow specific traits?
>
> **stop reflect**

nomothetic approach: an approach to explanation in which we seek to identify relationships between variables across many cases

The psychodynamic theory of personality

Many social psychologists and organizational theorists believe that personality emerges from complex processes too dynamic to be captured by factor analysis. The Austrian physician Sigmund Freud (1856–1939) developed the influential psychoanalytic theory of personality, which claims that the dynamic interplay of inner psychological processes determines ways of thinking, feeling and acting. Freud's work introduced such terms as 'ego', 'fixation', 'libido', 'rationalization' and 'repression' into Western popular discourse, as well as having a profound effect on twentieth-century personality research. The significance of psychoanalytic theories of socialization pioneered by Freud has been recognized by sociologists.

When treating patients with the French neurologist Jean Charcot, Freud became convinced that conversion hysteria, a disorder in which physical symptoms such as paralysis and blindness appeared suddenly and with no apparent physical cause, was connected to painful memories, which were often sexual or aggressive in nature, and seemed to have been repressed by the patient. When his patients were able to re-experience these traumatic memories, their physical symptoms often markedly improved or disappeared.

Freud experimented with various techniques, including hypnosis and dream analysis, to unearth the buried contents of the unconscious mind. His research convinced him that personality develops out of each person's struggle to meet her or his basic needs in a world that often frustrates those efforts. Freud suggested that an individual's personality is determined by conscious, preconscious and unconscious brain activity, with the unconscious part of the mind exerting great influence on consciousness and behaviour. He proposed that most psychological events are located in what he termed the subconscious, a vast repository of traumatic events that a person apparently can no longer consciously recall without the use of hypnosis. The conscious mind, which consists of mental events of which people are presently aware, represented just the 'tip of the iceberg' (Figure 4.4).

Go to www.freud.org.uk, a site dedicated to Sigmund Freud and his work

weblink

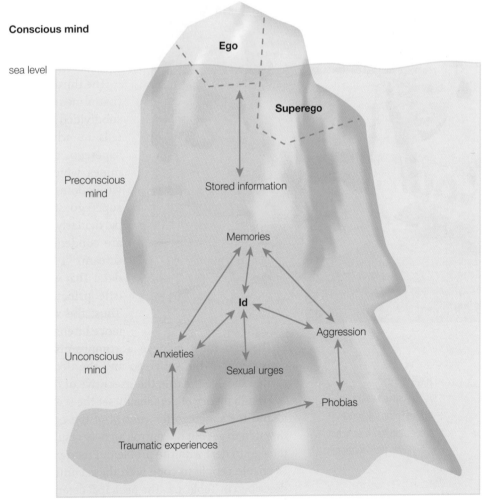

figure 4.4 Freud's conception of the personality structure: 'the Freudian iceberg'

The structure of personality: id, ego and superego

According to Freud, personality is made up three separate but interacting parts: the id, the ego and the superego. In Figure 4.4, the pointed arrows inside the 'Freudian iceberg' are meant to show the connections and the dynamic nature of the structure of personality. Freud saw the id (the Latin word for 'it') as the unconscious portion of the personality, where the libido, which is the primary source of life instincts, resides. The id is the only structure present at birth, and it functions in a totally irrational manner. The id operates on the pleasure principle, seeking the immediate gratification of impulses produced by two innate drives, sex and aggression.

For Freud, the id is:

> the dark, inaccessible part of our personality ... It is filled with energy reaching it from the instincts, but it has no organization, produces no collective will, but only a striving to bring about the satisfaction of the instinctual needs subject to the observance of the pleasure principle.[14]

id: Sigmund Freud's term for the component of personality that includes all of the individual's basic biological drives and needs that demand immediate gratification

ego: according to Sigmund Freud, the rational, reality-oriented component of personality that imposes restrictions on the innate pleasure-seeking drives of the id

superego: Sigmund Freud's term for the human conscience, consisting of the moral and ethical aspects of personality

The ego (Latin for 'I') is the thinking, organizing and protective self. It functions primarily at a conscious level, it controls and integrates behaviour, and it operates according to the reality principle. It negotiates a compromise between the pressures of the id and the demands of reality, deciding when and under what conditions the id can safely discharge its impulses and satisfy its needs. For example, the ego would seek sexual gratification within a consenting relationship rather than allow the pleasure principle to dictate an impulsive sexual assault.

The third component of personality is the superego (Latin meaning 'beyond' or 'above' the ego), which is subdivided into the conscience and the ego ideal, and tells us what we should and should not do. The superego, the moral arm of the personality, determines which actions are permissible and punishes wrongdoing with feelings of guilt. Like the ego, the superego strives to control the instincts of the id, particularly the sexual and aggressive impulses that are condemned by Western society. Whereas the id screams 'I want!', the superego replies, 'Don't you dare! That would be wicked!' For the superego, moralistic principles take precedence over realist ones. Thus, the superego might cause a person to experience intense guilt over sexual deviance.

plate 15 Research into the genetic basis of personality suggests that traits such as extroversion may be inherited.

Source: Getty Images

The ego must achieve a compromise between the demands of the id, the constraints of the superego and the demands of reality. This mediating role has earned the ego the title the 'executive of the personality'.[1]

Freud's theory of personality set the scene for a never-ending struggle between the id and the superego for control of the ego. When the ego confronts id drives that threaten to get out of control, anxiety results. Anxiety serves as a signal and motivates the ego to deal with the problem. Freud proposed a number of defence mechanisms to enable people to cope with these conflicts. Examples of defence mechanisms are described in Table 4.2. The principal defence mechanism is repression.

Have you ever found yourself using any of Freud's defence mechanisms? If so, what was the situation?

**stop
reflect**

table 4.2 Psychoanalytic defence mechanisms

Defence mechanism	Description	Example
Repression	An active defensive process through which anxiety-arousing impulses or memories are pushed into the unconscious mind	A sports celebrity who was sexually abused in childhood develops amnesia for the event
Denial	A person refuses to acknowledge anxiety-arousing aspects of the environment. The denial may involve either the emotions connected with the event or the event itself	A young man who is told he has terminal cancer refuses to consider the possibility that he will not recover
Displacement	An unacceptable or dangerous impulse is repressed, and then directed at a safer substitute target	A female employee who is harassed by her boss experiences no anger at work, but then goes home and abuses her husband and children
Rationalization	A person constructs a false but plausible explanation or excuse for an anxiety-arousing behaviour or event that has already occurred	An employee caught stealing justifies the act by pointing out that the company can afford the loss, and besides, other employees are stealing too

Source: Adapted from Passer et al. (2003)¹

Freud believed that, in repression, the ego uses some of its energy to prevent anxiety-arousing thoughts, feelings and impulses from entering consciousness. Defence mechanisms operate unconsciously, so people are unusually unaware that they are using self-deception to ward off anxiety.

In Freud's theory, personality develops through seven psychosexual stages: oral, anal, phallic, Oedipus complex, Electra complex, latency and genital – which involve seeking pleasure from specific parts of the body called erogenous zones. A major shortcoming of psychoanalytic theory is that many of its concepts are ambiguous and difficult to define and measure operationally. A second major criticism is that Freud laid too much emphasis on the events of early childhood as determinants of adult personality.

Go to http://pandc.ca
for books and theorists
on personality and
consciousness

weblink

Sociocultural theories of personality

In this section, we present an introduction to the work of prominent social psychologists and sociologists who, in different ways, are interested in understanding personality from a sociocultural perspective. According to the trait and psychodynamic approaches, personality consists of traits that shape thoughts, feelings and actions. In contrast, those taking a sociocultural approach understand personality to be fundamentally rooted in life experience, communities of practice and relationships. This **idiographic approach** posits that personality is acquired through learning in an immediate social milieu – the social setting that is directly open to an individual's personal experience. In essence, its central tenet is that personality should not be located within typologies but be understood as a complex social entity, closely related to self-image and identity.

idiographic approach: an approach to explanation in which we seek to explain the relationships among variables within a particular case or event; it contrasts with nomothetic analysis

Sociocultural researchers examine how personality is connected with social experience and the society in which people live: the culture, socialization and social dynamics of social interaction and situations. To illustrate this broad sociocultural perspective, we consider significant *social-cognitive* and *phenomenological* approaches to personality.

phenomenological approach: a philosophy concerned with how researchers make sense of the world around them, and whose adherents believe that the social researcher must 'get inside people's heads' to understand how they perceive and interpret the world

The social-cognitive approach, sometimes called the social-learning approach, emphasizes the development of personality through people interacting with a social environment that provides learning experiences. The **phenomenological approach** to personality suggests that the way people perceive and interpret social experience forms their personalities and influences their thoughts, feelings and actions.

The social-cognitive approach to personality

social-learning theory: a theory stating that much learning occurs by observing others and then modelling the behaviours that lead to favourable outcomes and avoiding the behaviours that lead to punishing consequences

The most influential social-cognitive or social-learning theories are those of Julian Rotter and Albert Bandura.[15–17] These theorists have developed an approach that views personality as the sum total of the cognitive habits and behaviours that develop as people learn through experience in their social setting.

Julian Rotter (pronounced like 'motor') argued that a person's decision to engage in a behaviour in a given situation is determined by two factors:

- what the person expects to happen following the action
- the value the person places on the outcome, which is called the reinforcement value.

expectancy theory: a motivation theory based on the idea that work effort is directed toward behaviours that people believe will lead to desired outcomes

Expectancy is our perception of how likely it is that certain consequences will occur if we engage in a particular behaviour within a specific situation. 'Reinforcement value' is basically how much we desire or dread the outcome that we expect the action to produce. For example, candidates for a particular position may spend a lot of money on new clothes to attend a job interview because past learning leads them to expect that doing so will help secure the job, and they place a high value on having the job.

Rotter also argued that people learn general ways of thinking about their environment, in particular about how life's rewards and punishments are controlled. Differences in this generalized expectancy concerning the degree of personal control that individuals have in their lives produced Rotter's influential concept of the internal–external **locus of control**. People with an internal locus of control believe that life outcomes are largely under personal control and depend on their own efforts. In contrast, people with an external locus of control believe that the environment is largely beyond their control, and that their fate has less to do with their own efforts than with the influence of external factors, such as luck.

locus of control: a personality trait referring to the extent to which people believe events are within their control

Research suggests that the locus of control that people develop has important implications for personality in later life. For example, in the workplace, there is evidence that an internal locus of control is positively related to self-esteem and feelings of personal effectiveness, and the internally focused are less likely to experience depression or anxiety, and tend to cope with stress in a more active and problem-focused manner than do externally focused people.[18] One study has shown that because locus of control is fashioned by people's social experience, this aspect of personality can change.[19] In the workplace, for example, experiencing participative decision-making arrangements may cause a shift towards an internal locus of control in managers and non-managers alike.

According to Albert Bandura, neither personal traits nor the social context alone determines personality. Instead, he argues that the environment, the person and the person's behaviour interact in a pattern of two-way causal links to determine personality. In short, personality is determined by what Bandura calls *reciprocal determinism* (Figure 4.5).

Go to http://sociologyindex.com for major ideas in the sociological study of socialization

weblink

figure 4.5 Bandura's model of reciprocal determinism

self-efficacy: the beliefs people have about their ability to perform specific situational task(s) successfully

One personal variable in this web of influence is particularly important in Bandura's view: **self-efficacy** refers to a person's beliefs about her or his ability to perform the actions needed to achieve desired outcomes. People whose self-efficacy is high have confidence in their ability to do what it takes to overcome obstacles and achieve their goals.

Self-efficacy not only determines whether a person will engage in a particular behaviour, but also determines the extent to which he or she will sustain that behaviour in the face of adversity. For example, if you believe that you are qualified for a job at the BBC, you are likely to apply for an interview. Even if you are turned down for the job, you are apt to apply for an interview at another TV company because you are confident of your abilities. High self-efficacy can facilitate both the frequency and the quality of behaviour–environment interactions, and low self-efficacy can hamper both.[7]

For Bandura, self-efficacy beliefs are always specific to particular situations. Thus, we may have high self-efficacy in some situations and low self-efficacy in others. For example, those who have mastered sophisticated computer software skills do not feel more generally capable in all areas of their life, despite their enhanced computer abilities. Efficacy beliefs are strong predictors of future performance and accomplishment. In short, they become a kind of self-fulfilling prophecy. We present more of Bandura's work in Chapter 6.

Which environmental factors do you feel may be more important for shaping personality? What kinds of personality difference between males and females have you observed? Are these differences genuine or a product of your culture? How do you know?

**stop
reflect**

The phenomenological approach to personality

The most influential phenomenological theories, also known as humanistic theories, of personality are those of Abraham Maslow (1908–1970) and Carl Rogers (1902–1987). These theorists emphasize the positive, fulfilling experiences of life, and argue that the way people perceive and interpret their social experiences forms their personality. Maslow believed that human motivation is based on a hierarchy of needs, and that understanding personality requires an understanding of this hierarchy of needs.[20] According to Maslow, personality is the expression of a basic human tendency towards growth and self-actualization. The innate drive for self-actualization, the realization of a person's true intellectual and emotional potential, is not specific to any particular culture. Maslow considered it as being a fundamental part of human nature: 'Man has a higher and transcendent nature, and this is part of his [sic] essence' (ref. 21, p. xvi).

Like Maslow, Carl Rogers saw personality as the expression of a basic human tendency towards growth and self-actualization.[22] However, unlike Maslow, he did not view personality development in terms of satisfying a hierarchy of needs. Rogers argued that personality development centres on a person's self-concept, the part of social experience that a person identifies as 'I' or 'me'. He believed that people who accurately experience the self – with all its preferences, approval, love, respect and affection – are en route to self-actualization.

The key to forming a psychologically positive personality is to develop a positive self-concept or image of oneself. How does a person do this? According to Rogers, people are happy if they feel that others are happy with them. Similarly, people are unhappy when others are dissatisfied or disappointed with them. People's feelings towards themselves depend significantly on what others think of them. From early childhood, we learn that there exist certain criteria or conditions that must be met before others give us positive regard. Rogers called these criteria 'conditions of worth'. In Rogers's view, rewards and punishment from others are important in personality development because they influence behaviour and shape self-perceptions. In short, personality is formed partly by the actualizing tendency and partly by others' evaluations.[8]

The social-self approach to personality

The traits (nomothetic) approach to understanding personality prevails in organizational behaviour literature, but the sociological concept of the *self* offers an

looking-glass self: Cooley's term
for the way in which a person's
sense of self is derived from
the perceptions of others

alternative conception of the individual. For sociologists, the processes of socialization, the life-long social experience by which people learn culture and develop their human potential, has great relevance for understanding personality. A century ago in 1902, sociologist Charles Cooley (1864–1929) introduced the phrase the 'looking-glass self' in his book *Human Nature and the Social Order* to mean a conception of self based largely on how we imagine we appear to others, and imagine judgements likely to be made about that appearance.[23]

Writing almost 30 years before the psychologist Carl Rogers, sociologist George Herbert Mead (1863–1931) expounded the concept of the looking-glass self, and developed a *process-relational theory* to explain how personality is formed through social activity and interaction with other people. Mead's writings have some similarities to those of Maslow and Rogers. Central to Mead's theory of personality is the concept of the 'self', that part of a person's personality composed of self-awareness and self image.[24] Mead believed that people form a personality by internalizing – or taking in – their locale. He rejected the notion that the self is inherited at birth and that personality is formed by biological inner impulses or drives, as argued by Sigmund Freud. According to Mead, the self develops only with social activity and social relationships, and if there is social isolation, as in the case of isolated children, the human body may develop but no self emerges.

After a self is formed, people usually, but not always, manifest it. For example, the novelist Daniel Defoe's character Robinson Crusoe developed a self while he was living in his own culture, and he continued to have a self when he was alone on what he thought was a deserted island. Thus, Crusoe continued to have the ability to take himself as an object.

The self is dialectically related to the human mind. The body, therefore, is not a self but becomes a self only when the mind has developed and engaged in reflexiveness. While Freud concentrated on the denial of the id's drives as the mechanism that generates the self's objective side, Mead drew attention to the source of the 'me' – how we become self-aware – by taking 'the role of the other'. People are interpretative creatures who must make sense of the world they live in. We learn to play different roles in this process. We are at different times children, students, friends, workers, parents and so on, and we do not behave in the same way in every situation. This process of role taking demonstrates that personality is a social product, and that 'group or collective action consists of aligning of individual actions, brought about by individuals' interpreting or taking into account each other's actions'.[25]

Language is an important aspect of socialization and the development of the self. As children learn to understand words and later to use them, they simultaneously learn to categorize their experience and evaluate their own behaviour and that of others. The first words many English or German children say is 'No' or 'Nein'. The use of language is one way individuals emphatically gauge different cultural meanings in disparate social situations and act accordingly. The self is reflexive, in that a person can become the object of her or his thought and actions. Language is central to the development of individual identity, the self. Moreover, 'the dynamics of the self and others are open to complex layers of interpretation and reflexive distancing' (ref. 24, p. 160).

Mead believed that the self has two parts: the 'I' (the unsocialized self) and the 'me' (the socialized self). The 'I' is the spontaneous, incalculable, impulsive, unsocialized and creative aspect of the self. Mead emphasized the 'I' because it is a key source of creativity in the social process, an individual's values are located in the 'I', it holds something that all individuals seek – self-realization – and finally, as society develops, people become increasingly dominated by the 'I' and less by the 'me'.

Make a list of the personality traits you think characterize you. Share your list with others who know you well, and ask what they think. To what extent, if at all, do you think your own personality originates from the interaction between you and your environment? Can you give examples?

**stop
reflect**

OB in focus   Psychometric testing: ensuring the right fit

In spite of their best efforts, many organizations struggle with consistently finding and hiring successful job candidates. To make better selection decisions, many firms are turning to a less traditional tool: psychometric assessments. Psychometric assessments are scientifically designed to provide a standardized measure of a candidate's general intellectual ability, competencies and personality traits. While there are many different tests available, they can generally be classified into two broad types: ability and personality.

Ability is a measure of 'can do'. An ability assessment measures a person's current level of knowledge and her or his capability to acquire further knowledge and skills. It also reveals a candidate's capabilities and learning potential. Examples of assessments that fall in this area include measures of intelligence, verbal ability and mechanical aptitude. Ability assessments are among the best predictors of job performance.

Personality is a measure of 'will do'. A personality assessment measures typical behaviour, and discloses what candidates are likely to do on a daily basis. It is designed to measure a person's preference for behaving in certain ways. Personality measures also reveal whether the individual is easy to manage, works hard, offers innovative solutions and works well with others.

Psychometric tests are also used for assessing characteristics that cannot be developed through training but are acquired over long periods of time, such as personality traits or in-depth knowledge of a profession. The use of well-constructed assessments can improve organization fit and address counterproductive behaviours.

Shawn Bakker, a psychologist at Psychometrics Canada (www.psychometrics.com). Source: *Canadian HR Reporter*, March 27, 2006, p. 7.

The 'me' is the social part of the self that is developed as the object of others' attitudes, beliefs and behaviour, including one's own reflections on one's self; it is 'the organized set of attitudes of others which one himself assumes' (ref. 23, p. 197). All social interaction has both parts: individuals initiate action (the 'I' phase of the self), and individuals continue their action based on how others respond to their behaviour (the 'me' phase of the self). Whereas the 'I' is associated with creativity, change and reconstruction of the self, the 'me' has a self-control aspect, in that it serves to stabilize the self. The combining of the 'I' and the 'me' leads to the formation of individual personality.[26] This reflexive process is invariably a social one, in which people form their sense of self in the context of family, peers and the mass media.[27] Thus, a person's personality will change across her or his life course as she or her participates in a community and interacts with different pervasive agents of socialization – family, school, peer group and mass media.

Mead's concept of the 'I' and the 'me' should not be confused with Freud's concept of the id and superego. As others have pointed out, Freud believed that the id and superego were firmly embedded in the biological organism, whereas Mead, on the other hand, rejected any biological element of the self. Furthermore, whereas the id and superego are locked in constant struggle, the 'I' and the 'me' work cooperatively.

Detractors argue that Mead's theory of personality is completely social, neglecting any biological element at all. Moreover, Mead's analysis of personality is rooted in the tradition of symbolic interactionism, a sociological perspective that focuses on the subjective meanings that people create through face-to-face communication in micro-level social settings. This was a perspective that resonated deeply in the North American individualistic culture and early US sociology.[28]

peer group: a group of people who are linked by common interests, equal social position and (usually) similar age

interactionism: what people do when they are in one another's presence, for example in a work group or team

individualism: the extent to which a person values independence and personal uniqueness

Identity and personality

The term 'identity' is derived from the Latin root *idem,* implying sameness and continuity. Its precise meaning is contested, but here we define identity as a complex fusion of the interplay between the inner self and the outer communal culture and social interaction.[29] The identity approach to understanding personality is located within a process-relational view of the subject or individual. According to this perspective, individuals are conceived as having emerging identities that are developed by, and also develop, the institutions and processes of modernity.[30] As children develop, they identify social roles, first within their family and later in the community. They also develop an understanding of status differences, and the ways in which roles interact with class, gender, ethnicity and race to create complex patterns of social behaviour. This process of socialization is therefore affected by whether they are the son or daughter of a neurosurgeon or a hospital porter; whether they grow up in a two-parent or a single-parent household; whether they grow up in London or Londonderry; whether they speak English or Hindi; and whether they worship at a mosque or a synagogue. As a result of socialization, most people acquire a set of attitudes, values, skills and behaviours that enable them to form and sustain relationships with others, work cooperatively with co-workers, avoid deviant behaviour and form a sense of self and identity.

plate 16 As children develop, they identify social roles, first within their family and later in the community. They also develop an understanding of status differences, and the ways in which roles interact with class, gender, ethnicity and race to create complex patterns of social behaviour.

Source: iStockphoto

The difference between personality and identity can be understood by answering the question, 'Who am I?' You could respond to this question with a list of personality traits such as 'I am an introvert, thoughtful, and reliable person.' Alternatively, your response could be, 'I am a parent, I work part-time at the Body Shop, and I am a university student.' The second set of responses, unlike the first, makes no reference to personality traits, but portrays a sense of identity on the basis of how we are related to others (for example, partner, mother, employee or student), and as such is deeply contextualized within the multiple social relations within which we are embedded. Identity speaks to social relations, to a fluid process of 'becoming' rather than an end state of 'being'. Identity is not something we are born with: it is structured or shaped by, and also shapes, societal influences. For Peter Berger, identity is defined clearly to be 'socially bestowed, socially sustained and socially transformed' (ref. 31, p. 98; see also ref. 32).

The concept of identity is complex and multifaceted. The main sources of identity include social class, gender, disability, sexual orientation and race and ethnicity. Anthony Giddens[33] identifies two types of identity: personal identity and social identity. Personal identity (or self-identity) refers to the ongoing process of self-development through which we construct a unique sense of ourselves and our relationship to the world around us. Identity is constructed through both social relations and discourses around, for example, gender (woman versus man), sexuality (straight versus gay) and race (black versus white). So, for example, ethnocultural factors may define identity. If I am Jewish, my religion may play a larger role in my identity than if I am agnostic, by virtue of the fact that Jewish people have been historically stigmatized. Identity draws upon the work of symbolic interactionists.[34]

personal identity: the ongoing process of self-development through which we construct a unique sense of ourselves and our relationship to the world around us

social identity: the perception of a 'sameness' or 'belongingness' to a human collective with common values, goals or experiences

If self-identity sets people apart as distinct individuals, social identity is the perception of 'sameness' or 'belongingness', the ways in which individuals are the same or members of some human collective – signs that denote who, in a basic sense, that person *is*.[33] Examples of social identities might include occupation, trade unionist, feminist, environmentalist, mother, Asian, disabled, Muslim and so forth. Social identities have a collective dimension and are predicated on a set of common values or goals or experiences. An individual can have multiple identities, some of which may be more dominant depending on a specific situation. What makes our identity dynamic, rather than static, is our capacity as self-conscious, self-reflexive human beings to constantly construct and reconstruct our identities.

Individuals spend a significant amount of time in work organizations and, unsurprisingly, derive a sense of identity from their occupation or from the organization or a work team within the organization. When a person says, 'I love my work; I am my work,' it connotes a sense of identity and its power to influence proactive behaviours. Each occupation, work group or organization will have a set of shared beliefs,

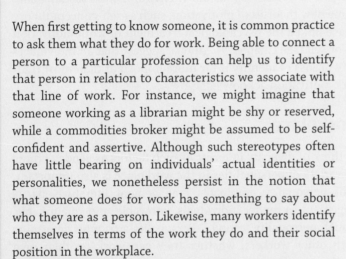

OB and globalization
Identity and instability in an uncertain economy

When first getting to know someone, it is common practice to ask them what they do for work. Being able to connect a person to a particular profession can help us to identify that person in relation to characteristics we associate with that line of work. For instance, we might imagine that someone working as a librarian might be shy or reserved, while a commodities broker might be assumed to be self-confident and assertive. Although such stereotypes often have little bearing on individuals' actual identities or personalities, we nonetheless persist in the notion that what someone does for work has something to say about who they are as a person. Likewise, many workers identify themselves in terms of the work they do and their social position in the workplace.

For workers in today's uncertain economy, the prospect of being made redundant generates stress not only about lost income, but also about the threat of an unmooring of their personal identities. Psychologists specializing in organizational behaviour note that, for many workers, their sense of self is inseparable from the work they do and the social environment of the workplace. The inability to engage in those familiar practices can leave them feeling ungrounded and even depressed. In a *Financial Times* article (Jacobs, 2008) dealing with redundancy and depression, a former banker explains how an organizational culture that promotes hard work, high achievement and an 'alpha male' approach can position workers for a long fall should they be made redundant:

> *Some think the world revolves around them, in good times and bad. When things are good they feel like masters of the universe, but when the bubble bursts they take it very hard. It can be devastating.*

In such situations, workers can stake their sense of self almost entirely on their work and, more specifically, on their place within the structure of the organization. Being unseated from their position within the organization can be equated to losing the reference point from which they are able to make sense of the world and their place in it.

According to London therapist Christine Martin, 'Redundancy demands existential questions alongside the financial worries' (Jacobs, 2008).

Anthropologist Dorothy Holland and her colleagues (Holland et al., 1998) describe identity as a sense of self that is actively and continually constructed, tested and refigured through daily social practices. They explain that these social practices take place in particular cultural realms that provide resources and structures that individuals can draw on to formulate personal identities which reproduce (or resist) those cultural realms. The importance of improvisation, agency and creativity – within defined social worlds – is also central to identity formation.

Using Holland et al.'s approach to identity, we can consider workplace culture in the UK as a cultural realm that provides workers with a set of practices and social relations that they use to position themselves vis-à-vis their work tasks, relationships with colleagues and the world at large. Understanding the links between organizational culture, personal identity formation and economic stability (or instability) can help managers to provide appropriate support services to workers when redundancies are deemed necessary.

stop! Do you think it is a positive or a negative thing for workers to have identities closely entwined with – even dependent upon – their work? Would such close links between identity and work benefit or hinder the workplace? How might they benefit or hinder other areas of workers' lives?

Sources and further research

Holland, D., Lachicotte, W. Jr., Skinner, D. and Cain, C. (1998) *Identity and Agency in Cultural Worlds*, Cambridge, MA: Harvard University Press.

Jacobs, E. (2008) 'Redundancy and a depression', *Financial Times*, August 19, 2008. Available at: www.ft.com; www.journalisted.com/article?id=763449.

Sheedy, B. (2005) 'All is not lost', *Management Today*, November/December 2005. Available at: www.aim.com.au/DisplayStory.asp?ID=571; www.doningtongroup.com/UserFiles/Media/0905-allisnotlost-SB-AIMmag.pdf.

Note: This feature was written by Gretchen Fox, PhD, Anthropologist, Timberline Natural Resource Group, Canada.

values, norms and demands particular to the group. Organizational goals and processes, such as sustainable products and practices, job design or rewards, can shape the relative value that individuals attach to joining and retaining their membership of groups or organizations. Equally, the termination of the employment relationship can lead to a loss of identity. The advocacy for a 'strong' organizational culture as a motivational strategy in an historical context of high-performance work systems underscores the importance of identity. Cultural control aims to have employees possess direct links to the values and goals of top managers in order to activate the emotion and create an identity that might elevate loyalty and commitment to the organization (see Chapter 12).

The power of social identity to define an occupation or organization's status relative to others can pose significant challenges to managers. For example, individuals may avoid or disassociate from a low-status organization considered to be managed without due regard to social responsibility, environmental sustainability and ethical practices. Some new theories of motivation, such as self-concept theory and whole-self theory, have linked the psychological treatment of work motivation to the notion of identity or self (see Chapter 7). Studies suggest that an individual's coherent sense of identity or loss of identity is far more important than most traditional treatments of work motivation acknowledge.[35,36]

Applying personality theories in the workplace

While managers tend to think of diversity in terms of such factors as gender, ethnic origin and disability, the variety of personalities in the workplace is also important. The nomothetic view of personality dominates management literature, partly because it enables management to render individuals 'knowable' and 'quantifiable' by identifying traits through personality testing.[37] Personality attributes determine how people interact with other workers, whether they can work on their own without supervision, whether they are conscientious or just do the minimum to 'get by', how they respond to change, whether they behave ethically or unethically, and much more.[38] For these reasons and others, organizations have developed an array of human resource management techniques to identify personality differences to help them to admit the 'right' people into the organization, and, once staff have been selected, this knowledge will help to identify those with the personality traits said to be required of an effective leader (see Chapter 13).

John Holland best articulated the view that organizations should consider aligning the requirements of the job and the characteristics of the workplace with personality characteristics.[39] In recent years, the awareness that organizations should focus on the degree of congruence between the individual and her or his work environment has expanded because of the need for workers to change and adapt to new work structures and employment relations. These include team working, individual-oriented performance-related compensation and a 'learning-oriented' organizational culture. Holland's personality–job fit model identifies six personality types – realistic, investigative, social, conventional, enterprising and artistic – each of which has a congruent occupational environment. Holland proposes that high congruence leads to satisfaction and the propensity to remain in that job or career. Table 4.3 defines these personality types and their personality attributes, and gives examples of congruent work environments.

Holland developed a model shaped like a hexagon that shows the relationships among occupational personality types, based on his Vocational Preference Inventory questionnaire, which contains 160 occupational titles. Respondents were asked to indicate which of the occupations they liked or disliked, and their answers were used to construct personality profiles. The closer two fields or orientations are in the hexagon, the more compatible they are. For example, the enterprising and social personality types are adjacent to each other in the hexagon model so, according to Holland's theory, individuals with both enterprising and social personalities have high compatibility (Figure 4.6).

There are three key points we should note about Holland's model:

- Intrinsic differences in personalities exist based on the restrictive Big Five personality model.
- Different types of occupation and work environment are better suited to certain personality types.
- Workers in workplaces and occupations congruent with their personality types should be more satisfied and more likely to remain with the organization than workers in incongruent occupations.

table 4.3 Holland's typology of personality and congruent work environments, and occupations

Personality type	Traits	Workplace characteristics	Congruent occupations
Realistic	Practical, shy, persistent, conforming, stable	Prefers physical activities that require skills and coordination	Mechanical engineer, farmer
Investigative	Analytical, creative, independent, reserved	Work involves thinking and analysing	Mathematician, biologist, systems analyst
Social	Sociable, friendly, outgoing, cooperative	Work involves helping and developing others	Social worker, teacher, counsellor, nurse
Conventional	Dependable, orderly, self-disciplined	Work is unambiguous, rule-regulated, orderly	Accountant, banker, administrator
Enterprising	Confident, ambitious, assertive, energetic	Prefers leading others, verbal activities, result-oriented setting	Lawyer, entrepreneur, salesperson, financial planner/consultant
Artistic	Creative, disorderly, impulsive	Thrives on ambiguous and unstructured activities	Musician, architect, painter, designer

Source: Based on information from Holland (1985)[39] and Greenhaus (1987)[53]

figure 4.6 Holland's individual–occupation hexagonal model

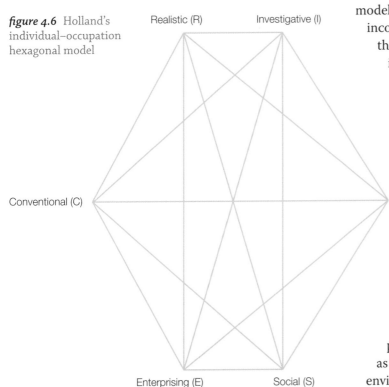

Research appears to strongly support the hexagonal model, but critics have pointed out that the model only incorporates the Big Five personality dimensions, and there are doubts whether the model can be generalized across cultures.[40–42]

With the resurgent interest in recruiting the 'right' people for the 'new' work regimes, and the 'discovery' of the Big Five personality model, research examining the relationships between personality traits and job performance, personality and social integration, and the efficacy of personality measuring instruments, has flourished. According to the new management parlance on knowledge work, workers are expected to create their own opportunities for innovation and positive change in the organization. Underlying the research on the relationship between personality traits and job performance is a presumption that a proactive personality – defined as a disposition to take action to influence one's environment – promotes job performance.[43] This is achieved by building a network of social relationships within an organization in order to gain access to information, wield influence and effect positive change – a process referred to as social capital. In short, the social capital approach advocates a view that individual power within a work organization is predicated on developing a network of relationships, which in turn enhances job performance (Figure 4.7).

social capital: the value of relationships between people, embedded in network links that facilitate trust and communication vital to overall organizational performance

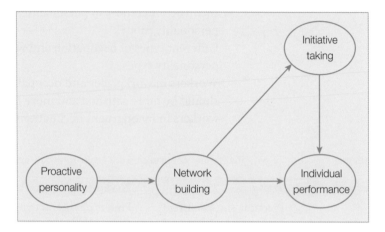

figure 4.7 A model of proactive personality and individual job performance

What do proactive employees do? By definition, employees with a proactive personality are inclined to construct their own environment. Proactive individuals are likely to seek ways to build a network of contacts in the organization that is conducive to their own self-interest. Proactive types, therefore, tend to seek allies and build alliances with other co-workers to support personal initiatives, and actively strive to become friends with people who occupy positions of influence and power. Thompson's quantitative study found a direct positive relationship between a proactive personality, network building and individual performance, suggesting that 'network building may occupy a critical stage in the process by which proactive personality engenders performance' (ref. 43, p. 1015).

Organizational behaviour theorists have long been interested in the connection between personality and innovative behaviours, and between personality and social integration. Henry Moon and his colleagues[44] identified personality and procedural fairness within a work organization as antecedents to proactive behaviour or 'taking charge'. Interestingly, the results show that the antecedents to proactive behaviour are based more on concerns about others than on self-interest. This suggests that getting employees to take charge within the firm may be more about 'we' than it is about 'me'.[44] An important aspect of the current wave of interest in self-managed work teams is the cultural dimension. In addition to changing methods of job performance, work teams demand changes in workers' attitude and behaviour.[45] Accordingly, organizational theorists are devoting increased attention to whether people with similar personalities make up more effective work teams.

The argument is that similar personalities might facilitate social integration among team members, increase the likelihood that co-workers will cooperate with each other, and foster trust between team leaders and members. Employment recruitment practices that create a homogeneous workforce of people with similar personalities and values may appear ideal in a team-based environment. As mentioned above, studies suggest that when employees hold similar personality characteristics, few rules, regulations and formal decision-making processes are needed to get work done. As a consequence, organizational leaders tend to choose people with personality traits similar to their own. The danger in top managers recruiting a workforce with similar personality traits is that homogeneity is a force potentially detrimental to change and long-term organizational survival.[5]

> If you were recruiting people to join you on an important work project, would you try to hire people with a personality profile similar to your own? If so, why? Can you think of any advantages and disadvantages of this approach?

**stop
reflect**

Work and Society: Why does she behave that way?

Many researchers who study work and personality stress the person–organization relationship. The assumption is that some personalities are a better 'fit' in particular organizational settings. Often, however, the question of person–organization fit is a complex one, and personality traits associated with highly skilled employees can sometimes be problematic.

One such personality trait is narcissism. A recent study suggests those with narcissistic personalities will have little to offer an organization:

> narcissists tend to lack empathy, engage in aggressive behavior and have self-serving motives ... narcissists should be especially unlikely to contribute positively to an organization's social and psychological climate by helping others, being courteous and a good sport, and going above and beyond the call of duty for the greater good. (Judge, et al., 2006, p. 765)

Narcissism would appear to be a personality trait that employers would want to avoid at all costs. However, it is important to realize that personality is only one of several factors that contribute to an individual's behaviour. Consider the following scenario. Sharon Smith had recently been hired by a mid-sized hospital as a specialist nurse practitioner – a new role situated midway between the physician and the traditional nurse. Those employed in more traditional nursing roles at the hospital resented the fact Sharon had taken over some of the more interesting and challenging aspects of their work. Sharon showed little sympathy for their concerns: 'Nurses need to understand that their education does not prepare them to perform these kinds of procedure safely.'

Sharon's interactions with physicians were also problematic. On one occasion, she clashed with Dr William Grant, a senior physician at the hospital. Dr Grant had questioned Sharon's recommendation that a particular patient could benefit from 'lifestyle changes'. Sharon responded without hesitation, 'There is no conclusive diagnosis for this patient, so why not proceed with the treatment the patient believes is best for him?' Later, in a conference with the ward manager, Sharon expressed her anger: 'Dr Grant has no right to question my judgement. In a situation like this, lifestyle changes are a perfectly reasonable course of action.'

Clearly, the idea of personality could prove useful in this context. Recognizing that Sharon exhibited many of the characteristics of a narcissistic personality might help managers make sense of a situation that seems to be getting out of control. However, it is possible to view Sharon's behaviour in a more positive light.

Perhaps Sharon's actions were the function of a conscientious rather than a narcissistic personality. Supporters of this more optimistic view might argue that Sharon was anxious to prove herself as an invaluable member of the healthcare team. But rather than working patiently to secure the trust and respect of her colleagues, she wanted immediate and unqualified validation. With the right 'coaching', however, Sharon could become aware of her personality traits, refine her social skills and make a genuine contribution to the hospital.

It is important to bear in mind that personalities are composed of a complex blend of 'traits' and, with appropriate mentoring, an individual may learn to manage various aspects of his or her personality. Issues of workplace design are also relevant here. When a new occupation is introduced into a well-established, hierarchical division of labour, conflicts are inevitable. Managers need to provide a clear rationale for change well in advance of the actual change. They must also create opportunities for dialogue among different members of the work team as the new occupation is integrated into established work roles and routines.

stop! What do you think? Is Sharon 'programmed' by her personality to be an endless source of conflict at the hospital? Are there steps that could be taken help her become a productive member of a relatively harmonious work team?

What about the role of gender? Is the clash between Sharon and Dr Grant aggravated by the fact that healthcare workplaces have traditionally been dominated by men?

Sources and further information:

Austin, E. and Deary, I. (2002). 'Personality dispositions', pp. 187–211 in R. Sternberg (ed.), *Why Smart People Can Be So Stupid*, New Haven, CT: Yale University Press.
Judge, T., LePine, J. and Rich, B. (2006) 'Loving yourself abundantly: relationship of the narcissistic personality to self- and other perceptions of workplace deviance, leadership and task and contextual performance', *Journal of Applied Psychology*, **91**(4), pp. 762–76.
For more information on the nurse practitioner, see the *Journal for Nurse Practitioners*.

Note: This feature was written by David MacLennan, Assistant Professor at Thompson Rivers University, BC, Canada.

Personality testing

The increased focus given to personality attributes, and how such attributes predict job performance and social integration, has led to increased research on selection methods in general, and personality testing in particular. Recent studies, for example, have explored the predictive validity of the Big Five personality model in relation to job performance through a meta-analysis of 36 studies that related validity measures to personality factors.[46] The empirically based research concluded that 'conscientiousness and emotional stability showed most validity for job performance, and that openness to experience was valid for training proficiency' (ref. 47, p. 239).

If you were a manager and had the task of writing within a week a complete personality description of an applicant you did not know for an important position in your organization, what would you do? Most likely you would seek information in a variety of ways. You might start by interviewing the applicant to elicit information about her strengths and weaknesses, interests and opinions. Based on the theories we have reviewed in this chapter, what questions would you ask? Would you ask questions related to the kinds of trait embodied in the Big Five model? Would you want to know about the person's early childhood experiences? Would you ask how she sees herself with others? Would you be interested in knowing how she responds to problems in various situations? You might ask her to complete a questionnaire that indicates her values, interests and preferences. You might also want to ask other people who know her well and obtain their views of what she is like. Finally, you might decide to ask her to perform job-related tasks and observe how she behaves in a variety of situations. As a manager or potential manager, your answers to these questions would tend to reflect your own view of what is important in describing personality.

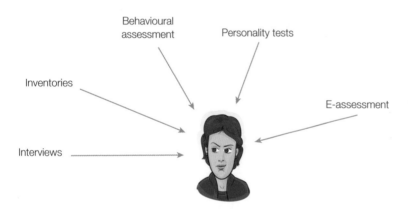

figure 4-8 Measurement approaches used to assess personality

reliability: in sociological research, the extent to which a study or research instrument yields consistent results

validity: in sociological research, the extent to which a study or research instrument accurately measures what it is supposed to measure

The major methods used by organizations to assess personality and predict work behaviour are shown in Figure 4.8. These consist of the interview, inventories, behaviour assessment, personality tests and e-assessment.

The task of devising valid and useful personality measures is anything but simple, and it has taxed the ingenuity of psychologists for nearly a century.[1] To be useful from a managerial perspective, personality tests must conform to the standards of reliability and validity. Reliability refers to the extent to which a technique achieves consistency in what it is claiming to measure over repeated use. For example, a selection test that measures a stable personality trait should yield similar scores when administered to the same individuals at different times (test–retest reliability). In addition, different managers should score and interpret the test in the same way (interjudge reliability). Validity refers to the extent to which a test actually measures what it sets out to measure – in this case, the personality variable. A valid test allows us to predict a person's performance in work that is influenced by the personality variable being measured.

The interview is the oldest and most widely used method of personality assessment. For centuries, people have made judgements about others by talking with them and observing them. Structured selection interviews contain specific questions that are administered to every interviewee in order to obtain information about a candidate's thoughts, feelings and other internal states, as well as information about current and past relationships, experiences and behaviour.

Personality inventories, or scales, are used for assessing personality. These are usually self-completed questionnaires that include standard sets of questions, usually in a true/false or rating scale format, which are scored using an agreed-upon scoring key. Their advantages include the ability to collect data from many people at the same time, the fact that all people respond to the same items, and ease of scoring. Their major disadvantage is the possibility that some participants will 'fake' responses by choosing not to answer the items truthfully, in which case their scores will not be valid reflections of the trait being measured.[48]

Human resource practitioners can observe the behaviours they are interested in rather than ask participants about them. In behavioural assessment, psychologists devise an explicit coding system that contains the behavioural categories of interest. Trained human resource recruiters then observe candidates until there is a high level of consensus (interjudge reliability) about how to describe their behaviour.

On of the most widely used personality tests in North America is the **Myers–Briggs Type Indicator (MBTI)**. The test contains 100 questions to participants about how they usually feel or act in certain situations. This personality test then labels participants as introverted or extroverted (I or E), intuitive or sensing (N or S), feeling or thinking (F or T) and perceiving or judging (P or J).

Online personality testing is also being used for personnel selection, a technique known as e-assessment. This form of assessment provides managers with the ability to conduct personality tests at any time and any place in the world, with the added advantage of the rapid processing of applicants.[47]

Whether the use of MBTI personality tests in fact accurately predicts future work performance is problematic.[49] It has been argued, for example, that broad traits such as Eysenck's 'Big Two' and the Big Five may be useful instruments for predicting behaviour across a whole range of work situations, much as a wide-beamed floodlight illuminates a large area. However, like a narrowly focused and intense spotlight, an analysis of specific traits such as Cattell's 16PF may be a better instrument in specific situations that call for the behaviours measured by the narrower traits. Personality testing provides organizations with insights into people's thoughts, feelings and behaviour. In other words, it makes aspects of personality quantifiable, and this allows the inner feelings of workers to be transmitted into measurements, about which management decisions can be made.

Myers–Briggs Type Indicator (MBTI): a personality test that measures personality traits

---

Critical insight

For many managers, personality tests such as the Myers–Briggs Type Indicator are useful instruments for measuring personality variables and helping to select suitable candidates to join the organization. Read pages 239–42 in Chapter 7, 'Recruitment and selection', in John Bratton and Jeff Gold's *Human Resource Management: Theory and Practice*,[50] for more information and discussion on psychometric testing. Also obtain a copy of Barbara Townley's *Reframing Human Resource Management: Power, Ethics and the Subject of Work*,[37] and read pages 83–98. What role, if any, does psychometric testing play in making workers known and manageable? Do you think Townley overstates her case? If so, why?

Some critical organizational theorists argue that psychometric testing measures what is effectively a stereotype of an 'ideal' worker or manager. It provides management with new ways of 'knowing' and managing managers and non-managers alike. It also represents a shift in management practices from the coercion of bodies through, for instance, time and motion and other Tayloristic techniques, to the attempted construction of self-regulated minds.[37,51,52] It is argued, for example, that 'The minutiae of the human soul – human interactions, feelings, and thoughts, the psychological relations of the individual to the group – [have] emerged as a new domain for management' (ref. 52, p. 72). Finally, personality assessment based on limited information can be damaging to the organization. For example, the over-emphasis on traits to identify 'ideal' personality types in which employees 'fit' into the workplace potentially reinforces the notion that workplace problems are embedded only in the personality characteristics of people, rather than being embedded in the organization at large and the inner tensions associated with managing the employment relationship.

Chapter summary

- Personality is the distinctive and relatively enduring pattern of thinking, feeling and acting that characterizes a person's response to her or his environment. In this chapter, we have examined a number of different approaches to personality. Each of these theories offers a view of how personality forms.

- Trait theorists try to identify and measure personality variables. They disagree concerning the number of traits needed to adequately describe personality. Raymond Cattell suggested a 16-factor model to capture personality dimensions, Eysenck offered a two-factor model, and McCrae and Costa suggested the Big Five factor model. Traits have not proved to be highly consistent across situations, and they also vary in consistency over time.

- We went on to examine Freud's psychoanalytic theory, which views personality as an energy system. He divided the personality into three structures: the id, the ego and the superego. According to Freud, the dynamics of personality involve a continuous struggle between the impulses of the id and the counterforces of the ego and superego.

- Sociocultural theorists emphasize the social context, the subjective experiences of the individual, and deal with perceptual and cognitive processes. We examined the theory of Albert Bandura, a leading social-cognitive theorist, who suggests that neither personal traits nor the social context alone determines personality. A key concept is reciprocal determinism, relating to two-way causal relations between personal characteristics, behaviour and the environment.

- Phenomenological theories, also known as humanistic theories, of personality were also examined. Influential humanist theorists such as Abraham Maslow and Carl Rogers emphasize the positive, fulfilling experiences of life, and argue that the way in which people perceive and interpret their social experiences forms their personality. Self-actualization is viewed as an innate positive force that leads people to realize their positive potential, if they are not thwarted by their social context.

- In addition, the chapter examined Mead's theory of personality and his key concept of the self. He argues that people develop a personality by internalizing – or taking in – their immediate environment. He rejected the notion that the self is inherited and that personality is the product of biological inner impulses or drives, as argued by Sigmund Freud. According to Mead, the self develops only with social activity and social relationships.

- The chapter has examined the role that an individual's identity (or identities) plays in determining behaviour in the workplace. Whereas personality is based on a cluster of traits, some of which are believed to be genetic and evident from birth, identity is perceived as socially constructed: it is developed by, and also develops, the institutions and processes of modernity. Identity is fluid and multiple, and emerges through our relationships with others.

- Managers use a variety of instruments and techniques to assess personality. These include the interview, inventories, behaviour assessment, personality tests and e-assessment. We noted also that, to be useful to the organization, personality assessment instruments must conform to standards of reliability and validity.

Key concepts

extroversion	106
factor analysis	105
Freudian iceberg	109
introversion	106
personality	103–104
personality traits	104–106
personality types	106–108
phenomenological approach	111
self-identity	116
social identity	116

Vocab checklist for ESL students

- ☐ Ego
- ☐ Expectancy theory
- ☐ Extrovert, extroverted
- ☐ Factor analysis
- ☐ Id
- ☐ Idiographic
- ☐ Individual, individualism
- ☐ Interactionism
- ☐ Introvert, introverted
- ☐ Locus of control
- ☐ Looking-glass self
- ☐ Nomothetic
- ☐ Peer group
- ☐ Phenomenology, phenomenological
- ☐ Phlegmatic
- ☐ Psychodynamic
- ☐ Psychometric
- ☐ Reliable, reliability
- ☐ Sanguine
- ☐ Self-efficacy
- ☐ Social capital
- ☐ Social learning theory
- ☐ Superego
- ☐ Valid, validity

Chapter review questions

1. What is personality, and why is the concept difficult to define?
2. What is meant by the trait theory of personality? Choose one trait theory, and explain the strengths and weaknesses of this approach to personality assessment.
3. Drawing on your knowledge of Freud's psychoanalytic theory, explain why the ego is sometimes referred to as the 'executive of the personality'. What do you understand by 'defence mechanism', and what relevance has this concept to understanding behaviour in the workplace?

4. Assess critically the importance of understanding the terms 'social self' and 'socialization', and explain how attitudes and values are developed and changed.

5. How are the concepts of personality and identity different?

❓ Chapter research questions

1. Form a diverse study group including, if possible, an international student(s). Discuss the following questions: In what ways has socialization bestowed, sustained and transformed your own sense of identity? What is the relationship between personality, self-identity and social identity? Discuss the power of agents of socialization. Use examples from your work experience or family, or from workplaces you have studied.

2. Read Anthony Giddens' opening chapter, 'The contours of high modernity' in *Modernity and Self-identity*.[30] After reading pages 10–15, how do you think Giddens links modernity to identity? Thinking about your own biography, how important, and why, are lifestyle choices in forming your self-identity?

3. Retrieve a copy of Cameron Anderson and others' (2008) article, 'Personality and organizational culture as determinants of influence' (see Further Reading, below), investigating personality as a determinant of influence in work organizations. How plausible is the evidence that individual effectiveness in initiating change and innovation depends largely on personality?

▣→ Further reading

Anderson, C., Spataro, S. and Flynn, F. (2008) 'Personality and organizational culture as determinants of influence', *Journal of Applied Psychology*, **93**(3), pp. 702–10.

Arthur, W., Woehr, D. J. and Graziano, W. (2001) 'Personality testing in employment settings', *Personnel Review*, **30**(6), pp. 657–76.

Bandura, A. (1997) *Self-Efficacy: The Exercise of Control*. New York: Freeman.

Giberson, T. R., Resick, C. and Dickson, M. (2005) 'Embedding leader characteristics: an examination of homogeneity of personality and values in organizations', *Journal of Applied Psychology*, **90**(5), pp. 1002–10.

Institute of Personnel and Development (1997) *Key Facts: Psychological Testing*. London: IPD.

Moon, H., Kamdar, D., Mayer, D. and Takeuchi, R. (2008) 'Me or we? The role of personality and justice as other-centered antecedents to innovative citizenship behaviors within organizations', *Journal of Applied Psychology*, **93**(1), pp. 84–94.

Sternberg, R. (1999) 'Survival of the fit test', *People Management*, **4**(24), pp. 29–31.

Tucker, K. H. (2002) 'Freud, Simmel, and Mead: aesthetics, the unconscious, and the fluid self', pp. 193–227 in *Classical Social Theory*, Oxford: Blackwell.

Wiggins, J. S. (ed.) (1996) *The Five-Factor Model of Personality: Theoretical Perspectives*. New York: Guilford Press.

Chapter case study 1

Identifying leaders in Nigeria

Setting

Nigeria is Africa's most populous country, with over 140 million people. In 2004, the United Nations Development Index, which measures a country's life expectancy, literacy, educational attainment and gross domestic product (GDP) per capita, ranked Nigeria 151 out of 177 countries. Devastating poverty affects 57 per cent of its population, and of the 57.2 million people who make up the labour force, over 10 per cent are unemployed. It struggles to cope with an inadequate infrastructure and under-developed human capital.

Nigeria's economy also has a detrimental over-dependence on a capital-intensive oil sector. At the beginning of the twenty-first century, Nigeria's crude oil production was averaging around 2.2 million barrels per day and providing 20 per cent of GDP, 95 per cent of foreign exchange earnings, and about 65 per cent of government revenues. It is Africa's top oil producer.

In recent years, with a new civilian government taking over from the former military rulers, there have been attempts to diversify the economy. The government has strived to attract foreign investors, citing locally available raw materials and the large national market as opportunities for long-term investments and joint ventures. However, these efforts have been stalled by foreign investors' fears of continued corruption, weak regulations, poor surveillance and inefficiencies.

For those willing to deal with such market impediments, investment advisors recommend that companies thoroughly educate themselves on local conditions and business practices, and establish a local presence. Researchers point out the importance of blending African work principles, such as an emphasis on work group activities and assigning leadership positions based on age (which is associated with experience and wisdom), into the workplace. Instead of front-line supervisors being held responsible for hiring, Nigerian workers expect and respect the involvement of senior managers in the process. Despite this knowledge, contrary foreign management methods still dominate human resource management practices in the multinational companies based in Nigeria. This has resulted in confusion, frustration and malaise among the Nigerian workforce.

The problem

A leading gas company in Europe, German-owned Lebenskraft is one of 200 multinational companies settled in Nigeria. In its over 80-year history, Lebenskraft has developed from a German regional distributor to an international gas company. As Germany has relatively few natural resources, it must import large quantities of energy, and the company has found ample supplies through its operations in Nigeria, where it first became established nearly a decade ago.

Since its arrival in Nigeria, Lebenskraft's middle- and upper-level positions have been filled by candidates who have been educated and have lived in Germany. As a way of broadening its choice of candidates, Lebenskraft's senior management has decided to consider employees from the Nigerian operations to fill a recent management vacancy.

The company has always used personality testing when assessing individuals for promotional opportunities as part of an overall succession plan. The test they normally use, Review, was developed in Germany and has been previously applied within that country with great success. For this latest management recruitment, it has been suggested that a previously used tailored job benchmark, identifying the desired characteristics for leadership roles, should be used. The test would then be applied to compare the abilities, interests and personality traits of multiple Nigerian candidates to the benchmark to identify the best candidate for the current vacancy.

The company has created the customized benchmark using the characteristics of assessed top performers in their German operations as well as current management input. They hope that by using their Nigerian employees' assessment results, in conjunction with the benchmark, they will successfully fill the management vacancy and perhaps create an effective local succession plan. However, since the personality testing has never been used outside Germany, the company is hesitant to rely on its results. The human resources department in the Nigerian operations has been given the task of making recommendations on the selection process before the local management are asked to proceed.

Tasks

As a member of the human resources department, prepare a short report including answers to the following questions:
1. What advantages do you see in using the testing?
2. What cultural aspects of Nigeria should be considered by the Lebenskraft management team when considering the use of the test's benchmark and in developing the selection process?

Essential reading

Anakwe, U.P. (2002) 'Human resource management practices in Nigeria: challenges and insights', *International Journal of Human Resource Management*, **13**(7), pp. 1042–59.

Cooper, D. and Robertson, I. (1995) 'Selection methods – psychometrics', Chapter 8 in *The Psychology of Personnel Selection*, London: Routledge.

Jackson, T. (2002) 'Reframing human resource management in Africa: a cross-cultural perspective', *International Journal of Human Resource Management*, **13**(7), pp. 998–1018.

Note

This case study was written by Lori Rilkoff, MSc, CHRP, Senior Human Resources Manager at The City of Kamloops, and Lecturer in HRM at Thompson Rivers University BC, Canada

 Chapter case study 2

Building Anna's self-esteem

 Visit www.palgrave.com/business/brattonob2e to view this case study

 ## Web-based assignment

Form a group of three to five people, and visit the websites of any of the following organizations: Microsoft (www.microsoft.com/uk/graduates), Sainsbury's (www.sainsburys.co.uk), British Airways (www.britishairways.com), and Santander (www.santander.com). What personality attributes are these organizations seeking when they recruit new employees?

Go to www.queendom.com/tests.html and www.psychometricadvantage.co.uk (search for psychometrics) and examine the psychometric tests. Some of these you may take yourself without applying for a job. How accurate, in your view, is your personality profile as revealed by any of the psychometric tests? Do your close friends agree with the assessment? Which kind of psychometric tests do you suppose would be more effective in revealing the more important aspects of your personality? Why? How much weight should organizations give to psychometric test results in employment selection? Explain your reasoning. Write a report detailing your findings.

 ## OB in film

American Beauty (1999) follows the last few days in the life of Lester Burnham, an advertising space salesman with a mid-life crisis. The film is particularly good at showing the multiple factors influencing Lester's behaviour. Some of these reside in his personality and some in the environment. Interestingly, there are many instances when Lester's interaction with events surfaces his personality.

Drawing upon Bandura's model of reciprocal determinism, map Lester's descent into a mid-life crisis in terms of his personality, his environment and his behaviour. How does this analysis of Lester shape your understanding of personality and its role in shaping behaviour?

Note: This feature was written by Professor Jon Billsberry, Senior Research Fellow, Open University Business School, UK.

 Bonus OB in Film feature!

Visit www.palgrave.com/business/brattonob2e to see how *The Odd Couple* (1968) can be considered in relation to the subject of leadership.

 ## References

1 Passer, M., Smith, R., Atkinson, M., Mitchell, J. and Muir, D. (2003) *Psychology: Frontiers and Applications*, Toronto: McGraw-Hill Ryerson.

2 Curtiss, S. (1977) *Genie: A Psycholinguistic Study of a Modern-day 'Wild Child'*, New York: Academic Press.

3 Davis, K. (1940) 'Extreme social isolation of a child', *American Journal of Sociology*, **45**(4), pp. 554–65.

4 Rymer, R. (1994) *Genie*, New York: Harper Perennial.

5 Giberson, T. R., Resick, C. and Dickson, M. (2005) 'Embedding leader characteristics: an examination of homogeneity of personality and values in organizations', *Journal of Applied Psychology*, **90**(5), pp. 1002–10.

6 Adler, S. and Weiss, H. (1988) 'Recent developments in the study of personality and organizational behavior', in C. Cooper and I.

Robertson (eds), *International Review of Industrial and Organizational Psychology*, New York: Wiley.

7   Carlson, N., Buskist, W., Enzle, M. and Heth, C. (2005) *Psychology* (3rd edn), Toronto: Pearson Education.

8   Bernstein, D. A., Clarke-Stewart, A., Penner, L. Roy, E. and Wickens, C. (2000) *Psychology* (5th edn), New York: Houghton Mifflin.

9   Eysenck, H. J. (1970) *The Structure of Human Personality* (3rd edn), London: Methuen.

10 Goldberg, L. R. (1990) 'An alternative "description of personality": the Big-Five factor structure', *Journal of Personality and Social Psychology*, **59**, pp. 1216–29.

11 McCrae, R. R. and Costa, P. T. (1995) 'Toward a new generation of personality theories: theoretical contexts for the five-factor model', pp. 51–87 in J. S. Wiggins (ed.), *The Five-Factor Model of Personality: Theoretical Perspectives*, New York: Guilford Press.

12 Dalton, M. and Wilson, M. (2000) 'The relationship of the five-factor model of personality to job performance for a group of Middle Eastern expatriate managers', *Journal of Cross-Culture Psychology*, March, pp. 250–8.

13 Paunonen, S. V. (1996) 'The structure of personality in six cultures', *Journal of Cross-Culture Psychology*, May, pp. 339–53.

14 Freud (1933). Quoted in Carlson, N., Buskist, W., Enzle, M. and Heth, C. (2005) *Psychology* (3rd edn), Toronto: Pearson Education, p. 462.

15 Rotter, J. B. (1966) 'Generalized expectations for internal versus external control of reinforcement', *Psychological Monographs*, **80**(1): 1–28.

16 Bandura, A. (1978) 'The self system in reciprocal determinism', *American Psychologist*, **33**, pp. 344–58.

17 Bandura, A. (1997) *Self-Efficacy: The Exercise of Control*, New York: Freeman.

18 Jennings (1990), quoted in Passer, M., Smith, R., Atkinson, M., Mitchell, J. and Muir, D. (2003) *Psychology: Frontiers and Applications*, Toronto: McGraw-Hill Ryerson, p. 565.

19 Frese, M. (1982) 'Occupational socialization and psychological development: an underemphasized research perspective in industrial psychology', *Journal of Occupational Psychology*, **55**, pp. 209–24.

20 Maslow, A. H. (1954) *Motivation and Personality*, New York: Harper.

21 Maslow, A. H. (1964) *Religions, Values, and Peak-Experiences*, New York: Viking.

22 Rogers, C. R. (1961) *On Becoming a Person*, Boston, MA: Houghton Mifflin.

23 Mead, G. H. (1934) *Mind, Self and Society*, Chicago: University of Chicago Press.

24 Ray, L. J. (1999) *Theorizing Classical Sociology*, Buckingham: Open University Press.

25 Blumer, H. (1969), quoted in Tucker, K. H. (2002) *Classical Social Theory*, Oxford: Blackwell, p. 218.

26 Pfuetze, P. (1954). *Self, Society and Existence: Human Nature and Dialogue in the Thoughts of George Herbert Mead and Martin Buber*, New York: Harper.

27 Tucker, K. H. (2002) *Classical Social Theory*, Oxford: Blackwell.

28 Brym, R., Lie, J., Nelson, A., Guppy, N. and McCormick, C. (2003) *Sociology: Your Compass for a New World*, Scarborough, ON: Thomson Wadsworth.

29 Mills, A. and Tancred, P. (eds) (1992) *Gendering Organizational Analysis*, Newbury Park, CA: Sage.

30 Giddens, A. (1991) *Modernity and Self-Identity*, Palo Alto, CA: Stanford University Press.

31 Berger, P. (1966) *Invitation to Sociology*, New York: Anchor Books.

32 Kellner, D. (1992) 'Popular culture and the construction of postmodern identities', pp. 141–77 in S. Lash and J. Friedman (eds), *Modernity and Identity*, Oxford: Blackwell.

33 Giddens, G. (2009) *Sociology* (6th edn), Cambridge: Polity Press.

34 Ravelli, B. and Webber, M. (2010) *Exploring Sociology*, Toronto: Pearson.

35 Fulop, L. and Linstead, S. (2009) 'Motivation and meaning', pp. 411–72 in S. Linstead, L. Fulop and S. Lilley, *Management and Organization: A Critical Text* (2nd edn), Basingstoke: Palgrave.

36 Herriot, P., Hirsh, W. and Reilly, P. (1998) *Trust and Transition: Managing Today's Employment Relationship*, Chichester: Wiley & Sons.

37 Townley, B. (1994) *Reframing Human Resource Management: Power, Ethics and the Subject of Work,* London: Sage.

38 Lee, S. and Klein, H. (2002) 'Relationships between conscientiousness, self-efficacy, self-description, and learning over time', *Journal of Applied Psychology*, **87**(6), pp. 1175–82.

39 Holland, J. L. (1985) *Making Vocational Choices: A Theory of Vocational Personalities and Work Environments* (2nd edn), Englewood Cliffs, NJ: Prentice Hall.

40 Brown, D. (1987) 'The status of Holland's theory of career choice', *Career Development Journal*, September, pp. 13–23.

41 Furnham, A. F. (1997) 'Vocational preference and P-O fit', in J. Arnold (ed.), 'The psychology of careers in organizations', *International Review of Industrial and Organizational Psychology*, **12**, pp. 1–37.

42 Young, R. A. and Chen, C. P. (1999) 'Annual review: practice and research in career counselling and development – 1998', *Career Development Quarterly*, December, p. 98.

43 Thompson, J. A. (2005) 'Proactive personality and job performance: a social perspective', *Journal of Applied Psychology*, **90**(5), pp. 1011–17.

44 Moon, H., Kamdar, D., Mayer, D. and Takeuchi, R. (2008), 'Me or we? The role of personality and justice as other-centered antecedents to innovative citizenship behaviors within organizations', *Journal of Applied Psychology*, **93**(1), pp. 84–94.

45 Procter, S. and Mueller, F. (2000) *Teamworking*, Basingstoke: Palgrave Macmillan.

46 Salgado, J. F. (1997) 'The five factor model of personality and job performance in the European Community', *Journal of Applied Psychology*, **82**, pp. 30–43.

47 Bratton, J. and Gold, J. (2003) *Human Resource Management: Theory and Practice* (3rd edn), Basingstoke: Palgrave.

48 Dalen, L. H., Stanton, N. A. and Roberts, A. D. (2001) 'Faking personality questionnaires in personal selection', *Journal of Management Development*, **20**(8), pp. 729–41.

49 Robertson, I. T., Baron, H., Gibbons, P., MacIver, R. and Nyfield, G. (2000) 'Conscientiousness and managerial performance', *Journal of Occupational and Organizational Psychology*, **73**(2), pp. 171–81.

50 Bratton, J. and Gold, J. (2007) *Human Resource Management: Theory and Practice* (4th edn), Basingstoke: Palgrave.

51 Hollway, W. (1991) *Work Psychology and Organizational Behaviour*, London: Sage.

52 Rose, N. (1990) *Governing the Soul: The Shaping of the Private Self*, London: Routledge.

53 Greenhaus, J. H. (1987) *Career Management*, Chicago: Dryden.

54 Eysenck, H. (1973) *The Inequality of Man*, London: Temple Smith.

chapter 5
Perception and emotion

chapter objectives

After completing this chapter, you should be able to:

- understand the basic nature of human perception and its far-reaching influence on the nature of decision making, behaviour and relationships in organizations
- identify and define the elements of the perception process, how they relate to each other, and why the sequence in which they occur will affect how individuals view people and situations
- understand how our emotions affect, and are affected by, our perception of people and situations
- explain the influence on perception of information-processing limitations and existing knowledge and expectations, including those arising from cultural background
- discuss how a knowledge of perception processes can generate insight into phenomena of particular significance in the workplace, such as human error, interpersonal conflict, stereotyping, performance expectations and intergroup relations

Introduction

If one manager's idea of creativity (or enthusiasm, or intelligence) is in his or her head and different from another's, how can employees know for sure that their potential and performance at work are being assessed fairly? If it happened to be another manager making the judgement, would that person have viewed things differently and given a particular employee that job, or that promotion, rather than turning her or him down? It is these types of concern about the accuracy and consequences of individuals' perceptions that drive the use of systematic assessment procedures in many organizations.

Systematic, formal procedures are used to make judgements in personnel selection and performance appraisals, and sometimes structured systems are used to assess the strategic options and risks that organizations face. In order to minimize the reliance on what is 'in the head' of one individual when important decisions are made, formal procedures usually aim to include multiple viewpoints rather than that of one person, and to use concrete definitions of the criteria by which a person or situation is to be assessed (for instance, 'creativity is defined as the number of brand new ideas generated'). But why is it necessary to employ complicated assessment procedures? Can we not just train each individual manager to be more objective so that managers will all make the same judgements when faced with the same decision?

perception: the process of selecting, organizing and interpreting information in order to make sense of the world around us

We show in this chapter how subjectivity in the way we perceive the world around us arises from the fundamental nature of human perception processes. It is not simply the result of lazy thinking, meanness or belligerence on the part of some individuals (although that is not to say that some people are not sometimes guilty of these things!). Subjectivity is the normal state of affairs in human judgement because of the particular way our senses gather information from the world, and the way our brains go about making sense of that information. So the task of ensuring a fair and good-quality assessment of people and situations in organizations is not about training individuals to see things as they 'really are'. Instead, the task is to understand how and why multiple realities will always exist in any given scenario, and to gain the benefits of them, or at least avoid the negative consequences of actions based on limited perspectives. In other words, the task is to understand perception.

The purpose of this chapter is to outline and discuss the psychological basis of perception: that is, what happens 'in the head' that leads us to perceive people and situations in particular ways. After introducing some examples of how individuals' perceptions can be consequential in organizational life, we explore the central features and processes of human perceptual systems that allow us to experience a seamless view of our world, through the use of cognitive efficiencies such as time- and energy-saving mental short cuts and the packaging of information for convenient retrieval.

In order to structure our discussion, the issues that arise from the workings of perception are grouped into two main themes: those relating to selective attention and those relating to the influence of existing knowledge. The central importance of context, and the background and characteristics of perceivers in determining what is perceived, will be emphasized throughout this discussion.

The final three sections of the chapter each focus on an aspect of perception that has particular significance in the workplace. First, we shall see how perceptions formed about the causes of behaviour and events experienced have an important influence on individuals' future behaviour and motivation to pursue particular courses of action. We then look at the role of emotions in perception. Finally, in the last section, focusing on perception, emotion and employee relations, the broader impact of individuals' perceptions on the social climate of organizations is highlighted.

The topic of perception lies at the heart of the study of human experience and behaviour, whether it occurs inside or outside work organizations, because it is through our perception that we decide what the reality of the world is. The truth is that perceptions, and therefore views of reality, are far more dependent on the perceiver than on what is actually 'out there'. The implication of this is that there is not one 'true' reality at any given moment waiting to be discovered, because what each of us believes to be the basic reality of the world around us is 'mostly convenient, internally generated fiction' (ref. 1, p. 95). Based on our goals, experience and personal qualities, we each create and then act upon our own unique perceptual worlds. Crucially, this creative work is mostly automatic, so we tend to act confidently upon our perceptions while remaining blissfully unaware that there might be alternative ways of seeing things.

The topic of perception is particularly important in organizational behaviour because work organizations represent a real challenge to our perceptual abilities; to use Weick's words, they are inherently 'puzzling terrain'.[2] So much of what occurs in organizations is both constantly changing and ambiguous, especially because workplaces are social settings, and interpreting other people's behaviour is rarely straightforward. Changing market conditions and competitors, diverse people with multiple roles and motivations, multiple communications in various media, organizational politics – all of these things contribute to the complexity of what people must make sense out of when they go to work each day. Because 'the way things are' in an organization is rarely indisputable, the particular perceptions formed by its members become important influences on the nature of individuals' behaviour and relations with each other, as well as on the nature and fate of the whole enterprise.

Take, for example, the role of employees' perceptions, particularly of fairness, in the smooth running and performance of organizations, as illustrated by a spate of so-called 'boss-napping' in France in the Spring of 2009. As the downturn in the global economy took its toll on French businesses, French trade unions and workers reacted angrily to news of job losses at a time when they perceived that company executives were receiving large bonuses or generous early retirement packages. Employees at 3M, Scarpa adhesives and Sony expressed their anger by taking the law into their own hands and holding senior company executives for ransom in their company offices overnight in an effort to force the company to reconsider its position. Large demonstrations were also held in the centre of Paris by employees of Total who were angry about the announcement of significant job losses just days after the company had announced the biggest annual profit in French corporate history (€13.9 billion).

These collective responses to perceived unfair treatment also serve to highlight the social dimension of human perception. Our perceptions do not just form in isolation and then remain in our heads. The way we view ourselves, others and the world around us will shape our behaviour, and our behaviour influences the perceptions and behaviour of others. Although this interdependence underlies many of our actions, the social dynamics of perception become more obvious in situations such as giving a presentation, conducting a negotiation or joining a new work team.

A good example of the social (and emotional) dynamics of perception is a lecturer giving a lecture to students. The lecturer may quickly lose confidence if he or she perceives signs from the audience that things are not going well. Now lacking confidence and feeling anxious, he or she becomes self-conscious, begins to speak far too quickly and forgets some of the key points. It is entirely possible that the lecturer has misread the earlier signs from the watching students – they may have been whispering to each other because they were actually very interested in the talk. But ironically, the lecturer's dive in confidence and collapse in performance may themselves have created the negative audience perceptions he or she feared had occurred earlier. The point is that our perceptions are formed in part on the basis of information or cues picked up from the environment, to which we must then attach meaning. The way we interpret the situation will then shape what we do next, which will affect our environment and the cues we pick up next, and so on and so on.

These examples all illustrate the significance of understanding the links between individuals' perceptions and their behaviour in the work context. For one thing, different perceptions have different consequences for the performance and success of individuals and their organizations. But also, gaining an insight into how and why people form particular and differing perceptions in given circumstances means we have more chance of avoiding or preventing the escalation of conflict between people and groups of people. In order to discover why, like our poor anxious lecturer, we can be blind to our own perceptual processes, and why, like the employees at Total, we can find it extremely difficult to comprehend and accept the validity of alternative viewpoints, it is necessary to consider the basic workings of human perception. The rest of the chapter will explore the nature and consequences of perception in detail.

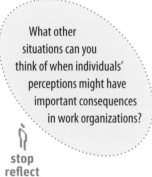

What other situations can you think of when individuals' perceptions might have important consequences in work organizations?

stop reflect

The basic features and process of perception

The basic features of perception

Before we explore the component processes involved in perception, it may be helpful to set the scene by highlighting some inherent features of the way we deal with information from the world. These features seem to provide good explanations for the phenomena highlighted in the introduction. Perception is selective, subjective, and largely automatic rather than conscious.

To function in the world, we need to gain information about the world around us. This information is gained through our six bodily senses of sight, hearing, touch, smell, taste and proprioception (the sense of the position and movement of our own body). Having sensed something, we then endeavour to make sense of what we are seeing, hearing, touching, tasting, smelling and/or feeling. This process is not always simply a matter of information processing of the kind carried out by a computer because we often experience an emotional reaction to the information we receive. This is most obvious when the primary information comes from our senses of smell or taste (certain odours and tastes provoking powerful feelings of disgust or nausea, for example), but, as our earlier example of 'boss-napping' illustrates, emotional feelings such as injustice and anger can be triggered by information gained from any of our senses. We will return to the role of emotion in perception later in this chapter.

We usually feel very certain about what we experience, and this certainty is actually helpful and adaptive because it allows us to go about our daily lives without having to think about every single thing we encounter. Our surroundings often make perfect sense to us without any conscious effort. We seem to need this feeling of order, but we actually have to work hard to create it, because the environment is not nicely ordered and organized. For one thing, there is just too much information available from the external environment for our senses to take it all in, and, to make things more difficult, this information comes in the form of raw data such as light and sound waves. So the basic ingredients of our perceptions are highly ambiguous sensory stimuli, and it takes a lot of 'brain work' to sift, organize and interpret them.

It is only possible for us to deal with the continuous bombardment of sights and sounds, smells and sensations because we employ **selective attention**. An obvious example is being able to focus on a companion's conversation in a busy cafe despite a myriad of sensory distractions such as others talking and laughing, background music, clattering plates, icy draughts or an uncomfortable chair. But the target of attention is determined by factors inside the person, as well as what stands out in the immediate context or setting. Individuals' preoccupations, emotional state and motivation will cause them to focus attention on specific aspects of people or situations. A professional salesperson meeting a client will probably be monitoring his or her speech and body language specifically for buying signals such as precise questions about the product. A manager who suspects an employee of time wasting may start particularly to notice whenever he or she is away from his or her desk, or talking to colleagues.

So it is that two perceivers can genuinely capture different aspects of the very same situation through selective attention. We do not have unlimited capacity for taking in information, so focusing on some environmental cues necessarily means ignoring others. And because this process is automatic rather than conscious, we are usually not too aware that we have been selective. When it comes to perception, rather than acting as neutral receivers of signals, we select the part of the environment to which we attend by acting as 'motivated tacticians'.[3] The motivation at a particular time may be to prioritize speed, as when we scan information to 'get the gist of it'. We may perceive defensively, as when we 'block out' information that we do not want to receive, or we may be looking for specific types of information to support a particular theory, as when we think someone is lying to us. The point is that our intentions and emotions colour our perceptions, playing a large part in determining what we draw from the environment.

Beyond selective attention, another central feature of perception is that the interpretation or meaning we attach to the external information we receive is strongly influenced by our existing knowledge: our ideas, experiences and backgrounds, including our ethnic and cultural origins. In other words, what we experience is subjective because others are unlikely to base their perceptions on exactly the same mix of motivations and prior knowledge. This principle applies to individuals who share cultural backgrounds, but culture-based assumptions will add an additional and powerful source of difference. So in the event that two individuals of different nationality, for instance, did manage to attend to exactly the same aspects of a

selective attention: the ability of someone to focus on only some of the sensory stimuli that reach them

Source: iStockphoto

plate 17 It is estimated that 80 per cent of the information we perceive comes through our sense of sight. Even when someone is talking to us, we still rely heavily on a host of additional non-verbal, visual information when we attend to and interpret what is being said.

shared situation, their cultural differences would mean that they would probably still not share the same thoughts about the meaning and relevance of the information.

It is estimated that 80 per cent of the information we perceive comes through our sense of sight. Even when someone is talking to us, we still rely heavily on a host of additional non-verbal, visual information when we attend to and interpret what is being said. The way we interpret much of this non-verbal communication is dependent on our cultural upbringing. Hand gestures offer a good example of this. Raising your hand and placing the tip of your index finger against the tip of your thumb so that the fingers form a circle is known as the 'ring gesture'. In English-speaking countries and in Indonesia, this gesture means 'everything is okay'. However, in France it can also mean zero or 'worthless', in Japan it can mean 'money', and in some Mediterranean countries it is used to infer that a man is homosexual. In Tunisia, the ring gesture means that the signaller feels extreme personal animosity towards you!

So existing knowledge, which includes culture-, gender- and age-related assumptions and expectations, as well as what we have learned and emotionally experienced in our lives, will influence how we interpret what we perceive. The key point is that existing factors specific to the perceiver will determine in good part the picture that he or she creates from the available information. So individuals' perceptions are likely to differ in the meaning attached to the information, as well as in the information picked up from the environment in the first place.

Critical insight

Get a copy of a paper by Dunkerley and Robinson, 'Similarities and differences in perceptions and evaluations of the communication styles of American and British managers',[4] and read about the different communication styles, perceptions and comments of the British and American managers in the study. What do you think we can do about the tendency to perceive our own cultural style as better than, rather than just different from, that of others?

The basic sequence and key factors in perception that we have discussed so far are shown in Figure 5.1. From the bombardment of sensory stimuli, the perceiver selects some of the information for attention and processing. Based on prior knowledge and current motivations, the perceiver then works out what the information means and responds accordingly. Once the person has responded in some way, her or his actions become part of the environment, and so influence the person's own and others' ongoing perceptions of what is happening.

In summary, human perception can be characterized as a process that is largely automatic, subjective and selective. Perception is not just something inside an individual; it has an emotional and a social dimension because perceptions affect our behaviour, which influences others. Although highly effective in helping us to easily and quickly make sense of the world around us, this amazing capability also has a downside. Our perceptions are most certainly providing only a limited perspective, because there will almost always be another point of view – and, dangerously, we are often 'blind' to this simple fact. By understanding how perception works, which means recognizing the inevitability of different world views, we become more able to understand and effectively manage our own and others' behaviour in organizations. The next section will examine the nature of perception processes in more depth.

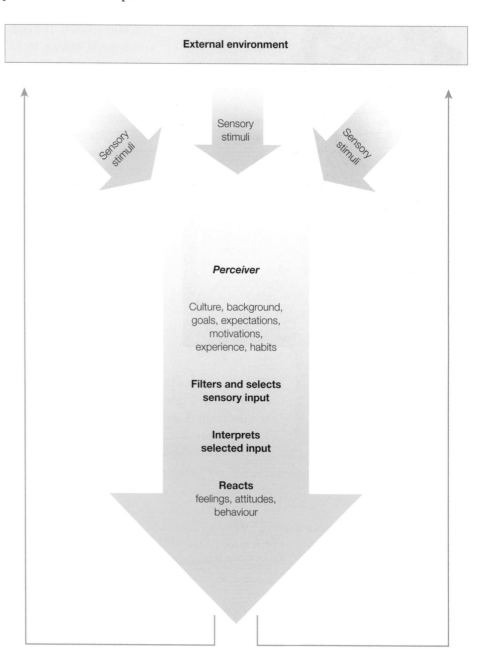

figure 5.1 The link between perception, behaviour and the environment

The process of perception

Perception is, then, a topic of significance in organizational behaviour because people's decision making and behaviour depend on how they interpret situations, and different interpretations are usually possible. But what exactly does the term 'perception' cover?

In truth, a definitive and comprehensive definition of human perception is not easy to find. The reason for this definitional difficulty is that perception is not really one topic or issue. Instead, the term 'perception' may be used in discussions about any one of a number of topics or issues, which can be placed at a number of different levels of analysis, from the physiological to the social. Research studies about human perception range from investigations of the inner workings of the human eye, to the impact of individuals' stereotypes on cross-cultural communication, to how others' perceptions affect people's choices about which careers to pursue. Nonetheless, it is still possible to identify a working definition to help us explore in more detail the psychological part of the perception process – the bit that happens inside our heads.

According to the cognitive psychologists Eysenck and Keane, 'At the very least, perception depends upon basic physiological systems associated with each sensory modality, together with central brain processes which integrate and interpret the output from these physiological systems' (ref. 5, p. 43). So our ability to 'perceive' depends upon three things:

1. *receiving:* being physically able to attend to and receive signals from the environment (for instance, having sight, hearing, touch, taste and smell, and being able to control which we employ at a given moment)
2. *organizing:* being able to mentally organize and combine those signals (which is what is happening when we see and hear speech in perfect synchronization, or see objects separate from their surroundings rather than as a mass of light patterns)
3. *interpreting:* being able to assign meaning or make sense of what we experience (for instance, attaching personal significance to particular combinations of sensory signals, like knowing when we are in a conversation and we need to talk back, or a person is threatening us, or a bus is approaching).

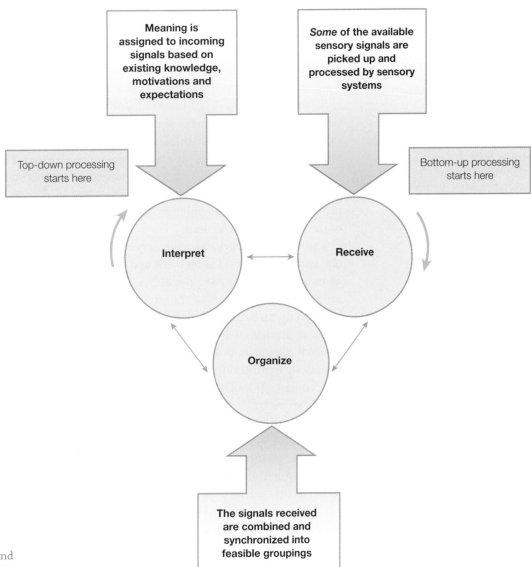

figure 5.2 The elements and process of perception

Figure 5.2 shows how these three elements are connected to each other.

To return to the features of perception already introduced, it is at the *receiving* stage that selective attention 'happens', and at the *interpreting* stage that subjectivity has its major influence. The *organizing* stage of perception is perhaps the most mysterious, in that our brains somehow work out those combinations of signals which are likely to go together, and those which are just not feasible. In this way, speech is attached to the face that is making the right movements even when there are other faces to choose from. This is how we know when we are looking at an image that is 'wrong' in some way, such as when the perspective is manipulated so the relative size of objects is unusual.

The sequence of perception: top-down or bottom-up?

Although it is helpful to separate the three elements of perception from one another so that we may better understand them, in reality they do not occur separately or in sequence; instead, they overlap and sometimes even occur in parallel. In addition, all three stages can be, and often are, influenced by our emotional reactions and dispositions. As we have discussed, our perceptions are actually constructed in a process that combines external information with our existing ideas about the world. Rarely do we start from scratch by piecing together the external 'clues' one by one. We have already attached some meaning to what we are in the process of perceiving while we are still receiving and organizing the external information. That is how we 'know' what someone is about to do or say, and why we are frequently surprised. The weight of evidence suggests that we almost always engage these three processes simultaneously.[5] Our relative reliance on external and existing information is not fixed, however, but will depend on the specific context.

When perception is led predominantly by gathering external sensory data and then working out what they mean, it is called 'bottom-up' or 'data-driven' information processing. When we think there may be consequences in getting it wrong, we are likely to rely more heavily on bottom-up processing. For instance, the requirement in most assessment centres that assessors explain and justify the ratings they award to candidates is thought to exert a 'press of accountability'.[6] The need to justify their judgements publicly leads assessors to pay extra attention to all aspects of the candidates' behaviour.

Rather than always ensuring accuracy, 'thinking too much' can actually hinder our attempts at sound judgement and decision making. If we try too hard to take in as much information as possible, it can interfere with our ability to focus on the most important aspects of the situation. If that happens, irrelevant pieces of information end up being included in the decision-making process.

Some studies of the use of magnetic resonance imaging (MRI) technology in medical diagnosis bear this out. MRI scanners offer doctors incredibly detailed images of the interior of the body. However, research suggests that these images may contain so much misleading information that the accuracy of a doctor's diagnosis can be badly affected. In one study, the spinal regions of 98 people with no back pain or back-related problems whatsoever were scanned by an MRI machine. The pictures were then sent to doctors without any other information. After examining the pictures, the doctors reported that two-thirds of the scans revealed serious spinal problems, and many recommended immediate surgery.[7] The MRI pictures showed so much information that the doctors found it harder to know what they should be looking at. In fact, the serious problems they diagnosed were a normal part of the ageing process.

In contrast to the 'bottom-up' approach, perception being led predominantly by existing knowledge and expectations is called 'conceptually driven' or

bottom-up processing: perception led predominantly by gathering external sensory data and then working out what they mean

top-down processing: perception
led predominantly by existing
knowledge and expectations rather
than by external sensory data

top-down processing. In this case, our working theory and expectations about what is happening will shape what we look for. We may fill in the scene from memory after perceiving a tiny number of cues that we think confirm our theory. Take a look at Figure 5.3. Can you see a black and white dog in this picture? If you can, you have just conformed to what psychologists called the 'law of closure', which states that if something is missing in an otherwise complete figure or object, we tend to try and complete it ('close the gaps') by adding additional information. In this case, our existing ideas of what a dog 'should' look like lead us to see a more complete picture of a dog than is actually there.

figure 5.3 The law of closure

Researchers have found that we tend to rely on top-down processing in circumstances that are very familiar. For instance, Roth and Woods reported that novice operators in nuclear power plants relied heavily on feedback from monitoring the environment to guide their interventions – a bottom-up strategy.[8] Experienced operators, by contrast, relied much more on their existing knowledge of the operating systems, making much less frequent checks of environmental information.

However, there is a danger of relying too much on existing knowledge. The danger is that changes in the environment that really require a response from us may simply go unnoticed. This can happen because we are focused on the picture of the situation that already exists in our heads, so we fail to perceive the signals that the actual situation actually looks somewhat different from what we expected. When the cognitive task in question is making a judgement about someone or something, rather than maintaining a work system, we may never become aware of the failure to consider key bits of information. Sadly, there are no system alarms that go off when we judge people on their mistakes and forget about the things they did really well.

perceptual bias: an automatic tendency to attend to certain cues that do not necessarily support good judgements

primacy effect: a perceptual error in which we quickly form an opinion of people based on the first information we receive about them

recency effect: a perceptual error in which the most recent information dominates our perception of others

halo and horns effect: a perceptual error whereby our general impression of a person, usually based on one prominent characteristic, colours the perception of other characteristics of that person

The dangers of 'thinking too little'[9] when making judgements have been well researched in the field of decision making (see Chapter 15). We have some **perceptual biases**, or automatic tendencies to attend to certain cues that do not necessarily support good judgements. The '**primacy effect**' is the term used to describe our tendency to pay too much attention to our first perceptions about someone. Although many people are aware of the power of first impressions, and try to avoid 'judging a book by its cover', it can be surprisingly difficult to change our initial perceptions. On the other hand, if we are not careful, we may be prone to the opposite bias, overemphasizing the last things we perceived about someone, called the '**recency effect**'.

Another general tendency in person perception is making broad-based assumptions about a person's qualities on the basis of one or a small number of observations, the so-called '**halo and horns effect**'. For instance, if an employee makes a mistake on one job task that is considered to be very important, it may bias a manager's overall perceptions, so that he or she

Source: London Fire Brigade

plate 18 Some people would be surprised to learn that this woman is a firefighter. The stereotype is of men doing such hazardous work.

assumes that the person is incompetent in every aspect of the job. It is always useful to guard against such biases in dealing with others, but it becomes particularly significant in the context of selection and appraisal interviewing, or indeed any situation at work where we are evaluating a person in order to make a consequential decision. It is for this reason that good design is so crucial in assessment procedures.

The key point about our use of perception strategies is that there is a trade-off or balance to be struck between avoiding the risk of holding inaccurate perceptions that comes with top-down processing, while at the same time minimizing the mental effort of perceiving everything from the bottom up.

Perceptual tricks, manipulations and illusions

The goal of human perception seems to be to make sense of the environment as quickly as possible, even if a bit of accuracy is sometimes lost along the way. As a result, it is quite easy to trick our brains by 'setting off' these tendencies to seek meaning and certainty using various common tricks and illusions. These tricks make it possible for us to get some brief glimpses of some of the usually automatic, non-conscious, workings of our perceptual systems. Indeed, history suggests that we are endlessly amused by having our senses duped. Magicians capitalize on our selective attention when they use sleight of hand in card tricks and disappearing acts. Ventriloquists amuse us because we cannot stop our brains organizing, or associating the ventriloquist's voice with the dummy's mouth movements despite knowing the truth. There appears to be something pleasing

Are you able to remember situations when you have used mostly a top-down or mostly a bottom-up perception strategy? Was this a conscious decision or did you become aware of it afterwards?

stop reflect

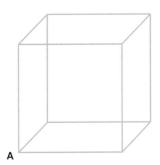

A

figure 5.4 The Necker cube

figure 5.5 The Mueller–Lyer illusion

linguistic relativity: the theory that the language we speak has such a fundamental influence on the way we interpret the world that we think differently from those who speak a different language

> The Exploratorium, a museum of science, art and human perception based in San Francisco, has an excellent website where you can explore a number of classic visual illusions online. Go to: www.exploratorium.edu/exhibits
>
> **weblink**

for us about being perceptually confused, although – paradoxically – only as long as we know it is happening.

Some 'serious' artists such as Salvador Dali and M. C. Escher have also produced work that plays with a feature of visual perception that means we can visually reverse the figure and the background of an image. So, in a painting such as *The Great Paranoiac* by Dali, it is possible to see the image as being made up of many small scenes, or to 'phase out' the detail and see one large image of a man's head, which is actually made up of the smaller images. The simplest demonstration of figure-ground reversal is the Necker cube (Figure 5.4), which is named after Louis Albert Necker, who discovered in 1832 that the perspective of the cube spontaneously changes if it is looked at continuously. So the front face becomes the back one, or, if you prefer, the corner marked A 'moves' from being at the front to being at the back of the cube. This is a demonstration of what is called 'multistability' in perception.[10] When there are multiple possible interpretations of something, and they are equally good or feasible, we will sometimes choose one, sometimes another, but never two at the same time.

Using the same principles as illusionists, perception researchers manipulate sensory inputs in a controlled way in order to explore how the elements of the perception process work and how they relate to each other. A simple and now classic experimental image, the Mueller–Lyer illusion, is shown in Figure 5.5. The straight lines are actually the same length, but the placement of the arrowheads makes them appear to be different: the line on the left appears longer that the one on the right. Curiously, researchers have found that the Mueller–Lyer illusion tricks our eyes but not our hands. There was no illusory effect when the lines were made into three-dimensional figures and people were asked to reach out and grab them between their thumb and index finger.[11] In other words, the study participants positioned their fingers at the right distance apart to grab the figures in each case. The illusory effect also seems to depend to some extent on the cultural background of the perceiver. When the illusion is depicted in the form of the rectangular corners of walls, people from cultures where the built environment does not include these angular features are less likely to perceive the lines as being of different lengths.

In fact, the exact relationship between culture, particularly language, and thought or cognition is the subject of much research and debate among psychologists. Followers of the theory of **linguistic relativity** argue that the language we speak has such a fundamental influence on the way that we interpret the world that we actually think differently from those who speak a different language. There is a difference, for instance, between English and Nepalese speakers in the way that the relative position of two people or objects is described.[12] In English, the positions would be described egocentrically, in relation to one's own body (for example, 'He is on my left and she is on my right'). In Nepalese, however, an environmentally centred description would be given instead (such as 'He is on the west side and she is on the east side').

The question that researchers have been trying to answer is whether such linguistic differences are linked to basic differences in the way that people raised in different cultures select and interpret environmental information. The contrasting view to linguistic relativity is that language plays a much less fundamental role in perception and cognition. From this standpoint, it is our thoughts that come first, and we use the language available to us to express those thoughts. As is often the case in the social sciences, there seems to be good evidence to support both viewpoints. The 'compromise view' as explained by Bloom,[13] is that there are some universal perceptions and interpretations of the world that all people

Source: Nick Tutton

plate 19   We know the fork is all in one piece, but our eyes deceive us.

perceptual set: describes what happens when we get stuck in a particular mode of perceiving and responding to things based on what has gone before

share, but that other distinctions in the meanings we attribute to what we experience are shaped by our native language.

The question of whether culture and language shape thought and perception clearly has important implications for our understanding of cross-cultural communication in organizations. Stated simply, the notion of linguistic relativity suggests that, for people attempting to live and work internationally, learning the language of the host country as an adult may not be enough to ensure that shared perceptions, understandings and ideas can be automatically developed with colleagues.

To focus on the context of organizational behaviour, not all of the perceptual tricks and illusions aimed at demonstrating the fundamental principles of perception, interesting as they are, can be applied directly to organizational life. One perceptual manipulation that has been used in a work context, however, is the old sales technique of the 'agreement staircase'. The technique involves making a series of requests to a customer to which he or she is highly likely to agree. The salesperson then immediately follows this with the main question – will the customer go ahead and buy? The idea is that the customer will instinctively say yes because he or she has fallen into the habit of doing so. Although, this technique sounds a bit naive, it can work if executed subtly because we do develop what are known as **perceptual sets**.

A perceptual set describes what happens when we get stuck in a particular mode of perceiving and responding to things based on what has gone before. The same effect can occur if you read a list of French words followed by an English one, for instance. You will tend to pronounce the English word as if it were French – which can be stupidly amusing if it is a particularly unromantic word like 'cabbage'! These experiments and manipulations do raise an important point that needs to be included in our exploration of perception. They demonstrate the significant effect of context on how we interpret even apparently straightforward information that we receive from the environment. When that information becomes more complex, as in social encounters, that point becomes even more significant.

The processing limitations underlying selective attention

We have already established that we attend to environmental information selectively. One central reason for selective attention is that there are actually physiological limits on how much information we can take in at once, as well as on how much mental work or processing we can do in a given time-frame. In other words, there are capacity constraints on two of the three elements of the perception process – receiving and organizing. Perception researchers have sought to understand how much of the different kinds of sensory information we can absorb, as well as what gets priority under different conditions.

An example of research in this area is the study of what is called 'dual-task interference', or when the attentional demands of one perceptual task limit our ability to do another at the same time. Put very simply, it is easier for us to do two tasks simultaneously if they involve different kinds of information input and require different kinds of response. Doing two computer screen monitoring tasks, each requiring a key stroke response, is more difficult than doing one visual and one auditory monitoring task simultaneously, for instance. As an example of the practical significance of this kind of knowledge, consider the controversy about the use of mobile cell phones while driving. This issue is of very real practical concern to the large number of people whose work involves driving, as well as to their employers.

One argument against their use is that mobile phones are a cause of road accidents because holding a phone and dialling numbers distracts motorists' attention from the road ahead and interferes with their ability to operate the vehicle's controls. In fact, two separate studies provide evidence that the interference with driving arises not from operating the phone, but rather from the amount of attention taken up by having a conversation. Whereas a passenger is aware of what is happening and will stop talking if the driver needs to act or concentrate, a person on the end of the phone cannot see what is happening in the car or on the road, so the conversation becomes more demanding for the driver. The findings reported in the studies included the statistic that drivers using mobile phones were four times more likely to be in an accident,[14] had slower reactions, and were two times more likely to miss traffic signals than those who were not on the phone.[15]

Other kinds of research study concerned with the limitations of information processing have identified two perceptual phenomena called 'change blindness' and 'inattentional blindness'. In these experiments, researchers test the focus of people's attention during various 'realistic' encounters by either changing the situation in some way, or introducing something unexpected and then finding out whether the manipulation was spotted. Change blindness refers to the fact that we simply do not seem to notice even large or obvious changes to things if they are not central to our concerns. In one experiment, somewhat reminiscent of a comedy sketch, members of the public who were giving directions to a researcher failed to spot that they were talking to a different person after two men carrying a door had walked in between them![16]

weblink

Have a look at the gorilla video and other videos too, and find out about other studies in inattentional blindness and change blindness at the researchers' websites. For the gorilla video, go to http://viscog. beckman.illinois.edu/djs_lab/demos. html. See also www.nelliemuller.com/ inattentional_blindness.htm

Another amusing experiment in the same vein, conducted by Simons and Chabris, involved a man in a gorilla suit.[17] Study participants were asked to watch a group of people passing a basketball between them and to count the number of passes that were made in a given time period. Amazingly, around 50 per cent of participants did not even see the man in the gorilla suit who walked among the ball players while they were counting the passes. This phenomenon has been termed 'inattentional blindness', because it seems we do not perceive even unusual or obvious things when we have focused our attention elsewhere. We appear to be very effective in automatically filtering out information that is not needed for the current task or goal. This propensity to reduce mental workload led to the characterization of human perceivers as 'cognitive misers',[18] using various short cuts to deal with limited processing capacity.

The influence of existing knowledge in perception

So far we have emphasized the idea of perceivers as 'cognitive misers', seeking the quickest, most energy-efficient route to decisive perceptions with the use of a bit of external information and a lot of expectation and existing knowledge. Because existing knowledge is so influential, questions about what we store and how we store it are important in understanding perception. How we store knowledge matters as well as what knowledge we hold, because it affects how quickly and how often we are able to bring specific thoughts to mind in a particular circumstance. Our brains have the same basic architecture, so all individuals will go through the same perception process – receiving, organizing and interpreting information in some order. But similarities and differences in the content of the mental models held, and when they are used as a basis for perception, will help to determine the degree to which two or more people will form overlapping views of the same experience.

The reason that we are able to bring information to mind so quickly is because our knowledge is organized into packages of related content. This means that it is necessary to stimulate only one piece of information for all the related knowledge that is held with it to come to mind. These knowledge packages are ready-made 'mental models' or simplified representations of the world, which provide the frameworks and theories against which we then 'test' and place incoming data. Cognitive psychologists call these mental models 'schemas', or 'schemata', to be accurate. A **schema** can be described as:

> a set of interrelated cognitions (for example, thoughts, beliefs, attitudes) that allows us quickly to make sense of a person, situation, event, place and so forth on the basis of limited information. Certain cues activate a schema, which then fills in missing details. (ref. 19, p. 48)

Individuals have a large number of schemata, each of which will contain more or less information depending on how much exposure they have had to the phenomenon in question. Our schemata will include those for people (such as a close friend or your mother), for situations (such as a job interview or eating at a restaurant) and for roles (like managing director or student). Schemata about people, roles and places we have not experienced may contain very general, simplified information. For instance, we may hold snapshot, idealized images of exotic countries we have not yet visited, and also associate those images with particular moods, feelings and personal goals. Even without having been there or read anything about it, a place like Zanzibar may, for someone from Northern Europe, conjure up images of golden beaches and sun-speckled blue seas that stimulate emotional feelings of warmth and relaxation, along with thoughts about winning the national lottery! By contrast, self-schemata, those which contain our thoughts and feelings about ourselves, will be both numerous and complex, and will include much more detailed information.

Schemata are based on our previous knowledge of and expectations about the world gained through the perceptual processes of receiving, organizing and interpreting information. Figure 5.6 shows how our schemata are activated and become progressively more accurate as they interact with the world. In the top-down processing mode, when perception begins with a clear theory or expectation, relevant schemata have already been activated and drive attention selectively towards external stimuli or cues that match or confirm the mental model in use. If I expect my boss to be angry, I will be selectively looking for signs of anger. So in the event that he or she smiles welcomingly at me, I might consider the possibility that I am seeing sarcasm in action, and look for other signs of anger rather than assume that my theory was wrong.

stop
reflect

Can you map the mental associations that you make in relation to some familiar roles, situations and people, including yourself?

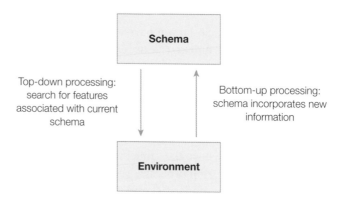

figure 5.6 The schema activation process

When people perceive in bottom-up mode, it is, as the diagram indicates, the cues that are noticed in the environment which drive the process. If I am going to see my boss and have no idea what mood he or she is in, I will start with the smile I see and build a theory based on all the signals I am getting. We tend to use distinctive and easily detected features such as a person's physical appearance as cues for choosing schemata.[19] The stimuli that grab our attention, those which are most salient, are received and organized, and these salient cues activate relevant schemata. The organization element of this process includes the basic categorization of the object, person or situation in question into a class or type before any meaning is attached. As an example, some person categories might be police woman, elderly foreign man or young trendy woman. This categorization process then determines which schema will be activated, and in turn how the perceiver will evaluate and respond to the encounter.

It is quite difficult to gain any mental control over the process of schema activation because it is so automatic. The associations between environmental cues, categories and schemata are not easily broken once formed. In fact, perhaps you have had personal experience of the research finding that trying to stop yourself having a particular thought actually has the opposite effect. It appears that we suffer 'post-suppression rebound' when we try to block thoughts from our heads.[20] The effect has been found in experiments where people were asked, and failed, to suppress thoughts of white bears, sex and past romantic relationships among other things.

One explanation for this effect is that, in order to suppress thoughts, we first have to detect them and then replace them with an alternative. Whereas the 'ironic monitoring process' that scans our thoughts to check for 'forbidden' content is automatic, the replacement process is not automatic, and takes mental effort. So when we have a lot to think about and the amount of mental processing capacity available to us is diminished, the replacement process breaks down, but the monitoring process continues, making the unwanted thoughts more rather than less accessible to conscious awareness.

Like most aspects of perception, schema activation is not a neutral process. For each person, some schemata are more easily accessible than others as a result of previous experiences, one's emotional state and personality characteristics (see Chapter 4). These more accessible schemata will then be brought to mind and used more often, making them even more easily retrieved as time goes on. In this way, we develop habitual tendencies to perceive the world in particular ways. When certain schemata are frequently used by an individual, they are said to be 'chronically accessible schemata'. An expatriate for instance, accustomed to living and working within different nations, may be prone to make sense of social misunderstandings in terms of cultural differences rather than the personality of the other person involved. An extrovert may interpret a wide range of situations as opportunities for social contact, as anyone cornered on a long journey with one will testify!

The use and misuse of perceptual cues

Differences in schema accessibility and use also mean that some environmental cues will be routinely more salient for some people than others. This is because schemata drive the selectivity in our attention, and lead us to notice what we expect or hope to see. In the last section, we gave the example of physical appearance as a cue for activating schemata. However, there is evidence that some aspects of physical appearance can trigger the kind of perceptual biases we discussed earlier in the chapter. For example, research has shown that taller people are often perceived as more authoritative and more physically attractive than people of below average height. Indeed, in 2007 a survey found that 58 per cent of all CEOs of the Fortune 500 companies were over 462 cm (6 feet 2 inches) tall, whereas only 4 per cent of adult US males are this tall.[21] In addition, an analysis of 8590 people found a significant correlation between height and income.[22] It would seem that people receive higher evaluations and higher pay even when the job involved has nothing whatsoever to do with height. This is a good example of the 'halo effect' in action.

The fact that people routinely make judgements about people based on such cues has motivated many people to attempt to manage the way they are perceived by others. Indeed, the research just described suggests that, if you are of average height, your career prospects may be improved by the simple expedient of wearing shoes with higher heels. In fact, as individuals, we happen to be very good at influencing what others think of us, and seek to do so much of the time. **Impression management** (IM) is 'the process whereby people seek to control or influence the impressions that others form'.[23] We are motivated to manage the way we are perceived in order to make real the image of ourselves we prefer, and to exert some control over how others respond to us.

impression management: the process of trying to control or influence the impressions of oneself that other people form

Presenting the best possible picture of ourselves to others requires us to do two things: enhance our positive attributes, and minimize those which might be perceived negatively. Self-promotion techniques such as describing our actions or qualities in a selective and favourable way, as well as non-verbal behaviour such as eye contact and walking and dressing in a certain style, can serve to enhance the positive in a given situation. Techniques such as providing excuses and justifications for less desirable facts about us serve to meet the goal of minimizing negative aspects. Further IM behaviours are directed towards the other people involved, such as flattery and agreement, but these still serve to create a particular image of the actor.

Relating these techniques to what we know about perception processes, we can describe IM as the way in which individuals seek to actively direct others' selective attention towards the cues that will stimulate the desired interpretation. For example, by wearing a smart business suit and walking into an interview room assertively, we seek to stimulate a 'professional, confident applicant' schema in the mind of the interviewer. Actually, we are not always even aware we are managing our image, but when we know we are being evaluated, as in the case of a job interview, the process becomes more of a conscious effort.

The workplace presents many evaluative situations, both formal and informal, which makes IM an important concept in organizational behaviour. The significance of self-presentational techniques and their effects are perhaps most obvious in the formal setting of personnel selection and appraisal procedures. However, given that the point of paid work is to perform a specified role and set of tasks, workers' performance and behaviour will often be under a good deal of scrutiny from their peers, superiors and employees on an ongoing basis, which will motivate positive self-presentation.

One concern is that some people are just better at using IM techniques, so will be perceived more favourably than those with equal or greater talents who are less skilful or less motivated in their self-presentation. This is a key concern in relation to the accuracy and fairness of decisions about people at work and the resulting opportunities made available to them. In one study, women managers were less willing than male colleagues to use IM behaviours such as networking, self-promotion and ingratiation to get ahead in their organizations, preferring instead to rely on doing an excellent job.[24] The difficulty with the women's approach is that promotion decisions are affected by seniors' perceptions of potential and promotability, as well as actual performance. Because male managers tend to be more accepting of the need to 'play politics' to secure promotion, they are more willing to actively manage their image with their seniors, so may have an advantage over the women when it comes to promotion.

IM is not restricted to individual behaviour. Organizations also try to influence the way in which people perceive them. Corporate advertisements in the mass media are an obvious example of this, but researchers have discovered that many companies employ IM techniques in their design of annual reports to shareholders, particularly in the design of graphs of financial data. One of the most common used types of IM technique in financial graph design is called 'proportionality measurement distortion'. A basic principle of graph design is that the physical measurements of the graph should be in direct proportion to the numerical values displayed on the graph – for example, if sales have doubled in one year, the length of the bar representing current sales should be twice as long as the bar representing sales a year earlier. Unfortunately, not all company reports follow this principle, and empirical evidence reveals that annual reports of companies in the US, Canada, UK, France, Australia and Hong Kong frequently contain graphs that distort financial information in this way.[25] Researchers have found that such measurement distortion tended to overemphasize the growth in sales and income and to underemphasize losses. In other words, the data were presented in such a way as to reinforce a favourable impression of the company's annual performance. Such an IM technique can be effective, as experimental studies reveal that people were significantly more likely to invest in companies with low growth rates when graphs of its performance were inaccurately drawn in this way than when the graphs were accurately drawn.[26]

The studies discussed above serve to highlight the controversial and ambiguous nature of IM behaviour. The line between simply highlighting one's best points and 'false advertising' is very difficult to determine, and each of us will have a different view about how far it is acceptable to 'manage' others' perceptions. Such controversy also surrounds IM behaviours that management stipulate as a contractual

Work and Society: Smile to save the company

In the service sector, paid work involving direct contact with customers requires workers to provide more than just physical labour; it requires them also to manage their emotions in order to create a publicly observable facial display.

Faced with depleted profits, Air Canada (the country's largest carrier) vowed to restore competitive advantage by placing a renewed focus on customer service and by encouraging their cabin crew to display a smile. The aim was to follow the lead set by low-cost carrier WestJet, which had long prided itself on courteous staff. In an internal message to Air Canada staff, the company's CEO Montie Brewer wrote, 'While Air Canada has the lead in hard attributes, it's up to each and every one of us to work together to be sure that we're also out in front in the soft attributes such as a ready smile, eagerness to help customers and simply perform jobs well' (Brewer, 2006).

Arlie Hochschild (1983) has called this aspect of paid labour 'emotional labour'. Emotions are strong feelings that individuals express and experience, such as anger, love, joy and friendship. For front-line service workers, such as flight attendants, she argues that the emotion accompanying the service is part of the service itself. Moreover, this service must be delivered not only with a smile, but also, in an emergency, with reassurance. She quotes a flight attendant:

Even though I'm a very honest person, I have learned not to allow my face to mirror my alarm or my fright. I feel very protective of my passengers. Above all, I don't want them to be frightened. If we were going down, if we were going to make a ditching in the water, the chances of our survival are slim, even though we [the flight attendants] know exactly

what to do. But I think I would probably – and I think I can say this for most of my fellow flight attendants – be able to keep them from being too worried about it. (p. 107)

For those employed as front-line service workers, the service cannot be separated from the mode of delivery. Hochschild's pioneering work emphasized that emotions are social and can be symbols that are widely recognized and form part of the way in which individuals manage and express themselves in social interaction. As social actors, workers' ability to manage emotions is based on their expectations of others and the expectations of others towards them. In understanding organizational behaviour, emotions become part of the social self and are one means that we use to interpret stimuli and develop an appropriate response.

stop! Can you identify occupations where emotional labour might apply?

How important is emotional labour in organizations?

Sources and further information

Ashforth, B. and Humphrey, R. (1993) 'Emotional labour and authenticity: views from service agents', pp. 184–203 in S. Fineman (ed.), *Emotion in Organizations* (2nd edn), London: Sage.
Brewer, M. *Globe and Mail*, November 11, 2008, p. B1.
Hochschild, A. (1983) *The Managed Heart: Commercialization of Human Feeling*, Berkeley, CA: University of California Press.
Morris, J. A. and Feldman, D. C. (1996) 'The dimensions, antecedents and consequences of emotional labour', *Academy of Management Review*, 21(4), pp. 986–1010.

requirement of employee behaviour. In some organizations, the desire to create a favourable impression leads management to require some employees, especially those employees who regularly engage in face-to-face contact with customers, to carefully manage their emotional behaviours. Hochschild calls this behaviour *emotional management* – the management of employees who are paid to adjust their emotions to the needs of the customer and the requirement of the work situation.[27]

Hochschild conducted research to explore how attendants on board commercial passenger aircraft are trained to manage their 'real' emotions in order to present a pleasant, smiling demeanour to passengers regardless of how afraid, tired, irritated or angered they may actually feel. From the passengers' perspective, such a demeanour is perceived as pleasant and can enhance their enjoyment of the flight (and the likelihood of flying with that particular airline again). However, looking at it from the employees' perspective, Hochschild argued that such behaviour represents a distortion of their feelings of self-esteem and self-identity.

Critical insight

Get a copy of Dominique Moisi's book *The Geopolitics of Emotion* (2009) and read Chapter 1, 'Globalization, identity, and emotion'.[28] Moisi contends that it is possible to draft a global map of emotions because dominant emotions, like dominant colours in paintings, do exist. One task of governments, he argues, is to study the emotions of their respective peoples, to capitalize on them if they are positive, and to try to reverse or contain them if they are negative. What relevance, if any, is Moisi's thesis to understanding organizational behaviour? Do you think managers should attempt to diagnose the emotional state of the workforce? Why?

The stability of schemata

Schemata develop over time through learning and experience, and, once formed, can be remarkably resistant to significant change. Although we add complexity to our mental models as we experience new examples of a particular phenomenon, wholesale revision of a schema is less likely. This is because a schema acts as a lens through which relevant new information is interpreted. Data that are inconsistent with what we 'know' to be the case are just reinterpreted so that they do not challenge our existing views. As numerous recent reality television shows demonstrate, if you strongly believe yourself to be a very promising singing talent, even the most uncompromising feedback to the contrary can be easily discounted and fully explained by the nasty personality of the judge.

Some failures to take on board feedback and change mental models do, however, have more serious consequences than wounded pride. A serious fire in 1949 in the USA called the Mann Gulch disaster claimed many lives despite the fact that skilled firefighters were in attendance.[2] A central point to come from the analysis of the incident pointed to the failure of the fire crew to acknowledge quickly enough that this was not the type of fire they thought it was. As a result, the men did not respond appropriately to the situation they were actually in, because they reinterpreted discrepant information about what they were experiencing and continued to respond according to the routine for the wrong type of fire. Tragically, some of the men could have kept their lives if they had listened seriously to one of their colleagues, who was engaging in bottom-up processing and understood the need for different behaviour.

Most of what happens inside organizations is not a life-and-death matter, of course, but it does nonetheless affect people's livelihoods and well-being. The consequences of senior managers failing to adjust their schemata about the organization's competition and strategy quickly enough in response to new information has been a topic of interest to researchers. For instance, Hodgkinson[29] investigated UK estate agents' (realtors') perceptions of the competitive environment in the industry just before a recession hit the property market and again once the slump was established. The estate agents demonstrated 'cognitive inertia'. Their perceptions of the environment in which they were operating remained stable even though there was clear evidence of a downturn in the market. In other words, the estate agents were overly dependent on their schemata of the situation, failing to monitor and interpret environmental cues appropriately. As a consequence, their ability to respond effectively to the real threat to the organizations' viability posed by the downturn was seriously compromised.

Apart from demonstrating the stability of schemata, this study also illustrates that schemata are not always specific to an individual, but can be shared between groups of people. In this case, the estate agents' shared perceptions were a result of similar work roles and industry context. Broad similarities between people, such as gender, ethnicity, national culture and educational background, can also increase the chances that there will be some similarity in their perceptions about some things. A study found that two people randomly paired are likely to share only about 10 per cent of their chronic mental constructs, that is, their stable knowledge.[30] However, people who live or work together are not random pairings; they will share some common roles, backgrounds or experiences. **Stereotypes** are a class of schemata that appear to be shared between people, and are of particular consequence in organizational life because of their effects on perceptions of, and subsequent behaviour towards, individuals.

Stereotypes are a form of schema containing generalized ideas about the qualities and characteristics of individuals within particular groups,[19] for example people with financial worries make motivated salespeople, stock market traders are usually privately educated men in their 20s and 30s, Chinese men and women are the best mathematicians, and taller people are more authoritative. These are all examples of stereotypical beliefs about groups of people because they make an assumption that the characteristics in question will be true of all or most of the individuals in the category. Not all stereotypes are negative or unflattering, of course. But when assumptions about certain groups are automatically applied to individuals in the work context, unfair, potentially discriminatory and probably ineffective judgements and decisions can result.

A case in point is the issue of age discrimination by employers. In countries where this is prevalent, the exclusion of skilled and capable older workers from the workforce based on negative stereotypes of their potential to contribute is laying to waste a sizeable portion of that nation's available labour. As well as denying opportunities and income to the older workers, this exclusion of capable individuals based on non-performance-related characteristics is making it harder for organizations to recruit enough people, leading to reduced performance and profitability.

It is also known that people do not perform as well as they are able when they feel they are being stereotyped.[31] So even when given an opportunity, a worker who is a member of a minority group in an organization may not be able to contribute fully if he or she feels that the group membership is uppermost in others' minds. Gender-based stereotypes are of particular concern in organizations, because women still do not get the same rewards for paid work as their male counterparts, and some occupations appear to be 'gendered', or occupied predominantly by one or other sex.

The phrase 'think manager, think male' was coined by Virginia Schein[32,33] to describe the effect of sex-role stereotypes on the perceptions of what it takes to be a successful manager. Many studies have shown that both men and women, and people of different nationalities, describe successful managers as having characteristics that they also associate more with men than women, such as competitiveness, decisiveness and ambition.[34] As well as affecting women's motivation and expectations, such perceptions may create a bias in the evaluation of potential and existing managers by decision makers if they are unaware of or unconcerned about the effect of gender-based stereotypes on their judgements.

As we have already discussed, it is actually very difficult to intervene in the automatic processes by which we associate people or situations with particular thoughts and feelings, even if we become aware of them. Trying to suppress stereotypical thoughts will probably result in 'thought rebound', bringing them even more to the forefront of our minds. We can, however, be vigilant about questioning and exploring our perceptions, reactions and decisions about people, in order to actively counter the inevitable biases and assumptions to which we would otherwise be prone.

It is hard to imagine a person who could not be stereotyped on some dimension, so we are all potentially at risk of being judged inaccurately at some point. Why then do we form stereotypes about people? We have already discussed the marvellous efficiency of schemata for making sense of the world quickly with minimum effort. Stereotypes allow us to size up people with the same efficiency, and apparently that includes ourselves. According to self-categorization theory, which is an extension of **social identity theory**,[35] stereotyping people occurs from the same process we use to categorize and understand the kind of person we are in relation to others. The basis of these influential theories is that part of our self-concept is defined in terms of the series of social groups to which we belong. Such groups include demographic ones based on age, gender and socioeconomic status, as well as those we have some choice about, including student, work, sports or more loosely defined groups such as 'clubbers' or classical music fans.

In order to decide whether an individual is a member of a particular group, we use as a basis what we consider to be the defining features or stereotypical attributes of members of that group. The effect of this process is to simplify the picture by maximizing the distinction between groups and minimizing any differences between individuals within groups. So we can then easily work out whether they, or we, have the key features necessary for membership. It has been suggested that one of two sources of motivation for this social comparison is to reduce uncertainty about the social world and how to behave in it, which, as we have discussed, is what our basic perceptual processes also appear to achieve.[36]

A second motivation for making these social distinctions concerns our need to maintain self-esteem, and this is crucial in relation to stereotyping. Although we categorize ourselves in the same way as others, this need to view ourselves positively means that we have an inherent tendency to evaluate the characteristics of the groups we belong to (**in-groups**) favourably, and those of other groups and their members (**out-groups**) negatively. So it is possible to see how perceptions of difference and negative stereotypes can form through basic social perception processes.

The ideas of self-categorization and social identity theories can be applied to try to understand some troublesome issues in contemporary organizations.[37] For instance, the evidence from reports of mergers and acquisitions is that 'people issues' are cited as one of the most difficult aspects of integrating two previously distinct firms.[38] From the perspective of social identity theory, the hostility and culture clashes that are a feature of firm integration can be explained by the tendency to favour our own groups and view others as both distinct or different, and less desirable. It is further suggested that events such as organizational restructuring may actually stimulate people to identify even more strongly with their in-groups as they seek to reduce the uncertainty that surrounds such events.[36] On the more positive side, the comparison groups we use are dynamic and flexible. So

Have you ever become aware you were being stereotyped? How did you feel about it? How did it affect your behaviour?

stop reflect

social identity theory: the theory concerned with how we categorize and understand the kind of person we are in relation to others

How would you define your social identity? Think about the types of people you identify positively with (your in-groups) and the types of people you are sure you are different from (your out-groups)

stop reflect

in-groups: groups to which someone perceives he or she belongs, which he or she accordingly evaluates favourably

out-groups: groups to which someone perceives he or she does not belong, which he or she accordingly evaluates unfavourably it may be possible to intervene in situations where there is unhelpful rivalry or hostility between work groups, by trying to subtly change individuals' identity perceptions. Focusing all groups' attention on external competitors rather than each other is one example.

Perceiving causes

As well as perceiving and judging people and situations, we are also naturally inclined to form perceptions about what has caused the behaviour and events we encounter. From the pursuit of religion to the public's fascination with getting 'into the mind' of serial killers, it is a human tendency to assume that there must be some meaning in all things, and some motive behind all people's actions. Hence, we develop ideas and expectations about causes and effects, and general ideas about how things happen and relate to each other, based on experience.

Broadly speaking, we distinguish between stable causes for things and transitory or changeable ones, and between two sources of explanation: those which are about the person (internal), and those which are about the situation (external). The explanations an individual chooses to use, '**causal attributions**' as they are called, are important because they can have a significant influence on his or her expectations and behaviour. This applies to expectations about ourselves, as well as about other people.

> causal attribution: the explanations an individual chooses to use, either internal (about the person) or external (about the situation), and either stable or transitory

Consider the experience of being shortlisted but then not selected for a prestigious and challenging job. The reaction of many people is to spend some time thinking about why they were not considered to be the most suitable candidate. If the rejected applicant puts the result down to a lack of preparation on his or her part – an attribution to an internal but changeable cause – he or she might well consider applying for a similar job in the future, but make changes in his or her preparation for the interview. If on the other hand, the person perceives the main cause of the rejection to be a lack of the required level of intelligence – an internal, stable attribution – he or she will probably believe that such prestigious jobs are simply out of reach, and apply only for less challenging jobs in the future. Of course, the applicant might make an external attribution, deciding that the outcome was nothing to do with him or her at all, but was caused by the personal connections of the successful job seeker. In this case, the person's perceptions create no reason to reduce his or her ambitions based on this rejection, or indeed to make changes in approach.

This example demonstrates the way in which our perceptions about what causes things to happen can shape the options for any action that we consider, and our beliefs about what will result from that action. **Perceived self-efficacy** is the term used to describe the 'beliefs in one's capabilities to organize and execute the courses of action required to produce given attainments' (ref. 39, p. 3). Levels of self-efficacy for a specific activity or goal will determine what goals people actually attempt, how much effort they exert to achieve those goals, and how willing they are to persevere in the face of difficulty.

> perceived self-efficacy: a person's belief in his or her capacity to achieve something

By definition, in order to develop high self-efficacy in an area, it is necessary to make at least some internal causal attributions for relevant outcomes, because efficacy requires us to believe in our ability to personally control what happens. The exception to this is the attribution of failures to stable, unchangeable personal qualities, which will naturally work to lower expectations of success. Of course, efficacy-lowering attributions are sometimes accurate, and in that sense they are useful. Failing to recognize appropriately when we do not have the skills or qualities required for a certain pursuit can be damaging in that it causes us to direct our effort in unproductive ways. It is when individuals' low expectations are not based on a realistic assessment of their capabilities that they constrain their ability to reach their potential.

There is solid evidence that efficacy beliefs are an important factor in determining many performance outcomes over and above actual ability.[39] An important example is in early study choices made at school, because these choices work to constrain the career options available to students later on. The sex-role stereotyping of subjects and occupations appears to affect girls' and boys' interests and expectations early on, through the subtle feedback and encouragement for different pursuits that children get from their social environments. From a young age, girls tend to have lower perceived self-efficacy for male-typed subjects such as maths and quantitative skills, regardless of their actual capabilities. For this reason, girls are less likely at school to choose and continue to study maths, which means they are not then well equipped to enter occupations for which continued exposure is required, such as science.

The case of girls and study choices shows how individuals' expectations can become **self-fulfilling prophecies**. That is, if we think that it is unlikely we can achieve a particular goal, we tend not to bother even trying, or to give up easily if we do try. This means we do not actually give ourselves the opportunity to succeed, so end up reinforcing our original expectation. Of course, this process can also work in a positive direction, where expectations of success can lead to engagement with, and increased effort to achieve, the goal in question. The implication of this information for organizational behaviour is that we cannot always assume that an individual's performance and attainment directly reflects her or his basic abilities. When setting goals, and when motivating and appraising performance, it may be helpful for individuals and their managers to examine causal beliefs and self-efficacy levels in order to identify potential barriers to achievement.

Given its practical significance, there is a good deal of theory and research focused on the ways in which we might come to make one type of causal attribution over another, but the ideas of Kelley are particularly influential.[19] In his 'co-variation model', Kelley suggested that we use information about the co-occurrence of the person, behaviour and potential causes to work out an explanation.[40] Specifically, three aspects of the occasion are considered:

- *Distinctiveness*: Does the person behave this way in other situations, or is the behaviour uncommon for them and specific to this situation?
- *Consistency*: Does the person always behave this way in this type of situation?
- *Consensus*: Does everyone behave this way in this type of situation, or is this person's behaviour different?

The pattern of answers to these three questions will rule out some potential causes and suggest others. Imagine that a colleague has just been very rude to you when passing on information. If this person is always rude to you (high consistency) but also rude to others (low distinctiveness), and everyone else in the organization is very friendly (low consensus), you will probably think that the person, and not you, is the cause of the problem. In the event that there is a lack of consistency in the person's behaviour in the situation – in this case, he or she is sometimes rude and sometimes friendly – we tend to discount the immediate possibilities and assume that there must be some other explanation.

One of the issues with Kelley's model is that it does not make too much sense unless we have experienced the person and situation more than once. If this is our only experience, we must use different criteria because we do not have the same information. In such cases, Kelley suggested that we use causal schemata as guiding frameworks for making attributions. There is supporting evidence for the

self-fulfilling prophecy: an expectation about a situation that of itself causes what is anticipated to actually happen

co-variation model: Kelley's model that uses information about the co-occurrence of a person, behaviour and potential causes to work out an explanation

co-variation model, but it is not actually clear whether we always or exclusively use this particular process to attribute causation. Nonetheless, the framework has proved a useful tool for understanding the implications of these perceptions.

As with the other aspects of perception discussed in this chapter, causal attribution is not a purely rational process free of selectivity and the workings of motivation. Just as we display biases towards perceiving some environmental cues over others, we are also subject to some general tendencies in the way we attribute causes to things. One bias that has been noted in our perception of causes is the **false consensus effect**, which is the tendency to over-estimate the degree to which other people will think and behave in the same way as we do. We also have a tendency to favour internal attributions for the behaviour of others but external ones to explain our own behaviour. So we are likely to assume that a colleague misses a deadline because she or he is unreliable or disorganized, whereas we miss our own deadlines because of unavoidable constraints. This is called the **fundamental attribution error**.

Actually, the error is not really fundamental in the sense of applying to all people. The extent to which people fall prey to this tendency appears to depend on their cultural background, because those from non-Western cultures are more likely to use external attributions.[41] It is also the case, mirroring the phenomenon of the chronic accessibility of certain schemata discussed earlier, that individuals appear to adopt particular 'explanatory styles', or have a predisposition to employ some types of explanation over others.

Two familiar explanatory styles are optimism and pessimism. Most of us have met someone who is unfailingly optimistic about life regardless of the circumstances, and someone for whom every silver lining has a cloud. Although we often treat such differences light-heartedly, they do have serious consequences. Optimism has been linked to achievement across life domains as well as physical health and psychological well-being, whereas pessimism has been linked with depression and lack of success.[42] It has been suggested that optimists are those who habitually favour external, unstable and specific (only affecting one part of their life) explanations for bad events.[43] By contrast, pessimists attribute bad results to internal, stable and global (affecting all aspects of their life) causes.

false consensus effect: the tendency to over-estimate the degree to which other people will think and behave in the same way as we do

fundamental attribution error: the tendency to favour internal attributions for the behaviour of others but external ones to explain our own behaviour

To find out more about learned optimism and other similar work, browse the website www.ppc.sas.upenn.edu. You will see that the researchers have made a number of questionnaires available for download, such as the Subjective Happiness Scale, which you could use for a research project of your own

weblink

Perception and emotion

Much has been written in recent years on the role that emotion plays in human perception and decision making. Like perception, emotions involve processes outside our conscious awareness, and research now shows that emotion plays a much bigger role in perception and thinking than was previously believed. Our schemata are not simply internal models of the world; they also contain emotional information and biases. Indeed, we have already seen in this chapter how feelings of anger, injustice, attractiveness, pessimism, wanting to belong, and desire to make a good impression on others can all influence how we interpret and interact with the world. We will also see in later chapters how emotional factors are important in motivation (Chapter 7), team working (Chapter 9), leadership (Chapter 13) and communication (Chapter 14).

But it is not just our perception of other people that is coloured by our emotions. Take, for example, our perception of risk. Findings from neuroscientific research suggest that our emotions have a key part to play in the creation of a perceptual bias against risk taking.[44] Our emotional brain would appear to be 'pre-programmed' to maximize feelings of pleasure and minimize feelings of pain. In modern societies, these feelings are commonly associated with the gain and loss of

Source: iStockphoto

plate 20 Our emotional brain is impulsive and not well equipped to look into the future. This is why decision making based on emotion and intuition is fraught with danger. What is your view on the safety or otherwise of 'tombstoning' (see picture)? To what extent is that view based on emotions, and to what extent on rationality?

something we value. We have an aversion towards loss because of the negative emotions this generates. Such loss aversion can seriously affect how we perceive and evaluate the riskiness of a particular situation. As a consequence, our desire to avoid feeling a sense of loss or regret can sometimes lead us to make very poor decisions. This may explain why investors put money into government bonds rather than corporate stocks even though the latter have historically out-performed the former by quite some margin[45] – bonds are perceived to be safer. It may also help us to understand why people sometimes continue on a particular course of action (for example, a large investment in a new organizational information system) even when that action is clearly failing: we don't want to regret wasting our 'sunk costs' even if the longer-term costs of continuing may end up being greater.

The neuroscientist Jonah Lehrer suggests that the emotional bias in our schemata to maximize pleasurable feelings lies at the heart of our irrational impulsive decision making.[46] He gives the example of the US subprime mortgage lending market (the collapse of which many economists blame for the onset of the 2009 global economic recession). The most common type of subprime mortgage is the 2/28 loan, which offers a very low fixed-interest rate for the first 2 years and a much higher variable rate for the next 28 years. This type of mortgage accounted for 20 per cent of all US mortgages before the housing market collapse in 2007. Clearly, for many people, the short-term benefits of these mortgages proved too tempting to resist. They were driven by the pleasurable feelings of getting a 'cheap deal' and overlooked the longer-term risk of rising interest rates. Our emotional brain is impulsive and not well equipped to look into the future. This is why decision making based on emotion and intuition is fraught with danger, and why so much research has been conducted on how to enhance the rationality of the decision-making process (see Chapter 15).

Perception, emotion and employee relations

There is one final topic that needs to be included in this discussion about perception and organizational behaviour, namely the role that perception plays in shaping the tone of relations that exist in the workplace. Throughout the chapter, we have discussed how it is that two people can share an experience but form altogether different perceptions about what has happened and what it means. The reasons have included differences in attentional focus, expectations, emotional reactions and prior knowledge. We have also seen how unalterable factors such as gender and cultural background will influence these elements of perception processes, both by shaping the nature of individuals' learning and experiences, which impacts on expectations and knowledge, and through the social categorization and stereotyping processes by which we work out where we and others fit into the social world.

As we explained in Chapter 1, there is in the work domain another basic distinction between people that is of some importance in understanding behaviour in organizations: that between employers (and managers as the agents of employers), and employees or workers. The relations between these two groups are referred to as the employment relationship, and managing these relations is a central concern of human resource management (see Chapter 17). The relevance here is that the differences in roles, responsibilities, motivations and rewards associated with being

OB and globalization

Emotional intelligence in the international oil and gas sector

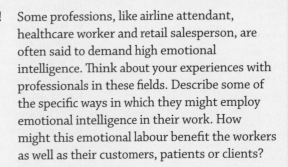

International business relationships and partnerships are becoming more and more common in the natural resource sector. As the worldwide population grows and new industrialized economies, such as China, Brazil, India and Russia, emerge, there is increasing pressure on nations – and private companies within their borders – to secure access to the resources that literally fuel their economies.

One means of doing this is through the formation of international business partnerships to ensure that resources that exist only in certain locations can be extracted, transported and sold around the world. Such partnerships have become increasingly common in the oil and gas sector, and industry leaders must be savvy to the challenges of managing a global network of colleagues, clients and workers, many of whom have different, culturally based ideas about proper business relationships and effective organizational management.

In a recent industry publication, Weijermars et al. (2008) explain that the challenges of successful business relationships between Western European and Russian oil companies extend beyond the technical and political aspects of business and contract management. Whereas managerial culture in Russia has traditionally tended to be hierarchical and centralized, Western European business culture is more decentralized and reliant on networking. Building management tools to effectively address these different cultural expectations is integral to the success of the partnerships. According to Weijermars et al.:

> The hiring of a multicultural workforce from a range of countries, distinct company cultures and different age groups poses a challenge in itself through the increased risk of communication barriers or gaps … The common aim is to establish an emotionally balanced relationship between the two partners and to narrow the communication gap. This results in better alignment of cultural values, skill sets and common goals, which is important to overcome the residual Cold-War impediments of the past.

Such partnerships highlight the role of *emotional intelligence* as a management tool in international business. Emotional intelligence describes the ability to manage one's own emotions and, through verbal and non-verbal performance, to identify and manage the emotions of others (Goleman, 1995). Emotions, or emotional responses, are often linked to cultural experiences and worldviews, and in order for managers to effectively develop their emotional intelligence, they must recognize the cultural paradigms within which their partners' emotions are operating. This is the challenge facing the oil and gas sector today. In the increasingly global economy, strong emotional intelligence can be just as crucial to the success of business relationships as technical or fiscal intelligence.

stop! Some professions, like airline attendant, healthcare worker and retail salesperson, are often said to demand high emotional intelligence. Think about your experiences with professionals in these fields. Describe some of the specific ways in which they might employ emotional intelligence in their work. How might this emotional labour benefit the workers as well as their customers, patients or clients?

Have you ever been in a situation where a friend or colleague from a different cultural background found it difficult to understand your emotional reaction to a situation, or vice versa? Describe how acquiring emotional intelligence about this person's culture might have helped you (or them) to understand and address the situation.

watch Watch the BBC 2 television series *The Office* (2001–03), paying specific attention to how emotional intelligence is (or is not!) used by different characters, and to what effect.

Sources and further research

Goleman, D. (1995) *Emotional Intelligence: Why It Can Matter More Than IQ*, New York: Bantam Books.

Harwood, M. (2008) 'Relationships critical to overseas personnel protection'. Available at: www.securitymanagement.com/news/relationships-critical-overseas-personnel-protection (accessed September 2009).

Lorz, M. (2006) 'Leadership styles'. Available at: www.management-issues.co.uk/2006/8/8/opinion/leadership-styles.asp?section=opinion&id=3435&is_authenticated=0&reference=&specifier=&mode=print (accessed September 2009).

Weijermars, R., De Jong, V. and Van Der Kooi, K. (2008) 'Cultural challenges in oil and gas industry management', *World Oil*, **229**(4), pp. 223–8.

Note: This feature was written by Gretchen Fox, PhD, Anthropologist, Timberline Natural Resource Group, Canada.

either an employer or an employee mean that individuals in these two groups are likely to perceive and emotionally respond to what happens in the organization somewhat differently. This is significant because there is evidence that the extent of the agreement between employers' and employees' perceptions about key aspects of work will have consequences for employees' work attitudes and performance.

Perceived unfair treatment can lead to industrial disputes, such as that highlighted earlier involving workers from Sony and Total in France. More broadly, such perceptions have been found to predict employees' feelings of job satisfaction and trust in managers, as well as their willingness to engage in discretionary behaviour such as staying to complete tasks beyond contracted hours and helping colleagues.[47] In fact, the notion of fairness or justice can be separated into two components: fairness of outcomes, or distributive justice, and fairness of procedures, or procedural justice. People tend to be concerned with the process by which decisions are made as well as the decision itself, and may in fact be willing to accept a personally disappointing outcome if the procedures used are perceived to have been equitable.

The importance of employees' perceptions about fairness or justice is not, however, restricted to how specific aspects of employment such as formal contract terms are viewed. The employment relationship is best seen as a series of agreements about a number of elements that are all of importance to the parties involved, such as working conditions, job security and commitment, management style, and pay and benefits. It is also an ongoing, dynamic interaction between the parties made up of a sequence of exchanges over time, each of which will influence the thoughts and perceptions of those involved. The psychological contract, a concept we introduced in Chapter 2, has become important in organizational behaviour and human resource management. It is a term used to capture individuals' general perceptions of the overall nature and balance of the employer–employee exchange.

A well-accepted definition of the psychological contract is provided by Rousseau, who describes it as 'individual beliefs, shaped by the organization, regarding the terms of an exchange agreement between individuals and the organization' (ref. 48, p. 14). In other words, it consists of employees' ideas about what they are expected to contribute to the organization and what they can expect to get back in return for their efforts. Two key points to note are that the psychological contract is unwritten and often unspoken, and that these are the perceptions formed by individual employees of the 'deal' promised by the employer. These expectations are formed during the recruitment process and when inside the organization, from what managers say and do, as well as the communications and culture of the company.

For all the reasons we have discussed for why people's perceptions may differ, one person's ideas about what the organization has promised and expects may not be fully or even partly shared by managers or indeed other employees. Much potential exists, then, for organizations to fall short of employees' expectations and vice versa, leading to feelings that agreed promises have been broken. The results from a number of studies suggest that violations of individuals' psychological contracts are linked to outcomes such as intentions to quit, reduced job performance and lower levels of commitment.[49]

Evidence from a study of supervisors and those they managed showed significant differences in relative perceptions of the extent to which aspects of the psychological contract related to pay, advancement opportunities and a good employment relationship were fulfilled.[50] Perhaps unsurprisingly, the supervisors felt that the employer's obligations had been fulfilled more fully than did their subordinates. This study also allows us to relate the issue of psychological contract violation to the process of causal attribution discussed earlier, and particularly the phenomenon of the fundamental attribution error. Where both parties agreed that some expectations were unmet, the employees were more likely to perceive the cause as intentional disregard by the employer, while the supervisors tended to see the cause as situational constraints, or events beyond the organization's control. Here then is another example of the very real and concrete organizational consequences of individuals' perceptions.

---

distributive justice: justice based on the principle of fairness of outcomes

procedural justice: justice based on the principle of fairness of the procedures employed to achieve outcomes

psychological contract: an individual's beliefs about the terms and conditions of a reciprocal exchange agreement between that person and another party

Chapter summary

❑ Perception is important in organizational behaviour because the fundamental nature of perceptual processes means that individuals usually interpret other people and situations differently and so routinely hold different views of reality, which in turn strongly influence their attitudes and actions. This means that avoiding conflict and ensuring that important workplace decisions are based on sound judgements is not a matter of training people how to see things as they 'really are', because multiple realities always exist. More can be gained from understanding how perception works, and shaping organizational activity so that the possibilities for negative outcomes (both emotional and behavioural) are minimized.

❑ 'Perception' refers to the process by which our senses gather information from the environment and our brains make sense of that information. The perception process is characterized as inherently selective, subjective and largely automatic rather than conscious. It can be broken down into three steps or elements – receiving, organizing and interpreting – representing the path by which we mentally transform sensory stimuli from the environment into meaningful information.

❑ The three elements of the perception process do not occur separately or in sequence, but overlap and sometimes occur in parallel. When perception proceeds from the sensory data received from the environment, it is called 'bottom-up' information processing. In contrast, when perception begins with existing knowledge that is used to interpret the incoming data, it is called 'top-down' processing. Whereas bottom-up processing requires a lot of mental effort, top-down processing carries the risk of assumptions and jumping to the wrong conclusions, so some balance is required between in the use of these two perception strategies.

❑ The processing limitations of our brains mean it is only because we employ selective attention that it is possible for us to experience the mass of sensory stimuli in the environment as orderly and meaningful. Our choice of what to attend to is driven by the environmental cues that are most salient, or by our own motivations, expectations, emotions and goals. This selectivity is highly resource efficient, but the downside is that we can miss crucial bits of information and form misleading perceptions of what we are experiencing. If we then act on those perceptions, we may suffer serious consequences.

❑ Existing knowledge has a powerful effect on how we perceive new experiences. We store knowledge in the form of mental models, or schemata: packages of related content (for instance, thoughts, emotions and attitudes) about people, situations and roles. Schemata do develop over time, but do not change much once formed because they act as lenses by which we view new information. New data that are inconsistent with what we 'know' are simply reinterpreted to fit. In perception, when one bit of information related to a schema is brought to mind, everything else in the package comes to mind also, so we can very quickly make sense of something on the basis of a small bit of information. But these stable, automatic linkages between thoughts can be unhelpful, as in the case of stereotypes. Although we can choose not to act upon stereotypes, it may not be possible to stop them coming to mind in the first place.

❑ Two specific classes of perception were identified that hold particular significance for organizations. The causes that people perceive (or attribute) for particular outcomes will significantly affect their future expectations and behaviour. If a person sees a failure to meet a goal as the result of stable, internal causes – such as intelligence – she or he is less likely to try again than if the cause of the failure is perceived to be more about his or her circumstances at the time. This knowledge is important for understanding individual performance and motivation. The second class of perception – employees' views of justice and fairness in the workplace – is significant because these impact on the employment relationship. If employees perceive that they are being treated unfairly by the organization, it will negatively influence their work attitudes and motivation. The difficulty is that employees and employers are very likely to perceive things differently by virtue of their respective roles and experiences, so it is a particular challenge for organizations to ensure that employees feel fairly treated.

Key concepts

causal attribution	149
chronic accessibility	151
cognitive inertia	147
explanatory styles	151
false consensus effect	151
fundamental attribution error	151
mental models	141
perceived self-efficacy	149
perceptual biases	138
perceptual errors	139
perceptual sets	140
psychological contract	154
salient cues	143
schemata	142
selective attention	132
social identity theory	148
stereotypes	147

Vocab checklist for ESL students

- ☐ Bottom-up processing
- ☐ Causal attribution
- ☐ Co-variation model
- ☐ Distributive justice
- ☐ Emotional management
- ☐ False consensus effect
- ☐ Fundamental attribution error
- ☐ Halo and horns effect
- ☐ Impression management
- ☐ In-groups
- ☐ Linguistic relativity
- ☐ Out-groups

- ☐ Perceived self-efficacy
- ☐ Perception, perceiver, perceptive, perceive
- ☐ Perceptual bias
- ☐ Perceptual set
- ☐ Primacy effect
- ☐ Procedural justice
- ☐ Psychological contract
- ☐ Recency effect
- ☐ Schema, schemata, schematic
- ☐ Selective attention
- ☐ Self-fulfilling prophecy
- ☐ Social identity theory
- ☐ Stereotype, stereotyping
- ☐ Top-down processing

Chapter review questions

1. Describe the basic features of human perception processes, and why these features explain the fact that people generally perceive the same situation differently.
2. Identify and explain two consequences of selective attention that can occur in the workplace.
3. Outline the pros and cons of the mental packaging of information into schemata.
4. What is causal attribution? Outline one scenario that might occur in an organization where a person's perceptions about the causes of things affect her or his motivation to achieve a goal.
5. In what ways can individuals' perceptions affect other people, groups of people and the social climate of an organization?

Chapter research questions

1. Get a copy of Jonah Lehrer's (2009) book, *The Decisive Moment*[45] and read the section entitled 'The danger of debt' in Chapter 3. This section argues that the 2008/09 world economic downturn had as much to do with the way we perceive and emotionally respond to offers of credit cards and subprime loans as it had to do with broader political and economic forces.
   - How far do you agree with this argument?
   - Do you think the 'Save More Tomorrow' programme discussed at the end of the section could work? What might be the likely reactions of employers and employees if such a programme were to be introduced into an organization?
2. Get a copy of Stuart Sutherland's (2007) book *Irrationality*,[51] and read Chapter 11, 'Distorting the evidence'. This chapter reveals how we often distort new evidence that disconfirms our current beliefs. What are the implications of this perceptual bias for a manager trying to explain to employees that long-established (and popular) working practices need to be fundamentally changed in order to achieve cost savings?
3. Get a copy of the paper 'The use of impression management tactics in structural interviews: a function of question type?' by Ellis et al. (2002),[52] and read about their study of the IM tactics used by job applicants in interviews using different types of question. Do you think organizations should try to prevent IM? Given that the way in which interviews are conducted seems

to make a difference, do you consider it to be the responsibility of interviewers or of job applicants to check the accuracy of what applicants say?

 Further reading

Bandura, A. (1997) *Self-Efficacy: The Exercise of Control*, New York: Freeman.

Eysenck, M. W. and Keane, M. T. (2005) *Cognitive Psychology: A Student's Handbook* (5th edn), Hove: Lawrence Erlbaum.

Haslam, S. A. (2001) *Psychology in Organizations: The Social Identity Approach*, London: Sage.

Hogg, M. A. and Vaughan, G. M. (2004) *Social Psychology* (4th edn), Hemel Hempstead: Prentice Hall.

Lehrer, J. (2009) *The Decisive Moment: How the Brain Makes up its Mind*, Edinburgh: Canongate.

Rosenfeld, P., Giacalone, R. and Riordan, C. A. (2002) *Impression Management: Building and Enhancing Reputation at Work*, London: Thomson Learning.

Chapter case study

The blame game

Setting

This case is set in medium-sized factory specializing in the manufacture of metal boxes and cases. The factory workers employees are semi-skilled but receive a good wage. Employee relations are generally good.

Problem

It began as a normal day on the shop floor in the metal working factory of Chidi Manufacturing. By mid-morning, the manufacturing process was in full swing and Morenike, the factory manager, was able to take a short break to enjoy a well-earned cup of tea. However, just as she had sat down in her office, Daren (one of two line managers in the factory) came rather timidly into her office.

'I'm afraid we have a serious quality problem, boss,' he said apologetically. 'Edwin is turning out sub-standard work that is threatening to disrupt the whole production run.'

'Can't you sort this out, Daren?' Morenike replied. 'After all, this falls firmly within your remit as line manager.'

'That's true, but Edwin is adamant that he is not the cause of the problem, and he is getting quite angry about it,' Daren replied. 'I'd be grateful if you could help out.'

The two managers walked swiftly through the busy factory until they came to Workstation 42. Edwin stood by his machine, which appeared to be switched off despite the fact that the production run was in full flow all around him. A stockpile of work was building up by the side of his workstation.

'Okay, Edwin,' Morenike said quietly, 'would you like to tell me what is going on and why you're not working?'

'Good morning, boss' he replied. 'About an hour ago I realised that my workstation was beginning to produce material that was falling below quality standards. I told Daren and he just told me to "put things right" and maintain production speed. But it isn't my fault that the machine is faulty. I was working at Workstation

18 all last week, and there was never any problem with my work there. This Workstation 42 machine needs overhauling or something, and so there's no point in carrying on using it if it's not up to the job.'

'Oh, I see,' Daren interjected, 'you're saying that it is the machine's fault and not yours. How do you explain the fact that Workstation 42 was working perfectly well on the night shift and then started misbehaving only once you came to work? A bad worker always blames his tools.'

'I don't see how you know how well the machine was working last night. You weren't here and neither was I!', Edwin replied angrily.

'Gentlemen, let's keep our tempers here,' Morenike insisted. 'Edwin, your job is to operate Workstation 42, and if your line manager tells you to keep working then you darn well should. Please get back to work immediately or I'll be forced to enforce disciplinary procedures.'

Edwin shrugged his shoulders and muttered something under his breath. Nevertheless, he turned round and switched the machine back on. The two managers stayed for a few minutes to ensure that everything was working smoothly and then Morenike returned to her office. However, less than 10 minutes later, the line manager was back in her office complaining bitterly that Edwin had deliberately 'sabotaged' his workstation so that it now appeared incapable of functioning. 'Never mind disciplinary procedures. I want him sacked,' Daren declared. 'He's trying to undermine my authority and make me look as if I'm in the wrong and not him. I want your support on this matter.'

Tasks

1. Which theory or theories of perception best help us understand the causes of the conflict described in the case?
2. What should the factory manager do next?

Note

This case study was written by Martin Corbett, Associate Professor of Industrial Relations and Organisational Behaviour, Warwick Business School, UK.

 ## Web-based assignment

What attracts you to some organizations and not others?

Get a copy of the recruitment pages of a national newspaper or a professional publication, such as *People Management* or *The Economist*. From the advertisements, identify a selection of the recruiting organizations that differ from each other and provide details of their websites. Browse each of the sites, particularly looking at the pages aimed at potential job applicants. It would be ideal if you could do this with a colleague or friend so you can have a discussion about it.

Consider these questions:

- What are your perceptions of each organization as a potential employer? Are they your kind of place?
- Try to identify what perceptual cues from the advertisement and websites captured your attention, and the prior knowledge and expectations that led you to your conclusions. To what extent can you apply social categorization theory to explain your attraction or aversion to each organization?

 ## OB in film

Scottish cyclist Graham Obree is one of the greatest cyclists of all time. His fame does not stem from becoming world champion or breaking the 1-hour record twice, great though these feats are, but from the fact that he did so on a home-made bike made from washing machine parts. This aspect of his story was made all the more curious given the contrast with his closest rival, Chris Boardman, who rode a state-of-the art bicycle engineered by Lotus. In addition, Obree's story is all the more compelling because he has suffered from clinical depression and twice tried to commit suicide. The film revolves around the apparent contrast of psychological illness and sporting success.

In the hands of most directors, Obree's story would be a typical biopic capturing an interesting and complex life story. But the director of *The Flying Scotsman* (2006), Douglas Mackinnon, did quite something different with Obree's story. Not only did he create an engaging story, but he also critiques the whole way in which biopics are portrayed. He does this by playing a perceptual trick with the audience. After following convention and telling Obree's story, Mackinnon challenges the audience at the end when the camera looks straight into the cyclist's eyes. At this point, the viewer is forced to question whether or not they really understand what is going on inside the hero's head. As you watch the film, try to pick out how the director is influencing and manipulating your perception of Graham Obree.

Note: This feature was written by Professor Jon Billsberry, Senior Research Fellow, Open University Business School, UK.

 Bonus OB in Film feature!

Visit www.palgrave.com/business/brattonob2e to see how *A Beautiful Mind* (2001) can be considered in relation to the subject of perception.

References

1 Ramachandran, V. S. and Rogers-Ramachandran, D. (2005) 'How blind are we?', *Scientific American Mind*, **16**(2), p. 96.

2 Weick, K. E. (2001) *Making Sense of the Organization*, Oxford: Blackwell.

3 Fiske, S. T. and Taylor, S. E. (1991) *Social Cognition* (2nd edn), New York: McGraw Hill.

4 Dunkerley, K. J. and Robinson, P. (2002) 'Similarities and differences in perceptions and evaluations of the communication styles of American and British managers', *Journal of Language and Social Psychology*, **21**, pp. 393–409.

5 Eysenck, M. W. and Keane, M. T. (2005) *Cognitive Psychology: A Student's Handbook* (5th edn), Hove: Lawrence Erlbaum.

6 Tetlock, P. (1983) 'Accountability and complexity of thought', *Journal of Personality and Social Psychology*, **45**, pp. 74–83.

7 Jensen, M. C., Brant-Zawadzki, M. N., Obuchowski, N., Modic, M. T., Malkasian, D. and Ross, J. S. (1994) 'Magnetic resonance imaging of the lumbar spine in people without back pain', *New England Journal of Medicine*, 331, pp. 69–73.

8 Roth, E. M. and Woods, O D. (1988) 'Aiding human performance. I: Cognitive analysis', *LeTravail Humain*, **51**, pp. 39–64.

9 Highhouse, S. (2001) 'Judgment and decision-making research: relevance to industrial and organizational psychology', in N. Anderson, D. Ones, H. K. Sinangil and C. Viswesveran (eds), *Handbook of Industrial Work and Organizational Psychology*, Volume 2: *Organizational Psychology*, London: Sage.

10 Attneave, F. (1971) 'Multistability in perception', in R. Held and W. Richards (eds), *Recent Progress in Perception*, San Francisco: W. H. Freeman.

11 Haart, E. G. O.-de, Carey, D. P. and Milne, A. B. (1999) 'More thoughts on perceiving and grasping the Mueller–Lyer illusion', *Neuropsychologica*, **37**, pp. 1437–44.

12 Mishra, R. C., Dasen, P. R. and Niraula, S. (2003) 'Ecology, language, and performance on spatial cognitive tasks', *International Journal of Psychology*, **38**, pp. 366–83.

13 Bloom, R. (2004) 'Children think before they speak', *Nature*, **430**, pp. 410–11.

14 Redelmeier, D. A. and Tibshirani, R. J. (1997) 'Association between cellular-telephone calls and motor vehicle collisions', *New England Journal of Medicine*, **336**, pp. 453–8.

15 Strayer, D. L. and Johnston, W. A. (2001) 'Driven to distraction: dual-task studies of simulated driving and conversing on a cellular telephone', *Psychological Science*, **12**(6), pp. 462–6.

16 Simons, D. J. and Levin, D. T. (1998) 'Failures to detect changes to people in a real-world interaction', *Psychonomic Bulletin and Review*, **5**, pp. 644–9.

17 Simons, D. J. and Chabris, C. F. (1999) 'Gorillas in our midst: sustained inattentional blindness for dynamic events', *Perception*, **28**, pp. 1059–74.

18 Nisbett, R. and Ross, L. (1980) *Human Inference: Strategies and Shortcomings of Social Judgement*, Englewood Cliffs, NJ: Prentice Hall.

19 Hogg, M. A. and Vaughan, G. M. (2004) *Social Psychology: An Introduction* (4th edn), Hemel Hempstead: Prentice Hall.

20 Macrae, C. N., Bodenhausen, G. V., Milne, A. B. and Jetten, J. (1994) 'Employee involvement management practices, work stress and depression in employees of a human services residential care facility', *Human Relations*, **54**(8), pp. 1065–92.

21 Gladwell, M. (2005) *Blink: The Power of Thinking Without Thinking*, Harmondsworth: Penguin.

22 Judge, T. A. and Cable, D. M. (2004) 'The effect of physical height on workplace success and income: preliminary test of a theoretical model', *Journal of Applied Psychology*, **89**, 428–41.

23 Rosenfeld, P., Giacalone, R. and Riordan, C. A. (2002) *Impression Management: Building and Enhancing Reputation at Work*, London: Thomson Learning.

24 Singh, V., Kumra, S. and Vinnicombe, S. (2002) 'Gender and impression management: playing the promotion game', *Journal of Business Ethics*, **37**, pp. 77–89.

25 Beattie, V. and Jones, M. J. (2000) 'Impression management: the case of inter-country financial graphs', *Journal of International Accounting, Auditing and Taxation*, **9**, 159–83.

26 Arunachalam, V., Pei, B. K. W. and Steinbart, P. J. (2002) 'Impression management with graphs: effects on choices', *Journal of Information Systems*, **16**, 183–202.

27 Hochschild, A. (1979) *The Managed Heart: Commercialization of Human Feeling*, Berkeley, CA: University of California Press.

28 Moisi, D. (2009) *The Geopolitics of Emotion: How Cultures of Fear, Humiliation, and Hope are Reshaping the World*, New York: Doubleday.

29 Hodgkinson, G. (1997) 'Cognitive inertia in a turbulent market: the case of UK residential estate agents', *Journal of Management Studies*, **34**, pp. 921–45.

30 Bargh, J. A., Lombardi, W. J. and Higgins, E. T. (1988) 'Automaticity of chronically accessible constructs in person × situation effects on person perception: it's just a matter of time', *Journal of Personality and Social Psychology*, **55**, pp. 599–605.

31 Steele, C. M., Spencer, S. J. and Aronson, J. (2003) 'Contending with group image: the psychology of stereotype threat and social identity threat', pp. 102–15 in M. P. Zanna (ed.), *Advances in Experimental Social Psychology*, San Diego: Academic Press.

32 Schein, V. E. (1973) 'The relationship between sex role stereotypes and requisite management characteristics', *Journal of Applied Psychology*, **57**, pp. 95–100.

33 Schein, V. E. (1975) 'The relationship between sex role stereotypes and requisite management characteristics among female managers', *Journal of Applied Psychology*, **60**, pp. 340–4.

34 Schein, E.A. (1996) 'Culture: the missing concept in organization studies', *Administrative Science Quarterly*, **41**, pp. 229–40.

35 Tajfel, H. and Turner, J. C. (1979) 'An integrative theory of intergroup conflict', in W. G. Austin and S. Worchel (eds), *The Social Psychology of Intergroup Relations*, Monterey, CA: Brooks/Cole.

36 Hogg, M. and Terry, D. J. (2000) 'Social identity and self-categorization processes in organizational contexts', *Academy of Management Review*, **25**, pp. 121–40.

37 Haslam, S. A. (2001) *Psychology in Organizations: The Social Identity Approach*, London: Sage.

38 Chartered Institute of Personnel and Development (2000) *People Implications of Mergers and Acquisitions, Joint Ventures and Divestments: Survey Report*, London: CIPD.

39 Bandura, A. (1997) *Self-efficacy: The Exercise of Control*, New York: Freeman.

40 Kelley, H. H. (1973) 'The process of causal attribution', *American Psychologist*, **28**, pp. 107–28.

41 Morris, M. W. and Peng, K. P. (1994) 'Culture and cause: American and Chinese attributions for social and physical events', *Journal of Personality and Social Psychology*, **67**, pp. 949–71.

42 Peterson, C. (2000) 'The future of optimism', *American Psychologist*, **55**, pp. 44–55.

43 Seligman, M. E. P. (1991) *Learned Optimism*, New York: Knopf.

44 Montague, R. (2007) 'Neuroeconomics: a view from neuroscience', *Functional Neurology*, **22**, 760–67.

45 Zweig, J. (2008) *Your Money and Your Brain*, New York: Simon Schuster.

46 Lehrer, J. (2009) *The Decisive Moment: How the Brain Makes up its Mind*, Edinburgh: Canongate.

47 Gilliland, S. W. and Chan, D. (2001) 'Justice in organizations: theory, methods and applications', in N. Anderson, D. Ones, H. K. Sinangil and C. Viswesveran (eds), *Handbook of Industrial, Work & Organizational Psychology*, Volume 2: *Organizational Psychology*, London: Sage.

48 Rousseau, D. M. (1995) *Psychological Contracts in Organisations: Understanding Written and Unwritten Agreements*, Thousand Oaks, CA: Sage.

49 Taylor, M. S. and Tekleab, A. G. (2004) 'Taking stock of psychological contract research: assessing progress, addressing troublesome issues, and setting research priorities', in J. A.-M. Coyle-Shapiro, L. M. Shore, M. S. Taylor and L. E. Tetrick (eds), *The Employment Relationship: Examining Psychological and Contextual Perspectives*, Oxford: Oxford University Press.

50 Lester, S. W., Turnley, W. H., Bloodgood, J. M. and Bolino, M. (2002) 'Not seeing eye to eye: differences in supervisor and subordinate perceptions of and attributions for psychological contract breach', *Journal of Organizational Behavior*, **23**, pp. 39–56.

51 Sutherland, S. (2007) *Irrationality*. London: Pinter & Martin.

52 Ellis, A. P. J., West, B. J., Ryan, A. M. and DeShon, R. P. (2002) 'The use of impression management tactics in structured interviews: a function of question type?', *Journal of Applied Psychology*, **87**, pp. 1200–8.

chapter 6
Learning and innovation

chapter objectives

After completing this chapter, you should be able to:

- explain the importance of learning in organizations
- define learning and discuss the difference between formal, non-formal and informal learning
- discuss the contested nature of behavioural, cognitive and social learning theories
- articulate how adult learning theories add to our understanding of learning processes
- identify the effects of social class, ethnicity and gender on learning and training opportunities in the organization
- discuss how learning facilitates and enhances the potential for innovation

Introduction

In traditional bureaucratic organizations, the majority of employees had limited opportunity to engage in work-related learning. The orthodox view saw the factory or office as a place to work, not to learn. Learning mainly occurred at school, college and university before people joined the organization, as part of a formal programme of study or perhaps a hybrid system of on-the-job and off-the-job apprenticeship training.

As notions of 'knowledge work', core competencies and sustainability have entered the contemporary management discourse, there has been a growing interest in the 'learning organization' and 'workplace learning'.[1-4] The reliance on intellectual capital has led to the realization that corporate leaders need to foster learning-rich environments.[5,6] Advocates have asserted that there is no place for managers who do not appreciate their own vital role in fostering learning.[7]

In this chapter, we emphasize that an inclusive understanding of learning needs to acknowledge the general nature of capitalist employment relations, the way in which organizational control systems generate and express internal contradictions, and the tension between managerial control and learning. We begin by explaining the importance of work-related learning, and then proceed to examine competing classical theories of learning and contemporary approaches to adult learning. The final section discusses some practical applications of adult learning theories.

stop reflect

The notion that education should serve business and the economy has been fiercely debated among adult educators. See Bruce Spencer's *The Purpose of Adult Education: A Guide for Students*[8] for an introduction to the debate. Look at the two opening quotes. Is it reasonable to assume that education should serve business? What are your views on this?

The nature of workplace learning

If you have worked in a paid job, can you recall how you felt on your first day? Like many young workers, you might have been nervous, even bewildered, as an environment filled with new faces and names, new tasks and new rules replaced the familiarity of school or college. But like most young workers, you probably adjusted to this new environment within a few days or weeks. This adjustment, or adaptation, to paid work can take many forms. Some are simple, as when buzzers sound to permit morning and lunch breaks from work.

New employees acquire explicit knowledge about the organization and working conditions in orientation workshops. New information and skills needed for various aspects of the work are acquired from manuals, training workshops and co-workers. New employees also develop knowledge about which aspects of their work behaviour are likely to be punished and which are likely to be rewarded. Some behaviours are appropriate only at certain times and in certain circumstances, and those circumstances must be identified and differentiated. Critical questioning, for example, might not be as acceptable at work as at school or college, but working collaboratively and sharing information – perhaps forbidden by college academic rules – might be rewarded at work.

Workers also learn that there are things they can do to prevent unwanted consequences. For example, observing practices such as working at the pace set by the work team, sometimes referred to as 'norms', can prevent people from being ostracized by other members of the group. In a similar way, workers sometimes learn *not* to learn because of perceived negative outcomes. For example, an individual employee or workers collectively may be reluctant to embrace learning and self-development because the resultant changes might undermine the collective interests of the learners.[9]

norms: the informal rules and expectations that groups establish to regulate the behaviour of their members

We can define learning as a relatively permanent change in behaviour or human capabilities resulting from processing new knowledge, practice or experience. These capabilities are related to specific learning outcomes, including cognitive skills, motor skills, attitudes and verbal information.[10] Learning plays a central role in most aspects of individual and collective behaviour in the workplace, from the knowledge and skills workers need to perform work tasks and the communication skills managers use to motivate subordinates, to clarifying the expectations, aspirations and understandings that managers and others have of each other (the psychological contract). Learning is people's primary mode of adaptation to change.[11] People learn in organizations and other different settings: in educational institutions, in families, through community activities, through recreation events, through union activities and through political campaigns and action.

learning: the processes of constructing new knowledge and its ongoing reinforcement

The quality of the learning experience in the workplace will depend upon a range of situational factors. The way work is designed – giving workers high or low autonomy – and the number of management levels in the organization affect work-related learning.[12] Clearly, different work regimes will affect how individuals engage, interact and construct knowledge from work situations.[1] In this context, learning can take any one of four forms: formal, non-formal, informal and incidental:

- *Formal learning* is associated with college and university studies or professional programmes (such as study for accountancy qualifications).
- *Non-formal learning* involves some form of systematic instruction, but takes place in a one-off situation (such as a workshop on workplace violence) and typically does not lead to any formal qualifications.
- *Informal learning* occurs when people consciously try to learn from their context and everyday life experiences. It does not involve formal instruction, but does involve individual or collective (for instance, by a work team or trade union) critical reflection on experience. Over the last few decades, the conceptualization of informal learning in the workplace has undermined the supremacy of formal instruction and learning organized by educational institutions.[13]
- *Informal and incidental learning* are interconnected, but are not necessarily the same.[14] Incidental learning occurs through an activity or as a result of trial and

explicit knowledge: knowledge that is ordered and can be communicated between people

tacit knowledge: knowledge embedded in our actions and ways of thinking, and transmitted only through observation and experience

error, and is seen as a by-product of direct experience. Whereas people acquire explicit knowledge through formal, non-formal and informal learning processes, through incidental learning people acquire tacit knowledge.

Explicit knowledge is ordered and can be communicated between people. **Tacit knowledge**, on the other hand, refers to information that cannot easily be captured, measured or codified and communicated from one individual to another individual or group; it is therefore more subtle.

OB and globalization

London calling ... from Delhi

Over the last decade, many large companies based in Western countries have made the decision to move all or part of their telephone-based customer service operations overseas to save money. This 'offshoring' or 'outsourcing' of work often results in call centres being established in developing countries such as India, the Philippines and Egypt, where companies can pay workers substantially lower wages than those made by workers in the European Union or North America. The cost savings associated with offshoring mean that the practice is likely to become an enduring feature of the global economy.

Through this process, companies have found that successful offshoring involves more than simply setting up an office and hiring workers. Their customers have culturally based expectations about what call centre workers representing British, American or Canadian companies should sound like, how they should manage business transactions, and the types of general knowledge they should have.

In a 2004 article from *The Independent*, British auto insurance salesperson Rajashree Sisodia describes his experiences as a customer service trainer at an Automobile Association call centre near Delhi, where he taught salespeople how to relate to their customers in the UK. Mr Sisodia's job extended beyond simply training Indian employees to speak with a UK accent; he also educated them in British culture, including popular television programmes and holidays. He explained:

I will explain and test them on the food British people eat, the pubs they drink in, the schools they send their children to, where they do their shopping, the political parties they could vote for and how to say the names of places and famous people.

Workers in offshore call centres are engaged in what Taylor and Bain (2005) refer to as 'culturally mediated emotional labour'. This means that they are using their newly acquired cultural knowledge of far-away places like the UK to convey a series of emotions – like empathy, humour or optimism – designed to put their customers at ease and gain their confidence. Just as important as the

technical aspects of call centre operations, the emotional labour of call centre workers is essential to the success of offshore operations. Sisodia's experience training Indian call centre employees highlights the (often overlooked) importance of cultural knowledge and expectations in organizational behaviour, and the emotional labour that goes into creating and maintaining an organization's corporate identity and customer satisfaction.

stop! Have you ever spoken with a call centre representative located offshore? How could you tell that they were located in another country? What types of cultural knowledge, behaviour and expectation might be common in an organization in your home country?

How would you react if you were asked by an employer to alter your accent or even use a pseudonym in the course of your work? (As an example, at the Indian call centre where Mr Sisodia worked, employee Anil Singh introduced himself as Alex Smith when speaking with customers in the UK.)

Would you say that training employees in the manner outlined above represents an organizational 'investment in training and learning' that indicates 'intention to develop intellectual capital'?

Sources and further information

Beaumont, N. (2009) 'Gidday, yur talkin to Manulla', *The Dominion Post*, February 7, p. 7.

Sisodia, R. (2004) 'India's John Smiths speak perfect English. Now they have a month to become British', *The Independent*, May 2.

Taylor, P. and Bain, P. (2005) 'India calling to the far away towns', *Work, Employment and Society*, **19**(2), pp. 261–82.

View the film *Outsourced* (2006), a comedy about an American call centre manager who is sent to India to train customer service employees to take over his job.

Note: This feature was written by Gretchen Fox, Anthropologist, Timberline Natural Resource Group, Canada.

intellectual capital: the sum of an organization's human capital, structural capital and relationship capital

reflexive learning: a view of adult learning that emphasizes learning through self-reflection

life-long learning: the belief that adults should be encouraged, and given the opportunity, to learn either formally in education institutions or informally on or off the job

From a managerial perspective, it is suggested that an organization's investment in training and learning acts as a powerful signal of its intentions to develop its **intellectual capital**. This can help to develop employees' commitment to the organization rather than simply their compliance. With the wave of interest in flexible 'high-performance work systems' in the 1990s, it is not surprising that some academics and management gurus claimed that **reflexive learning** was a means to promote flexibility and achieve competitive advantage over rivals.[15] Those subscribing to this view on sustainable competitive advantage advised companies to gain 'mutual commitment' by investing in their workforce and encouraging **life-long learning**.[16] This belief in the efficacy of continuous work-related learning is linked to a broader debate about 'progressive' human resource management practices, in which it is argued that work-related learning should be encouraged in order to enhance employee performance.

Research has focused on evaluating the effectiveness of particular managerial or leadership styles in specific contexts, for achieving specific learning outcomes. The classic work of Peter Senge[5] seeks to yield an understanding of how leadership practices can help bring about change and renew organizations through learning. He advocated that organizational leaders play the roles of teachers, designers and stewards in order to facilitate employee learning. Senge argued that 'leaders are responsible for building organizations where followers continually expand their capabilities to understand complexity, clarify vision, and improve shared mental models – that is, they are responsible for learning' (ref. 5, p. 340).

A case study of 'leadership activity' that promoted work-related informal learning found evidence of leaders exhibiting the three roles Senge outlined: designer, steward and teacher. The followers' perception of their leaders highlighted the role of gender and power (see refs 17 and 18 for information on leaders' activities that promote follower learning). For the most part, however, mainstream studies of leadership have given little attention to how leadership activity actually encourages individual or group learning.[19]

The emergence of critical studies on workplace learning has certainly added to the debate on the role of life-long learning. Contributions to the debate have emphasized that 'cultural control' can be reinforced through learning.[20] Critical accounts have exposed the potential of competency training to make work more 'visible' in order to make it more manageable.[21] Others have criticized popular accounts of work-related learning for adopting a conflict-free managerialist perspective, in which it is assumed that the goals of managers and workers are shared, and inherent tensions in the employment relationship are largely ignored.[22]

Critical organizational theorists share a deep scepticism for popular prescriptive publications such as Senge's *The Fifth Discipline*,[5] which discount the influence of power and political activity on workplace learning. For critical theorists, the likely effect of new learning regimes is to reshape organizational culture and strengthen the power of managers over the managed. In fact, if learning is synonymous with change, then attempts to manage a culture of learning, through either formal or informal processes, can be regarded as a management strategy to promote a change in structures, attitudes and behaviour. It is argued that, in adopting a 'learning strategy', managers therefore hope to unfreeze traditional attitudes and work practices and foster creative thinking and new ways of doing, or innovation. Neglecting these wider socioeconomic dynamics, tensions and contested aspects of learning might mean that learning practices become a managerial tool for work intensification and control in the workplace.[23–25]

Despite the increasing diversity and feminization of the paid workforce in most economies of the Organisation for Economic Co-operation and Development (OECD), another notable feature of the contemporary learning discourse is the tendency for the academic research to be blind to race, ethnic and gender issues. Recently, some writers have focused critically on gender issues in workplace learning. The emergence of feminist accounts of workplace learning adds depth to our understanding of how sexuality and gender relations in the paid workplace can shape learning. As these writers point out, the recent explosion of workplace learning practices still privileges men, and 'it is worth recognizing the continuities in women's unequal access to and benefit from workplace learning' (ref. 26, p. 112).

It should be apparent from this introduction that, as a field of study, learning can be explored and interpreted from different perspectives. Now that we have examined *why* learning is important to people and organizations, we go on to address two central questions: *how* do individuals learn, and *how* is work-related individual learning interconnected to collective learning in the organization?

Visit www.
managementhelp.org/
trng_dev/trng_dev.htm
for more information on
training and development
in the workplace

weblink

OB **in focus**   **The Learning Age: a renaissance for a New Britain**

Learning is the key to prosperity – for each of us as individuals, as well as for the nation as a whole. Investment in human capital will be the foundation of success in the knowledge-based global economy of the twenty-first century. This is why the Government has put learning at the heart of its ambition. This Green Paper sets out for consultation how learning throughout life will build human capital by encouraging the acquisition of knowledge and skills and emphasising creativity and imagination. The fostering of an enquiring mind and the love of learning are essential to our future success.

To achieve stable and sustainable growth, we will need a well-educated, well-equipped and adaptable labour force. To cope with rapid change and the challenge of the information and communication age, we must ensure that people can return to learning throughout their lives. We cannot rely on a small elite, no matter how highly educated or highly paid. Instead, we need the creativity, enterprise and scholarship of all our people. As well as securing our economic future, learning has a wider contribution. It helps make ours a civilized society, develops the spiritual side of our lives and promotes active citizenship. Learning enables people to play a full part in their community. It

strengthens the family, the neighbourhood and consequently the nation.

To realize our ambition, we must all develop and sustain a regard for learning at whatever age. For many people this will mean overcoming past experiences which have put them off learning. For others it will mean taking the opportunity, perhaps for the first time, to recognize their own talent, to discover new ways of learning and to see new opportunities opening up.

That is why this Green Paper encourages adults to enter and re-enter learning at every point in their lives, whatever their experience at school. There are many ways in which we can all take advantage of new opportunities: [1] as parents we can play our part in encouraging, supporting and raising the expectations of our children by learning alongside them; [2] as members of the work force we can take on the challenge of learning in and out of work; and [3] as citizens we can balance the rights we can expect from the state, with the responsibilities of individuals for their own future, sharing the gains and the investment needed.

The Learning Age will be built on a renewed commitment to self-improvement and on a recognition of the enormous contribution learning makes to our society. As President John F Kennedy once put it, 'Liberty without learning is always in peril and learning without liberty is always in vain.'

David Blunkett, Secretary of State for Education and Employment

---

Classical learning theories

Explicit and tacit knowledge is acquired in many different ways. The rest of this chapter gives an overview of both psychologically driven and socioculturally driven perspectives of learning. We begin by examining what can be called the 'classical' theories of learning. As in other areas of the discipline, they are considered classical partly because they represent the early contributions to our understanding of how children and adults learn, and also because some of the ideas recur in contemporary adult learning theories. It should be noted, however, that the explanations found in these different approaches are contested, and that no one theory – classic or contemporary – offers a 'correct' account of the learning process in the work-place. We would also suggest that the theories outlined here, and the organiza-tional practices that derive from them, are not appropriate to all forms of adult learning in all situations.

The classical behavioural approach: learning through reinforcement

What factors stimulate or inhibit the learning process, and what types of learning do people engage in? Our working definition of learning – that it is a relatively permanent change in behaviour or human capab-ilities – emphasizes the importance of experience and reinforcement. The best-known *behaviourist* psychologists, Ivan Pavlov (1849–1936) and B. F. Skinner (1904–90), explained learning in terms of the interac-tion of the human being with his or her environment. They discounted the significance of internal cognitive or mental activities – characterized by behaviourist psychologists as 'black box' activity – in the learning process. They argued that since it was impossible to measure such mental activities objectively, they had no place in the science of psychology.

The Russian Ivan Pavlov is often referred to as the 'father of behaviourism'. Pavlov and his colleagues held that all kinds of learning, human and animal, could be explained by the phenomenon of **classical conditioning**.[27] Working with dogs as his experimental subjects, Pavlov trained them to salivate in response to a variety of stimuli, such as the sound of a bell. This was achieved by continually pairing the sound of the bell or other stimulus, which originally produced no increase in saliva, with food. Salivation was the normal physiological response to food near or in the dog's mouth, and the repeated pairing of the bell with the food caused the dog to salivate simply upon hearing the bell, even when food was not available. Pavlov described the food as the 'unconditional stimulus' (UCS) and the sound of the bell as the 'conditional stimulus' (CS). Similarly, he described the dog's salivation when given food as the 'unconditional response' (UCR), and its salivation at the sound of the bell as a 'conditional response' (CR) (Figure 6.1). One way to distinguish between these two types of stimulus and response are to remember that 'uncondi-tioned' means 'unlearned' and 'conditioned' means 'learned'.

---

stop reflect

Think about the way learning happens on your course. What pedagogical techniques do your professors use – for instance, role playing, group discussions, case analyses, questions and answers, and video – to help you learn? What approaches help or hinder your learning? Given that we all have different learning styles, what norms should your instructor and co-students establish on the course to ensure maximum learning?

---

classical conditioning: a view of 'instrumental' learning whose adherents assert that the reinforcement is non-contingent on the animal's behaviour, that is, it is delivered without regard to the animal's behaviour. By contrast, in instrumental conditioning, the delivery of the reinforcement is contingent – dependent – on what the animal does

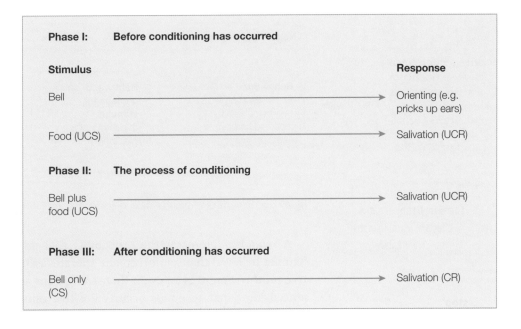

figure 6.1 Classical or Pavlovian conditioning

For more
information on
Pavlovian conditioning
and other theories of
learning, go to http://tip.
psychology.org; http://
ccs.mit.edu/LH

weblink

For Pavlov, learning was nothing more than 'a long chain of conditioned reflexes'.[28] The thought of using his findings in work situations, and dangling stimuli or rewards to elicit employee salivation, may seem offensive, but there are several reasons that Pavlov's research is considered important to learning in organizations. His research illustrates how internal mental events such as learning might be measured and studied. The American John Watson (1878–1958) developed Pavlov's work to demonstrate how relationships between two variables – environment and human behaviour – could be built into an objective and testable general theory of learning.[29]

The American Burrhus Skinner is another well-known advocate of behavioural psychology who has made an important contribution to our understanding of the learning process.[30] Skinner explained human behaviour in terms of the phenomenon of operant or instrumental conditioning, and he believed that reinforcement was a necessary part of this process.[31,32]

operant conditioning: a technique for associating a response or behaviour with a consequence

An **operant** is a response that has some effect on the situation or environment. For example, when an animal pulls a lever and food pellets are delivered, the animal has made an operant response that influences when the food will appear. Over time, the animal acquires the lever-pulling response as a means of obtaining food. In other words, the animal learns to pull the lever. Similarly, when a child cries and is then fed, the child has made an operant response that influences when food will be served. The kind of learning is called operant learning, because the subject learns to operate on the environment to achieve certain outcomes. Figure 6.2 illustrates operant or instrumental conditioning.

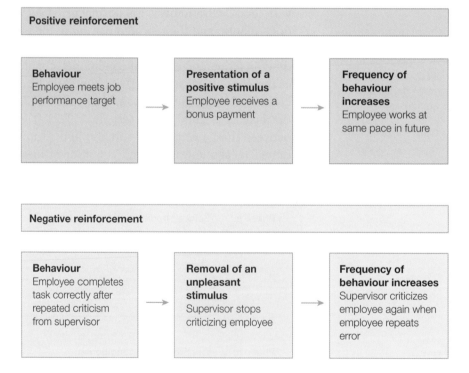

figure 6.2 Examples of positive and negative reinforcement

positive reinforcement: occurs when the introduction of a consequence increases or maintains the frequency or future probability of a behaviour

A *reinforcer* increases the probability that an operant response will reoccur. Skinner believed that reinforcement operates either positively or negatively. **Positive reinforcement** is an event that strengthens an operant response if it is experienced after that response occurs. Positive reinforcers are therefore a form of reward. In the context of a work organization, money, recognition, praise from a

Can there be any negative effects of learning in the workplace?

**stop
reflect**

Source: John Bratton

plate 21 Russian Ivan Pavlov is famous for his experiments with dogs, and is often referred to as the 'father of behaviourism'. Working with dogs as his experimental subjects, Pavlov trained them to salivate in response to a variety of stimuli, such as the sound of a bell.

negative reinforcement: occurs when the removal or avoidance of a consequence increases or maintains the frequency or future probability of a behaviour

manager and promotion can all act as positive reinforcers, since they all increase the likelihood of the preceding response being repeated. **Negative reinforcers** are unpleasant stimuli, such as a disapproving frown, a verbal reprimand or a threat, which strengthen a response if they are withdrawn after the response occurs. For example, a manager applies negative reinforcement when he or she stops criticizing an employee whose substandard job performance has improved. Reinforcements shape behaviour, and intermittent reinforcements also maintain established behaviours.[33]

Skinner also investigated the effect of punishment in shaping human behaviour, defining punishment as either the presence of an unpleasant stimulus or unpleasant outcome, or the removal of a pleasant one. Threatening an employee with disciplinary action or dismissal for verbally abusing another co-worker is an example of an unpleasant stimulus. When an employee is forced to forfeit a company car because of a poor annual appraisal, this is punishment by removing a pleasant stimulus.

Most behavioural psychologists would agree with Skinner that punishment is a less powerful means of shaping behaviour than positive reinforcement or reward. Punishment only indicates what response an individual should suppress; it cannot guide an individual towards desired behaviour. Moreover, punishment can cause anxiety and resentment, and might impact negatively on the psychological contract. Reward, on the other hand, has the virtue of indicating what desirable behaviour is required.

Skinner believed that learning in the organization was also influenced by what he called 'schedules of reinforcement'. The simplest schedule is *continuous reinforcement*: that is, every desired response behaviour is followed by a reward. A more complex schedule involves *intermittent reinforcement*, which involves applying the reinforcer after fixed or variable time intervals. For example, an employee is not rewarded each time he or she performs a desired behaviour, such as servicing a car, but the employee experiences the fixed-interval reinforcement schedule when he or she receives his or her weekly pay cheque. Likewise, when a supervisor is promoted to manager for outstanding performance, he or she experiences a variable interval reinforcement schedule, because promotion only occurs at relatively long time intervals.

The American psychologist Edward Thorndike (1874–1949) did much of the groundwork for Skinner's observations of the effects on learning of different reinforcement schedules. Thorndike developed the 'law of effect',[34] which states that if a response made in the presence of a particular stimulus is accompanied or closely followed by a satisfying state of affairs (such as a reward), that response is more likely to be made the next time the stimulus is encountered. Conversely, responses that produce unpleasant experiences are less likely to be repeated.[27]

The behaviourist theory of learning has been applied extensively in education and training institutions. For example, they often use learning objectives or outcomes framed in behavioural language, acknowledge the significance of giving immediate feedback on learners' achievements, use 'chaining' (the linking together of simpler tasks to create more complex ones), and appreciate the value for educators and trainers of positive reinforcement rather than punishment.[35]

Examples of operant conditioning pervade all formal organizations. Any manager who either explicitly or implicitly suggests that rewards (reinforcements) are dependent on some behaviour on your part is applying operant learning theory. However, the behaviourist approach to learning has been widely criticized for neglecting the individual's 'internal' mental states, for assuming that on occasion no learning occurs because others cannot 'observe' any change in behaviour, and for ignoring cognitive processes.

The cognitive approach: learning through feedback

An alternative theory of learning is the *cognitive approach*. Cognitive theorists believe that cognitive processes – how individuals perceive, evaluate feedback, represent, store and use information – play an important role in learning. Cognitive psychologists explicitly attempt to develop an understanding of the internal mental state – the 'black box' – of the learner.

The origins of the cognitive approach to learning can be traced back to research by three prominent European psychologists, Max Wertheimer (1880–1943), Wolfgang Köhler (1887–1967) and Kurt Lewin (1890–1947). At the University of Berlin's Psychological Institute, Wertheimer and Köhler became known as the Gestalt theorists, proposing that human consciousness cannot be investigated adequately by unscrambling its component parts, but only by investigating its overall shape or pattern.

There are many variants of cognitive learning theory; the aim here is to provide the reader with an introduction to the work of the Gestalt psychologist Wolfgang Köhler. His work with chimpanzees made a significant contribution to the understanding of the learning process through his explanation of the phenomenon of *insightful learning*. In contrast to the behaviourist psychologist Edward Thorndike, who believed that animals learn gradually through the consequences of trial and error, Kohler argued that animals' problem solving does not have to develop incrementally through stimulus–response associations.[36]

Köhler supported his assertion with three observations. The first observation was that once a chimpanzee solved a problem, it would immediately repeat the action in a similar situation. In other words, 'it acted as if it understood the problem' (ref. 30, p. 201). The second observation was that chimpanzees rarely tried a solution that did not work. Finally, Köhler observed that they often solved the problem quite suddenly. Through these observations, Köhler concluded that learning involves insight into the problem as a whole, occurs suddenly, is retained and is transferred readily to new situations.

More recent interpretations, however, suggest that insight might not occur as suddenly as Köhler assumed. Insightful learning might only occur after a mental 'trial and error' process in which individuals envisage a course of action, mentally evaluate its results, compare it with logical alternatives, and choose the option that is most likely to aid decision making.[30] The notion that learning involves mentally processing feedback has led others to compare cognitive-driven learning processes to cybernetics and information-processing theories.[37]

The main differences between the behaviourialist and cognitive theories of learning are summarised in Table 6.1.

Gestalt: a German word that means form or organization; Gestalt psychology emphasizes organizational processes in learning. The Gestalt slogan, 'The whole is greater than the sum of the parts,' draws attention to relationships between the parts

decision making: a conscious process of making choices between one or more alternatives with the intention of moving toward some desired state of affairs

feedback: any information that people receive about the consequences of their behaviour

table 6.1 Approaches to learning theory

Behaviourist approach to learning	Cognitive approach to learning
Learning in terms of responses to stimuli, 'automatic' learning	Feedback must be processed
Pavlovian (respondent) conditioning	Thinking, discovering, understanding. observing practices, relationships and meaning, dialoguing
Skinnerial (operant or instrumental) conditioning. Negative or positive reinforcement	Reframing of previously learned concepts and principles
Schedules of reinforcement	Insightful learning

Source: Adapted from Bratton and Gold (2003),[119] p. 343

The social-learning approach: learning through observation

This section examines a number of social-learning theories. Following the work of Albert Bandura,[38,39] social-learning theorists explain human development as the interaction between internal processes and the external social context. Learning is characterized as a reciprocal process that happens through indirect observation and modelling (Figure 6.3). Individuals learn by observing others whom they believe are credible and knowledgeable (so they can act as 'models'). What the observer acquires are symbolic representations of the model's actions. What is learned is then encoded into memory to serve as a guide for later behaviour. Observational learning involves four interrelated processes: attention, memory, motor activity and motivation.[39]

Before an individual can learn much from a more knowledgeable person (a model), she or he must actively attend to the other person. Attention is affected by characteristics of both the observer and the model. Memory is an important element because we may learn how to perform a behaviour, but then forget what we have learned. A motor process is another component in social learning. The observer may need to practise one or more of the motor actions required in order to perform the behaviour. Remember learning to ride a bike or snowboard? These behaviours were learned by observing others, but needed to be perfected through practice – hence the importance of hands-on experience.

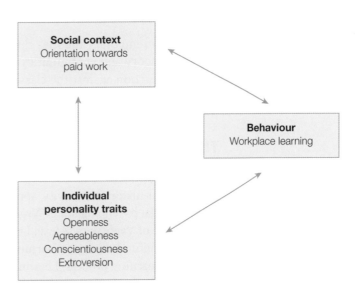

figure 6.3 Three aspects of reciprocal learning

Source: Adapted from Bamber and Castka (2006),[120] p. 75

The fourth component of observational learning is motivation. Social-learning theorists believe that whether or not an individual performs a behaviour depends on whether she or he expects to be reinforced or punished for doing so. Observational learning suggests that learning new knowledge and skills comes from:

- actively attending to the behaviour of the relevant other (the 'expert')
- remembering the observed behaviour
- practising the observed behaviour and directly experiencing the consequences of using knowledge or skills.

Finally, social-learning theorists believe that adult learning is influenced by a person's 'self-efficacy', that is, a person's judgement about whether he or she can successfully learn new knowledge and skills, and the influence of verbal persuasion by relevant others who encourage a person to believe that she or he can accomplish a behaviour, hence the importance of expert–learner social relations.[39]

plate 22 Social-learning theory suggests that when an individual observes a 'model' performing a particular behaviour, this leads them to expect that if they perform the same behaviour, there will be a favourable result. For example, if a child observes their mother or father performing a task successfully, they will expect the same outcome when they perform the task.

Source: Getty Images

Contemporary learning theories

The two contemporary theories that we have chosen to focus on here – cultural-historical theory and communities of practice – draw upon social-learning theory and are a reaction against the classical psychologically driven theories of learning. They have been chosen because both approaches have informed much of the research and scholarly inquiry on workplace learning during the last 10 years.

The cultural-historical approach: learning through social exchange

The cultural-historical activity approach to learning was first developed by the Russian social psychologist Lev Vygotsky in the 1920s and early 1930s.[40] A colleague and protégé of Vygotsky's, Alexei Leontiev, further developed the theory.[41,42] Vygotsky's sociocultural theory of learning emphasized the importance of social interaction in the learning process. Learning is not just about what happens internally, but is rather a product of interactions from the social to the individual.

According to Vygotsky, learning occurs through a dynamic social exchange between a mature practitioner or expert (a more capable and knowledgeable individual) and the learner (novice) in the learning community. The relationship is not passive but dynamic, and is defined by the needs of the learner, by the forms of social practice that 'relate' the learner (novice) to the objective context, and by what that context means for the learner. Such a 'relational' view also focuses on '**semiotic** mechanisms' including diagrams, cultural tools (such as language), mnemonic techniques (such as multiple-choice questions), works of art and writing, which are used to mediate the learning process and shape thinking. The acquisition of cultural tools enables knowledge to be transmitted. These semiotic mechanisms will vary across different activity contexts and cultures.

Another aspect of Vygotsky's theory is the importance of identifying the learner's lower and upper limits of ability. The learner's optimal performance level, called the zone of proximal development (ZPD), is achievable only with support or 'scaffolding'.[43] The concept of the ZPD exemplifies Vygotsky's concern with the role of

semiotics: the systematic study of the signs and symbols used in communications

assistance, assessment and feedback. With support, the mature practitioner bridges gaps so that the novice can act 'as if she or he is already able to complete the given task'.[44,45] The 'scaffold' allows learners to perform at a level beyond what they would be capable of on their own.

Vygotsky's approach to learning is, however, still a psychological model, since it focuses on the process of *internalization*. The psychological nature of his model is apparent in the clear boundary between self and social implied by Vygotsky's notion of internalization, and by the way in which sociocultural phenomena become psychological phenomena as they cross that boundary.

The community of practice approach: learning through socially embedded activity

communities of practice: informal groups bound together by shared expertise and a passion for a particular activity or interest

situated learning: an approach that views adult learning as a process of enculturation, where people consciously and subconsciously construct new knowledge from the actions, processes, behaviour and context in which they find themselves

The concept of a **community of practice** has antecedents in the work of Vygotsky and in social-learning theory. More recently, the approach has been articulated in the work of Lave and Wenger,[46] and Rogoff.[45] Whereas classical psychologically driven theories of learning developed primarily either in the laboratory or in classroom settings, **situated learning** theories have emerged out of studies of learning in workplace settings. Jean Lave,[47] for example, used the term 'situated learning' to focus attention on the development of knowledge and expertise through activity, and the context and culture in which learning occurs (that is, within which it is situated). Situated learning places greater emphasis on people learning in context, and as such has expanded key notions of the sociopsychological paradigm. Learning in context has become increasingly a matter for research and application in higher education. For example, students on professional programmes, such as nursing, increasingly spend a large proportion of their learning in a 'practicum' – actually in a hospital. A critical constituent of situated learning is social interaction and the concept of a community of practice.

Wenger further developed the notion that learning is a process of participation in a community of practice.[48] A community of practice can be defined as 'a unique combination of three fundamental elements: a domain of knowledge, which defines a set of issues; a community of people who care about this domain; and the shared practice that they are developing to be effective in their domain' (ref. 49, p. 27). The domain creates a sense of common identity for the members, the community creates the social fabric for the learning, and the practice is a set of ideas, information, stories, documents and tools that community members share. All communities of practice share this three-dimensional structure, and a set of relations among the members is central to the process. Moreover, the concept of community of practice is an intrinsic condition for learning, 'not least because it provides the interpretative support necessary for making sense of its heritage' (ref. 46, p. 98).

Examples of a community of practice include systems of apprenticeships in manual trades (such as carpentry, plumbing and mechanics). As the novice moves from the periphery of the community to its centre, he or she becomes more engaged within the culture, eventually assuming the role of 'master' or 'expert'. The apprenticeship system includes instances of formal and informal learning in various situated work activities.

Lave and Wenger's central concept in explaining the process and the path individuals take as they progress from 'apprentice' or novice to 'master' or expert is what they call legitimate peripheral participation. The authors explain the process like this:

By this we mean to draw attention to the point that learners inevitably participate in communities of practitioners and that the mastery of knowledge and skill requires newcomers to move toward full participation in the sociocultural practices of a community. 'Legitimate peripheral participation' provides a way to speak about the relations between newcomers and old-timers, and about activities, identities, artifacts, and communities of knowledge and practice. It concerns the process by which newcomers become part of a community of practice. (ref. 46, p. 29)

In developing their argument, Lave and Wenger emphasize the need for taking a holistic view of learning involving the whole person, and for activity in and with the world rather than 'receiving' a body of knowledge. Other theorists have built upon the situated learning model by the notion of 'cognitive apprenticeships', which focuses on how the learner acquires, develops and uses cognitive tools in authentic settings.[50] For example, architects, lawyers and physicians complete cognitive apprenticeships. Physicians, for instance, acquire the situated experience and knowledge on which they build their practice in their internships and residencies in hospitals.[51]

As a model for understanding how employees learn in the workplace, the community of practice approach has been the subject of some debate in the adult learning literature. An extreme position would be that there is little need for formal classroom-based learning because effective learning only occurs through the engagement of community membership. Thus, it is suggested, the learner (the new employee) is a valued member of the community, and expected to make contributions, as he or she 'learns the ropes'. The role of participants (novice and master or expert) evolves over time, as levels of mastery are achieved.

Feedback from expert members of the community (for example, managers) is formative and non-evaluative, is supportive and encourages risk taking. The 'scaffolding' provided by the expert may involve a modification of the task so that learning and success is possible. Another aspect is that the interaction between members of the community reflects the style of discourse appropriate for the context and environment. Furthermore, the notion of movement across contexts becomes a key concept when the theory of situated learning is applied to complex work organizations.[52]

For individuals, the perspective highlights the importance of finding the dynamic set of communities they should belong to, and of fashioning a meaningful pathway of experience through these communities over time.[1,53] Finally, situated learning assumes that the learner (novice worker) is motivated to learn, and that she or he develops and achieves the knowledge, expertise and value system that make up the community of practice.

The work of Engeström and Rogoff has built on Lave and Wenger's situated learning model.[54] Whereas Lave and Wenger downplay the importance of formal training and learning, Engeström emphasizes its necessity and value. While recognizing the central nature of social interaction in the mediation of adult learning, Engeström also emphasizes the value of structured instruction in developing knowledge and expertise. He argues that day-to-day learning consists of 'conditioning, imitation, and trial and error', but to reach a higher plane, that of 'investigative' and 'expansive' learning, instruction is necessary.[55] For Engeström, teacher-centred training practices complement, rather than negate, learner-centred approaches to individual development.

Barbara Rogoff's early laboratory research[54,56] emphasized the importance of the social milieu in which learning is embedded, arguing that 'context is an integral aspect of cognitive events, not a nuisance variable' (ref. 56, p. 3). In later work, she extended Lave and Wenger's theoretical approach by identifying two interrelated social processes, in addition to apprenticeships, that are important to learning – participatory appropriation and guided participation.

Andragogy

andragogy: the processes associated with the organization and practice of teaching adults; more specifically, various kinds of interaction in facilitating learning situations

A German teacher, Alexander Kapp, originally used the term 'andragogy' in 1833 to describe the educational theory of Plato.[60] But it was Malcolm Knowles[61,62] who, over 25 years ago, popularized the concept of andragogy, 'the art and science of helping adults learn', which he contrasted with pedagogy, the art and science of helping children learn.[62] Knowles took the view that knowledge is activity constructed by the learner, and learning is the construction of meaning through experience. In his early work, Knowles characterized adult learners as:

- independent and 'self-directing'
- mature and experienced
- motivated by 'what they need to know'
- problem centred
- internally motivated.

In his seminal book, *The Modern Practice of Adult Education: From Pedagogy to Andragogy*, Knowles focuses upon and portrays the two forms of education as polar opposites. The key five assumptions of andragogy are summarised in Table 6.2. As can be seen from this table, andragogy as it is conceived is an amalgam of description and prescription. It describes the motivation and assumption of adult learners in these terms: 'As a person grows and matures his [sic] self-concept moves from one of total dependency (as is the reality of the infant) to one of increasing self-directedness' (ref. 63, p. 45). It follows logically from this assumption that adult learning practitioners should embrace methodological techniques that focus on an adult's needs and life experiences, facilitation and internally driven motivation to learn.

table **6.2** A comparison of the assumptions of pedagogy and andragogy

	Pedagogy	Andragogy
The learner	The role of the learner is a dependent one. The teacher directs what, when, how a subject is learned	The learner moves from dependency toward increasing self-directedness. Teacher encourages and nurtures this movement
The learner's experience	Of little worth. Hence learners will gain most from the teacher, textbooks, assigned readings, AV presentations	A rich resource for learning. Hence teaching methods include discussion, problem solving and simulation exercises
Readiness to learn	Learners learn what society expects them to, so the curriculum is standardized	Learners learn what they 'need to know', so learning activities are designed around life application
Orientation to learning	Learners see education as a process of acquiring subject matter organized by content	Learners see education as a process of developing increased curriculum competence to achieve their full potential in life. Learners want to be able to apply new knowledge and skills. Hence learning activities are centred around competency-development categories

Source: based on Jarvis (1985, 1991)[60, 64]

Criticism from other adult educators caused Knowles to revise his original position that andragogy characterizes only adult learning. Many school teachers were using 'learner-centred' pedagogy that advocated problem-centred and 'discovery' learning strategies. In his later work, Knowles contended that pedagogy and andragogy represent a continuum ranging from teacher-directed to learner-directed learning, and that both approaches are appropriate with children and adults, depending on the situation.[59] It has been suggested elsewhere that self-directed learning principles became the vogue among professional adult educators because, in the mid-1960s, the philosophy underlying andragogy mirrored the 'Expressive

Revolution' and the social and political climate of the time.[64] Since then, the methodology of self-directed learning has been uncritically adopted as a technology of adult instruction[65] and incorporated into mainstream formal adult education settings, from basic adult literacy through to professional development.[66]

Andragogy's detractors maintain that self-directed learning as it is conceived, and deployed, in formal work organizations justifies an individualized and psychological approach to adult learning that is based exclusively on the perceived individual needs of the learner, and downplays the importance of social purpose and context. Furthermore, it is argued, Knowles's conception of andragogy is not so much an explanatory theory about the process of adult learning as a philosophical position with regard to the relationship of the individual to society. Drawing on Daniel Pratt's *Five Perspectives on Teaching in Adult and Higher Education*,[67] it is apparent that the language of andragogy is that of individual triumphalism.

Individuals are unique, they desire self-improvement, they have the power to achieve self-fulfilment in the face of social, political, cultural and historical forces, they are at the centre of adult education and their private goals dominate over collective goals, they are autonomous and capable of directing their own learning, and this self-direction and self-reliance is the true mark of mature adulthood within society. In the interests of achieving private ends, each individual must take responsibility, become self-directed, for his or her own idiosyncratic education and learning. Parallels may be drawn here with the business axiom 'The customer is always right'. In this case, the adult learner is always right. The values underpinning andragogy echo the influence of the white middle-class American belief system. The concept, it is argued, 'is saturated with the ideals of individualism and entrepreneurial democracy'.[8]

Liberatory adult educators are concerned that the social purpose and context of adult education might be relegated to the periphery.[65] Because it describes the individual in psychological terms, separate from social, political, economic, cultural and historical contexts, andragogy does not acknowledge the vast influence of these social structures on the formation of the individual's identity and ways of interpreting the world, much of which is received and accepted without conscious consideration or reflection. The learner is portrayed simply 'as an uncritical and unwitting member of institutions and structures that generate rules about meaning, dominance, and judgment in society' (ref. 65, p. 18). Nonetheless, the notion of self-directed learning continues to play an important role in adult learning in higher education and in the workplace. Education and training programmes continue to assume that adults continually learn from their experience through reflection, and that the adult learner prefers to identify her or his own learning needs, and prefers to join other learners to address real-life problems as laboratories of learning.[11,62,68–70]

The self-directed approach

The literature on self-directed learning has helped to define the unique characteristics of adult learning. Three main ideas are incorporated into the 'cult-like' concept of self-directed learning:

- a self-initiated process of learning that emphasizes the need for and ability of individuals to control and manage their own learning
- individual empowerment as far as learning is concerned
- a way of organizing instruction that allows for greater learner autonomy and control over the individual's learning.[71]

The individual learner is expected to assume primary responsibility for his or her own learning, and the learning process focuses on the individual and self-development. Carl Rogers,[72] an influential writer on adult learning theory, believed empowerment through a process of 'self-directed' learning was important for personal growth. The learner's life experience is central to the learning process, which critically assumes that learning is pragmatic in nature.[73] Parallels can be drawn with the humanistic psychology of Maslow,[73] and the North American philosophical orientation of individualism (see Chapter 7).

In terms of practice, the practitioner emphasizes the importance of specifying learning objectives, facilitating as opposed to 'teaching', negotiating the content of what is learned, empowering learners, and encouraging the learner to develop plans for personal growth, often in the form of learning contracts. Others, linking adult learning to incremental social change, emphasize the need for learners to reflect on conceptions of knowledge, and question commonly held assumptions about the world in which they live and work. This internal change of consciousness occurs when process and reflection are jointed in the individual's pursuit of meaning.

This mode of adult learning represents the most complete form of self-directiveness: 'one in which critical reflection on the contingent aspects of reality, the exploration of alternative perspectives and meaning systems, and the alteration of personal and social circumstances are all present' (ref. 72, p. 26). Proponents of the learning organization emphasize reflective thinking as a key part of life-long learning in professions, including management, medicine and architecture, learning in work teams, and small-group problem-solving activity in a learning organization.[74,75] They assume (or hope) that reflective processes enable workers to jettison their dysfunctional and taken-for-granted assumptions, and thus enhance their work performance in an unproblematic manner.

Assuming that workers are permitted to engage in critical reflection, critics argue that learning at work is bounded by capitalist employment relations, and the voice of the architects building the learning organization nurtures only superficial critical reflection that improves the organization's financial bottom line. From a critical perspective, 'The objects for critical focus are carefully delineated to exclude the fundamental structures of capitalism … employees' minds are expected to remain colonized and loyal to the imperial presence of their employing organization' (ref. 76, p. 149). Critical reflection does not extend to questioning the power structures and the more dysfunctional aspects of corporate governance.

The transformational approach

The theory of transformational learning is another perspective that attempts to articulate what is unique about learning in the workplace. Various theorists in adult education use the term 'transformational' to describe a learning process that is said to shape people by producing far-reaching changes in the learner. The individual learner is different after the experience, and the learner and others can recognize these differences. These changes have a significant impact on the learner's subsequent experiences. The transformational learning process can be sudden or incremental, and it can occur in a structured training and development situation or informally through experience in a workplace.[77]

Learning in the sense being used here is most often associated with the work of Jack Mezirow.[78,79] His view of transformational learning emphasizes the 'psychocultural' and cognitive restructuring of the self. Thus, the concept of perspective transformation is defined as:

> The emancipatory process of becoming critically aware of how and why the structure of psycho-cultural assumptions has come to constrain the way we see ourselves and our relationships, reconstituting this structure to permit a more inclusive and discriminating integration of experience and acting upon these new understandings. (ref. 78, p. 6)

learning contract: a learning plan that links an organization's competitive strategy with an individual's key learning objectives. It enumerates the learning and/or competencies that are expected to be demonstrated at some point in the future

transformational learning: a view that adult learning involving self-reflection can lead to a transformation of consciousness, new visions and new courses of action

A set of core beliefs underscores Mezirow's conceptualization of transformational learning: philosophical assumptions about the nature of human beings, beliefs about knowledge, and ideas about the relationship between the individual and society. Each of the three core beliefs of transformational learning has its own function. At the centre of Mezirow's theory is the concept of the autonomous, responsible and rational adult. Although social forces might limit individual choices, Mezirow believed that the goal of transformational learning is to gain 'a crucial sense of agency over ourselves and our lives' (ref. 78, p. 20). In the workplace, this core assumption is often associated with individuals reflecting on a dysfunctional operational system or company policy, and taking action to change it.

A second core belief of transformational learning relates to knowledge creation. Mezirow's theory of knowing is *constructivist*. In this view, reality is a subjective construction by individuals rather than an objective fact. In other words, human beings are active participants in the process of making meaning and are the creators of knowledge. Through this process, individuals in the organization engage in critical reflection, through which the underlying premises of ideas are assessed and critiqued. A number of conditions are required for critical reflection to take place, including full information, the ability to objectively evaluate arguments, and freedom from self-deception or coercion.

The third main belief of Mezirow's transformational learning has relevance to social theory, which facilitates explanations of social order, conflict and change, and the relationship between the individual and society. For Mezirow, society is made up of autonomous, responsible individuals who can act to bring about incremental change to their world. He assumes that the individual learner is free to act upon any new understanding he or she may have gained. Most of the critical attention that Mezirow has received is in this area.[8,80] He puts forward a vision of society in which individuals are responsible for their collective futures. Critical theorists, however, point out that class divisions and power relations in both society at large, and the work organization in particular, may severely limit the capacity of the individual learner to change his or her world. As they comment, 'the lower in the social hierarchy learners may be the more inhibiting they may find the social structures, if they seek to be socially mobile' (ref. 64, p. 103).

What contribution does this specific type of learning make to our understanding of learning in the workplace? According to Clarke,[77] the work of Mezirow expands the definition of adult learning, and emphasizes the importance of sense making, and of going beyond notions of learning as behavioural change. The approach focuses on the mechanism of internalization, highlighting the changes in consciousness within the learner, and this, it is argued, adds a new dimension to the definition of adult learning and 'carries theory to a new level' (ref. 77, p. 53). Transformational learning also makes a contribution to our understanding of learning by construing learning in terms of making sense of life experience: 'No need is more fundamentally human than our need to understand the meaning of our experience' (ref. 79, p. 11). Learning through an engagement of life experience means that adult learning can be conceptualized as the vehicle of individual development.

Transformational learning also encourages a more multidimensional approach to learning. The notions of reflection and changes in consciousness mean that the learning process cannot be understood solely in behavioural terms: it challenges researchers and practitioners 'to attend to multiple psychological factors' (ref. 77, p. 53). While some theorists consider Mezirow's contribution to learning theory invaluable, others find that it is incomplete. For instance, the issue of how exactly the social context, and in particular gender, race and ethnicity, affect the learning process would seem to require elaboration.

Class, ethnicity, gender and learning

In Chapter 1, we emphasized the importance of understanding the effect of societal factors such as social class, ethnicity and gender on human behaviour in the work organization. The same is true with learning at work. In a multicultural society like Canada or the UK, we need to understand that social class, ethnicity, culture, gender, sexual orientation and power relations affect access to learning opportunities and educational achievement. This will give us a more inclusive picture and a better understanding of the process of learning in the organization. Sociocultural perspectives of adult learning shift us from focusing on individual internal processes to an acknowledgment of the importance of social forces.[26,81–85]

Over the last half century, one focus of UK educational sociology has been on demonstrating the effects of social class on educational attainment, and explaining the conscious and unconscious mechanisms by which these effects occur, particularly in the field of secondary education, where public policy aims to promote equality of opportunity. An early significant study of secondary education found that, despite educational reforms to promote equality in education, 'Middle-class pupils have retained, almost intact, their historic advantage over [the] manual working class.'[86] Studies have revealed a number of social mechanisms that serve to reproduce class differentials, including the effect of teacher expectations on student performance.

The stereotypes of the society in which teachers and trainers work influence their professional work.[87–89] Many teachers tend to have a preconceived idea of what constitutes the 'ideal' student, in terms of appearance, ability and conduct. Those students who fit this ideal image tend to come from 'middle' and 'upper' class groupings, and those outside this ideal image tend to come from 'lower' class groupings. They can be perceived by educators as being uninterested in learning. The underachievement of many students from working-class or 'blue-collar' social groups may be explained by the effect of teacher expectations on student performance. The effects of social class on educational achievement, career and life experience have been vividly captured in the epic television documentary series *49 Up*.

Other social mechanisms that function to promote inequality of opportunity and reproduce social class differentials include differences in the types of language – referred to as 'linguistic codes' – used by middle-class and working-class students and their teachers,[81] and differences in the patterns of socialization between middle-class and working-class families.[81] These same social mechanisms operate in the workplace. For example, managers and trainers may perceive that workers falling into the 'blue-collar' class are not trainable for certain tasks or jobs, or are less interested in developing their learning skills. In addition, those students who perform well at secondary school and experience university education enter the professional occupations, where the opportunities for career and work-related learning are greatest.

In most industrialized societies, differential access to education and workplace learning is influenced by ethnicity. Social 'exclusionary' or discriminatory mechanisms that produce differences in the learning opportunities of ethnic groups are thought to operate to a greater or lesser extent in both developed and developing societies. Research data provide evidence of variations between ethnic groups in terms of educational achievement, but the differences are not always in the same direction for students from different ethnic groups, suggesting that the social mechanisms promoting underachievement in education and training are complex.[90] Additionally, globalization has tended to encourage researchers to focus on cultural diversity to explain differences in adult educational achievement in the workplace. Comparatively little research has been undertaken on cross-cultural differences in the meaning of learning in organizations, and in learning style.[91]

Critical insight

Obtain a copy of *Understanding Adult Education and Training*, edited by Griff Foley,[92] and read Chapter 1, 'A framework for understanding adult learning and education'. Also read Chapter 1, 'Understandings of workplace learning',

in *Understanding Learning at Work*, edited by D. Boud and J. Garrick.[7] How do these authors characterize the adult learner, and from a leadership perspective, do you agree with the statement that learning has become too important to be left to in-house training departments? What are the implications of the different learning theories for leaders?

Much of the earlier literature examining the links between gender and under-achievement in educational settings focused on female students, particularly working-class female students, in UK secondary schools. The basic feminist theory and feminist pedagogy is that gender differences and inequality are constructed by complex socialization processes, involving sex-role socialization in the family, gender-specific curriculum subjects that affect the trajectory of boys and girls going into science-related and arts-related careers, gender-specific occupational training, and consequent progress into gendered occupations.[82,93–97]

More recently, however, there has been a gravitation of research interest towards gender inequality in workplace learning.[26,97] Women have been socialized to occupy the more 'feminine' jobs, to take care of people, to be in support roles and to defer to men. Men, on the other hand, have been socialized to occupy leadership roles, and they benefit from greater privilege and power in our society. The liberatory or emancipatory model of feminist pedagogy deals with the nature of interlocking systems of oppression based on gender, and seeks to understand and deal with why women are often silenced or absent, or their contributions are discounted, in the public arenas of our society and in the classroom at all educational levels.[98–102] For example, Tisdell, drawing on feminist research, argues that examples used in learning material are created by and are primarily about the white middle-class male experience, and therefore white middle-class males are more likely to be successful both in the education system and in a society that accords greater value to that cited experience.[98] While male privilege is reproduced by the system, feminist theorists suggest that the oppression of women in both paid and unpaid domestic work is reproduced by events in the educational system.

Sociocultural perspectives on learning in organizations say little about the process of learning, but provide important insights into the barriers to equality in learning. Moreover, when gender and asymmetrical power relations enter the analysis, research that seeks to investigate workplace learning strategy independently of the sociology of gender or work becomes exclusive and problematic. A growing body of research demonstrates that being born into a working-class family, or being born black, or being female, severely limits life experience, power and access to knowledge acquisition. For example, there is well-documented evidence that young men and women from working-class backgrounds have been persistently under-represented in UK and North American universities. Survey findings also suggest that those holding more routine, highly supervised manual working-class jobs are more likely to pursue community-related informal learning.[103]

Feminist learning theory calls attention to these issues, and underscores the importance of dealing directly with them. In addition, feminist pedagogical theory can offer new insights both to the field of adult learning and to those educators and trainers interested in educating for social and individual transformation. Consequently, a sociocultural perspective on adult learning encourages reflectivity among adult educators and trainers. Adult educators who are interested in challenging unequal power relations based on class, gender and race need to address the ways in which their own ideologies and practices in the learning environment either challenge or reproduce society's inequitable distribution of power.[98]

Learning for innovation

The association between learning and innovation has been well documented. Studies suggest that learning in organizations mediates creativity, innovation and change.[104–108] As notions of knowledge work, core competencies and innovation have entered the contemporary management lexicon, there has been a growing interest in 'strategic' learning to mobilize workers' creativity.[3,7] The efficacy of continuous reflexive learning is linked to a broader discourse on employment practices that attempts to encourage functional flexibility and organizational cultural change.[109] In this section, we explore the links between learning, creativity and innovation that shape the future of organizations.

plate 24 Seeking to attract creative individuals, some organizations have sought to develop multifaceted centres designed to encourage innovation. This photo shows an interesting and innovative office space in Madrid, which is partially underground.

Source: Iwan Baan

Here we conceive informal learning as a potential key 'lever' for creativity and 'sustainable innovation'.[110,111] *Creativity* in the workplace has been defined as the development of ideas about products, services, processes or practices that can potentially enhance individual and organizational performance. It is posited that the different forms of creativity (technological creativity, economic creativity, artistic creativity and cultural creativity) are significantly interrelated: 'Not only do they share a common thought process; they reinforce each other through cross-fertilization and mutual stimulation' (ref. 105, p. 13). Seeking to attract creative individuals, some organizations have sought to develop multifaceted centres designed to encourage innovation. In a minority of cases, this has involved attracting artists, and an openness to explore the complementary relationship between the arts and sustainable creative behaviours in workplaces.[111–113]

Work and Society: **Keeping your distance**

How do people learn to think in creative ways about the problems they encounter in work settings? New research on human learning has generated some fresh insights into this fundamental issue. Central to these insights is the idea of 'representational competence'. People represent the world in various ways – through diagrams, maps and language – and their ability to create these representations (their 'representational competence') can play a key role in how well they are able to solve problems and innovate. As one summary of new research (Bransford et al., 2000) on learning puts it:

> An important way that knowledge affects performances is through its influences on people's representations of problems and situations. Different representations of the same problem can make it easy, difficult or impossible to solve. (p. 226)

Knowledge plays a role in representational competence, because prior knowledge of a particular situation or process influences the quality of the representations people construct. However, prior knowledge is not the only factor influencing representational competence; also important are the 'styles of thinking' that people bring to bear on problematic situations.

It is in relation to this idea of different thinking 'styles' that the idea of distancing, developed by psychologist Irving Siegel (Siegel and de Lisi, 2003), becomes relevant. Distancing may be defined as follows:

> In the distancing situation the ... [addressor] makes a cognitive demand that requires the addressee ... to separate himself or herself mentally from the here and now and transcend the ongoing present either by orienting self into the past or the future ... cognitive demands ... could be in the form of a question, a statement, a directive and a request for alternative solutions to a problem. Such strategies were hypothesized as helping to generate representational competence. (p. 700)

Defined in this way, distancing refers to thinking style rather than to any specific body of factual knowledge. The idea of distancing captures what many researchers consider to be the hallmark of sophisticated thinking – abstraction, or the capacity to move beyond what is perceptually present (in this regard, Piaget once suggested that, in abstract or formal thinking, 'reality is secondary to possibility'). Distancing, many would contend, is essential to innovation and effective problem solving. Without distancing, there is a tendency to become overwhelmed by the complexity of the immediate situation – to fail to see the forest for the trees. Distancing provides a way to escape this trap and to move beyond habitual or impulsive responses to situations in order to solve problems and innovate.

Although it would be tempting to view the thinking style associated with distancing as something equivalent to IQ

(a thing-like entity one inherits), this would be a mistake. Distancing is an acquired skill, and Siegel's work investigates both the skill and the work that parents and teachers might do to nurture the skill in children. Unfortunately, however, many people are not exposed to learning environments that foster distancing on a regular basis, and, as a consequence, they find it difficult to respond thoughtfully and creatively to situations they encounter at work.

One way to think about distancing is to imagine a continuum of possible representations: at one end of the spectrum lies a representation that closely resembles the existing situation (indicating a lack of distance); at the other lies a representation where many features of the existing situation have been changed (indicating distance). This is illustrated by recent work of researcher Engeström (2007), who studied workplace change in the Finnish Post Office. Workers produced two representations: one focused on work processes as they currently existed and identified various problems, the second – distanced representation – describing improved work processes as they might appear at some future date. Among the changes proposed by the postal workers and included in their representation of the future was an extension of the services they provided to include selling stamps and running a programme for checking up on seniors living alone.

Given opportunities to practise distancing in a supportive environment, employees can learn to construct multiple representations, to evaluate various hypothetical scenarios, and to respond creatively to problematic situations.

stop! Try the distancing process for yourself: pick a real or imagined workplace, and then create multiple representations of how it works now and how it could work in the future.

Use these representations as a focus for a discussion about workplace change.

Sources and further information

Bransford, J. D., Brown, A. L. and Cocking R. R. (2000) *How People Learn: Brain, Mind Experience and School*, Washington, DC: National Academy Press.

Cocking, R. and Renninger, K. (eds) (1993) *The Development and Meaning of Psychological Distance*, Hillsdale, NJ: Lawrence Erlbaum.

Engeström, Y. (2007) 'Putting Vygotsky to work: the change laboratory as a an application of double stimulation', in H. Daniels, M. Cole and J. Wertsch (eds), *The Cambridge Companion to Vygotsky*, Cambridge: Cambridge University Press.

Siegel, I. and De Lisi, A. (2003) 'Rod Cocking's legacy: the development of psychological distancing', *Applied Developmental Psychology*, **24**, pp. 697–711.

Note: This feature was written by David MacLennan, Assistant Professor at Thompson Rivers University, BC, Canada.

Although employees might develop novel and potentially useful ideas, it is only when the ideas are implemented successfully in the workplace that they can be considered to be innovation.[114,115] *Innovation* is the creation of any new service, product or process that is new to an organization. As such, innovation is a major driver of change. It means more than R&D, most effective innovations being based on the creative combination of existing ideas or techniques, or the cumulative effect of incremental change in processes or products.

Using Figure 1.2, we can identify some practices related to structure, technology and people that can be used to create a new product or service. Structural arrangements provide systems and procedures that direct and motivate behaviour. Innovation may occur if organizations encourage collaboration and problem solving by developing internal linking networks that bridge or connect disparate functions (for example, diverse project teams). One key behaviour in the innovation process is 'getting ideas' and 'matching up' idea generators with change agents. When building exchange networks, creating a common physical space can improve the process of getting ideas. The variations of such events are endless, but this line of inquiry is based on the belief that creative workers, coupled with learning opportunities, can improve the odds of 'match-ups' between idea generators, innovation and sponsors. New technology and the redesign of jobs to allow greater empowerment can also have important effects on employee creativity.

Of particular relevance to the learning/innovation debate is that certain *people* practices increase the creative agency and the organization's ability to innovate.[112] The assumption is that prospective innovators possess certain psychological attributes, including irreverence for the status quo – thus having a great need to achieve and to take risks. Idea generators 'often come from outcast groups or are newcomers to the company; they are less satisfied with the way things are and have less to lose if there's a change' (ref. 112, p. 176). The notion of innovative personality traits has its roots in Weberian sociology. Weber gave recognition to the role of intangibles – beliefs, values, aspirations – in business development.[116] A similar argument resolving around personality traits and innovation can be found in recent entrepreneurial studies.[117] There is evidence that artists 'embedded' in an organization can have innovative outcomes.[118] The central premise is straightforward: a learning environment provides fertile conditions for developing and validating new ideas or, to use the old cliché, 'out-of-the-box' thinking, for fostering innovation.

The quality of the learning experience, and with it the concomitant potential for developing reflexive behaviour that would harness 'creative capital', will necessarily depend upon, not least, the design of the potential learning experience. In this

learning cycle: a view of adult learning that emphasizes learning as a continuous process

context, the notion of a **learning cycle** is popular within the formal learning canon, possibly because it contains elements of cognitive, behaviourist and andragogical concepts that can potentially encourage innovation.[11] The learning model depicts learning as a circular process with no start or finish (Figure 6.5). The model emphasizes the centrality of experience in the learning process, the role of individual needs and goals in determining the type of experience sought, and the importance of completing all stages of learning before learning can occur.

The experiential learning cycle should be viewed as a holistic perspective that seeks to integrate behaviour, cognition, perception and authentic experience. Accordingly, the process of learning is concrete and abstract, active and passive. Others have plausibly argued that the four moments in the learning cycle may not be totally discrete. Experience should not be viewed in isolation, reflection contextualizes the learning, and any action arising from the 'testing'

When was the last time you felt that you had really learned something? Recall that occasion, reflect on it, and try to relate it step by step to the experiential learning model

stop
reflect

For more
information on the
learning organization, go
to www.ahrd.org; www.
cipd.co.uk/HRD; www.
elearningnetwork.org

weblink

may be contrary to power relations.[64] The 'good practices' and recommendations in Table 6.3 can be traced to the learning theories reviewed in this chapter. Conflict theories of work, however, remind us that the application of learning theories in work organizations is never straightforward given the nature of the employment relationship, the network of power and control, and the persistence of inherent tensions in the management of learning and innovation.[103]

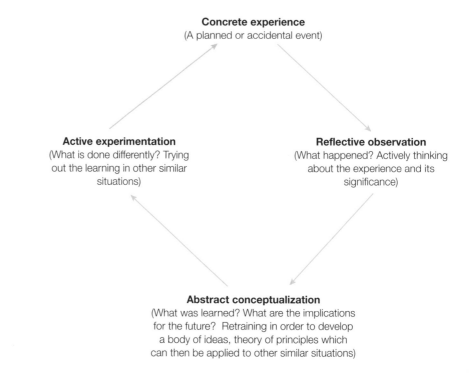

figure 6.5 Kolb et al.'s experiential cycle of learning

table 6.3 Applying learning theory in the organization

Social learning and adult learning concepts	Recommendations
Zone of proximal development	Expose learners to authentic tasks
Scaffolding	Encourage learners to interact with others
Communities of practice	Design work to allow knowledge to be applied
Participatory appropriation	Provide space and time for reflectivity
Guided participation	Develop mentoring skills to managers/experts
Andragogy	Develop communities of practice through partnerships
Self-directed	Encourage learner to move towards self-directedness
Transformation	Draw on learners' life experience
	Encourage critical thinking
	Design learning activities around learners' needs

Source: Based on Mezirow (1981)[78], Knowles (1980)[69] and Fuller and Unwin (1998)[121]

Chapter summary

- There has been a growing interest in learning in organizations, as contemporary management thinking and practice emphasize notions of knowledge work, flexibility, core competencies and sustainable competitive advantage through learning.

- Learning can be defined as a relatively permanent change in behaviour or human capabilities resulting from processing new knowledge, practice or experience. In organizations, the quality of this learning experience may depend on how the organization is structured, how work is designed, how individuals engage, interact and construct knowledge from these paid work situations, and how managers lead their subordinates. Learning in organizations can take any one of the following four forms: formal, non-formal, informal and incidental.

- We examined classical approaches to learning that focused on how internal mental events such as learning might be measured and studied through Pavlovian conditioning, and the importance of reinforcement in the learning process.

- The cognitive approach to learning was also examined. The Gestalt theorists, as they were known, proposed that human consciousness could not be investigated adequately by unscrambling its component parts, but only by investigating its overall shape or pattern. Proponents of this school of thought believe that cognitive processes – how individuals perceive, evaluate feedback, represent, store and use information – play an important role in learning.

- The third classical approach we examined related to social-learning theories. This suggests that individuals learn and develop through observational learning. That is, people learn by observing others – role models – whom they believe are credible and knowledgeable.

- We examined some contemporary approaches to learning – activity theory and community of practice – and explained that social-learning theory underpins the concept of a community of practice, which has been the subject of some debate in the adult learning literature. For example, an extreme position is that there is little need for formal classroom-based learning because effective learning occurs only through the engagement of community membership.

- We also discussed how psychologically driven learning theories began to give way to learning theories that articulated the unique characteristics of adult learning, and examined four perspectives that attempt to understand adult learning in general and adult learning in work: the andragogy, self-directed, transformational and sociocultural approaches.

- We defined creativity as the development of ideas about services, products or processes that can potentially increase individual and organizational performance. And innovation is the *creation* of any new service, product or process that is new to an organization.

- Finally, we examined Kolb's well-known learning cycle model and discussed the awareness that a learning environment provides fertile conditions for developing and validating unconventional ideas and behaviours, in other words, for fostering innovation.

Key concepts

andragogy	175–176
behaviourist approach	165–167
cognitive approach	168
creativity	181
innovation	183
learning process	164–165
negative reinforcement	167
Pavlovian conditioning	165–166
positive reinforcement	166
self-directed learning	176–177

Vocab checklist for ESL students

- ☐ Abstract
- ☐ Activity theory
- ☐ Andragogy
- ☐ Behaviour, behaviourism, behave
- ☐ Classical conditioning
- ☐ Cognition, cognitive
- ☐ Communities of practice
- ☐ Concept, conceptualization, conceptualize
- ☐ Concrete
- ☐ Decision making
- ☐ Experiment, experimentation, experimental
- ☐ Explicit knowledge
- ☐ Feedback
- ☐ Gestalt
- ☐ Intellectual capital
- ☐ Learner, learning, learn
- ☐ Learning contract
- ☐ Learning cycle
- ☐ Life-long learning
- ☐ Negative reinforcement
- ☐ Norm, normal, normative
- ☐ Operant conditioning
- ☐ Organizational learning
- ☐ Pedagogy
- ☐ Positive reinforcement
- ☐ Reflexive learning
- ☐ Semiotics
- ☐ Situated learning
- ☐ Stimulus, stimulate
- ☐ Tacit knowledge
- ☐ Transformational learning

Chapter review questions

1. Why is workplace learning important for managers and workers?
2. What are the main differences between the cognitive and behaviourist perspectives on learning?

3. Why is a psychologically driven approach to workplace learning controversial?
4. What is the difference between creativity and innovation?
5. What can managers do to encourage creativity and innovation?
6. Can art or artists 'embedded' in the organization contribute to the innovation process? How?

❓ Chapter research questions

1. A good way to understand the learning process is to consider your own experience as a student. Form a study group and examine Kolb's experiential learning cycle. This cycle has four moments. The point on the cycle in which a person is likely to spend most time is called a learning style. Reflecting on your own classroom experience, can you give examples of how your professors may have been influenced by this cycle when designing classes/seminars? What is your preferred learning style, and why? If, within your group, there are diverse learning styles, what implications does this have for professors/managers?

2. Obtain a copy of *Inside the Workplace: Findings from the 2004 Workplace Employment Relations Survey* (2006). After reading pages 82–7, what proportion of workplaces provided 'off-the-job' training to employees? Do all employees receive the same amount of training? What are the advantages/disadvantages of off-the-job training compared with informal learning?

3. Read Mark Easterby-Smith's (1997) 'Disciplines of organizational learning: contributions and critiques' (see Further Reading, below). What key ideas have psychology, sociology and cultural anthropology contributed to our understanding of workplace learning? What key problems have these disciplines addressed? How useful are these disciplinary approaches to your understanding of workplace learning?

▣→ Further reading

Billett, S. (2001) *Learning in the Workplace: Strategies for Effective Practice*, Crows Nest, NSW: Allen & Unwin.

Bratton, J., Helms Mills, J., Pyrch, T. and Sawchuk, P. (2004) *Workplace Learning: A Critical Introduction*, Toronto: University of Toronto Press.

Collin, K. (2009) 'Work-related identity in individual and social learning at work', *Journal of Workplace Learning*, 21(1/2), pp. 23–35.

Easterby-Smith, M. (1997) 'Disciplines of organizational learning: contributions and critiques', *Human Relations*, 50(9), pp. 1085–113.

Evans, K., Hodkinson, P. and Unwin, L. (2002) (eds) *Working to Learn: Transforming Learning in the Workplace*, London: Routledge.

Fulop, L., Marechal, G. and Rifkin, W. (2009) 'Managing knowledge and learning', pp. 35–88 in S. Linstead, L. Fulop and S. Lilley (eds), *Management and Organization: A Critical Text* (2nd edn), Basingstoke: Palgrave.

Guidice, R. M., Thompson Heames, J. and Wang, S. (2009) 'The indirect relationship between organizational-level knowledge worker turnover and innovation', *The Learning Organization*, 16(2), pp. 143–67.

Livingstone, D. W., Mirchandani, K. and Sawchuk, P. (2008) (eds) *The Future of Lifelong Learning and Work*, Rotterdam: Sense Publishers.

McIlroy, J. (2008) 'Ten years of New Labour: workplace learning, social partnerships and union revitalization in Britain', *British Journal of Industrial Relations*, 46(2), pp. 283–313.

Ramstad, E. (2009) 'Developmental evaluation framework for innovation and learning networks', *Journal of Workplace Learning*, 21(3), pp. 181–97.

 Chapter case study 1

Learning to be green in New Zealand

Setting

In the twenty-first century, New Zealand is facing environmental issues similar to those of many countries: a more sustainable use of water, managing marine resources, reducing waste and improving energy efficiency. New Zealand is particularly concerned about the decline of its unique plants, animals and ecosystems. The country is striving to build a positive image of New Zealand through exporting sustainable products and maintaining a reputation of being sustainable at home and abroad. The government has recognized that there is a need to increase reporting on sustainable practices among New Zealand businesses to raise the profile of New Zealand globally on this important issue.

Recently, the Ministry for the Environment announced the Sustainable Management Fund, which provides funding to support community groups, businesses and local government in taking practical actions that produce long-term environmental benefits, encourage proactive partnerships and promote community action. Eligible environmental projects would be considered for a minimum of $10,000 and up to a maximum of $200,000 of funding per financial year.

The problem

Capital Health Hospital, located near the city of Auckland, provides a wide range of complex medical, surgery and mental health services, and is not only one of New Zealand's largest healthcare centres, but its oldest. The hospital has a poor reputation in terms of its human resource management and struggles with adversarial union relations. Workers are given low autonomy in their jobs, and the organizational structure contains several layers of management.

The hospital's administration recently became aware of the funding provided by the government's sustainability initiative. Subsequently, in a public meeting, Chief Executive Officer Heath Nicol announced the creation of a Sustainability Innovation Committee, comprising staff members chosen from the various hospital departments: 'Environmental stewardship is a key component of our hospital's strategic and operational planning, and through this new committee we will be contributing to our organization's and the country's goals to become more sustainable.' The committee would, he said, recommend and develop projects that would meet the funding criteria outlined by the government.

This new and revolutionary approach by the hospital administration took most of the staff by surprise. While many were eager to learn about the environmental issues and contribute their ideas through this experience, others were suspicious of management's motives in involving staff members when they had never been asked to participate in such a public initiative before.

Shortly before the initial meeting of the selected group, the Human Resources Department received an angry call from the union executive questioning why they had not been asked to sit on the committee. The union demanded a meeting with management to discuss how workloads and jobs would be impacted by the employees' involvement.

Tasks

In small groups, discuss the following:

1. How does the work of the critical organizational theorists explain the situation the hospital administration now faces?
2. What do you think is really the union's concern about the initiative?

Sources of further information

Billet, S. (2001) *Learning in the Workplace: Strategies for Effective Practice*, Sydney: Allen & Unwin.

Steiner, L. (1998) 'Organizational dilemmas as barriers to learning', *The Learning Organization*, 5(4), pp. 193–201.

For more on New Zealand's Sustainable Management Fund and its other environmental initiatives, go to www.mfe.govt.nz

Note

This case study was written by Lori Rilkoff, MSc, CHRP, Senior Human Resources Manager at the City of Kamloops, and lecturer in HRM at Thompson Rivers University, BC, Canada.

Chapter case study 2

Coronation Bank, a transfer of learning dilemma

 Visit www.palgrave.com/business/brattonob2e to view this case study.

 Web-based assignment

There are competing views on the purpose of work-related learning. One school of thought believes that creativity and innovation are more likely to be fostered in organizations where learning is valued and of high quality. In this sense, workplace learning has an instrumental purpose: to 'unfreeze' employee work attitudes and practices to bring about change. Learning can also enhance an organization's performance and increase a nation's productivity. (See OB in Focus on 'The Learning Age', page 164)

Specifically, this assignment requires you to critically evaluate these assumptions. First, go to the following websites for more information on life-long learning: www.lifelonglearning.co.uk; www.lifelonglearning.co.uk/llp/index.htm. Second, choose two companies, enter their websites, and evaluate how each company provides for continuous work-related learning. What are

the company's objectives with regard to work-related learning? How does the company's learning strategy relate, if at all, to its business strategy? Is there any evidence that work-related learning benefits both individual employees and the company? What role should work-related learning play in the workplace?

 OB in film

The film *Erin Brockovich* (2000) is based on a true story. In the film, Brockovich (played by Julia Roberts), a legal assistant and a single mother of three children, investigates how a US company is illegally depositing cancer-causing chemicals in an unlined pond, causing high rates of cancer among the local community. The film raises questions about corporate crime, as well as about the education and training of lawyers, and access to university education.

Watch the scenes between Brockovich and the three lawyers discussing files, and look at how Brockovich deals with the cancer victims on a personal level. Do these scenes show informal learning? How does Brockovich's work-related learning differ from the formal legal training of the lawyers? Can the lawyers learn anything from Brockovich? What does the film reveal about the opportunity for energetic and intelligent women from low-income social groups to enter higher education?

 References

1 Billett, S. (2001) *Learning in the Workplace: Strategies for Effective Practice*, Crows Nest, NSW: Allen & Unwin.
2 Bratton, J., Helms Mills, J., Pyrch, T. and Sawchuk, P. (2004) *Workplace Learning: A Critical Introduction*, Toronto: Garamond Press.
3 Foley, G. (2001) *Strategic Learning: Understanding and Facilitating Organizational Change*, Sydney: Centre for Popular Education.
4 Mabey, C., Salaman, G. and Storey, J. (1998) *Human Resource Management: A Strategic Introduction* (2nd edn), Oxford: Blackwell.
5 Senge, P. (1990) *The Fifth Discipline*, New York: Doubleday.
6 Watkins, K. E. and Cervero, R. M. (2000) 'Organizations as contexts for learning: a case study in certified public *accountancy*', *Journal of Workplace Learning*, **12**(5), pp. 187–94.
7 Boud, D. and Garrick, J. (eds) (1999) *Understanding Learning at Work*, London: Routledge.
8 Spencer, B. (1998) *The Purposes of Adult Education: A Guide for Students*, Toronto: Thompson.
9 Bratton, J. (2001) 'International strategic human resource management: integrating human intelligence and strategic management', pp. 18–43 in J. Kidd, Xue Li and F. J. Richter (eds), *Maximizing Human Intelligence Deployment in Asian Business*, Basingstoke, Palgrave Macmillan.
10 Gagne, R. M. and Medsker, K. L. (1996) *The Conditions of Learning*, Fort Worth, TX: Harcourt Brace.
11 Kolb, D. (1984) *Experiential Learning: Experience as the Source of Learning and Development*, Englewood Cliffs, NJ: Prentice Hall.
12 Bratton, J. (1999) 'Gaps in the workplace learning paradigm: labour flexibility and job design', in Conference Proceedings of Researching Work and Learning, First International Conference, University of Leeds, UK.
13 Sawchuk, P. H. (2008) 'Theories and methods for research on informal learning and work: towards cross-fertilization', *Studies in Continuing Education*, **30**(1), pp. 1–16.
14 Marsick, V. and Watkins, K. (1990) *Informal and Incidental Learning in the Workplace*, London: Routledge.

15 Dixon, N. (1992) 'Organizational learning: a review of the literature with implications for HRD professionals', *Human Resource Development Quarterly*, **3**, pp. 29–49.

16 Kochan, T. and Dyer, L. (1995) 'HRM: an American view', in J. Storey (ed.), *Human Resource Management: A Critical Text*, London: Routledge.

17 Agashae, Z. and Bratton, J. (2001) 'Leader-follower dynamics: developing a learning organization', *Journal of Workplace Learning*, **3**(3), pp. 89–102.

18 Driver, M. (2002) 'Learning and leadership in organizations', *Management Learning*, **33**(1), pp. 99–126.

19 Knights, D. and Willmott, H. (1992) 'Conceptualizing leadership processes: a study of senior managers in a finance services company', *Journal of Management Studies*, **29**(6), pp. 761–82.

20 Legge, K. (2005) *Human Resource Management: Rhetorics and Realities* (2nd edn), Basingstoke: Palgrave.

21 Townley, B. (1994) *Reframing Human Resource Management: Power, Ethics and the Subject of Work*, London: Sage.

22 Coopey, J. (1996) 'Crucial gaps in the learning organization', in K. Starkey (ed.), *How Organizations Learn*, London: International Thomson Business Press.

23 Forrester, K. (1999) 'Work-related learning and the struggle for subjectivity', in K. Forrester, N. Frost, D. Taylor and K. Ward (eds), *Proceedings of First International Conference: Researching Work and Learning*, Leeds, UK: University of Leeds.

24 Spencer, B. (2001) 'Changing questions of workplace learning researchers', pp. 31–40 in T. Fenwick (ed.), *Socio-cultural Perspectives on Learning through Work*, San Francisco: Jossey-Bass.

25 Thompson, P. and McHugh, D. (2006) *Work Organizations: A Critical Introduction* (4th edn), Basingstoke: Palgrave.

26 Probert, B. (1999) 'Gendered workers and gendered work', pp. 98–116 in D. Boud and J. Garrick (eds), *Understanding Learning at Work*, London: Routledge.

27 Walker, J. T. (1996) *The Psychology of Learning*, Englewood Cliffs, NJ: Prentice Hall.

28 Pavlov (1927), quoted in Walker, J. T. (1996) *The Psychology of Learning*, Englewood Cliffs, NJ: Prentice Hall, p. 20.

29 Watson, J. B. and Rayner, R. (1920) 'Conditional emotional reactions', *Journal of Experimental Psychology*, **3**, pp. 1–14.

30 Bernstein, D. A., Clarke-Stewart, A., Penner, L., Roy, E. and Wickens, C. (2000) *Psychology* (5th edn), New York: Houghton Mifflin.

31 Skinner, B. F. (1953) *Science and Human Behavior*, New York: Macmillan.

32 Skinner, B. F. (1954) 'The science of learning and the art of teaching', *Harvard Educational Review*, **24**, pp. 86–97.

33 Nye, R. (2000) *Three Psychologies: Perspectives from Freud, Skinner and Rogers* (6th edn), Belmont, CA: Wadsworth/Thompson Learning.

34 Thorndike, E. L. (1913) *The Psychology of Learning*, New York: Teachers' College.

35 Tennant, M. (1997) *Psychology and Adult Learning* (2nd edn), London: Routledge.

36 Köhler, W (1925) *The Mentality of Apes*, New York: Harcourt Brace.

37 Wiener, N. (1954) *The Human Use of Human Beings: Cybernetics and Society*, New York: Avon.

38 Bandura, A. (1971) 'Psychotherapy based upon modeling principles', pp. 173–83 in A. E. and S. L. Garfield (eds), *Handbook of Psychotherapy and Behaviour*, New York: Wiley.

39 Bandura, A. (1977) *Social Learning Theory*, Englewood Cliffs, NJ: Prentice Hall.

40 Vygotsky, L. (1978) *Mind in Society: The Development of Higher Psychological Processes*, Cambridge, MA: Harvard University Press.

41 Leontiev, A. N. (1978) *Activity, Consciousness, and Personality*, Englewood Cliffs, NJ: Prentice Hall.

42 Leontiev, A. (1981) *Problems of the Development of the Mind*, Moscow: Progress Publishers.

43 Wood, D. J., Bruner, J. and Ross, G. (1976) 'The role of tutoring in problem solving', *Journal of Child Psychology and Psychiatry*, **17**, pp. 89–100.

44 Hung, D. (1999) 'Activity, apprenticeship and epistemological appropriation: implications from the writings of...', *Educational Psychologist*, **34**(4), pp. 193–205.

45 Rogoff, B. (1990) *Apprenticeship in Thinking: Cognitive Development in Social Context*, Oxford: Oxford University Press.

46 Lave, J. and Wenger, E. (1991) *Situated Learning: Legitimate Peripheral Participation*, Cambridge: Cambridge University Press.

47 Lave, J. (1993) 'The practice of learning', in S. Chaiklin (ed.), *Understanding the Practice: Perspectives on Activity and Context*, Cambridge: Cambridge University Press.

48 Wenger, E. (1998) *Cultivating Communities of Practice*, New York: Cambridge University Press.

49 Wenger, E., McDermott, R. and Snyder, W. (2002) *Cultivating Communities of Practice*, Boston, MA: Harvard Business School Press.

50 Brown, J. S., Collins, A. and Duguid, S. (1989) 'Situated cognition and the culture of learning', *Educational Researcher*, **18**(1), pp. 32–42.

51 Wilson, A. L. (1993) 'The promise of situated cognition', pp. 71–9 in S. Merriam (ed.), *An Update on Adult Learning Theory*, No. 57, San Francisco: Jossey-Bass.

52 Østerlund, C. (1997) 'Sales apprentices on the move: a multi-contextual perspective on situated learning', *Journal of Nordic Educational Research (Nordisk Pedagogik)*, **17**(3), pp. 169–77.

53 Wenger, E. (2000) 'Communities of practice and social learning systems', *Organization*, **7**(2), pp. 225–46.

54 Rogoff, B. (1995) 'Observing sociocultural activity on three planes: participatory appropriation, guided participation, and apprenticeship', pp. 139–63 in J. V. Wertsch, P. del Rio and A. Alvarez (eds), *Sociocultural Studies of Mind*, Cambridge: Cambridge University Press.

55 Engeström, Y. (1994) *Training for Change: New Approaches to Instruction and Learning*, Geneva: International Labour Office.

56 Rogoff, B. (1984) 'Introduction: thinking and learning in social context', pp. 1–8 in B. Rogoff and J. Lave (eds), *Everyday Cognition: Its Development in Social Context*, Cambridge, MA: Harvard University Press.

57 Beyer, J. and Trice, M. (1987) 'How an organization's rites reveal its culture', *Organization Dynamics*, **15**(4), pp. 4–24.

58 Hoeve, A. and Nieuwenhuis, L. (2006) 'Learning routines in innovation processes', *Journal of Workplace Learning*, **18**(3), Emerald, pp. 171–85.

59 Merriam, S. (ed.) (1993) *An Update on Adult Learning Theory*, San Francisco: Jossey-Bass.

60 Jarvis, P. (ed.) (1991) *Twentieth Century Thinkers in Adult Education*, London: Routledge.

61 Knowles, M. (1975) *Self-Directed Learning*, New York: Associated Press.

62 Knowles, M. (1980) *The Modern Practice of Adult Education: From Pedagogy to Andragogy* (2nd edn), New York: Cambridge Books.

63 Knowles, M. (1973) *The Adult Learner: A Neglected Species*, Houston, TX: Gulf.

64 Jarvis, P. (1985) *The Sociology of Adult and Continuing Education*, London: Routledge.

65 Pratt, D. D. (1993) 'Andragogy after twenty-five years', pp. 15–23 in S. Merriam (ed.), *An Update on Adult Learning Theory*, No. 57, San Francisco: Jossey-Bass.

66 Collins, M. (1991) *Adult Education as a Vocation: A Critical Role for the Adult Educator*, London: Routledge.

67 Pratt, D. (1998) *Five Perspectives on Teaching in Adult and Higher Education*, Malabar, FL: Krieger.

68 Brooks, A. and Watkins, K. E. (1994) 'The emerging power of action inquiry technologies', *New Directions for Adult and Continuing Education*, **63**, pp. 131–43.

69 Marsick, V. J. (1988) 'Learning in the workplace: the case of reflectivity and critical reflectivity', *Adult Education Quarterly*, **4**, pp. 18–29.

70 Mezirow, J. (1991) *Transformative Dimensions of Adult Learning*, San Francisco: Jossey-Bass.

71 Rogers, C. R. (1983) *Freedom to Learn for the 80s*, Columbus, OH: Merrill.

72 Caffarella, R. (1993) 'Self-directed learning', *New Directions for Adult and Continuing Education*, **57**, pp. 25–35.

73 Maslow, A. H. (1954) *Motivation and Personality*, New York: Harper.

74 Argyris, C. (1993) *Knowledge for Action: A Guide to Overcoming Barriers to Organizational Change*, San Francisco: Jossey-Bass.

75 Watkins, K. and Marsick, V. (1993) *Sculpting the Learning Organization*, San Francisco: Jossey-Bass.

76 Fenwick, T. (1998) 'Questioning the concept of the learning organization', pp. 140–52 in S. Scott, B. Spencer and A. Thomas (eds), *Learning for Life*, Toronto: Thompson Educational.

77 Clarke, M. C. (1993) 'Transformational learning', pp. 47–56 in S. Merriam (ed.), *An Update on Adult Learning Theory*, San Francisco: Jossey-Bass.

78 Mezirow, J. D. (1981) 'A critical theory of adult education', *Adult Education Quarterly*, **32**(1), pp. 3–24.

79 Mezirow, J. D. (1990) *Fostering Critical Reflection in Adulthood: A Guide to Transformative and Emancipatory Learning*, San Francisco: Jossey-Bass.

80 Scott, S. M. (1998) 'Philosophies in action', pp. 98–106 in S. M. Scott, B. Spencer and A. Thomas (eds), *Learning for Life*, Toronto: Thompson Educational.

81 Bernstein, B. (1971) *Class Codes and Control*, Volume 1, London: Routledge & Kegan Paul.

82 Farmer, H. S. (1997) *Diversity and Women's Career Development: From Adolescence to Adulthood*, Thousand Oaks, CA: Sage.

83 Hayes, E. and Flannery, D. D. (2000) *Women as Learners: The Significance of Gender in Adult Learning*, San Francisco: Jossey-Bass.

84 Hofstede, G. (1984) *Culture's Consequences: International Differences in Work-Related Values*, Beverley Hills, CA: Sage.

85 Sharpe, S. (1976) *Just Like a Girl: How Girls Learn To Be Women*, London: Penguin.

86 Douglas, J., Ross, J. and Simpson, H. (1968) *All Our Future*, London: Peter Davies.

87 Ashton, D. and Field, D. (1976) *Young Workers*, London: Hutchinson.

88 Becker, H. S. (1971) 'Social change variations in the teacher-pupil relationship', in B. Cosin, I. R. Dale, G. M. Esland and D. F. Swift (eds), *School and Society*, London: Routledge & Kegan Paul.

89 Becker, H.S. (1984) 'Social class variations in the teacher-pupil ratio', in A. Hargreaves and P. Woods (eds). *Classrooms and Staff Rooms: The Sociology of Teachers and Teaching*, Milton Keynes: Open University Press.

90 Craft, M. and Craft, A. (1983) 'The participation of ethnic minorities in further and higher education', *Educational Researcher*, **259**(1), pp. 45–51.

91 Martin, J. and Nakayama, T. (2000) *Intercultural Communication in Contexts* (2nd edn), Mountain View, CA/Toronto: Mayfield.

92 Foley, G. (ed.) (2000) *Understanding Adult Education and Training* (2nd edn), London: Allen & Unwin.

93 Bradley, H. (1986) 'Technological change, management strategies, and the development of gender-based job segregation in the labour process', pp. 54–73 in D. Knights and H. Willmott (eds), *Gender and the Labour Process*, Aldershot: Gower.

94 Cockburn, C. (1983) *Brothers: Male Domination and Technological Change*, London: Pluto.

95 Cockburn, C. (1991) *In the Way of Women: Men's Resistance to Sex Equality in Organizations*, Basingstoke: Macmillan.

96 Stanworth, M. (1981) *Gender and Schooling*, London: Hutchinson.

97 Rowbotham, S. (1973) *Woman's Consciousness, Man's World*, London: Penguin.

98 Tisdell, E. (1993) 'Feminism and adult learning: power, pedagogy and praxis', pp. 91–103 in S. Merriam (ed.), *An Update on Adult Learning Theory*, San Francisco: Jossey-Bass.

99 Belenky, M. F., Clinchy, B. M., Goldberger, N. R. and Tarule, J. (1986) *Women's Ways of Knowing: The Development of Self, Voice, and Mind*, New York: Basic Books.

100 Chafetz, J. (1988) *Feminist Sociology: An Overview of Contemporary Theories*, Itasca, IL: Peacock.

101 Wilson, F. M. (1992) 'Language, power and technology', *Human Relations*, **45**(9), pp. 883–904.

102 Gherardi, S. (1994) 'The gender we think, the gender we do in our everyday organizational lives', *Human Relations*, **47**(6), pp. 591–606.

103 Livingstone, D. and Sawchuk, P. (2004) *Hidden Knowledge: Organized Labour in the Information Age*, Toronto: Garamond/Washington, DC: Rowman & Littlefield.

104 Arora, A., Florida, R., Gates, G. and Kamlet, M. (2000) *Human Capital, Quality of Place and Location*, Pittsburgh: Carnegie Mellon.

105 Florida, R. (2002) *The Rise of the Creative Class*, New York: Basic Books.

106 Florida, R. (2005) *Cities and the Creative Class*, New York: Routledge.

107 Guidice, R. M., Thompson, J. T. Heames, and Wang, S. (2009), 'The indirect relationship between organizational-level knowledge worker turnover and innovation', *The Learning Organization*, **16**(2), pp. 143–67.

108 Hughes, H. (2000) *Arts, Entertainment and Tourism*, Oxford: Butterworth-Heinemann.

109 Bratton, J., Helms Mills, J. and Sawchuk, P. (2003) *Workplace Learning: A Critical Introduction*, Toronto: Garamond.

110 Dougherty, D. (1999) 'Organizing for innovation', in S. Clegg, C. Hardy and W. Nord (eds), *Managing Organizations: Current Issues*, Thousand Oaks, CA: Sage.

111 Tushman, M. and Nadler, D. (1996) 'Organizing for innovation', pp. 135–55 in K. Starkey (ed.), *How Organizations Learn*, London: International Thomson.

112 Galbraith, J. R. (1996) 'Designing the innovative organization', pp. 156–81 in K. Starkey (ed.), *How Organizations Learn*, London: International Thomson Business Press.

113 Bratton, J. A. and Garrett-Petts, W. (2008) 'Art in the workplace: innovation and culture-based economic development in small cities', pp. 85–98 in D. W. Livingstone, K. Mirchandani and P. Sawchuk (eds), *The Future of Lifelong Learning and Work*, Rotterdam: Sense Publishing.

114 Amabile, T. M. (1996) *Creativity in Context*, Boulder, CO: Westview Press.

115 Shalley, C. E., Ehou, J. and Oldham, G. R. (2004) The effects of personal and contextual characteristics on creativity: where should we go from here?', *Journal of Management*, **30**(6), pp. 933–58.

116 Weber, M. (1905/2002) *The Protestant Ethic and the 'Spirit' of Capitalism*, London: Penguin.

117 Bratton, J., Grint, K. and Nelson, D. (2005) *Organizational Leadership*, Mason, OH: Thomson-South-Western.

118 Rasminsky, L. (2001) 'Hire an artist, it's good for business', *Globe and Mail*, July 14, p. A13.

119 Bratton, J. and Gold, J. (2003) *Human Resource Management: Theory and Practice* (3rd edn), Basingstoke: Palgrave.

120 Bamber, D. and Castka, P. (2006) 'Personality, organizational orientations and self-reported learning outcomes', *Journal of Workplace Learning*, **18**(1&2), pp. 73–92.

121 Fuller, A. and Unwin, L. (1998) 'Reconceptualising apprenticeship: exploring the relationship between work and learning', *Journal of Vocational Education and Training*, **50**(2), pp. 153–71.

chapter 7
Motivation at work

chapter outline

- Introduction
- The nature of work motivation
- Content theories of motivation: workers with needs
- Process theories of motivation: workers with choices
- The sociological analysis of motivation: alienation, culture and self
- Integrating the approaches
- Applying motivation theories
- Summary and end-of-chapter features
- Chapter case study 1 : Equity at FindIT
- Chapter case study 2: Motivation at Norsk Petroleum

chapter objectives

After completing this chapter, you should be able to:

- define motivation and explain how motivation reflects the exchange embodied in the employment relationship
- compare and contrast needs-based theories of motivation at work
- describe the expectancy and equity theories of motivation
- discuss the managerial implications of process-based motivation theories
- understand the complexity of motivation at work through sociological insights, including alienation, culture and self-identity

Introduction

As you interact with other people,
travelling on buses and trains, entering offices,
banks, hospitals, schools, daycare facilities, shops or
university lecture theatres, you might observe that in any
group of workers who are performing identical jobs, some do
the work better than others. What is it that causes some people to
exert much more effort than others in what they do in the workplace?

motivation: the forces within a person that affect his or her direction, intensity and persistence of voluntary behaviour

organizational commitment: the employee's emotional attachment to, identification with and involvement in a particular organization

The observed differences in effect among people doing identical work reflect differences in individual knowledge, skills and abilities, or can reflect differences in the extent to which individuals are prepared to direct their energies. Work-related effort is thus contingent upon two different kinds of variable: the ability and skill of the individual, and his or her motivation to make use of personal endowments in the performance of paid work within a given social context.[1]

The issue of motivating workers underscores the nature of the employment relationship. At its most basic, the employment contract represents the exchange of effort or knowledge for pay. This effort–pay contract is, however, typically indeterminate: whereas the contract specifies pay, benefits, hours to be worked and so on, a workers' capacity to work – in Marxist terminology, his or her labour power – is indefinable with regard to the amount of effort and commitment the employee will apply to the job. The contract implies that workers are 'free' to decide whether to accept the pay on offer, free to internalize about their work situation and develop positive or negative attitudes toward their employment, and free to seek employment elsewhere.[2] In other words, employees have, as Peter Drucker once wrote, 'control over whether they work, how much and how well' (ref. 3, p. 14).

The indeterminate nature of the typical employment contract makes motivation (working harder) a running theme of management. Managers find themselves in positions of subordination as well as superordination, and, as a result, they themselves also have to be motivated in order to be able to motivate others. Top managers are often mystified on a daily basis by what motivates middle managers and what motivates male and female knowledge workers; in turn, middle managers are frequently mystified by what motivates male and female front-line employees.

Why do highly paid managers and knowledge workers resign or not perform as expected? Why do low-paid manual and front-line non-manual workers baulk at resigning even when they receive better job offers? For both managers and some organizational behaviour theorists, the task of discovering what motivates different categories of employee in different work settings is of the same magnitude as finding the Holy Grail.

The mainstream theories of work motivation that emerged during the last century as part of the hoped-for movement to employee commitment and enhanced effort focus on what are called *content theories of motivation* and *process theories of motivation*. Critical theories of motivation are more attentive to the contradictory nature of capitalist employment relations, to power relations, to the meanings men and women attach to paid work and to the ways through which management practices are expressed and reproduced.[4–8] As a result, they tend to emphasize the need for a societal analysis of work motivation. This chapter therefore has two broad aims. The first is to examine the mainstream theories of motivation, the second to provide a more holistic understanding of work motivation by expanding beyond notions of individual needs and cognitive processes to incorporate an awareness of the effects of complex interconnecting levels of domination stemming from class, gender and race relations in society.

> Before reading on, you may wish to ask yourself what motivates *you*. In doing your current or planned paid work, are you motivated primarily by money, or by something else? Go to our website and click on the 'Motivation questionnaire'. Alternatively, go to the website www.myskillsprofile.com/tests.php?test=20 and complete the questionnaire – it should take you about 20 minutes. Consider your response to the questions in the context of your current employment or previous work experience, and of what you have read in this book so far
>
> **stop reflect**

The nature of work motivation

After the Second World War, Western economies invested in education, and people experienced relatively full employment. In this social context, workers' fear of unemployment was no longer an individual or a collective motivation for work performance. If workers became dissatisfied with the effort levels expected by managers, or with another aspect of the job, they could find alternative employment relatively effortlessly. As management guru Peter Drucker wrote, 'fear no longer supplies the motivation for the worker in industrial society' (ref. 3, p. 303). This post-Second World War phenomenon led to an interest in the question, 'What motivates workers to perform effectively?' 'Effectively' meant closing the gap between the workers' potential to work and their willingness to maximize their effort towards the attainment of work objectives.

The indeterminacy of the employment contract is interpreted by both managers and pro-management theorists as the problem of motivation. Management concern with discovering the motivation elixir is a direct response to the constant pressure on management to employ people even more efficiently, thoroughly and rationally.[9] Most of the scholarship is primarily *normative*, directed at providing prescriptions for motivating workers. It tends to emphasize what it is that managers *should* do to ensure that subordinates close the gap between potential and actual performance.

The word 'motivation' comes from the Latin *movere*, 'to move', and work psychologists have traditionally focused on identifying factors that move workers towards accomplishing organizational **goals**. Motivation from a psychological perspective may be defined as a cognitive decision-making process that influences the effort, persistence and direction of voluntary goal-directed behaviour.

goals: the immediate or ultimate objectives that employees are trying to accomplish from their work effort

The first element in this definition is '*effort*', which is a measure of intensity that maximizes workers' potential capacity to work in a way that is appropriate to the job. The second characteristic of motivation is '*persistence*', which refers to the application of effort to work-related tasks that employees display over a time period. The third characteristic of motivation is '*direction*', which emphasizes that persistent high levels of work-related effort should be channelled in a way that benefits the organization. Whereas effort and persistence refer to the *quantity* of paid manual or knowledge work, direction refers to *quality* of work done.

Intrinsic versus extrinsic motivation

intrinsic motivator: a wide range of motivation interventions in the workplace, from inner satisfaction from following some action (such as recognition by an employer or co-workers) to intrinsic pleasures derived from an activity (such as playing a musical instrument for pleasure)

extrinsic motivator: a wide range of external outcomes or rewards to motivate employees, including bonuses or increases in pay

Theorists distinguish between **intrinsic** (inside) and **extrinsic** (outside) motivators. An intrinsic motivator stems from a person's 'internal' desire to do something, and is therefore usually self-applied. Outside the workplace, avid participation in hobbies or sports is typically intrinsically motivated. For example, we may be willing to exert a considerable amount of effort over many months with the aim of climbing a mountain, without any thought of financial reward, because we expect it to provide personal satisfaction: that is, we are intrinsically motivated. In the workplace, pure interest in a project, or a sense of professional accomplishment or positive recognition from our peers, is an example of intrinsic motivators. 'No single phenomenon,' Ryan and Deci argue, 'reflects the positive potential of human nature as much as intrinsic motivation.'[10] Intrinsically motivated people tend to seek out new challenges and explore new ways of doing things and learning. Extrinsic motivators, on the other hand, stem from outside the individual, and are generally applied by others higher in the organization's hierarchy. Extrinsic motivators include such tangible rewards as pay, bonuses and promotion (Figure 7.1).

Visit the following websites: www. higbee-schaffler.co.nz/Portals/0/ Documents/TOGETHERNESS%20IN%20 PERFORMANCE.pdf for information on team-based rewards; www.berr.gov.uk for data on profit-related pay in Britain (search '2004 employee relations survey') – this site gives a summary of the UK 2004 survey, including a section on work teams; and www.inc.com/guides/hr/20678. html for information on the role of stock options in motivating employees

weblink

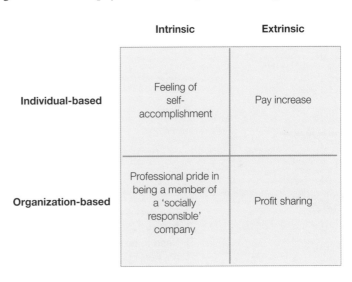

figure 7.1 Examples of intrinsic and extrinsic motivators

We should be aware that there is disagreement on these definitions and the relationship between intrinsic and extrinsic motivators, and even more disagreement on whether organizations can categorize all work motivators as precisely as these definitions suggest. For example, an employee might receive a promotion that also results in more interesting and satisfying work and additional pay. Thus, some potential motivators have both intrinsic and extrinsic qualities.[11] It should also be apparent from these examples that intrinsic and extrinsic motivators are strongly influenced by the values, ways of thinking, behaviours and social factors typical of a society. North American and European theories of motivation are embedded in management practices, as such practices offer the means to render workers and their behaviour predictable and measurable.[12]

Motivation theories attempt to explain how employee behaviour is initiated and shaped, as well as the different factors that contribute to directing and sustaining that goal-directed behaviour. Models show the variables believed to be important, but remember that these are a simplification of the phenomenon. Bearing in mind this caveat, there is no shortage of theorizing and modelling. Students of management should know that there are no quick solutions for releasing the motivation genie. Next we focus on theories that have been categorized in the literature as *content* and *process* theories of work motivation.

Content theories of motivation: workers with needs

needs: deficiencies that energize or trigger behaviours to satisfy those needs

Content theories of motivation assume that all workers possess a common set of basic 'needs'. Five of the better-known need theories are (1) Maslow's hierarchy of needs, (2) McGregor's Theory X and Theory Y, (3) McClelland's 'three learned needs' theory, (4) Alderfer's ERG theory, and (5) Herzberg's 'two-factor' need theory.[13-16]

Maslow's hierarchy of needs

In what is probably the most well known of the content theories, psychologist Abraham Maslow proposed that people have a built-in set of five basic needs, which can be arranged in a hierarchy as shown in Figure 7.2.

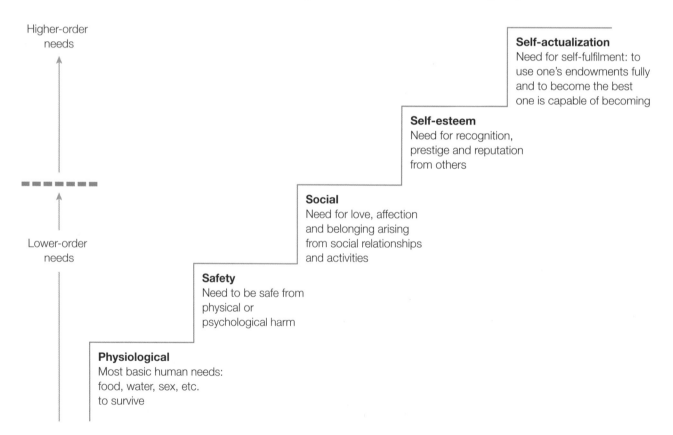

figure 7.2 Maslow's hierarchy of needs

needs hierarchy theory: Maslow's motivation theory of five instinctive needs arranged in a hierarchy, whereby people are motivated to fulfil a higher need as a lower one becomes gratified

The so-called lower-level needs in the **needs hierarchy** (the physiological and safety needs) are at first predominant: people's behaviour is directed towards satisfying these needs until they are met, at which point the next higher-order need comes to dominate, and so on. For example, only once an individual's physiological needs for the basic necessities of life – food, water and shelter – are satisfied will that individual focus on the next higher need. Once lower-order needs are addressed, the theory assumes that people direct their behaviours towards satisfying their needs for companionship, love and positive social regard by other people. The progression ultimately leads to behavioural change motivated principally by people's need to realize their full potential, which Maslow termed the **self-actualization** need.

According to Maslow, the self-actualization need, which involves people directing their behaviour towards work learning opportunities, is the ultimate motivator, because unlike the other needs it is insatiable. The second key aspect of Maslow's theory is that a satisfied or satiated need is not a motivator of behaviour. Once a person satisfies a need at one level in the hierarchy, the need ceases to motivate him or her. Only the need at the next level up the hierarchy will motivate the person and influence her or his behaviour.

Although it was not originally intended as an explanation of employee motivation, Maslow's needs hierarchy theory has been influential in mainstream management texts. It was seen as offering predictions about what directs behaviour in different contexts. In a context of relatively high unemployment, when jobs are relatively scarce and people do not automatically feel secure about meeting their basic needs, workers are motivated strongly by the need to satisfy their lower-level needs. In contrast, in a context of relatively full employment, when lower-order needs are more easily satisfied, social, self-esteem and self-actualization needs become important motivators in the workplace.

One implication of Maslow's theory is that, if workers are to continue to be motivated once their social needs have been satisfied, managers have to find ways to offer them self-actualization, which implies a focus on the intrinsic aspects of paid work. This might mean reconfiguring work structures and processes to challenge both manual and knowledge workers, and offer them a degree of autonomy. To apply Maslow's theory to the current management practices of organizational re-engineering and outsourcing, it might be feasible to motivate part-time or other 'peripheral' workers by appealing to their lower-order needs, while knowledge-based 'core' workers are motivated by satisfying their higher-order needs. The prescription offered by Maslow's theory is that managers need to know where their employees are located on the needs hierarchy, and ensure that their lower-order needs are satisfied before appealing to their higher-order needs.

Source: iStockphoto

plate 25 Will a person really focus on satisfying physiological needs before safety needs? Is this construction worker likely to stop to eat or drink before making sure the swinging girder is secured?

Maslow's needs hierarchy appears to offer common-sense advice to managers, but how valid is this theory of work motivation? One of the major problems with Maslow's theory is that it is extremely difficult to identify which need is predominant at any given time. Without this information, managers cannot confidently redesign the workplace or emphasize work-based learning to appeal to their employees' self-esteem or self-actualization needs, for instance, as these might not in reality be their main motivators.

To take a simple example, is it really true that a person will focus on satisfying physiological needs such as hunger and thirst before he or she attends to matters that threaten his or her security or safety? Does a construction worker have a bite to eat before checking that the scaffolding she is standing on is safe?

The significance of Maslow's work, it is suggested, might lie in its rhetorical value. Tony Watson, for example, offers a scathing critique of Maslow's theory, arguing that it has little scientific validity and that its main role has been as 'a propaganda device: propaganda in a good and humanistic cause, but propaganda nonetheless' (ref. 17, p. 110). Maslow's theory is still worth reviewing, however, because of its influence on the subsequent alternative motivation theories developed by Douglas McGregor, David McClelland and Clayton Alderfer.

McGregor's Theory X and Theory Y

Whereas Maslow focused on defining a hierarchy of needs that influence work-related behaviour, Douglas McGregor, a human psychologist, drew heavily from Maslow to argue that managers need a greater understanding of and attention to employees' needs. McGregor contrasts two opposite theories of employees and management: Theory X and Theory Y. According to McGregor, managers can be classified in terms of how they believe others (and perhaps they themselves) behave towards paid work, and how managers approach the issue of work motivation is strongly influenced by their assumptions about human nature. The two extreme sets of propositions are shown in Table 7.1.

McGregor suggests that underpinning the Theory X propositions is the conventional Tayloristic belief that the average employee is indolent, lacks ambition, dislikes responsibility, is inherently self-centred and is not very bright. These basic assumptions, he suggestions, shape and become embedded in organizational structures, culture and practices. McGregor's Theory Y offers an alternative set of assumptions about the essence of human nature and work motivation.

table 7.1 McGregor's Theory X and Theory Y of motivation

Theory X	Theory Y
1. Management is responsible for organizing the elements of productive enterprise – money, materials, equipment, people – in the interest of economic ends	1. Management is responsible for organizing the elements of productive enterprise – money, materials, equipment, people – in the interest of economic ends
2. With respect to people, this is a process of directing their efforts, motivating them, controlling their actions, modifying their behaviour to fit the needs of the organization	2. People are *not* by nature passive or resistant to organizational needs. They have become so as a result of their experience in organizations
3. Without this active intervention by management, people would be passive – even resistant – to organizational needs. They must therefore be persuaded, rewarded, punished, controlled – their activities must be directed. This is management's task in managing subordinate managers or workers	3. The motivation, the potential for development, the capacity for assuming responsibility, the readiness to direct behaviour towards organizational goals are all present in people. Management does not put them there. It is a responsibility of management to make it possible for people to recognize and develop these human characteristics for themselves
	4. The essential task of management is to arrange organizational conditions and methods of operation so that people can achieve their own goals *best* by directing *their own* efforts toward organizational objectives

Source: McGregor (1957/1970/1966)[18]

The problem of motivation lies not in the subordinate, but in the beliefs and resulting behaviour of the manager. Theory Y supports Maslow's higher-level needs by advocating a clear shift towards 'self-control and self-direction', and towards allowing self-esteem and self-actualization needs to be satisfied.[19] Despite the fact that many managers publicly support Theory Y, there may be a significant gap between the rhetoric and the practice, especially during an economic downturn.

McClelland's theory of needs

According to David McClelland's learned needs theory,[15] workers are motivated by the need to satisfy six basic human needs: achievement, power, affiliation, independence, self-esteem and security. In contrast to preceding theories, McClelland argued that these needs are not inherent, but learned from national culture. Employees are said to accomplish the most when they have a high need for achievement. Employees with a strong need for achievement tend to set goals that are moderately difficult, to seek out feedback on their performance, and to be generally preoccupied with accomplishment.

Unlike Maslow, McClelland did not become preoccupied with specifying a hierarchical relationship between needs. Instead, he argued that employees differ in the extent to which they experience needs for achievement, affiliation and power. McClelland and Burnham addressed the issue of power as the 'great motivator'.[20] They argued that, in practice, managers with a need for power might be more effective motivators than those with a need for achievement. The work of Harrel and Strahl[21] suggests that assessing the strength of these learned needs can be helpful in identifying employees who will respond positively to different types of work context. The advice that follows from this alleged insight is that it might be important for managers to consider the extent to which employees possess these needs, and to design motivational strategies that permit workers to satisfy those needs which are strongest for each individual.

Alderfer's ERG theory

Clayton Alderfer's ERG theory is closely related to Maslow's work. Based upon an alternative set of assumptions, it suggests that employee needs can be divided into three basic categories: existence (E), relatedness (R) and growth (G). Existence needs include nutritional, safety and material requirements. Relatedness needs involve an individual's relationships with family and friends, and colleagues at work. Growth needs reflect a desire for personal psychological growth and development.

As can be seen in Figure 7.3, Alderfer's ERG theory is not a major departure from Maslow's theory. Unlike Maslow, however, ERG theory does not assume a progression up a hierarchy. Alderfer suggests that all three levels might be important at the same time, and he believes that it is better to think in terms of a continuum, from existence needs to growth needs, with workers moving along it in either direction. Consequently, if, for example, growth needs are not satisfied, an inner state of frustration regression occurs, causing the person to focus on fulfilling her or his relatedness needs. For example, a supervisor unable to satisfy his or her growth needs by accepting greater responsibility might respond by demanding an increase in pay, thereby satisfying his or her existence needs. Therefore, unsatisfied needs become less rather than more important. This is the opposite of what Maslow assumed.

Furthermore, ERG theory emphasizes the importance to employees of satisfied needs. Alderfer's work suggests that growth needs are actually more important when satisfied, whereas Maslow argued that, when it is fulfilled, a need becomes less important to an individual. One implication of Alderfer's work is that work designs that satisfy workers' relatedness needs can continue to motivate workers, and that these are not necessarily superseded by growth needs. If this theory is correct, it would make it easier for managers to motivate their employees.

stop reflect

Can you think of managers you have encountered who were influenced by these two sets of assumptions about your attitude to work and motives?

ERG theory: Alderfer's motivation theory of three instructive needs arranged in a hierarchy, in which people progress to the next higher need when a lower one is fulfilled, and regress to a lower need if unable to fulfil a higher one

growth needs: a person's needs for self-esteem through personal achievement, as well as for self-actualization

weblink

Go to the following websites for more information on motivation theories: http://academic.emporia.edu/smithwil/oofallmg443/eja/tuel.html; http://www.accel-team.com/motivation/index.html for details on Maslow's hierarchy of needs; and http://psychology.about.com/ for links to motivation theories

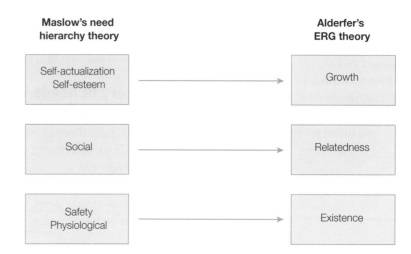

figure 7.3 Comparison of Maslow's needs hierarchy and Alderfer's ERG theory

A recent study by Arnolds and Boshoff[22] provides data to support a key hypothesis associated with Alderfer's ERG model. Unlike many conventional studies, it incorporates personality (see Chapter 4) in the motivation conundrum, and is sensitive to potential social factors affecting motivation at work. The study investigates to what extent a personality trait (self-esteem) impacts on the relationship between need satisfactions – as modelled by Alderfer – and the performance intentions of senior managers and white-collar 'front-line' employees in the banking, legal and retail sectors (Figure 7.4).

The model hypothesizes that employee need satisfaction, based upon Alderfer's theory, exerts a positive influence on self-esteem, which in turn exerts a positive influence on work behaviour in the form of job performance intentions (H). Arnolds and Boshoff argue that their data show that self-esteem significantly influences the performance intentions of senior managers, and conclude that 'top managers are primarily motivated by growth needs, in other words, higher order needs' (ref. 22, p. 712). The empirical results suggest that front-line white-collar workers are primarily motivated by the satisfaction of relatedness needs from co-workers, by existence needs and particularly by monetary reward.

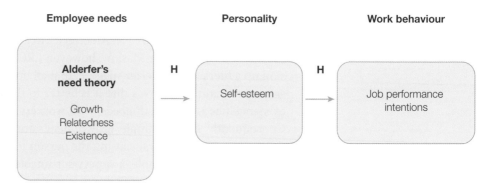

figure 7.4 Employee needs, personality and work behaviour

Source: Adapted from Arnolds and Boshoff (2002),[22] p. 702

Interestingly, and in contrast to Maslow's belief that growth needs do not motivate lower-level workers, Arnolds and Boshoff's sophisticated study suggests that higher-order needs such as growth needs can motivate front-line workers through increasing their self-esteem, 'provided that the motivation strategies directed at these higher-order needs are correctly implemented' (ref. 22, p. 713). The importance of this study is that it provides a plausible explanation, with supporting empirical data, of the relationship between needs satisfaction, an individual personality trait (self-esteem) and job performance intentions. More generally, by differentiating between different categories of employee, the analysis affirms the importance of avoiding the common tendency to generalize about managers' motivation interventions.

How helpful are Maslow's and Alderfer's theories in explaining why chief executives and car assembly workers might be predisposed to respond to different ways of motivating them to work?

stop reflect

Although Maslow's, McClelland's and Alderfer's needs theories of work motivation have been popularized in mainstream organizational behaviour texts, detractors have identified several important limitations. It is posited that these less than robust theories are conceptually flawed; they do not provide managers with a clear, unambiguous basis for predicting specific workers' behaviour to satisfy a particular need. Recent critics have also pointed out that the needs theories are strongly informed by the Anglo-American cultural paradigm of individualism – other societal cultures might have different hierarchies of needs. Finally, there is an assumption that needs motivate regardless of the age, sex or ethnicity of those involved. As a result, it can be argued that these theories are androcentric and reflect the values of a hierarchical social order.[23–25]

OB in focus   Money is the key incentive to work motivation

Most organizational behaviour theorists and behavioural scientists have consistently downplayed the importance of money as a motivator. They prefer to point out the value of challenging jobs, goals and participation in decision making to stir the motivation genie. We argue otherwise here: that money is the crucial incentive to work motivation. As a medium of exchange, it is the vehicle by which employees can purchase the numerous need-satisfying things they desire. Money also performs the function of a scorecard, by which employees assess the value that the organization places on their services and can compare their value with that of others.

For the vast majority of the workers, a regular pay cheque is absolutely necessary in order to meet their basic physiological and safety needs. Money has symbolic value in addition to its exchange value. People use pay as the primary outcome against which they compare their inputs to determine whether they are being treated equitably. In addition, expectancy theory attests to the value of money as a motivator. Specifically, if pay is contingent on performance, it will encourage workers to put in high levels of effort. Consistent with expectancy theory, money will motivate to the extent that it is seen as being able to satisfy an individual's personal goals, and reward is perceived as being dependent on performance criteria. The evidence demonstrates that money may not be the only motivator, but it is difficult to argue that it does not motivate!

Money doesn't stir the motivation genie!

There is no doubt that money can motivate some people under some conditions, so the issue is not really whether money can motivate. The more relevant question is, does money motivate most employees in the workforce today to higher performance? The answer, some organizational theorists argue, is 'No.' For money to motivate an employee's performance, certain conditions must be met. First, money must be important to the employee. Second, the employee must perceive the money as being a direct reward for performance. Third, the employee must consider the marginal amount of money offered for the performance to be significant. Finally, management must have the discretion to reward high performers with more money.

Since not all these conditions apply in all employment situations, money is not important to all employees. High achievers, for instance, are intrinsically motivated. Money should have little impact on these people. Money is relevant to those individuals with strong lower-order needs, but the lower-order needs of many employees are substantially satisfied. Money would motivate if employees perceived a strong link between performance and rewards in organizations. However, pay increases are far more often determined by levels of skills and experience, the national cost of living index, union–management pay bargaining and the firm's overall financial prospects, than by individual performance. In theory, money might be capable of motivating employees to higher levels of performance, but most managers do not have much discretion to match individual pay with individual performance levels.

Sources: K. O. Doyle (1992) 'Introduction: money and the behavioural sciences', *American Behavioural Scientist*, July, pp. 641–57; S. Caudron (1993) 'Motivation? Money's only no. 2', *Industry Week*, November 15, p. 33; B. Filipczak (1996) 'Can't buy me love', *Training*, January, pp. 29–34.

Herzberg's motivator–hygiene theory

exchange value: the price at which commodities (including labour) trade on the market

Frederick Herzberg's motivation research was designed to test the concept that a worker has two different needs: the need stemming from a human being's nature to avoid pain from the environment, and the need thought to stem from a unique

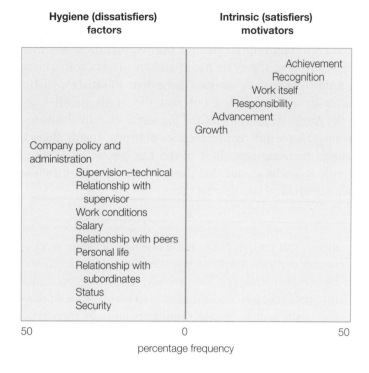

Hygiene (dissatisfiers) factors	Intrinsic (satisfiers) motivators
	Achievement
	Recognition
	Work itself
	Responsibility
	Advancement
	Growth
Company policy and administration	
Supervision–technical	
Relationship with supervisor	
Work conditions	
Salary	
Relationship with peers	
Personal life	
Relationship with subordinates	
Status	
Security	

50   0   50

percentage frequency

figure 7.5 Herzberg's motivator–hygiene model

Source: Adapted from Hertzberg (2003),[26] p. 90

characteristic to grow psychologically. Samples of workers were asked to describe events that resulted in either a significant increase or a significant decrease in their job satisfaction. After analysing the data, Herzberg found that the factors identified as sources of job satisfaction (called 'satisfiers', and later 'motivators') were different from those identified as sources of dissatisfaction (called 'dissatisfiers' or 'hygiene' factors). The strong *motivators* were achievement, recognition, work itself, responsibility and advancement. The strong *hygiene* factors causing work dissatisfaction were company policy and administration, supervision, salary, interpersonal relations and working conditions at work. Figure 7.5 summarises the major findings of his study.

Herzberg's model predicts that managers can motivate subordinates if they are aware of and incorporate 'motivators' into job design. His motivator–hygiene theory has clear parallels with other content theories of motivation. For example, Herzberg's motivators are similar to Maslow's higher-order needs and Alderfer's growth needs, and his hygiene factors resemble Maslow's lower-order needs, as well as Alderfer's existence and relatedness needs. Empirical studies on the motivator–hygiene theory have had mixed results, but are credited with stimulating research on the association between job design and performance, including the later work of Hackman and Oldham (see Chapter 9).

Process theories of motivation: workers with choices

Process theories of motivation focus on how employees make conscious choices that lead to a specific work behaviour; they emphasize the role of an individual's cognitive processes in determining her or his level of work motivation. Organizational leaders using process theories to motivate employees do so by clarifying the link between effort and reward. The three process theories of work motivation examined here are equity theory, expectancy theory and goal-setting theory.

Equity theory

equity theory: the theory that explains how people develop perceptions of fairness in the distribution and exchange of resources

Equity theory is one of the most influential process theories and is best known through a series of studies by J. Stacey Adams, and his colleagues (1963). Its basic premise is that there is one important cognitive process that involves employees comparing what effort other employees are putting into their work and what rewards they receive, with their own experience. This 'social comparison' process results in feelings of equity or inequity, and leads employees to form judgements on the value or 'valence' of a reward or outcome. According to equity theory, employees perceive effort and reward not in absolute but in relative terms, in the form of a ratio:[27]

$$\frac{\text{Outcome (self)}}{\text{Inputs (self)}} : \frac{\text{Outcome (other)}}{\text{Inputs (other)}}$$

When employees perceive others receiving a similar ratio of inputs (such as hours worked, time studying for qualifications and relevant work experience) to outcomes (such as pay, status and promotion) as they receive themselves, they experience equity. When workers perceive an input–outcome ratio that favours other workers in the organization (underpayment) or relevant others (such as workers in a similar company) or themselves (overpayment), they experience inequity, which is assumed to be a sufficiently unpleasant experience to motivate changes in behaviour (Figure 7.6).

	Self	**Other**
Equity	Outcomes (100) Inputs (100)	Outcomes (100) Inputs (100)
Inequity (under-rewarded)	Outcomes (100) Inputs (100)	Outcomes (150) Inputs (100)
Inequity (over-rewarded)	Outcomes (150) Inputs (100)	Outcomes (100) Inputs (100)

figure 7.6 Adams's conditions of equity and inequity

One practical application of equity theory is in the area of *reward management*. Managers must be careful to avoid setting pay rates that cause employees to feel underpaid relative to others either in the same workplace (internal equity) or in comparison groups outside the organization (external inequity). It should be noted that the reward system is part of a diverse range of interlocking control techniques that contain internal tensions and inconsistencies. For instance, a performance-related reward system might become discredited in the eyes of employees because of perceived 'procedural injustices' caused by subjective and inconsistent appraisals by managers who did not have the skills needed to judge performance fairly. As a result, the employees would experience internal inequity, and instead of the reward system motivating them, their commitment would be weakened.[28] The nature of the internal inequity can generate negative feelings such as anger, which results in reduced employee commitment or even in acts of sabotage in the workplace. Collectively, if the perception of external inequity is strong and is shared by a sufficient number of workers, unionization and strike action can occur. Most recent studies are most conclusive about perceived negative inequity and 'relative deprivation' in conditions of underpayment.[29]

In this context, a classic study by Baldamus of the 'wage–effort exchange'[30] is still relevant to understanding conflict behaviour in the workplace, because it links the notion of external inequity to inherent tensions and workplace conflict. A fuller understanding of this relationship between effort levels or inputs, and rewards or outcomes, is provided by the expectancy theory of motivation.

Expectancy theory

The role of the employee's perception of the link between levels of effort or performance and desirable reward is further reinforced in the **expectancy theory** of work motivation. The theory assumes a rational model of decision making whereby employees assess the costs and benefits of alternative courses of inputs and outcomes, and choose the course with the highest reward.

expectancy theory: a motivation theory based on the idea that work effort is directed toward behaviours that people believe will lead to desired outcomes

The first formulations of expectancy theory are found in the work of Kurt Lewin in 1935. The theory was popularized, however, by the work of Vroom, and further developed by Porter and Lawler.[31–34] Psychologist Victor Vroom proposed that work motivation is contingent upon the perception of a link between levels of effort and reward. Perceiving this link is a cognitive process in which employees assess:

- whether there is a connection between effort and their performance, labelled *expectancy*
- the perceived probability that the performance (such as higher productivity) will lead to those valued outcomes (such as higher pay), which is labelled *instrumentality*
- the expected net value of the outcomes that flow from the effort, labelled *valence*.

Expectancy theory, therefore, has three basic parts:

1. the **effort–performance expectancy** ($E{\rightarrow}P$)
2. the **performance–outcome expectancy** ($P{\rightarrow}O$)
3. the attractiveness or valence of the outcomes (V).

According to expectancy theory, work motivation can be calculated if the expectancy, instrumentality and valence values are known. The formula for the calculation is:

$$\text{Effort} = E \, \Sigma \, I \times V$$

where *effort* is the motivation of the employee to exert effort in her or his paid work, E is expectancy, I is the instrumentality of job performance, and V is the valence of an outcome(s). The Σ (capital sigma: the summation sign) indicates that effort is affected by a range of possible work and non-work outcomes that might result from job performance.

Expectancies are probabilities, ranging from 0 to 1, that effort will result in performance. An expectancy of 0.5 means that the person perceives only a 50 per cent probability of increased effort leading to increased performance. **Instrumentalities** can range from –1 to +1. An instrumentality of +1 means that performance is certain to lead to the desired outcome. For example, an insurance agent selling a home insurance policy is certain to receive a commission. The instrumentality between the two events is therefore +1. **Valence** is defined to vary between +10 and –10. A large anticipated satisfaction (high positive valence) and large anticipated dissatisfaction (high negative valence) will, when multiplied by associated instrumentalities and performance expectancy, have a large effect on work motivation.

As an example of the operation of expectancy theory, consider an employee – let's call him Joe – who perceives important work-related outcomes to be an increase in pay, promotion, longer vacation time and job-related stress. Figure 7.7 shows his expectancy theory calculations.

effort-to-performance ($E{\rightarrow}P$) expectancy: the individual's perceived probability that his or her effort will result in a particular level of performance

performance-to-outcome ($P{\rightarrow}O$) expectancy: the perceived probability that a specific behaviour or performance level will lead to specific outcomes

instrumentality: a term associated with process theories of motivation, referring to an individual's perceived probability that good performance will result in valued outcomes or rewards, measured on a scale from 0 (no chance) to 1 (certainty)

valence: the anticipated satisfaction or dissatisfaction that an individual feels toward an outcome

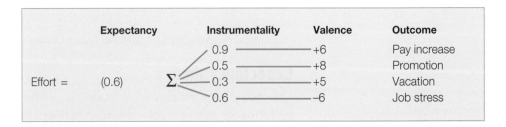

figure 7.7 Sample expectancy theory calculations

Joe has ranked four outcomes on a +10 to −10 scale, and has estimated the probability of increased effort producing each of these outcomes. He sees both positive and negative expected outcomes from increased job effort. He reckons there is only a 60 per cent chance that any increased effort on his part will lead to increased performance.

The motivational force of the job – the effort the individual is willing to expend on it – is calculated by multiplying the expectancy value (0.6) by the products of the instrumentality and valence estimates. Thus:

$$\text{Effort} = (0.6) \times [(0.9)\,(+6) + (0.5)\,(+8) + (0.3)\,(+5) + (0.6)\,(-6)] = 4.38$$

Summing the expectancy theory variables, the overall motivation to exert increased job effort is positive. Therefore, for Joe in this case, the rewards of putting in increased effort outweigh the costs.

To use expectancy theory in an attempt to increase job effort by each employee, a manager can focus on each element of the theory. For example, a manager can aim to increase the employee's perception that her or his expenditure of effort will result in completing the task successfully. The effort–performance expectancy (E→P) for Joe could increase from 60 per cent to 80 per cent, perhaps through additional training. In addition, a manager can help the employee to re-evaluate the performance–outcome expectancy (P→O). For example, the chances of promotion might be higher than is anticipated by the employee. To go back to the example of Joe, his manager might use the experiences of other employees to persuade him to increase his estimated probability of promotion if he does the job successfully from 50 per cent to 90 per cent.

Finally, a manager can attempt to increase the attractiveness of the outcome, the valence (V). Thus, in our example, Joe could perhaps be persuaded that the outcomes from exerting additional effort (a pay increase, a promotion, a longer vacation) would be more important or have more value to him than he had previously thought.

A development of the expectancy theory of work behaviour is to be found in research by Porter and Lawler.[33–35] In their models, the determinants of each element are incorporated to provide a more comprehensive explanation of both the *what* and the *how* of the work motivation process. The effort–performance expectancy is, for example, moderated by past experiences of similar situations and communications from other people. The assumption here is that what employees learn from past experiences contributes significantly to their effort–performance expectancies. If employees have had a series of past successes at similar work tasks, they will have a strengthened belief in their ability to perform those tasks, and to that extent their effort–performance expectancies will be high. The informal learning – learning that is embedded in work activities – need not be only from personal past experiences. Employees can and do learn from their observations of relevant others in similar situations, and from others communicating their past experiences to their peers. If I see Sally, for instance, succeed at a work task, and she has qualifications and work experience similar to mine, I am more likely to calculate that I too will succeed at that task. This informal learning operates at individual and group level, as well as in the opposite direction.

The performance–outcome expectancy link is contingent upon past experiences, communications from others and the attractiveness of the outcomes. The past experiences determinant refers to the experience in relation to outcomes. Suppose, for example, that a manager introduces a reward system that is performance based, and that her appraisal ratings of her staff are known to be arbitrary. With knowledge of this past experience, it is unlikely that her subordinates will believe that the

Work and Society: Finding 'flow' at work

Motivation can be defined as a willingness to expend effort on a particular activity or task. Defined in this way, its importance to the study of organizational behaviour is obvious. Managers want to know what makes employees work hard, and the study of motivation promises to answer this question.

What makes the study of motivation challenging is the fact that prevailing views of motivation have changed dramatically over the last two decades. Following the Second World War, the study of motivation was dominated by behaviourist models. Many readers will be familiar with the behaviourist view that human behaviour is motivated by 'reinforcement contingencies'. Behaviourists maintain that people will expend effort on an activity if they believe they will be rewarded for that effort.

The behaviourist view of motivation has been challenged by new perspectives. One of the most influential of these devotes attention to the emotions and thought processes of individuals engaged in activities of various kinds. Researchers have discovered that, under certain conditions, individuals involved in activities reported experiencing intense feelings of satisfaction and enjoyment. These individuals expended high levels of effort when appropriate, but they were not motivated by the anticipation of a future reward. Their motivation appeared to spring from another source: they were experiencing what has been called 'intrinsic' (as distinct from 'extrinsic') motivation. For these individuals, the act of doing something produced a positive experience that was rewarding in itself.

Pioneering research in this area was conducted by psychologist Mihaly Csikszentmihalyi, who used the word 'flow' to describe the positive experiences of persons fully immersed in the pleasure of various activities. What were the characteristics of the activities typically associated with flow experiences? Crucial to these experiences is the relationship between the challenge associated with a particular activity and the skill a person brings to the activity. In the ideal situation, there is a 'balance between high levels of challenge and high levels of skill' (Csikszentmihalyi and Schneider, 2000, p. 97). Csikszentmihalyi elaborates:

> Enjoyable experiences are usually described as having a cluster of related subjective dimensions. [In addition to a balance] of challenges and skills, enjoyable experiences provide clarity of goals: knowing what must be done from one moment to the next. Another dimension is immediacy of feedback: a person always knows how well he or she is doing. For instance, if a young boy enjoys fixing a bicycle, it is likely that he will say he knows exactly what he has to do – the chain must be tightened just so – and that he can

> test as he goes along whether the chain is working as it should. (Csikszentmihalyi and Schneider, p. 97)

This example has much to tell us about motivation. No doubt the boy fixing the bicycle may be motivated by an anticipated future reward: the opportunity to ride a bicycle with a properly functioning chain. But the fact that he gives the task his full attention, and is willing to expend whatever effort is required, does not depend primarily on this future reward. Because the task carries within it its own reward, the boy is fully engaged in his 'work' and yet is hardly aware of the effort he is expending.

Much of Csikszentmihalyi's work is relevant to a new model of motivation, a model that takes intrinsic motivation as its central idea. This new model of motivation is fascinating, and its implications for work design seem profound. But it is difficult to extract specific lessons for managers. We might begin by asking why, in the contemporary workplace, do so few employees report flow-like experiences? The reasons for this are complex. Some might argue that behaviourist models of human motivation are themselves to blame. Guided by the principles of the behaviourist model, managers have sought to motivate workers using a range of rewards external to the work process.

But the causes for the transformation of work lie deeper. Macrosociologists Chris and Charles Tilly suggest that over the last 300 years there has been a trend towards increased 'time-discipline' in the world of work, defining time-discipline as 'the extent to which other persons decide the disposition of a worker's effort within the working day' (1998, p. 30). It could be argued that as time-discipline increases opportunities for flow-like experiences decrease.

stop! Is this a valid argument in your view? How do employers justify the need for increased time-discipline? In what ways might the idea of flow lead employers to rethink their emphasis on time-discipline?

Sources and further information

Bakker, A. and Schaufeli W. (2008) 'Positive organizational behavior: engaged employees in flourishing organizations', *Journal of Organizational Behavior*, **29**, pp. 147–54.

Csikszentmihalyi, M. (2008) *Flow: The Psychology of Optimal Experience*, New York: Harper Perennial.

Csikszentmihalyi, M. and Schneider, B. (2000) *Becoming Adult: How Teenagers Prepare for the World of Work*, New York: Basic Books.

Tilly, C. and Tilly C. (1998) *Work Under Capitalism*, Boulder, CO: Westview Press.

Note: This feature was written by David MacLennan, Assistant Professor at Thompson Rivers University, BC, Canada.

plate 26 Expectancy theory can be used to better understand student motivation. It would predict that studying for an examination (effort) is conditioned by its resulting in answering questions in exams correctly.

Source: Getty Images

reward system will be truly performance based in practice. The past experience will influence employees' performance–outcome expectancies for the system. This assessment is, however, considerably affected by another determinant – communications from others – which represents an array of social interactions between employees, and between the supervised (employees) and their supervisors (managers), on a variety of outcomes, both positive and negative.

The valence of the outcomes (V) is moderated by the perceived *instrumentality* of the outcome to satisfy needs, and the perceived fairness or equity of the outcome. An outcome that is instrumental in satisfying an important need would have greater valence. Which outcome will an employee use to satisfy which need? Expectancy theorists suggest that it depends on the way the person has been socialized. Research suggests that, for Anglo-American employees at least, pay is most instrumental for satisfying physiological, security and ego-status needs, and not at all instrumental in satisfying social and self-actualization needs.[35]

The findings also explain why pay is important to both low-paid and high-paid employees. To the former, pay is instrumental in satisfying their physiological needs; to the latter, a high monthly pay cheque is instrumental in satisfying their ego-status needs.[36] The value of the outcome is also determined by the perceived equity of the reward. As we discussed earlier, employees compare their own input–reward ratio with the input–reward ratio of relevant others. If the two ratios are perceived to be equal, equity exists and the reward's valence increases. Thus, the valence of an outcome is affected by employees' perception of its equity, considering their overall effort level relative to the effort level and reward of their co-workers.

By recognizing the importance of informal workplace learning and social comparisons, the Lawler model provides an insightful refinement of expectancy theory. The model enables managers to better understand the complexity of managing people, and in particular, how the elements of work motivation relate to one another in the motivation process.

Goal-setting theory

The theory of **goal setting** assumes that participatory goal setting and communicating accurate information on work performance can be positive motivators for employees. One version of this theory of motivation contains four major assumptions:

1. *Challenging* goals will produce higher performance than less challenging goals.
2. *Specific* challenging goals will produce higher performance than no goals or vague or general goals, such as 'do your best'.

Based on your understanding of process theories, why are some managers more effective at motivating people than others?

stop reflect

goal setting: the process of motivating employees and clarifying their **role perceptions** by establishing performance objectives

role perceptions: a person's beliefs about what behaviours are appropriate or necessary in a particular situation, including the specific tasks that make up the job, their relative importance, and the preferred behaviours to accomplish those tasks

management by objectives: a participative goal-setting process in which organizational objectives are cascaded down to work units and individual employees

3. Goal setting with *feedback* on goal attainment will produce higher performances than goal setting alone.
4. *Employee participation* in goal setting will produce higher performances than no participation.[37]

Research conducted in several countries over the years has been consistent in demonstrating that goal-setting techniques do have a positive influence on work motivation.[38,39] The management technique of management by objectives is one of the best-known applications of goal-setting theory, and has been extensively used by Anglo-American management. Under management by objectives, a manager sets specific and challenging goals for a specified time period, periodically reviews progress towards goals that have previously been set, and provides feedback on goal accomplishment before setting goals for the next performance time period. In non-unionized workplaces, management by objectives also provides a mechanism for the appraisal of employee performance pay awards.

Go to the following websites for more information on management by objectives: www.1000ventures. com/business_guide/ mgmt_mbo_main.html; www.managepro.com/ MBOtoPM.html

weblink

The sociological analysis of motivation: alienation, culture and self-identity

Sociologists have developed a very different approach to understanding motivation in the workplace. Using concepts such as alienation, culture, orientation to work and the 'self', they challenge the adequacy of mainstream psychological theories of work motivation. Sociological theories remind us of the complex connection between the patterns of people's lives shaped by the societal configuration of class, gender and race that lie outside the workplace environment, and the pattern of social relations with others inside the work organization. This analysis of motivation also incorporates what critical theorists call 'antagonisms' or 'contradictions' inherent in capitalist employment relations.

Alienation

The problem of alienation as a condition of capitalist modernity is found in many novels. Witness Dr Robyn Penrose, a central character in David Lodge's novel *Nice Work*, set in the early 1980s, condemning the mindless, repetitive work and brutalizing conditions in Vic Wilcox's factory. As we discussed in Chapter 3, the concept of alienation was developed by Karl Marx. For most sociologists today, alienation is seen as residing in the social structure of paid work rather than in personality traits. In other words, its causes are rooted in capitalist employment relations, and are *social* rather than psychological.[40,41]

What do you think of this explanation of work motivation? To what extent, if at all, can work be designed to reduce alienation in the workplace?

stop reflect

When we refer to alienation in this book, we mean a phenomenon in which people have little or no control over the products or services they produce or offer, the organization of work, and the immediate work process itself. As James Rinehart writes:

alienation is objective or structural in the sense that it is built into human relationships at the workplace and exists independent of how individuals perceive and evaluate this condition. Alienations can be viewed broadly as a condition of objective powerlessness. (ref. 41, p. 14)

Much of the psychology-based research on work motivation appears entirely indifferent to, possibly even ignorant of, the concept of alienation.[9] For sociologists, a major source of alienated labour is division of labour or specialization (see Chapter 2). Critical analysts have argued that workers are alienated because the nature of the work progressively wears away their self-esteem, and consequently their commitment to work and the organization.[41] Consistent with need and expectancy theories of motivation, alienating work obstructs higher-level needs and valent outcomes (instrumentalities), causing low commitment and low work motivation.

Critical insight

Few of the early content theories of motivation acknowledge personality, class, gender, race or age as factors influencing work motivation. Few of the popular theories provide empirical data to substantiate their claims. Arnolds and Boshoff state that the impact of personality traits was ignored in earlier studies of motivation, and acknowledge the need to include variables such as age, gender, cultural background and so on in motivation models.

Obtain a copy of Arnolds and Boshoff's article, 'Compensation, esteem valence and job performance: an empirical assessment of Alderfer's ERG theory'.[22] What are the strengths of this approach to investigating work motivation? Look back at research strategies in Chapter 1. What would be the advantages and disadvantages of gathering qualitative data from top managers and front-line employees on their views on what motivates them?

Culture

The concept of culture refers to the tangible and intangible aspects of human society including material objects, technology, language, beliefs and values that are shared and learned, rather than inherited, from person to person and from one generation to the next. How does culture determine work motivation? A national culture can shape individual work values and patterns of behaviour in the workplace. The study of organizational culture, which draws upon concepts from sociology, examines the connections between both tangible and intangible aspects of the organization and behaviour in the workplace. We look at organizational culture in more detail in Chapter 12, but here we can emphasize that it can act as a form of managerial control, prescribing and prohibiting certain activities to shape and reshape worker behaviour in a way that is consistent with top management's expectations.[42,43] A perceptual analysis, however, should remind us that a 'strong' culture that motivates one employee will not necessarily motivate another employee.[44]

Work orientation

work orientation: an attitude towards work that constitutes a broad disposition towards certain kinds of paid work

Work orientation refers to the meaning that individuals give to paid work and the relative importance they assign to work within their lives as a whole. This perspective to understanding workplace behaviour encourages a greater awareness of the connections between work attitudes, values and behaviour patterns, and the structure and culture of society. As mentioned above, people's working and non-working lives are shaped by the societal configuration of class, gender and race that lies outside the workplace, as well as the behaviour of managers and non-managers inside the organization. Interest in individual differences to work orientation has led some researchers to investigate the connection between work motivation and social factors. These social factors include, but are not limited to, class, gender and race.[45]

A classic British study[46] focused on the relationship between work orientation and social class. The researchers argued that if individuals enter an impoverished work situation in the full knowledge that intrinsic rewards are not available, their work motivation is not likely to be significantly influenced by the absence of such rewards. In essence, they suggested that, for a majority of workers in their study, extrinsic rewards – such as pay or what they called the 'cash nexus' – were much more important than intrinsic rewards. The majority of workers, they explained, had decided 'to give more weight to the instrumental at the expense of the expressive aspects of work' (ref. 46, p. 33).

Source: iStockphoto

Source: iStockphoto

plate 27 The task of discovering what motivates different categories of employee in different work settings is of the same magnitude as finding the Holy Grail. For example, what factors motivate each of these men at work?

Numerous studies have investigated possible gender-related differences of work orientation, and the determinants of work satisfaction.[23,47–50] Testing the hypothesis that men and women have different expectations from paid work, results show that although women are more likely to enter an impoverished work situation than men, they have lower expectations and hence are as satisfied with their paid employment as men are. When men and women in management positions are compared, it has been found that both have very similar orientations to work.[47] One possible explanation for gender-related work orientation is differences in sex-role socialization. In support of this argument, there is well-documented evidence that women are socialized to pursue occupations reflecting their stereotyped sex-roles, regardless of individual abilities and talent. Studies affirm that women's employment aspirations and choices are frequently far lower than the aspirations of men with comparable ability.[51]

The work orientation approach was seen as an alternative to needs theories of work motivation. It adds support to expectancy theory, in that it emphasizes the need to focus on the expectations that individuals bring to the workplace in order to understand behaviour *inside* the workplace. As others insist, the conundrum of how to motivate workers cannot usefully be considered until we know their needs and expectations relative to their employment.[46] Although the orientation to work thesis is a useful corrective to the psychological universalism of needs and process motivation theories, it is important not to be drawn into a determinism about the possibilities for work motivation.[17] More importantly perhaps, orientations to work are ever-changing and can alter with the particular circumstances in which they become relevant to shaping behaviour. Examples of major change include attitudes to work–life balance, job insecurity arising from global economic recession or precarious employment relationships, and employers' coercion of employees.[17,52–57] The notion of 'dynamic orientations' suggests factors that will motivate the individual can be seen to be embedded in both the social and the individual's psychological contract with the employing organization.[53]

The 'self' at work

The sociological concept of the 'self' informs new theories of work motivation. When we are born, we have no idea that we are separate beings. Through life experiences, we develop a sense of *self*, the perceptual picture we have of ourselves, our view of what kind of person we are. The concept of self is most often held to derive from the influential work of American sociologists George Herbert Mead and Charles Cooley (see Chapter 3). In Mead's philosophy, the self-identity develops through the process of social interaction with others.

The *self-concept theory* of motivation is derived from the concept of the self-identity as an underlying force that motivates non-calculative-based behaviour in the workplace. The self-concept, the totality of our beliefs and emotions about ourselves, is an inner source of energy that gives direction to our behaviour. As such, the self-concept theory of motivation connects the individual's personality with paid work.[58] The theory is based on a number of assumptions about human nature: (1) people are motivated to retain and enhance their self-esteem and self-worth; (2) they are not only goal oriented but also self-expressive; (3) they are driven to maintain and increase their sense of self-consistency; (5) self-concepts are composed, in part, of social identities; and (5) self-concept behaviours are not necessarily related to specific calculative instrumental goals. So, for example, a person may volunteer to do unpaid work at a shelter for the homeless out of a sense of self-esteem and responsibility. And a young person may choose to enter the family business or to enter a profession because it has since early childhood always been expected of her by significant others and has become an important part of her social identity.

The *whole-self theory* of motivation posits an association between an individual's needs for spirituality and work. It assumes that human beings are motivated by more than financial rewards – by spiritual needs. According to this theory, people are looking for their work to provide deeper significance and self-meaning. So, as one advocate of the theory explained, 'the pressure many of us feel to recognize and respond to the sacred in us must find outlet in the secular workplace'.[59] The whole-self theory is a variant of Maslow's higher-order self-actualization need. The self-concept theory and whole-self theory of motivation imply that employee motivation is less susceptible to managerial initiatives and control. It seems intuitively plausible that there are significant individual differences based on self-concept that strongly influence motivation in the workplace. However, research is needed to support the hypothesis and establish a direct link between self-concept and workplace behaviour.

Integrating the approaches

The integrated motivation model shown in Figure 7.8 goes beyond notions of individual motivational drive, and takes into account other theories of motivation. It presents a dynamic framework that incorporates into it expectancy theory and some sociological concepts influencing motivation.

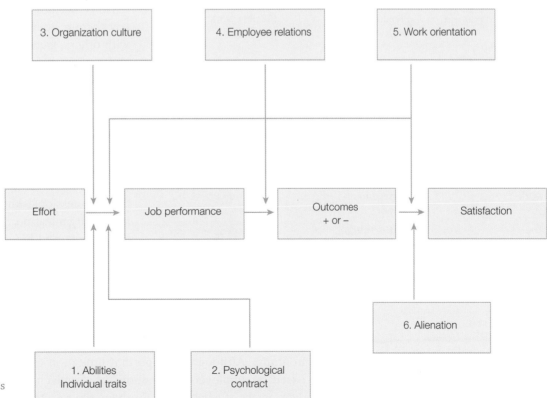

figure 7.8 Integrating psychological and sociological approaches to work motivation

The model portrays individual work motivation that is based on the three expectancies – effort-to-performance, instrumentalities and valence – and is also influenced by individual abilities and personality traits (such as self-esteem) (Box 1), by the psychological contract (Box 2), by organizational culture (Box 3), by employee relations (Box 4), by work orientation (Box 5) and by the alienating aspects of work (Box 6). We believe that this integrated model of work motivation has several advantages. It is informed by the work of psychologists and sociologists, incorporates expectancy theories, and emphasizes the importance of complex social processes in shaping individual and group behaviour. For an alternative integrated theory model, see the work of Klein.[60]

Applying motivation theories

Implementing motivational theory successfully in the workplace is challenging, and managers cannot simply transplant one of the theories discussed in this chapter and apply it in its 'pure' form. Every individual is unique and will respond differently to attempts to motivate him or her. What factors motivate a 56-year-old computer engineer? What factors motivate working mothers with young children? What factors motivate Muslin women at work? Managers need to be sensitive to the differences in individual needs and values among the people they manage. They need to avoid viewing their 'employees' as a homogeneous group. People are different in what they need and what they value, and in how they perceive and judge their work situation. For this reason, managers' motivation interventions must take into account the occupation (for example, managers, knowledge workers and first-level employees) and the employees' age, gender, race, ethnicity and disabilities (if any). This is only possible when managers know their employees.

People engage in paid work for many reasons besides the weekly or monthly pay cheque. They work so that they can be with others, gain respect, form an identity and realize their human potential. As an illustration, consider possible motivation interventions for knowledge workers. When we examined the changing nature of work in Chapter 2, we said that knowledge work is 'ambiguity intensive' and that knowledge workers are defined in terms of the requirement to share and apply their professional knowledge with others in the organization. Drawing on a study by Horwitz and his colleagues,[61] Table 7.2 shows the most popular, highly effective and least effective motivation interventions for managing knowledge workers.

As column 2 indicates, the most highly effective motivation interventions for knowledge workers included employment practices that allow them the freedom to plan work independently (in other words, autonomy). Although an important limitation of the research data is that they are based on employers' perceptions of effectiveness rather than on knowledge workers' views of what motivates them, the results are consistent with other

table 7.2 Most popular, highly effective, and least effective motivation strategies for knowledge workers

Most popular		Highly effective		Least effective	
Strategy type	**Rank**	**Strategy type**	**Rank**	**Strategy type**	**Rank**
Freedom to plan and work independently	1	Freedom to plan work	1	Flexible work practices	1
Regular contact with senior executives	2	Challenging work	2	Large cluster of knowledge workers	2
Incentive bonuses	3	Access to state-of-art technology and products	3	Generous funding for conferences	3
Challenging work	4	Top management support	4	Cash awards for innovations	4
Top management support	5	Ensure fulfilling work	5	Recruit people who fit organizational culture	5

Note: These rankings are based on the number of responses that were marked as the five most frequently used motivation interventions, and the five most highly effective and ineffective in motivating knowledge workers.

Source: Adapted from Horwitz et al. (2003),[61] pp. 31–2

OB and globalization

Dressing for success: control and agency in an offshore office

Many of us are familiar with media images of factory floors and data entry workspaces in places like India, Mexico, China and the Caribbean, where local workers complete low-skilled, low-paying jobs outsourced from large companies headquartered thousands of miles away. These images of self-contained workspaces can give the impression that the work carried out there remains separate from the local social, economic and cultural worlds that exist outside the factory or office doors. A closer look, however, reveals the complex ways in which outsourced work intersects with local lives.

In a study of the impacts of outsourced work on female workers at Data Air, an overseas company operating in Barbados, anthropologist Carla Freeman (2002) notes the ways in which local cultural values associated with womanhood and the middle class were evoked by Data Air managers, and by the company's female staff, to achieve different goals. Managers drew on these values to shape organizational behaviours deemed favourable for a data entry office, namely docility, conformity and attention to detail. The workers, on the other hand, viewed their office-based work as a way to improve their social and gender status in the community. A local observer explained to Freeman (2002, p. 93) how the modern office environment shaped employees' behaviour at work and beyond the office environment:

> *When you see a group of the young ladies, like the ones from Data Air, you can see that they're much better dressed than the ones from the assembly plant … They're probably not getting paid much better but their work environment is a cleaner one, a purer one … the young ladies working in there perceive that they are working in an office and they dress like it and they live like it.*

This 'professionalism' – and the behaviours and status that accompanied it – was cultivated at the Data Air office and was valued by both the company *and* the workers. Through policies such as a dress code, the company was able to manage its image and the behaviours deemed necessary to uphold that image. Likewise, the workers valued the dress code for its role in helping them shape new 'professional' or 'middle-class' identities. One worker explained:

> *Our policy is governed by a dress code … We are not a factory. We call ourselves an 'open office' and if you were*

> *working in an office, you wouldn't go in a jean skirt or jean pants or short skirts. You would dress as if you were an executive. That's what we expect our persons to do. And we instil that in our people, so by practice and counselling, we have reached the stage where people recognize us for the way we look. (Freeman 2002, p. 93)*

Rather than interpreting the management of foreign workers through policies like a dress code as simply the exercise of institutional power over low-wage workers, Freeman urges us to consider the workers' complicity and participation in the management of organizational behaviour and culture at Data Air. In this instance, the workers themselves recognized policies governing dress and behaviour as resources they could use to exert agency and improve their social and economic positions in local Bajan society. Through this example, we can begin to see the complexities inherent in the flows of capital, labour, culture and power associated with the outsourcing of work.

stop! Do you think that too much – or too little – emphasis is placed on how one dresses in the workplace? Are there particular types of work where dress matters more than in other types of work? Is there a relationship between dress and behaviour in the workplace? What is it?

Data Air management recognized the high value that Bajan women place on dressing well, and evoked this existing local value to manage workplace behaviour in the service of the company. What issues might arise when organizations doing business overseas capitalize on – and possibly change – local values and behaviours?

Sources and further information

Freeman, C. (1993) 'Designing women: corporate discipline and Barbados's off-shore pink-collar sector', in J. X. Inda and R. Rosaldo (eds), *The Anthropology of Globalization: A Reader*, Malden, MA: Blackwell Publishing.
Freeman, C. (2002) *High Tech and High Heels in the Global Economy: Women, Work, and Pink-Collar Identities in the Caribbean*, Durham, NC: Duke University Press.
Metters, R. and Verma, R.. (2007) 'History of offshoring knowledge services', *Journal of Operations Management*, **26**(2), pp. 141–7.

Note: This feature was written by Gretchen Fox, Anthropologist, Timberline Natural Resource Group, Canada.

studies surveying knowledge workers themselves.[61] There is a sizeable literature indicating that work motivation strategies need to consider carefully appropriate rewards and job design.

Reward design and motivation

In the context of mobilizing the motivation of employees in order to achieve the organization's objectives, rewards emphasize a core facet of the employment relationship: it constitutes an economic exchange or relationship. The reward is typically a package made up of pay, extended health plans, pension plans, vacation time and so on. Since the early 1980s, a 'new pay' agenda has been imported into UK workplaces moving from pay for time – show up and get paid – to pay for individual or team outputs – show up and perform to a satisfactory standard and get paid, perform to a highly satisfactory standard and cooperate with co-workers and receive more pay.[62] This individualized performance model is undoubtedly associated with the decline of trade union influence, neo-liberal economics and market deregulation, topics too large to examine in detail here. Table 7.3 classifies types of reward and behaviour objectives of the new pay paradigm.

table 7.3 New rewards and behaviour objectives

Type of reward	Examples	Behaviour
Individual rewards	Pay Overtime Performance standard Commission Bonuses Merit Paid leave Benefits	**Time:** maintain work attendance **Outputs:** perform assigned tasks **Competence:** complete tasks without error
Team rewards	Team bonuses	**Cooperation** with co-workers, sharing information and knowledge
Organizational rewards	Profit sharing Share ownership	**Commitment** to culture and goals

Here, we will be concerned with pay – money paid for work done – as an essential factor in work motivation. The motivational characteristics of pay are controversial, not least because of the fundamental tension between the economic, sociological and psychological theoretical frameworks or perspectives. Orthodox economic theory takes as its starting point the free labour market, which is based on the assumption that individuals are rational economic maximizers. Thus, other things being equal, higher pay will increase the number of people willing to work for the organization, and pay incentives will generate superior performance. Sociological thinking emphasizes that varying amounts of power relationship can be of central importance in determining work motivation. Furthermore, as previously discussed, sociology proposes that gender differences, culture and social inequality have a major influence on work motivation. The major psychological theories focus on the individual employee's perception, needs and expectations.

We began this book by noting the effects of the global recession on the *psychological climate*. The analysis of the motivational characteristics of pay cannot ignore a whole range of important contextual variables such as economic recession, culture and pay inequality. Evidence from international studies indicates that the perceived importance of pay as a motivator is bound up in the 'cultural clothes of masculinity'.[63–65] On one important aspect of social inequality – economic inequity – the statistics are truly breathtaking. Over the last 25 years in both Britain and North America, it has become socially acceptable for the income gap between rich and poor to widen. In Canada, for example, 99 per cent of working Canadians will work full time throughout 2010 to earn an average income of around $39,000 (£19,500). But by 10.33 am on January 2, 2010, the top 100 CEOs in the country will have already earned that amount. On average, the top 100 CEOs make more than 218 times as much as an average employee working full time for a full year.[66] Global capitalism has widened the gap between executive pay and the rest.

Organizational psychology uses a distinctive range of concepts, and emphasizes individual employees' perceptions, needs and expectations. Pay is considered to be one of the most noticeable employment practices through which the psychological contract can be established, changed, or violated.[67] Pay shapes the psychological contract by signalling to employees the behaviour that the organization values. A violation refers to the feelings of anger, fear, helplessness and betrayal experienced when the employee perceives that a breach of contract has occurred. This may occur when a promise on the nature of the contract turns out to be less favourable (for example, lower payment) than the employee expected, or as a result of job loss when the employee expected long-term security. The nature of the psychological contract means that every employee will put a somewhat different valuation on the pay provided and on the value of their contribution depending on their individual traits and situational circumstances.

The motivational characteristics of pay are multifaceted as a result of the conflict between intrinsic and extrinsic motivators. According to Maslow's and Alderfer's need theories, pay addresses lower-level needs as it can be exchanged for basic necessities of life. Adam's equity theory posits that pay is an important motivator because workers compare their performance and pay with their peers. And pay should prove motivational to the extent that it is highly valent and is clearly tied to performance, according to Vroom's expectancy theory.

So is pay an effective tool to motivate workers? Motivation is the nexus of character and circumstance. This observation takes account of both human perception, needs and expectations in motivation and the fact that human behaviour always happens within a particular time and situation. Empirical research has found that pay is not always an effective motivator as it will only motivate some people at some points in time, whereas with other people and at other times, it will actually demotivate them.

Research by Horwitz and his colleagues highlights the contradictions and controversy over pay–performance systems.[61] Pay contingent upon performance in this case had a detrimental effect on highly paid knowledge workers because, arguably, these individuals considered additional extrinsic rewards to be less important than intrinsic motivators. A study by Benabou and Tirole suggests that, in the short term, an emphasis on pay may act as a stimulus for effort, but in the long term, money may have a detrimental effect by reducing intrinsic motivation.[68] Finally, we can note in this discussion on motivation the role that reward has played in the recent global economic recession. A key contributor to the crisis leading to the pandemic criticism of executive bankers is that, in a 'culture of easy reward', they engaged in excessive risk-taking behaviour in their quest for huge bonuses.[69,70]

Empowerment and job satisfaction

Employment is a social activity, and for many people it is not regarded simply as a means to an end. Jobs are central to the lives of most people, in that they provide identity, status and experienced meaningfulness. The motivation theories discussed in this chapter suggest that the design of work can be the most effective motivator for many employees (see Table 7.2). *Job design* (see also Chapter 9) refers to the process of assigning tasks to a job, including the interdependency of those tasks with other jobs. Redesigning work to enlarge the number of tasks performed and allow greater decision making can be effective in motivating the individual employee to superior performance and an enhanced sense of achievement and self-worth. The concept of *empowerment* is one term used to describe motivational job design practices designed to allow employees some 'voice' in group or/and organizational decision making, either in their day-to-day work or through formal managerially driven mechanisms that enlist workers' skills, experience and **creativity**.[71]

creativity: the capacity to develop an original product, service or idea that makes a socially recognized contribution

self-efficacy: the beliefs people have about their ability to perform specific situational task(s) successfully

Empowering job design initiatives are predicated on the social psychology theory that individuals have a cognitive need for self-actualization and self-determination and, as such, can heighten **self-efficacy**. The cognitive concept of self-efficacy or a 'can-do' mentality refers to the beliefs people have about their ability to perform specific situational task(s) successfully.

Contrary to Theory X precepts, higher-level growth needs have been shown to have a significant influence on the self-esteem of first-level employees as well as of higher-level employees (see Figure 7.4, above). As Arnolds and Boshoff put it, 'frontline employees … also like to make one or more important decisions every day, use a wide range of their abilities and have the opportunity to do challenging things at work' (ref. 22, p. 715). However, although the job design motivation strategy focuses on notions of self-fulfilment, identity and employee perceptions of task characteristics, the way in which two employees view a particular job and perceive an identical task may be quite different depending on such factors as their age, personality and orientation to work, so achieving this is not straightforward.

Gender, for example, influences identity formation among women. Josselson, in her work on identity, found that 'in comparison to men, women orient themselves in more complicated ways, balancing many involvements and aspirations, with connections to others paramount; their identities are thus compounded and more difficult to articulate' (ref. 72, p. 8). Following on from this and the requirement for differentiation between occupational groups, it is insufficient to make objective changes in skill variety, autonomy or other job dimensions. Managers need to also appreciate and monitor how those objective changes influence the perceptions of different employees (see Chapter 5).

Herzberg's motivator–hygiene theory, described above, supports motivator empowerment strategies to increase job satisfaction. Hackman and Oldham's job characteristic theory[73] identifies five core job characteristics – **skill variety**, **task identity**, **task significance**, autonomy and feedback – as critical factors to produce a high job satisfaction (Figure 9.8). Overall job satisfaction refers to a collection of feelings or emotions that an employee has about her or his job as a whole.

skill variety: the extent to which employees must use different skills and talents to perform tasks in their job

task identity: the degree to which a job requires the completion of a whole or an identifiable piece of work

task significance: the degree to which the job has a substantial impact on the organization and/or larger society

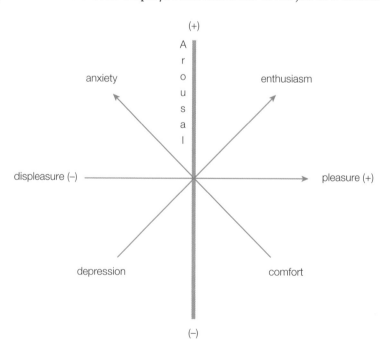

figure 7.9 Three poles for the measurement of well-being

Source: Adapted from Warr (2002),[74] p. 3

Peter Warr's three-dimensional model (Figure 7.9) portrays the range of emotional responses to paid work.[74] Central to this model is the horizontal pole illustrating emotions of high or low pleasure. In research on job-related well-being, this horizontal pole is traditionally indexed as job satisfaction. The second pole runs between anxiety and comfort. In the top left quadrant, feelings of anxiety combine high mental arousal with low pleasure. The third pole runs from depression to enthusiasm. In the top right quadrant, feelings of positive motivation combine high mental arousal with enthusiasm. An employee's location on each of the three poles can be determined through a standard questionnaire. This model has been extended with a fourth pole describing feelings of fatigue or vigour.[75]

That job satisfaction is essentially an affective rather than a cognitive response means that the concept is integral to the wider context of emotional labour, job-related stress and psychological well-being. It is important to bear in mind that job satisfaction is not a totally individualistic notion. Employees' accounts of their job satisfaction given to researchers will be influenced by their life experiences and orientation to paid work. Finally, research on job satisfaction has proved mixed results on the correlation between job satisfaction and workplace behaviour.[76,77]

Job satisfaction seems a crude measure for the almost infinitely complex array of social disparities in work-related stress and psychological well-being. A growing consensus points to wider life experiences, in particular the quality of people's social relationships in society. In some workplaces, employment relationships are supportive, helping individuals deal with life's challenges. In other workplaces, these relationships are toxic, putting health-damaging stresses on workers. Here we have identified a number of factors influencing whether employment relationships are supportive or toxic. For example, Warr's research highlights the importance of job designs that foster a sense of autonomy and trust rather than powerlessness and distrust. Recent research by Wilkinson and Pickett,[78] by contrast, suggests that people's health depends on the quality of their social relationships, and the most important determinant of the quality of relationships is the level of inequality. This is not a new idea, but if it is true, the effects of income inequality extend well beyond individual motivation and the work domain.

OB in focus   Anxiety and stress in the workplace

It is a well-established that depression is associated with a significant burden of illness and immense costs to organizations. However, anxiety disorders are more common and responsible for at least as much personal suffering, disability and economic loss. Anxiety disorders encompass six main categories: phobias, panic disorder with or without agoraphobia, generalized anxiety disorder, obsessive-compulsive disorder, acute stress disorder and post-traumatic stress disorder. One in four individuals suffers an anxiety disorder sometime in their life and one in 10 is likely to have had an anxiety disorder in the past 12 months.

Workplace stress occurs when we perceive the challenges and demands of work as excessive and don't think we can cope. Anxiety in the workplace is associated with: elevated fatigue; exhaustion; increased stress; irritability;

attention or concentration problems; increased worrying and anxious thoughts; emotional and physical symptoms such as moodiness, agitation, restlessness, irritability; muscle tension; abdominal distress; feeling isolated; decreased well-being; as well as behavioural symptoms such as changes in appetite and sleep and nervous habits such as nail biting or pacing.

In order to promote a healthy workplace, employers need to recognize factors contributing to work-related stress and anxiety. Effective managers could provide workshops on various health-related topics, including stress reduction. Attention to individual needs such as role definition, flexible work hours, learning opportunities, advancement and regular feedback on job performance are also essential elements of a healthy workplace.

Source: Extract from 'High cost of anxiety' by Katy Kamkar, psychologist with the Work, Stress and Health Programme at the Centre for Addiction and Mental Health, Toronto, *Canadian HR Reporter*, December 15, 2008, p. 34.

Chapter summary

- This chapter has emphasized the centrality of motivation in the employment relationship. Motivation is the driving force within individuals that affects the direction, intensity and persistence of their work behaviour in the interest of achieving organizational goals.

- We discussed Maslow's famous needs hierarchy. It assumes that when a person's need is not satisfied, that person experiences internal tension or states of deficiency, and this motivates the person to change behaviour to satisfy that need.[79] All the need theories tend to be heavily prescriptive in nature.

- We explained how process theories of work motivation place emphasis on the actual psychological process of motivation. According to the equity theory, perceptions of equity or inequity lead employees to form judgements on the value (or valence) of a reward or outcome. When an employee perceives a reward item to be inequitable, the individual will be dissatisfied, which will result in the individual not finding the outcome attractive; thus, reward will not be an effective motivator.

- Expectancy theory is based on the idea that motivation results from deliberate choices to engage in certain behaviours in order to achieve worthwhile outcomes. Its most important elements are the perception that effort will result in a particular level of performance (E→P), the perception that a specific behaviour will lead to specific outcomes (P→O), and the perceived value of those outcomes, the valences. The attractiveness of work activities (their valence) depends on an employee's individual differences, cultural factors and orientation to work.

- This chapter also suggested that if we are to understand what motivates people, we must go beyond psychological notions of individual needs and cognitive processes. We need to incorporate into any analysis the psychological climate, the culture, the dynamics of employment relations, orientation to work, and the effects of complex interconnecting levels of domination, which stem from the class and gender relations in society.

Key concepts

alienation	206–207
equity theory	200–201
expectancy theory	201–202
extrinsic motivator	193
goal setting	205–206
instrumentality	202
intrinsic motivator	193
motivation	191
needs	194
organizational culture	207
orientation to work	207–208
the self	208–209
self-concept theory	208–209
valence	202
whole-self needs	209

Vocab checklist for ESL students

- ☐ Alienation
- ☐ Creativity, create, creative
- ☐ Equity theory
- ☐ Exchange value
- ☐ Existence, exist
- ☐ Expectancy theory
- ☐ Extrinsic motivator
- ☐ Goals
- ☐ Goal setting
- ☐ Growth needs
- ☐ Inequity
- ☐ Instrumentality
- ☐ Intrinsic motivator
- ☐ Motivation, motivational motivate
- ☐ Needs
- ☐ Needs hierarchy theory
- ☐ Organizational commitment
- ☐ Orientation
- ☐ Self-actualization
- ☐ Skill variety
- ☐ Task identity
- ☐ Task significance
- ☐ Valence
- ☐ Work orientation

Chapter review questions

1. To what extent is motivating workers increasingly more or less challenging for managers in the early twenty-first century? Explain your answer.

2. Compare and contrast Maslow's needs hierarchy theory and Alderfer's ERG theory. How are they similar? How are they different? What do both theories imply for managerial practice?

3. Identify two different types of expectancy referred to in the expectancy theory of work motivation. What can a manager do to influence these expectations?

4. What are the limitations of expectancy theory in predicting an employee's work behaviour and performance?

Chapter research questions

1. One way to understand different motivation theories is to interview your peers on what is important to them when choosing a job. Form a diverse study group including, if possible, an international student(s). Discuss the following questions: How important is pay in choosing a job when you graduate? To what extent are needs theories of motivation culturally based? Give examples. Is personal autonomy important to your work motivation? Why? How helpful are self-concept and whole-self theories in thinking about your own choice of job and work motivation?

2. Obtain a copy of *Inside the Workplace: Findings from the 2004 Workplace Employment Relations Survey* (2006). After reading pages 196–201, how important is pay to overall job satisfaction?

3. Read Evert Van de Vliert's (2008) article investigating whether pay is perceived to be more important in poorer countries.[65] After looking at Figure 17.7, 'The international HRM cycle', in this book, what insights does the research provide for managing international rewards?

 Further reading

Corby, S., Palmer, S. and Lindop, E. (2009) *Rethinking Reward*, Basingstoke: Palgrave.

Horwitz, F. M., Chan Teng Heng and Quazi, H. A. (2003) 'Finders, keepers? Attracting, motivating and retaining knowledge workers', *Human Resource Management Journal*, **13**(4), pp. 23–44 (see p. 33).

Lawler, E. E., Mohrman, S. and Ledford, G. (1998) *Strategies for High Performance Organizations*, San Francisco: Jossey-Bass.

Pfeffer, J. (1998) *The Human Equation: Building Profits by Putting People First*, Boston, MA: Harvard Business School Press.

Van de Vliert, E., Van Yperen, N. W. and Thierry, H. (2008) 'Are wages more important for employees in poorer countries with harsher climates?', *Journal of Organizational Behavior*, **29**, pp. 79–94.

 Chapter case study 1

Equity at FindIT

Setting

FindIT is a US-based company, founded in 1989. In 2009, it has become the leader in publishing print and online directories for local and regional markets in the country. With the realization that their customers were looking to diversify their advertising outside the traditional channel of print, the company recently announced an expansion into the digital media market, including online and mobile platforms. At the same time, senior management began planning to introduce a new job evaluation scheme to simplify the pay structure.

Background to the case

To understand how management's plans affect people's experience of work, it is necessary to recognize the core features of job evaluation. First practised in the 1920s and 1930s, job evaluation is a systematic approach to establishing pay rates. Although variations have existed since its development, one popular method, the point system, attempts to create a more equitable process by ranking jobs based on a number of key factors (each assigned a number of points), such as required education, working conditions and supervision of others. Comparable jobs are grouped into different pay levels, creating a 'hierarchy of jobs': higher rated jobs are paid at the higher pay rates on the hierarchy. Although the actual pay rates are determined by comparing key jobs to the external market, the process of measuring jobs relative to each other within the organization creates a system focused on internal equity.

This approach was suited to the narrow and tightly structured jobs and job descriptions favoured by the classical organizations and unions of the first part of the twentieth century. Later, emerging human relations firms also embraced the method,

believing that it established fairness and equity in a pay system. Job evaluation was perceived to minimize subjectivity, favouritism and management bias in the distribution of pay. Despite changing approaches to how work is organized and the increasing complexity of work since then, job evaluation as a means of determining base pay is still widely practised in unionized and government organizations in North America.

With the change in focus, many of FindIT's 600 employees whose work duties had been routine now argued that their jobs had became more complex. Several approached management and asked to have their jobs evaluated under the new system. The company agreed to first evaluate those jobs most directly impacted by the digital media initiative. A small group consisting of management and selected employees helped to gather the job information through worker questionnaires and conducted the evaluations.

The problem

The evaluations took 6 months to complete. When the results were released with the revised job descriptions, a number of employees were shocked to discover that their jobs had been overgraded under the old system, and they would not receive any salary increases, despite the new responsibilities and skills now required in their jobs. Of these employees, 25 per cent left the company, stating that their contributions or personal performances were not recognized. For the rest, there was a distinct drop in their productivity and a rise in absenteeism. Interpersonal conflicts became more common, as employees began to argue over the value of their jobs relative to others. On the shop floor, employees began to share notes on how to influence the evaluation results through the questionnaires they were asked to fill out.

Tasks

Working either alone or in a small group, prepare a report for FindIT's senior management on the employees' reaction to the new job evaluation scheme. Your report should address the following questions:

1. How do equity theory and expectancy theory help to explain the reaction of the employees to the evaluation results?
2. What role should managers play in ensuring the acceptance of a job evaluation system by the organization's employees?
3. What would be the challenges in using job evaluation for today's more complex jobs, such as in research or information technology?

Further reading

Armstrong, M. and Baron, A. (1995) *The Job Evaluation Handbook*, London: CIPD Publishing.

Bratton, J. and Gold, J. (2007) 'Job evaluation', pp. 383–90 in *Human Resource Management: Theory and Practice*, Basingstoke: Palgrave.

Lawler, E. E. (2000) *Rewarding Excellence*, San Francisco: Jossey-Bass.

Note

This case study was written by Lori Rilkoff, MSc, CHRP, Senior Human Resources Manager at the City of Kamloops, and lecturer in HRM at Thompson Rivers University, BC, Canada.

Chapter case study 2

Motivation at Norsk Petroleum

 Visit www.palgrave.com/business/brattonob2e to view this case study

Web-based assignment

Form a study group of three to five people, and go to the website of any of the following organizations, or a similar one that interests members of the group:

- Compaq Computers (www.compaq.com)
- Apple (www.apple.com)
- Airbus Industrie (www.airbus.com)
- Walmart (www.walmart.com)
- General Electric (www.ge.com)
- Virgin Airlines (www.virgin.com).

When there, go to the 'Company overview' and the human resource management section of the site, and look at the language, assumptions and espoused values. Evaluate the organization's dominant culture in the light of our discussion in this chapter. Write a report that draws out the common features.

Alternatively, go to the websites of a number of universities, and compare and contrast your own university with others in the UK or abroad. As a guide to your search, ask the following questions: What artefacts are displayed that expresses the institution's culture? (Hint: do departments display the publications of the teaching faculty?) In the advertising material, does the institution emphasize teaching excellence, research or both? What are the President's espoused values? What rituals and ceremonies dramatize the institution's culture? What practices shape the university's culture? (Hint: ask your lecturer what is the most important criterion for promotion – excellence in teaching or the number of articles/books published.) Do the visible artefacts and processes provide a guideline for behaviour at the university? If so, why?

OB in film

The film *Dangerous Minds* (1995) centres on a former US Marine turned teacher, LouAnne Johnson (played by Michelle Pfeiffer). Ms Johnson accepts a teaching position at an inner-city high school and tries to motivate her students. The school principal, however, does not approve of her unorthodox motivation methods.

Watch the scene, starting with a shot of the school hallway, after the principal has reprimanded Johnson for taking students to an amusement park without signed permission. The film raises cognitive and behaviour motivation issues. Ask yourself, what methods does Ms Johnson use to motivate her students? Do the students change their behaviour as a result of her teaching approach? What lessons can be drawn from the film for motivating young workers in the workplace?

References

1 Vroom, V. H. and Deci, E. L. (eds) (1970) 'Introduction: an overview of work motivation', pp. 9–19 in *Management and Motivation: Selected Readings*, London: Penguin.

2 Legge, K. (2005) *Human Resource Management: Rhetorics and Realities* (2nd edn), Basingstoke: Palgrave.

3 Drucker, P. (1954/1993) *The Practice of Management*, New York: Harper Collins.

4 Fox, A. (1974) *Beyond Contract, Power, and Trust Relations*, London: Faber & Faber.

5 Friedman, A. (1977) *Industry and Labour: Class Struggle at Work and Monopoly Capitalism*, London: Macmillan.

6 Salaman, G. (1979) *Work Organizations: Resistance and Control*, London: Longman.

7 Clegg, S. and Dunkerley, D. (1980) *Organization, Class and Control*, London: Routledge & Kegan Paul.

8 Thompson, P. (1989) *The Nature of Work* (2nd edn), London: Macmillan.

9 Salaman, G. (1981) *Class and the Corporation*, London: Fontana.

10 Ryan, R. M. and Deci, E. L. (2000) 'Self-determination theory and the facilitation of intrinsic motivation, social development, and well-being', *American Psychologist*, **55**(1), pp. 68–78.

11 Vallerand, R. J. (1997) 'Toward a hierarchical model of intrinsic and extrinsic motivation', *Advances in Experimental Social Psychology*, **29**, pp. 271–360.

12 Townley, B. (1994) *Reframing Human Resource Management: Power, Ethics and the Subject of Work*, London: Sage.

13 Maslow, A. H. (1954) *Motivation and Personality*, New York: Harper.

14 Herzberg, F., Mansner, B. and Snyderman, B. (1959) *The Motivation to Work* (2nd edn), New York: Wiley.

15 McClelland, D. (1961) *The Achieving Society*, Princeton, NJ: Van Nostrand.

16 Alderfer, C. P. (1972) *Existence, Relatedness and Growth*, New York: Free Press.

17 Watson, T. (1986) *Management, Organization and Employment Strategy*, London: Routledge.

18 McGregor, D. (1957/1970), 'The human side of enterprise', pp. 306–19 in V. H. Vroom and E. Deci (eds), *Management and Motivation*, London: Penguin. McGregor, Douglas. Edited by Rob Roy McGregor, Martha McGregor, and Gregory N. Colvard, *Leadership and Motivation: Essays of Douglas McGregor*, figure from essay "The Human Side of Enterprise", © 1966 Massachusetts Institute of Technology, by permission of the MIT Press.

19 Pitsis, T. S. (2008) 'Theory X and Theory Y', pp. 1545–9 in S. R. Clegg and J. Bailey (eds), *The Sage International Encyclopedia of Organizational Studies*, Thousand Oaks, CA: Sage.

20 McClelland, D. C. and Burnham, D. H. (1976) 'Power is the great motivator', *Harvard Business Review*, March–April, pp. 100–10.

21 Harrel, A. M. and Strahl, M. J. (1981) 'A behavioral decision theory approach to measuring McClelland's trichotomy of needs', *Journal of Applied Psychology*, **66**, pp. 242–7.

22 Arnolds, C. and Boshoff, C. (2002) 'Compensation, esteem valence and job performance: an empirical assessment of Alderfer's ERG theory', *International Journal of Human Resource Management*, **13**(4), pp. 697–719.

23 Cullen, D. (1994) 'Feminism, management and self-actualization', *Gender, Work and Organization*, **1**(3), pp. 127–37.

24 Gordon, J. R. and Whelan, K .S. (1998) 'Successful professional women in midlife: how organizations can more effectively understand and respond to the challenges', *Academy of Management Executive*, **12**(1), pp. 8–27.

25 Wajcman, J. (1998) *Managing Like a Man: Women and Men in Corporate Management*, Cambridge: Polity Press/Penn State University Press.

26 Herzberg, F. (2003) 'One more time: how do you motivate employees?', *Harvard Business Review*, **81**(1), pp. 87–96.

27 Adams, J. S. (1965) 'Inequality in social exchange', pp. 267–99 in L. Berkowitz (ed.), *Advances in Experimental Social Psychology*, New York: Academic Press.

28 Bratton, J. and Gold, J. (2007) *Human Resource Management: Theory and Practice* (4th edn), Basingstoke: Palgrave.

29 Feldman, D. C., Leana, C. R. and Bolino, M. C. (2002) 'Underemployment and relative deprivation among re-employed executives', *Journal of Occupational and Organizational Psychology*, **75**(4), pp. 453–88.

30 Baldamus, W. (1961) *Efficiency and Effort*, London: Tavistock.

31 Lewin, K. (1935) *A Dynamic Theory of Personality*, New York: McGraw-Hill.

32 Vroom, V. H. (1964) *Work and Motivation*, New York: Wiley.

33 Porter, L. W. and Lawler, E. E. (1968) *Managerial Attitudes and Performance*, London: Irwin.

34 Lawler, E. E. (1973) *Motivation in Work Organizations*, Monterey, CA: Brooks-Cole.

35 Lawler, E. E. (1971) *Pay and Organizational Effectiveness*, New York: McGraw-Hill.

36 Kanungo, R. and Mendonca, M. (1992) *Compensation: Effective Reward Management*, Toronto: Butterworth.

37 Locke, E. A. (1968) 'Towards a theory of task motivation and incentives', *Organization Behavior and Human Performance*, **3**, pp. 152–89.

38 Tubbs, M. E. (1986) 'Goal-setting: a meta-analytic examination of the empirical evidence', *Journal of Applied Psychology*, **71**, pp. 474–83.

39 Latham, G. P. and Locke, E. A. (1990) *A Theory of Goal Setting and Task Performance*, Englewood Cliffs, NJ: Prentice-Hall.

40 Mandel, E. and Novack, G. (1970) *The Marxist Theory of Alienation*, New York: Pathfinder.

41 Rinehart, J. W. (2006) *The Tyranny of Work: Alienation and the Labour Process* (4th edn), Scarborough, ON: Nelson Thomson.

42 Roddick, A. (1991) *Body and Soul*, New York: Crown.

43 Tichy, N. and Sherman, S. (1993) *Control Your Destiny or Someone Else Will*, New York: Doubleday.

44 Hofstede, G. (1998) 'Organization culture', pp. 237–55 in M. Poole and M. Warner (eds), *The Handbook of Human Resource Management*, London: International Thomson Business Press.

45 Mottaz, C. J. (1985) 'The relative importance of intrinsic and extrinsic rewards as determinants of work satisfaction', *Sociological Quarterly*, **26**(3), pp. 365–85.

46 Goldthorpe, J., Lockwood, D., Bechhofer, R. and Platt, J. (1968) *The Affluent Worker: Industrial Attitudes and Behaviour*, Cambridge: Cambridge University Press.

47 Mottaz, C. J. (1986) 'Gender differences in work satisfaction, work-related rewards and values, and the determinants of work satisfaction', *Human Relations*, **39**(4), pp. 359–78.

48 Murry, M. A. and Atkinson, T. (1981) 'Gender differences in correlates of job satisfaction', *Canadian Journal of Behavioural Sciences*, **13**, pp. 44–52.

49 Metcalfe, D. (1989) 'Water notes dry up', *British Journal of Industrial Relations*, **27**(10), pp. 1–32.

50 Hodson, R. (1999) 'Management citizenship behavior: a new concept and an empirical test', *Social Problems*, **46**(3), pp. 460–78.

51 Wilson, F. M. (2003) *Organizational Behaviour and Gender*, Farnham: Ashgate.

52 Daniel, W. W. (1973) 'Understanding employee behaviour in its context', in J. Child (ed.), *Man and Organization*, London: Allen & Unwin.

53 Rousseau, D. M. (1995) *Psychological Contracts in Organisations: Understanding Written and Unwritten Agreements*, Thousand Oaks, CA: Sage.

54 Kelly, J. (2005) 'Industrial relations approaches to the employment relationship', pp. 48–64 in J. A.-M. Coyle-Shapiro, Shore, L. M., Taylor, M. S. and Tetrick, L. E. (eds), *The Employment Relationship*, Oxford: Oxford University Press.

55 Kersley, B., Alpin, C, Forth, J., Bryson, A., Bewley, H., Dix, G. and Oxenbridge, S. (2005) *Inside the Workplace: First Findings from the 2004 Workplace Employment Relations Survey (WERS 2004)*, London: Department of Trade and Industry.

56 Vosko, L. (2000) *Temporary Work: The Gendered Rise of a Precarious Employment Relationship*, Toronto: University of Toronto Press.

57 Charles, N. and James, E. (2003) 'The gender dimensions of job insecurity in the local labour market', *Work, Employment and Society*, **17**(3), pp. 531–52.

58 Leonard, N. H., Beauvais, L. L. and Scholl, R. W. (1999) 'Work motivation: the incorporation of self-concept-based processes', *Human Relations*, **52**(8), pp. 969–98.

59 Fairholm, G. W. (1996) 'Spiritual leadership: fulfilling whole-self needs at work', *Leadership and Organizational Development*, **17**(5), pp. 11–17.

60 Klein, H. J. (1989) 'An integrated control theory model of work motivation', *Academy of Management Review*, **14**, pp. 150–72.

61 Horwitz, F. M., Chan feng Heng and Quazi, H. A. (2003) 'Finders, keepers? Attracting, motivating and retaining knowledge workers', *Human Resource Management Journal*, **13**(4), pp. 23–44.

62 Corby, S., Palmer, S. and Lindop, E. (2009) *Rethinking Reward*, Basingstoke: Palgrave.

63 Hofstede, G. (1998) *Masculinity and Femininity: The Taboo Dimension of National Cultures*, Thousand Oaks, CA: Sage.

64 Hofstede, G. (2001) *Culture's Consequences: Comparing Values, Behaviors, Institutions, and Organizations across Cultures*, Thousand Oaks, CA: Sage.

65 Van de Vliert, E., Van Yperen, N. and Thierry, H. (2008) 'Are wages more important for employees in poorer countries with harsher climates?', *Journal of Organizational Behavior*, **29**, pp. 79–94.

66 Mackenzie, H. (2007) *The Great CEO Pay Race: Over Before it Begins*, Toronto: Canadian Centre for Policy Alternative.

67 Rousseau, D. M. and Ho, V. T. (2000) 'Psychological contract issues in compensation', pp. 273–310 in S. L. Rynes and B. Gerhart (eds), *Compensation in Organizations: Current Research and Practice,* San Francisco: Jossey-Bass.

68 Benabou, R. and Tirole, J. (2003) 'Intrinsic and extrinsic motivation', *Review of Economic Studies*, **70**(3), pp. 489–520.

69 Perkins, T. (2009) 'Financial watchdog tightens leash on banker pay', *Globe and Mail*, March 6, p. A1.

70 House of Commons Treasury Committee Report (2009) *Banking Crisis: Dealing with the Failure of the UK Banks*, London: Stationery Office.

71 Marchington, M. (2008) 'Employee voice systems,' pp. 231–50 in P. Boxall, J. Purcell and P. Wright (eds), *The Oxford Handbook of Human Resource Management*, Oxford: Oxford University Press.

72 Josselson, R. (1987) *Finding Herself: Pathways to Identity Development in Women*, San Francisco: Jossey-Bass.

73 Hackman, J. and Oldham, G. (1980) *Work Redesign*, Reading, MA: Addison-Wesley.

74 Warr, P. B. (ed.) (2002) *Psychology at Work* (5th edn), London: Penguin.

75 Daniels, K. (2000) 'Measures of five aspects of affective well-being at work', *Human Relations*, **53**, pp. 275–94.

76 Patterson, M. and West, M. (1998) 'People power: the link between job satisfaction and productivity', *Centrepiece*, **3**(3), pp. 2–5.

77 Somers, M. J. (2001) 'Thinking differently: assessing nonlinearities in the relationship between work attitudes and job performance using a Bayesian neutral network', *Journal of Occupational and Organizational Psychology*, **74**(1), pp. 47–62.

78 Wilkinson, R. and Pickett, K. (2009) *The Spirit Level: Why More Equal Societies Almost Always Do Better*, London: Allen Lane.

79 Kanter, R. (1990) 'Motivation theory in industrial and organizational psychology', pp. 75–170 in M. D. Dunnette and L. Hough (eds), *Handbook of Industrial and Organizational Psychology*, Palo Alto, CA: Consulting Psychology Press.

chapter 8
Gender, race, disability and class

chapter outline

- Introduction
- Equity and justice in work organizations
- Gender
- Race and ethnicity
- Disability and work: an emerging focus for research?
- Social class
- Summary and end-of-chapter features
- Chapter case study 1: Equity challenges in
- South African police service organizations
- Chapter case study 2: The glass ceiling commission

chapter objectives

After completing this chapter, you should be able to:

- understand and explain how equity affects organizations
- describe some of the principal means by which equity issues are handled in organizational practices
- compare and contrast the current status of gender, race/ethnicity, disability and class policy in organizational life in major English-speaking countries
- outline relevant areas where further investigation is needed in the many areas relating to equity in the workplace

Introduction

Understanding issues of **equity** across the major social divisions of society as it relates to work is vital for a deep understanding of organizational behaviour. The institution of paid work brings together people of all kinds. Indeed, with increased global migration, the workplace is becoming ever more diverse. Over the last 50 years, remarkable changes have occurred, beginning with the movement of women into paid work in greater and greater numbers. Civil rights movements around the world have affected how all people think about visible minority status. And more recently, people with disabilities are more effectively demanding the full rights of citizenship, which involve among other things the freedom to participate in paid employment, as is signalled by the increased efforts of the United Nations, for example, to help them achieve this.

employment equity: a strategy to eliminate the effects of discrimination and to make employment opportunities available to groups who have been excluded

These broad social changes help to set the stage for our discussion, but interwoven with them all is a particularly broad concern that is not often addressed in textbooks on organizational behaviour. This concern is for the role of 'social class'. The fact that work is implicated in the production and reproduction of class divisions has been understood for at least 150 years. Indeed, this connection between work and social class may have become so taken for granted that it has slipped off the radar screens of many organizational analysts. In addition, we might say that if class divisions are a necessary component of paid work, how can we problematize these divisions if we do not at the same time problematize the way work itself is organized and understood?

Ironically, outside organizational behaviour literature, a large proportion of literature up until the 1970s on work and inequities focused exclusively on issues of social class. Over the last 30 years, however, there has emerged a great deal of practical concern, policy and research about issues of gender, race and ethnicity. This, of course, should not be understood as making a case for the irrelevance of social class: clearly, social class is a major factor that shapes the work experience. Rather, it means that people's general understanding, as well as academic analyses, of work must become more sophisticated and nuanced to bring to light the relationships between race, gender, disability and social class.

In general terms, this chapter provides a systematic exploration of several of the key areas of equitable/inequitable practice in organizational behaviour, as well as more broadly in the institution of work,

Before getting started, take a moment to ask yourself how you understand the term 'equity' now? After you have considered this, take a moment to explore the web for sites devoted to equity across different countries. Two sites you might like to compare and contrast are: www.mtholyoke. edu/offices/comm/csj/040700/gender.html; www.publicservice.co.uk/pdf/dfid/ winter2003/DfID1%20MMS%20 Mdladlana%20ATL.pdf

stop reflect

including labour markets. We begin with a general section on the subfield of 'organizational justice', which has been developing for almost a quarter of a century.

Equity and justice in work organizations

organizational justice: in organizational behaviour literature, the perceived fairness of outcomes, procedures and the treatment of individuals

> Take a moment to come up with a list of key factors that could be used to compare different jobs for their relative 'value'. Now, using your set of factors, analyse some occupations. How did your system of comparison measure up? Do you think it produced a fair outcome?
>
> **stop reflect**

human rights: the conditions and treatment expected for all human beings

The concept of 'organizational justice' will serve as the starting point for this chapter because, although we explore a variety of other forms of research literature, it is the topic that most firmly connects us to the field of organizational behaviour, organizational psychology and the like. In other words, this discussion is essential, although not sufficient, for the full development of a broad and useful theory of equity in the context of organizational behaviour. But first it is perhaps relevant to look briefly at the general issues of pay and employment equity, a subfield of legal and social studies of work that is well established but that stands quite separate from the literature on organizational justice.

Pay and employment equity legislation is defined as laws intended to eliminate established inequalities in the pay received by women and (often specifically identified) members of minority groups working for a given employer.[1] Different forms of this type of legislation exist across many countries. In social democratic countries such as those of northern Europe, it is linked with general work environment legislation. In countries without these types of centralized legislative framework, such as the USA, Canada and the UK, it appears in stand-alone legal frameworks where litigation (as opposed to collective bargaining) is central.

In such countries, pay and employment equity laws do not, as such, focus on the broader experiences of workers and inequity, even though employers found to be in violation of the legislation are often required to identify and eliminate many of the factors that have produced the violation. Instead, the focus is on comparisons based on the principle of equal pay for work of equal value. Establishing this value is not easy, of course, and it reveals the many presumptions that infuse the world of work, which most of us take for granted. Generally speaking, however, such legislation has been shown to increase equity in the workplace in comparison to forms of self-regulation. For a good, recent example of this type of policy research analysis, see Peetza et al.,[2] whose work focuses on Australia but can be used to reflect on such issues elsewhere.

A broader set of concerns, both in the work-based literature and in practice, revolves around **human rights** legislation. Here, the concern is again discrimination, but the focus is much broader than that seen in pay and employment equity legislation. First, more personal characteristics are taken into account (that is, more than just gender and visible minority status), including disability, sexual orientation, age and even political or religious beliefs. Any analysis of human rights violation necessarily explores the full range of forms of discrimination and the factors involved, including those examined in the context of pay and employment equity. Here, we might look at issues of the conditions of employment, harassment, mental duress, legal expenses (as well as pay) and so on. Employers found to be in violation of the legislation are often required by law to make employees 'whole' by restoring them to the circumstance they would have been in had the discrimination not occurred.

This brief introduction to the legal dimensions of equity law provides a lead-in for a broad and introductory exploration of the issue of equity, and specifically organizational justice, in the research literature on organizational behaviour. Indeed, as we shall see, the two basic legal frameworks outlined above (as well as case research on collective bargaining) offer examples of the many different forms of organizational justice. First, however, we must ask what is known about how the issue of justice and the perceptions that surround it affect the actual behaviour of and within organizations.

Valuable work has recently been completed on these issues, in the form of general reviews of research and theory.[3–8] This research comes in a variety of forms: field research, experimental research and 'action' (or 'proactive') research. Each form and method has made important claims about the relations between different types of justice and variables such as job satisfaction, employee commitment and evaluation of authority.

We can identify three basic lines of inquiry in the area of organizational justice: the distributive, procedural and interactional approaches. (Some researchers identify four or more approaches, for instance distributive, procedural, interpersonal and informational, but here we use a three-type model.) Briefly, the types can be roughly defined as follows:

- *Distributive justice* refers to the outcomes and allocations emerging from processes.
- *Procedural justice* refers to the procedures set in place to produce the perception of fairness.
- *Interactional justice* refers to the interpersonal treatment of people using these procedures.

In general, it is important to note that 'justice', in this field of research, is understood to be socially constructed. It concerns practices and organizational structures, and the policies and procedures that shape them. Note too that justice is typically understood to be subjective, in the sense that 'fairness' is what the majority perceives it to be.[6] However, justice can also be understood in more objective terms – involving proportional shares of resources, outputs and so on – and we use this understanding in this discussion. We feel it is necessary to include both the subjective and objective dimensions of justice at work because, when the focus is on subjective formulations of justice – what people think is just – it is easy to sidestep many contentious issues regarding rights, responsibilities and social justice in a broader, more politicized sense.

Critical insight

The writings of G. S. Leventhal are important original attempts to define 'organizational justice'. Early on, Leventhal and his colleagues generated six criteria for procedures to be perceived as 'fair'. How many criteria can you come up with? After your attempt, read Leventhal, Karuza and Fry's article, 'Beyond fairness: a theory of allocation preferences'.[9]

Some of the research that has been carried out certainly sheds light on behaviour in work organizations. As in most sciences, the researchers tend to be preoccupied with how powerful the effects they identify are, and which specific theories are the most powerful predictors. Interested readers can look at the primary sources, but, for our purposes, we can say that organizational justice (or at least perceptions of it) correlates highly with positive outcomes and experiences of work as follows. Not only do we see that certain dimensions of personality shape organizational justice,[10,11] but we also see that increased organizational justice is found to be correlated with higher job satisfaction,[12] higher organizational commitment,[13] higher levels of trust,[14] more positive evaluations of managers,[15] enhanced organizational citizenship behaviour,[16] lower turnover and absenteeism,[17] as well as lower levels of workplace sabotage and revenge.[18,19] The literature on work performance is mixed, but overall it shows a positive correlation between forms of justice and better work outputs.[17]

Source: iStockphoto

plate 28 Women continue to be over-represented in the care-giving professions.

horizontal tension: tensions and contradictions that emerge in terms of people's participation in group endeavours irrespective of hierarchical institutional relationships

vertical tension: tensions and contradictions that emerge in terms of hierarchical institutional relationships

appropriation: the process through which, in capitalist workplaces, a proportion of the value produced in work activities – above investment in raw materials, equipment, health benefits, facilities and so on – is retained under the private control of owners, ownership groups and/or investors. A more critical perception of this process sees it as 'exploitation' of collective activities of the organization for private use

For our purposes, perhaps the most important point to be taken from all this is that the concept of 'justice', and with it 'equity', emerges and takes on personal relevance only in the context of the existence of systematic injustices and inequities. That is, it occurs in a system of tension and conflict. Work, in other words, is contentious; and it is this fact that makes it reasonable for any of us to notice or care about justice and equity in this context. What makes work contentious is, of course, the subject of whole bodies of literature across a wide range of disciplines from political economy to industrial relations, including women's studies, sociology and so on. For this chapter, however, we can say that this system of conflict and tension can be understood in two major dimensions, **horizontal** and **vertical**, which bear directly and distinctly on each of the social variables of gender, race and ethnicity, disability and class that we examine later in the chapter.

The tension in the employer–employee relationship should not be confused with tension in the relationships between groups and individuals. Although in reality they coexist with each other, analytically they represent two relatively distinct sets of dynamics, structures and determinants. This distinction is essential if we are to understand the different dynamics of justice and equity across different social groups that feature a mix of characteristics. Tensions that emerge from individual participation in group, team or organizational contexts are related to human individuality, the burdens of negotiating scarce resources, and conflicts arising from interdependency within work structures and processes. Organizational theorists call these *horizontal* tensions. They tend to emerge from the relationship between the individual and the group or organization, where individual agency meets forms of collective need and social structure. Strictly speaking, these tensions can emerge in any form of collective activity, both in and beyond the workplace (such as in social movements, community groups, families, non-profit work and trade unions).

The tensions that arise in the context of employer–employee (or capital–labour) relationships necessarily involve these tensions, which are inherent in individual and group/organizational relationships, but there is a distinct set of further tensions that are more or less unique to economic life under capitalism. These tensions revolve around a specific class-based form of what could be called *vertical* tensions, which appear both within specific work organizations and in society generally. This set of relationships and tensions is rooted in the processes of **appropriation**. By this is meant the process by which the capital accumulation that defines the success of a business firm requires control to be placed in private hands, in ways that are shaped by market exchanges, technological development and intercapitalist competition in the last instance.

It is true that the vast majority of decisions by firms in capitalist economies revolve around the satisfaction of projected, rather than direct, human needs. This may or may not be a problem, depending on your viewpoint, but what is generally not disputed is that the employer–employee relationship that emerges is full of vertical tensions and contradictions. These and other distinctions draw our attention to the essence of the central contradiction and lines of tension that define the employer–employee relationship under capitalism. The distinction between vertical and horizontal tensions also provides a foundation for understanding some of the more specific discussions about equity across different social groups. We present these below, beginning with the issue of gender.

Gender

gender bias: behaviour that shows favouritism towards one gender over the other

gender identity: a person's perception of the self as female or male

gender role: attitudes, behaviour and activities that are socially defined as appropriate for each sex and are learned through the socialization process

gender socialization: the aspect of socialization that contains specific messages and practices concerning the nature of being female or male in a specific group or society

glass ceiling: the pattern of employment opportunities that disproportionately limits the achievement of top administrative posts by certain social groups

sticky floor: the pattern of employment opportunities that disproportionately concentrates certain social groups at lower-level jobs

patriarchy: a hierarchical system of social organization in which cultural, political and economic structures are controlled by men

sexual harassment: the unwelcome conduct of a **sexual** nature that detrimentally affects the work environment or leads to adverse job-related consequences for its victims

sex: a term used to describe the biological and anatomical differences between females and males

To understand organizational behaviour and the various aspects of gender, we must take time to understand the aggregated results of organizational behaviours from the specific standpoint of women. Over the last 30 years, women have come to account for approximately half the labour force in most core capitalist countries (such as the G10 countries). At the same time, however, the wage gaps between men and women have hardly narrowed. Indeed, reports from as recently as 2007 have shown the degree to which these gaps exist in all countries, and the degree to which they have perhaps even widened. In fact, countries displaying the largest gender wage gaps are also the same countries displaying among the highest rates of economic growth.[22] It is clear, when we look at the available statistics, that differential wages as well as differential occupational distributions persist.

Two phrases seem to best describe the status of women in the workplace. One is 'glass ceiling', the concept that, despite their equal or greater educational training and performance, women remain systematically excluded from top corporate jobs. The other is the idea of 'sticky floors' on which women workers appear to be disproportionately glued. In other words, while women participate in paid work in numbers equal to men, they appear to be excluded from the top jobs, while vast numbers are clustered in low-paying, low-prestige jobs with little or no opportunity for advancement.[23,24] This appears to happen through a combination of outright discrimination along with educational and occupational segregation; the mechanisms that produce these persisting inequities can together be referred to as patriarchy. To take a specific example, in the USA the median wage for women continues to be only three-quarters that of men.[25] Studies of hiring practices in the USA have found that women are more likely to be found working in firms that are owned or managed by other women.[26]

Finally, gender-based harassment at workplaces both persists and has recently been shown to be much more broad than had originally been thought. This harassment undermines efforts to develop career progression and decent working conditions for women.[27]

A significant amount of research over the last decade has looked at the dynamics of gender and management. 'Good news' stories are occasionally seen in the media about the burgeoning numbers of business and governmental leaders who are women. However, these are not necessarily representative of the contemporary reality. For example, in 1999, there were only two female CEOs of Fortune 500 companies (the largest 500 companies in the USA), and a mere 4 per cent of all senior corporate officers in the USA were women. Similar statistics show that, in the UK, less than 4 per cent of corporate leaders were women.[28] Yet another sobering comparison: in the USA, at the current rate of change, it will take approximately 300 years for women to reach the representative 50 per cent mark in corporate leadership, and a remarkable 500 years for them to provide 50 per cent of political leaders.[29]

It is not just a matter of fairness. Gender inequities in the workplace have recently been shown to have important, and underexamined, effects on the health of women. One researcher who has examined this issue explicitly shows that, at both the macro (large-scale) and the micro (individual) levels, there is a close correlation between gender inequality at work, itself shaped by organizational practices, legal infrastructures and cultures of specific countries, and the overall mental and physical health of women.[30]

Some studies have effectively conceptualized gender effects in small-group behaviour,[31] and a variety of key researchers have linked general changes in work to a critical discussion of the emergence of new managerial styles that, on the surface, might seem to favour women.[28,29,32] Of course, as Wajcman points out, we need to consider to what degree these claims are based on gender stereotypes that may or may not be warranted:

> Traditionally, men have been seen as better suited than women to executive positions. The qualities usually associated with being a successful manager are 'masculine' traits such as drive, objectivity and an authoritative manner. Women have been seen as different from men, as lacking the necessary personal characteristics and skills to make good managers. The entry of women into senior levels within organizations over the last decade or so has brought such stereotypes into question. (ref. 28, p. 55)

At the same time, of course, denying the essential validity of stereotypes does not prevent stereotypes from having real material effects in people's lives (see, for example, Yoder on 'gender tokensim'[33]). In the majority of workplaces, these stereotypes flourish, and through this and other factors, major barriers to female advancement are constructed.

Is there a really a 'male' and a 'female' style of management? According to Wajcman's careful studies, the answer is no. Perceptions of difference persist, for example in the area of 'risk preferences,'[34] and certainly some variation is to be expected,[35] but assessments of managerial practices show that there are far more similarities between female and male managers than there are differences, particularly in the areas that are seen as the most definitive of managerial work.

Wajcman's conclusions are not particularly hopeful, but there are some positive proposals in Meyerson and Fletcher's 'A modest manifesto for shattering the glass ceiling.'[32] While Meyerson and Fletcher do not question the basic principles of the capitalist model, which may very well be an important source of this and many other forms of inequity, they nevertheless build on the type of argument that Wajcman[28] provides by seriously questioning both the efficacy of the current legislative structures and the reality behind the apparently increased 'sensitivity' of corporations. Meyerson and Fletcher are particularly harsh critics of attempts merely to change attitudes. They prefer to change the very way in which work organizations operate, while arguing for an incremental approach of what they call 'small wins' within firms.[32]

In Canada, authors like Falkenberg and Boland offer a slightly different prescription.[36] Their careful research of employment equity programmes in workplaces reveals that negative stereotypes are strongly persistent. They go on to show that employment equity programmes have probably created a significant backlash, which is led by males targeting, in particular, those women who have successfully

Does success for women in corporate leadership mean becoming 'more like a man'? Should it? Do feminist critiques such as Wajcman's offer a threat to 'male identity' that undermines reforms? Why or why not? And is this a significant barrier to equitable changes to the workplace?

stop reflect

feminist perspective: the sociological approach that focuses on the significance of gender in understanding and explaining the inequalities that exist between men and women in the household, in the paid labour force and in the realms of politics, law and culture

overcome the barriers. For Falkenberg and Boland, the solution is to be found not in regulation of the workplace, but rather through government-led education programmes. A variety of other research, however calls these conclusions seriously into question.[28,32]

There is also a very clear business case against gender inequity, and this makes the reasons for the persistence of discrimination even more complex. Several researchers highlight the tendency for team decision-making processes to be male dominated, and argue that it is highly ineffective for men to dominate team-based work.[37] Others outline the negative effects of gender stereotypes on mixed-gender negotiations at the bargaining table. They draw on fascinating experimental work that builds on the general 'stereotype threat' theories.[38]

An article by Ngo et al. reports, among other things, on the way in which such inequity leads to a decline in morale and performance levels, which ultimately erodes the capacity of firms to retain top women (and, in some cases, top men too).[39] On the surface, this would seem to be an issue in which the very principles of 'market competition' would bear progressive fruit, but this is not the case; that is, the market does not seem to be very effective at 'weeding out' weak firms on this basis. Ngo and colleagues provide a review of the literature, and also a case study suggesting that changes to organizational structures, rather than individual attitudes, are most important for addressing perceived inequities.

plate 29 Gender inequality is in many ways felt most strongly by women workers who are stuck to the 'sticky floor', from Chinese garment workers in Canada and the USA, to women across the world who labour in sweatshops.

Source: Impactt Limited

Although the glass ceiling issue is clearly important, in many ways the greater problem of gender inequity – at least in terms of the pure number of workers affected – is experienced by women who are stuck to the 'sticky floor'. They range from Chinese garment workers in Canada and the USA[40,41] to women across the world who labour in sweatshops.[42] Few surfaces are stickier than those to which domestic workers are fixed, and a recent study by Parrenas sheds light on just why this is. Her focus is on Filipinas, labouring across more than 130 countries, who represent one of the largest and widest flows of female migrant labourers on the contemporary scene.[43] She shows the incredible difficulties these particular women face. They appear to be unable to take advantage of what legislation there is to prevent discrimination.

In many ways, Parrenas's study highlights the difficulties in separating out different types of discrimination. Gender, race, disability and class issues are generally highly interwoven in an interactive complex of effects. How, we might ask, can we approach the issue of gender inequities and work in such as way as to encompass the fantastically diverse experiences of both those on the floor *and* those pushing against the ceiling?

Race and ethnicity

In autumn 1998, a fascinating article in the *Guardian* newspaper in the UK reported a pronounced pessimism about the future of race relations.[44] It outlined how most young people in the UK (in this context, those aged 18 to 24) felt that race relations would worsen rather than improve over the coming years. Excellent historical texts add depth to our understanding of the landscape of ethno-racial inequities and work.[45,46] Since there seems to be an incredible persistence in a wide range of ethno-racial injustices in the context of work, it is appropriate to ask ourselves several important questions to begin with. What are we to make of this suggestion that young people in the UK see a growing, rather than narrowing, schism between ethno-racial groups? Is this pessimism well founded? And how does it involve the workplace?

General research over the last three decades has confirmed that, although some progress has been made in achieving greater equity for ethno-racial minority groups, it is relatively minor and the results are mixed internationally. In 2002, for example, black and Hispanic individuals in the USA held just 13 per cent of all managerial and professional positions.[47] In a parallel with women's experience, studies of hiring practices in the USA have found that black workers are more likely to be employed in firms that are owned or managed by other black people.[48,49]

In the UK, Labour Force Surveys show that, during the 1980s and 90s, there was some upward mobility among ethno-racial minorities.[50] Figure 8.1 compares the levels of income enjoyed by different ethno-racial groups in the UK, again in the 1990s.

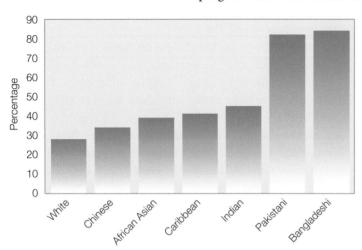

figure 8.1 Proportion of people living in households in the UK with less than half the national average income, 1994

Source: Modood et al. (1997)[51]

According to some researchers, in the workplaces of the UK, ethno-racial minorities are greatly under-represented in the highest positions and over-represented in the lowest ones.[51] Modood et al. note how there are also significant differences between minority ethno-racial groups. For example, in the UK, the earnings of Chinese men are on par with those of white men, while Caribbean and South-East Asian immigrants are the worst off. According to the most recent UK Labour Force Survey, the unemployment rate in 2001 for people of Bangladeshi origin was 24.6 per cent and for Pakistanis it was 16 per cent, compared with 5.4 per cent for white people. Since these latter groups have been in the UK in significant numbers for generations now, this too suggests that if conditions *are* changing, they are changing very slowly indeed. For a more expansive discussion and more recent statistical information in Britain, see Modood.[52]

As we have begun to suggest, there are differences in the experiences of different non-white groups, and there are also systematic distinctions between groups with the same skin colour. Phillips and Loyd, for example, have shown how there is not always a clear match between race and ethnicity, and attitudes, opinion and values. They go on to show that diversity in general seems to promote more effective decision making, and in particular encourages the voicing of dissent in organizations.[53]

In general, any exploration of different ethno-racial work experiences needs to bear in mind the cultural background. This includes both the history and culture of a group's country of origin, and the relationship between that country and the country where the group is now resident. We need to consider the effects of colonialism and imperialism, and how these continue to impact migrants from formerly colonized countries. Different groups have different varieties of diaspora (patterns of dispersion of émigré communities), and different cultural and material resources available to them. These same issues help to illuminate the processes by which stereotypes are produced, for example of African-Americans, Caribbean-Canadians and South-Asian British.

Another leading researcher on these types of question, Robinson, brings into play a range of other possible factors with the potential to deeply inform the types of inequity that occur in and through specific forms of organizational behaviour.[54] For example, we can look at the degree of general social integration or marginalization of specific ethno-racial minority communities and at their 'desire for social mobility'. We need to consider whether these groups are excluded generally from all forms of mobility, or whether they are 'segmented' into and isolated in specific industries, where they may experience some partial upward mobility. Often, the difference pivots on groups' differential success in schooling and their English language skills, but economic isolation is a factor not explained completely by these factors alone.

Modood et al. go beyond the concepts of exclusion and segmentation to explore how ethno-racial groups experience work differently.[51] They look at aspects of communities such as how 'tightly knit' they are, the degree of hierarchy in communities and between families, and the strength of connections to the country of origin, which have grown immensely with advanced telecommunications. All this makes it clear that we cannot ignore the background of home and community life when we try to assess equity in the context of work.

Much empirical research provides us with details of practices within organizations. There are obvious inequities associated with segmentation, exclusion, promotion and earnings, but there is also recent evidence explaining the processes that reproduce inequity across virtually every element of the workplace experience, from hiring practices to the labour process. There are some fascinating and highly instructive case studies that look at ethno-racial dimensions of the experience of work processes (see, for example, Dombrowski[55] on aboriginal workers in the lumber industry of Alaska, Davis[56] and Nelson[57] on black longshoremen, and Bao[58] on Chinese garment workers). In searching for an organizational perspective on issues of inequity, we can begin with the research of Brief et al., which looks at the experience of black applicants for jobs.[20] Drawing on an interesting experimental methodology, they highlight the complex web of relationships between managerial justifications, ethno-racial prejudice and decisions to employ individuals. They show convincingly that the concentration of authority in firms is a key factor in inequitable hiring.

Other researchers have provided a solid analysis of how African-Americans are systematically excluded and 'tokenized' in public services such as firefighting, and some of them focus specifically on women ethnic minority workers.[21] Participation in training programmes is obviously key for workers who want to obtain promotion and greater earnings. Some researchers have shown how non-English-speaking immigrants typically experience great difficulties in getting access to this kind of training.[59]

Recent studies in the USA have confirmed that, through the last decade, black and Hispanic individuals have typically earned 22 and 32 per cent less, respectively, than white workers; when combined with the findings of the previous section on gender, this can produce power combinational effects given that women in the USA also earn approximately 25 per cent less than men. See, for example, Bielby[60] and more recently Penner[61] for more on this. Penner goes on to make invaluable additional points regarding not merely the distribution of income, but also how the pooling of racialized groups in particular occupations explains a significant proportion of these wage disparities. For other countries where we find similar dynamics, the reader is referred to other sources such as Galabuzi in Canada,[46] Smyth in Australia,[62] and Modood[52] in Britain.

weblink

Throughout the world, there are many ethno-racial organizations, advocacy groups and so on doing important and interesting work. www.irr.org.uk/employment gives a sense of the activity in the UK. To further expand your ability to understand the linkages between racism and economic life, explore the following lecture available on the web, which provides an historical and international overview: mp3.lpi.org.uk/resistancemp3/marxism-and-race.mp3. Explore these and other relevant sites, and report back to your class on what you find

Disability and work: an emerging focus for research?

It is vital to assess gender and ethno-racial issues in the workplace in order to generate a broad and critical view of organizational behaviour and its context in contemporary society. Later, we look at one of the major sources of difficulty that is so pervasive as to have become invisible – social class – but first we explore an important, understudied, although perhaps emerging area of equity studies in the workplace: disability.

The category of disability is broad and diverse. By convention, it is divided into five subgroupings: sensory disability (such as blindness), physical disability, mental and psychiatric problems (such as depression), intellectual and developmental problems (like those experienced by individuals with Down syndrome), and learning difficulties (such as dyslexia). Beyond these categories, in a recent committee session of the United Nations on disability, Kevin McLaughlin put forth this definition for consideration:

Impairment + Disenabling factor = Disability

Disability is defined differently across countries, but available statistics confirm that, in general terms, a large number of people experience some form of disability, and that many of these people experience difficulty in obtaining and retaining paid work. In the USA, for example (where the American Disability Act [ADA] is a key piece of legislation), some researchers estimate that 31 per cent of non-institutionalized citizens aged between 18 and 64 who are considered to have a disability are employed. In other words, there is a 60–69 per cent unemployment rate among people with disabilities.[63] In the UK (where the Disability Discrimination Act is in force), the Labour Force Survey longitudinal database in 2003 reported the unemployment rate among disabled people to be 58 per cent. There were more than 2.4 million people in the UK who were disabled, out of work and wanting to work.

Recent research suggests that people who are disabled have difficulty finding work in which they can effectively apply their skills and talents. They also find difficulty in keeping paid employment. Research suggests that this is largely because of stereotyping and discrimination.[64] Once employed, workers with disabilities report a range of other difficulties, including issues of getting to and from work, movement within the workplace, a lack of adaptation of workstations, low flexibility in work arrangements, a lack of job coaches and a lack of Braille or other forms of text translation assistance. Bruyere has done further research into employer work practices, and reports that the most important challenges disabled workers faced involved the attitudes of supervisors and employees in the firms sampled.[65] Specifically, it is reported that changing co-workers' and supervisors' attitudes remains the primary barrier to making positive workplace change with regards to disability. Ranked as slightly less important are things like 'modifying return to work policy', 'creating flexibility in performance management systems' and 'change in leave policy'. Interestingly, Bruyere's research also allows us to see that there are inconsistent differences when comparing the private with the public sector regarding the importance placed on these concerns. While a concern for changing attitudes is roughly equal in these terms, return to work policy would seem to be more of a problem in the private sector, whereas additional issues such as 'ensuring equal pay and benefits' appear to be a greater concern in the public sector.

stop reflect

The World Health Organization's International Classification of Functioning, Disability and Health website (www.who.int/features/2005/disability/en) features a photo contest entitled 'Images of health and disability'. Go to the website and examine the images you find there. There are several entries that deal with work. What kinds of question do they raise for you? How does this relate to issues of equity?
The Internet also includes a range of quizzes on disability knowledge and attitudes. Many are specific to particular countries, so take a moment to look for one applicable to your country and report back to the class. If you cannot locate one for your area, why not consider creating one based on examples from elsewhere you find? Finally, take a moment to explore an important paper by one of the leaders in the field of disability studies, Mike Oliver, found at www.independentliving.org/docs4/oliver.html

OB and globalization

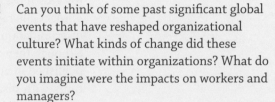

The Paralympic effect: changing the culture of disability and work in China

The 2008 Paralympics in Beijing, China, showcased the talent and charisma of the world's top athletes with disabilities. Billboards and posters featuring Paralympians were displayed prominently throughout the city, and events were televised around the clock. For many Beijingers, this public attention to and celebration of people with disabilities during the Paralympics was unusual to say the least. Although it is estimated that over a million people in Beijing live with a disability, a culture of shame and discrimination – not to mention a lack of infrastructural and social support – has largely prevented them from participating in public life, including work life. On the eve of the Paralympics, many disabled Beijingers and their allies were optimistic that the positive exposure of the Games would translate to improved access to work and supportive services.

Deng Pufang, president of the China Disabled Persons' Federation, expressed hope that the Games would initiate 'a great improvement on the career of the disabled in China and the level of civilization for the whole society' (Xinhua News Agency, 2008). He linked these possibilities for career development to the improvements in social and work life experienced by South Koreans with disabilities following the 1988 Seoul Paralympics. Special education professor Qian Zhiliang of Beijing Normal University echoed Mr Deng's hopes that the Games would reshape public opinion: 'The Paralympics are a platform for ordinary people to accept the disabled and for the disabled to accept themselves' (Demick, 2008).

In the year since the world tuned in to watch the Games, the city of Beijing has instituted policies to assist its disabled residents secure meaningful work, including a government funding programme to help disabled Beijingers access job training and provide incentives to companies to hire disabled workers (Wang, 2009). Although there is enthusiasm for such programmes at home, sceptics have questioned whether the spirit of the Paralympics will indeed be powerful enough to transform Chinese organizational culture (Eimer, 2008). Organizational culture is,

after all, in many ways a reflection of the values and practices of the larger society in which it operates. This case study provides an opportunity to consider the impact of global events on local cultural attitudes towards the proper social roles of particular groups of people. Linked as they are, shifts in organizational culture are possible as well when local cultural meanings are called into question. Paying attention to cultural relationships such as this one can shed light on the particular ways in which changes to organizational culture are enacted and experienced.

stop! Can you think of some past significant global events that have reshaped organizational culture? What kinds of change did these events initiate within organizations? What do you imagine were the impacts on workers and managers?

What types of step could organizations in your country take to ensure an equitable work environment for workers with disabilities? Think about infrastructural steps, as well as adjustments to organizational culture.

Sources and further information

Demick, B. (2008) 'Paralympics boon to China's disabled', *Los Angeles Times*. Available at: http://articles.latimes.com/2008/sep/05/world/fg-para5; http://en.chinaelections.org/newsinfo.asp?newsid=19045 (accessed September 28, 2009).

Eimer, D. (2008) 'Paralympics come to Beijing but little to celebrate for disabled Chinese', *Telegraph*. Available at: www.telegraph.co.uk/news/worldnews/asia/china/2651895/Paralympics-come-to-Beijing-but-little-to-celebrate-for-disabled-Chinese.html; http://hnn.us/roundup/entries/53997.html (accessed September 28, 2009).

Wang, Q. (2009) 'Career boost for disabled Beijingers', *China Daily*. Available at: http://www.chinadaily.com.cn/china/2009-04/01/content_7637958.htm; www.specialolympicseastasia.org/English/News/articles/0904%20Career%20boost%20for%20disabled_en.html (accessed September 28, 2009).

Xinhua News Agency (2008) 'Paralympics a boost for career development of disabled'. Available at: http://en.chinaelections.org/newsinfo.asp?newsid=19011; http://www.chinadaily.com.cn/paralympics/2008-09/08/content_7008821.htm (accessed September 28, 2009).

Note: This feature was written by Gretchen Fox, Anthropologist, Timberline Natural Resource Group, Canada.

Importantly, these statistics point towards a view of disability that moves away from the (unfortunately still prevalent) view that 'disability' is a problem that an individual *has* (that is, he or she is a 'disabled person'), and towards the view that disability is a problem that individuals face *in society*. In other words, it is a problem of how we organize society, including workplaces. This is exemplified by a statement by the Society for Disability Studies in 1993, that its field 'examines the policies and practices of all societies to understand the social, rather than the physical or psychological, determinants of the experience of disability'.[66] This is a crucial shift in how people, including academic researchers, can best understand the phenomenon of disability.

There are various overviews available of international disability policies, including comparative employment policies.[67] The journal *Disability and Society* is perhaps the most accessible English-language source of information on research in this area. However, its discussions of work and employment tend to focus on policy issues (see, for example, Shang on recent changes in China,[68] and Kitchin et al. on the experience of workers with disabilities in Ireland[69]). The issue that is of greatest interest in an organizational behaviour context is the dynamics of behaviour towards those with disabilities, but there is comparatively little literature on this.

MacGillivray et al. provide a look at managerial perspectives and practice on discrimination claims, including a comparative look at the USA and the UK, although they do not focus on disability alone.[70] In addition, an article by Premeaux published in 2001 provides a provocative discussion of the hiring process for applicants with disabilities (in particular, mental disabilities).[71] An important determinant of equitable access to jobs and promotion is access to training, and Tharenou's article on organizational development reported significant barriers in this context.[72]

An interesting case that raises complex questions for organizations can be found in the recent work of Reed,[73] who looks at litigation under the ADA over the last 30 years in the USA, and notes that the consideration of personal risk through employment is something that can now legitimately be taken into account. However well intentioned this legislation, in effect it provides grounds for discrimination. The duty to provide a safe work environment opens the door for important questions for human resources departments. Reed asks whether employer 'paternalism' should take precedence over the rights of a person with disability, as established under the ADA. A related question is how the kind of social definition of disability offered by the Society for Disability Studies relates to these legal structures, but Reed does not specifically consider this point.

Social class

Should issues of social class be included in a discussion of equity and organizational behaviour? Should we bother to resuscitate the term 'class society' from the apparently bygone industrial era? And (even if our answers are 'yes' and 'yes', respectively), what is the relationship of social class to other dimensions of equity, and why would we position it at the end of a chapter?

We would suggest that class is indeed highly relevant. In fact, we position this section at the end of the chapter to emphasize that although each of the dimensions we discuss above involves substantial proportions of the population, relationships of social class underpin the most damaging effects of each of them.

Class can be defined in a variety of ways. It can be understood in terms of culture (such as a bourgeois or working-class culture), status (seeing people as a 'wage earner' or 'owner/manager', for example), or through highly segmented classifications based on occupational and socioeconomic status (with categories such as professional, unskilled, upper-middle class and underclass). These definitions emerge respectively from cultural studies theory, from Marxist theory and from theories of class inspired by the sociologist Max Weber and others (see Chapter 3). There is an excellent, concise and accessible discussion in Milner's *Class*.[74] In

stop reflect

Do you think that disability is more about a disabling environment than a physical impairment? Why have employers largely ignored the legislation aimed at securing equal employment rights for disabled people? A leading activist in Canada (David Lepofsky) frames these issues in terms of challenging our ideas about the meaning of legitimate workplace 'accommodation': (as a lawyer who is blind) he remarks, 'lights are an accommodation for people who see'. See also http://atwestern.typepad.com/convocation_addresses/2006/10/october_19_pm_d.html

Source: Getty Images

plate 30 In male (main) stream organizational behaviour, the interests and ideas of women, racial minorities and people with disability are largely neglected or marginalized.

all cases, however, class involves hierarchy, the means of generation of this hierarchy, and the resulting different experiences and different levels of power, control, resources, sensibilities, behaviours and forms of practice.

Differences in class are generated by the full range of activities in the world (such as consumption, politics and education), but they are typically thought to be rooted in economic and employment experiences. In this chapter, our focus is on those who find themselves at a disadvantage (such as women in our discussions of gender, and minority groups in our discussions of race and ethnicity), so here we deal primarily with those who are subordinated by class processes – that is, the working classes. It should be emphasized that class issues interrelate with other issues of discrimination, so those at a disadvantage because of their gender, disability, race or ethnic origin find themselves doubly (triply, quadruply) disadvantaged if they are waged workers.

We can introduce our discussion of how class hierarchies work under a capitalist system by looking at the pay rates of corporate CEOs and the average workers in the same firms. According to the *New York Times*, the average CEO of a major corporation in the USA in 2002 received US$10.8 million in total compensation. That was 400 times as much as the average worker in those corporations, a proportion that has grown from a relatively modest 42 times in 1980. The available statistics suggest that the ratio is tighter in most other countries, but this is still evidence of considerable and growing differentials rooted in the world of work.[75] Streek's international comparison shows the following ratios regarding average CEO earnings and those of manual workers as follows: Japan, 7.8 to 1; Germany, 10.2 to 1; UK, 15.5 to 1; and USA, 25.8 to 1. For an informative and more recent look at the structure of executive compensation with a focus on the USA (but prior to the global recession that started in 2008/09), see Martin.[76] Again with a focus primarily on the USA but with a wide range of international examples, see also Gilbert,[77] which deals with executive compensation ratios and with other measures of inequality as well.

If we look at the major international journals on organizational behaviour, human resource development and organizational studies, or at most major textbooks in each of these fields, we discover something interesting, as we mentioned in Chapter 1: there is little mention in them of social class as such. Why is this? As we suggested earlier, perhaps it is because class relationships are so fundamental to the institution of work under capitalism that they have effectively become invisible. However, class is discussed in a wide range of indirect ways – perhaps most prevalently in discussing the role of **trade unions**. Why should *this* be the case?

trade union: an organization whose purpose is to represent the collective interest of workers

Trade unions can be seen as an institutional expression of the class interests of subordinate groups. They operate on the principle that workers need to act collectively to balance the playing field of negotiation with employers. They are certainly not perfect. It is hardly controversial to acknowledge that trade unions, like society more broadly, show fairly consistent patterns of inequity and hierarchy in relation to gender, race and ethnicity, and disability, although these organizations have in the recent past shown an enormous capacity to face up to these challenges.[78] It can be said, then, that unions pursue generalized class interests, but until recently they had not been very effective vehicles for supporting the interests of specific disadvantaged groups. In this sense (to return to a theme introduced at the start of the chapter), we might say that unions pursue the problem of 'vertical' tensions and conflicts, but tend to leave issues related to more 'horizontal' tensions and conflicts to fester. For all their inadequacies, however, unions remain for the average worker perhaps the only consistent vehicles for bettering conditions and increasing their say, or 'democracy', in the realm of work. As such, they are valuable institutions for addressing inequities in the context of organizational life.

In the 1960s, 70s and 80s, many women, ethno-racial minorities and progressives held out great hopes that equity and antidiscrimination legislation would improve equity in the workplace. (This was similar to the struggle that has moved on to advocates for those with disabilities today.) As the statistics bear out, their hopes have, however, been only marginally satisfied. Although small shifts have taken place, minorities continue to experience widespread and multiple forms of discrimination, and the fortunes of women are not much different. For both groups, it has become increasingly clear that labour unions are an important means of helping the majority of women and people of colour to overcome barriers in the workplace.[79] Indeed, perhaps disability advocates will soon realize this too.

While racism and sexism are seen in labour unions, increasingly unions have actively addressed these issues, for the sake of both social justice and their own survival. Some have done so with considerable success. In general, we believe that unions are vital for alleviating some of the major difficulties that it seems neither legislation nor corporate antidiscrimination programmes can adequately address. According to the US Bureau of Labor Statistics, for example, unions continue to play the most significant role in closing the gender wage gap. Unionized women earn an average of 31 per cent more than non-unionized women. Wage inequality in Canada is much lower than in the USA, but in Canada, according to the national statistics service, unionized women earned 38 per cent more than non-unionized women in 2002. When race and ethnicity are factored in, the 'union advantage' drops only marginally, to 34 per cent.

In general terms, in the USA, the UK and Canada, where there is greater working-class representation (through unions), there is a less ethno-racial and gender pay inequity. According to an Organisation for Economic Co-operation and Development (OECD) report in 1996, in the social democratic countries of Scandinavia, in countries with related 'social market' policies such as Germany and the Netherlands, and in France and Italy, where union coverage is very high (50–90 per cent), the same basic correlation holds true. However, we can usefully ask how exactly class representation, equity in the workplace and economic activity are related in broader terms.

Most mainstream economists see unions as almost exclusively concerned with raising the wages of their members. This, we are told, is a bad thing that 'distorts' the 'proper' functioning of labour markets and the economy. In this mainstream approach, the gains of unionized workers come at the expense of other workers, and perhaps even of society as a whole. In fact, however, this mainstream view does not hold water. While there are any number of ways of alleviating class inequities, the most developed economic literature recognizes that unions may in fact increase overall wage levels (across all workers, unionized and non-unionized) without detrimental effects on the economy. At the same time, unions provide a host of other mechanisms for challenging ethno-racial and gender inequities, giving a greater democratic say to employees, and providing a portion of human dignity at work.

It is sometimes claimed that unionization is detrimental to economic success, but this too is not borne out by the facts. For example, a large-scale study by the World Bank (itself no union partisan) showed no relationship between levels of unionization and the economic or employment performance of a country.[80] Likewise, in 1996, the OECD (looking at the 1980s and 90s) found no valid statistical proof that unionization was related to the greater or poorer economic/employment performance of industrialized countries. The International Labour Organization similarly demonstrated in 2001 that high unionization is quite compatible with good economic and employment performance.

Equity is as compatible with a flourishing economy as it is with a fair and just society, and this is true in class terms as well as for ethno-racial minorities, women and those who are disabled.

Work and Society: **Does diversity pay?**

Debates about diversity at work typically address the question of discrimination and the exclusion of certain categories of person on the basis of arbitrary criteria such as gender, religion or skin colour. Arguments against discriminatory practices can rest on moral principles such as the right of all people to be treated fairly and without prejudice. Arguments against discrimination can also rest on more narrowly economic considerations. For example, one might ask: what would be the impact on a firm's 'bottom line' if discrimination were decreased and diversity increased. Answers to questions like this form the basis of what might be called 'the business case for diversity'.

Using sophisticated quantitative methods, sociologist Cedric Herring (2009) set out to examine critically the business case for diversity. His research was organized in relation to a number of hypotheses. He tested these hypotheses against the data to determine whether the case for diversity could be justified on both moral and economic grounds. Among the hypotheses were the following propositions:

As racial workforce diversity increases, a business organization's profits relative to its competitors will increase. (p. 213)

As gender workforce diversity increases, a business organization's profits relative to its competitors will increase. (p. 213)

Herring's approach to diversity is interesting for a number of reasons. At the most general level, Herring wants to convince his audience that he is not biased and that he is approaching the topic in an objective, scientific way. He makes sure that his hypotheses are formulated explicitly, and he identifies clearly the data he will use to test those hypotheses. He also identifies different possible explanations for the place of diversity in business organizations and notes that decisions about diversity may vary in relation to the kind of business organization one is considering. Finally, he notes that the business case for diversity is not straightforward: there are some complicating factors that must be considered.

However, despite various complicating factors, Herring concludes that there is a strong business case for diversity. As he puts it:

Critics assert that diversity is linked with conflict, lower group cohesiveness, increased employee absenteeism and turnover, and lower quality and performance. Nevertheless,

results show a positive relationship between racial and gender diversity of establishments and their business functioning. It is likely that diversity produces positive outcomes over homogeneity because growth and innovation depend on people from various backgrounds working together and capitalizing on their differences. Although such differences may lead to communication barriers and group conflict, diversity increases the opportunities for creativity and the quality of the product of group work. (p. 220)

 stop! What kinds of creativity are likely to be unique to high-diversity organizations? Provide an example of a business organization in which diversity-related creativity is likely to exist, and develop a detailed description of how this creativity might be linked to improvements in that organization's bottom line relative to its competitors.

Herring refers to the possibility of 'communication barriers and group conflict' in organizations with higher levels of diversity. What might cause this conflict, what forms would it take, and how could it be averted?

Many large firms have introduced programmes to increase the amount of diversity among managers. Why do you think they have done this? Among the programmes introduced are diversity training, diversity evaluations, mentoring programmes and diversity managers (Dobbin et al., 2007). In your view, which programmes would be most effective and why?

Sources and further information

Dobbin, F., Kalev, A. and Kelly, E. (2007) 'Diversity management in corporate America', *Contexts*, **6**(4), pp. 21–7.

Herring, C. (2009) 'Does diversity pay?: race, gender and the business case for diversity', *American Sociological Review*, **74**(2), pp. 208–24.

Padavic, I. and Reskin, B. (2002) *Women and Men at Work* (2nd edition), Thousand Oaks, CA: Pine Forge Press.

Note: This feature was written by David MacLennan, Assistant Professor at Thompson Rivers University, BC, Canada.

Chapter summary

- We began this chapter with the claim that understanding issues of equity across the major social divisions of society is vital for a full understanding of organizational behaviour. We explored the general and specific tensions in organizations that make the issues of equity, inequity and justice a relevant topic for learning and research. Vertical and horizontal conflicts were shown to help us understand the complex forms of power that play out across organizations.

- Some suggest that the institution of work, including practices in work organizations, divisions in pay, and related issues such as access to training and employment, has become fundamentally more equitable over the years. We argue that this is only partially correct. There is still much to be done.

- Women, people from ethno-racial minorities, those who are disabled, and members of the working class (and all the combinations of these categories) continue to face major difficulties in gaining just and equitable treatment in relation to paid work. Students and scholars of organizational behaviour will benefit from a broader appreciation of these dynamics to inform the direction of future learning and research. Taken together, the vast majority of people in our society are subject to some form of discrimination. This begs the question of why, if the vast majority of people experience systematic inequities in relation to work, it is so difficult to realize significant, positive change. Some of the answers to this question lie within the realm of existing organizational behaviour research, but many others have not yet been addressed. To address these questions of equity, it is necessary to take a fundamental look at how work and society are organized. Through some of the interdisciplinary dimensions of this chapter, we hope readers will start on that journey of further exploration.

Key concepts

disability	230–232
ethnicity	227–229
femininities/masculinities	225–227
gender	225–227
institutional racism	234
labour market segmentation	224
patriarchy	225
race	227–229
sexual division of labour	225–227
sexuality	225
social class	232
social exclusion	229

Key vocab for ESL students

- ☐ Appropriation
- ☐ Disability, disable, disabled
- ☐ Employment equity
- ☐ Equity, equate, equable
- ☐ Ethnicity, ethnic
- ☐ Feminist perspective
- ☐ Gender bias
- ☐ Gender identity
- ☐ Gender role
- ☐ Gender socialization
- ☐ Glass ceiling
- ☐ Horizontal tension
- ☐ Human rights
- ☐ Justice
- ☐ Patriarchy
- ☐ Race, racism, racist
- ☐ Sex, sexuality
- ☐ Sexual harassment
- ☐ Sticky floor
- ☐ Vertical tension

Chapter review questions

1. What are the meaning and value of 'equitable practices' in organizations?
2. What is the relationship between the different dimensions of organizational justice and the specific social differences we explored in this chapter?
3. What do the terms 'sticky floors' and 'glass ceiling' have to do with gender, as well as with other forms of social difference?
4. How do these forms of social difference relate to one another to intensify or reduce inequities in organizations?

Chapter research questions

1. As we have been reminded of in this chapter, issues of equity and inequity come in a host of forms. A basic principle underlying each is the matter of inclusion and exclusion. All organizations produce patterns of inclusion and exclusion in both subtle and not-so-subtle ways. Take a moment to think about these processes in either your prior work experiences or your current study experiences. Can you identify some key ways in which different people come to be included and excluded from experiences and opportunities? Is there something systematic or patterned about these instances? Are there some forms of exclusion that matter more than others? Share your ideas with a fellow student and then test the hypothesis concerning whether or not – and if so, how – the effects of social differences such as the ones discussed in this chapter may be mutually reinforcing.

2. A relevant issue that has not been explicitly addressed in this chapter is the role that education and work-based training play in supporting equity or inequity. Training is typically thought of by most people as one of the great equalizers: through training people are provided with a chance at success and advancement. However, even workplace training systems can play in a role in reproducing existing inequities. A good collection of reflections on the role of equity in training can be found in a book edited by Marjorie Griffin Cohen entitled *Training the Excluded for Work: Access and Equity for Women, Immigrants, First Nations, Youth and People with Low Income*

(published by University of British Columbia Press in 2003). Its 14 chapters provide a series of case studies on training and its role in equity/inequity. Although based on nationally specific research (Canada), the same or remarkably similar insights can undoubtedly be applied to virtually any developed country. Take time to skim this collection, select a chapter and then report back to your class on it. What are the ways in which social differences play a role in work life chance through training systems? How different or similar might these dynamics be in other countries? If training is not quite the 'great equalizer', how might it be made so in your and your classmates' view?

3. A keystone that links employees' lives and organizational behaviour is the idea of careers and career development. Obviously, the very idea of a 'career' encapsulates not simply one's job, but one's past and future employment as well. Since equity in organizations likewise depends on the past, present and future of one's work experiences and opportunities, examining how equity and inequity are interwoven with career development makes a good deal of sense. There is a variety of written works that discuss equity in relation to careers, but a good one is Baruch's *Managing Careers: Theory and Practice* (published by Prentice-Hall, 2004). In particular, its discussion of diversity management and equity gives us additional food for thought for their effects on careers. Review Baruch's chapter on equity and career development, and select from this book's set of case studies an example that you feel is particularly important in terms of equity. What does the chapter and/or the selected case study suggest about how organizations need to change in order to be more equitable?

 Further reading

Brief, A., Dietz, J., Cohen, R., Pugh, S. D. and Vaslow J. (2000) 'Just doing business: modern racism and obedience to authority as explanations for employment discrimination', *Organizational Behavior and Human Decision Processes*, **81**(1), pp. 72–97.

Folger, R. and Cropanzano, R. (1998) *Organizational Justice and Human Resource Management*, Thousand Oaks, CA: Sage.

Jackson, A. (2000) *The Myth of the Equity–Efficiency Trade-off*, Ottawa: Canadian Council on Social Development.

Loprest, P. and Maag, E. (2001) *Barriers and Supports for Work among Adults with Disabilities: Results from the NHIS-D*, Washington, DC: Urban Institute.

Chapter case study 1

Equity challenges in South African police service organizations

Background

Dramatic events transformed South African society with the end of apartheid and democratic change in 1994. The new government officially proclaimed goals of representativeness, including plans to eventually have workplace organizations become representative of the population as a whole from top to bottom. Informed by principles of organizational justice as well as democracy, Employment and Human Rights legislation was

developed and put into initial practices across a majority of the economic sectors. One such sector was the police services in South Africa. Historically, these services remained dominated largely by white males with black male and black female officers (as a significant portion) only to be found in the lower third-class ranks, and the majority of women generally located in administrative work. Since the implementation of a range of laws and organizational policies, the police services in South Africa have shown slow progress.

The police officer

Lawrence Cooper, a white South African man and 10-year veteran of the Public Order Police (POP) Service of South Africa (renamed as of 1995) had carefully cultivated a deep working understanding of what needed to be known and done in order to police effectively in Durban, the POP in Durban including over 800 employees.

Although the purposes and goals of the police services had been radically changed since the election of the African National Congress government in 1994, Officer Cooper knew for instance that cohesion among police officers was vital. He also knew that every effective police officer needed to have a vast working knowledge of the people, the places and events. While some now said that these forms of knowledge were tinged with stereotypes – gendered and racial and highly linked to a long history of politics as well – and Officer Cooper knew that there was some truth in this, he also felt that they were part of the skills of effective police work. In fact, officers from all races used stereotypes for their work, and he felt there was importance to knowing how whites (indigenous European descent), Indians (indigenous Asian descent), Africans (indigenous African descent) and the Coloured people (of mixed racial descent), both Africans and Coloured being generally referred to as black, behaved in different circumstances.

Moreover, the physical side of much police work, he felt, generally made it 'unsuitable' for women; they were emotionally fragile and, he felt, were prone to leave the service to care for a family before they could develop the necessary skills and advance in ability and status. And in any case, he knew of few women who wanted to do this type of work. These matters were things that were deeply intertwined in the quality of his work. In some cases, his life literally depended on these forms of what could be called the informal 'cultural knowledge' of his job. These were things that were hard and important to learn, and he felt proud of his ability to do his assigned tasks well. On a personal level, he had developed a particular understanding of his role, learned it well and developed status as an excellent officer.

By 2001, Officer Cooper had seen important changes in the Durban POP. It had an African man as its unit commander, for example, although as far as he knew there was not, nor had there ever been, a requirement for the commander (or middle management for that matter) to be trained or have specialized skills in race relations within the force, which Officer Cooper thought was strange, especially given this new political environment and new policies. There were two high-ranking African women in operational management. What was clear, however, was that these appointments had a trickle-down effect: at the very least, officers in general complained less openly about the equity or affirmative action changes. In fact, reading a report from 2001, Officer Cooper already knew that over 50 per cent of officers were Africans and a third were

Indian, while the proportion of white officers had dwindled to about 1 in 10.

At the same time, Officer Cooper also saw that many other things were much slower to change. Although not an official policy (the official policy in fact being to racially integrate the units), units in the Durban POP remained racially segregated as they had traditionally been, but, importantly, the changes had, in his view, somehow 'fragmented' the force in many ways. Non-white officers, for example, were now much more likely to complain of specialized treatment for the largely white-only units. Black officers had even formed their own 'POP Empowerment Committee' (a committee that nevertheless included only a very small number of black women officers), which was in Cooper's view an example of how changes were happening not just from the top down, but from the bottom up.

Officer Cooper knew that, separate from the citizens he dealt with as a police officer, matters of race and gender were part of working with other officers. His years prior to 1994 in policing had been built on a long tradition in which the black officers were for decades not only limited in terms of whom they could arrest, and where and what they could police, but also frequently could not read or write, although this had changed quite a bit. Officer Cooper blamed 'affirmative action' for moving too quickly to bring both women and black individuals into key positions throughout the organization. The working skills and principles he had cultivated so carefully were under threat, and he resented it. In particular, the principle of cohesion, so vital to the police services in Cooper's understanding, had declined, and the quality of his work, if not the unit as a whole, was in jeopardy. For cohesion, officers needed to know their place and role. For effectiveness, he felt that policing needed to have the right person with the right abilities in the right position.

Tasks

Organizational justice, equity and human rights policy and law, politics, history and social differences – in addition to how each of these factors shapes and is given life in the course of daily lives and working knowledge within organizations – are all essential issues to consider in cases of equity in organizational behaviour. Such matters are particularly pronounced in the case described here, but they are just as likely to be found in various forms and types in other sectors and national settings. Begin working on this case study by noting factors related to policy, politics and history affecting the events summarized in the case above. Then create a list of important everyday organizational practices and forms of knowledge that have played a role. Finally, note that, over the last decade and half, inequities have proven difficult to dislodge. Now turn to the following questions:

1. What were the organizational structures that resisted creating greater equity in the police services in this case study?
2. How did organizational behaviour in everyday life (forms of informal 'cultural knowledge') play a role in this circumstance?
3. Specifically, what is the role of forms of cultural knowledge in organizations in relationship to equity/inequity?
4. What theories of organizational justice are most applicable to this case?

Following your work on this task, be sure to explore the expanded description of this case in the source documents listed below.

Sources of additional information

Marks, M. (2005) *Transforming the Robocops: Changing Police in South Africa*, Durban: University of KwaZulu-Natal Press.

Marks, M. (2008) 'Looking different, acting different: struggles for equality within the South African Police Service', *Public Administration*, **86**(3), pp. 643–58.

Note

This case study was written by Peter Sawchuk, Associate Professor, University of Toronto, Canada.

 Chapter case study 2

The glass ceiling commission

 Visit www.palgrave.com/business/brattonob2e to view this case study

Web-based assignment

This chapter covered many areas of inequity in organizations, but it certainly did not cover them all. Issues of ageism (discrimination based on age) and discrimination based on sexual orientation are two of the key ones that were not explored. The latter forms the basis of this case study. With over 75,000 employees worldwide and 16 billion in revenue, one of the leading corporations in the area of support for employees who are lesbian, gay, bisexual and transgender (LGBT) is Raytheon.

First, take some time to think of some of the issues faced by LGBT employees. Then go to the following website and see Raytheon's perspective: www.raytheon.com/newsroom/feature/equal0606.

OB in film

In *Dirty Pretty Things* (2002), we get a glimpse into the intersection of race, ethnicity, immigration, gender and class, as characters Okwe and Senay, who have both recently emigrated to England, must cope with various inequities, injustice and violence. Although the examples represented in the film are extreme, we nevertheless see a modern portrayal of multiple forms of inequity and social difference in relation to the lower-tier service economy that is growing in all G8 countries.

References

1   Godard, J. (2005) *Industrial Relations: The Economy and Society* (3rd edn), Concord, ON: Captus Press.
2   Peetza, D., Gardner, M., Brown, K. and Berns, S. (2008) 'Workplace effects of equal employment opportunity legislation: the Australian experience', *Policy Studies*, **29**(4), pp. 405–19.
3   Greenberg, J. and McCarty, C. L. (1987) 'A taxonomy of organizational justice theories', *Academy of Management Review*, **12**, pp. 9–22.

4   Cropanzano, R. and Greenberg, J. (1997) 'Progress in organizational justice: tunneling through the maze', pp. 317–72 in C. L. Cooper and I. T. Robertson (eds), *International Review of Industrial and Organizational Psychology*, New York: Wiley.

5   Cohen-Charash, Y. and Spector, P. (2001) 'The role of justice in organizations: a meta-analysis', *Organizational Behavior and Human Decision Processes*, **86**(2), pp. 278–321.

6   Colquitt, J. A., Conlon, D. E., Wesson, M. J., Porter, C. O. L. H. and Ng, K. Y. (2001) 'Justice at the millennium: a meta-analytic review of 25 years of organizational justice research', *Journal of Applied Psychology*, **86**(3), pp. 425–45.

7   Sawyer, J., Houlette, M. and Yeagley, E. (2006) 'Decision performance and diversity structure: comparing faultlines in convergent, crosscut, and racially homogenous groups', *Organizational Behaviour and Human Decision Processes*, **99**(1), pp. 1–15.

8   Johnson, R., Selenta, C. and Lord, R. (2006) 'When organizational justice and the self-concept meet: consequences for the organization its members', *Organizational Behaviour and Human Decision Processes*, **99**(2), pp. 175–201.

9   Leventhal, G. S., Karuza, J. and Fry, W. R. (1980) 'Beyond fairness: a theory of allocation preferences', pp.167–218 in G. Mikula (ed.), *Justice and Social Interaction*, New York: Springer-Verlag.

10 Colquitt, J., Scott, B., Judge,T. and Shaw, J. (2006) 'Justice and personality: using integrative theories to derive moderators of justice effects', *Organizational Behaviour and Human Decision Processes*, **100**(1), pp. 110–27.

11 Roberson, Q. (2006) 'Justice in teams: the activation of role and sensemaking in the emergence of justice climates', *Organizational Behaviour and Human Decision Processes*, **100**(2), pp. 177–92.

12 McFarlin, D. and Sweeney, P. (1992) 'Distributive and procedural justice as predictors of satisfaction with personal and organizational outcomes', *Academy of Management Journal*, **35**, pp. 626–37.

13 Tyler, T. (1990) *Why People Obey the Law: Procedural Justice, Legitimacy and Compliance*, New Haven, CT: Yale University Press.

14 Folger, R. and Cropanzano, R. (1998) *Organizational Justice and Human Resource Management*, Thousand Oaks, CA: Sage.

15 Ball, G., Trevino, L. and Sims, H. (1993) 'Justice and organizational punishment: attitudinal outcomes of disciplinary events', *Social Justice Research*, **6**, pp. 39–67.

16 Organ, D. (1990) 'The motivational basis of organizational citizenship behavior', pp. 43–72 in L. Cummings and B. Staw (eds), *Research in Organizational Behavior*, Volume 12, Greenwich, CT: JAI Press.

17 Masterson, S., Lewis, K., Goldman, B. and Taylor, M. (2000) 'Integrating justice and social exchange: the differing effects of fair procedures and treatment on work relationships', *Academy of Management Journal*, **43**, pp. 738–48.

18 Ambrose, M., Seabright, M. and Schminke, M. (2002) 'Sabotage in the workplace: the role of organizational injustice', *Organizational Behaviour and Human Decision Processes*, **89**(1), pp. 947–65.

19 Aquino, K. and Douglas, S. (2003) 'Identity threat and antisocial behavior in organizations: the moderating effects of individual differences, aggressive modeling, and hierarchical status', *Organizational Behavior and Human Decision Processes*, **90**(1), pp. 195–208.

20 Brief, A., Dietz, J., Cohen, R., Pugh, S. D. and Vaslow, J. (2000) 'Just doing business: modern racism and obedience to authority as explanations for employment discrimination', *Organizational Behavior and Human Decision Processes*, **81**(1), pp. 72–97.

21 Yoder, J. and Berendsen, L. (2001) '"Outsider within" the firehouse: African American and white women firefighters', *Psychology of Women Quarterly*, **25**(1), pp. 27–36.

22 United Nations (2007) *The Employment Imperative: Report on the World Social Situation 2007*. New York: United Nations Department of Economic and Social Affairs.

23 Kim, J. (2002) 'Taking note of the new gender earnings gap: a study of the 1990's economic expansion in the US labor market', *Journal of American Academy of Business*, **2**(1), pp. 80–5.

24 Hirsch, B. and MacPherson, D. (2003) *Union Membership and Earnings Data Book: Compilations from the Current Population Survey*, Washington, DC: Bureau of National Affairs.

25 Hartmann, H. (2003) 'Closing the gap amidst ongoing discrimination: women and economic disparities', *Multinational Monitor*, **24**(5), pp. 25–7.

26 Carrington, W. and Troske, K. (1998) 'Sex segregation in U.S. manufacturing', *Industrial and Labor Relations Review*, **51**(3), pp. 445–65.

27 Glomb, T., Richmann, W., Hulin, C. and Drasgow, R (1997) 'Ambient sexual harassment: an integrated model of antecedents and consequences', *Organizational Behavior and Human Decision Processes*, **71**(3), pp. 309–28.

28 Wajcman, J. (1998) *Managing Like a Man: Women and Men in Corporate Management*, Cambridge: Polity Press/Penn State University Press.

29 Rubenstein, H. (2003) *Women and Leadership: Review of Recent Studies*, Washington, DC: Growth Strategies.

30 Moss, N. E. (2002) 'Gender equity and socioeconomic inequality: a framework for the patterning of women's health', *Social Science and Medicine*, **54**(5), pp. 649–61.

31 Colarelli, S., Spranger, J. and Hechanova, M. (2006) 'Women, power, and sex composition in small groups: an evolutionary perspective', *Journal of Organizational Behaviour*, **27**(2), pp. 163–84.

32 Meyerson, D. E. and Fletcher, J. K. (2000) 'A modest manifesto for shattering the glass ceiling', *Harvard Business Review*, **78**(1), pp. 127–37.

33 Yoder, J. (2002) 'Context matters: understanding tokenism processes and their impact on women's work', *Psychology of Women Quarterly*, **26**(1), pp. 1–8.

34 Siegrist, M., Cvetkovich, G. and Gutscher, H. (2002) 'Risk preference predictions and gender stereotypes', *Organizational Behavior and Human Decision Processes*, **87**(1), pp. 91–102.

35 Walters, A., Stuhlmacher, A. and Meyer, L. (1998) 'Gender and negotiator competitiveness: a meta-analysis', *Organizational Behavior and Human Decision Processes*, **76**(1), pp. 1–29.

36 Falkenberg, L. and Boland, L. (1997) 'Eliminating the barriers to employment equity in the Canadian workplace', *Journal of Business Ethics*, **16**(9), pp. 963–75.

37 LePine, J., Hollenbeck, J., Ilgen, D. and Colquitt, J. (2002) 'Gender composition, situational strength, and team decision-making accuracy: a criterion decomposition approach', *Organizational Behavior and Human Decision Processes*, **88**(1), pp. 445–75.

38 Kray, L., Galinsky, A. and Thompson, L. (2002) 'Reversing the gender gap in negotiations: an exploration of stereotype regeneration', *Organizational Behavior and Human Decision Processes*, **87**(2), pp. 386–409.

39 Ngo, H., Foley, S., Wong, A. and Loi, R. (2003) 'Who gets more of the pie? Predictors of perceived gender inequity at work', *Journal of Business Ethics*, **45**(3), pp. 227–41.

40 Bao, X. (1991) *Holding up More than Half the Sky: Chinese Women Garment Workers in New York City, 1948–1992*, Urbana/Chicago: University of Illinois Press.

41 Hanson, J. (2003) 'Fighting for the union label: the women's garment industry and the ILGWU in Pennsylvania', *Oral History Review*, **30**(1), pp. 143–58.

42 Brooks, E. (2002) 'The ideal sweatshop? Gender and transnational protest', *International Labor and Working-Class History*, **61**, pp. 91–111.

43 Parrenas, R. (2001) *Servants of Globalization: Women, Migration, and Domestic Work*, Stanford: Stanford University Press.

44 Ward, L. (1998) 'Ethnic minorities pessimistic over race relations', *Guardian*, September 10.

45 Linden, M. V. (1995) *Racism and the Labour Market: Historical Studies*, New York: Bern.

46 Galabuzi, G-E. (2006) *Canada's Economic Apartheid: The Social Exclusion of Racialized Groups in the New Century*, Toronto: Canadian Scholars' Press.

47 US Bureau of Labor Statistics (2002) US Bureau of Labor Statistics (2002) 'Employment and earnings'. Available at: www.bls.gov/cps/home.htm.

48 Bates, T. (1994) 'Utilization of minority employees in small business: a comparison of nonminority and black-owned enterprises', *Review of Black Political Economy*, **23**, pp. 113–21.

49 Raphael, S., Stoll, M and Holzer, H. (2000) 'Are suburban firms more likely to discriminate against African-Americans?', *Journal of Urban Economics*, **48**(3), pp. 485–508.

50 Jones, T. (1993) *Britain's Ethnic Minorities*, London: Policy Studies Institute.

51 Modood, T., Berthoud, R., Lakey, J. et al. (1997) *Ethnic Minorities in Britain: Diversity and Disadvantage*, London: Policy Studies Institute.

52 Modood, T. (2007). *Multiculturalism: A Civic Idea*, Cambridge: Polity Press.

53 Phillips, K. and Loyd, D. L. (2006) 'When surface and deep-level diversity collide: the effects on dissenting group members', *Organizational Behaviour and Human Decision Processes*, **99**(2), pp. 143–60.

54 Robinson, V. (1990) 'Roots of mobility', *Ethnic and Racial Studies*, **13**(2), pp. 274–86.

55 Dombrowski, K. (2002) 'Bill Budd, choker-setter: native culture and Indian work in the Southeast Alaska timber industry', *International Labor and Working-Class History*, **62**, pp. 121–42.

56 Davis, C. (2002) '"Shape or fight?": New York's black longshoremen, 1945–1961', *International Labor and Working-Class History*, **62**, pp. 143–63.

57 Nelson, B. (2001) *Divided We Stand: American Workers and the Struggle for Black Equality*, Princeton: Princeton University Press.

58 Bao, X. (2002) 'Sweatshops in Sunset Park: a variation of the late 20th century Chinese garment shops in New York City', *International Labor and Working-Class History*, **61**, pp. 69–90.

59 Vanden Heuvel, A. and Wooden, M. (1997) 'Participation of non-English-speaking-background immigrants in work-related training', *Ethnic and Racial Studies*, **20**(4), pp. 830–48.

60 Bielby, W. (2000) 'Minimizing workplace gender and racial bias', *Contemporary Sociology*, **29**, pp. 120–9.

61 Penner, A. (2008) 'Race and gender differences in wages: the role of occupational sorting at the point of hire', *Sociological Quarterly*, **49**, pp. 597–614.

62 Smyth, P. (2008) 'Closing the gap? The role of wage, welfare and industry policy in promoting social inclusion', *Journal of Industrial Relations*, **50**(4), pp. 647–63.

63 Houtenville, A. J. (2003) *Disability Statistics in the United States*, Ithaca, NY: Cornell University Rehabilitation Research and Training Center.

64 Loprest, P and Maag, E. (2001) *Barriers and Supports for Work among Adults with Disabilities: Results from the NHIS-D*, Washington, DC Urban Institute.

65 Bruyere, S. (2000) *Disability Employment Policies and Practices in Private and Federal Sector Organizations*, Ithaca, NY: Cornell University, School of Industrial and Labor Relations, Program on Employment and Disability.

66 Society for Disability Studies. See www.disstudies.org.

67 Thornton, R. and Lunt, N. (1997) *Employment Policies for Disabled People in Eighteen Countries: A Review*, York: University of York Policy Research Unit.

68 Shang, X. (2000) 'Bridging the gap between planned and market economies: employment policies for people with disabilities in two Chinese cities', *Disability and Society*, **15**(1), pp. 135–56.

69 Kitchin, R., Shirlow, P. and Shuttleworth, I. (1998) 'On the margins: disabled people's experience of employment in Donegal, West Ireland', *Disability and Society*, **13**(5), pp. 785–807.

70 MacGillivray, E., Fineman, M. and Golden, D. (2003) 'Roundup of employment related news', *Journal of Organizational Excellence*, **22**(3), pp. 83–102.

71 Premeaux, S. (2001) 'Impact of applicant disability on selection: the role of disability type, physical attractiveness, and proximity', *Journal of Business and Psychology*, **16**(2), pp. 291–98.

72 Tharenou, P. (1997) 'Determinants of participation in training and development', *Journal of Organizational Behavior*, **4**, pp. 15–28.

73 Reed, L. (2003) 'Paternalism may excuse disability discrimination: when may an employer refuse to employ a disabled individual due to concerns for the individual's safety?', *Business and Society Review*, **108**(3), pp. 417–24.

74 Milner, A. (1999) *Class*, London: Sage.

75 Streek, W. (1996) 'German capitalism: does it exist? Can it survive?', Working Paper No. 218, Department of Industrial Relations, University of Wisconsin-Madison.

76 Martin, J. (2005) 'Golf tournaments and CEO pay: unraveling the mysteries of executive compensation', *Journal of Applied Corporate Finance*, **14**(3), pp. 22–34.

77 Gilbert, G. (2008) *Rich and Poor in America: A Reference Handbook*. Santa Barbara, CA: ABC-CLIO Press.

78 Burke, B., Geronimo, J., Martin, D., Thomas, B. and Wall, C. (2003) *Education for Changing Unions*, Toronto: Between the Lines Press.

79 Bronfenbrenner, K. (2003) 'Organizing women: the nature and process of union organizing efforts among US women workers since the mid-1990s', paper presented at the Cornell ILR Conference on Women and Unions, Ithaca, NY, November.

80 Aidt, T. and Tzannatos, Z. (2003) *Unions and Collective Bargaining: Economic Effects in a Global Environment*, Washington, DC: World Bank.

In this part of the book, we examine some of the important social processes that take place in the context of work groups.

In Chapter 9, we explore the development, nature and behavioural implications of work groups and work teams. The nature of work groups is analysed through the concepts of size, norms, cohesiveness and group learning. Some core concepts associated with decision making in groups are also examined. We go beyond the popular rhetoric and present arguments and evidence to suggest that self-managed teams shift the focus away from hierarchical, bureaucratic control structures and processes, to flatter organizational structures with a culture of self-control.

chapter 9   **Work groups and teams**

chapter 9
Work groups and teams

chapter outline

- Introduction
- Work groups and work teams
- Group dynamics
- Work teams and management theory
- Work teams: ending bureaucracy and extending employee empowerment?
- Paradox in team-based work systems
- Summary and end-of-chapter features
- Chapter case study 1: Building cars in Brazil
- Chapter case study 2: Teams at Land Rock Alliance Insurance

chapter objectives

After completing this chapter, you should be able to:

- distinguish between informal and formal work groups
- explain the current popularity of teams in work organizations
- articulate how group norms and cohesiveness exert influence on individual and group behaviour
- describe and critically evaluate the theories of team development
- explain the pros and cons of using groups to make decisions
- identify the different theoretical perspectives and paradoxes related to work teams

Introduction

Without doubt, everyone will find him- or herself at some point in life to be a member of a group. You have probably already experienced group membership through participating in a sports team, climbing or caving club, jury service, church, political party or study group. In many organizations, people are called upon to work in groups. Work groups influence the behaviour of their members, often enhancing job satisfaction, promoting learning and increasing individual and unit productivity and more effective decision making.

Work groups are not something invented by management consultants. History shows that they have been part of human social development since ancient times. For thousands of years, men and women lived in small hunting and gathering groups, and later they lived in small farming or fishing groups. It is only in the last 200 years, with the advent of industrial capitalism, that small groups have become the exception rather than the rule.[1] The factory system ushered in a minute division of labour and close direct supervision, which substantially improved labour productivity and profits. By the late twentieth century, however, extensive specialization and hierarchical forms of work organization were identified as a 'problem' (see Chapter 2).

A host of mainstream management literature proselytized the notion that traditional work organization was an obstacle to innovation and competitiveness.[2-4] Team work as a system of paid work is intended to transcend the alleged problems of inflexibility, poor quality, low employee commitment and motivation associated with traditional work structures. Its increased prevalence in Europe and North America is a recognition by employers that competitive advantage comes from so-called lean organizations, the full utilization of their human capital, and a set or 'bundle' of 'soft' human resource management practices that form part of an integrated high-performance workplace (HPW).[5] In the critical literature, team work and HPW initiatives are a means of increasing work intensification, obtaining higher productivity, increasing workplace stress and controlling workers indirectly through a culture of self-control.[5-9]

Before reading on, consider your own experience of group membership. Do people behave differently in groups? You might have experienced working in a study group at college or university. Reflect on your experience, and consider what specific behaviours exhibited during the group sessions were helpful to the group. What specific behaviours exhibited were detrimental to the group? How did the group deal with a member who was constantly late or did not complete his or her assigned work for a group assignment?

stop reflect

If you paused and thought about the questions we asked in the 'Stop and reflect' box above, you should appreciate that understanding groups and teams in work organizations is important for several reasons. Team work has become a significant feature of organizational life. Individuals behave differently when in a work group from how they do when they work independently. Team synergy can potentially transform moribund productivity and improve organizational performance. Finally, understanding group dynamics is seen to be an important aspect of managing (controlling) people more effectively.

This chapter introduces the complex phenomenon of work groups and work teams in organizations. It begins by examining the background, nature and behavioural implications of work groups. We also explore the nature of work groups through the concepts of group norms, cohesiveness and learning. Finally, we go beyond management rhetoric, and present arguments and evidence to suggest that self-managed teams shift the focus away from the hierarchy, and direct and bureaucratic **control** processes, to a culture of self-control.

> control: the collection and analysis of information about all aspect of the work organization and the use of comparisons that are either historical and/or based on benchmarking against another business unit

Work groups and work teams

What are work groups?

The term 'group' can be used to describe a cluster of individuals watching a hockey game or queuing for a bank teller. When studying the behaviour of groups, it is important to distinguish between a mere cluster of individuals and what organizational theorists call a 'psychological group'. This term is used to describe individuals who perceive themselves to be in a group, who have a shared sense of collective identity, and who relate to each other in a meaningful way. We can define a **work group** as two or more people who are in face-to-face interaction, each aware of their membership in the group, and striving to accomplish assigned work tasks.

> work group: two or more employees in face-to-face interaction, each aware of their positive interdependence as they endeavour to achieve mutual work-related goals

The first part of this definition suggests that there must be an opportunity for people to interact socially with each other, that is, to communicate with each other, to behave in each other's presence, and to be affected by the other's behaviour. Over time, group members who regularly interact socially become aware of each other's values, feelings and goals, which then influence their behaviour. Although a work group can theoretically range from two members to an unspecified upper limit, the need to interact limits the size of the group.

The second part of the definition refers to group members' perceptions of the group itself. Members of the group are able to distinguish who is and who is not in the group, and are aware that an action affecting one member is likely to affect all. This part of the definition helps us to exclude mere clusters of people who are simply individuals who happen to be assembled at the same location at a particular time (such as soccer fans, bank customers or airline travellers). These individuals do not consider themselves a part of any identifiable unit, nor do they relate to one another in any meaningful fashion, despite their close proximity.

On the other hand, a soccer team, an airline crew or a project team at the Bank of Scotland would fulfil the criteria for a work group. In a situation of extreme danger – such as the hijacking of an airline – an aggregate of passengers could be transformed into a group. For example, several passengers on US United Airlines Flight 93, which crashed on September 11, 2001, apparently formed a group that stormed the cockpit to prevent the hijackers from carrying out any further terrorist acts.

The third part of the definition implies that group members have common goals, which they work collectively to accomplish. Six individuals drinking coffee in the company rest area at the same time would not necessarily be considered a group. They do not have common goals, nor are they dependent on the outcome of each other's actions. However, six union shop stewards drinking coffee together regularly to discuss health and safety issues or grievances would be considered a work group.

Groups in organizations can be formal or informal. Organizational decision makers create formal work groups to permit collective action on assigned task(s). In this sense, the rationale for creating work groups can be linked to an organization's competitive strategy. A manufacturing strategy that emphasizes flexibility can result in tasks and responsibilities being reassigned from individual employees and supervisors to a group of employees. This process of dividing up the tasks, assigning responsibility and so on, is called job design, and it is through the restructuring of work that formal work groups are created and consciously designed. Managers are interested in ensuring that the behaviour of the formal group is directed toward organizational goals. Not surprisingly, therefore, much of mainstream organizational behaviour research focuses on the dynamics of formal work groups.

In addition to formal work groups, organizations also contain informal work groups. Managers do not specifically establish these work-based groups; they emerge from the social interaction of workers. Although an organization employs people for their intellectual capital, unlike with other forms of capital, the organization gets the whole person. People bring their personal needs to the workplace. Organizational behaviour theorists suggest that informal work groups are formed as an outcome of psychological processes: the perception of a shared social identity and to fulfil social needs for affiliation and supportive relationships. A cluster of employees can become an informal work group when members influence others' behaviour and contribute to needs satisfaction. Informal work groups are important in that they can help shape communication flows in the organization.

What are work teams?

The words 'group' and 'team' are often used as substitutes. In the management literature, the word 'team' is more likely to be used in a normative sense as a special type of group with positive traits.[10] Like a soccer team, it has connotations of collaboration, mutual support and shared skill and decision making.[11] The observation and implied criticism that 'He is not a team player' or 'This group is not a team' expresses the difference in meaning between 'group' and 'team' in the management lexicon. A mainstream text defines a team as 'a set of interpersonal interactions structured to achieve established goals' (ref. 1, p. 539), and two popular writers define a team as 'a small number of people with complementary skills who are committed to a common purpose, performance goals, and approach for which they hold themselves mutually accountable' (ref. 2, p. 45).

Another variant of 'teams' has become part of current managerial rhetoric – the words 'self-managed work team' (SMWT). The SMWT, which suggests a new way of organizing work, is not the same as a 'work group': an SMWT is 'a group of employees who are responsible for managing and performing technical tasks that result in a product or service being delivered to an internal or external customer' (ref. 12, p. xiii). The difference between work groups and SMWTs is explained in terms of the degree of interdependency and accountability. The interdependence among SMWT members is typically high, and the accountability for the work focuses primarily on the team as a whole rather than the individual group member. Another distinguishing feature of SMWTs is their longevity: SMWTs are typically an integral part of a redesigned organizational structure, brought together for long-term performance goals.

Work teams can be classified according to their position in the organization's hierarchy and their assigned tasks. Figure 9.1 shows three types of work team most commonly found in organizations. Teams that plan and run things are positioned

job design: the process of assigning tasks to a job, including the interdependency of those tasks with other jobs

informal group: two or more people who form a unifying relationship around personal rather than organizational goals

teams: groups of two or more people who interact and influence each other, are mutually accountable for achieving common objectives, and perceive themselves as a social entity within an organization

self-managed work teams: cross-functional work groups organized around work processes that complete an entire piece of work requiring several interdependent tasks, and that have substantial autonomy over the execution of those tasks

plate 31 A self-managed work team allows employees in the core work unit to have sufficient autonomy to manage the work process.

Source: Getty Images

in the top echelon (senior level) of the organization, teams that monitor things occupy the middle levels, and teams that make things occupy the lower levels of the organization. It is important to emphasize, however, that the nature of teams varies considerably among organizations, depending on whether they are engaged in value-added activities in small batches or large batches, or whether they provide financial or other services.

The formal definitions of work teams are not so different from the definition of a formal work group, which might explain why both words are used interchangeably in the organizational behaviour literature. However, the conscious use of the word 'team' is not simply a question of semantics. As we discuss in Chapter 14, mainstream management rhetoric is awash with what Bendix called 'a vocabulary of motivation'.[13] In this instance, communication emphasizes the 'team' (with phrases like 'We must all pull together') and the 'family' (suggesting that employees are brothers and sisters and customers are family guests), using these metaphors to obfuscate the power differentials and conflicting interests between management and workers. Whether employees are organized into a 'work group' or a 'work team', the effectiveness of the work configuration will be the outcome of complex group behaviours and processes, which is the focus of the next section.

www.managementhelp.org/grp_skll/slf_drct/slf_drct.htm is an online library devoted to self-managed teams. At http://groups.yahoo.com, people form their own social groups to exchange ideas. Visit the site and see how 'virtual groups' work

weblink

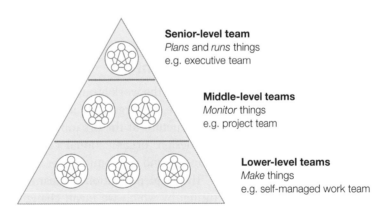

Senior-level team
Plans and *runs* things
e.g. executive team

Middle-level teams
Monitor things
e.g. project team

Lower-level teams
Make things
e.g. self-managed work team

figure 9.1 Classification of work teams

Group dynamics

group dynamics: the systematic study of human behaviour in groups, including the nature of groups, group development, and the interrelations between individuals and groups, other groups and other elements of formal organizations

Group dynamics is the study of human behaviour in groups.[1] The field studies the nature of groups, group development and the interrelations between individuals and groups. Group dynamics or processes emphasize changes in the pattern of activities, the subjective perceptions of individual group members and their active involvement in group life. Studies on group dynamics by mainstream researchers draw attention to two sets of process that underlie group processes: task-oriented activities and maintenance-oriented activities. Task-oriented activities undertaken by the group are aimed at accomplishing goals or 'getting the job done'. Maintenance-oriented activities, on the other hand, point to the subjective perceptions of group members and their active involvement in keeping acceptable standards of behaviour and a general state of well-being within the group. Conventional wisdom argues that the two processes constantly seek to coexist, and an overemphasis of one realm at the expense of the other leads to discontent and withdrawal. An effective group or team is one that creates a reasonable compromise between both realms.[10,14,15]

Some of the major factors influencing group dynamics are shown in Figure 9.2. The framework does not attempt to offer a theory of group dynamics, nor does it necessarily follow that all elements of the model must, or can, be applied to every work group. We offer it here as a useful heuristic for understanding the complexities of group dynamics. Four major elements are graphically depicted in the model: a context, team structure and processes, group effectiveness, and a feedback loop that links the outcomes back to the other main components. We look at each of the first three elements over the next few pages.

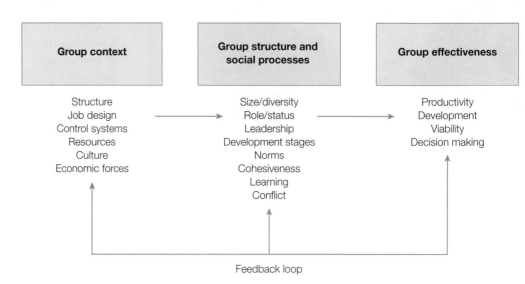

figure 9.2 A model of group dynamics

Group context

Although the work group or team is a structure in itself, it is also a subset of a larger structure, the organization. Thus, the work group is constrained to operate within the structure of the organization, and **group context** refers to organizational and job design, organizational control systems, resources and the external political economy and economic forces.

The implementation of team-based working requires organizational restructuring, by which we mean changing the core dimensions of the organization: its centralization, complexity and formality (see Chapter 10). Tasks and responsibilities must be designated within and between teams. Task interdependence, which refers to the level of relationship among members in the work activities, can affect group structure, processes and outcomes. Alternative work configurations are typically followed by alternative control systems. For example, when work groups are introduced, the direct supervisory control of employees is typically replaced by a computer-based control of group performance. The adoption of team work is normally contingent on management installing a system to control the redesigned work process.[6]

Resources are another contextual factor affecting group structure and processes. The amount of resources management is willing to commit to teams is directly

group context: refers to anything from the specific task a work group is engaged in to the broad environmental forces that are present in the minds of group members and may influence them

related to the organizational context. Specifically, the policies and procedures of the organization must provide for sufficient physical (such as computer software), financial and human resources to enable the team to function and complete the task. Inadequate resources, it is argued, will delay group development and have a negative impact on group outcomes.[3]

Group structure

Work groups and teams have a structure that influences the way in which members relate to and interact with one another, and makes it possible to explain individual behaviour within the group. Have you ever noticed that, when people come together in a new group, some listen while others talk? Such differences between group members serve as a basis for the formation of group structure. As differentiation takes place, social relations are formed between members. The stable pattern of relationships among the differentiated elements in the group is called **group structure**.

The group can be differentiated by a number of variables including size, roles, status and leadership. The *size* of the group plays a critical role in how group members interact with one another. The German sociologist Georg Simmel pointed out that increasing the size alters the group's dynamics, since the increased number of relationships results in different interactions.[16] Figure 9.3 shows the incremental impact of group size on relationships. Two individuals form a single relationship; adding a third person results in three relations; a group of seven, however, has 21 relationships. According to Simmel, as groups grow beyond three people, the personal attachments between individuals become looser, and coalitions emerge in which some group members align themselves against other group members. Thus, the more impersonal relationships need additional formal rules and regulations. At the same time, the group's growth allows it to become more stable, because the intensity of the interactions is reduced, and because it becomes better able to withstand the loss of some of its members.

> group structure: a stable pattern of social interaction among work group members created by a role structure and group norms

> **weblink**
> The notion of diversity and balance in teams is central to Belbin's team role theory. Visit www.belbin.com for more information and www.palgrave.com/business/brattonob2e for an activity on team roles

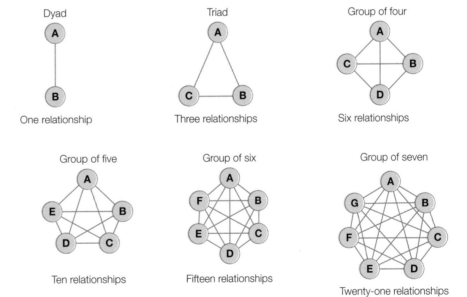

figure 9.3 The incremental effects of group size on relationships

The *composition* or diversity of work groups is another key variable that influences individual behaviour in a group setting. Work group composition can be diverse in terms of gender, ethnicity, age, hierarchical status, performance levels and educational background. Research suggests that group composition is a predictor of members' creative behaviour and the quality of decision making.

Gender and hierarchical status diversity tended to decrease a member's creative behaviour, and this negative effect appeared to be particularly strong for women members in a minority and 'low-power' group situation. The group's composition may also impede the shared exchange, discussion and integration of information, with negative effects on decision quality.[17,18]

All group members are expected to carry out certain functions. The set of expected behaviours associated with a position within the group constitutes the **role** of the occupant of that position. The role concept helps us understand how a member's behaviour is structured by the prescriptive dictates of the group and/or organization. A team-based culture will influence the roles individuals play within the organization. With HPW forms of organization, a premium is placed on values such as cooperative behaviour with team members, sharing information and expertise with others, and more generally on promoting a social network necessary for effective team performance. Role definition is often used as a diagnostic tool by management consultants to determine causes of poor team performance. Problems of **role ambiguity** – uncertainty on the group member's part about what exactly he or she is supposed to do – and **role conflict** – conflicting requests from more than one source – allegedly have far-reaching negative outcomes on group performance.[3] Role ambiguity and role conflict affect the socialization of new employees into existing work groups.[19]

Status is the relative ranking that a member holds, and indicates the value of that member as perceived by the group. Status is important because it motivates individuals and has consequences for their behaviour. Almost every work group has either a formal or an informal leader, who can influence communications, decision making, learning and similar processes, thereby playing an important part in group's outcomes.

It is necessary, but not sufficient for team efficacy, to have an organizational design strategy that incorporates adequate resources, effective control systems, role clarity and leadership. To be effective, managers and group members must learn to work in the new work structure. The group processes responsible for group development, norms, cohesiveness and learning are extremely important.

Group social processes

The term **group social processes** refers to the manner in which various aspects of group behaviour are constructed on a continuing basis, and the behaviour that serves to encourage or discourage group learning and to ameliorate or exacerbate group conflict. Understanding group social processes is important in so far as they are often considered to be key predictors of group effectiveness.

Group development

Organizational behaviour theorists typically highlight the importance of understanding the developmental stages that a group must pass through: groups are born, they mature and they die. It is suggested that a group must reach the mature stage before it achieves maximum performance. Of course, it is also acknowledged that not all groups pass through all these stages, and some groups can become fixed in the early stage and remain ineffective and inefficient. A good example of the life-cycle metaphor is Tuckman and Jensen's five-stage cycle of group development model: forming, storming, norming, performing and adjourning (Figure 9.4).[20]

In the *forming* stage, individuals are brought together and there tends to be ambiguity about roles and tasks. Group members are polite as they learn about each other and attempt to establish 'ground rules' for accomplishing the assigned task(s). Dependency on the group leader is said to be high at this stage.

role: a set of behaviours that people are expected to perform because they hold certain positions in a team and organization

role ambiguity: uncertainty about job duties, performance expectations, level of authority and other job conditions

role conflict: conflict that occurs when people face competing demands

status: the social ranking of people; the position an individual occupies in society or in a social group or work organization

group processes: refers to group member actions, communications and decision making

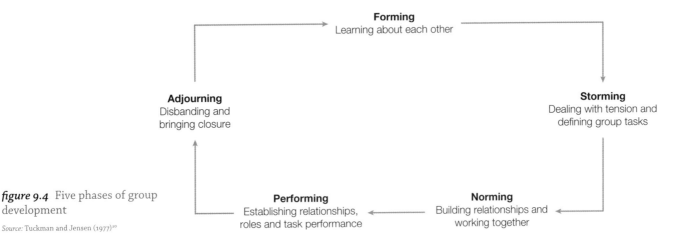

figure 9.4 Five phases of group development

Source: Tuckman and Jensen (1977)[20]

In the *storming* stage, individual members become more proactive by taking on specific roles and responsibilities. Members frequently compete for positions in the group, and conflict occurs between individuals, and/or alliances are formed between members. The group leader must be able to facilitate dialogue and handle conflict at this stage.

When group members begin to accept differences of opinion, conform to their roles and cooperate (for instance, sharing information), the group has reached what is called the *norming* stage. As a consensus forms around the group's goals and means of attainment, group cohesion grows.

High productivity is typically achieved at the *performing* stage of group development. A high level of trust in each group member is prevalent at this phase, and there is 'consensual validation' in the sense that members are positively valued for their specific attributes and qualities.

A work group does not exist infinitely. The *adjourning* stage refers to individuals leaving the group and being replaced by others, or to the group's disbandment. Social rituals, such as having a party, often accompany group disbandment.

Tuckman and Jensen's model is based on the premise that a group must go through each stage before being able to move on to the next, and every transition holds the potential risk of regression to an earlier stage. Organizational behaviour theorists taking a managerialist perspective have tended to interpret the five-stage model in terms of levels of performance, with group productivity being higher after the second stage. While this assumption may be correct, what makes a work group effective is more complex than this model acknowledges. Although the model has become entrenched in mainstream organizational behaviour texts and in management training, it has more recently been shown 'to be of little or no assistance in getting teams to perform better' (ref. 3, p. 34).

An earlier critique of Tuckman and Jensen's five-stage model found the phenomenon of 'punctuated equilibrium' to be a more useful concept to explain group development.[21] Specifically, a team does not accomplish a great deal up to about the halfway point to completion (this midpoint occurring regardless of the time-frame involved). At the midpoint, there is an acceleration of activity by members to accomplish their assigned work. In essence, the 'punctuated equilibrium' model characterizes work groups as exhibiting long periods of inertia interspersed with shorter bursts of activity, initiated primarily by their members' awareness of the impending completion deadline. This would suggest, therefore, that not all groups develop in a universal linear fashion.

The research on group development has drawn criticism because much of it has tended to be laboratory-based rather than workplace-based research. For example, old favourites like Tuckman and Jensen's model were developed from work with therapy, laboratory or training groups, not 'real teams in real contexts'. Group development models that predict linear sequential phases have particularly been criticized. As Kline graphically points out:

> Imagine the following situation. The cockpit crew of a 747 boards the plane twenty minutes before take-off. You are seated in seat 117B, and as the airplane rushes down runway nine you hope like hell that this team is past the storming stage of group development. (ref. 3, p. 5)

Kline argues that there is something, personalities aside, about the aircrew that enables them to fly the aircraft safely, even when they have just met one another. These 'contextual variables', she asserts, are powerful tools for understanding group dynamics and group performance.

Although alternative research suggests that every group does not go through all the development stages, Tuckman and Jensen's model can be a useful heuristic for understanding group dynamics and why some groups fail to perform. A group might be ineffective and inefficient because individuals are pulling in different directions, since the goals of the group have not been agreed. Alternatively, individuals might have a tendency to dismiss or ridicule others' thoughts, ideas and feelings, which leads to low trust among the group. For all these reasons, effective group functioning and learning might be hindered. The main conclusion drawn from the group development models presented here is that a team-based organizational structure does not imply an effective and efficient organization. Top managers introducing team-based work structures need to attend to the development of group interactions.

Group norms

Have you ever noticed that professors do not normally criticize other professors? Why? The answer is 'norms'. Groups significantly influence their members'

plate 32 Organizations send their employees to outdoor corporate training centres where they learn to work as teams.

Source: Getty Images

behaviour through the operation of norms. Social norms are a set of expected patterns of behaviour that are established and shared by the group's members. Norms inform members on what they ought and ought not to do under certain situations. A group's norms do not occur in a vacuum: they represent the interaction of historical, social and psychological processes. In the workplace, for example, a new employee joining a group will assess the norms for work effort from how most individuals in the group behave. In turn, members of the group observe the extent to which the new member's behaviour matches the group's norms. Norms develop in work groups around work activities (the means and speed), around attitudes and opinions that should be held by group members regarding the workplace, and around communications, concerning appropriate language.

group norms: the unwritten rules and expectations that specify or shape appropriate human behaviour in a work group or team

The Hawthorne studies[22] highlighted the importance of **group norms** to management theorists. The researchers identified three important norms: no 'rate-busting' (working too hard), no 'chiselling' (working too little) and no 'squealing' (telling the supervisor anything that could undermine the group). Group members who significantly deviated from these norms were subjected to either ridicule or physical punishment. Groups typically enforce norms that:

* facilitate the group's survival
* allow members to express the central values of the group
* reduce embarrassing interpersonal problems for group members – for instance, a ban on discussing religion or politics at work.[23]

Norms are communicated to new employees through a process called 'group socialization', whereby the new member learns the group's principal values and how these values are articulated through norms. Emergent group leaders differ from their peers in that they make more attempts to influence the group and play a role in forming team norms.[24]

Group cohesiveness

The term **cohesiveness** refers to the complex forces that give rise to the perceptions by members of group identity and attractiveness of group membership. The cohesiveness of a group has a major effect on the behaviour of its members, because higher cohesion amplifies the potency of group norms. A series of experiments conducted by Solomon Asch in 1952 and Stanley Milgram in 1963 suggested that group membership can engender conformity, and also that members are likely to follow the directions of group authority figures, even when it means inflicting pain on another individual. These psychological experiments can be used to help explain the brutalizing acts inflicted on prisoners by both male and female US guards at Abu Ghraib prison.[25]

A cohesive group can develop norms that can be a great asset to the organization, for example a norm that prescribes voluntary overtime working when required. Equally, a cohesive group can undermine organizational goals, for example by enforcing conformity to a work effort below what is considered acceptable by managers. Not surprisingly, therefore, sources of group cohesiveness are of considerable interest to mainstream organizational behaviour theorists and managers. For example, a recent study contends that humour can have a positive effect on a variety of group or team processes including group cohesiveness and the management of emotion.[26]

The attractiveness of a group is partly determined by its composition. Members of the group need to get along with each other, which might be difficult if members have very different values, attitudes towards work or interests. Research suggests that behaviour in work groups is shaped by a sex difference in aggressiveness, with male members engaging in more dominating behaviour than female members. Studies have found that, in groups, men talk more frequently, interrupt others and express anger more than women (see ref. 27, especially pp. 181–3). As a result, more men than women are chosen as group leaders. In institutions of learning, the experiences of work groups by women and faculty members from racial and ethnic minorities tend to differ significantly from the experiences of white male group members.[28]

Ensuring diversity in a work group or team is not only an equity matter – a lack of diversity might inhibit some of the benefits of group working. An early study suggests that moderate heterogeneity in a work group balances the requirements of cohesion and productivity.[29] As we will examine in the next section, one notable disadvantage of groups that are *too* cohesive is that their decision-making ability can be impaired by what Janis termed 'groupthink'.[30] He defined this group phenomenon as a psychological drive for consensus at any cost, which suppresses dissent and the evaluation of alternatives in cohesive decision-making groups.

---

cohesiveness: refers to all the positive and negative forces or social pressures that cause individuals to maintain their membership in specific groups

For more information on Milgram's classic psychological prison experiment, go to Stanford University's site: www.prisonexp.org

weblink

groupthink: the tendency of highly cohesive groups to value consensus at the price of decision quality

For more information on how 'groupthink' can influence decision making, visit www.afirstlook.com; www.abacon.com. Search for 'groupthink'

weblink

Group learning

We turn now to another aspect of social interaction within groups and teams: work-based learning. It will be apparent from this review of team theory and practice that expanding workers' skill sets and empowering workers to make prescribed decisions has significant implications for learning in the workplace. Rather than learning a narrow set of skills, the need for flexibility and interchangeability necessitates that workers acquire new knowledge and technical skills to perform the new repertoire of tasks. In addition, the experience of 'lived reality' – decision making, trial and error experimentation – and the social relations associated with teams create their own dynamic environment for enhancing informal work-based learning.

If the group or team is going to make its own decisions, control quality and control its own behaviour, members must engage in learning. Adult educators and human resource development theorists have suggested that, in order for a group or team to learn, individual members of the unit must be able to learn: that is, to experiment, reflect on previous action, engage in dialogue, and share and build on their individual knowledge.[31,32] As we pointed out in Chapter 6, adopting a culture of learning in the workplace impacts on innovation, employment relations and leadership style.

Group conflict

Work groups do not exist in isolation: they are located within capitalist workplace dynamics and linked by a network of relationships with other groups. Unsurprisingly, with the proliferation of teams in organizations, there is more research on behaviours that serve to ameliorate or exacerbate the effect that group conflict has on their effectiveness. In the critical studies, analysts have highlighted the inevitable tensions between team-based HPW rhetoric and the reality of work intensification and job insecurity.[33] Mainstream research on group conflict is, however, generally limited to investigating how dysfunctional behaviour at individual or group level affects the variance in groups' performance generally. There are many definitions for the term *conflict*. A broad definition describes conflict as 'that behaviour by organization members which is expended in opposition to other members' (ref. 34, p. 411).

Researchers widely recognize that group conflict is comprised of two dimensions: task and emotional conflict.[35] *Task conflict* refers to disputes over group members' tasks or the extent to which members disagree on the utilization of resources or ideas related to group tasks. *Emotional conflict*, which is also known as relational conflict, is more personal and involves personality clashes within groups and incompatibilities among team members, or the extent to which tension or verbal or non-verbal friction characterizes members' interaction within the group. Exemplars of specific types of behaviour associated with task and emotional conflict are shown in Table 9.1.

table 9.1 Task-related and emotion-related behaviours in groups

Task-related behaviours	Emotion-related behaviours
Goal setting	Criticizing
Integrating	Judging
Utilizing resources	Violence
Calculating	Bullying
Compromising	Favouritism
Decision making	Teasing
Evaluating	Sexual harassment

Source: Adapted from Proctor et al. (2009)[36]

empowerment: a psychological concept in which people experience more self-determination, meaning, competence and impact regarding their role in the organization

Psychological studies confirm the notion that individuals' personalities are part of the contributions that group members make to work groups, and, moreover, a mix of these individuals' personalities plays a key role in how intragroup conflict unfolds. It is well documented how many occupations regard team work and support from team members as 'lifelines' in coping with the various demands of work. For example, nurses and air cabin crew are known to rely upon support from fellow co-workers to help them deal with work-related emotion and difficult situations.[36] Studies on the consequences of members' emotions on team performance show that the team members' shared negative emotion, or what is called 'negative affective tone', is inversely related to team performance.[37] A conceptual framework for linking dysfunctional group behaviour and group effectiveness is shown in Figure 9.5.

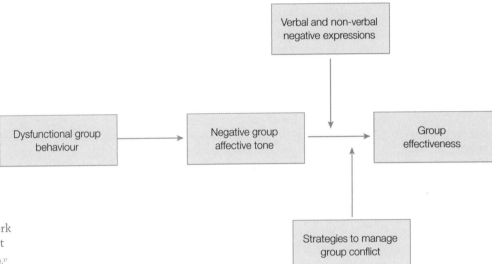

figure 9.5 A conceptual framework for examining intragroup conflict

Source: Adapted from Cole, Walter and Bruch (2008),[37] p. 946, itself based on Brown et al (2005),[91] p. 793

The proposed sequence of incidents depicted in the model begins with dysfunctional group behaviour causing an increase in what is labelled groups' 'negative affective tone' – groups' collective shared experience of negative emotions. In turn, it is hypothesized that that greater levels of negative group affective tone tend to reduce group effectiveness. It also proposes that 'display rules' capable of adjusting or varying the expression of negative emotions through verbal and non-verbal (for example, facial or body) cues is critical to groups' goal-directed behaviour and effectiveness. A study by Dunlop and Lee found that dysfunctional behaviour predicted 24 per cent of the variance in groups' performance.[38] With this assertion in mind, the model further proposes that emotion management strategies will mediate the effect of negative group affective tone.[37]

Research findings suggest that how well conflict resolution strategies address a group-level balance between task and emotion management is what yields superior group productivity and viability.[39] On the basis of reported results, when work groups withhold displays of negative emotionality, it seems they are better able to control the detrimental performance implications of dysfunctional behaviour.[37]

Intergroup conflict might also occur. One explanation for intergroup conflict is that when a group is successful, members' self-esteem increases, and conversely when group members' self-esteem is threatened, they are more prone to disparage members of other groups.[40-43] Another alternative explanation contends that intergroup conflict is the result of one group's perceiving another group as a threat to its goal attainment.[1,3,44]

The traditional managerial perspective tends to hold that conflicts between individuals and groups, and between workers and management, are a bad thing.

Work and Society: Making it work

With the emergence of the idea of 'positive psychology', there has been a pronounced effort to shift research attention away from its traditional focus on abnormal or problematic patterns of human functioning, and towards the study of optimal functioning and human flourishing. This shift in attention away from the problematic and towards the optimal is evident in many fields of study – from organizational behaviour research to studies of marriage. For example, in a pioneering analysis of marriage dynamics, Frank Fincham and his colleagues argue (2007) that the traditional preoccupation with conflict in marriage must be corrected. Their article focuses on 'naturally occurring marital self-repair processes' (p. 282) and seeks to understand the mechanisms that enable some couples to bounce back from conflict while others separate or continue to live together unhappily.

Does this research on marriages have anything to tell us about group dynamics? Obviously, the differences between small work groups and marriages are fundamental, and there is no need to review those differences here. The question is, are there enough similarities between work groups and marriages to derive some insights into group dynamics from recent research on marriages? You be the judge. Consider the following synopsis of the work of Fincham and his colleagues.

Inspired by the move toward positive psychology, Fincham and his co-investigators set out to identify what distinguishes marriages that endure (or 'bounce back' after trouble) from marriages that fall apart. They found that couples who stay together do not necessarily experience conflict-free relationships. What distinguishes these resilient couples from couples who separate are mechanisms that work to defuse conflict, often without the help of external interventions. One might say that spouses in these resilient couples exhibit capacities for 'self-regulation' and the couples themselves are capable of 'self-repair'.

To understand how this works, Fincham and his colleagues suggest we consider how conflicts unfold in time. An initial disagreement or problematic event will often escalate over time as couples become locked into cyclical patterns of 'tit-for-tat' responding. Resilient couples seem to be able to avoid this pattern. They do so by engaging in two kinds of regulation: they regulate both 'the degree to which a negative partner behaviour elicits a correspondingly negative response' and 'the extent to which negative partner behavior produces a change in the overall view of the relationship' (2007, p. 283). With regard to this second kind of regulation, one can imagine a wife (or husband) coming to the realization: this marriage is not worth saving. Spouses in resilient couples seem to be able to avoid these profound and irreversible changes of heart.

The two kinds of regulation associated with resilient couples are clearly relevant to work groups. Work groups experience internal conflict, and people in work groups become locked into cyclical patterns of 'tit-for-tat' responding. As with couples, the likelihood that members of work groups can resolve their conflicts without resorting to external mediation will depend on their capacity to engage in the kinds of regulation identified by Fincham and his colleagues.

Readers may feel comfortable with the analogy between marriages and work group thus far. But consider the proposed explanation of why some couples more than others are able to engage in effective self-regulation. Fincham and his colleagues offer the following list of factors that they believe enhance a couple's capacity for self-regulation and repair:

> Without methods for changing negative processes over time, or for changing direction once negative interactions begin, even the best marital skills for dealing with conflict may provide couples with insufficient basis for long-term marital satisfaction. The framework [described in this article has] ... the potential to help us understand the impact [on self-regulatory processes] of forgiveness ... commitment ... valuing sacrifice ... and sanctification. (p. 287)

stop!

Fincham and his colleagues associate this list of qualities – forgiveness, commitment, valuing sacrifice and sanctification – with couples who engage in effective self-regulation. Would these same qualities be associated with the optimal functioning of work groups? How would each of the four qualities contribute to higher levels of self-regulation among work group members?

Given its links to organized religion, the idea of sanctification may seem irrelevant to many work groups. Is there a secular version of sanctification that might be relevant to a broader range of work groups?

Sources and further information

Bakkle, A. and Schaufeli, W. (2008) 'Positive organizational behavior: engaged employees in flourishing organizations', *Journal of Organizational Behavior*, **29**, pp. 147–54.
Fincham, F., Stanley, S. and Beach, S. (2007) 'Transformative processes in marriage: an analysis of emerging trends', *Journal of Marriage and the Family*, **69**, pp. 275–92.

Note: This feature was written by David MacLennan, Assistant Professor at Thompson Rivers University, BC, Canada.

An alternative perspective, the *interactionist theory*, holds that conflicts in work groups are productive and can increase rather than decrease job performance.[45] The view holds that group leaders should encourage an ongoing 'optimum' level of conflict, which allows the group to be self-critical, creative and viable. But notions of 'win–lose' scenarios complicate estimates of what constitutes an 'optimal level' of conflict. It has been suggested, for instance, that the more the intergroup conflict is defined as a 'win–lose' situation, the more predictable are the effects of the conflict on the social relationships within the group and on relations between work groups.[1]

Group effectiveness

Most group theory examines group effectiveness or outcomes in terms of group performance and group decision making. Since the widespread proliferation of team work, much research has been occupied with investigating the link between work teams and performance. Two aspects of group effectiveness are examined in this section: perform-ance and decision making.

Group performance

Research on group performance has often drawn upon Hackman's normative theory of group effectiveness, where effectiveness consists of (1) productivity, (2) employee development, or the opportunity of the indi-vidual team member to learn from her or his experiences within the team as well as from other team members, and (3) team viability, or the degree to which members of the team are able to continue working together in the future.[46] The group literature contends that a combination of high-level cohesion and norms, consistent with organizational objectives, will have a positive effect on team productivity.[47–49] Figure 9.6 illustrates the relationship between group cohesiveness and group performance norms. Improved productivity of employees in SMWTs is said to stem from the fact that the interrelationship between the configuration of job design and employment practices inevitably leads to more intrinsic **job satis-faction**, higher team member commitment and the mobilization of greater discre-tionary effort from employees.[50,51]

Sociologists maintain that relationships formed in groups shape members' behaviour. Think about your own experience of working in a group. What norms and values did the group exhibit? Did any particular members challenge a particular group norm? If so, how did the other group members respond to the challenge? If they did not, why not?

stop reflect

job satisfaction: a person's attitude regarding his or her job and work content

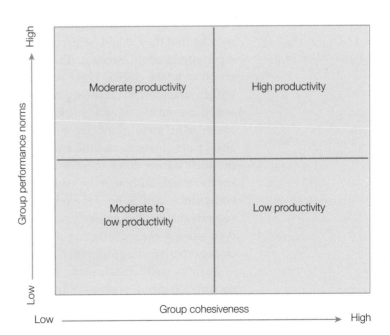

figure 9.6 Cohesiveness, norms and group performance

Group decision making

In theory, one advantage of cohesive groups is that, by combining member resources, they make better decisions than those made by a single individual. In mathematical logic, this phenomenon of groups, called synergy, suggests that 2 + 2 is greater than 4. The concept is used extensively in mainstream texts to understand group processes and to justify the implementation of work teams. The general assumption is that moderately cohesive work teams (sufficiently diverse to avoid groupthink), together with better communications and 'enlightened' leadership, are best able to encourage the sharing of information and group learning – which results in superior decision-making outcomes. Decision-making issues are discussed at length in Chapter 15. In terms of group decision making, here we examine some important concepts and empirical research on the decision-making performance of groups.

An important concept that might cause groups not to live up to their decision-making potential is *conformity* for people to change their behaviour to fit the norms of a group or team. It may make sense to follow others' behaviour or judgement when you are inexperienced or when the situation is ambiguous, but just how strongly do group norms influence individual behaviour and decision making when the situation is unmistakable?

Research by Solomon Asch and Stanley Milgram provided the answer to this question.[52,53] Asch recruited several groups of students, allegedly to study visual perception. Before the experiment began, he explained to all the students, apart from one student in each group, that the real purpose was to put pressure on the one selected student. Each group of students was asked to estimate the lengths of lines presented on a card. A sample line was shown at the left, and the group was to choose which of the three lines on the right matched it (Figure 9.7). Group members were seated so that the subject answered last. Group pressure did not affect the subjects' perception, but it did affect their behaviour. Initially, as planned, group members made the correct matches (B on Card 2). When, however, Asch's accomplices made incorrect responses, the uninformed subject became uncomfortable, and 76 per cent of the subjects chose to conform by answering incorrectly on at least one trial. The study shows how strong the tendency to conform can be, even when the pressure comes from people we do not know.

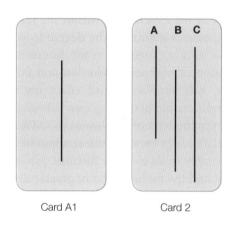

figure 9.7 An example of the cards used in Asch's experiment in group conformity

In Milgram's controversial study, a researcher explained to male recruits that they would be participating in an experiment on how physical punishment affects adult learning. The learner, actually an accomplice of Milgram's, was seated in a fake electric chair, with electrodes fastened to the wrist and secured by leather straps. In an adjoining room, the subject, playing the role of educator, was seated in front of a replica 'shock generator' with the capacity to administer an electric 'shock' of between 15 and 315 'volts' to the learner. The educator was directed to read aloud pairs of words, and the learner was asked to recall the second word. Whenever the adult learner failed to answer correctly, the educator was instructed to apply an electric shock. Although the educator heard moans and then screams as the level of voltage increased, none of the subjects questioned the experiment. Milgram's research suggests that people are likely to follow the directions of 'legitimate authority figures', even when it means inflicting pain on another individual. To learn about how this classic experiment by Milgram has been related to contemporary events, see ref. 54.

As previously mentioned, Irving Janis's study illustrates how 'experts' can succumb to group pressure.[30] Interestingly, to illustrate the concept of groupthink, Janis analysed the ill-fated attempt by President Kennedy's administrative team to invade Cuba in 1961. He argues that the executive group advising the US President displayed all the symptoms of groupthink: they were convinced of their invulnerability, and 'self-censorship' prevented members from expressing alternative views even when intelligence information did not align with the group's beliefs. There was, according to Janis, an illusion of unanimity, with silence being interpreted as consent. In other words, the pressures for conformity that can arise in a highly cohesive group can cloud members' judgement and the decision-making process. Table 9.2 outlines some symptoms of groupthink.

table 9.2 Symptoms of groupthink

Symptom	Description
Illusion of invulnerability	Group members are arrogant and ignore obvious danger signals
Illusion of morality	Groups decision(s) are not only perceived as sensible, they are also perceived as morally correct
Rationalization	Counter-arguments are rationalized away
Stereotypes of outsiders	Members construct unfavourable stereotypes of those outside the group who are the targets of their decisions
Self-censorship	Members perceive that unanimous support exists for their decisions and action
Mindguard	Individual(s) within the group shield the group from information that goes against its decisions

Obviously, groupthink results in low-quality decisions. More seriously, it has been implicated in the decision processes that led to NASA's fatal launch of the space shuttle Challenger in 2003, and the US and UK invasion of Iraq in 2003. Prior to the invasion, the US official position was that Iraq illegally possessed weapons of mass destruction in violation of UN Security Council Resolution 1441 and had to be disarmed by force. The decision to embark on the Iraq invasion, termed 'Operation Iraqi Freedom' was made by President George W. Bush and a small group of military and intelligence advisers. After investigating the events, which continue to shape the course of twenty-first century history as we write, a US Senate Committee found that the Central Intelligence Agency had dismissed alternative reports, and that the intelligence community as a whole suffered from 'collective group think'.[55] The research by Asch, Milgram and Janis tells us that groups influence the behaviour of their members, altering perceptions of reality and often promoting conformity, which can lead to imperfect and even catastrophic decisions.

The phenomenon of groupthink, therefore, has the potential to undermine the group's ability to appraise alternative choices and make quality decisions. Another phenomenon that has the potential to adversely affect decision making is group polarization. This refers to the tendency of groups to make more extreme decisions than managers and employees working alone. For example, suppose that a board of governors of a college meets to make a decision on the future of a new sports complex for the college. Individual board members might come to the meeting with various degrees of support or opposition to the project. However, by the end of the board meeting, it is highly possible that the board of governors will agree on a more ambitious (that is, a higher financial cost) plan than the average individual had when the board meeting began.

One reason for the more ambitious preference is that individual board members feel less personally responsible for the decision consequences because the entire board of governors makes the decision. Another reason is that board members become comfortable with more extreme positions when they realize that co-members also support the same position. Persuasive arguments favouring the dominant position convince doubtful members and help form a consensus around the most ambitious or extreme option. So persuasion, group support and shifting responsibility explain why groups make more extreme decisions.

OB and globalization

Power and culture in work team relations

The globalization of work has opened new opportunities for workers from different cultural backgrounds to work closely with each other – both in person and remotely. Diverse work teams can have positive effects on productivity and problem solving by generating a greater number of innovative ideas and approaches (Earley and Gibson, 2002). Many organizations with overseas operations, however, have also encountered challenges in managing multicultural work teams. These challenges are primarily related to team members' different cultural understandings about their role in the team (and within the larger organization) and how the work should be accomplished.

In an insightful study, Mutabazi and Derr (2003) explore the cultural and historical roots of a breakdown in work team relationships at a Franco-Senegalese organization the authors call Socometal, whose work teams were made up of French expatriates and local Senegalese workers. Mutabazi and Derr concluded that inefficiencies and misunderstandings in these multicultural work teams were, to a great extent, connected with the enduring legacy of colonialism. They explain:

the problem associated with multiculturalism [on work teams] comes from preexisting attitudes about relations between Africa and the West. This is a deeply-rooted relationship with perceptions distorted by historical consternation. On one side, the West as the dominant partner overemphasizes its own culture, ideals and conceptions of the world ... the resulting tendency is to impose this cultural determination upon the party that is considered inferior ... [and] this characteristic of multiculturalism becomes embedded in the relationship creating a vicious cycle of misunderstanding. (p. 3)

At Socometal, French managers and work team members did not understand the Senegalese community-based approach to team work, which relies on the circulation of people, goods, services and information through local social and economic networks. Likewise, the Senegalese workers did not understand the approaches of the French expatriate managers and workers, mistaking their focus on top-down decision making and individual competition as an assertion of superiority. The result was the reproduction of colonial power relationships between French and Senegalese workers, and work teams that were 'characterized by indifference toward the values and perspectives of fellow team members ... The professional and personal difficulties that [ensued led] to a breakdown of operations' (Mutabazi and Derr, 2003, p. 4).

This case highlights the centrality of power and culture in organizational behaviour. Gibson and Zellmer-Bruhn (2001) remind us that workplaces are culturally situated, and that relationships within organizations are shaped by culturally and historically embedded power relationships. Misunderstandings about work team relationships and responsibilities can be exacerbated in situations where team members make assumptions about their colleagues' capabilities and motivations based on preconceived notions. The potential of multicultural work teams to excel will remain untapped as long as they are managed according to a single cultural paradigm. Effective management approaches in these situations must address cultural misunderstandings and power imbalances head on, and provide enough flexibility to incorporate multiple approaches to team work and decision making into the organization.

stop! Have you ever worked on a project or a work team with members from different cultural backgrounds? Discuss any culturally based misunderstandings or 'disconnects' that you or your colleagues might have encountered while working on the project. How did you address your differences?

Can you think of any other examples of how historical relationships between nations or cultures could affect organizational behaviour if members of those groups were assigned to the same work team?

Sources and further information

Earley, P. C. and Gibson, C. B. (2002) *Multinational Work Teams: A New Perspective*, Mahwah, NJ: Lawrence Erlbaum Associates.

Gibson, C. B. and Zellmer-Bruhn, M. E. (2001) 'Metaphors and meaning: an intercultural analysis of the concept of teamwork', *Administrative Science Quarterly*, **46**(2), pp. 274–303.

Mutabazi, E. and Derr, C. B. (2003) 'The management of multicultural teams: the experience of Afro-Occidental teams', Research Paper 13, *European Entrepreneurial Learning*. Available at: www.em-lyon.com/%5Cressources%5Cge%5Cdocuments%5Cpublications%5Cwp%5C2003-13.pdf; http://cat.inist.fr/?aModele=afficheN&cpsidt=18098760 (accessed September 22, 2009).

Note: This feature was written by Gretchen Fox, Anthropologist, Timberline Natural Resource Group, Canada.

Research has repeatedly demonstrated that group decision making is not always superior. In reality, groups sometimes do perform better than the average group member but rarely do better than the best member.[56] One explanation is that even relatively homogeneous groups often fail to exchange their members' unique resources. One key assumption underpinning the enthusiasm for group-based decision making is the expectation to benefit from group members' distributed experiences and informational resources. This point is particularly important with regard to group diversity enhancing the quality of group decisions. Increasingly, diversity is an organizational fact of life, and many work groups are diverse in terms of the characteristics of their membership, bringing together members who may differ in gender, ethnicity, age, disability, hierarchical status, educational background and so forth.

Research on diversity in work teams has shown mixed results regarding the effects of group diversity on team decision making. On the one hand, the processing of decision-relevant information may benefit from a wider pool, variety of perspectives and life experiences in more diverse groups. On the other hand, diversity may actually impede the exchange, discussion and integration of decision-relevant information, with consequential negative effects on decision quality.[18] Others suggest that increasing diversity can have both positive and negative effects on group information processing and decision making contingent on 'individuals' beliefs about diversity'.[57] Thus, educating employees in diverse organizations to value diversity can improve the quality of decisions. Furthermore, the positive effects of diversity might be propagated through several structured group processes that are designed to improve the exchange of group members' unique information and the decision quality. These structured group decision-making processes include brainstorming, the nominal group technique and the stepladder technique, which are discussed in Chapter 15.

Clearly, group social processes are complex and contentious, and are strongly influenced by the individual characteristics of team members and by dominant gender, race and power patterns. The wealth of research and interest in work teams over the last decade is related to the changing fashion in US and European management theory on how to compete in conditions of globalized capitalism.

> **weblink**
> For examples of team working in European and North American companies, visit: www.honda.com; www.sony.com; http://ptcpartners.com/Team/home.htm; www.dti.gov.uk/employment/useful-links/index.html. Search for '2004 employee relations survey'. This site gives a summary of the UK 2004 survey, including a section on work teams

Work teams and management theory

The theoretical interest in work groups or teams draws upon human relations, sociotechnical and Japanese perspectives on organizational design.[5,6,12,58] Pioneering work on human relations by Roethlisberger and Dickson, Mayo, Maslow and McGregor focused top managers' attention on the importance of social relations within work groups.[22,59–61]

The collaborative research by Roethlisberger, an industrial psychologist from Harvard University, and Dickson, a manager at the Western Electric plant, involved studying the job performance of two groups of front-line workers doing identical work but in separate rooms. Each work group's productivity was carefully monitored. One work group – the study group – experienced ergonomic changes including increasing the intensity of the lighting in the workshop. The study group's productivity increased. The other work group – the control group – experienced no changes in lighting. However, to the astonishment of the researchers, its productivity increased also. Even more mystifying to the researchers, when the level of light intensity was lowered for the study group, the results showed that output continued to go up. After repeated experiments over many years, the researchers began to make connections between social interaction and job performance. In 1939, Roethlisberger and Dickson wrote:

stop reflect

Think about your experience of working in a group. Do Roethlisberger and Dickson's findings resonate with any aspect of your own view on group working? Why?

systems theory: a set of theories based on the assumption that social entities, such as work organizations, can be viewed as if they were self-regulating bodies exploiting resources from their environment (inputs) and transforming the resources (exchanging and processing) to provide goods and services (outputs) in order to survive

job enrichment: employees are given more responsibility for scheduling, coordinating and planning their own work

job rotation: the practice of moving employees from one job to another

job enlargement: increasing the number of tasks employees perform in their jobs

job characteristics model: a job design model that relates the motivational properties of jobs to specific personal and organizational consequences of those properties

stop reflect

What do you think of this job characteristics model? Think about any jobs you have had. Can you use this model to assess the 'quality' of the work you were paid for? What is missing from the model?

The study of the bank wiremen showed that their behaviour at work could not be understood without considering the informal organization of the group and the relation of this informal organization to the total social organization of the company. The work activities of the group, together with their satisfactions and dissatisfactions, had to be viewed as manifestations of a complex pattern of interrelations. (ref. 59, pp. 551–2)

After the Second World War, the work of Maslow and McGregor helped US human relations advocates to clarify their perspective, with its focus on the interrelations between workers and the quality of the employment relationship.

In Europe, much of the early research on work teams was conducted within the framework of sociotechnical **systems theory**. This theory developed from work in 1951 on autonomous work teams in the British coal-mining industry under the supervision of Trist and Bamforth. These researchers proposed that 'responsible autonomy' should be granted to primary work groups, and that group members should learn more than one role, so that an interchangeability of tasks would be possible within the group. The flexibility would permit the completion of sub-whole units. The studies showed that the labour process in mining could be better understood in terms of two systems: the technical system – including machinery and equipment – and the social system, including the social relations and interactions among the miners.

Later advocates of the sociotechnical systems approach to organizational design argued that work teams provide a work regime for achieving the 'best match' between technical and social considerations or 'systems'. The term 'best match' is used to describe the relationship between the social and technological systems of the organization, where each is sensitive to the demands of the other.[12]

Attempts to implement the sociotechnical systems approach have included work redesign to 'enrich' jobs. The concept of '**job enrichment**' refers to a number of different processes of **rotating**, **enlarging** and aggregating tasks. It increases the range of tasks, skills and control that workers have over the way they work, either individually or in teams. Job enrichment theory, also known as **job characteristics** theory, was given theoretical prominence by the work of Turner and Lawrence, and Hackman and Oldham.[29,62] As a counter to the thinking underlying Taylorism and Fordism, the job enrichment model has been influential in the design of work teams. It suggests a casual relationship between five core job characteristics and the worker's psychological state. If this relationship is positive, it leads in turn to positive outcomes. The five core job characteristics contained in the model are defined as:

1. *skill variety*: the degree to which the job requires a variety of different activities in carrying out the work, requiring the use of a number of the worker's skills and talents
2. *task identity*: the degree to which the job requires completion of a whole and identifiable piece of work
3. *task significance*: the degree to which the job has a substantial impact on the lives or work of other people
4. *autonomy*: the degree to which the job provides substantial freedom, independence and discretion to the worker in scheduling the work and in determining the procedures to be used in carrying it out
5. *feedback*: the degree to which the worker possesses information on the actual results of her or his performance.

The more that a job possesses the five core job characteristics, the greater the motivating potential of the job (Figure 9.8).

The model also recognizes the importance of learning to achieve motivation and outcome goals. Workers' work-related learning is implicitly linked to the existence of the 'moderators' – knowledge and skills, growth need strength and context satisfaction – contained in the model. The presence of moderators is used to explain why jobs that are theoretically high in motivating potential will not automatically generate high levels of motivation and satisfaction for all workers.

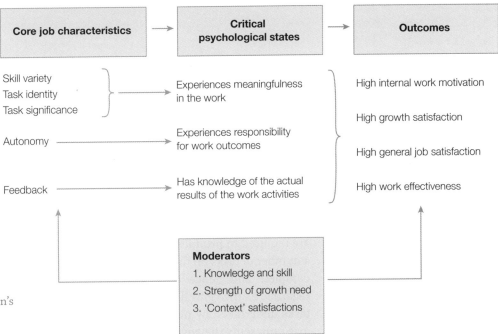

figure 9.8 Oldham and Hackman's job characteristics model

Source: Oldham and Hackman (1980)[59]

The argument goes that an employee with a low 'growth need' is less likely to experience a positive outcome when her or his work is 'enriched'. Thus, the neo-human relations approach to job design in general, and the job characteristic model in particular, emphasized the fulfilment of social or relatedness needs by recomposing fragmented jobs. In certain circumstances, self-managed teams could provide an alternative to individual job enrichment.

The quality of work and work-related learning in small SMWTs rests on five principles of 'good' job design:

- The first principle is *wholeness*: the scope of the job is such that it includes all the tasks to complete a product or process.
- The second principle involves individual and group *learning and development*. Opportunities exist to engage in a variety of fulfilling and meaningful tasks, allowing team members to learn a range of skills within a community of practice, and facilitating job flexibility.[63]
- The third principle relates to *governance and self-regulation*. With the focus on product differentiation and the rise of knowledge-based economies, the imperatives of work do not permit managers to master all the challenges. As a result, they must allow team and project members to assume responsibility for the pace of work, problem solving and quality control.
- The fourth principle involves occupational *wellness and safety*. Work is designed to maintain the safety and wellness of team members and to support a good work–life balance.[64]
- Finally, the fifth principle is *social interaction*. The job design permits interaction, cooperation and reflexivity among team members.

Drawing upon the work of Klein and McKinlay et al.,[65] the principles of 'good' job design are achieved by management interventions in the technical, governance and sociocultural dimensions of work (Figure 9.9).

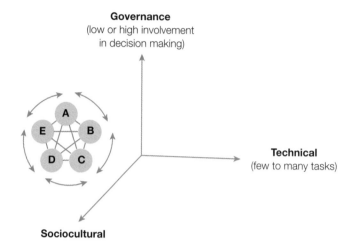

figure 9.9 The three dimensions of group work: technical, governance and social

The horizontal axis in Figure 9.9 represents the functional or technical tasks that are required to produce the product or service. Group working involves combining a number of tasks on the horizontal axis to increase the cycle times and create more complete and hence more meaningful jobs. The technical dimension is then regarded as the central purpose of work teams, and is concerned with the range of tasks undertaken by members, multiskilling and functional flexibility. The vertical axis represents the governance aspects of the labour process, and shows the extent of workers' autonomy on the job. The third axis, the diagonal, represents the sociocultural aspects of work, one of which is the social interaction that takes place in work groups. The sociocultural dimension is perhaps the most interesting as far as organizational behaviour is concerned, since it represents the behaviour or 'normative' considerations – what ought to happen – to secure effective team performance. This dimension of group work recognizes that employees' compliance and cooperation depend upon the complex interplay of social interactions in the group. It should be noted that, in a five-member team, there are 10 relationships (see Figure 9.3, above).

The SMWT represents an *ideal-type* work regime because it restores the craft paradigm by enlarging tasks on the horizontal axis and by giving members greater autonomy over how the work is accomplished on the vertical axis: a reversal of Taylorism. The movement along the diagonal axis represents the implications of group working in terms of group norms, group cohesion and organizational culture. The three dimensions of work organization in Figure 9.9 help to illustrate the point that top managers make strategic choices regarding how work is designed, and alternative work structures have an impact on social behaviour and organizational culture.

Critical insight

Workplace observers agree there is evidence that, in organizations that have been successful in devolving decision making to work groups, there have been benefits for management and workers: a 'win–win' situation. Visit www.jobquality.ca and 'High-performance working' at www.cipd.co.uk. Read also Andy Danford et al. (2008), 'Partnership, high-performance work systems and the quality of working life', *New Technology, Work and Employment*, **23**(3), pp. 151–66. Who are the prime beneficiaries of team-based working? Do SMWTs reduce workplace stress?

Chapter summary

◻ In this chapter, we have examined the background, nature and behavioural implications of work groups. We have suggested that the current wave of interest in work teams, often located within a cluster of other employment practices constituting what is called a 'high-performance workplace', is linked to lean forms of work organizations and the perceived shortcomings of large bureaucratic organizational structures.

◻ The chapter has emphasized that understanding group processes, such as groupthink, group leadership, informal group learning and intragroup conflict, is imperative for the successful management of the HPW system.

◻ Management tries to persuade workers of the need to work beyond their contract for the 'common' good and to engage in self-regulatory norms. The SMWT is said to be upskilling and empowering workers.

◻ However, we have also gone beyond management rhetoric, and presented arguments and evidence to suggest that self-managed teams shift the focus away from the hierarchy, directive and bureaucratic control processes, to a culture of self-control mechanisms.

◻ The discussion has emphasized that orthodox and critical accounts of team working provide very different views of this form of work organization and employment relations. Both perspectives, however, conceptualize team working as influencing individual behaviour and contributing to improved organizational performance. While both approaches make employee autonomy central to their analyses, each conceptualizes team membership as having a different influence. Additionally, autonomy is theorized as leading to different outcomes (such as growth need versus self-regulation) in each perspective.

Key concepts

group dynamics	247–248
group processes	250
group structure	249
job characteristic model	262
peer pressure	267
psychic prison	268
work group	245
work team	246–247

Vocab checklist for ESL students

◻ Cohesiveness
◻ Empowerment, empower
◻ Formal work group
◻ Group context
◻ Group dynamics
◻ Group norms
◻ Group processes
◻ Group structure
◻ Groupthink
◻ Increment, incremental
◻ Informal group
◻ Job characteristics model
◻ Job design
◻ Job enlargement
◻ Job enrichment
◻ Job rotation
◻ Job satisfaction
◻ Paradox, paradoxical
◻ Role
◻ Role ambiguity
◻ Role conflict
◻ Role perceptions
◻ Self-managed work teams
◻ Systems theory
◻ Status
◻ Teams
◻ Work group

Chapter review questions

1. How useful are group development models for understanding group or team behaviour?
2. What effect, if any, do you expect workforce diversity to have on group processes and outcomes?
3. Explain how the size of the work group might affect group dynamics and performance?
4. 'Self-managed work teams are simply attempts by managers to control individuals at work by mobilizing group processes.' Do you agree or disagree? Discuss.
5. Students often complain about doing group projects. Why? Relate your answer to group processes and the critique of self-managed work teams.
6. What is meant by 'group think', and how important is it in deciding group performance?

Chapter research questions

1. Diversity is an organizational fact of life. In a group, we would like you to examine your own beliefs about diversity and how people stereotype others. Form a study group. (a) Post each term from the following list on separate sheets of paper: Male, Roman Catholic, Asian, Generation Y, Disabled, American, Muslim, Female, Irish, Single mother, Over age 60, West Indian. (b) Circulate the sheets around the group, and write down one stereotype you have heard under each heading. Avoid repeating anything that is already written down. (c) After everyone has finished writing, each group member takes turns to read all the stereotypes under each category. (d) Group members should then discuss (i) their personal reaction, (ii) what they have learned about stereotyping others, and (iii) what managers can do to experience positive effects of diversity.
2. Obtain a copy of Bolton and Houlihan's book *Work Matters: Critical Reflections on Contemporary Work* (see Further Reading).

After reading pages 162–79, explain how team working was introduced into a major supermarket chain. How much autonomy did the teams have? How did the leadership style differ between the teams? How was team productivity measured? How did team work help members cope with work-related stress? How might team diversity impact on the team dynamics?

3. Read Rolf van Dick et al.'s article, 'Group diversity and group identification: the moderating role of diversity beliefs' (see Further Reading). Does group diversity positively or negatively affect group decision making? What can managers do to improve the quality of group decision making?

Further reading

Behfar, K., Peterson, R., Mannix, E. and Trochim, W. (2008) 'The critical role of conflict resolution in teams: a closer look at the links between conflict type, conflict management strategies, and team outcomes', *Journal of Applied Psychology*, **93**(1), pp. 170–88.

Belbin, R. M. (1993) *Team Roles at Work*, London: Butterworth/Heinemann.

Bolton, S. and Houlihan, M. (eds) (2009) *Work Matters: Critical Reflections on Contemporary Work*, Basingstoke: Palgrave.

Cole, M. S., Walter, F. and Bruch, H. (2008) 'Affective mechanisms linking dysfunctional behavior to performance in work teams: a moderated mediation study', *Journal of Applied Psychology*, **93**(5), pp. 945–58.

Cordery, J. (2002) 'Team working', pp. 326–50 in P. Warr (ed.), *Psychology of Work*, London: Penguin.

Danford, A., Richardson, M., Stewart, P., Tailby, S. and Upchurch, M. (2008) 'Partnership, high performance work systems and quality of working life', *New Technology, Work and Employment*, **23**(3), pp. 151–66.

Kasl, E., Marsick, V. and Dechant, K. (1997) 'Teams as learners', *Journal of Applied Behavioral Sciences*, **33**(2), pp. 227–46.

Kooij-de Bode, H. J. M., Hanneke J. M., van Knippenberg, D. and van Ginkel, W. P. (2008) 'Ethnic diversity and distributed information in group decision making: the importance of information elaboration', *Group Dynamics: Theory, Research and Practice*, **12**(4), pp. 307–20.

Proctor, S., Fulop, L., Linstead, S., Mueller, F. and Sewell, G. (2009) 'Managing teams', pp. 539–73 in S. Linstead, L. Fulop and S. Lilley (eds), *Management and Organization: A Critical Text* (2nd edn), Basingstoke: Palgrave.

Russell, N. and Gregory, R. (2005) 'Making the undoable doable: Milgram, the Holocaust, and modern government', *American Review of Public Administration*, **35**(4), pp. 327–49.

Sewell, G. (1998) 'The discipline of teams: the control of team-based industrial work through electronic and peer surveillance', *Administrative Science Quarterly*, **43**, pp. 406–69.

Taggar, S. and Robert Ellis, R. (2007) 'The role of leaders in shaping formal team norms', *Leadership Quarterly*, **18**, pp. 105–20.

van Dick, R., van Knippenburg, D., Hagele, S., Guillaume, Y. R. F. and Brodbeck, F. (2008) 'Group diversity and group identification: the moderating role of diversity beliefs', *Human Relations*, **61**(10), pp. 1463–92.

 Chapter case study 1

Building cars in Brazil

Setting

Founded in the earlier part of the century, the Cable Motor Company was a traditional, North American automobile manufacturer. They used Fordist management techniques and traditional assembly line production, and worked with a highly unionized workforce. By the mid-1980s, with their sales slumping, the company made the decision to purchase an obsolete automotive assembly plant in Brazil. The company quickly proceeded to upgrade the plant, resulting in a very large, modern, single-storey building of approximately 1.4 million square feet with four major manufacturing centres: stamping, body, paint and final assembly. The plan was to adopt the use of cooperative work teams, which had been used by Swedish car manufacturers such as Saab and Volvo, and to implement the Japanese lean production system originally created by Toyota and later adapted by Mazda.

The company spared no expense in planning for the workforce that would fit the plant's new approach to job design. There were extensive pre-employment screening and selection techniques used to recruit the 1200 people needed for the production run. Unlike the minimalist training normally provided under the Ford system, the company provided intensive classroom time and continuous on-the-job training for employees on the subject of self-managed work teams. Group decision making, integral to team success, was a strong focus.

The company found that the union representing the workers, the National Union of Cable Motor Company Workers, had little influence in the new Brazilian plant. This resulted in a much quicker implementation of the flexible production system. Production shifts of about 100 persons were scheduled with workers performing operations individually and in self-directed two-, three- or four-person teams. Any team member could pull a car off the line to check a quality issue. In such a case, a group walk-around decided if a car needed 'finessing'.

CEO John Miner was impressed with the initial look of the new production system. 'Minimal supervision and a self-directed workforce are what we strive to maintain and encourage,' he remarked. 'We will not get bogged down in traditional thinking, processes or paperwork. All workers are encouraged to be free-thinking and to get creative.'

The problem

The selection of the team leaders was conducted by the senior management group. Maria Lopez, a 30-year-old clerical worker, was moved from the administration office to head up one of the teams. Shortly after, production manager Clive Richards began to notice that Maria's team's production cycle times were increasing. He also noticed conflicts within her group. Clive decided to approach one of Maria's team members, Juan Fernandez, who had formerly worked in a team at another car company's assembly plant in Brazil. 'We can't work with Maria as our team leader,' Juan said. 'The team finds it hard because she is a woman. You have to remove her.'

While Clive struggled to decide what to do with Maria, other problems emerged. Employees were arriving to work late on a consistent basis. City buses, the main source of transportation for the plant workers, ran late if they ran at all. This was beginning to impact the continual on-the-job training as it required workers to arrive at work on time. Other employees were hesitant to do quality checks on their own work, saying that it would create the impression that the supervisors did not trust them.

Clive decided to meet with the CEO to let him know about the increasing issues so that action could be taken before the problems got worse. John was concerned when he heard what was happening at the new plant as he had just returned from a meeting where there were preliminary discussions on opening another in a different Brazilian location. 'I need you to do a presentation for the Board of Directors,' John said to Clive. 'We have to show what we've learned from this experience and how we can move forward.'

Tasks

Prepare a short presentation, incorporating the answers to the following questions:

1. How did Brazilian culture or work ideology contribute to the problems the company experienced with its use of teams?
2. In what alternative way could the team leader have been chosen which may have been more acceptable to the team members?
3. Should the conflicts in Maria's group only be viewed as a negative development?

Ask yourself:

4. Why do you think the use of teams could weaken a union's influence or power in the workplace?

Essential reading

Katz, H. C., Lee, W. and Lee, J. (2004) *The New Structure of Labour Relations*, New York: Cornell University Press.

Proctor, S., Fulop, L., Linstead, S., Mueller, F. and Sewell, G. (2009) 'Managing teams', pp. 539–73 in S. Linstead, L. Fulop and S. Lilley (eds), *Management and Organization: A Critical Text* (2nd edn), Basingstoke: Palgrave.

Note

Cable Motor Company is a fictitious company, but the background material for the case is derived from Muller, Rehder and Bannister (1998).[89] Some circumstances of the case organization have been altered. This case study was written by Lori Rilkoff, MSc, CHRP, Senior Human Resources Manager at the City of Kamloops, and lecturer in HRM at Thompson Rivers University, BC, Canada.

 Chapter case study 2

Teams at Land Rock Alliance Insurance

 Visit www.palgrave.com/business/brattonob2e to view this case study

Web-based assignment

Work groups and teams is one of the most important topics of organizational behaviour, and given that many students have experienced group working and will be called upon to work in groups in organizations, it is important to reflect on how groups influence human behaviour.

For this assignment, we would like you to gain more information on work teams by visiting www.workteams.org and www.berr.gov.uk. In addition, you are asked to explore examples of team working in European and North American companies by visiting the following websites: www.honda.com; www.sony.com; http://ptcpartners.com/Team/home.htm; www.berr.gov.uk.

What main principles can be identified as 'good' job design when applied to work teams? Looking at the companies that have introduced teams, what behaviours or 'norms' are expected of employees? How does the team-based model impact on other aspects of management such as human resource management? Discuss your findings with other students on your course.

OB in film

The film *Twelve Angry Men* (1957) examines the behaviour of 12 members of a jury who have to decide on the innocence or guilt of a young man from a working-class background. At the beginning, 11 jurors are convinced of the youth's guilt and wish to declare him guilty without further discussion. One member of the jury (played by Henry Fonda) has reservations and persuades the other members to review the evidence. After reviewing the evidence, the jury acquits the defendant.

A modern version of this film can be seen in a 2005 episode of the television series *Judge John Deed*, in which Judge Deed (played by Martin Shaw) serves as a member of a jury and persuades the other members to review the evidence in a sexual assault case.

What group concepts do the film or the *Judge John Deed* episode illustrate? What types of power are possessed by the characters played by Henry Fonda and Martin Shaw? What pattern of influencing behaviour is followed by Henry Fonda and Martin Shaw?

References

1. Johnson, D. W. and Johnson, F. P. (2000) *Joining Together: Group Theory and Group Skills* (7th edn), Boston: Allyn & Bacon.
2. Katzenbach, J. R. and Smith, D. (1994) *The Wisdom of Teams*, New York: Harper Business.
3. Kline, T. (1999) *Remaking Teams*, San Francisco: Jossey-Bass.
4. Orsburn, J. and Moran, L. (2000) *The New Self-directed Work Teams*, New York: McGraw-Hill.
5. Procter, S. and Mueller, F. (2000) *Teamworking*, Basingstoke: Palgrave Macmillan.
5. Bratton, J. (1992) *Japanization at Work*, Basingstoke: Macmillan.
7. Thompson, R and Ackroyd, S. (1995) 'All quiet on the workplace front: a critique of recent trends in British industrial sociology', *Sociology*, **29**(4), pp. 615–33.
8. Sewell, G. (1998) 'The discipline of teams: the control of team-based industrial work through electronic and peer surveillance', *Administrative Science Quarterly*, **43**, pp. 406–69.

9   Wells, D. (1993) 'Are strong unions compatible with the new model of human resource management?', *Relations Industrielles/Industrial Relations*, **48**(1), pp. 56–84.

10   Hertog, J. F. and Tolner, T. (1998) 'Groups and teams', pp. 62–71 in M. Poole and M. Watner (eds), *The Handbook of Human Resource Management*, London: International Thomson Business Press.

11   Buchanan, D. (2000) 'An eager and enduring embrace: the ongoing rediscovery of teamworking as a management idea', in S. Procter and F. Mueller (eds), *Teamworking*, London: Macmillan.

12   Yeatts, D. E. and Hyten, C. (1998) *High-performing Self-managed Work Teams*, Thousand Oaks, CA: Sage.

13   Bendix, R. (1956) *Work and Authority in Industry*, New York: Wiley.

14   Crawley, J. (1978) 'The lifestyles of the group', *Small Groups Newsletter*, **2**(1), pp. 26–39.

15   Gil, R., Rico, R., Alcover, C. M. and Barrasa, A. (2005) 'Change-oriented leadership, satisfaction and performance in work groups: effects of team climate and group potency', *Journal of Managerial Psychology*, **20**(3/4), pp. 312–29.

16   Simmel, G. (1908/1950) 'Subordination under a principle', pp. 250–67 in *The Sociology of Georg Simmel* (ed. and trans. K. Wolff), New York: Free Press.

17   Choi, J. N. (2007) 'Group composition and employee creative behaviour in a Korean electronics company: distinct effects of relational demography and group diversity', *Journal of Occupational and Organizational Psychology*, **80**, pp. 213–34.

18   Kooij-de Bode, H. J. M., van Knippenberg, D. and van Ginkel, W. P. (2008) 'Ethnic diversity and distributed information in group decision making: the importance of information elaboration', *Group Dynamics: Theory, Research and Practice*, **12**(4), pp. 307–20.

19   Slaughter, J. E. and Zicker, M. J. (2006) 'A new look at the role of insiders in the newcomer socialization process', *Group & Organization Management*, **31**(2), pp. 264–90.

20   Tuckman, B. and Jensen, M. (1977) 'Stages of small group development revisited', *Group and Organization Management*, **2**, pp. 419–27.

21   Gersick, C. J. (1988) 'Time and transition in workteams: towards a new model of group development', *Academy of Management Journal*, **31**, pp. 47–53.

22   Mayo, E. (1946) *The Human Problems of an Industrial Civilization*, New York: Macmillan.

23   Feldman, D. C. (1984) 'The development and enforcement of group norms', *Academy of Management Review*, **1**, pp. 47–53.

24   Taggar, S. and Ellis, R. (2007) 'The role of leaders in shaping formal team norms', *Leadership Quarterly*, **18**, pp. 105–20.

25   Zimbardo, P. (2008) BBC *Hardtalk* interview, April 22, 2008.

26   Romero, E. and Pescosolido, A. (2008) 'Humor and group effectiveness', *Human Relations*, **61**(3), pp. 395–418.

27   Wilson, F. M. (2003) *Organizational Behaviour and Gender*, Farnham: Ashgate.

28. Smith, J. W. and Calasanti, T. (2005) 'The influences of gender, race and ethnicity on workplace experiences of institutions and social isolation: an exploratory study of university faculty', *Sociological Spectrum*, **25**(3), pp. 307–34.

29   Hackman, J. and Oldham, G. (1980) *Work Redesign*, Reading, MA: Addison-Wesley.

30   Janis, I. L. (1972) *Victims of Groupthink*, Boston, MA: Houghton Mifflin.

31   Senge, P. (1990) *The Fifth Discipline*, New York: Doubleday.

32   O'Brien, D. and Buono, C. (1996) 'Building effective learning teams: lessons from the field', *SAM Advanced Management Journal*, **61**(3), pp. 4–11.

33   Jenkins, J. (2008) 'Pressurised partnership: a case of perishable compromise in contested terrain', *New Technology, Work and Employment*, **23**(3), pp. 167–80.

34   Thompson (1960). Cited in Robbins, S. P. (1990) *Organization Theory: Structure, Design, and Applications* (3rd edn), Englewood Cliffs, NJ: Prentice-Hall, p. 411.

35   Varela, O. E., Burke, M. J. and Landis, R. S. (2008) 'A model of emergence and dysfunctional effects of emotional conflicts in groups', *Group Dynamics: Theory, Research and Practice*, **12**(2), pp. 112–26.

36   Bolton, S. (2005) *Emotion Management in the Workplace*, Basingstoke: Palgrave.

37   Cole, M. S., Walter, F. and Bruch, H. (2008) 'Affective mechanisms linking dysfunctional behavior to performance in work teams: a moderated mediation study', *Journal of Applied Psychology*, **93**(5), pp. 945–58.

38   Dunlop, P.D. and Lee, K. (2004) 'Workplace deviance, organizational citizenship behavior, and business unit performance: the bad apples do spoil the whole barrel', *Journal of Organizational Behavior*, **25**, 67–80.

39   Behfar, K., Peterson, R., Mannix, E. and Trochim, W. (2008) 'The critical role of conflict resolution in teams: a closer look at the links between conflict type, conflict management strategies, and team outcomes', *Journal of Applied Psychology*, **93**(1), pp. 170–88.

40   Tajfel, H. (1978) 'Social categorization, social identity, and social comparison', pp. 61–76 in H. Tajfel (ed.), *Differentiation between Social Groups*, London: Academic Press.

41   Tajfel, H. (1981) 'Social stereotypes and social groups', in J. C. Turner and H. Giles (eds), *Intergroup Behaviour*, Oxford: Blackwell.

42   Turner, J. (1987) *Rediscovering the Social Group: A Self-categorization Theory*, New York: Basic Books.

43   Miller, N. and Brewer, M. B. (eds) (1984) *Groups in Contact: The Psychology of Desegregation*, New York: Academic Press.

44   Sherif, M., Harvey, O. J., White, B. J., Hood, W. R. and Sherif, C. W. (1961) *Intergroup Conflict and Cooperation*, Norman, OK: Oklahoma Book Exchange.

45   De Dreu, C. and Van de Vliert, E. (eds) (1997) *Using Conflict in Organizations*, London: Sage.

46   Hackman, H. R. (1986) 'The psychology of self-management in organizations', pp. 89–136 in M. S. Pallack and Perloff, R. O. (eds), *Psychology and Work: Productivity, Change and Employment*, Washington, DC: American Psychological Association.

47   Banker, R. D., Field, J. M., Schroeder, R. G. and Sinha, K. (1996) 'Impact of work teams on manufacturing performance: a longitudinal study', *Academy of Management Journal*, **39**(2), pp. 867–90.

48   Cohen, S. G. and Bailey, D. E. (1997) 'What makes team work: group effectiveness research from the shop floor to the executive suite', *Journal of Management*, **23**(3), pp. 239–90.

49   Steiner, I. D. (1972) *Group Processes and Productivity*, New York: Academic Press.

50   Horwitz, F. M., Chan feng Heng and Quazi, H. A. (2003) 'Finders, keepers? Attracting, motivating and retaining knowledge workers', *Human Resource Management Journal*, **13**(4), pp. 23–44.

51   Stewart, P. and Danford, A. (2008) 'Editorial: Union strategies and worker engagement with new forms of work and employment', *New Technology, Work and Employment*, **23**(3), pp. 146–50.

52   Asch, S. E. (1951) 'Effects of group pressure upon modification and distortion of judgements', in H. Guetzkow (ed.), *Groups, Leadership and Men*, New York: Carnegie Press.

53   Milgram, S. (1973) *Obedience and Authority*, London: Tavistock.

54   Russell, N. and Gregory, R. (2005) 'Making the undoable doable: Milgram, the Holocaust, and modern government', *American Review of Public Administration*, **35**(4), pp. 327–49.

55   Koring, P. (2004) 'Iraq war based on "flawed" reports', *Globe and Mail*, p. A11.

56   Winquist, J. and Franz, T. (2008) 'Does the stepladder technique improve group decision making? A series of failed replications', *Group Dynamics: Theory, Research and Practice*, **12**(4), pp. 255–67.

57   van Dick, R., van Knippenburg, D., Hagele, S., Guillaume, Y. R. F. and Brodbeck, F. (2008) 'Group diversity and group identification: the moderating role of diversity beliefs', *Human Relations*, **61**(10), pp. 1463–92.

58　Benders, J. and Van Hootegem, G. (1999) 'Teams and their context: moving team discussion beyond existing dichotomies', *Journal of Management Studies*, **36**(5), pp. 609–28.

59　Roethlisberger, F. J. and Dickson, W. J. (1939) *Management and the Worker*, Cambridge, MA: Harvard University Press.

60　Maslow, A. H. (1954) *Motivation and Personality*, New York: Harper.

61　McGregor, D. (1960) *The Human Side of Enterprise*, New York: McGraw-Hill.

62　Turner, A. N. and Lawrence, P. R. (1965) *Industrial Jobs and the Worker*, Boston: Harvard University, Graduate School of Business Administration.

63　Hoeve, A. and Nieuwenhuis, L. (2006) 'Learning routines in innovation processes', *Journal of Workplace Learning*, **18**(3), pp. 171–85.

64　Lowe, G. (2000) *The Quality of Work: A People-centred Agenda*, New York: Oxford University Press.

65　Klein, J. (1994) 'Maintaining expertise in multi-skilled teams', *Advances in Interdisciplinary Studies of Work Teams*, **1**, pp. 145–65.

66　'Volvo's radical new assembly plant: "the death of the assembly line"?', *Business Week*, August 28, 1989.

67　Cressey, P. (1993) 'Kalmar and Uddevalla: the demise of Volvo as a European icon', *New Technology, Work and Employment*, **8**(2), pp. 88–96.

68　Elger, T. and Smith, C. (eds) (1994) *Global Japanization?*, London: Routledge.

69　Thompson, P. and Wallace, T. (1996) 'Redesigning production through teamworking', *International Journal of Operations and Production Management*, **16**(2), pp. 103–18.

70　Baldry, C, Bain, P. and Taylor, P. (1998) '"Bright satanic offices": intensification, control and team Taylorism', pp. 163–83 in P. Thompson and C. Warhurst (eds), *Workplaces of the Future*, Basingstoke: Macmillan.

71　Manz, C. C. and Sims, H. P. Jr. (1993). *Business Without Bosses*, New York: Wiley.

72　Danford, A., Richardson, M., Stewart, P., Tailby, S. and Upchurch, M. (2008) 'Partnership, high performance work systems and quality of working life', *New Technology, Work and Employment*, **23**(3), pp. 151–66.

73　Thompson, P. and McHugh, D. (2006) *Work Organizations: A Critical Introduction* (4th edn), Basingstoke: Palgrave.

74　Piore, M. and Sabel, C. (1984) *The Second Industrial Divide*, New York: Basic Books.

75　Turnbull, P. (1986) 'The Japanisation of British industrial relations at Lucas', *Industrial Relations Journal*, **17**(3), pp. 193–206.

76　Sayer, A. (1986) 'New developments in manufacturing: the just-in-time system', *Capital and Class*, **30**, pp. 43–72.

77　Tomaney, J. (1990) 'The reality of workplace flexibility', *Capital and Class*, **40**, pp. 29–60.

78　Clarke, L. (1997) 'Changing work systems, changing social relations? A Canadian General Motors Plant', *Relations Industrielle/Industrial Relations*, **52**(4), pp. 839–65.

79　Malloch, H. (1997) 'Strategic and HRM aspects of kaizen: a case study', *New Technology, Work and Employment*, **12**(2), pp. 108–22.

80　Willmott, H., (1995) 'The odd couple?: re-engineering business processes: managing human relations', *New/Technology, Work and Employment*, **10**(2), pp. 89–98.

81　Thompson, P. (1989) *The Nature of Work* (2nd edn), London: Macmillan.

82　Burawoy, M. (1979) *Manufacturing Consent*, Chicago: University of Chicago Press.

83　Burawoy, M. (2002) 'What happened to the working class?', pp. 69–76 in K. Leicht (ed.), *The Future of the Market Transition*, New York: JAI Press.

84　Shalla, V. (1997) 'Technology and the deskilling of work: the case of passenger agents at Air Canada', in A. Duffy, D. Glenday and N. Pupo (eds), *Good Jobs, Bad Jobs, No Jobs: The Transformation of Work in the 21st Century*, Toronto: Harcourt.

85　Wood, S. (1986) 'The cooperative labour strategy in the U.S. auto industry', *Economic and Industrial Democracy*, **7**(4), pp. 415–48.

86　Kasl, E., Marsick, V. and Dechant, K. (1997) 'Teams as learners', *Journal of Applied Behavioral Science*, **33**(2), pp. 227–46.

87　Finn, R. (2008) 'The language of teamwork: reproducing professional divisions in the operating theatre', *Human Relations* **61**(1), pp. 103–30.

88　Morgan, G. (1997) *Images of Organization* (2nd edn), Thousand Oaks, CA: Sage.

89　Muller, H. J., Rehder, R. R. and Bannister, G. (1998) 'The Mexican–Japanese–U.S. model for auto assembly in Northern Mexico', *Latin American Business Review*, **2**(1), pp. 47–67.

90　Proctor, S., Fulop, L., Linstead, S., Mueller, F. and Sewell, G. (2009) 'Managing teams', pp. 539–73 in S. Linstead, L. Fulop and S. Lilley (eds), *Management and Organization: A Critical Text* (2nd edn), Basingstoke: Palgrave.

91　Brown, S. P., Westbrook, R. A. and Challagalla, G. (2005) 'Good cope, bad cope: adaptive and maladaptive coping strategies following a critical negative work event', *Journal of Applied Psychology*, **90**, 792–8.

In this final part of the book, we shift our focus once again, this time to explore how organizational design, technology, culture, leadership, communications, power and politics and human resource management (HRM) practices influence social relations and the behaviour of people in organizations.

In Chapter 10, we explain that organizational structure refers to the formal division of labour and the formal pattern of relationships that coordinate and control organizational activities. Several theoretical frameworks are examined around the notions of the bureaucratic and post-bureaucratic.

In Chapter 11, we suggest that students need to think of technology as a social phenomenon by recognizing both consent and conflict within processes of adoption. We aim to stimulate a variety of questions, but perhaps more importantly, students should after reading this chapter be better able to understand, evaluate and affect the current landscape and trajectory of new technology.

In Chapter 12, we explore the nature of organizational culture, which we define as a pattern of shared basic assumptions, beliefs, values, artefacts, stories and behaviours, and discuss how the concept has become closely associated with the notion of postmodern organizations and contemporary management theory.

In Chapter 13, we explain that organizational leadership is a dialectic process wherein an individual persuades others to do things they would not otherwise do. This is a result of the interaction of the leader and followers in a specific context, and is equated with power. We explain that leadership is not the same as management. Whereas management is associated with certain activities, the leadership process produces change or significant movement.

In Chapter 14, we
explore how the communication process
in the workplace reflects management style, the
degree of employee involvement and empowerment, and
organizational culture. We emphasize that people engage with
their world through symbols (verbal, non-verbal and written language).
Language creates the organizational concepts that define the culture of an
organization and give form to notions of control, delegation and rationality.
In Chapter 15, we examine the different models of decision making. Here we are
careful to explain that, in reality, decision makers must suffer from bounded rationality.
We go on to discuss ethics in business decision making and explain the concept of corporate
social responsibility.

In Chapter 16, we explore the abstract concept of power and, drawing on the work of Gramsci
and Foucault, examine the deep social roots of power systems.

Finally, in Chapter 17, we examine the developments in HRM practices, how these influence the
behaviour of people in organizations, and the growth of interest in international HRM as a spin-off
from globalization. We discuss how contemporary HRM practices are a product of our times, the
ascendancy of a new political and economic ideology. Paradox is an ongoing part of the
employment relationship, and we expose some internal paradoxes in HRM.

The Epilogue reviews the key contents of the book, draws some general conclusions
about organizational behaviour, and sets the scene for future developments in
organizational behaviour against the backcloth of global capitalism, organization
restructuring and governance.

chapter 10
Organizational design

chapter outline

- Introduction
- Organizational structure and design
- Dimensions of structure
- Typologies of organizational structure
- Determinants of organizational structure: making strategic choices
- Organizational restructuring: a conceptual framework
- Traditional designs of organizational structure: bureaucracy
- Emerging organizational designs: post-bureaucracy?
- Gender, sexuality and organizational design
- Summary and end-of-chapter features
- Chapter case study 1: Strategy and design in Australia's tourist industry
- Chapter case study 2: ABC's just-in-time supply chain

chapter objectives

After studying this chapter, you should be able to:

- identify and define the foundation concepts of organizational structure and design
- understand the meaning and significance of complexity, formalization and centralization
- explain the relationships between strategy, size, technology and capitalist development, and the different forms of organizational design
- describe the difference between classical and modern thinking about organizational design
- describe some of the emerging contemporary forms of organizational design and identify the potential impact on workplace behaviour
- explain and illustrate the basis of criticism of managerial thinking about organizational design with reference to power, gender and sexuality

Introduction

In his influential book *Beyond Reengineering*,[1] Michael Hammer cited the Ford Motor Company as an exemplar of how a few American corporations had restructured and transformed 'beyond recognition' their old ways of doing things in order to meet the challenges of global competition. In February 2009, Ford chairman and CEO Bill Ford and other CEOs from General Motors and Chrysler were publicly explaining to the US Senate banking committee why they needed US$17 billion of emergency financial infusion to prevent bankruptcy. And in March 2009, US President Barack Obama rejected General Motors' and Chrysler's restructuring plans that had been submitted in February, while demanding the resignation of General Motors' CEO, Rick Wagoner, as part of the government's offer to help General Motors to accelerate and deepen their restructuring plans (see OB in focus, below).

In the same period, corporate bail-outs and the restructuring of European companies such as Fiat SpA, Renault SA, Volvo and Opel were reported. These restructuring initiatives were not unique to the manufacturing sector. Accelerated by dysfunctional financial markets and deteriorating global trade, venerable financial firms such as American International Group, Fannie Mae, Freddie Mac, Citigroup, Bank of America, Northern Rock, Bradford and Bingley, Royal Bank of Scotland and HBOS have been bailed out, restructured or nationalized.

Organizational restructuring entails a significant decrease in the resources that it allocates to process activities or product markets in which it has previously engaged, or a reallocation of resources to new geographical locations.[2] A plethora of studies have analysed such a 'downsizing' as part of a process of 'outsourcing' many functions originally assigned to permanent employees. Restructuring has been wrapped in the mantra of flexibility, lean and mean and competitiveness.[3–12] These studies emphasize that 'corporate anorexia' can fundamentally change how work is performed as well as reshape employment relations. Thus, the study of organizational structure and design is essential for a deeper understanding of workplace behaviour. What exactly are senior managers 'restructuring'? What determines organizational design? What is the right relationship between the centre of a company and its periphery? How does the psychological contract between the worker and the employer change after restructuring? And how does organizational design and redesign modify behaviour?

The answer to these questions is the focus of this chapter. We begin by explaining the meaning and nature of organizational structure and design. To

formal organization: a highly structured group formed for the purpose of completing certain tasks or achieving specific goals

Think about an organization where you have worked or studied. Can you identify a set of characteristics that help to describe its structure?

stop reflect

help with our analysis of different organizational forms, we offer a conceptual framework of the various types of organizational reconfiguring. We then move on to examine some traditional **formal organizational** designs: functional, product/service, divisional and matrix. New organizational designs that have allegedly supplanted the traditional forms are also examined. We conclude this chapter with a discussion on the links between gender, sexuality and organizational design.

OB in focus   OB in focus: Corporate restructuring and the car industry

Since the start of the recession, downsizing has become the management trend around the world, and corporate restructuring has become key to survival. In just one week in November 2008, Britain's BT, Canada's Nortel and German-owned DHL were just three of many firms announcing massive job cuts. In addition to having to trim down the number of employees, businesses are having to rethink the organization of their headquarters. Many are struggling with the problem of maintaining the right relationship between the centre and the periphery. In the 1970s, large multinationals created large headquarters. In the 1990s, the fashion changed to modest, simple centres. In the twenty-first century, headquarters were beginning to expand again – but the recession will probably force organizations to revert to minimalism.

The car industry has been hit especially hard by the recent economic downturn. Three of the largest US car manufacturers – General Motors (GM), Chrysler and Ford – have been forced to make significant changes to how they operate, while the government has had to step in to help out. All three organizations were in the midst of implementing vast

restructuring and cost-cutting strategies when they were knocked back again by tightening credit and rising oil prices. The revelation that GM was in danger of running out of cash concentrated executive minds. Although not quite as desperate, Ford was in a similar position, while Cerberus Capital Management (which owned 80 per cent of Chrysler) sought to offload the car maker to another firm. So the struggling car manufacturers were left with just two options: either the US government would have to come to the rescue, or the biggest car companies in America would have to seek Chapter 11 bankruptcy protection.

Chrysler did in the end file for bankruptcy (despite evidence that customers would be likely to abandon the products of a car manufacturer that took this step). The US government bailed out GM, and President Obama expressed his hope that the company would emerge 'leaner and meaner' as a result of its financial woes. In some ways, it seems that the Obama administration's automotive task force holds the fate of the US car industry and its future structure in its hands.

Sources: Anonymous (2008) 'Centres of attention', *The Economist*, November 13; Anonymous (2008) 'Follow the money', *The Economist*, October 18, p. 72; Anonymous (2008) 'On the edge', *The Economist*, November 15, 2008, p. 75; Keenan, G. (2009) 'Losses force GM to question its future', *Globe and Mail*, February 27, p. B1; http://news.bbc.co.uk/1/hi/business/8065760.stm.

Organizational structure and design

As we briefly discussed in Chapter 1, organizations are created to produce goods or services and to pursue dominant goals that individuals acting alone cannot achieve. According to Peter Drucker, the purpose of the work organization 'is to get the work done'.[13] However, organizational structure is not easy to define because it is not a physical reality, but rather a conceptual one. Let us begin to explain the concept in this way. To accomplish its strategic goals, an organization typically has to do two things: divide the work to be done among its members, and then coordinate the work. **Organizational structure** refers to the formal division of work and the formal configuration of relationships that coordinate and control organizational activities. The **organizational design** is the planning and implementation of a structural configuration of roles and modes of operation. Arguably, theories of organizational structure are a product of modernity, because they are largely based on Weber's notions of rationality and bureaucratic specialization.

organizational structure: the formal reporting relationships, groups, departments and systems of the organization
organizational design: the process of creating and modifying organizational structures

plate 34 In a small restaurant, the horizontal divisions might be divided into three main work activities: preparing the food, service and running the bar. A vertical division of labour would describe the coordinating and directing work of the head chef, the restaurant supervisor and the head bar tender, all of whom report to the restaurant manager.

Source: iStockphoto

Thus, work is divided horizontally into distinct tasks that need to be done, either into jobs, subunits or departments. This horizontal division of labour is associated with specialization on the part of the workforce. The vertical division of labour is concerned with apportioning authority for planning, decision making, monitoring and controlling: who will tell whom what to do? For example, in a small restaurant, the horizontal divisions might be divided into three main work activities: preparing the food, service and running the bar. A vertical division of labour would describe the coordinating and directing work of the head chef, the restaurant supervisor and the head bar tender, all of whom report to the restaurant manager.

This small business has a simple structure. However, the structure could become more complex as more people were hired and as coordination and control became more difficult. As business expanded and management became more complicated, the manager might not have enough time to deal with the accounts and hiring and training of new staff. To solve these problems, the restaurant manager might hire an accountant and a human resource manager, which would increase the vertical division of labour. The growth of an organization might therefore lead to a greater degree of specialization of its workforce.

Alternatively, the restaurant manager might create work teams and allow the team members to coordinate their work activities and hire and train their members. This limited 'empowerment' of the workers would then free up time for the head chef, the restaurant supervisor and the head bar tender to handle the accounts for their departments.

Specialization occurs when people focus their effort on a particular skill, task, customer or territorial area. Our simple example of the restaurant illustrates two important points: managers have choices over how to divide labour, and different organizational configurations impact on people's work experience. (For instance, if teams were introduced, additional tasks would have to be learnt and the pace of work might intensify.)

An **organization chart** graphically shows the various parts as boxes, and the coordination and control by lines that connect the boxes. This system is used in Figure 10.1 to demonstrate the simple structure of the restaurant just described, and is used in the sample organization charts that follow. Organizational design refers to the process of creating a structure that best fits a strategy, technology and environment. For example, Ford Motor Company has created a structure on a product basis, with separate divisions for specific models. So why do managers redesign structures? Management designs new structures in order to reduce costs, to respond to changing customer buying patterns or business boundaries, to reset priorities, to shift people and align capabilities, to shift perceptions of service among users, or to 'shake things up'.[14]

Why is organizational structure important? From a managerial perspective, structure may make the task of managing employees more complex, bringing into play the questions of efficiency and consistency that are likely to arise more often when different groups report directly to departmental managers, rather than to a

specialization: the allocation of work tasks to categories of employee or groups. Also known as division of labour

organization chart: a diagram showing the grouping of activities and people within a formal organization to achieve the goals of the organization efficiently

single owner or manager in an organization employing relatively few people. Structure therefore defines lines of responsibility and authority. In terms of organizational performance, a 'good' structure is not a panacea, but it is very important, argues management guru Peter Drucker: 'Good organizational structure does not by itself produce good performance ... But a poor organization structure makes good performance impossible, no matter how good the individual managers may be' (ref. 15, p. 4). The structure of an organization also affects the ability of workers to learn, to be creative, to innovate and to participate in decision making.[16,17]

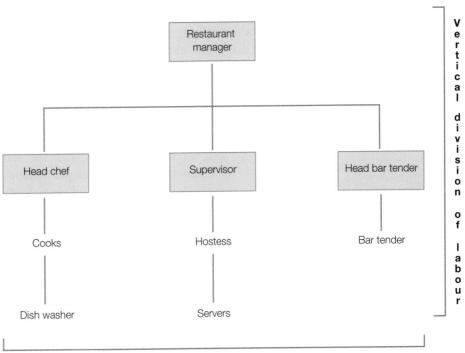

figure 15.1 An example of a simple organizational structure

Horizontal division of labour

From a worker's perspective, different structural configurations affect not only productivity and economic results, defined by the marketplace, but also job satisfaction, commitment, motivation and perceptions about expectations and obligations. Redesigning organizational structure will therefore affect the intangible 'psychological contract' of each individual worker (see also Chapter 2).

The concept of the psychological contract has an important implication for those redesigning organizational structures. Each individual employee will have different perceptions of his or her psychological contract, even when the structure within which he or she works is identical. Therefore, there will be no universal notion of mutual expectations and obligations.[18] Changes in the organization's structure also affect employee relations and organizational governance. All this serves to remind us that organizational success and failure depend on the behaviour of people, who work within the formal structure and who mould and imprint their personality into their work activities.

So far, we have given what could be described as the orthodox or mainstream position, in which organizational structure is rationally designed by managers to meet dominant organizational goals in as efficient a way as possible within the constraints they perceive. However, a critical approach to studying organizational behaviour examines the **informal aspects of structure**, which consist in part of unofficial working arrangements, social **networking** cabals and the internal **politicking** of people. Conceptually, it is argued that these two aspects of organizational structure – the formal and the informal – are dialectically related, in that they are

informal structure: a term used to describe the aspect of organizational life in which participants' day-to-day activities and interactions ignore, bypass or do not correspond with the official rules and procedures of the bureaucracy

networking: cultivating social relationships with others to accomplish one's goals

organizational politics: behaviours that others perceive as self-serving tactics for personal gain at the expense of other people and possibly the organization

influenced by each other, and activities in one encourage activities in the other.[19,20] For example, a team-based organizational structure designed by senior management to increase flexibility may invite unofficial strategies among line managers who choose to resist being relocated. An organizational structure reflects internal power relationships.[21,22]

Dimensions of structure

A variety of dimensions can be used to conceptualize organizational structure. There is a disagreement among theorists over what makes up the term 'structure', but a relatively recent way of thinking about organizations and structure is as 'discursive metaphors'. Advocates of this approach suggest that organizations are 'texts', created through discourses, which have symbolic meaning for managers and workers. These meanings are open to multiple readings even when particular meanings become sufficiently privileged and concrete. Here, we take a more orthodox approach to examine how researchers have analysed structure, before discussing how it affects organizational behaviour.[23] While we acknowledge the elastic definitions and various labels attached to organizational phenomena, here we examine three aspects: complexity, formalization and centralization.

Complexity

complexity: the intricate departmental and interpersonal relationships that exist within a work organization

Complexity is the degree of differentiation in the organization. Complexity measures the degree of division of tasks, levels of hierarchy and geographical locations of work units in the organization. The more tasks are divided among individuals, the more the organization is *horizontally complex*. The most visible evidence in the organization of horizontal complexity is specialization and departmentalization.

Specialization refers to the particular grouping of activities performed by an employee. Division of labour – for example, accounting activities – creates groups of specialists (in this case, accountants). The way these specialists are grouped is referred to as departmentalization. As the vertical chain of command lengthens, more formal authority layers are inserted between top management and front-line workers. In such circumstances, the organization becomes more *vertically complex*. Therefore, vertical complexity refers to the depth of the organization's hierarchy: the number of levels between senior management and the workers. Organizations with the same number of workers need not have the same degree of vertical complexity. Organizations can be 'flat', with few layers of hierarchy, or 'tall', with many levels of management between the top CEO and front-line employees (Figure 10.2).

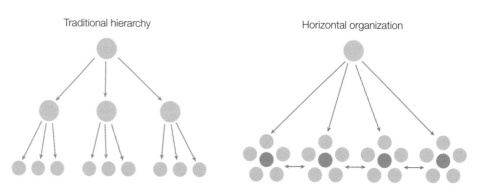

Traditional hierarchy   Horizontal organization

***figure* 10.2** A tall organization structure versus a flat (team-based) structure

During the last decade, organizations have moved towards flatter configurations by eliminating whole levels of middle managers and generally 'doing more with less'. This form of restructuring, commonly called 'downsizing', increases the span of control for the managers who remain. The **span of control** defines the number of subordinates that a single manager or administrator can supervise effectively. If this span is narrow, managers have few subordinates reporting to them. If it is wide, managers are responsible for many subordinates. The larger the span, the less potential there is for control by direct supervision. When work tasks are routine, the control of subordinates through technology and output performance substitutes for direct supervision. At lower operational levels, it is not unusual to have spans of control of up to 20 individuals. In the managerial ranks, work is less routine, and spans of control tend to be smaller. Thus, the complexity of the task often dictates the span of control.

Vertical complexity can also affect managerial behaviour by impacting on other factors such as communication networks and manager–worker dynamics. For example, a wide span of control makes it more difficult for a manager to hold face-to-face meetings.

An organization can perform the same work activities in geographically separate locations, a fact emphasized by globalization. The existence of multiple workplaces increases complexity. *Spatial complexity* refers to the degree to which the organization's operations and core workforce are geographically dispersed. As spatial complexity increases, managers face coordination, control and communication challenges relating to their subordinates.[24]

> span of control: the number of people directly reporting to the next level in the organizational hierarchy

Formalization

Formalization is the second core dimension of organizational structure, and describes the degree of standardization of work and jobs in the organization. It refers to the extent to which work is defined and controlled by rules. The more rules there are about what is to be done, when it is to be done and how it should be done, the more an organization is formalized. Where formalization is low, employees are given freedom to exercise discretion in their work. The degree of formalization can vary widely within and among organizations.

The extent of formalization typically varies with the nature of the work performed and the size of the organization.[25] The most complex and creative paid work is amenable to low degrees of formalization. Formalization also tends to be inversely related to the hierarchical level in the organization. Individuals lower in the organization are engaged in activities that are relatively simple and repetitive, and therefore these people are most likely to work in a highly formalized environment. Although formalization regulates workers' behaviour, it can also impose constraints on managers and subordinates. In a unionized workplace, for instance, contract rules negotiated by union and management can constrain managers' ability to mobilize the skills, creativity, commitment and values of their subordinates.[26]

> formalization: the degree to which organizations standardize behaviour through rules, procedures, formal training and related mechanisms

Centralization

Centralization, the third core dimension of organizational structure, refers to the degree to which decision making is concentrated at a single point in the organization. In essence, it addresses the question, who makes the decisions in the organization? A decentralized organization is one in which senior managers solicit input from members when making key decisions. The more input members provide or the more autonomy they are given to make decisions, the more decentralized the organization.

> centralization: the degree to which formal decision authority is held by a small group of people, typically those at the top of the organizational hierarchy

The degree of centralization affects workers' ability to make decisions, levels of motivation and the manager–subordinate interface. An ongoing challenge for managers is to balance the degree of centralization necessary to achieve control on the one hand, and to gain commitment through participation and work-related learning on the other.

Typologies of organizational structure

mechanistic organization: an organizational structure with a narrow span of control and high degrees of formalization and centralization

organic organization: an organizational structure with a wide span of control, little formalization and decentralized decision making

Can you identify organizations that have organic features and organizations that display mechanistic features?

stop reflect

The three core dimensions of formal organizational structure – complexity, formalization and centralization – can be combined into a number of different types or models. Two popular descriptive models have received much attention: the mechanistic model and the organic model.[27]

The **mechanistic organization** has been characterized as a machine. It has high complexity, high formalization and high centralization. A mechanistic organization resembles a bureaucracy. It is characterized by highly specialized tasks that tend to be rigidly defined, a hierarchical authority and control structure, and communications that primarily take the form of edicts and decisions issued by managers to subordinates. Communication typically flows vertically from the top down.

Organic organizations are the antithesis of mechanistic organizations. They are characterized by being low in complexity, formality and centralization. An organic organization is said to be flexible and informally coordinated, and managers use participative decision-making behaviours. Communication is both horizontal (across different departments) and vertical (down and up the hierarchy), depending on where the information resides.

Determinants of organizational structure: making strategic choices

competitive advantage: the ability of a work organization to add more value for its customers and shareholders than its rivals, and thus gain a position of advantage in the marketplace

Visit http://www.12manage.com/methods_contingency_theory.html and http://changingminds.org/disciplines/leadership/theories/contingency_theory.htm for more information on contingency theory

weblink

The underlying rationale for mechanistic and organic organizations is, according to conventional organizational theory, explained by the choice of competitive strategy. The mechanistic organization strives for **competitive advantage** by maximizing efficiency and productivity, whereas an organic organization's competitive strategy is based on maximum adaptability and flexibility. Thus, structural characteristics concern contextual factors within the organization and affect the management process. So far, although we have examined a number of core organizational design concepts, we have not provided much insight into why organizational structures vary so much, or into the forces behind corporate restructuring. The purpose of this section is to discuss theories of organizational design in terms of their relevance for understanding current restructuring endeavours.

Early management theorists put forward universalistic organizational structure theories: that is, the 'one size fits all' principle applied to organizations. Over the last 30 years, organizational analysts have modified the classical approach by suggesting that organizational structure is contingent (or depends) on a variety of variables or contextual factors. The contingency approach to organizational design takes the view that there is no 'one best' universal structure, and emphasizes the need for flexibility. The significant contingency variables are strategy, size, technology and environment.

Strategy and structure

As we discussed in Chapter 1, strategy can be viewed as a pattern of activity over time to achieve performance goals. The classical position that 'structure follows strategy' assumes that managers choose the structure they have: 'A new strategy required a new or at least refashioned structure' (ref. 28, p. 15). This hypothesis is represented in Figure 10.3.

For example, if top management chooses to compete through product and service innovation and high quality – a differentiation strategy – then managers need to adopt an organic or horizontal organizational structure. A cost leadership strategy, on the other hand, requires products or services to be standardized with minimum costs. A mechanistic, functional structure with more formalization and centralization is most appropriate with this strategy, so that managers can closely control quality and costs.

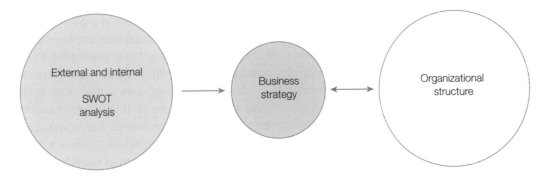

figure 10.3 The strategy-structure thesis

A counter-thesis sees strategy as related less directly to organizational design. In this view, 'strategy follows structure'.[29] The design of the organization is the context in which top managers form the business strategy. Thus, the existing organizational configuration affects top managers' perceptions of internal strengths, weaknesses, threats and opportunities (SWOT) outside the organization, and helps shape a strategy.

Empirical research offers support for both views of strategy affecting the design of an organization; this is illustrated in Figure 10.3 by a two-headed arrow between structure and strategy. This recognizes that the link between strategy and structure is affected by other contingency factors, such as size, technology and environment.

In her book *No Logo*, globalization critic Naomi Klein provides a more controversial account of the link between corporate strategy – a focus on 'branding' and the relocation of manufacturing capacity from the core capitalist economy to the periphery, where wage levels are low – and multifaceted structures spanning national frontiers:

> The astronomical growth in the wealth and cultural influence of multinational corporations over the last fifteen years can arguably be traced back to a single, seemingly innocuous idea developed by management theorists in the mid-1980s, that successful corporations must primarily produce brands, as opposed to products ... The very process of producing – running one's own factories, being responsible for the tens of thousands of full-time, permanent employees – began to look less like the route to success and more like a clunky liability.

> At around this time a new kind of corporation began to rival the traditional all-American manufacturers for market share; these were the Nikes and Microsoft, and later, the Tommy Hilfigers and Intels ... What these companies produced primarily were not things, they said, but images of their brands. Their real work lay not in manufacturing but in marketing. This formula, needless to say, has proved enormously profitable, and its success has companies competing in a race towards weightlessness: whoever owns the least, has the fewest employees on the payroll and produces the most powerful images, as opposed to products, wins the race. (ref. 30, p. 4)

Visit www.
corpwatch.org, a
US-based organization
that monitors and critiques
global capitalism through
education and social
action

weblink

Of course, as globalization theorists have observed, the notion of 'weightlessness' is only feasible because of the developments in transportation, namely containerization and the Internet.

Size and structure

Most studies define organizational size as the total number of employees, and researchers suggest that larger organizations have different structures from smaller organizations. As organizations increase in size, they tend to develop more written rules and procedures, and division of labour becomes more specialized. A number of theorists have argued that size is an important factor affecting organizational design.[31–33] It seems credible that there is a positive relationship between size and the degree of formalization, specialization and centralization.

Critics of the size imperative have countered that neither formalization nor complexity can be inferred from organizational size. An equally valid alternative interpretation of early empirical data is that size is the result, not the cause, of structure.[34] The key point here is that there are obvious structural differences between large and small organizations, but a statistically significant relationship between size and structural dimensions does not imply causation. For example, technology influences structure, which in turn determines size.

Technology and structure

Technological change is quintessentially a defining feature of the 'knowledge economy', and is also another important contingency variable explaining organizational structure. Researchers have adopted either a restrictive or an expansive definition of technology, and the early research on technology suggests a positive relationship between type of technology and organizational structure.[35,36]

The 'technology–structure' thesis has sought to analyse technology as an independent explanatory variable. The British academic Joan Woodward, for example, classified production technology into three main categories for analysis: unit production (as in a tailor's shop), mass production (as in an automotive plant), and continuous process production (like that of a pulp mill). Perrow classified four types of technology: routine, engineering, craft and non-routine. Routine technologies have few exceptions and easy-to-analyse problems (for example, pulp and paper mills or chemical plants belong to this category). Engineering technologies have a large number of exceptions, but can be managed in a systematic manner (as with the construction of bridges). Craft technologies deal with relatively difficult problems with a limited set of exceptions (such as in hand-crafted furniture making). Non-routine technologies are characterized by many exceptions and difficult-to-analyse problems (as with research and development).

The research found evidence of different types of technology being associated with different organizational designs. Non-routine technology, for instance, is positively associated with high complexity. So as the work becomes more customized, the span of control narrows. Studies also suggest that routine technology is positively related to formalization. Routine technologies allow leaders to implement rules and regulations because the work is well understood by their followers. It has been proposed that routine technology might lead to centralized decision making and control systems if formalization is low. Within this theoretical framework, it is suggested that technology mediates mechanical and integrated forms of management control, which are incorporated into the technology itself. Thus, employee performance is subject to control by technology rather than by direct human supervision.

Joan Woodward died in 1971, but her thesis that technology is a crucial contingency influenced the American sociologist Howard Aldrich. For Aldrich in 2002, as for Woodward, the technology in use in the organization had high priority in accounting for the degree of organizational structure.[37] Both structure and technology are multidimensional concepts, and it is not realistic to relate technology to structure in any simple manner. In addition, all the technological paradigms have their strengths and weaknesses. Conceptualizing technology by degrees of 'routineness' leads to a generalizable conclusion that technology will shape structure in terms of size, complexity and formalization. The strategic choice discourse also suggests that it is managerial behaviour at critical points in the process of organizational change – possibly in negotiation with trade unions – that is critical in reshaping managerial processes and outcomes, including organizational structure.

Environment and structure

The **environment** is everything outside the organization's boundary. The case for the environmental imperative argues that organizations are embedded in society, and therefore a multitude of economic, political, social and legal factors will affect organizational design decisions. The attack on the World Trade Center on September 11, 2001 and the global economic recession that began in 2008–09 are two catastrophes outside organizations that resulted in major restructuring within many airlines and banks.

An early study by Burns and Stalker in 1966 proposed an environment–structure thesis.[27] In essence, their study of UK firms distinguished five different kinds of environment, ranging from 'stable' to 'least predictable', and two divergent patterns of managerial behaviour and organizational structure – the organic and the mechanistic configurations. They suggested that both types of structural regime represented a 'rational' form of organization that could be created and sustained according to the external conditions facing the organization. For instance, uncertainty in the environment might cause top managers to restructure in order to be more responsive to the changing marketplace.

An organization's environment can also range from *munificent* to *hostile*. Organizations located in a hostile environment face more competition, an adversarial union–management relationship and resource scarcity.

These four distinct dimensions of environments shape structure. The more dynamic the environment, the more 'organic' the structure, and the more complex the environment, the more 'decentralized' the structure.[38] The explosive growth of e-commerce, for example, has created a dynamic complex environment for much of the retail book and clothing industry, and is therefore spawning highly flexible network structures. Despite the criticisms of contingency theory, it has provided insights into understanding complex situational variables that help to shape organizational structure.

Globalization and organizational restructuring

Our aim in this chapter is to offer a multidimensional understanding of organizational structure and restructuring. Existing organizational behaviour texts tend to be more narrowly focused, and give limited, if any, coverage to the causation and consequences of global capitalism.

As a field of study, the term **globalization** is controversial, as are its alleged effects. Clearly, a detailed study of globalization is beyond the scope of this chapter, but to ground the arguments on organizational structure we need to at least acknowledge the interplay of continuity, restructuring and the diversity of experiences of globalization.

For some, globalization involves the spread of transplanetary connections between people.[39] For others, globalization primarily revolves around two main

environment: refers to the broad economic, political, legal and social forces that are present in the minds of the organization's members and may influence their decision making and constrain their strategic choices, such as the national business system

Can you think of any developments in the UK or Europe that have changed organizational design?

stop reflect

globalization: when an organization extends its activities to other parts of the world, actively participates in other markets, and competes against organizations located in other countries

Work and Society: Fordism for doctors?

For those who study occupational change, the professions represent an interesting case. 'Professional' occupations span a broad range of areas – from established occupations such as doctor or lawyer, to so-called 'semi-professional' occupations such as teacher or social worker. What makes the professions unique is that they appear to have resisted many of the trends that have changed the face of work in the twentieth century. Although specialized, the professional worker is not alienated. He or she enjoys considerable discretion over how work is done, the settings in which it is done, and the ways in which it is evaluated. Traditionally, professional workers have maintained control over their work processes, despite efforts by managers and consumers to challenge that control.

The world of professional work has undergone significant change in the last two decades. Professional authority has been contested, and there have been efforts to subordinate professional authority to managerial authority. Some of the more dramatic instances of this kind of challenge have occurred in Britain's National Health Service (NHS). Referring to specific moments in this process of reform, David Hunter (1994), a Professor at the Nuffield Institute for Health, offers the following analysis:

> Much of the impetus beyond the 1989 reform proposals … can be seen as an attempt to secure a shift in the balance of power between doctors and managers in favour of the latter. They seek to achieve such a shift in the context of advocating improved efficiency in the use of resources and in the provision of services. Much of the management problem in the NHS has centered on the notion of undermanagement in respect of the medical side of the service. Getting a grip on the freedom enjoyed by clinicians and holding them to account for expenditure they incur is seen as the last unmanaged frontier in the NHS. (p. 6)

As Hunter suggests, the rationale behind this attempt to limit the professional power of doctors was efficiency. But what is the larger historical context of this managerial initiative? Richard Sennett argues that the rationale for reform of this kind can be traced back to Henry Ford's views on how work should be organized. In Sennett's view, 'Fordism' entails a particular perspective on the division of labour: 'each worker does one task, measured as precisely as possible by time-and-motion studies; output is measured in terms of targets that are … entirely quantitative' (Sennett, 2008, p. 47). Sennett goes on to suggest how Fordism has shaped reforms in the NHS: 'Fordism monitors the time doctors and nurses spend with each patient; a medical treatment system based on dealing with auto parts, it tends to treat cancerous livers or broken backs rather than patients in the round' (p. 47).

How effective has this approach been to managing the clinical world of healthcare? Hunter maintains that while the power of doctors was constrained in some ways, doctors continued to exert considerable influence over how health and disease should be understood, and consequently on how the work of producing health and preventing illness should be organized. Moreover, as Sennett notes, 'doctors create paper fictions' to circumvent the practice guidelines imposed by managers in the NHS: 'Doctors in the NHS often assign a patient a disease in order to justify the time spent exploring a puzzling body' (p. 49).

The challenge of how to organize and manage professional work remains a central issue in the field of organizational design. We have yet to answer the question of what might constitute the optimal balance between professional and managerial power. Perhaps the best way to approach this question is to attempt to envision a situation where shared power enhances productivity and quality in the provision of healthcare.

stop! Taking the doctor as an example, where would you position the threshold beyond which too much managerial power might erode productivity and decrease the quality of patient care? Provide some concrete examples to illustrate how a sharing of power between professionals (including allied professionals, such as nurses) and managers will enhance the overall effectiveness of the NHS and national health systems more generally.

Can you identify the major source of managerial authority in a system like that of the USA where private corporations play a key role in the delivery of healthcare?

Consider how these issues may apply to other professions, such as law and teaching.

Sources and further information

Freidson, E. (1998) *Professionalism Reborn*, Chicago: University of Chicago Press.

Hunter, D. (1994) 'From tribalism to corporatism: the managerial challenge to medical dominance', pp. 1–22 in J. Gabe, D. Kelleher and G. Williams (eds), *Challenging Medicine*, London: Routledge.

Sennett, R. (2008) *The Craftsman*, New Haven, CT: Yale University Press.

Note: This feature was written by David MacLennan, Assistant Professor at Thompson Rivers University, BC, Canada.

phenomena. First is the emergence of a capitalist global economy based on a sophisticated system of production, finance, transportation and communication driven by transnational corporations (TNCs). Second is the notion of global culture, which focuses on the spread of particular patterns of consumption and the ideology of consumerism at the global level.[40]

The more radical globalization literature helps us to locate the main driver of organizational design and restructuring in the dialectical development of global capitalism. This argument is based on the theory that organizational restructuring occurs because of systematic contradictions.[41] This approach, which has occupied an immense space in Marxist literature, searches for inherent tendencies in the global capitalist system that create tension and bring about their own conflicts, until such a system can no longer maintain itself without far-reaching structural adjustments. Thus, every phase of capitalist expansion is characterized by the particular model through which business organizations 'make their profits'. In Marxist literature, this is referred to as 'accumulation'.

To apply accumulation theory to the various restructuring initiatives shown in Figure 10.5, below, profit maximization was achieved in the first half of the twentieth century through the use of bureaucracies modelled on Fordist-style production and employment relations. The whole point about bureaucratic Fordism as a profitable undertaking is that it achieves economies of scale: the system produces standardized products at relatively low unit costs.

However, as we explained in Chapter 2, the downside to Taylorism and Fordism is that the success of the operation depends on an expanding market for the same standard product, and mass production cannot readily adjust to changing consumer tastes. The offer to consumers of 'Any colour of car provided it's black' is less compelling when the market is saturated with black cars and competitors are offering a choice of colours. It is perhaps not surprising that, in order to maintain profitability, an early response of employers to the catalogue of problems associated with bureaucratic Fordism was to decentralize and transplant assembly-line systems from core capitalist countries (such as Germany) to the periphery (for example, to Mexico), where wage levels were very low. The systematic contradiction of Fordism and corporate imperatives created divisionalized structures, including strategic business units, as manufacturing was relocated to the newly industrialized economies (NIEs) of South-East Asia, Brazil and Mexico.

In recent years, market changes compelled further restructuring and 'downsizing' towards 'horizontal' or 'lean' organizations. As two US management theorists write, 'American companies were weighted down with cumbersome organizational charts and many layers of management' (ref. 42, p. xiii). Critical accounts of organizational restructuring also describe the associated changes in social relations: non-standard or precarious employment, and a new 'international division of labour' in which a small number of NIEs participate in the global dispersal of manufacturing by TNCs.

Feminist scholars have highlighted the exploitative and patriarchal nature of the new international division of labour. The critics of global capitalism argue that, as the dominance of the capitalist global system spreads and deepens, it simultaneously sows the seeds of organizational restructuring by providing resources, forms of organizational capacity and the ideological rationale.[40]

Figure 10.4 is an adaptation of Figure 1.2 and offers a synthesis of current thinking. It suggests that organizational structure is influenced by business strategy, size, technology, environment and the economics of global capitalism. It is also influenced by internal situational variables, such as culture, managerial and worker behaviour, and the strategic choices available to dominant organizational decision makers. The end results include increased profits for corporations and a new international division of labour.

Visit https://www.cia.gov/library/publications/the-world-factbook for more information on the relative size, by revenue, of TNCs

weblink

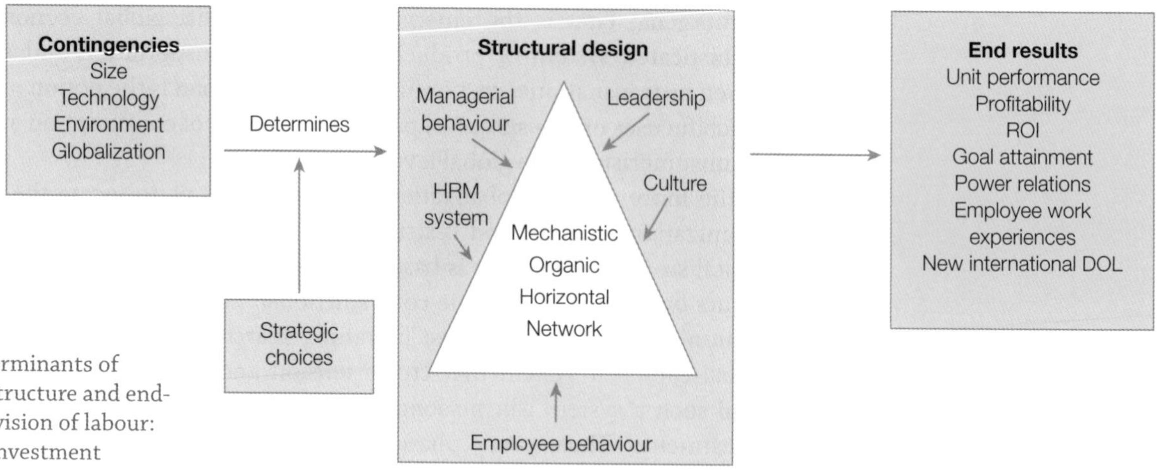

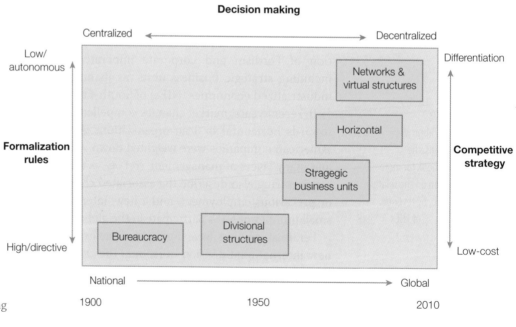

figure 10.4 Determinants of organizational structure and end-results. DOL, division of labour: ROI, return on investment

Organizational restructuring: a conceptual framework

Much discussion on organizational structure in standard organizational behaviour textbooks tends to be historically blind, economically shallow, culturally illiterate and politically naive. Although organizational structure and redesign are widely assumed to influence behaviour in the workplace, most treatment of the subject gives scant attention to the complex interplay of organizational structure, management strategies and changes in global capitalist development. To help the analysis of the interplay of different dimensions that appear to have been critical in recent organizational restructuring, we have drawn upon the work of Mabey and his colleagues[43] and constructed a conceptual framework using four interconnected dimensions. Each of these is shown in Figure 10.5.

figure 10.5 Types of organizational restructuring

Source: Adapted from Mabey, Salaman and Storey (1998),[43] p. 235

On the bottom horizontal axis is the dimension of capitalist global development over the last century, from national economies to a global scale. On the right vertical axis is the dimension of competitive strategy, covering the spectrum from low cost to differentiation. On the left vertical axis is the dimension of formalization, showing the contrast between high/directive and low/autonomous, and on the horizontal axis at the top of the figure is the dimension relating to decision making, which contrasts centralized and decentralized modes.

At the risk of oversimplification, some alternative structural designs are shown for illustrative purposes. In the first half of the twentieth century, at the lower left of Figure 10.5, the bureaucratic form is located to suggest a low-cost, mass-production competitive strategy, a high degree of formalization and direction, and a centralized decision-making mode. Ascending and moving to the right in the figure, from about the 1960s, we see the development of divisionalized configurations, to the development of strategic business units and then networks and virtual organizations.

In addition to the changes in conventional structural boundaries, organizations have recently undertaken other types of restructuring involving new commercial relationships. Manufacturing companies have outsourced the production of some parts – note the influence of just-in-time systems – and services (such as payroll, training and benefits handling), and in the public sector so-called non-core activities (such as laundry, catering and cleaning) have been privatized.

This framework is useful in illustrating the different organizational forms and design options facing top managers, when considered in relation to the core dimensions of formal organizational structure and in relation to each other. The argument of this book is that if we are to understand contemporary workplaces and explain what is happening in them, we need to locate restructuring initiatives in a multidimensional framework that includes capitalist global development. While we believe that the actions of TNCs and the international division of labour are intimately interconnected with organizational design and restructuring, the inclusion in the framework of capitalist global development does not suggest any inevitable linear progression.[39,43] We must remember that millions of people still work in 'sweatshops' and bureaucratic organizations in core economies and NIEs, and these traditional modes of organizing work exist alongside 'new' horizontal and process-based forms and 'frame-breaking' network-based organizations.

The next two sections review the traditional and contemporary types of organizational structure shown in Figure 10.5.

Traditional designs of organizational structure: bureaucracy

In Henry Mintzberg's *Structure in Fives: Designing Effective Organizations*,[44] he suggests that any work organization has five core parts, which vary in size and importance (Figure 10.6). Three line roles include senior management (the strategic apex), middle management (the middle line), and the production (operating, technical) core. The production core consists of those who do the work of the organization, making its products or servicing its customers. Two staff roles include technical support (technological structure) and clerical support (support staff). The model suggests that, given these five different parts, organizations can adopt a wide variety of structural configurations, depending on which part is in control.

At its simplest, work organizations must perform four essential functions to survive and grow in a capitalist economy:

1. A product or a service must be developed that has value.
2. The product must be manufactured or the service rendered by employees who rely on paid work as their only or major source of income.
3. The product or service must be marketed and made available to those who are to use it.
4. Financial resources are needed in order to develop, create and distribute the product or service provided.

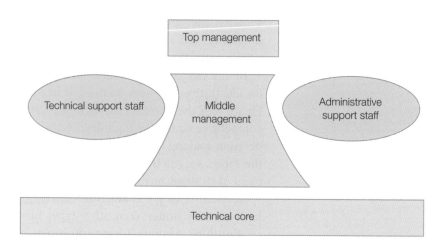

figure 10.6 Five basic elements of an organizational structure

Source: iStockphoto

These 'task' functions are the basic activities of the organization, and are undertaken within each of Mintzberg's five basic elements: developing (support), manufacturing the product or providing the service (technostructure and operating core), marketing the product and service (support), and financing the organization (strategic apex and support).

The process of developing, manufacturing the product or providing the service, and marketing it in a capitalist economy also results in a number of organizational imperatives (an imperative being something that dictates something) that centre on issues of control. For those who sit at the strategic apex and for middle-line managers, producing for a market creates pressures to control costs and control uncertainties. Organizations that compete in the marketplace typically face two types of competitive pressure: pressure for cost reductions and pressure to be responsive to changing customer tastes.

Responding to pressures for cost reductions means that managers must try to minimize unit costs by, for example, producing a standardized product and achieving economies of scale. On the other hand, responding to pressures to be responsive to customers requires that managers differentiate the firm's product offering in an effort to accommodate differences in consumers' tastes and preferences. These two types of competitive pressure are even more intense in the global marketplace.[45]

Additionally, the indeterminacy of employees' job performance creates pressures to render individual behaviour predictable and manageable. The control imperatives inherent in capitalist production and employee relations create a need for other managerial behaviour that is supportive of the operating functions of the organization, including human resource management (HRM), industrial relations and public relations. Together, the pressures arising from 'task' functions and 'control' functions shape formal organizational structure as a hierarchy, where decision making is top-down, with subunits or departments, and with managers hired to control employee behaviour.

In the industrial technology era, the organizational dynamics just described caused managers to adopt one of four common structural configurations. They could structure the organization by:

- function
- product/service
- division
- function and product, a matrix.

No formulas exist to guide the choices for organizational structure. Each structure has advantages and disadvantages. The guiding principle is that although there is no one right organizational structure, the right structure for top managers is the one that offers the most advantages and the fewest limitations, or, to put it another way, the one that 'makes their profits'.

Several newer contemporary forms of organizational design have evolved over the last two decades, and are well established in the organizational discourse. These new designs focus on processes or work teams, or the electronic connection of widely dispersed locations and people to form an extended 'virtual' organization. Understanding the strengths and limitations of each structural design helps us to understand what informs design choices, as well as the interplay between different structural configurations and organizational behaviour.

functional configuration: an organizational structure that organizes employees around specific knowledge or other resources

A **functional configuration** is one in which managers and subordinates are grouped around certain important and continuing functions. For example, in an engineering company, all design engineers and planners might be grouped together in one department, and all marketing specialists grouped together in another department (Figure 10.7). In a functionally designed organization, the functional department managers hold most of the authority and power. Key advantages of functional organizations include the development of technical expertise and economies of scale: it is the classic bureaucratic structure. Disadvantages can include the encouragement of narrow perspectives in functional groups, alienation and demotivation, and poor coordination of interdepartmental activities.

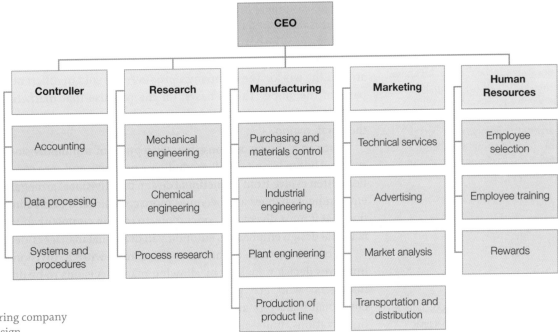

figure 10.7 Engineering company with a functional design

A product or service design arrangement is one in which managers and subordinates are grouped together by the product or service they deliver to the customer. For example, at Volvo Motors there is a car division, a truck division and so on (as schematized in Figure 10.8). Another example is a hospital where a medical team and support workers are grouped together in different departments or units dealing with particular treatments, such as maternity, orthopaedic surgery and emergencies.

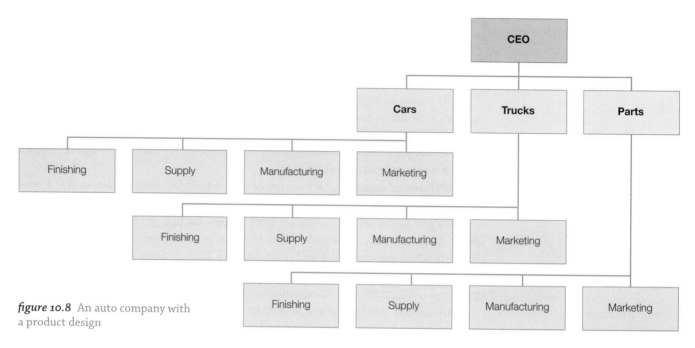

figure 10.8 An auto company with a product design

The advantages of product or service structures include increased coordination of functional departments, improvements in decision making, and the location of accountability for production and profit. Disadvantages of product or service structures can include a loss of economies of scale, the duplication of scarce resources and the discouragement of cooperation between divisions.

A **divisional structural** arrangement uses decentralization as its basic approach. The decentralized divisions can group employees together in one of three ways: by the products or services on which they work, by the sets of customers they serve, or by the geographical locations in which they operate. In the 1980s, these divisional structures developed into **strategic business units**, often with 20 levels of management between the corporate CEO and front-line employees in the business units.

The Body Shop uses a divisional structure based on its major operating regions around the world. The company's products are sold in different markets in different parts of the globe. This is based on the premise that marketing The Body Shop's products in Canada is different from marketing skin and hair products in the UK or the Asian region.

Figure 10.9 shows one possible conception of a multidivisional corporation with strategic business units, built around core products and core competencies. Organizations often evolve from a functional design to a divisional arrangement. As the external environment changes and becomes more complex and uncertain, management might find that it must diversify its operations to remain competitive.[24,45,46] Divisional organizational design emphasizes autonomy in divisional managers' decision making.

There are several advantages associated with a divisional configuration. It improves decision making by allowing many decisions to be delegated to divisional managers, who are generally more knowledgeable about the local markets. Divisional managers are more accountable for their decisions. In many divisional organizations, units are 'profit centres', and divisional managers are evaluated on the overall performance of their unit.

The disadvantages of a divisional structure come partly from its decentralized activities. Economies of scale are lost because many task functions of the organization, such as marketing, and control functions, such as accounting and HRM, are duplicated in each division. Specialists in one division may not be able or willing to share information with similar specialists in other divisions. Thus, the autonomy given to each division to pursue its own performance goals becomes an obstacle to

divisional structure: an organizational structure that groups employees around geographical areas, clients or outputs

strategic business unit: a term to describe corporate development that divides the corporation's operations into strategic business units, which allows comparisons between each strategic business unit. According to advocates, corporate managers are better able to determine whether they need to change the mix of businesses in their portfolio

Go to www.starbucks. com/aboutus/international. asp to examine Starbucks' matrix structure, which combines functional and product divisions, with employees reporting to two heads

weblink

achieving overall corporate goals. As a consequence, warn Hamel and Prahalad in *Competing for the Future*, 'corporate' strategy is little more than 'an amalgamation of individual business unit plans' and managerial strategic behaviour tends to be parochial, focusing only on existing business units (ref. 24, p. 309). From a worker's perspective, the outcome can be catastrophic: relocating to another geographical location means job loss as the firm's products or services are relocated to typically low-wage economies or outsourced and, in the case of public corporations, privatized.

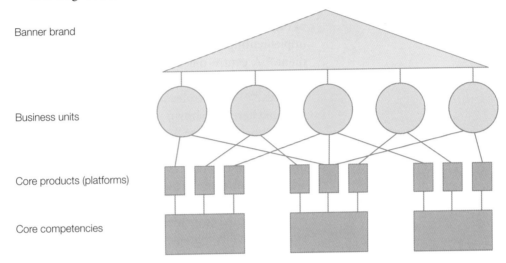

Banner brand

Business units

Core products (platforms)

Core competencies

figure 10.9 Divisional organizational structure based on strategic business units

Source: Hamel and Prahalad (1994),[24] p. 279

matrix structure: a type of departmentalization that overlays a divisionalized structure (typically a project team) with a functional structure

In the **matrix structure**, both functional specialities and product or service orientation are maintained, and there are functional managers and product managers. Functional managers are responsible for the selection, training and development of technically competent workers in their functional area. Product managers, on the other hand, are responsible for coordinating the activities of workers from different functional areas who are working on the same product or service to customers. In a matrix design, employees report to two managers rather than to one (Figure 10.10).

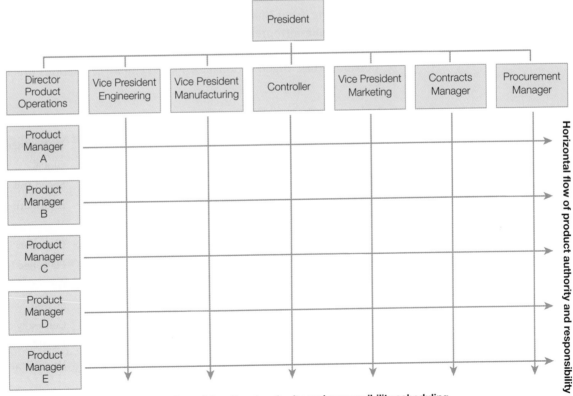

figure 10.10 An engineering company with a matrix design

Emerging organizational designs: post-bureaucracy?

Since the 1980s, faced with accelerated changes in global capitalism, the limitations of bureaucracy and new technologies, such as the Internet, new post-bureaucratic forms of organization have emerged in the management literature: the flexible firm,[47] the cellular configuration,[48,49] the adhocracy configuration,[38] the postmodern organization,[50] the individualized corporation,[51] the re-engineered corporation,[52] and the virtual[53] and the networked[54] organization. All the post-bureaucratic forms of organization are conceived as substituting a hierarchical model of structure and implementing a more flexible work regime that gives workers limited empowerment.[55] A centre-piece of employment relations in the post-bureaucratic organization is a 'new pay' paradigm linking individual or group performance to rewards.[56,57] Three leading-edge post-bureaucratic configurations, which we examine here, are shown in Figure 10.5, above: horizontal, virtual and network.

The **horizontal or 'lean' structure** is the division of work into teams or 'cells' that are responsible for completing a whole process. A team-based organization uses decentralization to move decisions to the work teams, and gives limited autonomy to those teams to decide about product and service design, process design, quality and customer service (see Chapter 9). Typically, work-based regimes are accompanied by other management techniques such as just-in-time and total quality management.

horizontal or 'lean' structure: an integrated system of manufacturing, originally developed by Toyota in Japan. The emphasis is on flexibility and team work

Business process re-engineering

One design methodology with a process emphasis in a horizontal structure is **business process re-engineering (BPR)**. According to the re-engineering guru James Champy, BPR is 'about changing our managerial work, the way we think about, organize, inspire, deploy, enable, measure, and reward the value-adding operational work. It is about changing management itself' (ref. 26, p. 3).

Structurally, the typical pyramid-shaped industrial model is stood on its head, management structures are leaner or 'delayered', and decision making is pushed down to the 'front line' to meet the contemporary demands for quality, flexibility, low cost and entrepreneurial autonomy. Some writers have described these anti-hierarchical characteristics in organizational design as a shift from 'modernist' to 'postmodernist' organizational forms and employee relations practices.[52]

business process re-engineering: a radical change of business processes by applying information technology to integrate operations, and maximizing their value-added content

table 10.1 The re-engineered and virtual organization

Characteristic	Bureaucratic model	Re-engineered model
Market	Domestic	Global
Competitive advantage	Cost	Speed and quality
Resources	Capital	Information
Quality	What is affordable	No compromise
Focal point	Profit	Customer
Structural design	Hierarchical	Flattened
Control	Centralized	Decentralized
Leadership	Autocratic	Shared
Labour	Homogeneous	Culturally diverse
Organization of work	Specialized and individual	Flexible and in teams
Communications	Vertical	Horizontal

The re-engineered organization allegedly has a number of common characteristics (Table 10.1). Central to these organizational forms is the 'reconceptualization' of core employees, from being considered to be a variable cost to being represented as a valuable asset; capable of serving the customer without the need for a directive style of organizational leadership.[58] With the ascendancy of 'customer democracy', employees are encouraged not only to exercise initiative, but also to display **emotional labour** in creating value for customers. According to BPR proponent Hammer, 'Loyalty and hard work are by themselves quaint relics ... organizations must now urge employees to put loyalty to the customer ... because that is the only way the company will survive' (ref. 1, pp. 158–9). Unlike earlier movements in organizational design, re-engineering is market driven – the 'dictatorship of the customariat' – and, by focusing on the social interaction between the buyer and seller of services, rather than the relationship between employer and employee, BPR emphasizes emotional labour as a key aspect of competitiveness.

Re-engineering has been criticized largely by academics.[58–63] It is argued, for example, that the 'leaner' organization actually gives more power to a few: 'Removing some of the middle layers of organizations is not the same as altering the basic power structure ... By cutting out intermediary levels [of management] ... the power resources of those at the top can be increased' (ref. 60, p. 192).

Virtual organizations

In the age of the Internet, it is not unsurprising that the **'virtual' organization** has captured the attention of organizational analysts. The virtual organization is a temporary or permanent arrangement of otherwise independent companies or individuals, with a lead firm, to produce a product or service by sharing costs and core competencies. This ever-changing constellation of organizations is connected not through formal rules, but rather through virtual networks. A **core competency** is a knowledge and expertise base that resides in the organization.[24] The Internet, the World Wide Web and information technology connect members of the network wherever they are in the world. Typically, data are electronically transferred around the virtual network and separate competency sets work on the data either sequentially or in parallel.[64] Several factors have driven organizations to adopt network-based modes of organizing: an increased requirement for flexibility and global learning, reducing market uncertainty, managing joint production, a high-tech base and the perceived need to manage cultural diversity.[65]

Corporate global network connections have forerunners in the eighteenth and nineteenth centuries, but they have figured as a pervasive, major aspect of organizational life in the twenty-first century.[39] A **networked organization** is a constellation of several independent organizations or communities of people, usually linked on a large project basis, such as aerospace alliances between specialist engineering firms. The firms or groups in the network have a more formal and long-term commercial relationship than in the virtual organization.[66] Hierarchy is sacrificed in order to speed decision making, and vertical integration is supplanted by horizontal integration across group boundaries. Each group in the network focuses on a set of competencies. This structure enables each community of people to be flexible and responsive to changes.[64]

Networks, argues Castells, have had a transformational effect on structures.[67] Examples of network structures exist at Amazon.com, Cisco Systems, Dell Computers and Mozilla Corporation. Perhaps the best-known company using a

---

emotional labour: the effort, planning and control needed to express organizationally desired emotions during interpersonal transactions

Visit www.wbs.ac.uk/faculty/research, the website at the University of Warwick, for information on publications on BPR. Alternatively, visit www.accenture.com and search for 'business process engineering'

weblink

'virtual' organization: an organization composed of people who are connected by video-teleconferences, the Internet and computer-aided design systems, and who may rarely, if ever, meet face to face

core competency: the underlying core characteristics of an organization's workforce that result in effective performance and give a competitive advantage to the firm

network structure: a set of strategic alliances that an organization creates with suppliers, distributors and manufacturers to produce and market a product. Members of the network work together on a long-term basis to find new ways to improve efficiency and increase the quality of their products

network structure is Amazon.com, a virtual bookstore with no inventory, online ordering and electronic links to its customers. Cisco Systems, another exemplar, produces 80 per cent of the world's Internet hardware using a global network of employees and suppliers using web-based technology. In a recent book, Clay Shirky argues that Internet technologies make it increasingly easy to create constellations of networked project groups (see the Critical Insight 'Business without Organizations', below).[68]

A virtual or network structure has neither a corporate head office nor an organizational chart. Mitchell Baker, the CEO of Mozilla Corporation, developer of the Firefox web browser, for example, describes her role not as head of the organization but as 'the coordinator and motivator of a group effort'.[69] Bartlett and Ghoshal describe an integrated global network structure with, for example, a firm in France receiving flows of components from across the globe.[70] The concept of an integrated networked structure emphasizes the shift from inflexible to permeable structures and processes, accompanied by significant flows of components, resources, information and people. Unilever is an example of a networked company that has pursued a transnational strategy, with 17 different and largely decentralized detergent plants in Europe alone.

The network structure offers employers access to wider markets, lower production costs, and the potential to respond quickly to new product and service developments and markets. The weakness of the network arrangement is that associates have little direct control over the functions done by other members of the network. The number of independent members in the network creates a high-dependency relationship between each company within the network. This requires new behaviours and a high trust in network members. Managers and knowledge workers need to radically modify their behaviours as strategic planning, for example, is no longer an independent activity, but a process needing coordination, information sharing and global learning.[70]

Although the networked organization may have been the favoured paradigm of the 1990s, the global economic recession of 2008/09 has caused firms to reassess the efficacy of the networked model. As *The Economist* reported, management wisdom had for two decades been to make companies as lean as possible, expanding just-in-time supplier networks around the globe and outsourcing all but core competencies, lubricated by cheap credit. In September 2008, the abrupt closure of the overnight commercial paper market to lubricate the system meant that most companies need to accumulate cash to meet such basic obligations as paying their employees. Thus, 'ultra-lean supply chains no longer look like a brilliant idea when you have to find cash to keep a supplier afloat that cannot get even basic trade credit' (ref. 71, p. 17). A case perhaps of 'just-in-time' being substituted for a 'just-in-case' network.

More sceptical analysts have found the 'dark side' of networks. A characteristic signature of networks is the exploitation of the less powerful by the more powerful members. Buttressing this assertion is evidence that employees experience 'uncertainty, ambiguity and frustration' in their attempts to enact their professional roles within this organizational form.[72] Countering the academic hype around 'post-bureaucratic' organizations is a recent study by Pulignano and Stewart. Analysing primarily qualitative data from global automotive companies, they persuasively argue that new employment arrangements have, paradoxically, revitalized Weber's typology of bureaucracy. According to the researchers, new employee performance-related incentives have generated behavioural rules that reinforce bureaucratic control at Fiat, VW and Renault: 'Thus, intriguingly, the use of bureaucratic control emerges as the main element of labour control in this type of workplace' (ref. 56, p. 104). Arguably, the binary bureaucratic/post-bureaucratic view of organizational design is a somewhat misleading analytical paradigm. In reality, new organizational structures are likely to be hybrids, new forms coexisting alongside some old enduring elements of bureaucracy.[73]

Critical insight

Business without organizations

The Internet and social networking sites are bringing people together like never before. Websites such as Facebook and Bebo make it extraordinarily easy to meet like-minded people, join groups and exchange ideas. What impact might this be having on business? Clay Shirky, author of the recent book *Here Comes Everybody: The Power of Organizing Without Organizations*,[68] argues that these new technologies could revolutionize the way in which businesses operate. But how? The story of rival web browsers Microsoft Internet Explorer and Mozilla Firefox provides an excellent example.

In the early 1990s, Internet Explorer appeared to have an unassailable lead in the web browser market, with an estimated market share of around 95 per cent in 2002. Microsoft's supremacy seemed assured when rival company AOL abandoned its own Netscape browser, leaving Internet Explorer with a near-monopoly. What happened next is a lesson in the growing power of informal networks and their increasing ability to take on big business. Former Netscape employees grouped together under the title The Mozilla Foundation and, using a small investment from AOL, began work on a new web browser. But The Mozilla Foundation was (and still is) no ordinary company: it is a non-profit-making organization, made up of not only staff, but also a network of volunteers and contributors – essentially, a community of Mozilla enthusiasts whose efforts are organized and coordinated electronically using the open-source model. In the words of Mozilla's CEO, Mitchell Baker, 'we build software, but we also build communities of people who build software and share a particular vision for what the future of the Internet should look like'.

This open-source model has enabled Mozilla to draw on a vast array of talent and creativity without having to become a huge, unwieldy corporation – and in this way, it gains competitive advantage over more traditional business set-ups. Any given individual might only contribute one idea to the development of the browser – their output could be very limited, but their input to the project could be crucial. Mozilla can harness the skills of such individuals without having to employ them full time – meaning that it can avoid becoming a vast, bureaucratic and hierarchical organization.

The success of Mozilla's model speaks for itself: Firefox's market share has increased to around 20 per cent since its foundation, and it now has over 100 million users worldwide – an incredible achievement and a very speedy growth rate, particularly given that it was pitting itself against the fearsome might of an established Microsoft product.

Consider the following question: Do you think that traditional corporations are the *solution* to our problems or *are* the problem? How can Facebook and Twitter transform organizational structure and design?

Source: Based on an article by Ken Hunt (2009), 'The chaos theory of organization', *Report on Business*, March, pp. 16–18.
Further research: Shirky, C. (2008) *Here Comes Everybody: The Power of Organizing Without Organizations*, New York: Penguin.[68]

Implications for organizational behaviour

The downsizing and restructuring to create 'lean and mean' high-performance workplaces hit employees across the globe with cataclysmic force in the global economic recession that emerged in 2008–09. By definition, downsizing and restructuring include both high and poor performers. Employees are therefore usually correct in predicting job losses, extensive changes in the way they perform their work, work intensification, skill changes and changes in employee relations (see Figure 2.3).

It is well documented that relocating operations to an NIE or outsourcing and privatizing a service in a public sector organization can have major employment implications. Downsizing has a chilling effect on the psychological climate, much as high levels of unemployment depress wage rates. Well-documented empirical research shows that, for the survivors of corporate restructuring, there can be detrimental effects on work motivation and commitment building, as well as fundamentally redefining the contours of employment relations.[43] The trauma of downsizing has predictable negative effects on the psychological well-being of individuals. 'Survivors typically are less loyal and less willing to provide service to customers and support for fellow employees,' opines Denise Rousseau (ref. 74, p. 212). The effects of the global recession and downsizing on the psychological climate also include negative perceptions about corporate leaders and decreased trust in management on the part of the survivors and the public generally.[75]

Gender, sexuality and organizational design

Alongside management debates on organizational structures, there is a body of critical literature that focuses on relationships between gender, sexuality and organizational design. The term 'sexuality' refers to sexual characters and sexual behaviour in the workplace. Sexuality pervades organizations through pornographic pin-ups, innuendo, gossip and sexist joking. While it serves to affirm men's sense of shared masculinity, sexuality can, in a male-dominated workplace, serve to make women feel uncomfortable (see also feminist perspectives on organizational culture in Chapter 12). Leaving the organization is often seen as the only alternative.[76,77]

Studies of the gendering of organizations emphasize that gender and sexuality make an overwhelming difference to organizational reality.[78–82] The studies draw attention to the double problem of women entering work organizations: discrimination and gender harassment. The first part of the problem is entering occupations and professions that have traditionally been occupied by men (for example, manual trades and white-collar professions).[83] The notion that 'gendered occupations', that is, ones that associate job requirements with the perceived qualities of a particular sex, has generated debate in organizational studies over the extent to which organizations and their hierarchical structures can be considered as gendered. The second part of the problem is that, once in the organization, many women face gender harassment, making it difficult for women to move into positions of authority. This is often referred to as a 'glass ceiling' – invisible, informal barriers to promotion to higher positions of authority in the organizational hierarchy.

Legislation making direct gender discrimination and harassment unlawful means that it is more common for male and even some female subordinates to hinder in indirect ways the promotion of women. Indirect gender harassment may be an identifiable element of an organization's culture, a feature of the workplace that we examine in more detail in Chapter 12. Gender analysis questions research findings and analysis that segregate studies of organizational behaviour from those of gender divisions in the labour market, patriarchal power, issues of workplace inequality and 'dual-role' work–family issues.[84] More importantly, however, including the 'gender and sexuality paradigm' in the study of the organizational structure and restructuring has pushed the boundaries of organizational behaviour by examining the people who are deemed to be the 'recipients' of organizational design.

As sociologist Judy Wajcman observes in her insightful study, the individual and the modern bureaucracy are not gender-neutral. Indeed, more controversially perhaps, she presents a powerful argument for gender-inclusive organizational theories if we accept her main premise that 'gender is woven into the very fabric of bureaucratic hierarchy and authority relations' (ref. 84, p. 47).

OB and globalization

Gender equality in times of economic transition: women workers in Russia

The late twentieth century brought significant changes to world of work in Eastern Europe and the former Soviet Union. The fall of Communist state governments was accompanied by a massive restructuring of national and local economies, and of the social lives of the workers who populated these institutions. While old-order policies and practices were pushed aside in favour of open markets, social and cultural attitudes about gender endured, often extending into the offices and boardrooms of organizations navigating this massive capitalist shift.

By the late 1990s, the new Russian economy was starting to look up, buoyed by successes in high-tech and natural resource sectors. Russian women, in particular, made strides in the new economy, creating successful businesses catering to the burgeoning Russian consumer culture. Two decades after this transition, scholars and journalists are turning a critical eye to how gendered experiences of work in post-Soviet Russia continue to be affected by enduring cultural attitudes about women in Russian society.

According to Russian *Vogue* magazine editor Alyona Doletskaya, although career opportunities for women in Russia have changed significantly over the past few decades, women workers continue to overpopulate sectors such as fashion, service and public relations (Weir, 2005). Furthermore, women's salaries are substantially lower than those of their male counterparts. Weir writes, 'A recent survey of living standards ... suggested that of the poorest 15 percent of Russians, 68 percent are women. Many of the poor are well-educated women who find their skills unrewarded in the new economic order.'

The contemporary experiences of Russian women in the workforce can be linked to the Soviet era, when women were often relegated to undesirable, low-wage work, a pattern that reflected state support for, and reproduction of, wider cultural attitudes about gender roles. Today, although the transition to a free market economy has resulted in access to new types of work for Russian women workers, enduring cultural attitudes about gender roles continue to affect women's abilities to participate fully in the new Russian economy. This period of economic, political and social transition in Russia provides us with an opportunity to consider how cultural attitudes about gender can span major systemic changes, influencing local people's experience of such transitions. It also raises questions about how, over time, the new economic and political orders in Russia will affect local constructions of gender.

stop! Using gender as an example, consider the often-entwined relationships between cultural beliefs and economic and governance systems. How do local attitudes about gender influence government and economic policy and practice? How do governments and economies influence local constructions of gender?

What kinds of societal attitude and practice related to gender extend into workplaces where you live? Who should be responsible for regulating gender roles and gender equity in the workplace?

How should 'gender equality' be defined? Are there different organizational approaches to achieving equity?

In times of political and economic upheaval, support for social conservatism can surge. How might this claim be used to explain – or dispute – the experiences of Russian women workers described above?

Sources and further information

Ashwin, S. (2005) *Adapting to Russia's New Labour Market: Gender and Employment Strategy*, New York: Routledge.

Brainerd, E. (1998) 'Winners and losers in Russia's economic transition', *American Economic Review*, **88**(5), pp. 94–115.

McGregor, C. (2003) 'Getting beyond the glass ceiling', *Moscow Times*, February 10. Available at: www.clumba.com/news.asp?ob_no=2927 (accessed October 2, 2009).

Weir, F. (2005) 'For Moscow's businesswomen, a powerful new role', *Christian Science Monitor*. Available at: www.csmonitor.com/2005/0308/p07s01-woeu.html; www.usatoday.com/news/world/2005-03-07-russsia-women_x.htm (accessed October 2, 2009).

Note: This feature was written by Gretchen Fox, PhD, Anthropologist, Timberline Natural Resource Group, Canada.

Chapter summary

- We have attempted to cover a wide range of complex issues in this chapter. Organizational structure refers to the formal division of work or labour, and the formal pattern of relationships that coordinate and control organizational activities, whereas organizational design refers to the process of creating a structure that best fits a strategy, technology and environment.

- The three core dimensions of formal organizational structure – complexity, formalization and centralization – can be combined into different types or models. Three descriptive models were examined: mechanistic, bureaucratic and organic. The mechanistic organization has been likened to a machine. It is characterized by highly specialized tasks that tend to be rigidly defined, a hierarchical authority and control structure, and communications that primarily take the form of edicts and decisions issued by managers to subordinates. Communication typically flows vertically from the top down. Thus, it has high complexity, high formalization and high centralization. A mechanistic organization resembles a bureaucracy. A bureaucratic organization is a rational and systematic division of work. Within it, rules and techniques of control are precisely defined. A bureaucratic design allows for large-scale accomplishments. The disadvantages associated with bureaucracy include suppression of initiative through overcontrol.

- Organic organizations are the antithesis of mechanistic organizations. They are characterized by being low in complexity, formality and centralization. A post-bureaucratic organizational structure, such as team-based structures and those produced by BPR, is organic and highly adaptable. However, the binary bureaucratic/post-bureaucratic view of organizational design may be a somewhat misleading analytical device.

- The contingency view of formal organizational design focuses on strategy, size, technology and environment. A change in business strategy may require changing the manufacturing process and the organizational design, for example moving from a functional to a team-based organizational structure. Large organizations will tend to be more centralized and have more rules and techniques of control. Organizations with complex non-routine technologies will tend to have more complex organizational arrangements. Organizations with routine technologies will tend to use written rules and procedures to control people's behaviour, and decision making will be more centralized than in establishments using non-routine technologies.

- An organization's external environment can range from 'stable' to' dynamic' and from 'hostile' to 'munificent'. Distinct external environments help to explain divergent patterns of managerial behaviour and organizational structure. For example, organic configurations are better suited to dynamic and hostile environments so that organizational members can adapt more quickly to changes.

- The external context has a significant impact on managerial and employee behaviour. The external domain influences the formal structure and functioning of a work organization, and in turn the organization's leaders influence the wider society. The linkage between external contexts and the search for competitive advantage through employee performance and managerial activities is complex. We have therefore emphasized that organizational behaviour studies must be able to deal with the new complexities and nuances. Caught up in the drama of severe economic recession, there is a need for a multidimensional approach to the study of organizational behaviour.

- The analysis offered here provides a guide to how formal organizational structure helps to shape the behaviour of managers and employees. The contingency elements identified – strategy, size, technology, environment, culture and HRM systems – are not separate, but are integrated and linked in complex ways. It is within this integrated framework that interpretations of competing resources, conversations and interests take place, and influence people's behaviour in many ways.

Key concepts

bureaucracy	291–292
horizontal	282
mechanistic	284
network structure	297
organic	284
technological change	286
virtual organization	297

Vocab checklist for ESL students

- ☐ Artefacts
- ☐ Business process re-engineering
- ☐ Capitalist, capitalism, capitalize
- ☐ Centralization, centralize, central
- ☐ Competitive advantage
- ☐ Complexity, complex
- ☐ Core competency
- ☐ Divisional structure
- ☐ Emotional labour
- ☐ Environment, environmental
- ☐ Formal organization
- ☐ Formalization
- ☐ Functional configuration
- ☐ Globalization, globalist, globalize, global
- ☐ Horizontal structure
- ☐ Information structure
- ☐ Lean structure
- ☐ Matrix structure
- ☐ Mechanism organization
- ☐ Networking, network
- ☐ Network structure
- ☐ Organic organization
- ☐ Organization chart
- ☐ Organizational design
- ☐ Organizational politics

- ☐ Organizational structure
- ☐ Span of control
- ☐ Specialization, special, specialize
- ☐ Strategic business unit
- ☐ Virtual organization

⟨⁈⟩ Chapter review questions

1. Compare and contrast a 'mechanistic' and a 're-engineered' organization. What is it like to be a manager making decisions in these two types of organization? What employees' behaviours are likely to be rewarded? What type of competitive strategy is each best suited to?
2. Why is there no 'one best way' to design an organization's structure?
3. What is the link between organizational structure and technology?
4. Why do organizations in fast-change and unstable environments have different structures from those in stable environments?
5. Review the 'new' forms of organizational design described in this chapter. Discuss the designs that you and other students finding appealing and challenging. Explain your reasons.
6. Does Internet web-based technology have the potential to demolish bureaucracy?

⟨?⟩ Chapter research questions

1. Read the Critical Insight 'Business without Organizations', above. Form a study group. Thinking about how you use Facebook and Twitter, sketch out how new social networking sites (a) provide an opportunity to change the form of organizational structure and design, (b) can create new services or products, and (c) can enhance the delivery of your orgnizational behaviour course and other courses in your university programme.
2. Obtain a copy of *The Oxford Handbook of Work and Organization* (see Further Reading). After reading Chapter 20, 'Post-bureaucracy?', discuss why the authors believe that emerging post-bureaucratic forms operate more as a means of *legitimating* change and innovation than as a concrete indicator of changing forms of work organization.
3. Read the article by Jonathan Morris et al. (2008), listed in Further Reading. What empirical evidence do the researchers provide of a shift towards new governance post-bureaucratic forms of work organization?

⟨📖→⟩ Further reading

Acker, J. (2008) 'Helpful men and feminist support: more than double strangeness', *Gender, Work and Organizations*, **15**(3), pp. 288–93.

Alvesson, M. and Thompson, P. (2006) 'Post-bureaucracy?', pp. 485–507 in S. Ackroyd, R. Batt, P. Thompson and P. Tolbert, (eds), *The Oxford Handbook of Work and Organization*, York New: Oxford University Press.

Armstrong-Stassen, M. and Schlosser, F. (2008) 'Taking a positive approach to organizational downsizing', *Canadian Journal of Administrative Science*, **25**, pp. 93–106.

Bakan, J. (2004) *The Corporation*, London: Penguin.

Currie, G., Finn, R. and Martin, G. (2008) 'Accounting for the "dark side" of new organizational forms: the case of healthcare professionals', *Human Relations*, **61**(4), pp. 539–64.

Du Gay, P. (2000) *In Praise of Bureaucracy*. London: Sage.

Fulop, L., Hayward, H., and Lilley, S. (2009) 'Managing structure', pp. 195–237 in S. Linstead, L. Fulop and S. Lilley (eds), *Management and Organization: A Critical Text* (2nd edn), Basingstoke: Palgrave.

Grey, C. (2005) *A Very Short, Fairly Interesting and Reasonably Cheap Book about Studying Organizations*, London: Sage.

Hammer, M. (1997) *Beyond Reengineering*, New York: Harper Business.

Lazonick, W. (2006) 'Corporate restructuring', pp. 577–601 in S. Ackroyd, R. Batt, P. Thompson and P. S. Tolbert (eds), *The Oxford Handbook of Work and Organization*, Oxford: Oxford University Press.

Morris, J., Hassard, J. and McCann, L. (2008) 'The resilience of institutionalized capitalism: managing managers under "shareholder capitalism" and "managerial capitalism"', *Human Relations*, **61**(5), pp. 687–710.

Pulignano, V. and Stewart, P. (2006) 'Bureaucracy transcended? New patterns of employment regulation and labour control in the international automotive industry', *New Technology, Work and Employment*, **21**(2), pp. 90–106.

Tyler, M. and Wilkinson, A. (2007) 'The tyranny of corporate slenderness: "corporate anorexia" as a metaphor for our age', *Work, Employment and Society*, **21**(3), pp. 537–49.

 Chapter case study 1

Strategy and design in Australia's tourism industry

Setting

Tourism is a strong contributor to Australia's economy, with over a half million people employed in the sector, and tourism spending reaching over $85 billion a year. The country promotes its beautiful landscapes, Aboriginal art and culture, coastal lifestyles and the outback as main attractions for visitors.

Australia's top five international tourism markets are New Zealand, the UK, Japan, the USA and China. Visitor numbers from the emerging markets of China and India have grown strongly, while the numbers of Japanese and Korean tourists have declined in the last few years. China is now Australia's fifth largest international tourism market, bringing it into second place with New Zealand, and this is set to grow over the next decade.

However, Australia's share of global tourism continues to drop, with a decrease of 14 per cent between 1995 and 2008. Since its peak in 2001, it has also declined as a proportion of Australia's gross domestic product. The Australian tourism industry continues to struggle from the effects of a series of crises, starting with a pilot strike in 1989 and the worldwide economic outfalls of the Iraq War and the SARS outbreak in more recent years. Skilled staff shortages are also contributing to the industry's troubles, with an estimated 42,000 employees needed by 2015.

The problem

Established in the early 1990s, Outback Inc. is an adventure-based tour company located in Sydney, Australia. The company offers a variety of services, including guided tours, accommodation and meals, to those wishing to visit remote and regional areas of Australia. Outback's comprehensive packages of services appeal to travellers from all over the world, particularly visitors from Japan, who typically make up over 80 per cent of their client base. However, despite increased marketing efforts aimed at the general Asian market, the company has seen a decrease in bookings from its traditionally reliable Japanese sector. Outback has yet to attract new clients from China or other Asian countries experiencing more favourable economic conditions.

Although Outback grew from a small, family-owned business in the early 1990s to a moderately sized company with sales of several million dollars a year, it still retains its original functional organizational structure. Outback's managers, typically members of the company's founding family, head up the various departments, which are structured around traditional functions such as marketing, finance and human resources. Although the company does have its own website, management has been hesitant to move away from using standard travel agencies for their client booking purposes.

As with most organizations in the hospitality field, the Outback management uses a traditional leadership style, with decisions made at the top levels of management and communicated downwards. The majority of Outback's employees are young, highly motivated and eager for learning opportunities, but the company struggles to retain them, facing a turnover rate higher than even what is expected in an industry with a notorious turnover culture.

Management recently made the decision to hire a consultant whom they hoped could make some recommendations to help attract new clients and stop the flow of employees walking out of the door.

Tasks

As a consultant hired by the Outback management, prepare a short presentation addressing the following questions:

1. Would you recommend a change in the company's functional structural arrangement? If yes, which of the other three common structural configurations (product/service, division, matrix) would you recommend? Why?
2. How does your recommended structure fit with a strategy that could help with Outback's goal to attract new clients?
3. Would you characterize Outback as a mechanistic organization? How might this contribute to a high turnover of its staff?

Essential reading

Navickas, V. (2007) 'The reasons and consequences of changes in organizational structures of tourism companies', *Economics and Management*, pp. 809–13.

Ogaard, T., Marnburg, E. and Larsen, S. (2008) 'Perceptions of organizational structure in the hospitality industry: consequences for commitment, job satisfaction and perceived performance', *Tourism Management*, **29**(4), pp. 661–71.

Tribe, J. (1997) *Corporate Strategy for Tourism*, London: International Thomson Business Press.

For more information on Australia's tourism industry and the challenges it faces, go to www.tourism.australia.com/home.asp

Note

This is a fictional case study. It was written by Lori Rilkoff, MSc, CHRP, Senior Human Resources Manager at the City of Kamloops, and lecturer in HRM at Thompson Rivers University, BC, Canada.

 Chapter case study 2

ABC's just-in-time supply chain

 Visit www.palgrave.com/business/brattonob2e to view this case study.

✒ Web-based assignment

This chapter discusses the different types of organizational design, and the interconnectedness between structure and restructuring, and organizational behaviour. Organizations can adopt a large number of structures to match their strategy, size, technology and profit-making imperative. Restructuring affects job design and individual workers' perception of the employer and work motivation.

This web-based assignment requires you to explore the web to find a site that displays an organizational chart, or that discusses a method of managing its structure. For example, enter the website of Dell Computers (www.dell.com), Canadian TV and media company Globalmedia (www.globalmedia.ca) or car manufacturer Saturn (www.saturn.com) for an example of a 'flatter' organizational structure.

Consider these questions:

- What kind of organizational structure does the company have (for example, in terms of decision making, is it centralized or decentralized)?
- In what ways is the organizational structure appropriate for the company?

🎞 OB in films

The documentary film *The Corporation* (2003) offers an excellent collection of case studies, anecdotes and true confessions from corporate elites, which reveal structural contradictions and behind-the-scenes tensions. The documentary also features many critical perspectives, including interviews with Noam Chomsky, Michael Moore, Maude Barlow and Naomi Klein.

What examples are given to substantiate the claim that corporations, if left unregulated, behave much like individuals with 'a psychopathic personality', creating destruction? What examples of corporate crime does the film illustrate?

📑 References

1 Hammer, M. (1997) *Beyond Reengineering*, New York: Harper Business.

2 Lazonick, W. (2006) 'Corporate restructuring', pp. 577–601 in S. Ackroyd, R. Batt, P. Thompson and P. S. Tolbert (eds), *The Oxford Handbook of Work & Organization*, Oxford: Oxford University Press.

3   Baumol, J. W., Blinder, S. A. and Wolff, N. E. (2003) *Downsizing in America*, New York: Russell Sage Foundation Press.

4   Delbridge, R. (1998) *Life on the Line in Contemporary Manufacturing*, Oxford: Oxford University Press.

5   Gowing, M. K., Kraft, J. D. and Campbell Quick, J. (eds) (1997) *New Organizational Reality: Downsizing, Restructuring, and Revitalization*, Washington, DC: American Psychological Association.

6   Hales, C. (2002) 'Bureacracy-lite and continuities in management work', *British Journal of Management*, **13**(1), pp. 51–66.

7   Innes, P. and Littler, C. (2004) 'A decade of downsizing: understanding the contours of change in Australia, 1990–99', *Asia Pacific Journal of Human Resources*, **42**(2), pp. 229–42.

8   Legge, K. (2000) 'Personal management in the lean organization', pp. 43–69 in S. Bach and K. Sisson (eds), *Personal Management*, Oxford: Blackwell.

9   Littler, C. and Innes, P. (2004) 'The paradox of managerial downsizing', *Organizational Studies*, **25**(7), pp. 1159–84.

10 Moody, K. (1997) *Workers in a Lean World*, London: Verso.

11 Womack, J., Jones, D. and Roos, D. (1990) *The Machine that Changed the World*, London: HarperCollins.

12 Tyler, M. and Wilkinson, A. (2007) 'The tyranny of corporate slenderness: "corporate anorexia" as a metaphor for our age', *Work, Employment and Society*, **21**(3), pp. 537–49.

13 Drucker, P. F. (1997) 'Toward the new organization', pp. 1–5 in F. Hesselbein, M. Goldsmith and R. Beckhard (eds), *The Organization of the Future*, San Francisco: Jossey-Bass.

14 Gadiesh, O. and Olivet, S. (1997) 'Designing for implementability', pp. 53–78 in F. Hesselbein, M. Goldsmith and R. Beckhard (eds), *The Organization of the Future*, San Francisco: Jossey-Bass.

15 Drucker, P. (1954/1993) *The Practice of Management*, New York: HarperCollins.

16 Galbraith, J. R. (1996) 'Designing the innovative organization', pp. 156–81 in K. Starkey (ed.), *How Organizations Learn*, London: International Thomson Business Press.

17 Bratton, J. (1999) 'Gaps in the workplace learning paradigm: labour flexibility and job design', in Conference Proceeding of Researching Work and Learning, First International Conference, University of Leeds, UK.

18 Herriot, P. (1998) 'The role of human resource management in building a new proposition', pp. 106–16 in P. Sparrow and M. Marchington (eds), *Human Resource Management: A New Agenda*, London: Financial Times Management.

19 Watson, T. (1995) *Sociology of Work and Industry* (3rd edn), London: Routledge.

20 Thompson, P. and McHugh, D. (2006) *Work Organizations: A Critical Introduction* (4th edn), Basingstoke: Palgrave.

21 Clegg, S. and Dunkerley, D. (1980) *Organization, Class and Control*, London: Routledge & Kegan Paul.

22 Hardy, C. and Clegg, S. R. (1999) 'Some dare call it power', pp. 368–87 in S. R. Clegg and C. Hardy (eds), *Studying Organization*, London: Sage.

23 Clegg, S., Hardy, C. and Nord, W. (eds) (1999) *Managing Organizations: Current Issues*, Thousand Oaks, CA: Sage.

24 Hamel, G. and Prahalad, C. K. (1994) *Competing for the Future*, Boston, MA: Harvard Business School Press.

25 Daft, R. (2001) *Organization Theory and Design* (7th edn), Cincinnati, OH: South-Western.

26 Champy, J. (1996) *Reengineering Management*, New York: HarperCollins.

27 Burns, T. and Stalker, G. M. (1966) *The Management of Innovation* (2nd edn), London: Tavistock.

28 Chandler, A. (1962) *Strategy and Structure*, Cambridge, MA: MIT Press.

29 Keats, B. W. and Hitt, M. (1988) 'A causal model of linkages among environmental dimensions, macro organizational characteristics, and performance', *Academy of Management Journal*, September, pp. 570–98.

30 Klein, N. (2000) *No Logo*, London: Flamingo.

31 Blau, P. M. and Schoenherr, R. A. (1971) *The Structure of Organizations*, New York: Basic Books.

32 Pugh, D., Hickson, C, Hining, R. and Turner, C. (1969) 'The context of organization structures', *Administrative Science Quarterly*, **14**, pp. 91–114.

33 Child, J. (1972) 'Organizational structure, environment and performance: the role of strategic choice', *Sociology*, **6**(1), pp. 331–50.

34 Aldrich, H. (1972) 'Technology and organizational structure: a re-examination of the findings of the Aston Group', *Administrative Science Quarterly*, **17**(1), pp. 26–43.

35 Woodward, J. (1965) *Industrial Organizations: Theory and Practice*, London: Oxford University Press.

36 Thompson, J. D. (1967) *Organizations in Action*, New York: McGraw-Hill.

37 Aldrich, H. E. (2002) 'Technology and organizational structure: a reexamination of the findings of the findings of the Aston Group', pp. 344–66 in S. R. Clegg (ed.), *Central Currents in Organization Studies*, London: Sage

38 Mintzberg, H. (1993) *Structure in Fives: Designing Effective Organizations* (7th edn), Englewood Cliffs, NJ: Prentice Hall.

39 Scholte, J. A. (2005) *Globalization: A Critical Introduction*, Basingstoke: Palgrave Macmillan.

40 Sklair, L. (2002) *Globalization: Capitalism and its Alternatives*, Oxford: Oxford University Press.

41 Hoogvelt, A. (2001) *Globalization and the Postcolonial World* (2nd edn), Basingstoke: Palgrave.

42 Orsburn, J. and Moran, L. (2000) *The New Self-Directed Work Teams*, New York: McGraw-Hill.

43 Mabey, C., Salaman, G. and Storey, J. (1998) *Human Resource Management: A Strategic Introduction* (2nd edn), Oxford: Blackwell.

44 Mintzberg, H. (1983) *Structure in Fives: Designing Effective Organizations*, Englewood Cliffs, NJ: Prentice Hall.

45 Hill, C. and Jones, G. (2004) *Strategic Management Theory*, New York: Houghton Mifflin.

46 Jacoby, S. M. (2005) *The Embedded Corporation: Corporate Governance and Employment Relations in Japan and the United States*, Princeton, NJ: Princeton University Press.

47 Atkinson, J. (1984) 'Manpower strategies for flexible organizations', *Personnel Management*, August, pp. 14–25.

48 Bratton, J. A. (1992) *The Japanization of Work*, London: Macmillan.

49 Miles R. E., Snow, C. C., Matthews, J. A. and Coleman, H. J. (1997) 'Organizing in the knowledge area: anticipating the cellular form', *Academy of Management Executive*, **11**(4), pp. 7–20.

50 Hassard, J. and Parker, M. (1993) *Postmodernism and Organizations*, London: Sage.

51 Ghoshal, S. and Bartlett, C. A. (1997) *The Individualized Corporation: A Fundamentally New Approach to Management: Great Companies Are Defined by Purpose, Process, and People*. New York: Harper Business.

52 Hammer, M. and Champy, J. (1993) *Reengineering the Corporation: A Manifesto for Business Revolution*, New York: Harper Business.

53 Goldman, S. L., Nagel, R. N. and Preiss, K. (1995) *Agile Competition and Virtual Organizations: Strategies for Enriching the Customer*, New York: Van Nostrand Reinhold.

54 Powell, W. W. (2003) 'Neither market nor hierarchy: network forms of organization', pp. 315–30 in M. J. Handel (ed.), *The Sociology of Organizations*, Thousand Oaks, CA: Sage.

55 Clarke, T. and Clegg, S. R. (1998) *Changing Paradigms: The Transformation of Management for the 21st Century*, London: Collins.

56 Pulignano, V. and Stewart, P. (2006) 'Bureaucracy transcended? New patterns of employment regulation and labour control in the international automotive industry', *New Technology, Work and Employment*, **21**(2), pp. 90–106.

57 Corby, S., Palmer, S. and Lindop, E. (2009) *Rethinking Reward*, Basingstoke: Palgrave.

58 Willmott, H., (1995) 'The odd couple?: re-engineering business processes: managing human relations', *New/Technology, Work and Employment*, **10**(2), pp. 89–98.

59 Reed, M. I. (1993) 'Organizations and modernity: continuity and discontinuity in organization theory', pp. 163–82 in J. Hassard and M. Parker (eds), *Postmodernism and Organizations*, London: Sage.

60 Thompson, P. (1993) 'Fatal distraction: postmodernism and organizational theory', in. J. Hassard and M. Parker (eds), *Postmodernism and Organizations*, London: Sage.

61 Craig, J. and Yetton, P. (1993) 'Business process redesigns critique of *Process Innovation* by Thomas Davenport as a case study in the literature', *Australian Journal of Management*, **17**(2), pp. 285–306.

62 Oliver, J. (1993) 'Shocking to the core', *Management Today*, August, pp. 18–21.

63 Grint, K. and Willcocks, L. (1995) 'Business process re-engineering in theory and practice: business paradise regained?', *New Technology, Work and Employment*, **10**(2), pp. 99–108.

64 Davidow, W. H. and Malone, M. A. (1992) *The Virtual Corporation: Structuring and Revitalizing the Corporation for the 21st Century*, New York: HarperCollins.

65 Ferlie, E. and Pettigrew, A. (1998) 'Managing through networks', pp. 200–22 in C. Mabey, G. Salaman and J. Storey (eds), *Strategic Human Resource Management: A Reader*, London: Sage.

66 Rocket, J. F. and Short, J. E. (1991) 'The networked organization and the management of interdependence', in M. S. Scott Morton (ed.), *The Corporation of the 1990s: Information Technology and Organizational Transformation*, Oxford: Oxford University Press.

67 Castells, M. (2000) *The Information Age: Economy, Society and Culture*, Volume 1: *The Rise of Network Society* (2nd edn), London: Blackwell.

68 Shirky, C. (2008) *Here Comes Everybody: The Power of Organizing Without Organizations*, New York: Penguin.

69 Baker, M. Quoted in Hunt, K. (2009) 'The chaos theory of organization', *Report on Business*, March, p. 18.

70 Bartlett C. A. and Ghoshal, S. (1989) *Managing Across Borders: The Transnational Solution*, London: Random House.

71 Anonymous (2008) 'All you need is cash', *Economist,* November 22, p. 17.

72 Currie, G., Finn, R. and Martin, G. (2008) 'Accounting for the "dark side" of new organizational forms: the case of healthcare professionals', *Human Relations*, **61**(4), pp. 539–64.

73 Dunford, R., Palmer, I., Benveniste, J. and Crawford, J. (2007) 'Coexistence of "old" and "new" organizational practices: transitory phenomenon or enduring feature?', *Asia Pacific Journal of Human Resources*, **45**(1), pp. 24–43.

74 Rousseau, D. M. (1995) *Psychological Contracts in Organizations*, Thousand Oaks, CA: Sage.

75 Clarke, J. and Koonce, R. (1995) 'Engaging organizational survivors', *Training and Development*, **49**(8), pp. 22–30.

76 Mills, A. and Tancred, P. (eds) (1992) *Gendering Organizational Analysis*, Newbury Park, CA: Sage.

77 Hearn, J., Sheppard, D., Tancred-Sheriff, R. and Burrell, G. (eds) (1989) *The Sexuality of Organization*, London: Sage.

78 Dex, S. (1988) 'Gender and the labour market', pp. 281–309 in D. Gallie (ed.), *Employment in Britain*, Oxford: Blackwell.

79 Witz, A. (1986) 'Patriarchy and the labour market: occupational control strategies and the medical division of labour', in D. Knights and H. Willmott (eds), *Gender and the Labour Process*, Aldershot: Gower.

80 Knights, D. and Willmott, H. (eds) (1986) *Gender and the Labour Process*, Aldershot: Gower.

81 Phillips, R. and Phillips, E. (1993) *Women and Work: Inequality in the Canadian Labour Market*, Toronto: Lorimer.

82 Wilson, F. M. (2003) *Organizational Behaviour and Gender*, Farnham: Ashgate.

83 Ledwith, S. and Colgan, F. (eds.) (1996) *Women in Organizations: Challenging Gender Politics*, London: Palgrave Macmillan.

84 Wajcman, J. (1998) *Managing Like a Man: Women and Men in Corporate Management*, Cambridge, MA: Polity Press/Penn State University Press.

chapter 11
Technology in work organizations

chapter outline

- Introduction
- Defining technology: a critical look at trends
- Historical and philosophical contexts of ICT and work
- Applications of ICT legislation, policy and programmes
- Skills and practices related to technology and workplace adoption
- Summary and end-of-chapter features
- Chapter case study: Technological change at the Observer–Herald newspaper

chapter objectives

After completing this chapter, you should be able to:

- outline current trends in the relationship between technology and work organizations
- understand and explain the following key concepts: participatory design, configurations, technology agreement, four key forms of technological thought, and Luddite revolt
- compare and contrast major theoretical approaches to technology and work organizations including the post-industrialism thesis and the deskilling/enskilling debates
- discuss possible implications of theories and research for workplace practice

Introduction

A recent report from the Society for Human Resource Management[1] tells us that information and communications technology (ICT) has become embedded in previously unheard of numbers of work organizations. While many professionals and other middle-class people in core capitalist countries now take such technologies as a given in their lives, it should give us pause to note that it took 74 years for telephones to reach the lives of 50 million people, and 13 years for television to do so. The Internet has achieved this and much, much more in roughly one-tenth the time, and the effects of this seemingly never-ending stream of technological change remain a thinly understood phenomenon for those who use and manage the use of such technologies in the workplace. Moreover, if national expenditures on technologies are any indication of their importance and the general need to understand their uses and effects, we might also note that these national expenditures on ICT have approached double digits as a percentage of gross domestic product, with the USA, Japan and the European Union countries breaking the 7.5 per cent mark: these expenditures represent over US$1.5 trillion per year.

At the same time, Organization for Economic Co-operation and Development policy analysts and an enormous array of others suggest this is not enough.[1–6] For them, it is clear that economic success is dependent on ICT – investment in the technology, its application and its diffusion. This thinking represents a type of orthodoxy that is rarely challenged. In this chapter, we shall look at it closely, alongside the many different, competing theories that are often left out of most work-based and government policy-based discussions.

The challenge of this chapter is to explore the relevance of this orthodoxy to a critical understanding of organizational behaviour. We can, and should, begin this in a simple way by asking how 'technology' itself is defined and understood. What are the presumptions made about the relationship between ICT development, organizational behaviour and ICT use? Hidden in the answers to such questions, we argue, are important possibilities for understanding a topic that has become all but taken for granted – a sure recipe for arriving at a destination not of our own collective choosing.

In this chapter, we include a discussion not often seen in organizational behaviour textbooks, which points to the broad work-based policy and practice surrounding ICT. National and international policy and programmes are examined with reference to the USA, Canada, the European Union and finally Sweden and Norway. We look at important types of policy and practice at the level of the firm, with a focus on, first, technology agreements, and second, the effect of scholarship on the practice of ICT innovation and its use in the labour process. There is an emphasis on what is known in the sociology

Before reading on, you may wish to think carefully about how you define 'technology' now, based on how you have seen it applied in the workplaces you are familiar with. Do you feel that this definition is narrow or broad? When is either type of definition useful? Important to the chapter generally will be the notions of conflict and consensus. From your experiences, is technological change at work associated with conflict, consensus or both?

stop reflect

of work field as the deskilling/enskilling debate for what it can teach us about organizational behaviour.

We begin, however, with a brief discussion of the key concepts, main literature and central ideologies of technological thought. Together, this review sets the stage for critical and creative thinking about the relationship between technology, work and organizational behaviour.

Defining technology: a critical look at trends

technology: the means by which organizations transform inputs into outputs, or rather the mediation of human action. This includes mediation by tools and machines as well as rules, social convention, ideologies and discourses

In the context of workplace organizations, **technology** is conventionally defined as 'the means by which an organization transforms inputs into outputs … [including] the techniques and process used to transform labour, knowledge, capital and raw materials into finished goods and services' (ref. 7, p. 178).

Classic post-Second World War researchers developed a research programme that looked carefully at the relationship between technology and work. For example, Woodward studied the relationship between production technology and the organizational structure of firms, testing also for the possible roles of

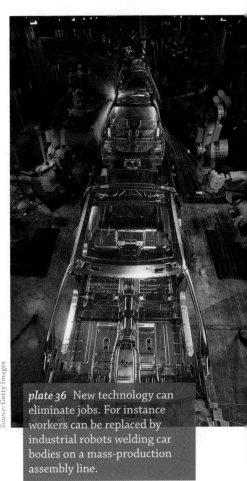

Source: Getty Images

plate 36 New technology can eliminate jobs. For instance workers can be replaced by industrial robots welding car bodies on a mass-production assembly line.

authority, control, division of labour and intrafirm communications.[8] She found that the type of organization corresponded to the (product or service) production technologies it used. This perspective has been criticized by a range of authors for the amount of influence granted to the technology, or rather its 'technological determinism', an influence that has probably grown increasingly as users become more and more resigned to constant change in this area. Other 'classic' researchers of this period added additional insights into the relationship between technology and organizational forms, stressing not simply the correlation between the two, but also causative relationships: that is, the 'why' and 'how' of the relationship.[9,10]

post-industrial economy: an economy that is based on the provision of services rather than goods

Around the same time, there emerged an influential series of arguments (which are, nevertheless, contestable) that organizational structures, organizational behaviour and technology were combining to form '**post-industrial**', 'knowledge' and/or 'information' economies, which were significantly different from the styles and structure of work to that point. Promoted by a variety of influential researchers (for example, Bell in the USA,[11] Porter in Canada,[12] Touraine in France[13] and Richta in Eastern Europe[14]), this school of thought is still with us today, trumpeting the collapse of workplace drudgery, low-skill jobs to be replaced by '**knowledge workers**', 'information workers' or 'symbolic analysts', all with an emphasis on the use of computerized technology. Even more recently, others have taken up the torch to perpetuate the tradition.[3,5,15]

knowledge worker: a worker who depends on her or his skills, knowledge and judgement established through additional training and/or schooling

The current argument of these gurus of the 'perpetually coming but never arriving good times' is, in brief, that technology with informating properties – that is, the capacity to provide relevant information and generate analytically based knowledge – encourages the development of computer, social and analytical skills, and hence contributes both to the emergence of new occupations (such as software developers) and to worker empowerment. Although consumers of electronics may in their non-work lives tend to see ICT as expanding their capabilities in and access to information and services, it is vital to note that, in the paid workplace, ICT often has additional effects that are less likely to be positive. It may alter management–employee relations by encouraging decentralized activities and new forms of 'panoptic' (that is, all-embracing) managerial control.

Work and society: Computers and work

In her major study of the role of computers in the workplace, Shoshanna Zuboff (1988) reviews the complex relations between technological innovation and work. She argues that it would be a mistake to view the process or impact of technological change as predetermined. Patterns of technological change are shaped by political factors. Those who introduce new technologies into the workplace must make choices. What happens at work depends, in part, on the choices they make.

Of particular interest to Zuboff is the question of how the computerization of the workplace will influence the foundations of managerial authority. She suggests that the foundations of managerial authority were traditionally connected to management's knowledge of work processes. Due to a knowledge gap (favouring managers), it was believed that management had a right and responsibility to control workers. According to Zuboff, the introduction of computers into the workplace has the potential to change this relationship between management and workers. One can imagine several possibilities, but one thing is certain: if the knowledge gap changed as a result of computerization – for example, if it were to shrink – this would have important implications for managerial authority.

What makes Zuboff's study so engaging is that she enables readers to view these issues through the eyes of the workers and managers at the pulping plants where she conducted her research. Some workers expressed concern that computerization had caused them to lose some of the sensory knowledge (sights, smells and sounds) they had used to run the plant effectively. Other workers expressed concern that they were not receiving the kind of training that would enable them to make decisions at the newly computerized plant:

> The technology lets us know a lot, but we need to know more. As a manager, you should teach everybody what you know – keep passing the knowledge on. But they do not give us the knowledge to think for ourselves. I think it is because it would do away with their jobs, or they would look stupid if we had the knowledge. (p. 278)

One of the managers Zuboff interviewed had this to say about his responsibility for 'passing the knowledge on':

> I am not willing to break things down real simply to explain something to the operators. I won't give up my terms that I learned as an engineer. The concepts are hard to understand. I am not here to teach those concepts. I went to college to learn these things, and so it proves I have a right to tell people what to do. (p. 281)

Zuboff is careful to make the case that the impact of computers at work is difficult to predict. She presents us with multiple scenarios, some that depict an almost Utopian future for workers and some that depict a darker outcome. Here is her optimistic account of the computerized workplace of the future:

> Organizational leaders recognize the new forms of skill and knowledge needed to truly exploit the potential of an intelligent technology. They direct their resources towards creating a work force that can exercise critical judgement as it manages the surrounding machine systems. Work becomes more abstract as it depends upon understanding and manipulating information. This marks the beginning of new forms of mastery and provides an opportunity to imbue jobs with more comprehensive meaning. A new array of work tasks offer unprecedented opportunities for a wide range of employees to add value to products and services. (p. 6)

stop! It is possible that both the worker and the manager described above have valid points. Write a dialogue for a conversation that might take place between this worker and this manager at an informal meeting convened by senior management.

Does Zuboff's optimistic scenario 'ring true' for you? In your experience, has the computerization of work increased or diminished worker autonomy and the quality of working life?

Sources and further information

McLoughlin, I. and Clark, J. (1994). *Technological Change at Work*, Philadelphia: Open University Press.

Zuboff, S. (1988). *In the Age of the Smart Machine: The Future of Work and Power*, New York: Basic Books.

Decentralized work activity can foster more collaborative work teams, even allowing them to function over the barriers of time and space, so it is viewed as a key enabler of new forms of work organization. There is an assumption that ICT and new forms of technology will lead to new firms, new products and new jobs. Some writers on the topic are particularly fascinated by the prospect of greater 'outsourcing', which is made easier since ICT reduces the transaction costs associated with contracting. This places a downward pressure on wages and employee control, but it is said to encourage innovation.

These accounts, however, tend to ignore the messy work through which real technological or economic change emerges in society. In sum, both people's everyday experience of ICT use in their non-work lives and the hyper-Utopian views of technology advocates for the workplace conspire to minimize the conflictual dimensions of change, and overplay the consensual or rather mechanistic dimension: the view that change is simply an anonymous, faceless force of nature.

As the old adage goes: we cannot know where we are going unless we know where we have been. In this sense, economic history teaches us that the claims of links between technology, productivity and the emergence of apparently 'new' phases in the economy are not as straightforward as they may seem, and a healthy scepticism is, in our view, an important response for students and scholars of organizational behaviour in this topic area.

The key technologies of modernism that are said to have defined the first, second and third industrial revolutions – that is, steam, electricity and ICT – have seen fascinating and complex pathways to application in the workplace.[4,16–19] Among these 'general-purpose technologies' (GPTs), electricity,[20] ICT[21,22] and in particular steam[17] clearly emerged, not out of some inventor's mind as much as from the push and pull of the forces of political and economic struggle. The details of the emergence and diffusion or transfer of GPTs provide important clues to the actual nature of technology as a phenomenon. Is technology a 'thing', or is it a social process? Lazonick seems to suggest the latter in his discussion of the meaning of 'technological transfer':

> Insofar as the utilization of technology requires complementary human inputs with specific cognitive capabilities and behavioural responses, the transferred technology will have to be developed in the new national environment before it can be utilized there. As a result, when 'transferred' technology is ultimately developed so that it can be productively utilized in a new national environment, it is in effect a new technology. (ref. 23, p. 194)

The type of description that Lazonick provides is aligned with Fleck's notion of 'configurations' (as opposed to 'technologies' as such).[24] **Configurations** are defined as complex mixes of standardized and locally customized elements that are highly specific to an organization. In fact, those who have been most insightful in considering the very nature of technology have defined the term quite broadly to reflect this broad set of considerations. These scholars tend to produce statements that are at first glance simple, but at a second glance can be seen to be deeply informed. Technology is not this or that tool, artefact or machine, and neither is it a GPT such as steam, electricity or ICT. Rather, it is 'the way we do things around here',[25] the 'organization of resources',[26,27] 'society made durable'[28] and so on. Students of work, technology and society gain the potential for valuable leadership when they break the bonds of conventional wisdom to explore its terms critically. In this chapter, we suggest that we must approach technology and organizational behaviour as a thoroughly social phenomenon.

configurations: defining technology as the combination of social and technical factors. Configurations are a complex mix of standardized and locally customized elements that are highly specific to an organization

Check out www. informationweek.com for the latest and most interesting business stories on the relationship between technology and work. Test your knowledge of this chapter by picking an article that interests you, and then trying to apply a critical, social approach to the technology issue

weblink

However, the question remains: what kind of social phenomenon are we talking about? We have already mentioned that steam, electricity and ICT all emerged from the push and pull of economic and political power. It is a contested terrain, or, as Feenberg says, 'technology is a scene of struggle … a parliament of things' (ref. 29, p. 14). Historically, as now, the intersection of work, learning and technological change has occasioned conflict: from the Luddite revolts of early nineteenth century to the countless more recent industrial conflicts caused by the imposition of technological change. More recently, this has involved the transformation of occupations including engineering,[30] textile work,[31] postal work,[32] computer programming[33] and – one of the more frequently documented occupations – printing.[34–37] Wallace and Kalleberg, working in the US context, summarise it like this:

> We have argued that while technology is the proximate cause of this transformation, the underlying and fundamental sources for these changes are found in historically developed social relations of production … The stated goal of automation in printing, as in other industries, is the rationalization of the labor process: the streamlining of production and elimination of costly sources of human error … However, efficiency is not a value-neutral goal in capitalist economies. (ref. 35, pp. 321–2)

Thus, it is the core point of departure in this chapter that our conceptions of ICT and work must be conditioned by an impulse to 'de-reify', to move beyond mere appearances. ICT as an isolated device, tool or machine is an abstraction; in reality, it is an elaborate historical process. It is both a social and highly conflictual phenomenon.

Historical and philosophical contexts of ICT and work

According to Theodore Roszak,[38] the word 'computer' entered the North American public vocabulary in the 1950s, at a time when the most advanced models were still room-sized beasts that burned enough electricity to present a serious cooling problem. Building on the principle of ICT, work and organizational behaviour as a conflictual social phenomenon, it is important to note that, as with the emergence of steam and electricity, historical scholarship has demonstrated that computers were not simply 'discovered' in the conventional sense of the term. Instead, ICT was brought into being by specific historical and political economic processes: by politics, policy and practice.

Noble provides the definitive analysis,[22] noting that contemporary ICT emerged through a series of concerted and contested activities by which companies like General Electric, Westinghouse, RCA, AT&T and IBM, relying upon private control over public funds for what could be called the 'university–industrial–military' complex of the post-Second World War era in the USA, developed specific forms of computer technology. These included numerical control, computerized numerical control, automated robotics and now advanced ICT including the Internet. Importantly, Noble makes it clear that, in fact, alternatives to computerized numerical control could have been just as efficiently developed, and that strategic choices revolved around issues of power and control over the organization of production.

Just as the **Luddites** of nineteenth-century Britain were in favour of technologies that supplemented rather than displaced human skills,[39] the key alternative during the early history of computers was 'record/playback' technology. This system was actively ignored largely because, as Noble puts it, 'to the software engineer, this places far too many cards in the hands of the lowly machinist' (ref. 22, p. 190). Such matters, in fact, raise invaluable questions still applicable today as technological

Luddites: a group of textile workers, led by General Ned Ludd in early nineteenth-century England, who systematically smashed new workplace technologies because they directly undermined their working knowledge and economic interests as workers

design continues to make presumptions about who should control what, and what features and purposes ICT should entail.

Although this historical background is important, it is equally important – if we are to understand the intersection of ICT, work and organizational behaviour as a contested as well as a consensual social phenomenon – to have a basic understanding of the competing ideologies or philosophical approaches that inform the development and use of ICT. As Williams and Edge remark, 'these debates are not merely 'academic': they relate to policy claims and objectives' (ref. 40, p. 2). We can categorize the different approaches into four basic categories: instrumental/technocratic, substantive, constructivist, and what Feenberg refers to as a 'critical theory' of technology.[29]

Instrumentalist or technocratic approaches tend to be the source of either the positive or neutral characterizations of ICT in the workplace. This is the dominant approach in government, business and mainstream policy sciences. Here the transfer of technology is inhibited only by cost, what works in one context can be expected to work equally well in another, and 'the only rational stance is an unreserved commitment to its employment' (ref. 29, p. 6). More discussions of the origins of this approach can be found in the work of a variety of leading sociologists of the immediate and later post-Second World War era, who wrote at length on the issues of technology and industrial progression.[11,41,42] More often than not under this approach, technology comes to take on a kind of autonomous, creative and deterministic role (and thus it makes sense that *Time* magazine can designate a computer 'person of the year'). This autonomous casting, in turn, gives rise to exaggerated tales of the emergence of 'knowledge workers' and 'symbolic analysts'.[3,11,43]

A contrasting approach to technocratic thought is said to be the **substantive approach**, represented best in the writings of Jacques Ellul or Martin Heidegger.[44,45] In a type of mirror image, however, this approach also attributes an autonomous force to technology, although it sees it as a 'cultural system' that orients the world as an 'object of control'. This approach tends to see the future as dark (for instance, 'Only God can save us now,' says Heidegger), and argues that a return to simplicity or primitivism offers the only viable alternative.

Standing in many ways separate from either of these approaches is the **constructivist approach**, exemplified (differently) by the likes of Latour,[28] Callon[46] and Suchman.[47] Such works emphasize how technology is rooted in human interaction and the local activation or use of technologies by human beings. The meaning and effects of technology are determined in their use by actors, and not necessarily in any prior way by designers. Among all the approaches to ICT, it is the constructivist approach that most clearly articulates how users implement and appropriate ICT, sometimes in keeping with the intentions of the designers and those who contracted them, sometimes not. Others have echoed the importance of this approach for technological development, emphasizing how design, implementation, use (and re-design) are interrelated, and opening up new ground in conventional understandings of 'choice' in the course of technological development.[48,49]

Finally, there is the **critical approach**. Its roots are largely in the Frankfurt School of critical social theory,[29] although a variety of work such as that of Lewis Mumford has relevant connections to this approach as well.[27] In general, the approach rejects the presumptions of both the technocratic and the substantive approach, charting a course, as Feenberg says, between the resignation and Utopian visions of efficiency.

To the degree that the approach is defined by its reference to issues of power, it might overlap with certain elements of the constructivist approach. Some constructivist researchers[28,46] overtly declare that there are inherent political dimensions to technological development (for instance, Latour's comment that 'Technologies are politics pursued by other means'[50]). However, central to the critical approach is

instrumentalist or technocratic approach: approaches to technology that are uncritical of its broader social, political and economic significance, viewing technologies as autonomous and positive

substantive approach: an approach that tends to see technologies as producing negative social and political effects

constructivist approach: an approach to technology that tends not to focus on social or political influences but instead sees technologies as defined strictly in how they are put to use

critical approach: an approach to technology that tends to focus on how the social and political effects are produced through contestation and negotiation

what Feenberg calls the 'democratic advance': that is, the democratic participation of citizens in the establishment of both the goals and means of technological development, implementation and diffusion.

Echoing this concern in terms of policy analysis, Gartner and Wagner[51] have carried out careful case studies in Europe, and drawn attention to the difficulties faced by design efforts situated in 'fragmented political cultures'. Mumford's pan-historic discussions also emphasize what he calls 'authoritarian and democratic technics'.[27] By 'authoritarian technics' he means a development that is 'system-centred, immensely powerful and yet unstable due to its centralization of control'. Indeed, he goes on to say that 'if democracy did not exist, we would have to invent it' (ref. 27, p. 21) if we were to deal effectively with the technologies of the modern era.

We suggest that these four basic approaches to technological thought will be useful for analysing policy and practice, providing us with a type of philosophical compass. In other words, they orient us to the more general directions and purposes that all too often remain hidden beneath the surface of the legislation, policy, programmes and practice that expresses them.

Applications of ICT legislation, policy and programmes

If we commit to understanding the intersection of ICT, work and organizational behaviour as a broad, conflictual social phenomenon, we are in essence seeking to understand a process of change. Both personal and organizational change can perhaps most usefully be studied as a process of 'learning', either individual, group or organizational. We benefit greatly by looking at work-based learning, whether it is organized as a training programme or undertaken informally in everyday participation in the labour process, as a phenomenon that sits above, gives meaning to, reacts upon and in turn affects legislation, policy and programmes regarding ICT.

Critical insight

The purpose and outcomes of the introduction of new technology in organizations have been assessed and reassessed many times in the literature over the years. Earlier in the chapter, we mentioned classic readings in this area, so now let us take a careful look at two of them.

Read Joan Woodward's *Industrial Organizations: Theory and Practice* and J. D. Thompson's *Organizations in Action*.[8,9] Compare and contrast their assessments. Be sure to note the research on which each set of arguments is based.

Research and development (R&D) is central to the efforts of leading firms, as well as being carried out on a national scale by the core countries of global capitalism,[6] although there is a considerable variation in the degree and focus that countries bring to it (see Mani[52] for a comparison of developed and developing countries). When it comes to the relationship between direct and indirect involvement in technology development and industrial relations, we see that Northern European governments are often the most directly involved, with other European governments such as France and Germany (as well as non-European countries such as Japan) being moderately involved, and the governments of countries such as the UK, the USA, Southern Europe, Australia and Canada being least directly involved on a regulatory basis.

The most 'interventionist' government responses are to be found in countries like Norway and Sweden, where issues from ICT research and application, as well as industrial relations more broadly, are shaped by a commitment to 'co-determination'. However, in general, the power of national or international governmental bodies to use regulation to influence the introduction and application of ICT in actual work processes and workplaces is quite limited. In the USA, for example, while Carnoy, Pollack and Wong have noted that the structures, policies and practices of labour relations are coming to the centre of the debate on the design and adaptation of new technologies,[53] the most common model of employer–employee negotiation and ICT adoption is adversarial and antagonistic.

We can, however, briefly note that a parallel system of private sector policy and (corporate-based) governance has blossomed. For example, there has been a growing number of international agreements between large corporations about various forms of the development and application of ICT. According to Archibugi and Coco,[55] international firm-to-firm technological development agreements doubled between the periods of 1981–86 and 1993–98. In particular, strategic technology partnerships (for R&D) between Europe and the USA rocketed in the 10 years to 2006. These partnerships may also involve collaborations with public research institutions and universities, which play an increasingly important role in the international dissemination of knowledge and ICT development.

Although this layer of ICT and work policy is important, a solid grasp of the range of governmental legislation, policy and programmes in this area remains the most relevant for our discussion here. To review these, we look at several selected examples involving different countries as well as different political levels of enactment.

The US system

The US system of training, ICT development and implementation is often set up as an ideal in the policy world, in terms of leading-edge practices of ICT-based innovation. However, closer examination reveals a complex, sometimes chaotic, mix of federal, state and regional efforts.

At the level of the firm and sector, the US system of industrial relations places decisions on technological change and work organization firmly under the 'management rights clause' of any company–union collective agreement.[56] In the context of a corporate culture that is hostile to unions, and of comparatively high levels of involvement in 'interfirm' technological development agreements, there is not a great deal of likelihood of a genuine 'co-determination' of organizations' technological direction in the USA.

In slightly broader terms, but directly bearing on the translation of technological policy and actual organizational behaviour and change, we can look at the vocational and work-based training policy in the USA. This too has come to be recognized to be a patchwork of state and federal programmes. Legislation began in 1962 with the Manpower Development and Training Act, which was followed by the Comprehensive Employment and Training Act of 1973, the Job Training Partnership Act (1983) and the School-to-Work Opportunities Act (1994–2001).[57]

A host of authors have lamented the general historical lack of industrial policy in the USA, and this is reflected in the arena of ICT R&D policy.[58] At the same time, however, Herman has documented some important examples of multilateral partnership agreements over the implementation and training of ICT.[59] These appear to hold a good deal of promise for the future. Based on 14 case studies of 'high-road' partnerships between employers, government, unions and local communities, Herman concludes that, in the USA, the most successful ICT/work/learning policy tends to be found at the sectoral rather than the state or federal level.

Canada

Canada provides an alternative to the type of decentralized, largely corporate-controlled policy models seen in the USA. Here there has been innovative experimentation with government policy. 'Sector Skills Councils' in Canada generally focus on technological change, and offer a unique model not seen elsewhere in the world. At the federal level, these councils have their roots in the industrial adjustment services established in 1963. Following the establishment of the Sectoral Partnership Initiative by the federal government in the early 1990s, they reached the level of 22 councils in the mid-1990s, 17 of which involved union participation. Related initiatives also emerged at the provincial level in Canada.

In general, the Skills Councils built on pioneering examples such as the Canadian Steel Trade and Employment Congress.[60] Both federally and provincially, Sectoral Skills Councils had their origins in the inability of the private sector to develop workable options for high levels of training and adjustment on their own, where a chief concern of corporate leaders was the **'free-rider' problem** – the fear that firms that trained workers well would simply lose those workers to other firms offering higher wages.

'free-rider' problem: the fear firms have that if they invest in training for workers, these workers might eventually leave the firm for one offering higher wages/benefits, thus losing the firm its investment

---

OB in focus
Mechanized high-tech workers?

It is often assumed that those with the greatest technical skills and education are most ideally situated on the labour market. Certainly, most people would not expect 'computer programmers' to have a difficult time, but business analysts are now saying otherwise. Charles Simonyi, former programmer with Microsoft and founder of Intentional Software Corp., claimed on www.informationweek.com that the:

outsourcing trend indicates that an ever-larger part of IT work has become routine, repetitive and low-bandwidth

– one might even say unexciting or boring ... Outsourcing has been historically a prelude to mechanization, and mechanization is a high-value domestic opportunity ... in the long run these jobs will be 90 per cent mechanized, with the help of senior domestic talent. (ref. 61)

Strangely, there are ever-increasing numbers of highly skilled programmers available from all over the world, yet there does not seem to be enough 'skilled work' for them to do. Why can't employers create enough jobs that allow skilled workers to apply their talents? Does it have anything to do with the wage level they would have to pay them at? How does 'outsourcing' play a role?

An important example at the provincial level was established in Canada's most industrialized province, Ontario. It followed a mixed governmental/firm/corporate model that, as in the USA, seems most effective at the sectoral level. The Technology Adjustment Research Programme was first envisaged by the first Premier's Council of Ontario in the late 1980s, and was later funded by the Ontario Federation of Labour and the provincial government's Ministry of Economic Development and Trade.[62] It involves the participation of 16 specific unions.

In connection with this programme, the government established sectoral strategic initiatives in areas including aerospace, steel, biotechnology, plastics and automotive parts. Sectoral Skills Councils emerged, a variety of sectoral initiatives were established, and a variety of innovative multilateral research efforts were undertaken. However, the results were mixed at the level of the workplace, ICT implementation and learning. After the withdrawal of the government, only remnants of the programme persist today.

These efforts made it clear that, without both broader legislative support as well as ongoing resources for developing the multilateral model (inclusive of a genuinely multilateral industrial policy), even the best efforts would be hampered. Frequently, those at the centre of policy implementation and programme research lamented a lack of a broader 'European' approach (and the funds to match).

Western Europe

One of the most comprehensive sets of studies of ICT, work and organizational change was conducted in Western Europe in the early 1990s. It was entitled Participation in Technological Change, and was undertaken by the European Foundation for the Improvement of Living and Working Conditions. Based on 64 case studies and a large (7326 participants) survey, the study showed that technological change was dependent on national industrial relations regimes as well as, in broader terms, the 'historical and cultural factors' associated with particular nations and sectors. In keeping with our discussion, two key factors for success were unionization and the skill level of workers.

The European Union is a key example of how international policy and programmes are created and carried out, and provides important information on the current status of the intersection of ICT, work and organizational behaviour in advanced capitalism. In general terms, this model of policy development contrasts starkly with the decentralized model in the USA. EU policies in the area of technology and training revolve around the principle that the circulation of knowledge is as important as a common currency. To put it more starkly, 'economic growth, employment and welfare in the old continent are strictly associated with its capability to generate and diffuse new technologies' (ref. 55, p. 1).

As a student of organizational behaviour, you should explore the outputs of such bodies to gain a sense of where practice, research and policy are headed. Perhaps as important as the centralized organization of ICT-related policy, however, is the willingness and ability of the European Union to carry out combined R&D, training and implementation research programmes that link corporations, research institutions and governmental resources.

The most relevant example in this regard is the European Commission's information technology program entitled European Strategic Programme of Research on Information Technology (ESPRIT, 1994–98).[63] ESPRIT represents an international example of an attempt at the policy/programme level to organize R&D- and ICT-based innovation, as well as work and learning outcomes, to respond to the needs of the workplace. Its outcomes have, however, remained partially ambiguous from a critical viewpoint. This is in part because of the phenomenon that Gartner and Wagner describe as narrow forms of 'agenda setting':

> What is politically and ethically legitimate and desirable cannot be simply solved by establishing participatory structures. The kind of close partnership between designers and users at which, e.g. situated design, aspires is not a sufficient answer to the core question of what makes a 'good system'. Our case analysis points at the importance of understanding agenda setting. Each arena has its own set of legitimate agenda, from questions of user interface design to quality of working life and privacy issues. (ref. 51, p. 203)

The ESPRIT programme and the associated European Commission policies on which it was built were largely democratic, but at the same time its agenda was largely predefined along technocratic lines. At the point of learning and ICT use, for example, its motive was tied, mostly although not exclusively, to serving markets and relatively narrow interests of profitability, rather than to more broad issues of quality of working life, sustainability, equity and so forth.

Scandinavia

In Northern Europe, however, there is a different tradition at the intersection between ICT, work and organizational behaviour. Again, Gartner and Wagner's work is instructive.[51] Their work looked closely at the role of formal national legislative frameworks, such as the Norwegian Work Environment Act (NWEA), which detail the relations between the various industrial partners and the norms of work, technological development and ICT use. The NWEA defines participation in work-related areas related to ICT systems (among other things), and suggests a much deeper form of participation in policy formation.

Specifically, the 1970s was a watershed decade for progressive policy and legislation around ICT design, implementation and work in Northern Europe. The Norwegians put the NWEA into place in 1977, giving workers formal participation in 'company assemblies' and the right to appoint trade union representatives in the area of technological change. Co-determination procedures were established, and a system of penalties was set in place.

Similarly, in the late 1970s, Sweden enacted a series of 'work democracy' regulations including the establishment of a legal framework for labour representatives on company boards, disclosure acts and other items under the Work Environment Act of 1978. This set of acts, described by some as the most important reform in Swedish society since the universal right to vote, also included the Joint Regulation Act of 1977, which guaranteed co-determination specifically around issues of the design and use of new technology. While management did retain certain rights of ownership, articles in these acts stipulated that employers must negotiate with local unions before making any major changes to work processes, that workers can initiate such negotiations as well, and that all parties have the rights to relevant documentation (financial and technical).

Significantly, in Sweden, these legislative and policy frameworks were complemented by specific ICT development research programmes, namely DEMOS and UTOPIA,[64] which had as their central goal to investigate how technical design could respond to this radical new legislative environment. Also complementing these legislative frameworks were innovative experiments in user-based design: Scandinavia's UTOPIA programme[65] as well as the Effective Technical and Human Implementation of Computer-based Systems (ETHICS) programme.[66] As a result, the network of policies, programmes and legislation was particularly thick with ideas and potential.

The conclusions from this exciting period in Northern Europe were that local participants must be deeply involved in the process, but also that **participatory design** is necessary but not sufficient for genuinely progressive socioeconomic outcomes surrounding technology design, implementation, learning and use.[67] It also became apparent that trade unions were often not prepared to adequately take advantage of their new powers and responsibilities. They lacked the resources and organizational structure to produce levels of expertise comparable to business.

> One critical scholar of technology puts forth the argument that, today, machines take precedence over people in the workplace.[51] He goes further, adding that such environments 'seriously upset the habits of mind applied to the work world', and that whether 'one conceives work in the capitalist model of costs of production or the Marxist one of the Organic composition of labor, information machines disrupt the models of comprehending work'. Do you think this is true? Why or why not? Reading the original article might help you to consider the issues
>
> **stop reflect**

participatory design: an approach to design and implementation of technologies that is premised on user participation

Skills and practices related to technology and workplace adoption

We have explored the conceptual, historical and philosophical context of ICT, and reviewed key legislative, policy and programmatic initiatives. We have also emphasized that policy takes on its meaning within the cycle of social processes that includes organizational behaviour and learning. With this in mind, in this section we review existing literature on workplace ICT, skill and learning to fill in an important gap in our discussion thus far. This section also completes our discussion on different theoretical approaches to ICT and organizational behaviour, by exploring different sociological and organizational theory approaches to work.

Technology agreements

technology agreements: agreements with legal standing that set in place rules for negotiation over technological selection, adoption and implementation

Clearly, one of the ways in which policy and practice intersect in the workplace is through what are known as 'technology agreements'. These agreements, often although not exclusively seen in unionized firms, establish a form of co-determination (jointly between management and workers) over issues of ICT adoption and use. In some ways, these agreements mirror on a smaller scale the kinds of national legislative framework seen in Norway and Sweden. However, they have appeared in a much wider range of countries.

Although technology agreements are not quite as common now as when they were first introduced in the 1970s and 80s, the basic technology agreement remains an important form of workplace-based policy concerning the adoption and effective use of ICT. In the early days of their emergence, according to some writers,[68,69] these agreements typically included two basic components. First, there were 'procedural' elements, which included broad statements on the need for new technologies and, arguably more importantly, agreements on the timely disclosure of information by employers. These were to include the likely effects of the changes and to set out options. The options often included procedures for the development of joint union–management committees and change-monitoring practices, the establishment of worker technology representatives, and arrangements for union and management to draw on outside experts or consultants. Unions were occasionally given veto powers if management clearly violated the agreed procedures.

A second component to technology agreements was what are called 'substantive' elements: specific statements on how various issues should be handled. The aspects covered included job security, retraining and adjustments, methods of sharing economic benefits, health and safety, and surveillance issues.

Small and Yasin[69] have noted the varied effects that technology agreements have on practice in the workplace, and also note the importance of the related industrial relations infrastructure in a firm. (Basically, they emphasize the importance of unionization.) Although many factors affect the overall success of technology agreements, evidence suggests that they tend to lead to better firm performance, a broader and more productive labour process, and a collective learning feedback loop that leads to a better choice and implementation of new technologies.

plate 37 Technology has the capacity to either deskill or enskill.

Source: iStockphoto

ICT and workplace skills

To complete the picture, we need to look carefully at specific discussions of ICT and workplace skills. For this, we turn to writings on adult education, industrial relations and the sociology of work to expand our understanding of organizational behaviour.

Skill and knowledge development in the workplace has regularly been associated with the introduction of new technology. In different historical phases of the labour process, this has been seen under the paradigms of craft production, Taylorism, Fordism, neo-Fordism, flexible specialization and virtual organizational design (also see the discussion in Chapter 2). Approaches to work, learning and policy

– for example, those associated with the technocratic approach – largely presume that ICT requires advanced skills.[3,6] However, many of those who have looked closely at skill and learning practice associated with workplace technological change have questioned this assumption.[70,71]

Poster,[67] for example, suggests that levels of learning may be reduced in some ways by the introduction of ICT, and that, either way, accurate assessments of performance and skill change remain elusive. Important empirical analyses in North America seem to support Poster's claim, with some suggesting that there may in fact be a surplus in computer literacy: that is, there are inadequate real opportunities for workers to apply their skills at work.[54,72–74] For example, Lowe studied computer literacy in Canada and specifically states that, typically, 'job structures deprive workers of opportunities to use their education and talents' (ref. 75, p. 77).

In research from both North American countries, the most powerful analysis shows that, despite calls from the corporate and government sectors to increase computer literacy, 'empirical evidence certainly suggests that there are now more people with basic computer literacy than there are jobs which need it' (ref. 73, p. 50). By all estimates, North American workplaces are not alone in this paradoxical situation of, on the one hand, the relatively widespread availability of ICT, and on the other, apparent barriers to effective diffusion, implementation, learning and use.

Kelley provides a useful review of sociological literature on the issue of work-based skills, as well as an empirical analysis of her own, which focuses on practice at the level of the firm.[56] She concludes that translating a firm's adoption of ICT into a skillful application of the new technology is dependent on a host of organizational as well as broader industrial relations policy and practice issues. In this, she builds on and broadens the observations of the 'classical' post-Second World War scholarship that we explored earlier in the chapter. According to Kelley, the 'least complex' firms are most effective at successful adoption. That is, the open participation of workers in all facets of production, including management operations, appears to be vital.

In some sense, the conditions that Kelley describes represent the spirit of the 'co-determination' legislation, policy and programmes we discussed earlier. Nevertheless, how any organization achieves this type of open participation remains an open question. Small firms seem to offer hope for translating the adoption of ICT into effective production outcomes, but typically lack the levels of capital for significant ICT investment. Large firms have the capital but may not have an industrial relations infrastructure (in the sense of recognized unions) to generate accountable, genuine, shared decision making across all levels of the organization. Unionized firms offer an infrastructure for shared decision making, but, given that in most countries workers must actively fight to obtain union representation, these firms can experience bitter management–labour relations. However, it has for some time been a demonstrated fact that union representation often provides the best chance for achieving effective technological adoption and skill-enhancing outcomes.[54,76,77]

Deskilling and enskilling

Research related to what is known as the 'deskilling/enskilling' debate provides a key conceptual approach for understanding questions surrounding the successful application of technology in the workplace. This debate was initiated in the work of Harry Braverman.[78,79] His ground-breaking research was based on an elaboration of Marxist theory through a critique of Taylor's scientific management (or Taylorism).

Braverman and other advocates of the deskilling thesis note that the goal of the labour process under capitalism is to generate managerial control for maximization of efficiency and profitability.[21,34,80,81] In seeking control, managers often dispense with the very employee capacities that are claimed to be so vital by today's managerial theories:

The focus on the labour process points also to the irremediable necessity of a coercive system of control and surveillance, leading to a critical perspective towards the role of 'management'. Of crucial importance, such a focus also helps deflate the ideology of 'technology' as a neutral, autonomous and irresistible force. (ref. 82, p. 93)

deskilling: a reduction in the proficiency needed to perform a specific job, which leads to a corresponding reduction in the wages paid for that job

In Taylorist, Fordist and neo-Fordist models of production, the deskilling argument focuses on the stark division of mental and manual labour, and the breaking up of complex tasks into smaller, more discrete ones. This is often, although not exclusively, achieved with the aid of new technologies. As Hyman suggests, there is often a significant growth in the surveillance of workers as well.[82] The classic assembly line, and the myriad of similar work design principles we see today across manufacturing as well as in many service sector workplaces, attempted to generate profit and managerial control by breaking up the knowledge and skill that was 'owned' (for lack of a better word) by individuals or groups of workers. It converted these skills into a feature of the work system itself, so they became 'owned' by the business owners/shareholders, and under the control of managers.

This classic form of deskilling still occurs widely, as you will know if you or your friends have worked in, for example, a fast-food or retail outlet, but the introduction of new forms of advanced ICT has redefined the deskilling process for a small number of occupational groups.[83,84] The classic separation of mental and manual has evolved into something more complex, although it remains difficult to argue that it is fundamentally distinct from the classic deskilling dynamics.

In other words, in some firms and among certain occupational groups, we now see a more nuanced form of the division between mental and manual labour, which is associated with the struggle over macro design (or 'agenda setting') and the creative micro, or local, design and use of ICT. Hosts of workers are now being asked to use the tools provided for them in creative and responsive ways, but in contexts and with goals that are pre-established and beyond their control. We can of course see this predicted by commentators such as Marx: more than a century ago, he noted that the capitalist labour process can (although it does not necessarily have to seek to) eliminate the mental capacities of labour in order to appropriate and control work outcomes.

enskilling: changes in work, often involving technology, that result in an increase in the skill level of workers. The issue of control is often implicated

The so-called 'enskilling' thesis claims the contrary: that increased technology leads to more, not less, worker skill. Its advocates point to niches in the economy (often involving small firms) where stark divisions between mental and manual labour are less often seen. A range of other researchers discussed earlier in the chapter are in this sense the forefathers of the enskilling thesis,[11,85,86] collectively suggesting that unskilled jobs will be simply be 'automated away', while Reich and a host of technocratic analysts can be viewed as more contemporary advocates.

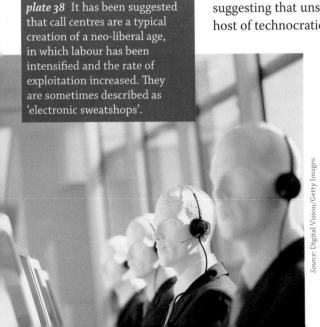

plate 38 It has been suggested that call centres are a typical creation of a neo-liberal age, in which labour has been intensified and the rate of exploitation increased. They are sometimes described as 'electronic sweatshops'.

Source: Digital Vision/Getty Images

Between these two camps are other researchers, including types of what are known as 'contingency' and 'institutionalist' theorists, who emphasize a range of organizational, institutional and market factors that shape the deskilling/enskilling outcomes of the introduction of new technology.[56,87–89] Burris sums things up nicely by noting that a commonly held corollary of technocratic restructuring is:

'skill restructuring' (Cockburn, 1983), 'skill disruption' (Hodson, 1988) and new types of alienation, stress and occupational hazards (see Hirschhorn, 1984) ... Both deskilling and reskilling occur, and the balance between the two depends upon both the design of the technology and the way in which it is implemented. (ref. 83, p. 40–1)

Adoption practices and outcomes

Invaluable as the deskilling/enskilling debate is for our understanding, it cannot help but gloss over the actual behavioural processes that surround technological change and organizational development. The 'how' of successful ICT adoption remains obscure.

Lam provides a good comparative international analysis of how institutions, legislation and policy in different countries (looking at Japan, the UK, the USA and Denmark) support or inhibit innovation in and the adoption of ICT.[90] At the centre of this analysis is the concept of 'tacit knowledge', rooted in the relationships of discretionary communities of practice (which can be established either within an organization or more widely across a specific occupational group).

In the USA, anthropologist Charles Darrah has exhaustively described this type of knowledge production process, with some specific attention to advanced ICT.[91–93] A host of detailed empirical studies of exactly how ICT and learning practice relate is provided by Luff, Hindmarsh and Heath[94] (see also selected contributors to Engeström and Middleton[95]). Each of these studies shows that ICT is not merely 'adopted' by a workplace, but rather is *activated*, and in some sense *reconfigured*, by users in the course of (learning) practice.

A particularly relevant piece of work in this area was carried out by Livingstone and Sawchuk.[54,96] Their collection of case studies provides an important complement to organizational behaviour scholarship, as well as the sociology of work and deskilling/enskilling debates. It is based on a comparative examination of workplaces across five sectors in the Canadian economy (auto assembly, garments, light manufacturing, chemicals and public service), and draws on in-depth 'learning life-history' interviews. These case studies demonstrate, among other things, how the adoption of ICT is shaped by the industrial relations climate and the dynamics of a specific sector, as well as by the struggle of workers for greater participation in the labour process. The analysis also makes it clear that issues of race, gender and age (see Chapter 8), as well as occupational type, are significant indicators of skill and knowledge development.

Some related work on computer literacy development among manufacturing workers in Canada[74] delves even more deeply into the types of linkage (cultural, economic and political) between ICT and skill at work. Providing a critical but complementary partner to the work of Darrah, it shows how learning as a dimension of organizational behaviour is rooted in collective, informal groupings of workers, and operates interactively across the workplace, home and community spheres. This learning is carried out in order to cooperate with the needs of industry and labour markets, as well as in order to satisfy individual needs that may diverge from the interests of business.

Overall in the work of Livingstone and Sawchuk, we see computer literacy skills among workers that far outstrip the actual needs of their workplace. Thus, as we saw in the context of previous sections, important assumptions informing mainstream, technocratic approaches to policy surrounding ICT, work and learning are questioned. These and other matters addressed in this chapter raise points that are, now more than ever, important to consider in a critical and careful manner. For whom and for what purposes should technology be directed? How is control over technological design, implementation and diffusion established, and for whom? What is technology's actual effect on productivity, skill and the quality of life in the workplace? As we noted at the beginning of this chapter, taking a common-sense view of technology that overlooks the many political, economic and even philosophical choices it entails will probably not result in arriving at destinations that we collectively choose.

OB and globalization

Plugged in: technology as a mediator of organizational culture

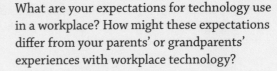

Do you rely on text messaging to coordinate meeting places with your friends? Do you use social networking sites to share and exchange information with an extended network of acquaintances – some of whom live halfway around the world? When confronted with a technical or logistic challenge, is your first approach to query an Internet search engine to learn how others have solved similar problems? If these scenarios sound familiar, the chances are that you belong to Generation Y, also called the Millennial Generation, the Net Generation or even the iPod Generation. This generational cohort includes those born between 1980 and the year 2000, the children of Baby Boomers and older members of Generation X. For this generation – the first raised with mobile phones and the Internet – engagement with applications and hardware that provide instant information sharing and feedback is second nature.

Over the past decade, Generation Y members have begun to enter the workforce, initiating some notable shifts in how work is perceived and carried out, and how organizations manage workers. These shifts are due in large part to the ways in which Generation Y workers use technology in their approaches to problem solving and interpersonal relationships. Much has been written about the impacts of Generation Y workers on more 'traditional' organizations, and how such organizations might adapt to accommodate the expectations and harness the potential of these bright new employees.

In a *Financial Times* article, Twentyman (2009) examines several ways in which Generation Y workers are transforming work. She notes that workers' aptitude at technology-mediated social networking allows them to tap into a wider pool of expertise for collective problem solving. They are also able to apply their social networking skills in novel ways to the realms of marketing, sales and business development. Furthermore, these workers are redefining the concept of the 'working day'. As task-oriented, rather than clock-oriented workers, Generation Y employees are likely to use mobile technology to complete work projects outside regular office hours and from remote locations. The expectations and work approaches of Generation Y present management challenges as well as opportunities for organizations willing to embrace change. Twentyman concludes that 'this new tribe of employees can only make its mark if the businesses they work for are able to accommodate and capitalise on a host of new attitudes, beliefs and ways of working'.

The entry of Generation Y into the workforce provides a good example of how technology can mediate – or influence – organizational behaviour and culture. This phenomenon is not new: technology has always mediated how work is done. Its role in mediating work becomes most apparent in moments of innovation and change. For instance, prehistoric advances in irrigation technologies had profound impacts on how food was grown and how nation-states developed around the world. Likewise, the machine-based technologies that spurred the Industrial Revolution in Western Europe and North America in the late eighteenth and early nineteenth centuries led to a major reordering of how workers were managed, and how they approached their work. The changes to organizational culture brought about by the arrival of Generation Y workers in the workforce can be understood as another node in the continuum of technological innovation and organizational culture.

stop! What are your expectations for technology use in a workplace? How might these expectations differ from your parents' or grandparents' experiences with workplace technology?

What are some advantages and disadvantages of relying on technology to mediate social relationships in the workplace?

Sources and further information

Dawe, T. (2008) 'Mutual trust and loyalty are the keys that will unlock the best results', *Times Online*. Available at: http://business.timesonline.co.uk/tol/business/related_reports/business_solutions/article5308939.ece; http://bx.businessweek.com/millennials-at-work/mutual-trust-and-loyalty-are-the-keys-that-will-unlock-the-best-results/16086575364626302333-09211a4fdf8f02d4326677101a2defe2.

'"New-Generation Workers" want technology their way, Accenture survey finds' (2008) *Business Wire*. Available at: www.reuters.com/article/pressRelease/idUS152519+05-Nov-2008+BW20081105; www.verticalnews.com/newsletters/Journal-of-Technology/2008-11-18/2986TE.html.

Sujansky, J. G. (2009) 'Spoiled, impatient and entitled: why you need strong Millennials in your workplace', *Exchange Magazine*. Available at: www.exchangemagazine.com/morningpost/2009/week30/Thursday/072406.htm.

Tapscott, D. (2008) *Grown Up Digital*. Columbus, OH: McGraw-Hill.

Twentyman, J. (2009) 'Skills: business must learn from the new tribe', *Financial Times*. Available at: www.ft.com/cms/s/0/497a9870-4a54-11de-8e7e-00144feabdc0.html.

Us Now, available at www.usnowfilm.com, a film about how the Internet and global collaboration is changing the way we share information, engage in social life and make sense of work.

Note: This feature was written by Gretchen Fox, PhD, Anthropologist, Timberline Natural Resource Group, Canada.

Chapter summary

- Comparative international analyses of concepts and theoretical debates, as well as policies and programmes, provide an important basis for understanding how technology is related to work and organizational behaviour. We propose a broad, multilevel approach suggesting that technology should be thought of as a social phenomenon, recognizing both consent and conflict in processes of adoption. In reviewing these areas, we are aided by a general understanding of the ideologies of technological thought, which we summarised early on. How do specific technologies and attempts at technological adoption relate to the technocratic, substantive, constructivist or critical approaches? For example, how do the substantive critiques of Heidegger or Ellul colour the messages offered by the likes of Negroponte, Castells and Reich?[3,5,97] And what can the constructivist approach of Suchman, Latour or Callon add to the deskilling/enskilling debates surrounding ICT, work and organizational behaviour, and so on?

- After reading this chapter, a variety of answers to these and other questions should begin to emerge, but perhaps more importantly you should be in a better position to understand, evaluate and perhaps even affect the current landscape and direction of ICT, work and related issues. These are all important matters in our society today.

Key concepts

co-determination	315
configurations	311
four key forms of technological thought	313
ICT and deskilling	321
ICT and enskilling	321
Luddite revolt	312
post-industrialism	309
technology agreement	319

Key vocab for ESL students

- ☐ Configuration, configure
- ☐ Constructivist approach
- ☐ Critical approach
- ☐ Deskilling
- ☐ Enskilling
- ☐ Free-rider problem
- ☐ Information and communications technology (ICT)
- ☐ Instrumentalist, instrumental
- ☐ Knowledge worker
- ☐ Luddites
- ☐ Participatory design
- ☐ Post-industrial, post-industrialism
- ☐ Substantive approach
- ☐ Technocrat, technocratic
- ☐ Technology, technological
- ☐ Technology agreements

Chapter review questions

1. What is the substance of the claims by authors since the Second World War, such as Woodward, Bell, Blauner and others, regarding technology and changes to society?
2. What are the four key modes of technological thought?
3. Explain the deskilling and enskilling debate in the context of technological change.
4. How do different nations compare in their approach to technological development and work-based adoption?
5. How can organizational behaviour research benefit from broad understandings of international policy regarding technological development and workplace change?
6. How is the use of technology in our non-work lives different from and/or the same as the use of technology in our paid work lives, and what definitions of technology covered in this chapter help us to explain these potential differences?

Chapter research questions

1. Much is made (often with good reason) of how technological literacy is strongly affected by age or generational cohorts. Take a moment to share your experiences with some classmates concerning how your generation is different from others in terms of technological literacy. Do you feel that your technological literacy will affect or has affected your future work opportunities in some way? Has the technological literacy of younger generations been effectively utilized in the workplace in your view? In what way?

2. Technology in organizations has many faces and just as many expected and unexpected effects on work. A book by Boreham, Parker, Thompson and Hall entitled *New Technology @ Work* (published by Routledge in 2008) provides a detailed and conceptually powerful overview of this diversity of forms and outcomes. Although the book addresses several of the topics dealt with in this chapter, two of the chapters address topics for which we have not made space: how technology is currently shaping the work of managers and professionals (Chapter 5), and how technology is related to contemporary distributed work and telework situations (Chapter 6). The authors give us plenty of food for thought on these topics. Review either Chapter 5 or 6 of this book (you might also want to take a moment to familiarize yourself with the terminology the authors use by looking at the two opening chapters as well), and discuss with a classmate whether you feel that current technologies are changing work for the better, for the worse, or a bit of both.

3. At first glance, it may not seem to be connected to the issues discussed in this chapter, but wiki technologies such as Wikipedia may have something important to teach us about the processes of technological development in organizations. It may seem even less obvious to suggest that one excellent starting point for understanding such linkages can be found in a book about patent-granting procedures. However, in a book entitled *Wiki Government: How Technology Can Make Government Better, Democracy Stronger and Citizens More Powerful* by Noveck (published by Brookings Institution Press, 2009), we can find information that has the potential to stimulate our thinking in this area very well indeed. Although the book is focused on how wiki technologies can be used in

government and civil society (as the title suggests), it can also, with some creative thinking, be used to help us re-imagine how various technologies can be developed at and for work as well. From YouTube and Mozilla's Firefox browser to Amazon's Mechanical Turk and the Internet Movie Database (IMDb), we see examples in the society of how technologies can be developed collectively (and usually voluntarily) in ways that undoubtedly have the potential to harness more, not less, human creativity: what Noveck refers to as 'unleashing the cognitive surplus' (p. 7). Indeed, if we pay attention, we can find similar attempts in the workplace. What exactly might such processes mean for the future of organizations? Take some time to review the sections of Noveck's book that interest you the most, and then take some time to creatively consider how such approaches might be used in work organizations, and what their likely effects would be, as well as the potential pitfalls. Is there a revolutionary transformation hidden in such approaches to technology – or are these approaches just as likely to produce the kind of uneven and occasionally contradictory outcomes we have seen in the past?

Further reading

Beirne, M. and Ramsay, H. (eds) (1992) *Information Technology and Workplace Democracy*, London: Routledge & Kegan Paul.

Bell, D. (1973) *The Coming of the Post-Industrial Society*, New York: Basic Books.

Ellis, V. and Taylor, P. (2006) '"You don't know what you've got till it's gone": recontextualising the origins, development and impact of the call centre', *New Technology, Work and Employment*, **21**(2), pp. 107–22.

Gee, J., Hull, G. and Lankshear, C. (1996) *The New Work Order: Behind the Language of the New Capitalism*, Boulder, CO: Westview.

Noble, D. (1984) *The Forces of Production: A Social History of Industrial Automation*, New York: Knopf.

Thomson, R. (ed.) (1993) *Learning and Technological Change*, New York: St Martin's Press.

Zersan, J. and Carnes, A. (eds) (1991) *Questioning Technology: Tool, Toy or Tyrant*, Philadelphia, PA: New Society.

Chapter case study 1

Technological change at the Observer–Herald newspaper

The setting for this case study is London, UK, in 1980. The Observer–Herald newspaper has been around for over a half a century, and printing workers there, as elsewhere, have been regarded as master craftworkers, building their skill, knowledge and judgement through distinctive apprenticeships. Over the years, they have earned high wages, exercised considerable control over their work environments, and by and large been indispensable to the production process. Relations between the printers and management at the newspaper are good. Each respects the other, and each views the product (one of the leading daily newspapers in the country) with a good deal of pride.

But the 1970s had seen growing unemployment. Industry all over Britain had seen the introduction on the shop floor of new automated computer technologies. Computers were being touted in manufacturing and even in office work as the way of the future. Workers all over feared for their jobs and their future. Printing industry trade journals had for several years been talking about technological change too. New 'computerized' presses were said to be able to save companies thousands of hours of labour.

James Armstrong, a master printer at the Observer–Herald, had decades of experience in the detailed work of typesetting the text of the newspaper. However, on a cool spring evening, James arrived at work to face a new challenge. Along with the other printers, he had been called to a meeting, at which he learned that the newspaper would be introducing new computer-based typesetting technology. He felt a stone in his stomach. His ideas about his work were transformed.

'Together, we've got over a hundred and fifty of years of knowledge,' James said to the manager. 'Do you really think a machine can replace that!'

Craig Withnall, the production manager, had known James and the rest of the print workers for a long time. He looked sympathetically toward them and then turned to James. 'I know what you're saying, Jim. But if the company didn't think it would work, they wouldn't be doing this. You'll all have a job here, rest assured. It will just be different. You'll have to learn some new things, that's all.'

Tasks

1. After reviewing the suggested readings below along with this chapter, what do you think will change in terms of skill level, control and sense of the job for James and his fellow printers?

2. What is gained and lost in technological change initiatives of this kind? Are there ways in which you can see the company building on the years of knowledge and experience of workers like James, or is the replacement of such skills and knowledge simply inevitable?

Sources of additional information

Gordon, D. (1976) 'Capitalist efficiency and socialist efficiency', *Monthly Review*, **28**, pp. 19–39.

Wallace, M. and Kalleberg, A. (1982) 'Industrial transformation and the decline of craft: the decomposition of skill in the printing industry, 1931–1978', *American Sociological Review*, **47**, pp. 307–24.

Website: see http://atschool.eduweb.co.uk/trinity/t_and_g.html for information on technology and gender.

Note

This case study was written by Peter Sawchuk, Associate Professor, University of Toronto, Canada.

Web-based assignment

There are few words that appear as often as the word 'technology' on the Internet today. In many ways computers, the Internet and technology are thought of as synonymous with one another. However, one of the goals of this chapter is build a more 'social' analysis of technology, and to encourage you to think carefully about what technology really means. Building a basic historical awareness of different sorts of tools, devices, machines and so on can be helpful in this respect.

Visit http://inventors.about.com/od/astartinventions/a/ FamousInvention.htm, which does not present a definitive historical account of the origins of different technologies (in the broader sense), but is worth exploring to begin to gain a sense of how technology developed. Based on this, you can then build a deeper and more critical appreciation for how and why specific forms of technology emerged, and in turn, why they affect organizations in the way that they do.

OB in film

The film *Enemy of the State* (1998) features a successful labour lawyer, Robert Clayton Dean (played by Will Smith), who without his knowledge is given a video that ties a top official of the US National Security Agency (NSA) to a political murder. NSA agents use sophisticated technology to target Dean and disrupt every aspect of his private life. Dean and his colleague (played by Gene Hackman) use their wits and computing skills to survive.

What does the film illustrate about the abuse of communication and surveillance technology in society? How is the Internet affecting our lives in the home and the workplace?

References

1 Patel, D. (2002) *Workplace Forecast: A Strategic Outlook 2002–2003*, Washington: Society for Human Resource Management.

2 Organization for Economic Co-operation and Development (1999) *The Knowledge-Based Economy: A Set of Facts and Figures*, Paris: OECD.

3 Reich, R. (1991) *The Work of Nations: Preparing Ourselves for 21ˢᵗ Century Capitalism*, New York: Knopf/London: Simon & Schuster.

4 Thomson, R. (ed.) (1993) *Learning and Technological Change*, New York: St. Martin's Press.

5 Castells, M. (1996) *The Rise of the Network Society*, Volume 1, Oxford: Blackwell.

6 Archibugi, D. and Lundvall, B. (eds) (2001) *The Globalising Learning Economy*, Oxford: Oxford University Press.

7 Anderson, A. H. and Kyprianou, A. (1994) *Effective Organizational Behavior: A Skills and Activity-based Approach*, Oxford: Blackwell.

8 Woodward, J. (1965) *Industrial Organizations: Theory and Practice*, London: Oxford University Press.

9 Thompson, J. D. (1967) *Organizations in Action*, New York: McGraw-Hill.

10 Perrow, C. B. (1970) *Organizational Analysis: A Sociological View*, Belmont, CA: Brooks Cole.

11 Bell, D. (1973) *The Coming of the Post-Industrial Society*, New York: Basic Books.

12 Porter, J. (1971) *Towards 2000: The Future of Post-Secondary Education in Ontario*, Toronto: McClelland & Stewart.

13 Touraine, A. (1971) *The Post-Industrial Society: Tomorrow's Social History: Classes, Conflicts and Culture in the Programmed Society*, New York: Random House.

14 Richta, R. (1969) *Civilization at the Crossroads*, White Plains, NY: International Arts and Science Press.

15 Kumar, K. (1978) *Prophecy and Progress*, Harmondsworth: Penguin.

16 Von Tunzelmann, G. N. (1978) *Steam Power and British Industrialization to 1860*, Oxford: Clarendon Press.

17 Devine, W. (1983) 'From shafts to wires: historical perspective on electrification', *Journal of Economic History*, **43**, pp. 347–72.

18 Gospel, H. (ed.) (1991) *Industrial Training and Technological Innovation: A Comparative and Historical Perspective*, London: Routledge & Kegan Paul.

19 Lipsey, R. G., Bekar, C. and Carlaw, K. (1998) 'What requires explanation?', in E. Helpman (ed.), *General Purpose Technologies and Economic Growth*, Cambridge, MA: MIT Press.

20 Hughes, F. (1983) *Networks of Power*, Baltimore, MD: Johns Hopkins University Press.

21 Noble, D. (1979) 'Social choice in machine design: the case of automatically controlled machine tools', pp. 18–50 in A. Zimbalist (ed.), *Case Studies on the Labour Process*, New York: Monthly Review Press.

22 Noble, D. (1984) *The Forces of Production: A Social History of Industrial Automation*, New York: Knopf.

23 Lazonick, W. (1993) 'Learning and the dynamics of international competitive advantage', pp. 172–97 in R. Thomson (ed.), *Learning and Technological Change*, New York: St Martin's Press.

24 Fleck, J. (1993) 'Configurations: crystallizing contingency', *International Journal of Human Factors in Manufacturing*, **3**(1), pp. 15–36.

25 Franklin, U. (1990) *The Real World of Technology*, Toronto: CBC Enterprises.

26 Hacker, S. (1991) *Doing it the Hard Way: Investigations of Gender and Technology*, Winchester, MA: Unwin Hyman.

27 Mumford, L. (1964) 'Authoritarian and democratic technics', *Technology and Culture*, **5**(1), pp. 1–8.

28 Latour, B. (2000) 'Technology is society made durable', pp. 41–53 in K. Grint (ed.), *Work and Society: A Reader*, Cambridge: Polity Press.

29 Feenberg, A. (1991) *Critical Theory of Technology*, New York: Oxford University Press.

30 Jones, B. (1988) 'Work and flexible automation in Britain: a review of developments and possibilities', *Work, Employment and Society*, **2**(4), pp. 451–86.

31 Lazonick, W. (1979) 'Industrial relations and technical change: the case of the self-acting mule', *Cambridge Journal of Economics*, **3**, pp. 231–62.

32 Louli, C. and Bickerton, G. (1995) 'Decades of change, decades of struggle: postal workers and technological change', pp. 216–32 in C. Schenk and K. Anderson (eds), *Re-Shaping Work: Union Responses to Technological Change*, Toronto: Our Times.

33 Kraft, P. (1977) *Programmers and Managers: The Routinisation of Computer Programming in the United States*, New York: Springer-Verlag.

34 Zimbalist, A. (ed.) (1979) *Case Studies on the Labor Process*, New York: Monthly Review Press.

35 Wallace, M. and Kalleberg, A. (1982) 'Industrial transformation and the decline of craft: the decomposition of skill in the printing industry, 1931–1978', *American Sociological Review*, **47**, pp. 307–24.

36 Cockburn, C. (1985) *Machinery of Dominance: Men, Women and Technical Know-how*, London: Pluto.

37 Smith, P. (1988) 'The impact of trade unionism and the market in a regional newspaper', *Industrial Relations Journal*, **19**, pp. 214–21.

38 Roszak, T. (1994) *The Cult of Information: A Neo-Luddite Treatise on High Tech, Artificial Intelligence and the True Art of Thinking*, Berkeley, CA: University of California Press.

39 Sale, K. (1995) *Rebels Against the Future: The Luddites and their War on the Industrial Revolution – Lessons for the Computer Age*, London: Addison Wesley.

40 Williams, R. and Edge, D. (1996) 'The social shaping of technology', *Research Policy*, **25**, pp. 856–99.

41 Dahrendorf, R. (1959) *Class and Class Conflict in an Industrial Society*, London: Routledge & Kegan Paul.

42 Kerr, C. (1962) *Industrialism and Industrial Man*, London: Heinemann.

43 Naisbitt, J. (1982) *Megatrends: Ten New Directions Transforming our Lives*, New York: Warner.

44 Ellul, J. (1964) *The Technological Society*, New York: Vintage.

45 Heidegger, M. (1977) *The Question Concerning Technology*, New York: Harper & Row.

46 Callon, M. (1992) 'The dynamics of techno-economic networks', pp. 72–102 in R. Coombs, P. Saviotti and V. Walsh (eds), *Technological Change and Company Strategy: Economic and Social Perspectives*, London: Harcourt Brace.

47 Suchman, L. (1987) *Plans and Situated Action: The Problem of Human–Computer Communication*, New York: Cambridge University Press.

48 Rip, A., Misa, T. and Schot, J. (eds) (1995) *Managing Technology in Society: The Approach of Constructive Technology Assessment*, London: Pinter.

49 Suchman, L. (2002) 'Practice-based design of information systems: notes from the hyperdeveloped world', *Information Society*, **18**, pp. 139–44.

50 Latour, B. (1988) 'How to write "The Prince" for machines as well as machinations', pp. 20–43 in B. Elliott (ed.), *Technology and Social Process*, Edinburgh: Edinburgh University Press.

51 Gartner, J. and Wagner, I. (1996) 'Mapping actors and agendas: political frameworks of systems design and participation', *Human–Computer Interaction*, **11**, pp. 187–214.

52 Mani, S. (2002) *Government, Innovation and Technology Policy: An International Comparative Analysis*, Cheltenham: Edward Elgar.

53 Carnoy, M., Pollack, S. and Wong, P. L. (1993) *Labour Institutions and Technological Change: A Framework for Analysis and a Review of the Literature*, Stanford University/International Labour Organization.

54 Livingstone, D. and Sawchuk, P. (2004) *Hidden Knowledge: Organized Labour in the Information Age*, Toronto: Garamond/ Washington, DC: Rowman & Littlefield.

55 Archibugi, D. and Coco, A. (2000) *The Globalisation of Technology and the European Innovation System*, Rome: Italian National Research Council.

56 Kelley, M. R. (1990) 'New process technology, job design and work organization: a contingency model', *American Sociological Review*, **55**, pp. 191–208.

57 Grubb, N. (1996) *Learning to Work: The Case for Reintegrating Job Training and Education*, New York: Russell Sage Foundation.

58 *Industrial Policy: Investing in America* (1993) Volume 5, Number 1.

59 Herman, B. (2001) 'How high-road partnerships work', *Social Policy*, **31**(3), pp. 11–19.

60 Sharpe, A. (1997) *Sectoral Skills Councils in Canada: Future Challenges*, Ottawa: Human Resources Development Canada.

61 Simonyi, C. (2003) 'Future view: software jobs will be mechanized in long run'. Available at: www.informationweek.com/news/global-cio/training/showArticle.jhtml?articleID=16100723 (accessed October 2, 2009).

62 Schenk, C. and Anderson, J. (eds) (1995) *Re-Shaping Work: Union Responses to Technological Change*, Toronto: Our Times.

63 Cressey, P. and Di Martino, V. (1991) *Agreement and Innovation: The International Dimension of Technological Change*, New York: Prentice Hall.

64 Ehn, P. (1988) *Work-Oriented Design of Computer Artifacts*, Stockholm: Arbetslivscentrum.

65 Bjerknes, G., Ehn, P. and Kyng M. (eds) (1987) *Computers and Democracy: A Scandinavian Challenge*, Aldershot: Avebury.

66 Beirne, M. and Ramsay, H. (eds) (1992) *Information Technology and Workplace Democracy*, London: Routledge & Kegan Paul.

67 Poster, M. (2002) 'Workers as cyborgs: labor and networked computers', *Journal of Labor Research*, **23**(3), pp. 339–54.

68 Evans, J. (1983) 'Negotiating technological change', pp. 152–68 in H. J. Otway and M. Pletu (eds), *New Office Technology: Human and Organizational Aspects*, London: Frances Pinter.

69 Small, M. and Yasin, M. (2000) 'Human factors in the adoption and performance of advanced manufacturing technology in unionized firms', *Industrial Management & Data Systems*, **100**(8–9), pp. 389–401.

70 Hyman, R. (1991) 'Plus ça charge? The theory of production and the production of theory', pp. 259–83 in A. Pollert (ed.), *Farewell to Flexibility?*, Oxford: Blackwell.

71 Gee, J., Hull, G. and Lankshear, C. (1996) *The New Work Order: Behind the Language of the New Capitalism*, Boulder, CO: Westview.

72 Berg, I. (1970) *Education and Jobs: The Great Training Robbery*, New York: Praeger.

73 Livingstone, D. (1999) *The Education Jobs Gap*, Toronto: Garamond.

74 Sawchuk, P. (2003) *Adult Learning and Technology in Working-class Life*, New York: Cambridge University Press.

75 Lowe, G. (2000) *The Quality of Work: A People-centred Agenda*, New York: Oxford University Press.

76 Doeringer, P. B. and Piore, M. (1971) *Internal Labor Markets and Manpower Analysis*, Lexington, MA: C. Heath.

77 Mishel, L. and Voos, P. (eds) (1992) *Unions and Economic Competitiveness*, New York: M. E. Sharpe.

78 Braverman, H. (1974) *Labor and Monopoly Capitalism: The Degradation of Work in the Twentieth Century*, New York: Monthly Review Press.

79 Penn, R. and Scattergood, H. (1985) 'Deskilling or enskilling?: an empirical investigation of recent theories of the labour process', *British Journal of Sociology*, **36**(4), pp. 611–30.

80 Glenn, E. and Feldberg, R. (1979) 'Proletarianizing clerical work: technology and organizational control in the office', pp. 51–72 in A. Zimbalist (ed.), *Case Studies on the Labor Process*, New York: Monthly Review Press.

81 Shaiken, H., Herzenberg, S. and Kuhn, S. (1986) 'The work process under more flexible production', *Industrial Relations*, **25**, pp. 167–83.

82 Hyman, R. (1982) 'What ever happened to industrial sociology?', in D. Dunkerley and G. Salaman (eds), *The International Yearbook of Organisation Studies 1981*, London: Routledge & Kegan Paul.

83 Burris, B. (1999) 'Braverman, Taylorism and technocracy', in M. Wardell, T. Steiger and P. Meiksins (eds), *Rethinking the Labor Process*, New York: SUNY.

84 Rothman, H. K. (2000) 'What has work become?', *Journal of Labor Research*, **21**(3), pp. 379–92.

85 Friedmann, G. (1961) *The Anatomy of Work*, Glencoe, IL: Free Press.

86 Blauner, R. (1964) *Alienation and Freedom: The Factory Worker and his Industry*, Chicago: University of Chicago Press.

87 Piore, M. and Sabel, C. (1984) *The Second Industrial Divide*, New York: Basic Books.

88 Sorge, A. and Streeck, W. (1988) 'Industrial relations and technical change: the case for an extended perspective', pp. 19–47 in R. Hyman and W Streeck (eds), *New Technology and Industrial Relations*, Oxford: Blackwell.

89 Form, W., Kaufman, R., Parcel, T. and Wallace, M. (1988) 'The impact of technology on work organization and work outcomes', pp. 303–28 in G. Farkas and P. England (eds), *Industries, Firms and Jobs: Sociology and Economic Approaches*, New York: Plenum.

90 Lam, A. (2002) 'Alternative societal models of learning and innovation in the knowledge economy', *International Social Science Journal*, March, pp. 67–82.

91 Darrah, C. (1994) 'Skill requirements at work: rhetoric versus reality', *Work and Occupations*, **21**(1), pp. 64–84.

92 Darrah, C. (1996) *Learning and Work: An Exploration in Industrial Ethnography*, New York: Garland.

93 Darrah, C. (1999) *Learning Tools Within a Context: History and Scope*, Washington, DC: US Department of Education, National Institute on Postsecondary Education, Libraries, and Lifelong Learning.

94 Luff, P., Hindmarsh, J. and Heath, C. (2000) *Workplace Studies: Recovering Work Practice and Informing System Design*, New York: Cambridge University Press.

95 Engeström, Y and Middleton, D. (1992) *Cognition and Communication at Work*, New York: Cambridge University Press.

96 Sawchuk, Peter H. (2006) '"Use-value" and the re-thinking of skills, learning and the labour process', *Journal of Industrial Relations*, **48**(5), pp. 589–613.

97 Negroponte, N. (1995) *Being Digital*, New York: Knopf.

chapter 12
Organizational culture

chapter outline

- Introduction
- National culture and culture dimensions
- Understanding organizational culture
- Perspectives on organizational culture
- Managing cultures
- Summary and end-of-chapter features
- Chapter case study: Changing the University of Daventry's culture

chapter objectives

After studying this chapter, you should be able to:

- explain the relationship between national culture and organizational culture
- define organizational culture and be aware of its importance for understanding behaviour in the workplace and organizational performance
- explain the three levels of organizational culture and notions of dominant culture, cultural diversity, subcultures and countercultures
- explain mainstream and critical theoretical perspectives on organizational culture
- describe how managers seek to manage cultures and how leaders strive to change the culture of their organization

an *individualist* culture in which the ties between individuals are loose and everyone is expected to look after themselves and their immediate family. In the West, assertiveness has been much advocated as a way for women to communicate, but communication scholars point out that the effectiveness of this means of communicating is culture related (see Chapter 14).

The work of Geert Hofstede and his core assumption that countries have a singular national culture has attracted considerable criticism. The empirical basis for his assertion that a national population shares a singular culture is based on a statistical averaging of the quantitative data – the survey responses from IBM's employees. An average of personal values claiming to measure the values of a national culture is about as meaningful as an average of personal income. As has been well established elsewhere, in the same way that there is a wide variance in personal income in any population, so there is wide dispersion in the personal values of that population.[10]

Among the developed countries in the global economy, few are likely to exhibit a single cultural orientation, but they are more likely to have a plural orientation with hyphenated identities such as African-American, Chinese-Canadian, Anglo-Indian and so on. The empirical evidence at the centre of Hofstede's claims is problematic, and the term 'national culture' is misleading. Nonetheless, deep cultural undercurrents structure human behaviour in subtle but highly regular ways, and managers and other employees carry their cultural heritage and ethnicity to the workplace.[11] Research on the relationships of national cultures, based mainly on values, to organizational cultures are, however, 'loose ones'.[6] Sociological research demonstrates that cultural diversity is a global fact of human life. In the face of such plurality, will this diversity be reflected at work?

The problem of identifying a national culture is soon apparent when we examine values. Taking Britain or Australia, for example, just what are core 'British values' or core 'Australian values'? How do we complete the phrases 'as British as . . .?' or 'as Australian as . . .?'

stop reflect

Understanding organizational culture

The notion of organizational culture is a complex concept because it lends itself to very different uses. In the literature, the terms 'corporate culture', 'organizational culture' and 'organizational climate' are common. The distinction between corporate culture and organizational culture is that the former is devised and transmitted down to subordinates by management executives as part of a strategy of mobilizing employee commitment, and emphasizes actors as 'culture-takers'. Organizational culture, on the other hand, is a product of members' creativity and emphasizes actors as 'culture-makers'.[12]

Schneider[1] notes that '*organizational climate*' is the 'elder child' in cultural scholarship, and the terms *culture* and *climate* are used interchangeably by some culture researchers. Others refer to the disagreements over whether the two concepts are distinguishable constructs as 'paradigm wars'.[13] Organizational culture and organizational climate are two complementary constructs, but reveal overlapping nuances in the social and psychological life of complex organizations. The former tends to take a sociological approach, using qualitative methodology derived from anthropology, to examine symbolic and cultural forms of organizations. Climate researchers, however, attempt to measure individuals' perceptions of autonomy, leadership, growth or whatever (see Critical Insight, p. 351), and the meaning they assign to them, using quantitative methods derived from the nomothetic traditions in organizational psychology. The distinction between culture research and climate research lies in the different methodological traditions, what they consider to be significantly meaningful and their agendas. The sociologist Martin Parker argues that the psychological treatment of culture largely reflects 'a neo-human relations agenda' (ref. 14,

p. 132).(For a discussion on epistemological and ontological issues, see Chapter 1, and for an introduction to the human relations movement, see Chapter 3.)

table 12.1 Some definitions of organizational culture

Social or normative glue that holds an organization together ... The values or social ideals and the beliefs that organization members come to share. These values or patterns of beliefs are manifested by symbolic devices, such as myths, stories, legends and specialized language. (Smircich, 1983, p. 344)[20]
Talking about organizational culture seems to mean talking about the importance for people of symbolism – of rituals, myths, stories and legends – and about the interpretation of events, ideas, and experiences that are influenced and shaped by the groups within which they live. (Frost et al., 1985, p. 17)[101]
The shared beliefs and values guiding the thinking and behavioral styles of members. (Cooke and Rousseau, 1988, p. 245)[102]
Culture is 'how things are done around here'. It is what is typical of the organization, the habits, prevailing attitudes and grown-up pattern of accepted and expected behaviour. (Drennan, 1992, p. 3)[103]
For me values are less central and less useful than meanings and symbolism in cultural analysis ... Culture is not primarily 'inside' people's heads, but somewhere 'between' the heads of a group of people where symbols and meanings are publicly expressed, for example in work group interactions, in board meetings but also in material objects. Culture then is central in governing the understanding of behaviour, social events, institutions and processes. Culture is the setting in which these phenomena become comprehensible and meaningful. (Alvesson, 2002, pp. 3–4)[36]

Writers have offered various definitions of organizational culture (Table 12.1), and a synthesis of these definitions captures most of the essential elements of organizational culture. It is about the importance of the shared values, beliefs and language that shape and perpetuate this network of values of organizational reality, so that employees behave predictably to achieve the organization's goals.

To help us understand organizational culture, we need to examine its parts, even though any organizational culture is greater than the sum of its parts. Drawing on the work of Edgar Schein,[15] Figure 12.2 shows three fundamental levels of organizational culture: *artefacts*, *values* and *basic assumptions*. These can be imagined as the skins of an onion, artefacts representing the less abstract and basic assumptions the deepest manifestations of organizational culture, with values lying in between. Here, we use an alternative image, the iceberg. The uppermost subtriangle might be viewed as the 'tip of an iceberg' representing observable parts of organizational culture, which are embedded in shared values, basic assumptions and beliefs that are invisible to the human eye. Each level of culture influences another level.

The first level shown in Figure 12.2 comprises visible culture, the *artefacts* and material objects such as buildings, technology, art and uniforms that the organization 'uses' to express its culture. For example, when a company only uses e-mail for internal communication, the cultural message is that IT is a highly valued resource. Displaying art on office walls signals to members and visitors that creating a stimulating cultural context in which employees can explore ideas and aesthetics is highly valued.[16] Other examples are the wearing of a professorial gown in universities and the doctor's white coat in the National Health Service.

The visible culture also includes *language*. How managers describe other employees is an example of using symbols to convey meaning to each other. For example, Walmart refers to its employees as 'associates', and at Disneyland they are known as 'cast members'. Social *behaviour* is another aspect of observable

Looking at Table 12.1, does your university have a culture? How does this differ within and between different faculties, schools or departments within the university?

stop reflect

rituals: the programmed routines of daily organizational life that dramatize the organization's culture

ceremonies: planned events that represent more formal social artefacts than rituals

organizational culture and includes rituals and ceremonies. **Rituals** are collective routines that 'dramatize' the organization's culture. For example, the office party can be viewed as a ritual for *integrating* new members into the organization. **Ceremonies** are planned and represent more formal social artefacts than rituals, for example the 'call to the bar' ceremony for graduating lawyers.

Visit http://en.wikipedia.org/wiki/Organizational_culture for more information on Edgar Schein

weblink

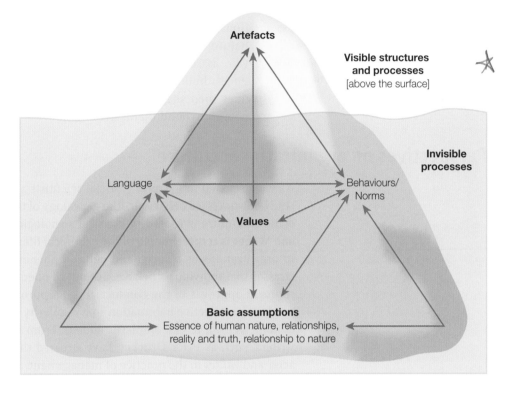

figure 12.2 The three levels of organizational culture

plate 40 Rituals are collective routines that 'dramatize' the organization's culture. For example, the office party can be viewed as a ritual for integrating new members to the organization. Ceremonies are planned and represent more formal social artefacts than rituals, for example the 'call to the bar' ceremony for graduating lawyers.

Source: Catherine Travers

The second level of organizational culture comprises shared work-related *values*, which are not visible, but which we recognize influence patterns of observable behaviour at work. For example, in healthcare, standard medical practice is influenced by a belief in evidence or a commitment to patient-centred care. In many universities, practice is influenced by the espoused value of 'We are a teaching-centred institution.' Employment-related espoused values possess six characteristics:

1. They involve moral or ethical statements of 'rightness'.
2. They pertain to desirable modes of behaviour at a given point in time.
3. They directly influence employee behaviour and experiences, and act as significant moderators.
4. They are typically associated with strategic goals and address questions like 'What are we doing?' and 'Why are we doing this?'
5. They guide the selection and evaluation of members.
6. They may vary in respect to male/female, demographic and cultural differences,[17] for example that women in the armed forces should not engage in combat roles.

The term 'shared' in cultural analysis implies that organizational members are a whole. Each member has been exposed to a set of dominant values, although not every member may internalize and endorse them.

The third level of organizational culture relates to *basic assumptions*, which are invisible, unconscious, taken for granted, difficult to access and highly resistant to change. These are the implicit and unspoken assumptions that underpin everyday choices and shape how members perceive, think and emotionally react to social events. For example, in healthcare, assumptions about the relative roles of doctors and nurses, about patients' rights or about the sources of ill-health underpin everyday decisions and actions.[18] The basic assumptions/beliefs about human nature, human relationships, relationship to nature and how the world works form the base from which employees, who as social beings enter the workplace with life histories and experiences, build their values of how the world *should* be. Assumptions and values then shape organizational behaviour and the artefacts with which members surround themselves.

> **stop reflect**
>
> Think about your own university or college. As a student, do you expect a student-centred focus? Are teaching and support staff helpful? Do teaching staff primarily focus on their teaching or on research interests? Try to assess your answer at three levels: observable artefacts, shared values and basic assumptions of the culture

Perspectives on organizational culture

As we discussed in Chapter 1, social scientists adopt different perspectives on the study of workplace behaviour. The genealogy of the different perspectives on organizational culture is rooted in classical sociological theory. The work of Durkheim and Weber is representative of the canonical literature on understanding behaviour in organizations as a social and cultural phenomenon. Here, for example, Weber stresses that individuals behave 'not out of obedience, but either because the environment approves of the conduct and disapproves of its opposite, or merely as a result of unreflective habituation to a regularity of life that has *engraved itself as a custom*' (ref. 19, p. 312, emphasis added). From the 1950s, influential management writers, such as Peter Drucker, have stressed the importance of *integrity* of character and *values* in the practice of management.

Contemporary culture analysis can essentially be divided into what by now should be two familiar schools of thought: managerialist and critical. The managerialist-oriented perspective on the topic is functionalist in that theorists in this school stress the value of culture from the premise that it can play a role in building organizational consensus, building harmony and improving performance. Organizational culture is viewed as a *variable* – an attribute that an organization possesses or '*has*', and as such can be produced by senior managers.[20] The critical-oriented school, on the other hand, focuses on describing and critically explaining cultural processes, how culture emerges through day-to-day social interaction, power relations, shaping communities of practice, emotion and norms of workplace behaviour. Viewed through a sociologist's lens, culture is something that a work organization '*is*' and emphasizes the symbolic, consciousness and subjective aspects of the workplace, the role of culture in strengthening management control over employees, and the interrelationships between organizational cultures *inside* and social inequalities *outside* the workplace.

The managerialist perspective on organizational culture

functional theory: a sociological perspective emphasizing that human action is governed by relatively stable structures

The **functionalist** perspective is based on the assumption that the organization is a stable, orderly system that serves specific functions. Organizational culture, in terms of attitudes, beliefs, values and norms, is generated and managed according to organizational goals and needs. Cultural analysis from a functionalist perspective is based on the theoretical insights of Emile Durkheim, whose sociological studies focus on the integrative and social stabilizing ability of culture.

Neo-management theorists primarily understand organizational culture as a unifying phenomenon, in which cultural processes can create organizational stability and consensus, focusing on how culture can be managed and disseminated downwards by senior management. Thus, mainstream theorists are said, in Martin's words, to follow an '*integration*' perspective. In this sense, management-inspired cultural processes and interventions attempt to mitigate the many forms of the ever-present conflict that arise from managing the labour process. This approach focuses on building a culture that binds members together around the same core values, beliefs and norms, which are considered prerequisites for achieving strategic goals. For integration or functionalism theorists, culture is conceptualized as 'organization-wide agreement with values espoused by top management'.[21] The notion of 'cultural engineering' – creating the 'right' kind of culture to align with strategic goals – is seen as a 'lever' for fostering commitment and loyalty in the workforce.

Searching for excellence and innovation

A cluster of functionalist writers put forward ideas about causality by attempting to demonstrate positive linkages between the 'right' corporate culture and performance.[3,22,23] Within this genre, Peters and Waterman's influential pop-management book, *In Search of Excellence*, is probably the best well-known example of the 'has' school. These gurus view culture as an elixir that binds together specific human qualities and skills that lead to organizational excellence and success. They write:

> What our framework has really done is to remind the world of professional managers that 'soft is hard'. It has enabled us to say, in effect, 'All that stuff you have been dismissing for so long as the intractable, irrational, intuitive, informal organization *can* be managed ... you [are] foolish to ignore it.' (ref. 22, p. 11)

What constitutes the 'right culture' for excellence is a matter of debate. A popular approach in functionalism is *contingency* theory (see Chapter 13). Based on the belief that senior managers need to consider a range of different external and internal variables when deciding what kind of culture best fits their particular organization, Deal and Kennedy[23] and Handy[24] identify a fourfold typology of culture, in which the choice of each culture depends on an assessment of organizational situations. Contingencies that have been identified as important include level of risk, size and design of the organization, ownership and governance, market preference, technology, national culture and need for innovation.

For functionalist theorists, leaders can create 'strong' corporate cultures. Leadership studies consider change as a situation-driven contingency that moderates the effectiveness of certain leadership styles. It is suggested that transformational leadership is especially effective in shaping and guiding organizations towards innovation-oriented cultures. Thus, in Rosabeth Moss Kanter's *The Change Masters*, she notes that employees 'find their stability and security not in specific organizational arrangements but in the *culture* and direction of the organization. It requires that they feel *integrated with the whole* rather than identified with the particular territory of the moment, since that is changeable' (emphasis added).[25] In turn, the 'right' culture is counterposed to bureaucratic cultures. In Hammer and Champy's *Reengineering the Corporation*, the authors contend that 'the reigning values and beliefs in an organization must support the performance of its design process' (ref. 26, p. 81). Similarly, in Champy's *Reengineering Management*, it is posited that 'values are our moral navigational devices', and for real change to occur, leaders need 'cultural warriors' at every level of the organization to communicate new values to their peers (ref. 27, p. 79).

Whereas modern management gurus like Ouchi, Peters and Waterman, Deal and Kennedy, and Hammer and Champy focus on values that foster 'strong cultures', Handy and Kanter are more sensitive to the complexities and problematic aspects of culture (Table 12.2).

table 12.2 Typologies of organizational culture

Deal and Kennedy's ideal types	Handy's ideal types
Process culture This type is concerned with ensuring that members follow uniform procedures, and is associated with low-risk hierarchical organizations; for example, hospitals	*Role culture* This type is mechanistic and highly formalized, abounds with rules, and is dominated by authority and the hierarchical structure; for example, utility services
Work hard/play hard culture This type is team- and customer-focused and stresses 'fun' at work; for example, Google	*Person culture* This type centres around 'star' performers who are loosely attached to the organization; for example, barristers, surgeons and architects
Bet-your-company culture This type characterizes high-investment, long-term, highly technical members; for example, the NASA space agency	*Power culture* This type exhibits a single power source, with centralized policy and decision making; for example, a family-owned and operated company
Macho culture This type is characterized by fast decision making and high risk; for example, traders in merchant banks	*Task culture* This type is organic, informal and product and project based, the opposite of role culture; for example, firms of management consultants

Subcultures and counter-cultures

As is the case with anthropological studies of national cultures, contingency literature draws attention to cultural heterogeneity. Martin[28] refers to such studies as the '*differentiated*' perspective. A large complex organization, for example British Airways, might have one dominant culture expressing senior management's core values, but they also have sets of *subcultures* typically defined by professional occupations, spatial separation and departmental designations. These work groups might share a distinctive set of values, beliefs and norms that differ in some significant way from that of the organization's dominant values and philosophy. The concept of cultural heterogeneity has been applied to distinctions ranging from professional identities associated with engineers, artists, healthcare practitioners, researchers and ethnic- and religion-based groups, to small reservoirs of employees presumed to be marginalized from the larger organization as a result of distinctive work paradigms or the particular demands of the occupation. A subculture emerges to bind members working intensely together, as a means of coping with common frustrations concerning the demands of emotional labour, or as a way to preserve their distinctive identity.[29]

In the context of healthcare organizations, a recent study revealed that 'complex multiple cultural values are often hierarchical and are commonly interpreted in ways that ascribe differentiated, fragmented and collective meaning' (ref. 30, p. 61). For example, healthcare professionals may collectively interpret the espoused value of providing the 'best possible care' for patients. But the delivered 'care' will be performed differently by the various professional groups, each with distinctive interpretations of what 'best care' means. For doctors, it may mean eradicating the cause of illness, whereas for occupational therapists it may mean helping patients to achieve greater mobility and improved quality of life.[31] In contrast, a macho and highly aggressive subculture might exist among male manual workers doing repetitive, mundane work or among abattoir workers slaughtering animals.[32,33]

The analyses of subcultures reveal a wide variation in values, norms and assumptions both within and across subcultures, which might cause conflict – but this is a normal part of organizational life.

Sociologically informed analysis of culture acknowledges the existence of *counter-cultures* in organizations. As others have observed, these create their own

Does a complex organization like the UK National Health Service have subcultures? What are the management implications if core subcultures exist?

stop
reflect

form of organizational reality through a subculture that actively opposes the dominant values and norms.[34,35] For example, a change in status of an education institution, from a college to a university, may produce counter-cultures. A particular teaching faculty may strongly reject university values on research and a 'publish-or-perish' culture. In the private sector, mergers and acquisitions may produce counter-cultures. There may be a 'clash of corporate cultures' when the values, beliefs and norms held by the members of an acquired organization are inconsistent with those of the acquiring organization. The debate surrounding the existence of subcultures and counter-cultures emphasizes the complexities and interwoven character of organizational culture, and avoids an overly static and monolithic picture of everyday organizational life.

Critical perspectives on organizational culture

Although all critical theorists share a similar view on the role of culture – that values and norms are deeply embedded but can change over time – they typically see organizational culture through somewhat different lenses as they are guided by different theoretical perspectives in their research. What do these critical perspectives tell us about organizational culture? In contrast to the mainstream functionalist perspective that understands culture as something that an organization 'has', critical perspectives proceed, as we saw earlier in the chapter, from the root-metaphor idea that the organization 'is' a culture. Therefore, critical-oriented perspectives promote a view of organizations as manifestations of human consciousness, as a source of power and as a socializing and controlling force, and are studied in terms of their networks of symbols and shared meanings. Moreover, advocates of the 'is' view of culture are likely 'to play down the pragmatic results that can help management increase effectiveness in favour of more general understanding and reflection as the major emphasis of cultural studies' (ref. 36, p. 25). Here, we look at three critical-oriented perspectives: the symbolic-interactionist, the conflict and the feminist. These perspectives will serve as alternative lenses through which to see organizational culture.

The symbolic-interactionist perspective

symbolic interactionism: the sociological approach that views society as the sum of the interactions of individuals and groups

The **symbolic-interactionist** approach, using a micro-level analysis, understands organizational culture as the sum of all its members' interactions. In this school of thought, culture plays the role of a vehicle for shared meaning (hence 'symbolic'), and is produced by workers and managers in face-to-face encounters (hence 'interactionist') as they go about their everyday workplace activities. Culture is constructed by organizational actors and reproduced by the networks of symbols and meanings that workers and managers share, and that make shared social behaviour possible. The analysis of organizational culture can therefore be through studying observable artefacts, language, action and the beliefs and values of organizational members.

In the realm of shared *artefacts*, displayed mission statements, framed photographs of individuals and ceremonies, technology, paintings and sculptures are all manifestations of culture. Space is an element of culture. For example, if senior management has allocated privileged parking within the organization's boundary while others park outside in the street, the cultural message is that hierarchy and status are highly valued by the organization. Symbolic interactionists explore how *language* and emotion are used to communicate effectively in order to make social action possible. Shared stories, myths and legends serve to construct a common ground for understanding social behaviour. For example, an account of a dramatic event in the past history of the company serves to create shared meaning of how

Source: iStockphoto

plate 41 If senior management has allocated privileged parking within the organization's boundary while others park outside in the street, the cultural message is that hierarchy and status are highly valued by the organization.

workers are expected to handle problems in the present. Also scrutinized is shared social *action. R*ites commonly found in the workplace are those of acceptance (for example, an invitation to the office party), of recognition (for example, the employee of the month award), of conflict (for example, a disciplinary hearing) and of severance (for example, dismissal to emphasize unacceptable behaviour).

Symbolic interactionists also examine shared *beliefs* and *values*. Beliefs are the dominant assumptions of the organization concerning the society and how it works, while values contain an 'ought to' implicit in them. In organizational talk, the assertion of 'values' is omnipresent, either of legislative provisions not always heeded (for example, antidiscrimination laws) or of espoused values not adequately funded. Groups in the organization will clothe their proposals around 'values' rhetoric to elevate these demands over more pedestrian ones, for example diverting resources from one department to another – from production to employee training – because a core 'value' is continuous work-related learning. This approach to cultural analysis highlights how members produce and reproduce the culture of an organization through day-to-day social interaction. However, symbolic interactionism tends to underemphasize how larger social structures cause disagreement on meanings.

The conflict perspective

conflict perspective: the sociological approach that views groups in society as engaged in a continuous power struggle for the control of scarce resources

Conflict perspectives are based on the assumption that conflict is a basic feature of organizational life as members seek to control scarce resources.[37] Unlike the integration perspective, critical theorists insist on treating conflict as a central concept in exploring how values, beliefs and norms develop to sustain the power and control of senior management. The conflict perspective sets out to develop an understanding of organizational culture by situating it in the context of capitalist relations of domination and control.

As early conflict theorist Karl Marx emphasized, ideas are the cultural constructs of a society's most powerful social elite. The creation of ideas, of conceptions of consciousness, is directly interwoven with work-related activity and the material interaction of people, the language of real organizational life. As Marx states, 'The production of ideas, conceptions, of consciousness is, to begin with, immediately involved in the material activity and the material interaction of men [sic], the language of real life.'[38] Many conflict theorists agree with Marx's

ideology: a term with multiple uses, but in particular referring to perceptions of reality as distorted by class interests, and the ideas, legal arrangements and culture that arise from class relations (a term taken from Marx)

assertion that social elites use **ideology**, a non-material element of culture, to shape the thoughts and actions of members of other social classes – the common idea, for example, that an unfettered market can best decide society's economic priorities because 'Governments cannot pick winners' or 'What's good for Ford is good for America'. Public discourse often supports these views, since no other alternatives are debated or offered.

Conflict views on culture emphasize perpetual tension, conflict and resistance between different groups in the organization. This emphasis on a structured antagonism between 'capital' and 'labour', and concomitantly on managerial control, focuses on motive – the 'who' of power and the 'how' of employee commitment. It tends to dismiss conceptualizing organizational culture as the 'organization's personality' or as an overarching catch-all to describe 'the way we do things around here'. Instead, the focus is on how corporate culture attempts to generate *real*, as opposed to hollow, employee commitment and self-control by mobilizing values, beliefs and emotions. The study by Ray is an example of cultural control as an employment strategy:

> The top management team aims to have individuals possess direct ties to the values and goals of the dominant elites in order to activate the emotion and sentiment which might lead to devotion, loyalty and commitment to the company. (ref. 39. p. 294)

For Ray, control by corporate culture did not rely on direct supervision, but primarily on an acceptance of values and peer enforcement. It was the 'last frontier', in that a 'strong' corporate culture had enabled top management to generate employee emotion and commitment, at the same time internalizing control by fusing individual with corporate identity. Shared social activities outside the organization's space and time, such as weekend 'retreats' or social events for employees' families, expand cultural controls by integrating both manual staff and managerial employees, and developing a sense of community or 'family' through what Thompson and McHugh describe as a form of 'compulsory sociability' (ref. 40, p. 203).

Around this thesis has developed a body of literature which argues that cultural control overlaps and exists alongside, rather than replaces, more traditional forms of management control strategies, such as bureaucracy (see Chapter 10), new technology (see Chapter 11) and human resource management (HRM) practices (see Chapter 17). Weberian internal bureaucratic control focuses on rules, internal labour market structures and reporting hierarchies. Computer-based technology can be used for the surveillance of employees by recording attendance, output or productivity and time logged after hours as measure of commitment. The HRM function plays a central role in the development of strong corporate cultures and in managing emotion by integrating a complex array of recruitment, training, reward and discipline practices, as well as policies to deal with trade unions, if necessary, that are designed to direct work processes, to secure commitment and to control the workforce. In this sense, faced with a complex set of internal and external forces, systems of cultural hegemony do not replace but *complement* other employment strategies adopted over time that are aimed at increasing the loyalty and control of employees, and ultimately their efficiency.

The picture represented by conflict theorists is more likely to be one that represents contradictory, fluid and unstable cultures. Drawing on the postmodernist discourse that characterizes modern life as ephemeral, fragmentary and contingent,[41] Joanne Martin describes this approach to understanding culture as the 'fragmentary' perspective.[28] Organizational culture is characterized by so much ephemerality, ambiguity and change, and so exposes the truth claims of monolithic and united corporate cultures, that, she argues, culture is 'a loosely structured and incompletely shared system that emerges dynamically as cultural members experience each other, events, and the organization's contextual features' (ref. 28, p. 152). The value of this fragmentary approach to organizational culture is in its exposure of the naivety of thinking that there is no ambiguity in what cultural members believe and do. For example, it exposes claims to the espoused truth that 'We are an equal opportunity employer' while masking gender or race inequality arising from the cultural values and beliefs of a male-dominant or white-dominant workplace.[42–44]

There are other contributions to debates on organizational culture that warn of a neo-Orwellian nightmare of creeping omnipresent cultural control. Whereas Weberian sociology laments about rationalization processes creating the 'iron cage' of the modern bureaucracy, insidious corporate culture apparently seeks the 'governance of the employee's soul'. Powerful cultural processes, it is argued, seek to

**stop
reflect**

Go back to Figure 1.2. What external and internal factors drive development in managerial employment strategies? To what extent will the financial and economic crisis facing the global economy cause managers to change the mix of strategies, including cultural control, with which they experiment?

replace the 'iron cage' of bureaucratic controls with a 'velvet cage' of managed emotion, self-surveillance and self-subordination.[45–48] Others rightly acknowledge that although corporate culture is a key ideological element in the labour process, its effectiveness as the ultimate means of moulding employees' acceptance of managerial initiative should not be exaggerated. Empirical studies show the limits of culture, and reveal that employees are not passive recipients of corporate social engineering. As one British Airways manager acknowledged: 'We know it's hype – they know it's hype. It's okay … But do I believe in it? – well that's a totally different question' (ref. 49, p. 205). Employees may comply with the demands for adherence to corporate language, and participate in organizational rites and obey cultural values as espoused through the mission statements, but '*without* internalizing the values and therefore generating the "real" commitment' (ref. 50, p. 205). However, this does not imply that interventions to change organizational culture have no effect, which we examine below.

The feminist perspective

feminist perspective: the sociological approach that focuses on the significance of gender in understanding and explaining the inequalities that exist between men and women in the household, in the paid labour force, and in the realms of politics, law and culture

As with all perspectives, a focus on conflict and control has the effect of silencing other ways of seeing. Thus, there is a body of literature that is rooted in a critical analysis of capitalism, but which draws attention to aspects of organizational life that other perspectives we have examined do not reveal. The **feminist perspective** argues that gender is a central aspect of organizational analysis. A gender perspective in organizational culture analysis is important for at least three essential reasons:

1. Membership of the organization through recruitment, selection and appraisal practices often conforms to and extends sex-biased societal values that discriminate against women.
2. Cultural values associated with notions of masculinity and femininity are often reflected in organizational processes, for example processes that privilege the rationality and 'objectivity' associated with masculine attributes while suppressing emotion, associated with family and 'natural' feminine attributes.
3. Some organizations (e.g. schools, media and popular culture) directly play a part in the socializing processes in which people acquire gender identities.[51,52] For example, the social association between masculinity and physical danger contributes to the gendered nature of 'the way things are done' in an organization, justifying 'masculine occupations'.

The deep-rooted assumptions about the nature of human nature have affected the manner in which society and organizations have been studied. In Western thought, the social arrangements have, since the European Enlightenment at least, been generally understood as the result of the 'rule of the mind and the rational element over the passionate'. Aristotle, for example, thought that 'the female was an incomplete version of the male' (ref. 53, p. 3). The view that male hegemony in human society is a 'natural' phenomenon, and gave rise to a resultant 'natural' superiority of men over women, continued in nineteenth-century Western classical sociological theory and twentieth-century organizational analysis.[54]

The argument is that, with notable exceptions, mainstream organizational analysis has generally reflected dominant social beliefs about gender roles, that men inhabit the 'public' domain of action, decision making, power and authority, and women the 'private' domestic world. Thus, feminist scholars have contended that the standard treatment of organizational culture neglects how gender, a patriarchal system and sexuality in organizations influence the dynamics of organizational culture. The term 'sexuality' refers to sexual characters and sexual behaviour in the workplace. Sexual harassment can be an entrenched feature of organizations through pornographic pin-ups, taunting and innuendo, and predatory conduct.

plate 42 Sexual harassment can be an entrenched feature of organizations through pornographic pin-ups, taunting and innuendo and predatory conduct. And organizational culture is a crucial determinant of sexual harassment. While sexuality serves to affirm men's sense of shared masculinity, it can serve to make women feel uncomfortable and leaving the organization is often seen as the only alternative.

Source: iStockphoto

And organizational culture is a crucial determinant of sexual harassment.[55,56]

Workplaces exhibit both heterogeneity and harassment, as we discussed in Chapter 10. After overcoming the challenge of the 'glass ceiling', female managers who progress into positions of authority have problems exercising that authority. Moreover, female managers and supervisors are significantly more likely to be sexually harassed in the workplace than are female subordinates because male co-workers target woman managers as a way to equalize power in the workplace.[57] One female manager, for example, recalled her subordinates joking: 'If we had somebody with balls in this position, we'd be getting things done.' As McLaughlin and her colleagues argue, 'By objectifying women, it strips them of any power or prestige that they hold in the workplace.'[57] While sexuality serves to affirm men's sense of shared masculinity, it can serve to make women feel uncomfortable, and leaving the organization is often seen as the only alternative.[58] Sexual harassment is less about sexual desire or innuendo than about control and male domination. Studies of the gendering of organizations emphasize that gender, sexuality and sexual harassment make an overwhelming difference to the reality of organizational life for women.[59,60] Gender analysis questions research findings and analysis that segregates studies of organizational culture from those of gender divisions in the labour market, patriarchal systems, the processes of male institutionalized power, workplace inequality and 'dual-role' work–family issues.

Observing Indian culture in 2009, journalist Stephanie Nolen illustrates the interrelation of a patriarchal system, sexuality and gendered work organizations. She describes the culture shock for a Western woman moving to work in India like this:

> I am reminded more incessantly of the sexism here. It started when I signed our lease, and had to provide either my father's name or my husband's. I've had to adjust to the fact that every repair person, shopkeeper and many potential staff members utterly ignore anything I say to them, waiting for the voice of authority, my male partner, to tell them what they really ought to do. (ref. 60, p. A13)

National culture with its societal value system and norms of behaviour and organizational culture are deeply intertwined in a **dialectical** relationship: each is fashioned and refashioned by the other. In an important way, by including the gender–sexuality paradigm in the study of the organizational culture, feminist writers have pushed the boundaries of organizational behaviour by examining the people who are deemed to be the 'recipients' of organizational culture. As sociologist Judy Wajcman observes in her insightful study, the individual, work groups and the modern organization are not gender neutral. Indeed, more controversially perhaps, she presents a powerful argument for gender-inclusive cultural theories if we accept her main premise that 'gender is woven into the very fabric of bureaucratic hierarchy and authority relations' (ref. 62, p. 47). The feminist perspective shares with the differentiation approach concerns with inequality and redressing discriminatory workplace practices.

dialectic: refers to the movement of history through the transcendence of internal contradictions that in turn produce new contradictions, themselves requiring solutions

Work and Society: 'Farmers' wives' working at Wal-Mart

Why is the idea of culture so important to the understanding of organizational behaviour? One reason is because it encourages us to move beyond narrowly individualistic accounts of what happens in organizations. To recognize the importance of culture in organizations is to recognize that there is a 'supra-individual' level of reality – shared values, for example – that influences what people in organizations do.

It makes sense to think about the ways in which cultural values influence behaviour, but we should never lose sight of the fact that people vary in the ways they respond to cultural values and the extent to which they care about those values. Sociologist Margaret Archer develops this point in a series of monographs on the complex interactions between structural factors like culture and another set of factors she groups under the heading 'agency' (the human capacity to act in, and on, the world). Given the powers and preferences that individuals bring to any given situation, they have the capacity to respond in various ways to different cultural values and different forms of cultural conditioning. We must take these variations into account when we develop cultural explanations of organizational behaviour.

Take the case of Wal-Mart, widely recognized as one of the most successful companies in the world. Critics have argued that Wal-Mart's success has come at the expense of some of its employees. A review of several major studies of Wal-Mart describes the 'harshness' of Wal-Mart's working conditions (compared with similar companies, such as Costco) and suggests that some Wal-Mart employees 'have … been subjected to relentless harassment' (Head, 2004, p. 4). Women are particularly likely to experience harassment at Wal-Mart, and the reviewer, Simon Head, refers to evidence from 'the Dukes case, a class-action lawsuit brought in 2001 by six female employees and named for one of the six, Betty Dukes' (p. 4).

Head goes on to offer the following cultural explanation of the problematic features of the Wal-Mart approach to management:

> Sex discrimination at Wal-Mart has a long history. Bethany Moreton, a doctoral candidate in history at Yale, has stressed the importance of Wal-Mart's origins in the rural, small-town culture of the Ozarks, where Wal-Mart's corporate headquarters at Bentonville, Arkansas, is still located. In the early years some of the women who worked at Wal-Mart were the wives of local Ozark farmers, and the women's earnings were a meagre supplement to their husbands'. The women in the Dukes case say that some of their store managers still often think of them as resembling those farmers' wives. Ramona Scott, a Dukes case petitioner who worked for Wal-Mart in the 1990s, was told by her store manager that "men are here to make a career and women aren't. Retail is for housewives who just need to earn extra money" (pp. 4–5)

This review of research on Wal-Mart contains a factual claim: the reviewer notes that some studies have discovered instances of harassment and discrimination at Wal-Mart. The review also makes reference to an explanatory claim: some researchers who study Wal-Mart have used a cultural explanation to account for documented cases of harassment and discrimination. In this context, the cultural explanation – the specific reference to rural, small-town culture – may seem persuasive.

However, bearing in mind Archer's more nuanced approach to culture, it is worth questioning whether all, or even most, managers at Wal-Mart see female employees as farmers' wives and therefore as deserving of the second-class status such a characterization supposedly entails. Perhaps this is typical only of male managers in certain geographical regions and would not be found, for instance, among female managers in Alaska.

Consider another possibility: perhaps many managers do not see women this way but are 'forced' to treat their employees harshly for other reasons. For example, earlier in the review, Simon Head notes that Wal-Mart typically fails to provide managers with the budgets they need 'to staff their stores at adequate levels' (Head, 2004, p. 3). Perhaps harsh treatment of employees is more the result of pragmatic managers seeking to keep their jobs than it is the result of the managers' internalization of rural, small-town values.

To conclude, the idea of culture provides a valuable perspective on organizational behaviour, but we must be careful not to portray people as 'cultural dopes' whose behaviour is wholly determined by the cultural values to which they have been exposed.

stop! Develop a cultural explanation of organizational behaviour, but be sure that your explanation recognizes the agentic powers of the people whose behaviour you are explaining.

Sources and further information

Archer, M. (2000) *Being Human: The Problem of Agency*, Cambridge: Cambridge University Press.
Head, S. (2004) 'Inside the Leviathan', *New York Review of Books*, **51**(20), pp. 1–8.

Note: This feature was written by David MacLennan, Assistant Professor at Thompson Rivers University, BC, Canada.

✻ *table 12.3* The major perspectives on organizational culture

Perspective	Analysis level	Primary concern	Nature of organizations
Functionalist	Macro level	Maximizing efficiency/loyalty	A system comprising interrelated parts/groups that work together with no inherent conflict. Power is not important. Culture is something that an organization '*has*'
Symbolic-interactionist	Micro level	How culture is learned/equity	Organizational culture is constructed and reproduced by symbols and shared meanings in interaction with members. Culture is a metaphor for the organization. It is something that an organization '*is*'
Conflict	Macro level	Elimination of power imbalances	Organization is characterized by economic/power inequality/conflict over scarce resources. Culture is fragmented in complex and conflicting ways. It is something that an organization '*is*'
Feminist	Macro level *and* micro level	Elimination of sexual inequality	Organization is characterized by pervasive sexuality/power inequality/sexual discrimination. Culture is fragmented, something that an organization '*is*'

Looking at Table 12.3, what are the key differences between the '*has*' perspective and the '*is*' perspective on organizational culture? Which of these perspectives do you consider most useful for understanding the nature of organizations and shared behaviour, and why?

stop reflect

Each of the four major ways of thinking about organizational culture we have examined involves different assumptions. As a result, each perspective leads us to ask different research questions and to view the realities of organizational life differently. Table 12.3 reviews the four perspectives in terms of three characteristics: (1) their primary level of analysis; (2) the primary concern of the theorists associated with each; and (3) how each understands the nature of organizations. These major perspectives can be used as a theoretical compass for navigating through the myriad competing views found in the organizational culture literature.

Managing cultures

Much management 'integrationist' theory identifies a robust corporate culture as an important factor in promoting work motivation. Proponents advocate that senior managers abandon bureaucratic 'command and control' regimes for a 'strong' corporate culture to win the commitment of their workers, much like a magnet will realign a chaotic collection of iron filings into a discernible pattern. A strong culture can help to activate latent employment-related values, which workers possess but have laid dormant or discouraged. In this narrative, corporate culture functions as the ultimate form of management control: self-control consistent with management expectations. Thus, developing a 'strong' culture in which members develop a fierce loyalty to the company is seen as central to modern management for its potential to close the 'gap' in the employment relationship and thereby release worker's creative capacity.[63–65]

As discussed in Chapter 5, it is considered central to 'soft' HRM practices to manage the *psychological contract*, to change the employment relationship from a binary, hierarchical, low-trust and low-commitment relation to a participatory, high-trust and high-commitment one,[66] and to capture, manage and control emotion in the organization.[29] Drawing on concepts from the sociologist Erving Goffman from the 1950s and 60s, work that analogizes the interactions between individuals to what goes on in drama, a robust corporate culture provides normative and behaviour 'scripts' for employees when management seeks to capture and manage emotional labour and introduce new initiatives, such as high-performance work systems and team-total quality control.[67,68]

Ways of managing culture

Cultural theorists and managers alike have tried to identify effective ways to change manifestations of organizational culture: visible *artefacts*, including language and shared behaviour, and work *values*, which are invisible but can be espoused. This section reviews strategies of planned culture change in three ways:

1. reframing social networks of symbols and meanings through artefacts, language, rituals and ceremonies
2. initiating new HRM practices to change behaviour and norms
3. leadership processes that aim to create the motivation to change behaviour, with particular emphasis on their symbolic content.

All three strategies implicitly adhere to Kurt Lewin's three-stage model of planned change, which involves 'unfreezing' present inappropriate behaviours, 'changing' to new behaviour patterns and positive reinforcement to 'refreeze' the desired changes.[69]

Reframing of social networks and meanings

The reframing of social networks of symbols and meanings to strengthen commitment to the organization and work-related values is manifested through changes in physical artefacts ranging from displaying a framed copy of the organization's new mission statement, and redesigning departments to create 'open-plan' office spaces or work teams with greater autonomy and new work uniforms, to establishing an R&D centre to emphasize the importance of research and innovation. Many organizations have reframed shared symbols and meanings by changing the language to promote the values of customers and quality. Stories and story telling are pervasive in culture management. Stories often contain, explicitly and implicitly, arguments for and against work-related values; they help members to locate work experiences and to develop new insights, which in turn promote sense making or sense giving and new ways of behaving.[70-72] Notable examples of language and narrative strategies to achieve cultural change are British Airways 'Putting People First' and Hewlett Packard's 'HP Way'. Others include the 'corporate' university, where students are increasingly conceptualized as 'clients' and professors as 'service providers' who must 'brand' their institutions and sell their 'products' to 'clients', as do car and beer manufacturers.[73]

Rituals aim to change behaviour. For example, the 3M Corporation has its own version of a Nobel Prize for innovative employees. The general gist of this change strategy is that, properly introduced, the reframing of cultural artefacts is seen to be potentially very effective in disconfirming the appropriateness of employees' present behaviours, providing employees with new behavioural models and affirming new ways of doing things.

HRM practices to change culture

The values that employees bring into the workplace may be identified through the selection process, and it is also posited that a particular culture can be created by a galaxy of HRM practices that select, retrain, reward or replace employees. Human resources selection techniques are an important means of 'knowing' and managing a culture change.[74] Personality- and competency-based tests are the psychological calculation of suitability that enables managers to find the 'best person' for the new culture. Changing and managing culture involves formal and informal work-related learning. This includes a process of socialization, through which employees learn the symbols and meanings and the shared practices: 'The fact that organizational cultures are composed of practices rather than values makes them somewhat manageable: they can be *managed* by changing the practices' (ref. 75, p. 240, emphasis added).

The performance appraisal system is a systematic HRM mechanism used to classify and rank employees hierarchically according to how well they integrated the newly defined set of beliefs, values and actions into their normal ways of doing things. The new espoused work values are incorporated into appraisal systems to allow employees to be compared with each other, to render them 'known' and to reinforce the desired change. The reinforcement effect is further secured when appraisals are linked to performance-related rewards. For example, given the general commodification of education, new contracts in university education reinforce a 'research culture' when promotion and pay are tied to research productivity rather than teaching. Such HRM initiatives help with 'cultural doping' so that employees exhibit new behaviours and attitudes.[76] Thus, a metaphorical 'glue' bonds employees and encourages each to internalize the organization's culture because it fulfils their need for social affiliation and identity.

commodification: in Marxist theory, the production of goods and services (commodities) for exchange in the marketplace, as opposed to the direct consumption of commodities

Leading cultural change

The role of leadership in generating employees' support for cultural change is rooted in the leadership literature (see, for example, Bass and Riggio[77]). There are sociologically informed writers who recognize that cultures can be changed to match strategic goals. In contrast to the crudely prescriptive functional approach, Morgan, for example, cautiously argues that:

> Managers can influence the evolution of culture by being aware of the symbolic consequences of their actions and by attempting to foster desired values. But they can never control culture in the sense that many management writers advocate ... An understanding of organizations as cultures ... [does] not always provide the easy recipe for solving managerial problems that many managers and management writers hope for. (ref. 78, p. 152)

The guiding maxim for implementing successful strategies for cultural change is that of meeting 'complexity with complexity'.[79]

One approach that subsumes Kurt Lewin's change model and recognizes complexity is John Kotter's either-step sequential model, which focuses on what specific behaviours leaders should engage in when leading change (Table 12.4).[80] Steps 1–4 represent Lewin's 'unfreezing' stage, steps 5, 6 and 7 represent the 'changing' stage, and step 8 represents the 'refreezing' process. Kotter's model attempts to change culture through a empiricist-rational strategy, that is, with the view that individuals will make rational choices if provided with 'correct' information. In an economic and political crisis, Canadian writer Naomi Klein reminds us that 'unfreezing' and organizational change may occur through 'shock therapy' as well as adroit management.[66,81] The practitioner approach offered by Kotter does not address whether the change-appropriate behaviours are less or more likely to be exhibited by certain types of organizational leader.[82]

Is managing culture desirable?

Assuming that senior managers are able to transform organizational cultures, is this necessarily desirable? If the central premise of the 'has' theory is that ideas within a social work group are homogeneous, unified and uncontested, a strong culture can be a double-edged sword. It can give members an organizational identity, facilitate collective commitment, provide social stability and influence behaviour without the need for bureaucratic controls. If fundamental changes are needed, however, a strong corporate culture can actually be an impediment to creative thinking, to informal learning, creativity and innovation, and to change, and may thus undermine organizational excellence and success. The learning–creativity paradigm as a decisive source of competitive advantage is based upon spontaneity, irrational and idiosyncratic rather than conventional ideas and solutions, risk taking and rule breaking; it celebrates the creative potential of deviant thinking and action.[83]

table 12.4 A strategy for cultural change

Step	Description of action
1. Establish a sense of urgency	Examine competitive realities. Identify and discuss realities, crises or opportunities relating to why cultural change is needed
2. Create the guiding coalition	Create a cross-functional group of people with enough power to lead the cultural change
3. Develop a vision and strategy	Create a vision and strategic plan to help direct the change process
4. Communicate the change vision	Develop and implement a communication strategy that consistently communicates the new behaviour expected of employees
5. Empower broad-based action	Eliminate obstacles to change, and use target individuals and groups to transform the organization. Encourage risk taking and creative thinking and problem solving
6. Generate short-term wins	Plan for and create visible short-term improvements or 'wins'. Recognize and reward people who contribute to the wins
7. Consolidate and produce more change	Consolidate gains. The guiding coalition uses credibility from short-term wins to create more change. Reinvigorate the change process with new change agents and new projects
8. Anchor new approaches in the culture	Create better customer- and productivity-oriented behaviours. Ensure a reconnection between new behaviours and processes and organizational success. Develop methods to ensure leadership development and succession

Source: Kotter (1996),[80] p. 21.

The much-vaunted 'learning organizations' in contemporary managerial lexicon meet the learning goals only if learners engage in critical reflection and open dialogue activities that may be considered deviant in organizations attempting to create cultural homogeneity.[84,85] The current managerial and political infatuation with Richard Florida's concept of 'creative economy' must be squared with the complexities of managing 'inherent tensions' between learning-creativity and control.[86,87] Furthermore, a strong corporate culture can undermine effective decision making because it encourages the phenomenon of group conformity or **groupthink** (see Chapter 9). Thus, although prescriptive literature presents organizational culture as a variable that can be manipulated at will to produce ideal types of coherence and integration to 'fit' new corporate aims, reservations exist on the appropriateness of such a strategy.

groupthink: the tendency of highly cohesive groups to value consensus at the price of decision quality

Evaluating cultural change strategies

Much cultural analysis is framed within an effort–performance relationship in which a 'strong' culture increases commitment, great loyalty to the organization and better all-round performance. Despite published accounts of 'culture change' initiatives, demonstrating an empirical relationship between a strong culture and organizational performance is problematic. To say that culture and perform-ance are correlated requires the measurement of particular attributes of one variable against particular attributes of the other. In addition, correlation in itself does not constitute a causal relationship between the two variables, although this is one criterion of causality. The methodology for ensuring high internal validity would ideally permit a calculation of how different cultures – 'weak' versus 'strong' – affect organizational performance while controlling the other factors that might influence those performance outcomes. The data must demonstrate the extent to which a stable group of employees have internalized the new value demands, and the extent of the successful socialization of new members into these values, compared with a particular set of performance variables over a period of time.

These measurement challenges underscore the importance of the statistical concepts of **reliability** and **validity**, which raises questions concerning the appropriateness of 'culture change' and performance measures. For example, there is the challenge of isolating external variables. Exchange rates can, for instance, significantly affect the financial bottom line, which makes it difficult to measure accurately the impact of a culture change. To be confident about the culture–performance link, we need credible evidence and a theory about how much of the variance can be explained by the culture factor. Otherwise, as two researchers have admitted, 'We cannot be sure of the extent to which the compa-nies we studied were actually successful in creating that commitment or whether that commitment contributed to their success. All we can say is that the managers in question reported that their efforts ... produced a significant improvement' (ref. 88, p. ix).

The arguments around lack of rigor in research methodology have been well rehearsed;[89–93] see also Bratton and Gold[94] for an overview of measuring the effect of human factors on organizational performance. A small sample size, the

reliability: in sociological research, the extent to which a study or research instrument yields consistent results

validity: in sociological research, the extent to which a study or research instrument accurately measures what it is supposed to measure

plate 43 Exchange rates can significantly affect the financial bottom line, which makes it difficult to measure accurately the impact of a culture change.

exclusion of unfavourable data and citing corporate leaders as incontrovertible evidence of a culture–performance linkage is evidence of allegedly deficient research. When CEOs project an image of the organization by espousing values to the outside world (for example, the researcher), the image and the values may be inconsistent with what they truly value – referred to as enacted values – and what internal stakeholders experience. In this respect, given the dynamics between employee insiders and community outsiders, incongruence between the corporate culture (or image) projected outwards and what is fed back into the organization is likely to breed cynicism, because the openly espoused values do not match the values and norms of the organization.[95] Additionally, it must be kept in mind that individuals within the same workplace will not necessarily internalize the culture of their workplace in the same way, and predictions of a 'strong culture' creating commitment and motivating one employee does not necessarily work with all employees. The evidence for a positive culture–performance link is tenuous. Indeed, it is so deficient that some have argued that it should not be dignified with serious attention.[47]

The most sceptical detractors argue that organizational culture *as a whole* cannot be 'created, discovered or destroyed by the whims of management' (ref. 96, p. 209). Organizational culture is embedded in potent informal shared interactions and norms. Hugh Willmott[47] – a deflater of the 'balloons of academic beliefs' – argues that resistance to strong cultures, or what he calls 'corporate culturalism', is found among powerful professional groups with considerable autonomy over how they perform their work. For example, Schein found that a strategy for cultural change that focused on the 'bottom line' and expected engineers to 'sell their services to clients' caused many to resist and threaten resignation.[97] Resistance to strategies for cultural change has also occurred in universities, healthcare and the BBC in the UK. This concept of 'misbehaviour' (see Chapter 16) emphasizes that acts of resistance to new cultural demands can be less overt, less familiar and barely observable to the 'outsider'. And in what Sharon Bolton[29] describes as 'small spaces of resistance', employees' misbehaviour is changing from the familiar acts of soldiering and absenteeism towards more subtle acts of resistance that are far more difficult for managers to manage.

Not surprisingly therefore, the critical school tend to be highly sceptical about claims of managing cultures, regarding such claims as naive and unethical. Moreover, a strong corporate culture does little to alter the nature of the employment relationship, at least not in any meaningful way. The preoccupation with culture may obscure enduring structural antagonism and conflict. It does nothing to obviate the need for top management to try to reduce labour costs, to intensify the pressure of work and, sometimes, to render employees redundant.[37]

The binary conflict of interest between capital and labour that exists within a 'negotiated order' of mutual cooperation and combinations of values and norms suggests that the significance of organizational culture cannot be grasped unless it is related to structures of power within a context of market exigencies. In other words, culture can never be wholly managed, argue detractors, because it emerges from complex processes involving how employees construct their sense of identity in ways that are beyond management's control. The scope for misbehaviour and indifference to values and the efficacy of culture change strategies is captured by Erving Goffman thus:

> We find that participants decline in some way to accept the official view of what they should be putting into and getting out of the organization ... Where enthusiasm is expected, there will be apathy, where loyalty, there will be disaffection;

where attendance, absenteeism; where robustness, some kind of illness; where deeds are to be done, varieties of inactivity … Wherever worlds are laid on, under-lives develop. (ref. 98, p. 267)

These arguments stress that participants' work values are shaped by outside variables such as class, gender, race and profession or trade. At the very best, culture change interventions are only successful at the observable behavioural level rather than the subconscious level.[99]

Finally, adding to the complexity of managing culture is the omnipresent Internet. It has, for example, been argued that the Internet adds both new operational capacities and a 'space dimension' that affects organizational culture in new ways.[100]

survey: a research method in which a number of respondents are asked identical questions through a systematic questionnaire or interview

Critical insight

Can quantitative measurements capture organizational culture?

Organizational culture is an important area of the organizational behaviour field, but academics disagree on the best way to measure it. Ashkanasy et al. undertook research in 2000 to investigate the question of how best to carry out research into organizational culture. They found that the best research method really depends on *where* organizational culture is considered to be 'based'. If it is founded in values, the best way to carry out research is to use a technique that is able to access these deep-rooted, qualitative aspects – such as observations and interviews. On the other hand, if organizational culture is seen as being 'rooted in perceived practices rather than values', more standardized, quantitative techniques, such as questionnaires, may have an important part to play. Such quantitative techniques have a number of benefits, as Ashkanasy et al. state: 'We note that self-report surveys allow respondents to record their own perceptions of reality, and quantitative techniques allow for replication, cross-sectional comparative studies and provide data that can be analyzed through multivariate statistical techniques.'

But how should these questionnaires be designed? Ashkanasy et al.'s work found a lack of consensus on this question – in part, perhaps, because many researchers lack valid and reliable research tools to investigate organizational culture. In an effort to investigate this problem and perhaps provide a solution, Ashkanasy et al. devised the 'OCP' survey, which produced an 'organizational culture profile' based on questions relating to 'leadership, structure, innovation, job performance, planning, communica-tion, environment, humanistic workplace, development of the individual and socialization on entry'. Initially, they surveyed 151 individuals using their OCP approach, but their results 'provided only mixed support for the reliability and validity of the OCP'. However, the results of a second OCP survey, using a larger sample, were more encouraging.

Ashkenasy et al.'s work investigating research methods for quantitative culture led them to conclude that 'multidimensional measures of organizational culture offer greater interpretive power and have a continuing role in advancing our knowledge of organizational culture.' They also provide the following advice to budding organizational culture researchers:

- Carry out research in order to establish a more theoretical basis for the measures being used in the questionnaire.
- Ensure that the dimensions being measured are clearly distinguishable.
- Use a wide spectrum of respondents.
- Gather qualitative data on the nature of the sample and subcultures.
- Apply controls for environmental stability, in order to establish that the culture measures are valid.
- Use longitudinal studies to establish causal relationships between the cultural dimensions and outcome the variables.

Do you agree? Do you think that surveys and questionnaires can capture the richness of organizational culture or deviant subcultures?

Source: Based on N. M. Ashkanasy, L. E. Broadfoot and S. Falkus (2000) 'Questionnaire measures of organizational culture,' pp. 131-45 in N. M. Ashkanasy, C. P. M. Wilderom and M. F. Peterson (eds), *Handbook of Organizational Culture and Climate*, Thousand Oaks, CA: Sage.

Chapter summary

- In this chapter, we have explored the nature of organizational culture – a unique configuration of shared artefacts, common language and meanings and values that influence ways of doing things in the workplace. The culture of an organization influences what employees should think, believe or value in this social discourse.

- The belief that organizational culture can be produced and managed has become closely associated with organizational redesign and management theories around HRM, the management of emotional labour and transformation leadership.

- Three fundamental levels of organizational culture comprise visible artefacts (buildings, technology, language and norms), underpinned by values, which are invisible, and basic assumptions, which are also invisible, unconscious and resistant to change.

- We explained that culture analysis can be divided into two schools of thought: managerialist and critical. The managerialist perspective is functionalist in that it stresses that culture can play a role in building consensus and harmony, and how culture can improve performance. It views organizational culture as a *variable*: it is something that an organization '*has*' and, as such, can be produced and managed.

- The prescriptive literature tends to present too uniform a view of organizational culture. Alternative approaches point out the existence of *subcultures* and *counter-culture*. These concepts are important if we believe that organizations consist of individuals and work groups with multiple sets of values and beliefs.

- The critical perspective focuses on a sociological concern to describe and critically explain cultural processes, how culture emerges through social interaction, power relations, social inequalities, influencing communities of practice, emotion and norms of individual and group behaviour. Viewed through a sociologist's lens, culture is something that a work organization '*is*'.

- The critical literature emphasizes the symbolic and subjective aspects of the workplace, the role of culture in strengthening management control, and the relationships between social inequalities and patriarchal systems *outside*, and work socialization and behaviour *inside*, the workplace.

- We have discussed how national culture and organizational culture are deeply intertwined, each influencing the other and with latter embedded in society. Gender refers to culturally specific patterns of human behaviour and is culturally learned or determined. Unarguably therefore, gender is a central facet of organizational analysis. Yet standard accounts of organizational culture have tended to neglect how gender, patriarchy and sexuality in society and in workplaces influence the dynamics of organizational culture.

- This chapter described a model for culture change. We emphasized that managers must be aware of the complexities of cultures. Finally, we discussed the problem of a strong corporate culture undermining decision making because it may encourage conformity or groupthink.

Key concepts

artefacts	330
corporate culture	333
counter-cultures	338–339
misbehaviour	350
national culture	330
organizational climate	333
organizational culture	333–334
rituals	335
stories	346
subcultures	338
values	335

Vocab checklist for ESL students

- ☐ Artefacts
- ☐ Assumptions, assume
- ☐ Commodification, commodity
- ☐ Culture, cultural
- ☐ Development, develop, developed, developing
- ☐ Differentiated, differentiate
- ☐ Dominance, dominate, dominant
- ☐ Fragment, fragmentary
- ☐ Functionalist
- ☐ Groupthink
- ☐ Ideology, ideological
- ☐ Integration, integrate
- ☐ Invisible structures
- ☐ Macho
- ☐ Mores
- ☐ Nation, nationalize, national
- ☐ Organizational climate
- ☐ Organizational culture
- ☐ Paternal, paternalistic
- ☐ Reliability, rely, reliable
- ☐ Ritual, ritualistic, ritualize
- ☐ Socialization, socialize, social
- ☐ Soldiering
- ☐ Subculture
- ☐ Taboo
- ☐ Validity, validate, valid
- ☐ Values, value, valuable
- ☐ Visible structures

Chapter review questions

1. What is meant by organizational culture, and how does it relate to national culture?
2. What are the three levels of culture, and how do they operate?
3. Review the 'mainstream' and 'critical' perspectives on organizational culture described in this chapter. Discuss the

perspectives that you and other students find appealing and plausible. Explain your reasons.

4. What mainstream interventions have been used for changing or reinforcing organizational culture? What are the strengths and weaknesses of each?

5. What impact do cultural values and expectations about gender have upon the design and operation of organizations, and how, in turn, does this impact on gender?

6. To what extent, if at all, do notions of masculinity and femininity reinforce or challenge traditional notions of organizational culture?

Chapter research questions

1. One way to understand organizational culture is to observe your own university or college and reflect on students' comments in class. What visible artefacts, ceremonies and practices of the teaching faculty indicate, for example, a 'strong' focus on research or on teaching students? Talk to other students and ask them what the distinctive facets of their national culture are. Give examples of their value statements that may be considered reflective of a national culture.

2. Obtain a copy of Peter Warr's article 'Work values: some demographic and cultural correlates'.[17] What does the World Values Survey tell us about work values in countries with a different cultural heritage? What are the implications of the findings for international managers?

3. Mats Alvesson's *Understanding Organizational Culture*[36] emphasizes the importance of avoiding 'quick fixes' when it comes to organizational culture. What are Alvesson's 'seven sins' in organizational culture thinking? How do these 'seven sins' compare with more traditional management texts on the subject?

Further reading

Aaltio, I. and Mills, A. J. (2002) *Gender, Identity and the Culture of Organizations*, Routledge: London.

Alvesson, M. (2002) *Understanding Organizational Culture*, London: Sage.

D'Amato, A. and Zijlstra, D. (2008) 'Psychological climate and individual factors as antecedents of work outcomes', *European Journal of Work and Organizational Psychology*, **17**, pp. 33–54.

de Cieri, H. (2008) 'Transnational firms and cultural diversity', pp. 509–29 in P. Boxall, J. Purcell and P. Wright (eds), *The Oxford Handbook of Human Resource Management*, Oxford: OUP.

Dennison, D. R. (1996) 'What is the difference between organizational culture and organizational climate? A native's point of view on a decade of paradigm wars', *Academy of Management Review*, **21**, pp. 619–54.

Linstead , S. (2009) 'Managing culture', pp. 149–94 in S. Linstead, L. Fulop and S. Lilley (eds), *Management and Organization: A Critical Text* (2nd edn), Basingstoke: Palgrave.

McSweeney, B. (2002) 'Hofstede's model of national cultural differences and their consequences: a triumph of faith – a failure of analysis', *Human Relations*, **55**(1), pp. 89–118.

Martin, J. (2002) *Organizational Culture: Mapping the Terrain*, Thousand Oaks, CA: Sage.

Martin, J., Knopoff, K. and Beckman, C. (1998) 'An alternative to bureaucratic impersonality and emotional labour: bounded emotionality at the Body Shop', *Administrative Science Quarterly*, **43**(3), pp. 429–69.

Morgan, P. I. and Ogbonna, E. (2008) 'Subcultural dynamics in transformation: a multi-perspective study in health care professionals', *Human Relations*, **61**(1), pp. 39–65.

Ogbonna, E. and Harris, L. (2006) 'Organizational culture in an age of the Internet: an exploratory case study', *New Technology, Work and Employment*, **21**(2), pp. 162–75.

Parker, M. (2000) *Organizational Culture and Identity*, London: Sage.

Schneider, B. (2000) 'The psychological life of organizations,' pp. xvii–xxi in N. M. Ashkanasy, C. P. M. Wilderom and M. F. Peterson (eds), *Handbook of Organizational Culture and Climate*, Thousand Oaks, CA: Sage.

Chapter case study 1

Changing the University of Daventry's culture

Setting

The UK higher education sector generally is facing uncertainty about a continuing national demand for higher education as the level of unemployment, caused by the global economic recession, is increasing. Other challenges facing higher education are changes to student fee regimes, changing political agendas and public funding, as well as the unpredictable demand from international students. The increase in student fees has sharpened students' focus on the value they receive from their universities. Combined with an increase in the number of new universities entering the sector, and at least a short-term reduction in student applications, this will increase the pressure on universities to make their programmes and services more attractive to students while maintaining their academic standards. Globalization has created a booming market in higher education, and, aided by new technologies and the dissolution of national market borders, international partnerships have developed to create 'super' universities with overwhelming competitive advantages over individual locally or regionally focused institutions.

Background

Located in central England, the University of Daventry, created from the amalgamation of Daventry College and Daventry Institute of the Arts, gained university status in 2009. Student numbers have grown steadily in the past few years, and it recruited to meet its target level or the first time in 2007/08. The headcount is 8500 full- and part-time students. The University's core activity is helping students succeed. The vast majority of students attend the University to improve their career prospects or to change career. Daventry offers programmes across a comprehensive range of disciplines. Historically, it has been strong in business studies, but more recently technology, health studies and the creative programmes have experienced significant growth. Daventry has always attracted a high proportion of mature students, and its geographical location, discipline mix and entrance policies have made it attractive and accessible to a diverse student population drawn from larger cities such as Coventry, Leicester, Bedford and Peterborough. Mature students account for 50 per cent of full-time undergraduates, and international students account for 9 per cent of the student population.

The University of Daventry must reduce its dependence on undergraduate students funded by the Higher Education Funding Council for England, and create a more diverse portfolio of income streams without putting its core activity at risk. The University's strategic plan is to deliver high-quality, innovative, flexible programmes both on and off the campus. It also aims to work closely with employers, schools, colleges and agencies in the region to offer excellence in research, scholarship and knowledge transfer, which will shape and support cultural and economic development in support of a sustainable agenda.

The University of Daventry has a number of identifiable strengths: a significant proportion of teaching staff with professional qualifications and experience in addition to their teaching qualifications; an increasing number of programmes with professional accreditation with recognition by over 30 professional bodies; and a high student satisfaction rate and reputation for excellent student support. The University also recognizes some weaknesses, including a low proportion of teaching staff engaged in research, a poor track record in attracting students with high qualifications upon entry, and a low number of departments with strong working partnerships with relevant professional employers. In setting a course to achieve its new strategic vision, the University has established five strategic goals: (1) helping all career-motivated students to achieve their career aspirations; (2) consistently delivering academic excellence; (3) building the University's track record in applied research and innovation; (4) developing the capacity to generate income; and (5) contributing to the cultural and economic prosperity of the region.

Ad Hoc Joint Committee Meeting: developing research capacity

The Ad Hoc Joint Committee established by the University's Board of Governors, which consisted of representatives from the teaching staff, deans, students' union and human resources, and was chaired by the President, Heather Gannon, was mandated to develop an action plan to build the University's track record in research (goal 3). At the first meeting, James Duncan, the Human Resource Manager for University of Daventry, presented data on external research funding and research-based activities gleaned from the websites of six medium-sized universities. In closing his presentation, he remarked that although Daventry's teaching staff were highly committed to teaching, few engaged in research, and this was unlikely to change any time soon because 'There is no incentive to do so,' he said.

Bill Warren from the Department of Management forcefully countered, 'Teaching staff don't have time to do research', going on to say that 'The strength of the University lies in the quality of our teaching, not research.' Dr Michael Peters, from the Department of Applied Sciences, then responded to this by saying, 'High-quality teaching and research go together. If the University is to attract and retain students with high qualifications on entry, they must have the opportunity to become involved in research with their professors. When our teaching staff and their undergraduate students learn with each other and from each other, the result is powerful.'

A perceptive contribution came from the mature undergraduate student representative, Alex Boxall: 'Students are worried that if teachers are promoted on the books they write, they will be less interested in teaching.' Dr Margaret Cinel, Dean of Social Sciences and recently recruited from a large 'research-intensive' university, added that, compared with her previous institution, few of the teaching staff discussed research: 'This is a teaching institution, and if we are to achieve the strategic goals, we have to change the culture,' she said.

The President, Heather Gannon, summed up the contributions from around the table. Finally, following extended discussion, it was agreed that Dr Margaret Cinel, Dr Michael McLennan, Bill Warren, Alex Boxall and Mr James Duncan would draft a discussion paper for the next meeting on what could be done to change the culture at the University of Daventry.

Tasks

Workings in a small group, and role playing the five members of the subcommittee, prepare a report for the Ad Hoc Joint Committee drawing on the material from this chapter and addressing the following:

1. What change interventions can senior administrators introduce in order to create a culture at the University of Daventry that is more aligned with the new strategic vision?
2. What role, if any, should members of the Ad Hoc Joint Committee play in the culture change programme?

Additional Information

Arthurs, H. (2007) 'Publish-or-perish culture at universities harm the public good', *Ottawa Citizen*, November 3. Available at: http://osgoode.yorke.ca/media2.nsf/

Levin, J. S. (2003) 'Organizational paradigm shift and university colleges in British Columbia', *Higher Education*, **46**, pp. 447–67.

Note

This case was written by John Bratton. Although the case draws upon material from UK and Canadian universities, the names of Daventry University and the individuals in the case study are fictitious.

 Web-based assignment

This chapter discusses the significance of culture in work organizations and the interconnectedness between national culture, and organizational culture and behaviour in organizations and businesses. The mainstream or managerialist perspective tends to focus on changing organizational culture to match business strategy and improve efficiency and profitability. This perspective focuses on achieving an organizational culture in which all members subscribe to one set of values and beliefs, normally decided by senior management. Critical perspectives tend to focus on how multiple viewpoints, values and beliefs are controlled or ignored by senior managers. This web-based assignment requires you to explore the Internet to find a website that provides insight into different cultures in organizations. For example, visit the websites of:

- Cosmetics retailer The Body Shop, at www.thebodyshop.com
- US entertainment corporate giant Disney, at http://disney.go.com
- Swedish homeware chain IKEA, at www.ikea-group.ikea.com
- South American agricultural and food giant Bunge, at www.bunge.com/about.html.

1. What kind of organizational culture do these organizations have (for example, what are their espoused values)?
2. What would critical theorists make of the cultures at these companies (or any others you have found)?

OB in Film

In recent years, there has been a growing backlash against corporate leaders accused and convicted of falsifying financial documents, misleading investors and engaging in fraudulent accounting practices. In 2002, American President George W. Bush's rhetoric promised harsh punishment for senior executives who 'cooked the books' and violated the public trust, the premise being that removing a minority of corporate malefactors could solve corporate white-collar crime. The American film *Wall Street* (1987), directed by Oliver Stone, offers an insight into the culture of financial corporations premised on greed. What examples of organizational culture does the film illustrate? What examples are given to substantiate the claim that a culture of anomie and avarice, not simply a few unscrupulous individuals or 'bad apples', contributed to the historic 2008/09 market crisis?

References

1 Schneider, B. (2000) 'The psychological life of organizations,' pp. xvii–xxi in N. M. Ashanasy, C. P. M. Wilderom and M. F. Peterson (eds), *Handbook of Organizational Culture and Climate*, Thousand Oaks, CA: Sage.

2 Ackers, P. J. and Black, J. (1991) 'Paternalist capitalism: an organization in transition', in M. Cross and G. Payne (eds), *Work and the Enterprise Culture*, London: Falmer.

3 Ouchi, W. G. (1981) *Theory Z*, Reading, MA: Addison-Wesley.

4 Wicken, P. (1987) *The Road to Nissan*, London: Macmillan.

5 Williams, R. (1983) *Key Words*, New York: Oxford University Press.

6 Hofstede, G. (1997) Cultures *and Organizations: Software of the Mind* (2nd edn), New York: McGraw-Hill.

7 Giddens, A. (2009) *Sociology*, Cambridge: Polity Press.

8 Ravelli, B. (2000) 'Culture', pp. 39–61 in M. Kanwar and D. Swenson (eds), *Canadian Sociology* (3rd edn), Dubuque, IA: Kendall-Hunt.

9 Hofstede, G. (1991) *Cultures and Organizations: Software of the Mind*, Maidenhead: McGraw-Hill.

10 McSweeney, B. (2002) 'Hofstede's model of national cultural differences and their consequences: a triumph of faith – a failure of analysis', *Human Relations*, **55**(1), pp. 89–118.

11 Adler, N. J. and Gundersen, A. (2008) *International Dimensions of Organizational Behavior* (5th edn), Mason, OH: Cengage Learning [formerly Thomson-South-Western].

12 Linstead, S. and Grafton-Small, R. (1992) 'On reading organizational culture', *Organization Studies*, **13**(3), pp. 331–55.

13 Payne, R. L. (2000) 'Climate and culture: how close can they get?', pp. 163–76 in N. M. Ashkanasy, C. P. M. Wilderom and M. F. Peterson (eds), *Handbook of Organizational Culture and Climate*, Thousand Oaks, CA: Sage.

14 Parker, M. (2000) 'The sociology of organizations and the organization of sociology: some reflections on the making of a division of labour', *Sociological Review*, **48**(1), pp. 124–46.

15 Schein, E. H. (1985) *Organizational Leadership and Culture*, San Francisco: Jossey-Bass.

16 Harding, K. (2003) 'Working with art', *Globe and Mail*, August 20, p. C1.

17 Warr, P. (2008) 'Work values: some demographic and cultural correlates', *Journal of Occupational and Organizational Psychology*, **81**, pp. 751–75.

18 Davies, H. T. O. (2002) 'Understanding organizational culture in reforming the National Health Service', *Journal of the Royal Society of Medicine*, **95**(3), pp. 140–2.

19 Weber, M. (1922/1968) *Economy and Society*, Los Angeles: University of California Press.

20 Smircich, L. (1983) 'Concepts of culture and organizational analysis', *Adminstrative Science Quarterly*, **28**, pp. 33–58.

21 Martin, J and Frost, P. (1996) 'The organizational cultural war games: a struggle for intellectual dominance', pp. 599–621 in S. R. Clegg, C. Hardy and W. Nord (eds), *Handbook of Organization Studies*, London: Sage.

22 Peters, T. and Waterman, R. (1982) *In Search of Excellence*, New York: Harper & Row.

23 Deal, T. E. and Kennedy, A. A. (1982) *Organization Cultures: The Rites and Rituals of Organizational Life*, Reading, MA: Addison-Wesley.

24 Handy, C. (1993) *Understanding Organizations*, London: Penguin.

25 Kanter, R. M. (1982) *The Change Masters*, New York: Simon & Schuster.

26 Hammer, M. and Champy, J. (1994) *Reengineering the Corporation*, New York: HarperBusiness.

27 Champy, J. (1996) *Reengineering Management*, New York: HarperCollins.

28 Martin, J. (1992) *Culture in Organizations: Three Perspectives*, New York: Oxford University Press.

29 Bolton, S. C. (2005) *Emotion Management in the Workplace*, Basingstoke: Palgrave.

30 Morgan, P. I. and Ogbonna, E. (2008) 'Subcultural dynamics in transformation: a multi-perspective study in health care professionals', *Human Relations*, **61**(1), pp. 39–65.

31 Fitzgerald, J. A. and Teal, A. (2004) 'Health reform and occupational subcultures: the changing roles of professional identities', *Contemporary Nurse*, **16**(1/2), pp. 9–19.

32 Collinson, D. L. (1988) '"Engineering humour": masculinity, joking and conflict in shop-floor relations', *Organization Studies*, **9**(2), pp. 181–99.

33 Ackroyd, S. and Crowdy, P. (1990) 'Can culture be managed? Working with raw material: the case of the English slaughtermen', *Personnel Review*, **19**(5), pp. 3–13.

34 Martin, J. and Siehl, C. (1983) 'Organization culture and counterculture', *Organizational Dynamics*, **12**, pp. 52–64.

35 Jones, R., Lasky, B., Russell-Gale, H. and LeFevre, M. (2004) 'Leadership and the development of dominant and countercultures: a narcissistic perspective', *Leadership and Organization Development Journal*, **25**(1/2), pp. 214–33.

36 Alvesson, A. (2002) *Understanding Organizational Culture*, Los Angeles: Sage.

37 Edwards, P. K. (1990) 'Understanding conflict in the labour process: the logic and autonomy of struggle', pp. 125–52 in D. Knights and H. Willmott (eds), *Labour Process Theory*, Basingstoke: Macmillan.

38 Marx, K. (with Friedrich Engels) (1845/6/1978) 'The German ideology', p. 154 in R. Tucker (ed.), *The Marx–Engels Reader* (2nd edn), New York: Norton.

39 Ray, C. A. (1986) 'Corporate culture: the last frontier of control?', *Journal of Management Studies*, **23**(3), pp. 287–97.

40 Thompson, P. and McHugh, D. (2002) *Work Organizations* (3rd edn), Basingstoke: Palgrave.

41 Harvey, D. (1990) *The Condition of Postmodernity*, Oxford: Oxford University Press.

42 Calás, M. B. and McGuire, J. B. (1990) 'Organizations as networks of power and symbolism', pp. 95–113 in B. Barry (ed.), *Organizational Symbolism*, Berlin: de Gruyter.

43 Martin, J. (2000) 'Hidden gender assumptions in mainstream organizational theory and research', *Journal of Management Inquiry*, **9**(2), pp. 207–16.

44 Mills, A. (1995) 'Managing subjectivity, silencing diversity: organizational imagery in the airline industry: the case of British Airways', *Organization*, **2**(2), pp. 243–69.

45 Deetz, S. (1998) 'Discursive formations, strategized subordination and self-surveillance', pp. 151–72 in A. Kinlay and K. Starkey (eds), *Foucault, Management and Organization Theory*, London: Sage.

46 du Gay, P. and Salaman, G. (1992) 'The cult(ure) of the customer', *Journal of Management Studies*, **29**(5), pp. 615–33.

47 Willmott, H. (1993) 'Strength in ignorance, slavery is freedom: managing culture in modern organizations', *Journal of Management Studies*, **30**(4), pp. 515–52.

48 Sewell, G. and Wilkinson, B. (1992) 'Empowerment or emasculation? Shopfloor surveillance in a total quality organization, in P. Blyton and P. Turnbull (eds), *Reassessing HRM*, London: Sage.

49 Höpfl, H. (1992) 'The challenge of change: the theory and practice of organizational transformation', presented to the Employment Research Unit Annual Conference, Cardiff Business School, September. Quoted in P. Thompson and D, McHugh (2009), *Work and Organizations*, Basingstoke: Palgrave-Macmillan, p. 205.

50 Thompson, P. and McHugh, D. (2009) *Work and Organizations*, Basingstoke: Palgrave Macmillan.

51 Mills, A. (1988) 'Organization, gender and culture', *Organization Studies*, **9**(3), pp. 351–69.

52 Helm Mills, J. C. and Mills, A. (2000) 'Rules, sensemaking, formative contexts, and discourse in the gendering of organizational culture', pp. 55–70 in N. M. Ashkanasy, C. P. M. Wilderom and M. F. Peterson (eds), *Handbook of Organizational Culture and Climate*, Thousand Oaks, CA: Sage.

53 Sydie, R. A. (1994) *Natural Women, Cultured Men*, Vancouver: UBC Press.

54 Bratton, J. , Denham, D. and Deutschmann, L. (2009) *Capitalism and Classical Sociological Theory*, Toronto: UTP.

55 Watts, J. H. (2007) 'Porn, pride and pessimism: experiences of women working in professional construction roles', *Work, Employment and Society*, **21**(2), pp. 299–316.

56 Chamberlain, L. J., Crowley, M., Tope, D. and Hodson, R. (2008) 'Sexual harassment in organizational context', *Work and Occupations*, **35**(3), pp. 262–95.

57 McLaughlin, H., Uggen, C. and Blackstone, A (2009) 'A longitudinal analysis of gender, power and sexual harassment in young adulthood', presented at the American Sociological Association's 104th annual meeting, August 8. Quoted in *Globe and Mail*, August 11, 2009, p. L1, L3.

58 Brewis, J. and Linstead, S. (2000) *Sex, Work and Sex Work: Eroticizing Organization*, London: Routledge.

59 Mills, A. and Tancred, P. (eds) (1992) *Gendering Organizational Analysis*, Newbury Park, CA: Sage.

60 Hearn, J., Sheppard, D., Tancred-Sheriff, P. and Burrell, G. (eds) (1989) *The Sexuality of Organization*, London: Sage.

61 Nolen, S. (2009) 'From Johannesburg to New Delhi', *Globe and Mail*, January 10, p. A13.

62 Wajcman, J. (1998) *Managing Like a Man: Women and Men in Corporate Management*, Cambridge: Polity Press/Penn State University Press.

63 Burns, J. M. (1987) *Leadership*, New York: Harper & Row.

64 Kirkpatrick, S. A. and Locke, E. A. (1996) 'Direct and indirect effects of three core charismatic leadership components on performance and attitudes', *Journal of Applied Psychology*, **81**(1), pp. 36–51.

65 Soder, R. (2001) *The Language of Leadership*, San Francisco: Jossey-Bass.

66 Legge, K. (2005) *Human Resource Management: Rhetorics and Realities*, Basingstoke: Palgrave.

67 du Gay, P. (1996) *Consumption and Identity*, London: Sage.

68 Thompson, P. and Findley, T. (1994) 'Changing the people: social engineering in the contemporary workplace', in A. Sayer and L. Ray (eds), *Culture and Economy after the Cultural Turn*, London: Sage.

69 Lewin, K. (1951) *Field Theory in Social Sciences: Selected Theoretical Papers*, London: Tavistock.

70 Boyce, M. E. (1997) 'Organizational story and storytelling: a critical review', *Journal of Organizational Change*, **9**(5), pp. 5–26.

71 Gold, J., Holman, D. and Thorpe, R. (2002) 'The role of argument analysis and story telling in facilitating critical thinking', *Management Learning*, **33**(3), pp. 371–88.

72 Taylor, S. S., Fisher, D. and Dufresne, R. (2002) 'The aesthetics of management storytelling', *Management Learning*, **33**(3), pp. 313–30.

73 Gingras, Y. (2009) 'Marketing can corrupt universities', *University Affairs*, February, p. 39.

74 Townley, B. (1994) *Reframing Human Resource Management*, London: Sage.

75 Hofstede, G. (1998) 'Organization culture', pp. 237–55 in M. Poole and M. Warner (eds), *The Handbook of Human Resource Management*, London: International Thomson Business Press.

76 Alvesson, M. and Willmott, H. (1996) *Making Sense of Management: A Critical Introduction*, London: Sage.

77 Bass, B. M. and Riggio, R. E. (2006) *Transformational Leadership*, Mahwah, NJ: Erlbaum.

78 Morgan, G. (1997) *Images of Organizations* (2nd edn), Thousand Oaks, CA: Sage.

79 Bate, P. (1995) *Strategies for Cultural Change*, Oxford: Butterworth-Heinemann.

80 Kotter, J. (1996) *Leading Change*, Boston: Harvard University Press.

81 Klein, N. (2007) *The Shock Doctrine: The Rise of Disaster Capitalism*, Toronto: Alfred Knopf.

82 Herold, D. M., Fedor, D. B., Caldwell, S. and Liu, Y. (2008) 'The effects of transformational and change leadership on employees' commitment to a change: a multilevel study', *Journal of Applied Psychology*, **93**(2), pp. 346–57.

83 Bratton, J. A. and Garrett-Petts, W. F. (2008) 'Art in the workplace: innovation and culture-based economic development in small cities', pp. 85–98 in D. W. Livingstone, K. Mirchandani and P. H. Sawchuk (eds), *The Future of Lifelong Learning and Work*, Rotterdam: Sense.

84 Fenwick, T. (1998) 'Questioning the concept of the learning organization', pp. 140–52 in S. Scott, B. Spencer and A. Thomas (eds), *Learning for Life*, Toronto: Thompson Educational.

85 Coopey, J. (1996) 'Crucial gaps in the "learning organization": power, politics and ideology', pp. 348–67 in K. Starkey (ed.), *How Organizations Learn*, London: International Thomson Business Press.

86 Thompson, P., Jones, M. and Warhurst, C. (2007) 'From conception to consumption: creativity and the missing managerial link', *Journal of Organizational Behavior*, **28**, 625–40.

87 DeFillippi, R., Grabher, G. and Jones, C. (2007) 'Introduction to paradoxes of creativity: managerial and organizational challenges in the cultural economy', *Journal of Organizational Behavior*, **28**, 511–21.

88 Martin, P. and Nichols, D. (1987) *Creating a Committed Workforce*, London: Institute of Personnel Management.

89 Antony, P. A. (1994) *Managing Culture*, Milton Keynes: Oxford University Press.

90 Guest, D. E. (1992) 'Right enough to be dangerously wrong: an analysis of the in search of excellence phenomenon', in G. Salaman (ed.), *Human Resource Management*, London: Sage.

91 Ogbonna, E. and Wilkinson, B. (1990) 'Corporate strategy and corporate culture: the view from the checkout', *Personnel Review*, **19**(4), pp. 9–15.

92 Silverman, J. (1987) 'The ideology of excellence: management and neo-conservativatism', *Studies in Political Economy*, **24**, pp. 105–29.

93 Smith, P. and Peterson, M. (1988) *Leadership, Organizations and Culture*, London: Sage.

94 Bratton, J. and Gold, J. (2007) *Human Resource Management: Theory and Practice* (4th edn), Basingstoke: Palgrave.

95 Herrbach, O. and Mignonac, K. (2004) 'How organizational image affects employee attitudes', *Human Resource Management Journal*, **14**(4), pp. 76–88.

96 Lynn Meek, V. (1992) 'Organizational culture: origins and weaknesses', pp. 192–212 in G. Salaman (ed.), *Human Resources Strategies*, London: Sage.

97 Schein, E. H. (2004) *Organizational Culture and Leadership* (3rd edn), San Francisco, CA: Jossey Bass.

98 Goffman, E. (1961) *Asylums*, London: Penguin. Quoted in S. Bolton (2005), *Emotion Management in the Workplace*, Basingstoke: Palgrave, p.267.

99 Ogbonna, E. (1992) 'Organization culture and human resource management: dilemmas and contradictions', pp. 74–96 in P. Blyton and P. Turnbull (eds), *Reassessing Human Resource Management*, London: Sage.

100 Ogbonna, E. and Harris, L. (2006) 'Organizational culture in an age of the Internet: an exploratory case study', *New Technology, Work and Employment*, **21**(2), pp. 162–75.

101 Frost, P. J. , Moore, L., Louis, M., Lundberg, C. and Martin, J. (1985) *Organizational Culture*, Newbury Park, CA: Sage.

102 Cooke, R. A. and Rousseau, D. M. (1988) 'Behavioural norms and expectations: a quantitative approach to the assessment of organizational culture', *Group and Organization Studies*, **13**, pp. 245–73.

103 Drennan, D. (1992) *Transforming Company Culture*, London: McGraw-Hill.

chapter 13
Leadership and change

chapter objectives

After completing this chapter, you should be able to:

- explain the meaning of leadership and how it differs from management
- explain the different perspectives on studying organizational leadership
- demonstrate how leadership influences organizational change and performance

Introduction

Now, it seems, leadership is out, and management is in. In 2004, when the Royal Bank of Scotland's Chief Executive Officer, Fred Goodwin, was knighted 'for services to banking', it was fashionable to elevate leadership over management. For more than two decades, management literature had shown a preference for, and interest in, 'leadership' that reflected a desire to move away from 'command-and-control' systems and style associated with management. Leadership is associated with vision, reformed cultures, empowering strategies and innovation – management with something less. Sir Fred Goodwin, deemed a failed banker, once revelled in his nickname 'Fred the Shred', which referred to his leadership role in cost-cutting and job purges.

On February 10, 2009, however, giving evidence to members of the British parliament Treasury Select Committee, the former CEO gave a 'profound and unqualified apology' for all the distress caused by the banking and financial crisis. Other former British bank executives, including Andy Hornby, CEO of HBOS, Dennis Stevenson, chairman of HBOS, and Tom McKillop, chairman of Royal Bank of Scotland, also gave public apologies. Former Labour minister Michael Meacher demanded that Sir Fred Goodwin, a symbol of corporate arrogance, incompetence and greed, be unceremoniously stripped of his knighthood for ruling over 'a culture of reckless spending' and to atone for his past profligate misdeeds. Similar acts of atonement occurred when US banking and automobile executives gave evidence to the Senate Committee. When asked what went wrong, Goodwin said, 'The dilemma has always been it's a highly competitive landscape and many of the practices have come from the United States.'[1]

How did the Royal Bank of Scotland and other European and US bank leaders not see the crisis coming? Laid-off workers in the banking sector know to their cost that poor leadership has consequences. So do the thousands of retirees and shareholders who lost their savings, pensions and investments when the Royal Bank of Scotland recorded losses of £28 billion, the biggest in UK corporate history, in February 2009. The scale of the British and US banking crisis and the reckless behaviour of its top leadership may surpass that of the US company Enron, which collapsed in May 2006, as the most analysed case study of leadership failure in corporate history.

The public atonement by bankers and automobile executives may be good political theatre, but the 2009 financial and economic crises emphasize that **leadership**

leadership: influencing, motivating and enabling others to contribute towards the effectiveness and success of the organizations of which they are members and 'managership' is more than a rhetorical issue. British, Irish, Icelandic and US bankers did everything leaders should do: exhibit vision, innovate and take risks. Their behaviour created what one British writer describes as the 'buccaneer culture' of trading and banking.[2] In contrast, the past limitations of 'managership' now seem like virtues: rigidity recast as 'meticulous processing', risk-aversion as prudence. Over the last century, there has been a plethora of research and scholarship devoted to 'leadership' and 'leaders'. Much of the debate is framed by a familiar conception of the subject: the effective leader is a hero possessing a variety of traits or attributes, competencies and charismatic powers that enable him or her (mostly it is a him) to bring about transformative effects.[3]

Not surprisingly, a key question asked by researchers and practitioners alike is, 'What makes an effective leader?' Some suggest that one factor is the charisma and ability of an individual to inspire others to fulfil the visions and goals of the organization. Others emphasize that leadership of an organization is a collective phenomenon: every leader needs competent followers. Indeed, organizations have had too much leadership and might need less leadership.[4] Leadership studies potentially offer a variety of explanations, including personal attributes, contingencies and the role of co-workers or followers.

This chapter examines the different ways in which academics have defined organizational leadership, and the difference between leadership and management. We explain the different perspectives on understanding leadership, and conclude by assessing the evidence on whether 'good' leadership can improve organizational performance.

The nature of organizational leadership

For information on organizational leadership, go to www.ccl.org

weblink

personality: the relatively stable pattern of behaviours and consistent internal states that explain a person's behavioural tendencies

Think about a position you have held in a voluntary organization or a work organization. To what extent were you a leader? To what extent were you a follower?

stop reflect

Leadership has been studied since the emergence of civilization, but in contemporary literature it has acquired extraordinary importance to organizations concerned with developing a 'strong' culture and building high-performance work systems. Over the last decade, voluminous articles on leadership have been published in English-language management journals. The vast amount of scholarship has, however, not resulted in a consensus on the substantive phenomenon itself, and the jury is still out on the effectiveness of leadership. Indeed, the extensive research has prompted one respected scholar to acknowledge that 'leadership is one of the most observed and least understood phenomena on earth.'[5]

Leadership as a concept permeates the theory and practice of management. Leadership has been conceived as a matter of **personality**, as particular behaviour, as a matter of contingency, as a power relation, as the focus of group processes, and as combinations of these variables. Most definitions of managerial leadership reflect the assumption that it involves a process whereby an individual exerts influence upon others in an organizational context. The notion of influence is central to Gary Yukl's 2006 definition:

> Leadership is the process wherein an individual member of a group or organization influences the interpretation of events, the choice of objectives and strategies, the organization of work activities, the motivation of people to achieve the objectives, the maintenance of cooperative relationships, the development of skills and confidence by members, and the enlistment of support and cooperation from people outside the group or organization. (ref. 6, p. 5)

Yukl's definition, while emphasizing many aspects of 'people skills', tends to focus on the dynamics and surface features of leadership as a social influence process. More critical accounts of leadership tend to focus on the hierarchical

classical and modern. Table 13.2 depicts this theorizing of leadership around traits, behaviours, contingencies, competencies and leader–follower relations. But we should note that modern is not necessarily better.

Trait perspective: the search for 'giants'

plate 44 Early research on organizational leadership focused on the notion that successful entrepreneurs like Sir Richard Branson possess superior qualities or attributes compared with the traits possessed by non-leaders.

Source: EMPICS

table 13.3 Selective leadership attributes according to Stogdill's 1948 and 1970 surveys

Attribute	Number of positive findings	
	1948	1970
Physical characteristics		
Energetic	5	24
Social background		
Social status	15	19
Cognitive ability		
Intelligence	23	25
Fluency of speech	13	15
Personality		
Dominant	11	31
Self-control	11	14
Self-confidence	17	28
Integrity	6	9
Task-related		
Determination	19	38
Social		
Sociability	14	35

Source: Based on Stogdill (1974)[12]

For information on leadership–performance links, go to www.orgdna.com/google/hbr.cfm for an article on stimulating organizational performance through leadership

weblink

Early research on leadership focused on the notion that individuals who occupy leadership positions possess superior qualities or attributes compared with the traits possessed by non-leaders. The so-called 'great man' theories therefore focused on identifying the innate qualities possessed by influential leaders among European monarchs, military generals or politicians. The subject matter for these studies was drawn from the corporate elite; little interest has been shown in identifying the traits of distinguished labour leaders or influential women. The focus was androcentric: 'great man' rather than 'great person' theories. In 1974, American researcher Ralf Stogdill found that leadership is based on complex groupings of traits and social interactions rather than on a single trait or a small cluster of traits (Table 13.3).[12]

The 1974 data showed that leaders tend to be endowed with a large supply of positive physical characteristics such as stamina. Socioeconomic factors were also important variables. In terms of 'class position', few corporate leaders had fathers who were manual wage earners. Intelligence and fluency in speech were found to be positively related to leadership. Task-related characteristics included such attributes as the desire to excel. Social attributes, such as the ability to exhibit tact and diplomacy, are another cluster of traits that 'successful' leaders appear to possess. Stogdill used these selective clusters of traits to differentiate leaders from followers, and effective from ineffective leaders. He concluded that specific 'patterns of traits' appear to interact in a complex way to give advantage to an individual seeking a leadership position. The trait approach to studying leadership still flourishes. For example, it has been asserted that 'it is unequivocally clear that leaders are not like other people' (ref. 13, p. 59), and that eight major traits (Table 13.4) and a strong internal locus of control orientation are positively related to leadership effectiveness.[6]

stop reflect

What do you think makes an effective leader? List three leaders you know about who are alive today, and write down the special attributes you believe each of these people possesses. Compare your list of special qualities with that of your peers, and see whether you can agree on a 'master list'

Evaluating the trait approach

The trait perspective has attracted several criticisms. First, the research has largely neglected the context within which the leaders find themselves. Second, it celebrates 'inequality' between the leader and others, and does not recognize the importance of followership in the leadership process.[14] Third, the research is culturally determined: Asian and Anglo-American scholars, for example, might not agree on what counts as a positive leadership trait. In spite of globalization, major cultural differences exist within as well as between regions. In Asia alone, people speak at least seven different major languages, and believe in a wide range of different religions, ranging from Buddhism and Hinduism to Islam and Christianity. Personal characteristics that appear as 'positives' in Anglo-American research might score negatively in other cultures.[15]

The behaviour perspective

Whereas trait theories emphasize the personal characteristics of leaders, behaviour leadership theorists focus on leaders' behaviour – that is, away from the notion that leaders are born, towards the investigation of what leaders *do*, and in particular how they behave towards followers. In the 1940s, two classic US research programmes at the University of Michigan and Ohio State University pioneered early research. Working independently, the researchers developed two similar analytical frameworks for followers' assessments of their leaders' behaviour, which was distilled into two core dimensions: concern to accomplish *task* and concern for *people*.

table 13.4 Major traits predicting leadership effectiveness

Energy
Internal locus of control
Self-confidence
Emotional maturity
Integrity
Power motivation
Achievement orientation
Low affiliation need

Source: Based on Yukl (2006)[6]

OB in focus

Richard Branson, chair of the Virgin Group since 1973, has attained cult status in the UK as the result of his business exploits, unique personal style and quests for high-risk adventure. By the late 1990s, the Virgin brand had become one of the top 50 brands in the world, and a poll of British consumers at the time showed that 96 per cent had heard of Virgin.

Through Richard Branson's leadership, the Virgin Group has become a diversified grouping of more than 200 privately held companies. The largest of these include Virgin Atlantic Airways, the number two airline in the UK; Virgin Holidays, a vacation tour operator; Virgin Rail, the second largest UK train operator; and Virgin Direct, which offers financial services. Although this is a disparate group of companies, the Virgin brand has under Branson's stewardship been associated with efficiency and high-quality services. According to Branson:

> Virgin is about doing things that really work, not just looking the part. We are passionate about running our businesses as well as we can, which means treating our customers with respect, giving them good value and high quality and making the whole process as much fun as it can be.

The Virgin Group has sales of over US$5 billion and employs 24,000 people.

Branson's entrepreneurial bent emerged during his childhood. At the age of 15, he started a magazine called *Student*, which sold 50,000 copies. The venture was so successful that Branson dropped out of school when he was 17 to run his business full time. In 1971, he opened a string of Virgin Records stores that was also successful. In 1984, Branson purchased a Boeing 747 and founded Virgin Atlantic Airways.

Virgin's success has been attributed to Branson's innovative entrepreneurial ideas and his leadership style, which was a radical departure from corporate norms in the 1980s. Branson operated his unwieldy holding company from his private boat, relying on telecommunications to keep him in touch with his managers. Branson's logic behind his remote office was that it gave his subordinates, spread out in more than 25 London buildings, greater autonomy. 'People always want to deal with the top person in the building. So somebody besides me takes complete responsibility. He becomes chairman of that company ... and I can be left to push the group forward into new areas.' Indeed, according to published accounts, one of Richard Branson's greatest virtues was his ability to delegate and allow managers to take control of the pet projects that he conceived and started.

For more information on Richard Branson and the Virgin Group visit Virgin's website at www.virgin.com.

task behaviour: focuses on the degree to which a leader emphasizes the importance of assigning followers to tasks, and maintaining standards – in other words, 'getting things done' – as opposed to behaviours that nurture supportive relationships

relationship behaviour: focuses on manager's activities that show concern for followers, look after subordinates' welfare and nurture supportive relationships with followers, as opposed to behaviours that concentrate on completing tasks

initiating: part of a behavioural theory of leadership that describes the degree to which a leader defines and structures her or his own role and the roles of followers towards attainment of the group's assigned goals

consideration: the extent to which a leader is likely to nurture job relationships, and encourage mutual trust and respect between the leader and his or her subordinates

plate 45 Army NCOs (junior officers) exemplify individuals who are high in initiating structure. In training, they give orders and structure recruits' activities throughout the day. Emphasis on task accomplishment takes precedence over the recruits' personal needs.

Source: Getty Images

The first dimension to consider, **task behaviour**, describes the extent to which the leader emphasizes productivity targets or goal accomplishment. These behaviours are also called 'production-centred' and task-oriented' leadership styles. The second, **relationship behaviour**, describes the extent to which the leader is concerned about his or her followers as people: their needs, development and problems. Around these two core dimensions, three studies provided the foundations of behavioural theories of leadership.

At the University of Michigan, researchers differentiated *production-oriented* and *employee-oriented* managers. The former were characterized by detailed work routines and close supervision, and subordinates were viewed as a factor of production – as a means for getting the work done. The latter gave special attention to subordinates' personal needs, valued their individuality, and generally approached subordinates with a strong human relations emphasis. With respect to effectiveness, the Michigan researchers found that employee-oriented leadership behaviours were associated with higher work group performance and higher satisfaction among group members.[16]

The Ohio State University studies suggested that two important dimensions underlie leader behaviours: an *initiating structure* and *consideration*. The first, an **initiating** structure, refers to the extent to which a manager is likely to define and structure his or her own roles and those of subordinates, and establish clear patterns of communication towards completing formal tasks and goals. In contrast, **consideration** refers to the extent to which a leader is likely to nurture job relationships, and encourage mutual trust and respect between the leader and his or her subordinates. The Ohio State researchers argued that high 'initiating structure' was associated with greater effectiveness, higher employee absenteeism, higher turnover rates and higher number of grievances. High 'consideration', on the other hand, was associated with higher subordinate satisfaction.

The Ohio State researchers regarded the initiating structure and consideration as being two independent dimensions. Thus, manager behaviour was flexible and could be changed as situations warranted. Leaders could score highly on the initiating dimension and not on the consideration dimension, but equally could score high on both or low on both. The high grievance levels declined when the manager was rated high on both initiating structure and consideration. The Ohio State results were interpreted as indicating that the most effective leader would score high on both dimensions, and that leadership could derive from individuals holding no formal position in the organization.[17] Subsequent research has tended to confirm the Michigan and Ohio State University results.[18]

Robert Blake and Jane Mouton's highly influential Managerial Grid, later renamed Leadership Grid, is based on an extended version of the production-oriented and employee-oriented theme found in the Michigan and Ohio State studies.[19] The Leadership Grid was designed for leadership training by allowing trainees to assess their current levels of task-oriented and people-oriented leadership styles. Not surprisingly, it has been noted that these two core dimensions of leadership styles parallel McGregor's Theories X and Y respectively (see Chapter 7). The later version, by Blake and McCanse, identifies five basic combinations of concern for production and concern for people, using a nine-point scale, where 9 shows high concern for people and 1 shows a low concern (Figure 13.2).[20]

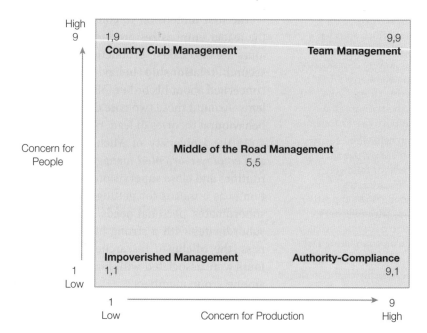

figure 13.2 The Leadership Grid™

From Blake, Robert R. and McCanse, Anne Adams (1991) *Leadership Dilemmas – Grid Solutions* (Formerly the Managerial Grid by Robert R. Blake and Jane S. Mouton), Houston: Gulf Publishing Company, p. 29. Copyright 1991 by Scientific Methods, Inc. Reproduced by permission of the owners

Go back to Chapter 7, on Motivation, and look-up Theories X and Y. In what way is production orientation reminiscent of Theory X, and employee orientation reminiscent of Theory Y? Using the X and Y classification, how would you rate 'team management'?

stop reflect

The styles are authority-compliance style (scoring 9,1), country-club (scoring 1,9), impoverished management (scoring 1,1), middle-of-the-road management (scoring 5,5) and team management (scoring 9,9). The Leadership Grid model advocates the team management style, which suited the popular human relations theory that high levels of performance and job satisfaction could be mutually achieved.

Evaluating the behavioural approach

The Leadership Grid approach has been tested many times, but mixed results have generated criticisms of behavioural style research. First, it has not adequately demonstrated how leaders' behaviours are associated with performance outcomes. The relationship between production and relationship behaviours and performance outcomes is tenuous. It is also argued that 'behaviour research, like the trait approach, suffers from a tendency to look for simple answers to complex questions'.[6] Furthermore, behavioural taxonomies suggest that the most effective leadership style is the so-called 'high–high' style: that is, high production and high people-oriented behaviour. Yet extensive research in Anglo-American countries found only limited support for the universal proposition that 'high–high' leaders are more effective. Researchers concluded that there is no 'one best way' to lead; rather, it is believed that the effectiveness of a given leadership style depends on situational factors.

The contingency perspective

Contingency leadership theories are based on the idea that the most effective leadership style depends upon the leader, the followers and the situation. In other words, whether a set of traits or behaviours will result in leadership success is contingent, that is, will depend, upon the situational variables, including the characteristics of co-employees, the external and internal environments, and the nature of the work performed. The assumption is that different trait patterns (or behaviour patterns) will be effective in different situations, and that the same trait pattern (or behaviour pattern) is not optimal in all situations.

Most contingency leadership theories assume that effective leaders must be flexible and able to adapt their behaviours and styles to match the situation. This challenges the notion of 'one best way' to manage or lead. For example, Winston Churchill, after exhibiting inspiring leadership throughout the Second World War, was defeated in the July 1945 general election. Thus, it is suggested that Churchill's wartime leadership qualities no longer fitted the new contextual situation. Fiedler's contingency theory, Evans and House's path–goal theory, Hersey and Blanchard's 'situational leadership' model, and Kerr and Jermier's substitutes for leadership theory are four examples of leadership theories that diagnose contextual factors.

Fiedler's leadership contingency theory

Fiedler's contingency model: suggests that leader effectiveness depends on whether the person's natural leadership style is appropriately matched to the situation

Fiedler's contingency theory is the oldest and one of the most widely known contingency models of leadership. It proposes that the fit between the leader's need structure and the favourableness of the leader's situation determines the team's effectiveness in work accomplishment. This theory assumes that leaders are either task oriented or relationship oriented, and that leaders cannot change their orientations.[21] Task-oriented leaders are focused on accomplishing tasks and getting work done. Relationship-oriented leaders are focused on developing good, comfortable interpersonal relationships. The effectiveness of both types of leader depends on the favourableness of the situation. The theory classifies the favourableness of the leader's situation according to the leader's leader–follower relations, the structure of the task and the leader's position power.

Fiedler classifies leaders using the least preferred co-worker (LPC) scale.[22] The LPC scale is an instrument to measure a manager's leadership style. Respondents are asked to think about the person with whom they can work least well (the LPC). Next, respondents are asked to describe this person using adjectives like pleasant versus unpleasant, and inefficient versus efficient. Fiedler argues that leaders who describe their LPC in positive terms (that is, pleasant, efficient, cheerful and so on) are classified as high-LPC, or relationship-oriented, leaders. Those who describe their LPC in negative terms (that is, unpleasant, inefficient, gloomy and so on) are classified as low-LPC, or task-oriented, leaders. The LPC score is a controversial element in contingency theory because of measurement biases and low measurement reliability.[23,24]

Fiedler's model is based on the assumption that the situation determining leadership style depends on three interrelated factors: (1) *leader–member relations*, which reflects the extent to which the leader has the support, respect and trust of subordinates; (2) *task structure*, the amount of structure contained within tasks performed by the work group, ranging from highly structured and detailed to low structure; and (3) *position power*, the degree to which the leader has the capacity to exercise formal authority through rewards or punishments to obtain compliance from subordinates. Based on these three dimensions, the situation is either 'favourable' or 'unfavourable' for the leader.

Fiedler's contingency model is shown in Figure 13.3. The row labelled 'Situation' shows that there are eight different leadership situations. Each situation represents a unique mix of leader–member relations, task structure and position power. Situations I, II and III represent the most favourable or high-control situations, where there is little need for relationship-oriented action, since leader–member relations are already good. Situations VII and VIII, on the other hand, represent the most unfavourable or low-control situations – here, the relationship-oriented leader may give insufficient attention to task-related problems. Figure 13.3 shows that task-oriented leaders are hypothesized to realize good group performance at these extremes, under favourable (high-control) and unfavourable (low-control) situations. The model also shows that in situations IV and V, in the centre, where the

To what extent are contingency theories of leadership bound by culture?

stop reflect

situation is moderately favourable (moderate control), the relationship-oriented leader achieves good group performance.

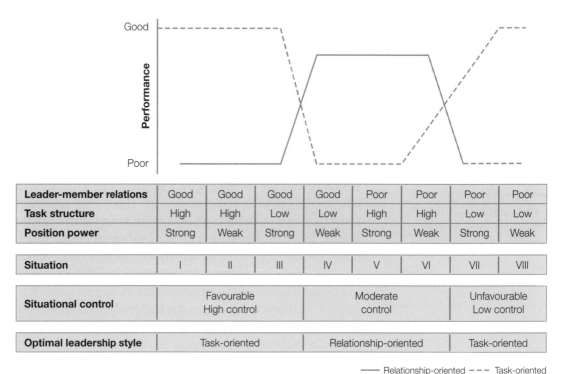

Leader-member relations	Good	Good	Good	Good	Poor	Poor	Poor	Poor
Task structure	High	High	Low	Low	High	High	Low	Low
Position power	Strong	Weak	Strong	Weak	Strong	Weak	Strong	Weak

Situation	I	II	III	IV	V	VI	VII	VIII

Situational control	Favourable High control			Moderate control			Unfavourable Low control	

Optimal leadership style	Task-oriented			Relationship-oriented			Task-oriented	

—— Relationship-oriented - - - Task-oriented

figure 13.3 A representation of Fiedler's contingency model of leadership

Source: Adapted from Fiedler (1974),[25] p.71.

What happens when a leader is in a moderately favourable or unfavourable situation? Fiedler argued that leader orientation is difficult, if not impossible, to change, so he recommends that leaders must learn to influence the leadership situation in order to create a match between their leadership style and the amount of situational control.[26] Thus, a moderately favourable situation could be altered to be more favourable and a better fit for the task-motivated leader. Similarly, the highly unfavourable situation would be changed to one that is moderately favourable, and a better fit for the relationship-motivated leader.

Evaluation of Fiedler's model

There is considerable debate about the validity of Fiedler's model, and research suggests that the model has been better supported in laboratory studies than in field studies.[24] Criticism has prompted others to examine the contingency nature of leadership.[27]

Path–goal theory

path–goal leadership theory: a contingency theory of leadership based on the expectancy theory of motivation, which relates several leadership styles to specific employee and situational contingencies

Robert House's **path–goal theory of leadership**, which draws upon the expectancy theory of motivation, hypothesizes that leaders can affect motivation, job satisfaction and the performance of work group members by their actions.[28,29] In the expectancy theory of motivation, the linkages between effort and performance, and between performance and valued rewards, are critical to employee motivation. Chapter 7 explores this notion further in relation to the motivation of employees. In path–goal theory, the main task of the leader is to smooth the follower's path to the goal. The leader uses the most appropriate of four leader behavioural styles to help followers clarify the paths that lead them to work and personal goals, as shown in Figure 13.4.

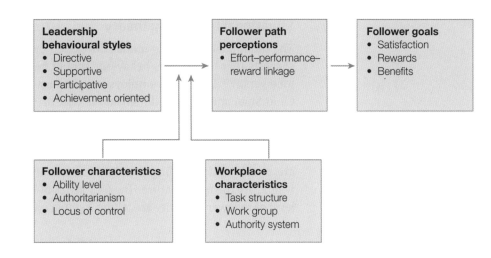

figure 13.4 The path–goal model

In contrast to Fiedler, who proposes that leaders have one dominant style, path–goal theory proposes that the leader behaviours are adjusted to complement the situational contingency variables in order to influence job satisfaction and work motivation for task performance. The four leadership styles identified in the model are directive, supportive, participative and achievement oriented. The *directive style* is used when the leader must communicate expectations, schedule work and maintain performance standards. The *supportive style* is used when the leader needs to express concern for followers and create a climate that demonstrates support. The *participative style* is used when the leader wants to share decision-making authority with followers. The *achievement-oriented style* is used when the leader must set challenging goals for followers, expect very high levels of performance and show strong confidence in the followers.

The contingency variables in path–goal theory are the characteristics of the work environment (situation) and those of the followers. Research has focused on matching leader behaviours to follower characteristics and environment characteristics. For example, when tasks are ambiguous, directive leader behaviour is appropriate. When the environment is stressful, supportive leadership is appropriate. When followers are ready to be empowered, participative leadership is appropriate.

When followers have high achievement orientations, achievement-oriented leadership is appropriate. These are just a few examples of the links between leader behaviour and contingency variables. The leader selects the leader behavioural style that helps followers achieve their goals. Leaders can use several different styles, and can diagnose the situation and apply the appropriate style.

Evaluation of path–goal theory

The research support for path–goal theory is mixed.[30] There is support for some of the model's predictions, for example the link between directive leader behaviour and job satisfaction for low-ability subordinates, and supportive leadership is shown to be related to subordinate satisfaction across situations. We can conclude that the full path–goal model has not been sufficiently tested.[31]

plate 46 The entry of more women into management positions has generated more research on gender and leadership, questioning, among other things, whether women lead differently from men.

Source: Getty Images

Situational leadership theory

The situational leadership model, developed by Paul Hersey and Kenneth Blanchard, suggests that the leader's behaviour should be adjusted to the maturity level of the followers.[32,33] The model employs two dimensions of leader behaviour as used in the Ohio State studies: one dimension is task or production oriented, and the other is relationship or people oriented. Follower maturity is categorized into four levels, as shown in Figure 13.5. Follower maturity is determined by the ability and willingness of the followers to accept responsibility for completing their work. Followers who are unable and unwilling are the least mature, and those who are both able and willing are the most mature. The four styles of leader behaviour associated with each level of follower maturity are telling, selling, participating and delegating.

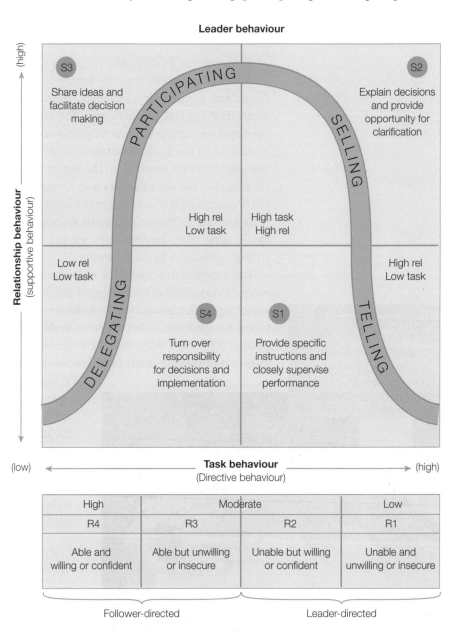

figure 13.5 The situational leadership model

According to the situational leadership model, a leader should use a *telling style* of leadership with immature followers who are unable and unwilling to take responsibility for completing their work. This style is characterized by high concern with the task and strong initiating structure behaviour, coupled with low concern with relationships and little consideration behaviour. For Warren Bennis,[34] an effective leader has to be able to *communicate meaning* to ensure that followers are inspired and support the organization's goals. This important characteristic of an effective leader is reflected in Hersey and Blanchard's model.

As followers mature to the second level, the leader should use a *selling style*, in which there is high concern with both the task and relationships. Able but unwilling followers are the next most mature, and require a *participating style* from the leader. This style is characterized by high concern with relationships and low concern with the task. Finally, the most mature followers are ones who are both able and willing, and these require a *delegating style* of leadership. The leader employing this style of leadership shows low concern with both the task and relationships, because the followers accept responsibility.

Evaluation of situational leadership theory

One key limitation of the situational leadership model is the absence of central hypotheses that could be tested, which would make it a more valid, reliable theory of leadership. Some partial tests of the model have indicated support, but others have found no support at all.[35,36] However, the theory has intuitive appeal and is widely used for training and development in corporations. In addition, the theory focuses attention on followers as important participants in, if not determinants of, the leadership process.

Critical insight

The Hersey and Blanchard model is a widely used prescriptive approach to leadership. Read Chapter 8, 'Situational leadership' in their book *Management of Organizational Behavior*.[33] What are the strengths and weaknesses of this model? Why do you think it is so popular among consultants and management trainers?

Obtain a copy of Mats Sundgren and Alexander Styhre's article, 'Leadership as de-paradoxification: leading new drug development work at three pharmaceutical companies'.[37] How, if at all, could the situational leadership model be used in a research-intensive creative work environment?

Substitutes for leadership

The mainstream leadership theories we have so far examined all assume that formal leadership is necessary, whatever the circumstances. This basic assumption is challenged by Kerr and Jermier,[38] who contend that there are a variety of situational variables that can substitute for, neutralize or enhance the effects of formal leadership. These situational variables are referred to as substitutes for leadership. Table 13.5 shows representative examples of these variables. Ability, experience and knowledge can serve as follower characteristics; a highly structured and routine job can serve as a job characteristic; and a bureaucracy with explicit directives, formalized areas of responsibility and inflexible application of rules and procedures can serve as an organizational characteristic.

A *leadership substitute*, Kerr and Jermier propose, can make a leader's behaviour unnecessary. For example, task-centred behaviour is less relevant for the experienced and well-trained employees often found in self-managed work teams or in professional occupations. These employees are more likely to be guided by their own initiatives or by their immediate peers, thereby replacing task-motivated behaviour. A similar prediction can be made for a highly structured job, in this instance the 'McDonaldization' approach, noted in Chapter 2, to designing workers' roles based on fragmented tasks and repetitive work routines, including worker–customer interaction. The theory predicts situations when any type of leadership is negated. This situation is referred to as a *leadership neutralizer*. For example, when rewards are not within

table 13.5 Substitutes for leadership

Characteristic	Affect on leadership	
	Task-oriented behaviour is unnecessary	Relationship-oriented behaviour is unnecessary
Of the follower		
1. Ability, experience, knowledge	O	
2. Professional orientation	O	O
3. Indifference to organizational rewards	O	O
Of the job		
4. Highly structured and routine	O	
5. Provides own feedback on performance	O	
6. Intrinsically satisfying		O
Of the organization		
7. Formalization/inflexibility	O	
8. Cohesive work groups/teams	O	O
9. Rewards not controlled by leader	O	O
10. Spatial distance between leader/followers	O	O

Source: Adapted from Kerr and Jermier (1978),[18] pp. 375–403

the leader's control, or if there is spatial distance between leaders and the work group, behaviour may negate these behaviours, but they are still necessary. Although the list of characteristics is not all-inclusive, it shows that there are more substitutes for task-oriented leadership than for relationship-oriented leadership. Theory suggests that managers should be attentive to the potential substitutes because they impact directly on intrinsic and extrinsic motivators (see Chapter 7).

Evaluation of substitutes for leadership theory

The research results on the substitutes for leadership approach have been mixed.[39] One study did find that combined attentiveness to leader behaviours and substitute variables significantly explained employee work attitudes and behaviours.[40] The theory assumes that the individual manager has the power and the discretion to change the situational variables. It also assumes that leadership is replaced by alternatives, but such variables may coexist alongside leadership.[41]

Modern leadership perspectives

Transformational leadership

Most of the leadership theories we have discussed so far in this chapter were developed at a time when Fordism was the dominant production paradigm in Western capitalism. Yet from the beginning, Fordism based on mass production and consumption was plagued by economic and social problems. The model became inextricably associated with deskilled workers, standardized products, hierarchical managerial structures and conflict between labour and management.

In the 1970s, Fordism entered a crisis. Among the many solutions adopted to solve the crisis was post-Fordism. This new industrial model involved reversing Tayloristic principles around the design and managerial control of work (see Chapter 2). The diagnosis was that US and European organizations had too much management. Thus, flexible specialization, the 'holistic assembly line' and Japanese cellular production necessitated new theories of leadership to enhance innovation and mobilize employee's underused intelligence and knowledge. For Burns, leaders could be separated into two types: the *transactional* and the *transformational*.[5]

The essence of classical leadership is concerned with an exchange or transaction. Leaders motivate their subordinates by clarifying role and task requirements. The defining features of *transactional leadership* are (1) that the leader uses contingent rewards and recognition to motivate employees towards an established goal or purpose, and (2) that the leader exerts corrective and possible punishment when subordinates do not reach performance expectations. At best, these leadership behaviours result in employee performance that meets expectations.

Transactional leadership is typically contrasted with *charismatic leadership* and *transformational leadership*. The Oxford Dictionary defines *charisma* as (1) 'the ability to inspire followers with devotion and enthusiasm', and (2) 'a divinely conferred power or talent'. By virtue of the leader's defining personal attributes, charismatic leadership creates respect for and trust in the leader. Whereas transactional leadership focuses on interpersonal exchanges, charismatic leadership emphasizes symbolic leader behaviour, visionary and inspirational messages, appeal to values and self-sacrifice. Leaders who can do all these things and produce profound social change, inspire others to transcend their own self-interests, and have an astonishing effect on followers are said to be charismatic leaders. Winston Churchill, Martin Luther King, Nelson Mandela and, to some, Barack Obama are examples of charismatic leaders in politics. In addition, Richard Branson (see above) and Lee Iacocca of Chrysler are the most cited examples of charismatic Anglo-American business leaders. But charisma is something that followers perceive: like beauty, it lies in the eyes of the beholder.[9]

The German sociologist Max Weber was the original writer on charismatic leadership. His contribution to charismatic leadership theory lies in his analysis of authority relations (see Chapter 3). Weber argued that people comply with a leader's demands based on three forms of authority: traditional, rational-legal and charismatic. In the case of charismatic authority, people obey because of the extraordinary endowments of charismatics, the 'bearers of specific gifts of body and mind' (ref. 42, p. 1112). For Weber, charismatic leadership emerged only during periods of social crisis. At such 'moments of distress', the charismatic leader 'seizes the task for which he [sic] is destined and demands that others obey and follow him by virtue of his mission' (ref. 42, p. 1112). Although Weber's work relates primarily to religious phenomena, the idea that social crises can act as catalysts for change developed into a theory. In the 1980s, the US economist Milton Friedman wrote the highly influential statement: 'Only a crisis – actual or perceived – produces real change' (ref. 43, p. ix). This became known as 'the crisis hypothesis'.

In the 1980s, in response to the crisis in modern industry, a model of leadership emerged from the recognition of the sparseness of charisma among industrial leaders that centred on the strategic influence of senior managers. Transformational leadership is a 'weaker' version of charisma,[9] as defined by Weber, which is more far more modest in its goals – changing or transforming organizations, not nation-states. Transformational leadership is sometimes identified separately from charismatic leadership in the literature, but the two formulations are not in fact different. Transformational is a weaker variant in which 'charisma is an important attribute of leaders who serve in the change agent or transformational role'.[7,44]

The essence of transformational leadership is about issues around the processes of transformation and change.[45] Figure 13.6 presents a summary of three key sets of leader behaviour. The first set of transformational leader behaviours involves responding to signals from the environment indicating change (stage I). The crisis event must be perceived and responded to by the leader. The second set of leader behaviours involves creating a vision that a critical mass of followers will accept as a realistic, credible and desirable change for the organization (stage II). The third set of leader behaviours involves three key elements: the transformational leader sets high performance expectations and standards, publicly communicates confidence in the followers' ability to meet high performance expectations, and acts as a role model for the desired new values, beliefs and behaviours needed to realize the new vision (stage III). These leader behaviours establish 'new realities, actions, and practices [that] must be shared so that changes become institutionalized' (ref. 46, p. 31).

plate 47 Barack Obama's communicative powers have been described as 'absolutely masterful' and, to some, speak to his charisma as a leader.

Source: Shutterstock

stop reflect

Can you think of people who illustrate charismatic leadership? Do you think that charismatic leadership was the answer to the economic and financial woes of 2008/09? Are there any 'risks' associated with following a charismatic leader?

stop reflect

To what extent do the three sets of transformational leader behaviour resemble Kurt Lewin's (1951)[47] model of change discussed in Chapter 12?

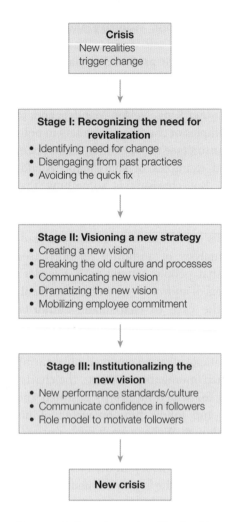

figure 13.6 Transformational leadership

Source: Adapted from Tichy and Devanna (1990),[46] p. 29

competencies: the abilities, values, personality traits and other characteristics of people that lead to a superior performance

Evaluation of transformational leadership theory

Empirical research has found support for transformational leaders with charisma. Evidence indicates that transformational leadership can enhance employee motivation and performance, and levels of satisfaction and organizational measures of effectiveness.[48–50] And those 'strong' transformational leaders are also likely to be strong transactional leaders; in other words, they are good 'all-rounders'. Some detractors insist that the most consistently successful organizations are led by individuals with an unorthodox combination of attributes, skills or abilities that falls outside the usual transformational leadership paradigm.[51] The research evidence underscores the importance of management development: individuals can be trained to be more transformational.

Shared/superleadership theories

Transformational leadership theory focuses on extraordinary individuals at the top echelons of the organization, rather than on work groups and teams. At the root of mainstream leadership thinking is employees' powerlessness, their lack of vision and creativity. Several leadership analysts have proposed that an exceptionally gifted leader is someone who leads others to lead themselves. Shared or distributed or superleadership theories propose that gifted leaders empower their subordinates by acting as teacher or coach, rather than an 'all-knowing' commandant. For example, Peter Senge insists that, in creative organizations, 'leaders are designers, stewards, and *teachers*' (ref. 52, p. 340, emphasis added). Underpinning this approach to leadership is the notion that leaders can actually have more power and control if they share power with their followers. In the practitioner literature, the concept of the high-performance workplace is heralded as a new management model in which the employment relationship is characterized by more socially consensual practices and leadership styles. In this context, the role of superleaders in sharing power with team members and developing team leadership takes on heightened importance.[53] The approach to leadership is also suggestive of substitutes for leadership theory.

Evaluation of shared/superleadership

Research has shown that superleadership has the potential to reduce indirect costs (fewer managers) and free up time for top executives to engage in strategic behaviours.[54] As in the case of substitutes for leadership, shared or superleadership is therefore likely to attract interest and further inquiry from practitioners and researchers.

Leadership competencies

The concept of leadership competency has become ubiquitous in the field of management development. The theory uses a taxonomy (a classification) of either criterion-related behaviours or standards of performance, which are referred to as **competencies**. We may define competency as 'the set of behaviour patterns that the incumbent needs to bring to a position in order to perform its tasks and functions with competence'.[55] A competency model applied to a leadership position specifies a set of desired values, behaviours and/or skills that organizational members feel their leaders need in order to be effective and to successfully meet current and future challenges. A competency model is very reminiscent of early behavioural leadership theories.

Studies in the UK underscore the importance of competency frameworks in management and leadership development programmes. For example, in the UK,

Work and society: Leadership and communityship

In a recent article, Henry Mintzberg (2009) offers some reflections on leadership. What is most interesting is the way he frames his analysis. Initially, it seems that the key concept of the article is not leadership but community. After reading further, Mintzberg's thesis is clarified: he is arguing that effective leadership rests on an understanding of the nature of workplace communities. For Mintzberg, the ideas of 'communityship' and 'leadership' go hand and hand.

Despite this provocative pairing of ideas, the Mintzberg article is short and does not do justice to the broad range of issues it raises. If we wish to explore further the link between worker community and leadership, one new idea stands out as particularly powerful – the idea of 'communities of practice' developed by Etienne Wenger (1998).

Communities of practice are based on a new way of thinking about worker knowledge. The theory is that workers possess many different kinds of knowledge, including tacit knowledge (tacit knowledge sometimes involves sensorimotor 'know how' that may be difficult to express verbally). Workers acquire this tacit knowledge gradually by working alongside more experienced practitioners or experts. The complex process of using, transmitting and acquiring knowledge is a source of community: it binds workers together and gives them a common identity.

In his first major statement on communities of practice, Wenger (1998) advised against 'top-down' approaches to leadership and change – approaches he characterized as too 'prescriptive' (p. 10). More recently (2002), he has worked with colleagues to develop an analysis of how communities of practice might be cultivated. Wenger and his co-authors suggest that communities of practice have three key elements: a domain (the topic the community focuses on); the community itself; and a practice (a body of shared knowledge). Although each element is an essential part of the whole, community is clearly central. Wenger and his colleagues offer the following definition of what they mean by community in this context:

The community creates the social fabric of learning. A strong community fosters interactions based on mutual respect and trust. It encourages a willingness to share ideas, expose one's ignorance, ask difficult questions and *listen attentively. Have you ever experienced this mixture of intimacy and openness to inquiry? Community is an important element because learning is a matter of belonging as well as an intellectual process, involving the heart as well as the head. (pp. 28–9)*

Wenger maintains that communities of practice are everywhere: they exist, for example, when people with common hobbies spend time together, when families cook together, when people participate in web-based activities and games. The theme that underlies these diverse situations is a weaving together of knowledge, identity and community. As leaders explore possibilities for change in the workplace, they need to take into account this complex web of relationships.

stop! You may want to reflect on your own membership of a community of practice and consider the following questions.

- What forms of knowledge and skill are valued in this community of practice? How is this knowledge stored, transmitted and applied?
- Who are the novices and experts in the community of practice? How does the identity of group members change as they acquire new levels of knowledge?
- In what sense does the group form a community? How would members of the group respond if an outsider were to question their knowledge and ask them to change their practices?

Sources and further information

Mintzberg, H. (2009) 'Rebuilding companies as communities', *Harvard Business Review*, (July–August), pp. 140–3.
Wenger, E. (1998) *Communities of Practice: Learning, Meaning and Identity*, Cambridge: Cambridge University Press.
Wenger, E. , McDermott, R. and Snyder, W. (2002) *Cultivating Communities of Practice: A Guide to Managing Knowledge*, Boston, MA: Harvard Business School Press.

Note: This feature was written by David MacLennan, Assistant Professor at Thompson Rivers University, BC, Canada.

competency frameworks were embraced in the National Occupational Standards for management. In the 1990s, in identifying inadequate leadership as the first and fundamental barrier to successful team-based re-engineering projects, a competency framework identified a cluster of 11 leadership competencies that were considered necessary for the successful implementation and maintenance of 'high-performance work systems'. These were delegator, visionary, change agent, inspirer, high-trust, coach, team builder, supporter, champion, facilitator and partner.[56]

Evaluating the competency approach

While competency models apparently dominate UK and US leadership development programmes, the approach also has several shortcomings. The competencies identified to promote an individual to a leadership role may be more likely to be exhibited by a particular gender or ethnic group. Another criticism is the distinction between actual and perceived competence. If an individual cultivates the correct 'office front', it may enable a relatively incompetent individual to be perceived by co-workers as competent.[57] A further limitation is that it gives insufficient attention to the value 'reflexivity' and emotion in the workplace.[58]

Power, gender and cross-cultural issues

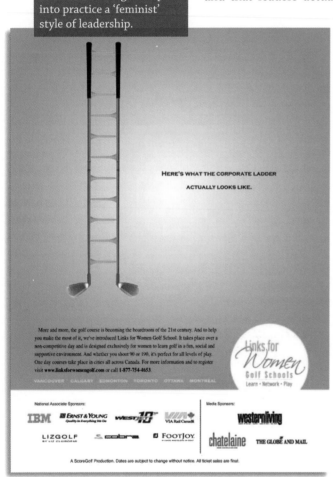

plate 48 Some argue that powerful economic and organizational imperatives do not permit opportunities for female managers to put into practice a 'feminist' style of leadership.

HERE'S WHAT THE CORPORATE LADDER

ACTUALLY LOOKS LIKE.

More and more, the golf course is becoming the boardroom of the 21st century. And to help you make the most of it, we've introduced Links for Women Golf School. It takes place over a non-competitive day and is designed exclusively for women to learn golf in a fun, social and supportive environment. And whether you shoot 90 or 190, it's perfect for all levels of play. One day courses take place in cities all across Canada. For more information and to register visit www.linksforwomengolf.com or call 1-877-754-4653.

VANCOUVER CALGARY EDMONTON TORONTO OTTAWA MONTREAL

Links for Women Golf Schools
Learn · Network · Play

National Associate Sponsors:

IBM   ERNST & YOUNG   WESTJET   VIA Rail Canada

LIZGOLF   cobra   FOOTJOY

Media Sponsors:

westernliving

chatelaine   THE GLOBE AND MAIL

A ScoreGolf Production. Dates are subject to change without notice. All ticket sales are final.

Source: SCOREGolf

As we have discussed in earlier chapters, critical organizational theorists are highly sceptical about the assumptions and motives upon which traditional accounts of management are based. The mainstream leadership literature assumes consensus in the workplace that socially consensual leadership increases employee commitment, and that leaders actually influence organizational performance. Critical analysts emphasize that leadership is intrinsically rooted in power. The assumption made in mainstream leadership literature is that if leaders can persuade their followers to act, then leaders appear to be powerful. The new popular rhetoric on leadership envisages the shifting from the old 'command and control' style of leading to 'shared leadership'. Thus, it is argued that, in the so-called knowledge economy, much of leadership is paradoxical: leaders gain more power by giving it away.

Power is related to leadership because it is part of the influence process. But what is power, where does it come from, and what do we know about the relationship between leaders and power? Some scholars interested in power–influence theories seek to explain leadership effectiveness in terms of the amount and type of power possessed by a leader, and how the leader exercises that power. One major issue addressed by scholars is the way power is 'acquired' and 'lost' by various individuals in the workplace. Team-based organizational designs and notions of power sharing through participative leadership styles have generated an interest in power–influence research.

Others scholars have emphasized the primacy of language and discourse in understanding power. According to this perspective, power is not a commodity possessed by leaders, but operates through discourses, which produce knowledge, and disciplinary techniques that define and constrain the identities of both followers and leaders. Michel Foucault's work on power-knowledge, which suggests that followers are deeply enmeshed in their own subordination, is prominent in this approach to power–influence.[59] Chapter 16 provides further discussion on the traditional and contemporary approaches to power in the organization, and their relationship to work behaviour.

Since the early 1990s, the topic of gender has entered leadership literature, and has generated much research and questioning on, among other things, whether women lead differently from men. Mainstream analysts argue that women managers have a

power–influence approach: an approach that examines processes of influence between leaders and followers, and explains leadership effectiveness in terms of the amount and type of power possessed by an organizational leader and how that power is exercised

How do you view feminist approaches to leadership? To what extent does the majority male culture of organizations shape gender relations in the workplace?

stop reflect

more interactive style, which includes more people-oriented, knowledge-sharing and participative leadership. Feminist leadership characteristics that have been identified include consensus building, shared power and the promotion of diversity.

Critical analysts have focused on the way in which jobs, occupations and organizations are themselves gendered, arguing that the processes and practices of gendering within the organization consolidate men's power in the workplace, and marginalize and exclude women from management positions. This is popularly referred to as the 'glass ceiling'. As we have already noted, numerous writers have pointed out that most leadership models are based on male behaviour.

Does gender make a difference? Do women managers have more people-oriented and participative leadership styles? Whereas some observers proposed that feminine characteristics, such as warmth, caring and empathy, allow women to succeed in organizational leadership roles because they are associated with a 'transformative' leadership style,[60] sociologists analysing from a critical perspective have argued that the belief that women are 'naturally' more consensual could be 'the expression of a relative lack of power rather than a characteristic of woman-hood per se' (ref. 61, p. 165). Data on practising managers suggest that workers tend to perceive female managers as having an 'inclusive' and 'soft' leadership style, and male managers as having a 'controlling' and 'hard' style. Some feminists argue that women leaders in organizations have the interactional leadership style needed to encourage and nurture worker commitment to organizational goals.

empathy: a person's ability to understand and be sensitive to the feelings, thoughts and situations of others

Sociological studies focus our attention on familiar antagonisms and imperatives, which avoid the tedious piety about female managers being inclusive and cooperative while male managers are competitive and controlling. Managers of both genders are competitive, and male managers are just as capable of being inclusive as women. The choice between different leadership styles is usually dictated by the situation and by economic and organizational imperatives. As Judy Wajcman compellingly argues:

The literature on women's management style ... has been concerned with the issue of whether women manage in the same way as men or have a distinct style of their own ... We are asked to celebrate an idealized femininity as demonstrated by women's greater caring, intuitive qualities. The trouble is that the qualities, characteristics and culture ascribed to women originate from the historical subordination of women ... in practice, senior women managers manage in much the same way as senior men within the same specific context. This is because styles of management are shaped more by organizational imperatives than by the sex or personal style of specific individuals. (ref. 61, pp. 258–9)

Thus, the organizational dynamics and culture might not provide opportunities for female managers to put into practice a 'feminist' style of leadership, but compel them to 'manage like men'.

Evaluating leadership: is leadership important?

Do leaders actually influence organizational performance? To begin to answer this question, we need a sense of the methodological challenges of measuring the leadership–performance link.

What types of performance variable should be measured? A variety of variables have been commonly employed, including employee job satisfaction, productivity, customer satisfaction and market share. Any analysis is of course very much dependent upon, among other things, the perspective that is used.[62,63] For example, shareholders may evaluate the organization's performance solely in terms of financial outcomes such as profits and share values. Employees may, however, judge the organization's performance in terms of a healthy and safe workplace, while community groups may focus on compliance with environmental regulations.

The argument that leaders influence performance seems plausible and is made by numerous writers. For example, one study found that 44 per cent of the profitability of the organizations studied was accounted for by changing the leader,[64] while another asserted that the driving force behind any successful change process is 'leadership, leadership, and still more leadership' (ref. 65, p. 31). Another study reported that leadership is associated with positive effects on the shared perceptions of group members regarding an organization's practices and the types of behaviour that are rewarded.[66] These results reinforce the findings that leadership has a fundamental role in shaping and guiding the cultural characteristics of their organization.[67]

The counter-argument is that leadership is of little consequence: more influential are the forces in which the leader is situated.[68] A dramatic example is the 2001 collapse of the North American airline industry, without any change in leadership, following the September 11 attack on the World Trade Center in New York. In some sectors, 'the leader is insignificant' hypothesis can be made following the global recession caused by the US financial crisis of 2008/09. Furthermore, as we have discussed, it is argued that leaders have limited discretion in their strategic behaviours, and ineffective leaders can be substituted by synergistic work teams and information technology.[69]

Evaluating organizational leadership presents tough methodological challenges for researchers. The research on leadership outcomes calls for the disclosure of commercially sensitive information on performance indicators, which many managers are unwilling or unable to provide to an independent researcher. The researcher has to isolate the relevant variables. For instance, even if an apparently causal relationship between leadership and market share is discovered, can it be assumed that nothing else has changed in the meantime? Exchange rates can significantly affect market share, and factors like this make it difficult to assess leadership effectiveness with complete confidence. In addition, the selection of appropriate criteria depends on the objectives and values of the person making the evaluation.[50] There is broad agreement, therefore, that it is difficult to evaluate the leader–performance relationship, as there are so many alternative measures of performance and it is uncertain which criterion is most relevant.

We started this section by asking the question, 'Do leaders actually influence organizational performance?' Arguably in the twentieth century, there was popular enthusiasm for the transformative outcomes attributed to the perceived charismatic leader. By 2009, however, in the throes of the worst economic slump since 1929, spectacular banking failures and an implosion of the global economy, enthusiasm for the popular 'heroic' theories of leadership had waned. Indeed, researchers have shown the 'dark side' of charismatic leadership, and some are scathing of the adulatory focus on so-called visionary leaders.[70–73]

Perhaps we need a model of leadership that celebrates mutual equality between the actors and the active visible hand of government – for a stronger regulation of global capitalism. Challenging the traditional notion of leadership, Keith Grint argues that critical to successful leadership:

> is not a list of innate skills and competences, or how much charisma you have, or whether you have a vision or a strategy for achieving that vision, but whether you have *a capacity to learn from your followers*. And that learning approach is inevitably embedded in a relational model of leadership. (ref. 9, p. 105, emphasis added)

The challenge for researchers is to locate leadership in a wider social context, and to provide empirical evidence to substantiate the emerging theories on the interconnectedness of leadership, learning, creativity and sustainability.

For further information and research reports on evaluating the leadership–performance linkage, go to www.nber.org/authors/casey_ichniowski; http://people.few.eur.nl/paauwe

stop reflect

Chapter summary

- Leadership is a dialectical process in which an individual persuades others to do something they would not otherwise do. It is a result of the interaction between the leader and followers in a specific context, and is equated with power.

- Leadership is not the same as management. Management is associated with functions such as planning, organizing, controlling and efficiency, whereas leadership is associated with vision making and significant change. Management processes produce a degree of order and consistency in work behaviour. Leadership processes produce significant change or movement.

- We observed that leadership theories are typically classified according to the types of variable emphasized in a theory or empirical study. We reviewed the major perspectives of leadership, including the trait, behaviour, contingency, transformational, shared and competency approaches. We showed how the systematic research on leadership has evolved from a narrow focus on the leader's traits to a multidimensional model of leadership, which looks at the exercise of leadership as a complex reciprocal process affected by the interaction between the leader, the followers and the opportunities and constraints afforded by the external and internal contexts in which they find themselves.

- We have drawn attention to issues of power and gender, as well as the limitations of individualistically oriented charismatic and transformative leadership models.

- In the context of twenty-first century corporate greed, irresponsibility, scandals and a single-minded focus on shareholder value, there is the danger that once people overalign themselves with a company, and invest excessive faith in the wisdom of its leaders, they are liable to lose their original sense of identity, tolerate ethical lapses they would have previously deplored, find a new and possibly corrosive value system taking root, and leave themselves vulnerable to manipulation by the leaders of the organization, to whom they have mistakenly entrusted many of their vital interests.[74]

Key concepts

behaviour perspective 364–366	
charismatic and transformational leadership 372–373	
contingency perspective 366–368	
integrative approach 379	
power- and gender-influenced perspectives 376–377	
shared/superleadership 374	
substitutes for leadership 371–372	
trait perspective 363	
transactional leadership 372	

integrative approach: explains the effectiveness of a leader in terms of influence on the way the followers view themselves and interpret the context and events around them

Vocab checklist for ESL students

- ☐ Agenda
- ☐ Attribute
- ☐ Competencies
- ☐ Contingency, contingent
- ☐ Delegate, delegation
- ☐ Dyad
- ☐ Empathy
- ☐ Integrative
- ☐ Initiate, initiating
- ☐ Leadership, leader, lead
- ☐ Least preferred co-worker
- ☐ Outcomes
- ☐ Path–goal theory
- ☐ Personality
- ☐ Power-influence approach
- ☐ Relationship behavior
- ☐ Task behaviour

Chapter review questions

1. Are management and leadership diametrically opposed?
2. What are the main differences between classical and modern theories of leadership?
3. In the context of recent corporate and banking failures, does the use of unethical methods negate the claim to be a leader?
4. What contribution do critical analysts make to our understanding of organizational leadership?
5. After reading this chapter, do you believe that leaders are born or made?
6. How do managers and leaders make a difference to organizational performance?

Chapter research questions

1. One way to understand different approaches to analysing leadership is to examine your own university or organization. Form a group to discuss how you would address the following questions: How important is the top leader to the overall performance of your university or organization? What leadership theory discussed in this chapter could you use to analyse the leadership of one of the leaders in your university or organization? What degree of diversity is there among the leaders in your university or organization? Why is there diversity or little diversity in your university or organization?

2. Obtain a copy of Gary Yukl's (2008) article 'How leaders influence organizational effectiveness'.[50] What does the flexible leadership theory tell us about the leadership–performance link?

3. Keith Grint's (2005) *Leadership: Limits and Possibilities*[9] emphasizes the contested nature of the leadership concept. Read Chapter 1, 'What is leadership: person, result, position or process?' Why does leadership remain contested? What are the implications of this for teaching and training leadership?

▣→ Further reading

Bolden, R. and Gosling, J. (2006) 'Leadership competencies: time to change the tune?', *Leadership*, **2**(2), p. 160.

Bratton, J., Grint, K. and Nelson, D. (2005) *Organizational Leadership*, Mason, OH: Thomson-South-Western.

Carroll, B., Levy, L. and Richmond, D. (2008) 'Leadership as practice: challenging the competency paradigm', *Leadership*, **4**(4), pp. 363–79.

Grint, K. (2005) *Leadership: Limits and Possibilities*, Basingstoke: Palgrave Macmillan.

Herold, D., Fedor, D., Caldwell, S. and Liu, Y. (2008) 'The effects of transformational and change leadership on employees' commitment to change: a multilevel study', *Journal of Applied Psychology*, **93**(2), pp. 346–57.

Jepson, D. (2009) 'Studying leadership at cross-country level: a critical analysis', *Leadership,* **5**(1), pp. 61–80.

Schnurr, S. (2008) 'Surviving in a man's world with a sense of humour: an analysis of women leaders' use of humour at work', *Leadership*, **4**(3), pp. 299–319.

Sundgren, M. and Styhre, A. (2006) 'Leadership as de-paradoxification: leading new drug development work at three pharmaceutical companies', *Leadership*, **2**(1), pp. 31–51.

Yukl, Y. (2008) 'How leaders influence organizational effectiveness', *Leadership Quarterly*, 19, pp. 708–22.

Chapter case study 1

Hitting the glass ceiling at Hotoke, Japan

Setting

Women have long held subservient roles in Japanese society, and Japan's 1986 law barring sex discrimination in the workplace did little to stem the societal perception about traditional gender divisions of labour. It established a social obligation not to discriminate, but does not impose penalties on those who breached the law. In 2004, only 2.7 per cent of division chiefs at Japanese companies of 100 employees or more were women. Japan's lack of external support for families, including daycare options, makes it difficult for married women to continue working once they start a family. Company expectations for workers to put in long days at the office, and attend social events in the evenings, also creates stress for women, who are typically responsible for the bulk of domestic responsibilities in the home. It is therefore not surprising that many Japanese women view having a long-term career and a life as a wife and mother as simply incompatible.

The problem

Hotoke is an international, well-established company based in Japan, where it has led the industry in producing a variety of information technology and security products, digital devices and parts, and power and industrial services for over half a century. This includes home electronics, audio/visual equipment, PCs, mobile phones and lifestyle services. The company also conducts advanced, wide-ranging research in fields ranging from parts and materials development to hardware, software and services, resulting in world-leading research achievements.

Shigeru Takahasi oversees the electronics business segment of the business. In recent years, it had become increasingly difficult to recruit for key positions within his division, and with the company's ageing workforce, Shigeru knew this problem would only become worse. When one of his lower-level managers became ill and had to leave the company, Shigeru decided to look at employees in the non-management pool to see who might be a viable candidate.

Shigeru's first response was to look among the male workers as they made up the overwhelming majority of employees in the electronics area, but one female worker, 26-year-old Hirose Takako, caught his eye. Unlike most of the female employees who held university degrees in the humanities, education or the social sciences, Hirose had studied engineering. She had been with the company since she had graduated, and although an obviously intelligent woman, she was still working in an assistant's role similar to that of the other female employees. She had been provided with only minimal training since her arrival.

Shigeru knew that he would face a challenge from upper-level management in recommending Hirose for the management vacancy. After all, there had never been a female manager in the entire history of the company. Shigeru felt the time was right to move in that direction. After preparing the background material, Shigeru made a presentation to the Board of Directors.

As expected, the Board was not initially impressed with the idea. 'We cannot promote women and give them more responsible jobs,' one Director remarked. 'She will be likely to quit to get married. We cannot invest in someone who will be leaving soon. We expect a lifetime commitment.' Another complained that female workers were not able to execute plans and lacked the socialization skills to be part of management.

Shigeru was persistent. 'We must become more diverse in our promotion process. It will help us to solve our demographic issue and to become more innovative.' After some persuasion and several meetings later, the Board agreed to provide Hirose with a trial period as the company's first female manager.

It did not take long for Shigeru to become disappointed. Although she was cooperative and demonstrated a consensus style of decision making, valued by the Japanese management, Hirose clearly lacked confidence and appeared uncomfortable at the thought of being the company's first female manager. She disliked socializing in the male-oriented bars with the other managers in the evenings. Hirose quit shortly after her promotion, telling Shigeru that she was stressed with the idea of being a role model for other women and was not willing to forego marriage and motherhood in exchange for such challenges. Shortly after Hirose's resignation, Shigeru's supervisor asked him to prepare a report on what the company, and Shigeru, had learned from the experience.

Tasks

Prepare a short report, including answers to the following questions:

1. How do the trait and gender perspectives help explain why Hirose may or may not have been the right choice for the management job?
2. How did the company's culture, which reflects Japanese society's as a whole, contribute to how Hirose reacted?
3. What could the organization have done to help prepare Hirose and the company itself for her new role?

Essential reading

Adler, N. and Izraeli, D. (eds) (1994) *Competitive Frontiers: Women Managers in a Global Economy*, Cambridge: Blackwell.

Imamura, A. (ed.) (1996) *Re-imaging Japanese Women*, Berkeley: University of California Press.

Shimada, H. and Rebick, M. (2005) *The Japanese Employment System: Adapting To a New Economic Environment*, Oxford: Oxford University Press.

Tanaka, Y. (1995) *Contemporary Portraits of Japanese Women*, Connecticut: Praeger.

Woods, G. (2005) 'Japan's diversity problem: women command too few posts', *Wall Street Journal*, October 24.

Note

This case study was written by Lori Rilkoff, MSc, CHRP, Senior Human Resources Manager at the City of Kamloops, and lecturer in HRM at Thompson Rivers University, BC, Canada.

 Chapter case study 2

The challenge of evaluating leadership development training

 Visit www.palgrave.com/business/brattonob2e to view this case study

 Web-based assignment

You can evaluate the extent to which leadership research has influenced management education and training by visiting the following websites: www.cmctraining.org (which includes self-assessment quizzes); www.ourcommunity.com.au/leadership (this Australian website including a selection of 'Great Leadership Speeches'). Select a particular professional group, such as engineers. What leadership competencies do individuals need to display to be effective in the profession? Do 'leadership competencies' appear to have a gender bias? If so, why? Report your findings to your seminar group.

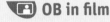 OB in film

The eleventh film spin-off from the legendary television series, *Star Trek* (2009) returns to tell the story of how Captain James T. Kirk became skipper of the *USS Enterprise*. His ascension to the chair is not straightforward, and he has to usurp Mr Spock, the more senior officer, who has been left in command when the previous captain, Captain Pike, is away from the ship and apparently lost.

1. Why was Kirk successful in the leadership battle with Mr Spock?
2. Using any system of classifying leadership style you choose, identify the dominant leadership styles of Captain Kirk and Mr Spock.
3. Identify key traits and behaviours of Captain Kirk and Mr Spock as illustrated in the film.

4. Why were other officers happy to accept Kirk as their new commanding officer?

Note: This feature was written by Professor Jon Billsberry, Senior Research Fellow, Open University Business School, UK.

 Bonus OB in Film feature

Visit www.palgrave.com/business/brattonob2e to see how the 2004 film *Master and Commander* can be considered in relation to the subject of leadership.

 **References**

1. Farrell, S. 'Bonfire of the bankers'. Available at www.independent.co.uk/news/business/analysis-and-features/treasury-select-committee-bonfire-of-the-bankers-1606332.html (accessed October 11, 2009).
2. Kay, J. Quoted in 'Praise for the steady', Editorial, *Globe and Mail*, February 13, 2009, p. A14.
3. Wood, M. and Case, P. (2006) 'Leadership refrains – again, again and again', *Leadership*, 1(2), pp. 139–45.
4. Mintzberg, H. (2004) 'Enough leadership', *Harvard Business Review*, 82(11), p. 22.
5. Burns, J. M. (1978) *Leadership*, New York: Harper & Row.
6. Yukl, G. (2006) *Leadership in Organizations* (6th edn), Englewood Cliffs, NJ: Prentice Hall.
7. Conger, J. A. and Kanungo, R. N. (1998) *Charismatic Leadership in Organizations*, Thousand Oaks, CA: Sage.
8. Apps, J. (1994) *Leadership for the Emerging Age*, San Francisco: Jossey-Bass.
9. Grint, K. (2005) *Leadership: Limits and Possibilities*, Basingstoke: Palgrave.
10. Adair, J. (2006) *Effective Leadership*, London: CIPD.
11. J. Kotter (1996) *Leading Change*, Boston, MA: Harvard Business School Press.
12. Stogdill, R. M. (1974) *Handbook of Leadership: A Survey of Theory and Research*, New York: Free Press.
13. Kirkpatrick, S. A. and Locke, E. A. (1991) 'Leadership: do traits matter?', *Executive*, 5, pp. 48–60.
14. Harter, N., Ziolkowski, F. and Wyatt, S. (2006) 'Leadership and inequality', *Leadership*, 2(3), pp. 275–93.
15. Granrose, C. S. (2001) 'The challenge of Confucius: the generalizability of North America career assumptions', in J. Kidd, X. Li and F.-J. Richter (eds), *Maximizing Human Intelligence Deployment in Asian Business: The Sixth Generation Project*, Basingstoke: Palgrave.
16. Kahn, R. L. and Katz, D. (1960) 'Leadership practices in relation to productivity and morale', in D. Cartwright and A. Zander (eds), *Group Dynamics: Research and Theory*, Elmsford, NY: Paterson.
17. Grint, K. (ed.) (1997) *Leadership*, Oxford: Oxford University Press.
18. Vecchio, R. P., Hearn, G. and Southey, G. (1996) *Organizational Behaviour*, Sydney: Harcourt Brace.
19. Blake, R. and Mouton, J. (1978) *The New Management Grid*, Houston, TX: Gulf.
20. Blake, R. and McCanse, A. A. (1991) *Leadership Dilemmas – Grid Solutions*, Houston, TX: Gulf.
21. Fiedler, F. E. (1964) *A Theory of Leader Effectiveness*, New York: McGraw-Hill.
22. Fiedler, F. E. (1970) 'Leadership experience and leader performance: another hypothesis shot to hell', *Organizational Behaviour and Human Performance*, 5, pp. 1–14.
23. McMahon, J. T. (1972) 'The contingency theory: logic and method revisited', *Personnel Psychology*, 25, pp. 697–710.
24. Peters, L. H., Hartke, D. D. and Pohlman, J. T. (1985) 'Fiedler's contingency theory of leadership: an application of the meta-

analysis procedures of Schmidt and Hunter', *Psychological Bulletin*, **97**, pp. 224–85.

25 Fiedler, F. E. (1974) 'The contingency model – new directions for leadership utilization', *Journal of Contemporary Business*, **3**(Autumn), p. 71.

26 Fiedler, F. E. (1965) 'Engineering the job to fit the manager', *Harvard Business Review*, **43**, pp. 115–22.

27 Schriesheim, C. A. and Kerr, S. (1977) 'R.I.P. LPC: a response to Fiedler', pp. 51–6 in J. G. Hunt and L. L. Larson (eds), *Leadership: The Cutting Edge*, Carbondale: Southern Illinois University Press.

28 House, R. T. (1971) 'A path goal theory of leader effectiveness', *Administrative Science Quarterly*, **16**, pp. 321–38.

29 House, R. J. and Mitchell, T. R. (1974) 'Path–goal theory of leadership', *Journal of Contemporary Business*, **3**, pp. 81–97.

30 Wofford, J. C. and Liska, L. Z. (1993) 'Path–goal theories of leaderships meta-analysis', *Journal of Management*, **19**, pp. 858–76.

31 Yukl, G. (2002) *Leadership in Organizations* (5th edn), Upper Saddle River, NJ: Prentice-Hall.

32 Hersey, P. and Blanchard, K. H. (1969) 'Life cycle theory of leadership', *Training and Development Journal*, **23**, pp. 26–34.

33 Hersey, P., Blanchard, K. H. and Johnson, D. (1977) *Management of Organizational Behavior: Utilizing Human Resources* (3rd edn), Upper Saddle River, NJ: Prentice Hall.

34 Bennis, W. G. (1985) *Leaders: Strategies for Taking Charge*, New York: Harper & Row.

35 Vecchio, R. P. (1987) 'Situational leadership theory: an examination of a prescriptive theory', *Journal of Applied Psychology*, **72**, pp. 444–51.

36 Blank, W., Weitzel, J. R. and Green, S. G. (1990) 'A test of situational leadership theory', *Personnel Psychology*, **43**, pp. 579–97.

37 Sundgren, M. and Styhre, A. (2006) 'Leadership as de-paradoxification: leading new drug development work at three pharmaceutical companies', *Leadership*, **2**(1), pp. 31–51.

38 This article was published in *Organizational Behaviour and Human Performance*, Vol. 22, Kerr, S. and Jermier, J. M., 'Substitutes for leadership: their meaning and measurement', pp. 375–403, Copyright Academic Press, Elsevier (1978).

39 Posakoff, P. M., Dorfman, P. W., Howell, J. P. and Todor, W. D. (1989) 'Leader reward and punishment behaviours: a preliminary test of a culture-free style of leadership effectiveness', *Advances in Comparative Management*, **2**, pp. 95–138.

40 Posakoff, P. M., MacKenzie, S. B. and Bommer, W. H. (1996) 'Meta-analysis of the relationship between Kerr and Jermier's substitutes for leadership and employee job attitudes, role perceptions, and performance', *Journal of Applied Psychology*, August, pp. 380–99.

41 Howell, J. P. and Dorfman, P. W. (1981) 'Substitutes for leadership: test of a construct', *Academy of Management Journal*, **24**, pp. 714–28.

42 Weber, M. (1978) *Economy and Society*, New York: Bedminster.

43 Friedman, M. (1982) *Capitalism and Freedom*, Chicago: Chicago University Press.

44 Bass, B. M. (1985) *Leadership and Performance Beyond Expectations*, New York: Free Press.

45 Bass, B. M. and Riggio, R. E. (2006) *Transformational Leadership*, Mahwah, NJ: Erlbaum.

46 Tichy, N. M. and Devanna, M. A. (1990) *The Transformational Leader* (updated edn), New York:: John Wiley.

47 Lewin, K. (1951) *Field Theory in Social Sciences: Selected Theoretical Papers*, London: Tavistock.

48 Conger, J. A., Kanungo, R. N. and Menon, S. T. (2000) 'Charismatic leadership and follower effects', *Journal of Organizational Behaviour*, November, pp. 747–68.

49 Lowe, K. B., Kroeck, K. G. and Sivasubramaniam, N. (1996) 'Effectiveness correlates of transformational and transactional leadership: a meta-analytic review of the MLQ literature', *Leadership Quarterly*, pp. 385–425.

50 Yukl, Y. (2008) 'How leaders influence organizational effectiveness', *Leadership Quarterly*, **19**, pp. 708–22.

51 Collins, J. (2002) 'Level 5 leadership'. Cited by Grint, K. (2005) *Leadership: Limits and Possibilities*, Basingstoke: Palgrave, p. 222.

52 Senge, P. M. (1990) *The Fifth Discipline*, New York: Currency/Doubleday.

53 Manz, C. C. and Sims H. P. Jr. (1989) *Superleadership: Leading Others to Lead Themselves*, New York: Berkley Books.

54 Bratton, J. A. (1992) *Japanization at Work*, London: Macmillan.

55 Woodruffe (1992). Quoted in Bratton, J. and Gold, J. (2003) *Human Resource Management: Theory and Practice* (3rd edn), Basingstoke: Palgrave, p. 227.

56 Oram, M. (1998) 'Re-engineering's fragile promise: HRM prospects for delivery', pp. 72–89 in P. Sparrow and M. Marchington (eds), *Human Resource Management: The New Agenda*, London: Pitman.

57 Price, K. H. and Garland, H. (1981) 'Compliance with the leader's suggestions as a function of perceived leader/member competence and potential reciprocity', *Journal of Applied Psychology*, **66**, pp. 329–36.

58 Bolden, R. and Gosling, J. (2006) 'Leadership competencies: time to change the tune?', *Leadership*, **2**(2), p. 160.

59 Foucault, M. (1977) *Discipline and Punish: The Birth of the Prison*, New York: Pantheon.

60 Rosener, J. (1990) 'Ways women lead', *Harvard Business Review*, December, pp. 199–225.

61 Wajcman, J. (1998) *Managing Like a Man: Women and Men in Corporate Management*, Cambridge: Polity Press/Penn State University Press.

62 Gaertner, G. H. and Ramnarayan, S. (1983) 'Organizational effectiveness: an alternative perspective', *Academy of Management Review*, **8**, pp. 97–107.

63 Zammuto, R. F. (1982) *Assessing Organizational Effectiveness*, Albany, NY: State University of New York Press.

64 Weiner, N. and Mahoney, T. A. (1981) 'A model of corporate performance as a function of environment, organization and leadership influences', *Academy of Management Journal*, **24**, pp. 453–70.

65 Kotter, J. P. (1996b) 'What leaders really do', in *Harvard Business Review on Leadership*, Boston, MA: Harvard Business School Press.

66 Zohar, D. and Tenne-Gazit, O. (2008) 'Transformational leadership and group interaction as climate antecedents: a social network analysis', *Journal of Applied Psychology*, **93**(4), pp. 744–57.

67 Berson, Y., Oreg, S. and Dvir, T. (2008) 'CEO values, organizational culture and firm outcomes', *Journal of Organizational Behavior*, **29**, pp. 615–33.

68 Pfeffer, J. and Salancik, G. (1977) 'Organizational context and the characteristics and tenure of hospital administrators', *Academy of Management Journal*, **20**, pp. 74–88.

69 Howell, J. P., Bowen, D., Dorfman, P., Kerr, S. and Podsakoff, P. (1990) 'Substitutes for leadership: effective alternatives to ineffective leadership', *Organizational Dynamics*, **19**, pp. 21–38.

70 Khurana, R. (2002) 'The curse of the superstar CEO', *Harvard Business Review*, **80**(9), pp. 60–6.

71 Huy, Q. N. (2001) 'In praise of middle managers', *Harvard Business Review*, **79**(8), pp. 72–9.

72 Morgan, N. (2001) 'How to overcome "change fatigue"', *Harvard Management Update*, July, pp. 1–3.

73 Thomas, A. B. (2003) *Controversies in Management Issues, Debates, Answers* (2nd edn), London: Routledge.

74 Tourish, D. and Vatcha, N. (2005) 'Charismatic leadership and corporate cultism at Enron: the elimination of dissent, the promotion of conformity and organizational collapse', *Leadership*, **1**(4), pp. 455–80.

75 Avolio, B. J. and Bass, B. M. (2006) *Multifactor Leadership Questionnaire* (3rd edn), Menlo Park, CA: Mind Garden.

76 Avolio, B. J. and Bass, B. M. (2005) 'Multifactor leadership questionnaire feedback report'. Available at www.destinysdoorcoaching.com/MLQ_Sample_11-05.pdf

77 Lewin, K., Lippitt, R. and White, R. K. (1939) 'Patterns of aggressive behaviour in experimentally created social climates', *Journal of Social Psychology*, **10**, pp. 271–99.

chapter 14
Communications

chapter objectives

After reading this chapter, you should be able to:

- discuss the importance of communication in the workplace
- discuss alternative perspectives on managing diversity in the organization
- explain the communication process, including non-verbal communication
- understand the use of communication in the leadership process
- understand the relationships between culture, gender and communication
- appreciate the existence of paradox in communication processes in the workplace

Introduction

The popular view of language is that it is simply a means of communicating ideas. However, rhetorical theorists are aware that language is a powerful force for getting people to do things, and cultural theorists emphasize that story telling is central to understanding our identity. People express themselves to each other in symbolic form. Language is a powerful force for moving people to action, which emphasizes its persuasive force. It is used by executive management as a means of shaping and controlling members' behaviour, for changing the culture of an organization (for example, eschewing the language of competition, embracing instead cooperation; see Chapter 12) and, in the current economic meltdown, to communicate the prospect of downsizing or budget cuts.[1] In the modern organization, where it is claimed that flexibility, learning and innovation are key issues, the processes of **dialogue** and communication have become critical core skills for managers and non-managers alike.[2,3] US President Barack Obama has 'shown the power of brilliant rhetorical force'.[4] His powerful speeches moved the people of the USA to vote for its first Afro-American president in 2009.

dialogue: a process of conversation among team members in which they learn about each other's mental models and assumptions, and eventually form a common model for thinking within the team

communication: the process by which information is transmitted and understood between two or more people

symbolic interactionism: the sociological approach that views society as the sum of the interactions of individuals and groups

language: a system of symbols that express ideas and enable people to think and communicate with one another

The exchange of information and the transmission of meaning are the very essence of formal work organizations. Information about the organization's products and services, its external competitors and its people is essential to management, workers, shareholders and customers. The string of accounting scandals that rocked the US business community in the summer of 2002 and the 2009 scandal of Satyam Computer Services in India illustrate how information that is communicated (or not communicated) helps to define a certain type of behaviour that we expect from the organizations we deal with. Communication in formal organizations, however, is a more complex process than simply information disclosure.

According to the behavioural perspective on **communication**, it is a symbolic process in which individuals act to exchange perceptions and ultimately to build a knowledge bank for themselves and for others, for the purpose of shaping future actions.[5,6] Language allows for the possibility of meaningful social interaction, and shapes the self – that part of an individual's identity composed of self-image and self-awareness. Language is also closely connected to power, and it shapes gender relations in organizations and the wider society. According to the **symbolic interactionism** thesis, identity is created through interaction with others. **Language** – broadly understood as a system of signification – is the most important source of symbolic meaning in human social life. Symbolic interactionism, which originates from the work of the American philosopher George Herbert Mead, is concerned with how language enables individuals to become self-conscious beings, aware of their own individuality.

The key element in this process is the symbol, something that represents something else. For example, the words that people use to refer to objects are in fact symbols that represent what we mean. The word 'cup' is the symbol we use to describe a receptacle that we use in Western society to drink coffee or tea. Non-verbal messages or forms of communication – such as hand signs, nods of the head or eye contact with others – can substitute for words. The use of symbols in social encounters both outside and inside the organization necessarily involves other people interpreting what they mean.

However, language is ambiguous and changes over time, and non-verbal symbols too can signify a multiplicity of meanings and ideas at any point in time. The phrases 'fat chance' and 'slim chance' might seem to be opposites, but they have the same meaning in English-speaking North America. Non-verbal symbols can signify different things depending on where they are used. For example, a thumbs-up sign is a gesture of approval in Britain, but in Ghana it is an insult. An open palm is an insulting gesture in Greece, while in West Africa it means you have five fathers, an insult akin to calling someone a bastard.[7]

Language has become important for the sociological exploration of contemporary societies. It is associated, for example, with power and gender relations. In this context, it is argued that writing is an ideological act in the process of gender redefinition.[8,9] The interplay of power and language comes through clearly in how people use masculine words to signify greater force, significance or value. For instance, the positive word 'seminal', meaning ground-breaking, is derived from the word 'semen' or 'male seed'. The positive adjective 'virtuous', meaning morally worthy, is derived from the Latin word *vir*, meaning man. By contrast, the disparaging adjective 'hysterical' comes from the Greek word *hystera*, meaning uterus or womb.[10]

Language plays a crucial role in establishing the status and power of a profession, particularly for high-status, knowledge-based occupations such as law and medicine.[11] A monopoly of esoteric knowledge is the essence or 'hallmark' of a profession: it marks out its members as 'privilege-knowing subjects' (and often seems to imply white male experience and a white male standpoint). The work of Erving Goffman demonstrates the importance of language and power in physician–patient relations, particularly when a patient is obliged to enter hospital for medical treatment.[12] Through the work of the historian and philosopher Michel Foucault, the relationship between language and knowledge has been turned 180 degrees. Far from language symbolizing original creative thought, Foucault argued that language as a social construct actually dictates the thoughts individuals have: 'Languages do not represent our meaning so much as construct them for us' (ref. 13, p. 509).

From a managerialist standpoint, 'effective' communications is one means by which managers 'get things done', for example by articulating a vision, informing workers of organizational rules, and giving feedback in face-to-face interviews. In this sense, it should be self-evident that the process of management, as shown diagrammatically in Figure 1.3, depends critically on communication between managers and non-managers. Not surprisingly therefore, management texts emphasize the importance of open, clear and precise communication. They also emphasize that managers cannot afford to underestimate the complex interconnections that can result in unanticipated face-to-face encounters. When managers fail to 'think in circles', they get into trouble.[14] The nature of the communication process established in the organization reflects the management style, degree of employee participation, culture and efficiency of the workplace. It is suggested that 'improving the communication of senior executives, especially the CEO, may be the most cost-effective way to improve employees' satisfaction with communication in their organizations' (ref. 15, p. 26).

Do you see language as a reflection of power in society?

stop
reflect

Theorists have implied that the two constructs of 'communication' and 'organization' are equivalent.[16,17] Thus, all organizational models contain implicit notions about communication theories, and all communication theories, in turn, provide important insights into managing the employment relationship.[18] From a critical standpoint, organizational communication is an important tool for shaping and controlling various aspects of workers' behaviour in the workplace. It is a means of gaining commitment to the organization's goals, a means of conveying the organization's disciplinary practices, and ultimately of making workers more governable.[19]

This chapter examines different approaches to studying communication: functionalist, interpretivist and critical. It describes the functions and directions of communications in the workplace. It also explores the communication implications of culture, gender and diversity in the workplace, as well as the importance of persuasion in the communication process.

> Look again at Figure 1.3, which shows the management process. Why is communication so important to the management process and leadership?
>
> **stop reflect**

Perspectives on communication

When reading about organizational communication, it is important to be alert to the different perspectives that authors and researchers select. We will consider three major perspectives for understanding organizational communications: the functionalist, interpretivist and critical approaches.

Functionalist approach

functionalist perspective: the sociological approach that views society as a stable, orderly system

The **functionalist** or mechanistic approach is the dominant perspective in management studies, and sees communication as intended or unintended action. The work organization is viewed as an entity, and different communication acts are variables that shape and determine the operations of that entity.[20] Communication occurs as a chain, the weakest link of which determines the effectiveness of the communication as a whole. Messages are concrete 'things' with properties that can be measured. Communication can be broken down into smaller and smaller units (known as message bits). The functionalist approach views communication as a metaphorical pipeline through which information is transmitted between a sender and a receiver. Organizational members have three basic methods of transmitting information, as shown in Figure 14.1.

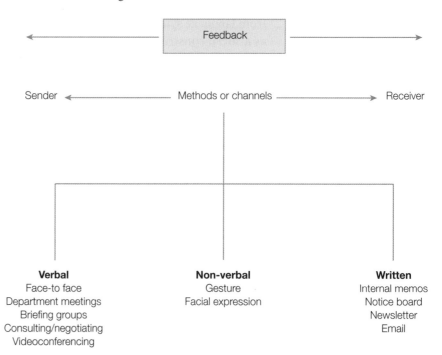

figure 14.1 Organizational communication as action

Source: Bratton and Gold (2007).[6a] Used with permission

Looking at Figure 14.1, consider what barriers to communication exist in organizations

stop reflect

Verbal communication ranges from a casual conversation between two employees to a formal speech by the managing director. In face-to-face meetings, the meaning of the information being conveyed by the sender can be reinforced through gesture or facial expressions – what is referred to as non-verbal communication. Written communication ranges from a casual note to a co-worker to an annual report. Electronic mail systems, videoconferencing and webcams have revolutionized written and verbal communication in organizations. Functionalists categorize behaviours or messages in terms of accomplishing goals and objectives.[20]

Mainstream authors suggest that aspects of organizational communications include mechanistic, interpretive-symbolic, and systems-interaction perceptual and psychological processes.[21] Another approach recognizes that the function of communication is to control, motivate and inform workers, and enable them to release emotional expression.[22] Thus, it is argued, the life-blood of the organization is communication: information is carried to all parts of the organization so that decisions and actions may be taken.

More critical authors (such as Putnam and his colleagues) identify seven clusters of metaphors or perspectives used in organizational communication theories – conduit, lens, linkage, performance, symbol, voice and discourse – which correspond to the theoretical approaches used in this chapter.[18] They look at how the organizational context affects communication, and at how communication shapes the organizational context. By privileging communication as the producer of organizations, and examining the metaphors used in organizational communication literature, they show that 'metaphors reveal alternative ways of thinking about the origin and nature of organizing, its processes, and the constructs that form its ontological roots' (ref. 18, p. 126).

Early organizational communication theories included classical or scientific management, and bureaucracy. The predominant metaphor applied to these organizations was the machine. Organizations were viewed as the primary vehicle through which lives were rationalized, 'planned, articulated, scientized, made more efficient and orderly, and managed by experts' (ref. 23, p. 57). The pipeline or chain images were absorbed into the conduit and lens metaphor clusters identified by Putnam and his co-workers. Communication was seen as the linear transmission of information. It was treated as a variable that influenced individual and organizational performance. The dominant interest was in the skills that make individuals more effective communicators, or factors that characterize system-wide communication effectiveness. Workers were viewed as a passive audience incapable of responding, interpreting, arguing or countering this form of control. Mainstream literature uses the words 'conduit', 'channel' and 'media' in descriptions of organizational communication.[24,25] The lens metaphor provides a different slant on the transmission of information. The assumption is that information is incomplete.

When a message is transmitted, the likelihood that the information will be converted, simplified, reduced or summarised increases if the senders and receivers have different cultural backgrounds and goals. The inevitability of misconception challenges traditional notions of accuracy, clarity and communication effectiveness by introducing meaning and interpretation into message transmission. One research domain that adopts a lens metaphor is media richness. Media richness theorists contend that managers will be more effective if they choose a communication medium that matches the ambiguity of their task.[26] Lean and rich media diagrams can be found in mainstream texts. Grint characterizes the functionalist approach, or the transmission model, in concrete terms: the 'language, technologies' are simply channels for telling somebody something. The manager chooses the most appropriate channel of communication to convey the information, accomplish goals and improve efficiency.[27]

media richness: refers to the number of channels of contact afforded by a communication medium, so, for example, face-to-face interaction would be at the high end of media richness, and a memorandum would fall at the low end of media richness

Interpretivist approach

interpretivism: the view held in many qualitative studies that reality comes from shared meaning among people in that environment

The **interpretivist** approach is a reaction against the functionalist perspective.[28] It attempts to understand human communication as something *in* the work organization, rather than something that *manages* the organization. Interpretivists argue that human beings do not behave as predictably as is suggested by the functionalist school. Thus, we may be able to predict that most people, or some people in the workplace, will react to a certain message in a certain way, but we cannot make the prediction for all workers. Some employees will do one thing and some another when presented with identical information. Interpretivist scholars argue that, because people are so complex in their behaviours and exhibit choice in responding to stimuli, functionalist explanations of organizational behaviour are inappropriate. The organism metaphor is associated with this approach. It is applied to a system of mutually connected and dependent parts constituted to share a common life.[29]

Communication is the transference and understanding of meaning. Most communication models convey this as a linear process (although they assume that both sender and receiver have an active role), but we need to be aware that the construction of meaning is affected by the skill, attitude and knowledge of the participants, and also by the sociocultural context in which the communication takes place. The creation of shared meanings is the basis of the interpretive-symbolic perspective. These shared meanings create the organization's **culture**, and can also serve to create and shape social reality. An organization's culture is partially created by the shared talk of its members. Organizational members capture complex experiences that are combinations of sense, emotion, reason and imagination, using narration and story telling to impart meaning.

culture: the knowledge, language, values, customs and material objects that are passed from person to person and from one generation to the next in a human group or society

Cultural factors are strong influences on the interpretive process. The definition and meaning of culture has been contested more than any other concept in the social sciences. Raymond Williams, the father of 'cultural studies', suggests that it has three core meanings:

- a general process of intellectual, spiritual and aesthetic development
- a meaning that relates to the works and practices of intellectual and artistic activity
- a meaning that refers to a particular way of life, whether of people, a period or a group.[30]

plate 49 Rituals such as handshakes, coffee breaks, gift giving and staff meetings are the norms and behaviours that embody the rites.

The prominent sociologist Anthony Giddens claims that the last of these is the definition used by sociologists. He claims that way of life is composed of 'the values the members of a given group hold, the norms they follow and the material goods they create' (ref. 30, p. 40), which may describe a work culture. An important part of work culture is the social interaction involved in the interpretation of narratives, rites and rituals. These symbolic 'shared meanings' serve to socialize newcomers, solve problems and impart organizational values and beliefs. Rites such as award ceremonies, retirement dinners and new member orientations are elaborate dramatic activities that consolidate cultural expressions into one event. Rituals such as handshakes, coffee

Source: Getty Images

breaks, gift giving and staff meetings are the norms and behaviours that embody the rites. The interpretive approach to organizational communication seeks to make sense of organizational members' actions as part of the social constructions of individuals that have become shared. These symbols are more than manifestations of an organization's culture: they are the means through which organizing is accomplished.

Metaphors have been used in organizational behaviour studies to understand the workplace. A metaphor is a particular linguistic expression that can link abstract social constructs to concrete things, and metaphors can be used to legitimize managers' actions, set goals and guide managers and non-managers' behaviour in the workplace.[18] Metaphors help theory building by enabling us to examine images at different levels of analysis. A theory is metaphorical if it suggests, through language, enlightening comparisons between organizational communication and other processes. For example, scientific management theory compares organizations with machines. The predominant metaphor used during the Summit of Americas in Quebec was the family of nations. Images of family and teams, the latter utilizing the language of sports, recur frequently in mainstream management texts on organizational design. The boxing metaphor has been adopted by some management analysts in response to the global economic crisis that began in 2008–09.[31] In the Western tradition, metaphor has the privilege of revealing unexpected truth. As Aristotle put it, 'Midway between the unintelligible and the commonplace, it is metaphor which most produces knowledge' (ref. 32, p. 151). Similarly, others believe that metaphors inform action and shape organizational practices.[29,33–35]

Many workplaces are pervaded by game and military metaphors, as well as metaphors of friends, family and home.[33,36] Accordingly, 'A metaphor works through invoking a concept originating from another field or level than the one that is being understood. The former modifies the latter and forms a specific image or gestalt' (ref. 35, p. 112). The knowledge of theories about organizational communications enables us to participate in a particular **discourse community**, which in this case is made up of individuals who share an interest in organizations and communication. To join in this ongoing conversation, as communication theorist Kenneth Burke describes it, we need to be aware of the previous and present conversations. Theories enhance our ability to understand and explain a variety of practical issues, such as where the idea of organization originated and what motivates people to work. Theories can show how communication and efficiency are linked. Because organizational communication theories are dynamic, we should view each theory as a participant in a larger, ongoing discourse. One theory should not be given prominence over another; rather, we should recognize its origins, bias and relationship to other theories.

Critical approach

The critical approach derives from the critical theory school, which seeks to expose the often hidden but pervasive power that post-industrial organizations have over individuals, while also challenging the assumed superiority of unfettered market capitalism. Whereas the functionalist approach is concerned with making the organization more efficient, the critical theorist is more concerned with examining organizational communication, such as myths, metaphors and stories, as a source of power. Critical theorists also try to understand why organizational practices that maintain strong controls over workers are considered legitimate, and so are not resisted.[37]

Organizational communication is thus studied in terms of hidden exercises of power and managerial influence. The metaphors of voice and discourse enable us to analyse the questions of who can speak, when and in what way. We need to consider

---

stop reflect

To what extent do social factors such as status differences, social conformity and cultural differences act as barriers to communication? Can you think of examples?

---

discourse community: a way of talking about and conceptualizing an issue, presented through ideas and concepts, spoken or written, within a social group or community (such as lawyers or physicians) communication as the expression or suppression of organizational members' voices. Morgan identifies a number of metaphors used to convey the perspectives of critical theorists.[29] We will consider the metaphors of culture, political system, language game and text/discourse in the next few pages.

Discourse analysis, inspired by Gramsci and Foucault, is a useful way of theorizing culture. Rather than seeing culture as something static and real that is common to all members of a nation or ethnic group, discourse analysis sees it as 'social processes operating in contested terrains in which different voices become more or less hegemonic in their offered interpretations of the world' (ref. 30, p. 40). Organizational culture is a set of meanings, ideas and symbols that are shared by members of a collective and have evolved over time. Talking about culture then means 'talking about the importance for people of symbolism – rituals, myths, stories, and legends – and about the interpretation of events, ideas, and experiences that are influenced and shaped by the groups within which they live' (ref. 35, p. 104).

Two critical theorists, Alvesson and Due Billing, argue that culture facilitates social life but also includes elements of constraint and conservatism.[35] It tends to freeze social reality in order to subordinate people to dominating ideas, beliefs and assumptions that are taken for granted. Wittgenstein's metaphor of a language game suggests that organizational activity is a game of words, thoughts and actions.[29] As individuals engage with their worlds, through specific codes and practices (using both verbal and non-verbal language), organizational realities arise as rule-governed symbolic structures. Language creates the organizational concepts that define the culture of an organization and give form to notions of control, delegation and rationality. Meetings, or 'technologies of power', are an example of the social reality created and controlled by management, which endorse and encourage certain understandings and feelings that reflect managerial interests and perspectives.[38]

empirical approach: research that attempts to answer questions through a systematic collection and analysis of data

Alvesson's empirical research suggests that the meeting is one element of the ongoing creation and recreation of the organization.[38] Management of meaning is part of everyday leadership. Attention is placed on some things and not on others. Language is carefully chosen. One example of simple, but powerful, word choice is the familiar 'them and us' concept being superseded by the use of 'we' and 'you'. During meetings, the phrase 'We did as you said' is frequently used. 'We' in this context is top management, and 'you' the collective workforce. This counteracts the idea that power is directed from the top downwards. It suggests that decisions are anchored in the workforce, and that top management is carrying out the wishes of the collective. 'We' is used to suggest a common identity among those present at the meeting; they are encouraged to consider themselves as part of the same unit, with common interests and objectives. As Frost puts it, 'Communication structures, channels, networks, and rules are avenues of power … Thus the communication medium is never neutral' (ref. 35, p. 68).

Critical theory draws attention to the political and exploitative aspects of organizational life. This perspective seeks to expose the 'order' that interpretive theory seeks to understand, and functionalist theory to enhance, as superficial. Critical theorists suggest that, like other aspects of organizational life, the organizational communication process is complicated by organizational characteristics such as hierarchy and power relations, and by the fact that individual managers and non-managers have idiosyncrasies, abilities and biases. They argue that organizational communication is central to the other processes of power, leadership and decision making. Organizational communication involves more than providing employees with information about their employment and wider issues relating to the organization in which they work. It is as complex as human behaviour itself.

According to this perspective, every human act, both conscious and unconscious, contains information that is then interpreted by a receiver. The three notions associated with communications – behaviour, meaning and context – are synthesized in this definition of organizational communication: 'Both behaviours and symbols, generated either intentionally or unintentionally, occurring between and among people who assign meaning to them, within an organizational setting' (ref. 5, p. 4).

In modern organizations, symbolic power is particularly noticeable compared with technical and bureaucratic means of control. The management of meaning is regarded as symbolic action. The creation of a managerially biased social reality reduces the number of available variations in the way things can be perceived, when the possibilities of describing, understanding and evaluating workplace conditions and objectives are being negotiated:

> Generally dominance is manifested not in significant political acts but rather in the day-to-day, taken for granted nature of organizational life. As such, the exercise of power and domination exists at a routine level, further protecting certain interests and allowing the order or organizational life to go largely unquestioned by its members. (ref. 35, p. 66)

Consequently, dominance is exercised chiefly by ensuring that the current reality in the organization is regarded as natural, rational, self-evident, problem-free, sensible and so on. Therefore, the power aspect is of crucial importance in organizational communication. Communication provides the means through which power can be exercised, developed, maintained and enhanced.

Communication and management

Now we have seen something of the different *perspectives* for studying organizational communications, it should not surprise us to find that the *function* of organizational communications is contested. Traditional approaches to organizational communication identify at least two functions of communication: to exchange information and to bring about change. Figure 14.1 illustrated the first function of communication, the process by which information is exchanged between a sender and a receiver. This function of organizational communication can be seen in studies of managers and their work. One classic study found that managers spend 80 per cent of their contact time on activities devoted exclusively to the transmission of information.[39] The second function of communication is to help those who manage the organization to bring about change, by persuading others to adopt a different work regime and/or behaviour.

Channels of communication

formal channels: a communication process that follows an organization's chain of command

informal channels: a communication process that follows unofficial means of communication, sometimes called 'the grapevine', usually based on social relations in which employees talk about work

Communication theorists refer to **formal and informal channels** of communication in a work organization. The three basic communication media – written, verbal and non-verbal – can be used in either of these types of channel. Formal channels are established by the organization and transmit messages relevant to job-related activities, using for example memos, voicemail, email and meetings. Informal channels, such as personal or social messages, contribute to the culture and social reality of an organization. Among those who have studied and researched these differences is Mikhail Bakhtin, a Russian literary and cultural critic. He was interested in language in actual use, the 'utterance', or primary speech genres. From these, the more complex 'secondary' genres of writing are derived.

genre: a term to describe the different kinds of writing and reading in the workplace, including, reports, letters and memoranda

In the workplace (as elsewhere), **genre** is the word used to indicate the different kinds of thing, in this case writing required to complete the communication loop and ensure efficient action is taken. Empirical studies of workplace writing reveal the complex social, cultural and institutional factors at play in the production of specific trends of writing.[40] Two researchers, Freedman and Medway, point to the interaction and interpersonal dynamics that are part of creating texts in an organization. The features of the text are often 'conventionalized by tacit agreement – the lore of the tribe' (ref. 41, p. 148). They can function as the social glue that helps an organization to establish its own culture. The interpersonal dynamics that surround and support the creation of texts in an organization reflect the levels of relative power, influence and access to information.[41]

Verbal and non-verbal aspects of communication are inextricably linked. Even a verbal message on a computer-generated voice telephone voicemail system has a 'gender' and 'ethnicity' and so has a non-verbal aspect. Verbal communication ranges from a casual conversation between employees to the company president's speech transmitted to branch offices throughout the country. Face-to-face interaction is the most effective form of verbal communication when the sender wants to persuade or motivate the receiver. Research has found that face-to-face talk is preferred because it provides for the maximum amount of information to be transmitted during a communication episode. That is, it offers multiple information cues (through words, postures, facial expression and gestures), and the personal touch of 'being there'. Non-verbal cues may be organized into several categories: the environment, personal space, postures, gestures, facial expressions, eye behaviour, and tone and pitch of voice.[21]

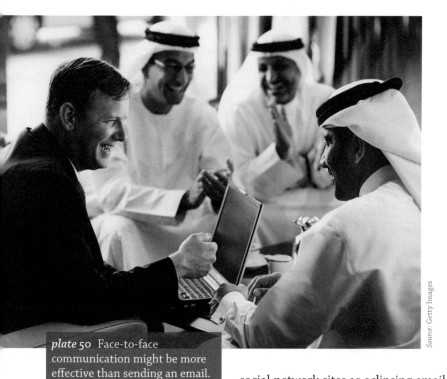

Source: Getty Images

plate 50 Face-to-face communication might be more effective than sending an email.

Face-to-face interaction is considered to be the richest medium on the communication channel continuum. Recent research in face-to-face conversations confirms that individuals engage in interactions to affirm themselves and express their relation to others. Conversations promote and share human knowledge.[42] It is most suitable for non-routine messages, whereas routine messages use the poorest media: flyers, bulletins or general reports. Marshall McLuhan's popular phrase 'The medium is the message' refers to the idea that the sender's choice of communication channel transmits meaning beyond the message content. The symbolic meaning of choosing one medium over another may vary from one manager to another. For example, some people might see the use of email as a sign of professionalism and/or efficiency, while others might view it as impersonal and inappropriate. A research report by Neilson Online identifies social network sites as eclipsing email. Carmi Levy, technology analyst at AR Communications Inc., concludes that email is yesterday's messaging platform. The social networking site Facebook, with 175 million users, shows that the website can be vital for business as well as personal use. As argued, 'This has serious implications for companies – they need to get with program quickly and learn how to leverage [social network sites], rather than shut-down or ban them.'[43]

One example of managerial insensitivity is the announcement on television that Canadian Airlines was shutting down: employees learned of their fate by listening

plate 51 Organizations send employees to indoor climbing centres where they learn to solve communication problems and work as a team.

Source: Nick Tutton

leadership for at least three reasons: the increasing use of teams, the rapid pace of globalization, and the growing need to retain talent. The social skill of managing leader–follower relationships is also closely linked to the powers of persuasion. Persuasiveness can be viewed as a social skill that is a component of emotional intelligence. Black contends that effective managerial communication involves taking responsibility for and ownership of the content (the message), ensuring recipients' understanding of the message, and knowing the organization's position on difficult issues and its rationale for decisions. To be competent, the leader–manager needs to create the right impact on her or his audience.[49]

Keith Grint, a prominent researcher in leadership, adopts classical rhetoric as his model to describe persuasive communication.[46] People's ethos – which includes their perceived expertise on the topic, their credentials and their experience – contributes to their ability to persuade. Their expertise in how they speak also greatly influences listeners. This concerns issues such as speaking confidently and relatively quickly, using some technical language, and avoiding pauses ('erm' or 'uh') and hedges ('you know' and 'I guess'). Establishing trustworthiness and respect enables a communicator to be more effective. If listeners perceive that the communicator will not benefit personally from the proposal he or she is putting forward, and the communicator acknowledges that the opposing position has one or two positive elements, this helps to convince listeners of the reasonableness of the argument.

The message content is of course a critical feature of persuasive communication. If the speaker expects the audience to be resistant to the message, he or she must first present viewpoints that validate the audience's viewpoint, before presenting his or her own position. If the issue is highly emotive, a good alternative is the Rogerian structure of presenting arguments.[50] This is appropriate if the leader wants to avoid threatening those who hold opposing views, since 'Rogerian persuasion basically aims at achieving consensus around a correct position. The objective is truth, not victory' (ref. 50, p. 397). Both classical and Rogerian rhetoric rely on emotional and logical appeals, which form Aristotle's three criteria of persuasiveness, as shown in Figure 14.3.

In organizational communications, it is often difficult to separate personal character and emotional appeal. Logical proof is seldom as effective as Aristotle maintains. This does not mean that appeals to rationality – to the 'truth' and to the 'facts' – are irrelevant. Far from it, they are crucial elements of persuasion, but they are not in and of themselves sufficient to persuade others on each and every occasion. This is blatantly clear when scientific 'experts' disagree on the 'facts', such as in the case of genetically modified foods or global warming. Effective communication involves a combination of speech (content), speaker, situation (context) and spectators (audience), and also the active roles of individuals and groups who socially shape the contents and contexts, rather than merely responding to them.[46] We must consider the rhetorical context of the communication process as including the social and collective forms of organization (that is, the culture) that generate persuasive interpretations of the message (Figure 14.4).

The rhetorical context of meetings designed to convey information, which was studied by Alvesson,[38] reveals the techniques of power and discipline that are used in effective managerial communication. The seemingly neutral conveying of information and use of language can reinforce asymmetrical power relations and contribute to the disciplinary function, which is so central to management and to many other manifestations of organizational culture. Symbolically charged activities, events and words condense important ideas and assumptions, and convey them forcefully to the audience. Using 'we' and 'you' in this specific situation may have considerable rhetorical appeal. Managers are therefore agents of power, creating or reproducing shared meanings, ideas and values through acts of communication, which suspend social reality, or at least counteract an open, questioning approach to how it should be negotiated.

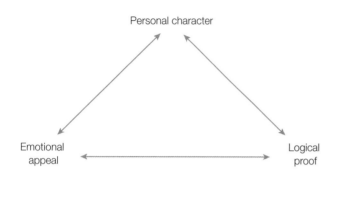

figure 14.3 Aristotle's model of rhetoric

Source: Grint (2001).[46] Used by permission of Oxford University Press

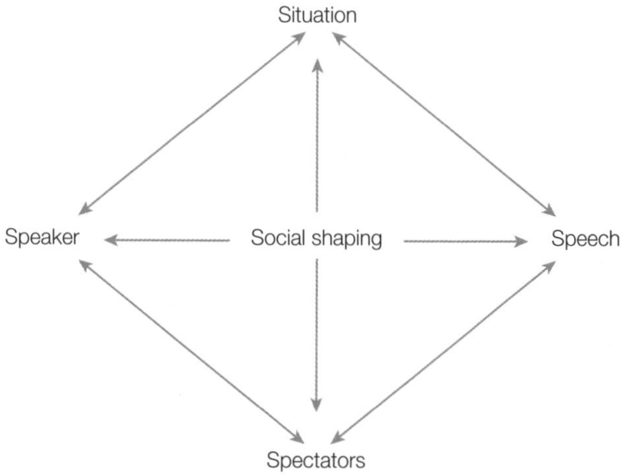

figure 14.4 The immutable four Ss model of speech making

Communication and cultural diversity

With the globalization of markets, and an increase in mergers and acquisitions, the workplace is seeing greater interaction and communication among peoples of different cultures and experiences.[51] The multicultural communication environment of organizations is an indisputable thriving reality. It can be argued that the way in which businesses manage cross-cultural communication between colleagues will determine their economic survival and competitiveness in the global marketplace. Managers who have a systematic understanding of the cultural and organizational dynamics of cross-cultural communication will enhance organizational effectiveness and performance. Managers and researchers need to guard against ethnocentrism, the tendency to judge other cultures by the standards of one's own.

Diversity in organizations

Narrow definitions of diversity emphasize race, ethnicity and gender. Broader definitions of diversity tend to focus on issues of 'racism, sexism, heterosexism, classism, ableism, and other forms of discrimination at the individual, identity group, and system levels' (ref. 52, p. 88). Broad definitions contend that everyone is different, and comply with the individualistic concept that structures thinking about organizations. Essentially, scholars are referring to 'diversity in identities' based on social and demographic groups: 'A mixture of people with different group identities within the same social system' (ref. 53, p. 88).

So the concept of identity is at the core of understanding diversity in organizations. This has implications for effective communication in the workplace. Studies of work teams reveal that people's identification with subgroups (*micro-identities* in the organizational context) takes precedence over their identification with the organization as a whole (their *macro-identity*). The ability of people to work together in teams composed of members from different group identities may be hampered by the consequences of group identification.[54]

The interpersonal communications model discussed earlier in this chapter (see Figure 14.1) ignores different cultures and how culture impacts on the communication process.[55] Critics of this linear communication model argue that people communicate differently because of their culture, their gender and how they have learned to perceive the world. Cultures differ in both their verbal and their non-verbal communications. A culturally diverse workforce has the potential to improve organizational effectiveness. It can provide improved decision making, creativity and innovation, and marketing knowledge to different types of consumer, all of which benefits the global organization. Employees must overcome their reluctance to communicate with co-workers from other cultural groups.

A Canadian study of cultural diversity in Toronto's major hotels found that language barriers made it difficult for managers to give non-English-speaking employees meaningful feedback to help them improve their jobs.[25] Even when people speak the same language, interpreting voice intonation can be problematic. In some cultures, the tone changes depending on the context, such as home, a social situation or work. Using a personal, informal style in a situation where a more formal style is expected affects the meta-meaning behind the message.

There was considerable research on racio-ethnicity and gender following the passing of equal opportunities and antidiscrimination legislation in the USA and Britain in the late 1960s and early 1970s. Taken as a whole, these studies suggest that black individuals and women face both access and treatment discrimination in organizations. However, it is important to note that assimilation theory underlies the questions studied and the solutions that are proposed. The successful integration of racial minorities and white women into organizations requires their loss of identity: they must adapt to the norms and behaviours of the dominant group.

The theory and research are dominated by dichotomous thinking about identity: that is, thinking that divides people into two opposed groups, such as black versus white, Anglo versus Latino, or male versus female. Oppositional thinking implies not only that there is a difference, but also that there is a hierarchy in which one group is superior to the other, the dominant group obtaining its privilege by suppressing the other group. In much of the research on diversity in organizations, the legitimacy and basic values of the organization are not questioned. Organizations are regarded as fundamentally sound and neutral sites. However, we argue that it is essential for attention to be paid to what sustains and maintains the pattern of power relations in organizations. Communication plays an essential role in the establishment and maintenance of these power relations.

Discourse theory and analysis, referred to above, also covers the study of all types of written text and spoken interaction (both formal and informal), with particular attention to the functions served by language. It asks how certain sorts of talk and writing can accomplish particular goals, such as exclusions, blamings or justifications. It is important to study the language we use to talk about diversity in identities because, as one researcher points out, 'Language is so structured to mirror power relations that often we can see no other way of being, and it structures ideology so that it is difficult to speak both in and against it' (ref. 56, p. 100).

In the globalized marketplace, international communication across political or national borders is an integral part of business negotiations. Success can depend on the implicit and explicit nature of the communication process (both verbal and non-verbal). The informational context and the degree of background data that has to be transmitted varies from culture to culture.

high-context culture: a culturally sanctioned style of communication that assumes high levels of shared knowledge and so uses very concise, sometimes obscure, speech

low-context culture: a culturally sanctioned style of communication that assumes low levels of shared knowledge and so uses verbally explicit speech

The anthropologist E. T. Hall developed a useful system for understanding the communication implications of culture.[57] He classified cultures on a scale that ranges from 'high context' to 'low context'. (These are also sometimes described as individualistic [low-context] and collectivist [high-context] cultures.) In low-context societies, people are less able to agree or solve disputes without resorting to written contracts or litigation than they are in high-context ones. Explicit written and verbal messages are the norm in, for example, the USA, Canada, Scandinavia, Germany and Switzerland. High-context cultures emphasize collaboration and personal relationships as important aspects of doing business. Informal and unwritten contracts are the norm, together with the non-verbal language that surrounds the explicit message. This happens for example in Korea, China, Japan and Arab countries.

These two types of culture also differ in their patterns of time usage. Low-context cultures are characterized by monochronic time patterns. This is a linear and compartmentalized view of time. These cultures value quick responses and a direct approach to the issue, without the use of much background information. High-context cultures tend to work with polychronic time, which is more contextually based and flexible. Oral and written communication is less direct and more circular in nature. Discussion in business meetings may go off at tangents; the direct approach, to refocus on the agenda, can be considered rude. In resolving conflicts in cross-cultural communications, all parties involved must not only know about their own culture, but also demonstrate a willingness to accept differences in other cultures.

For further details on the importance of being sensitive to different communication practices when travelling abroad or working in international organizations, visit the following websites: www. internationalbusinesscentre.org; www.deloitte.com/ca/diversity

weblink

OB in focus   Humour in the workplace

Recent research has illustrated that successful organizational humour can improve group processes and outcomes that contribute to overall group effectiveness. Group productivity is enhanced because humour can have a positive effect on group cohesiveness, communication, creativity and stress reduction. Anecdotal evidence from the popular press indicates that today's workers expect work to be enjoyable. Younger workers (aged 18–25) in particular want to have fun at work and are more likely to leave firms when work is boring. A positive use of humour can facilitate long-term group effectiveness by having an impact on individual learning and development within the group, and team viability, or on the degree to which members of the group are able to continue working together in the future.

Communication plays a critical role in both group productivity and overall group effectiveness. Humour makes people more receptive to the receiver and message, it can be used to build morale and maintain relationships, and it can encourage communication between group members by reducing social distance and facilitating the expression of emotion and values. Furthermore, engaging in more effective communication processes leads to group members being more informed about processes, requirements and externalities that might influence group effectiveness, which should in turn lead to a more informed collective goal-setting process.

Using humour to create stronger cohesion between group members promotes higher levels of psychological safety and reduces stress levels, both of which are strongly influenced by the development of trust, open communication and personal rapport at the individual level. Groups that develop an atmosphere of psychological safety are able to solve problems based on honest reflection, openness and mutual influence, which results in learning. The use of humour within groups leads to positive group emotions that influence the development of group cohesion, commonly defined as 'attraction to the group'. The group is therefore a more attractive (for example, fun) place to be for group members. Consequently, this has implications for group viability and will aid in reducing employee turnover.

Source: Adapted from Eric Romero and Anthony Pescosolido (2008) 'Humor and group effectiveness', *Human Relations*, **61**(3), pp. 395–418.

A variety of gestures are used only in certain cultures, or their meaning changes between cultures. In Canada and the UK, for example, nodding the head up and down signals 'yes' and shaking it back and forth means 'no'. In Bulgaria, parts of Greece, Turkey, Iran and Bengal, it is the reverse. The gesture where the thumb and forefinger form a simple circle means 'OK' or 'everything is fine' in Canada, the UK and the USA, but in France it means zero or worthless, and in Japan it is the signal for money. In many other countries, it is considered a sexually rude gesture.[21] Canadians are taught to maintain eye contact with the speaker to show interest and respect, yet this is considered rude to some Asian and Middle Eastern people, who are taught to show respect by looking down when a supervisor or older person is talking to them.

Gender and communication: 'She said, he said'

Just as culture affects interpretation, so research has demonstrated that gender plays a role in influencing what is considered to be the appropriate communication medium. There appear to be important differences between the conversational styles of men and women, which can be summarised in terms of 'report' and 'rapport' respectively.[24] A plausible explanation of why genders can create communication barriers is that men tend to see conversation as a tool: they use it to exchange information, accomplish a task, offer advice or advance their status. For many men, conversations are primarily a means to preserve independence. On the other hand, it is suggested that women talk in order to nurture, support and empathize. Women speak and hear a language of cooperation, connection and intimacy. Recent research suggests that female managers can mitigate the negative effects of being in a 'masculine' role by being able to perceive the non-verbal emotions of their subordinates. Also, male managers who were emotionally perceptive garnered more employee satisfaction.[58]

Studies have also indicated that female managers use an open communication style that centres on cooperation and request when dealing with personnel problems. However, male managers use their position in the organization's chain of command to resolve the problem. Interestingly, they tend to use their position of power when dealing with female employees, whereas when dealing with male employees they use communication strategies.

plate 52 Non-verbal messages can be a very powerful mode of conveying meaning.

Source: Getty Images

From a managerial perspective, gender issues play a part in the better utilization of human resources. An awareness of sex discrimination and conservative gender patterns enables recruiting, keeping, placing, training and promoting labour to be carried out in a more rational way. Embracing and welcoming diversity, and validating the viewpoints of women and men, may facilitate organizational learning and creativity. It is argued that managers need to address organizational cultures, structures and practices in terms of gender. We have used the term 'diverse' to convey cultural and gender differences between colleagues in a company, and cognitive and relational differences between Eastern and Western cultures. However, diversity is itself a contested term.

Critical insight

We have emphasized in this chapter the self-evident value of communications in the workplace, and also the interplay between gender, power and language. In many familiar ways, language both mirrors social attitudes and helps to perpetuate them. It also confers different value on the two sexes. An introduction to the issue of language and its importance for sociological research of contemporary societies is presented in *Introductory Sociology* by Bilton et al.[59] Obtain a copy and read Chapters 18 and 19. Explain the role of language in the construction of self. How does language define women and men differently?

Deborah Tannen has done extensive research on how language defines men and women differently, usually to the advantage of men. Obtain a copy of Tannen's book, *You Just Don't Understand: Women and Men in Conversation*.[60] In what ways do men define life experiences differently from women? What implications does Tannen's work have for organizational communication? How important is the social context in explaining the success or failure of particular forms and styles of communication?

Communication and paradox

Contradictions and paradoxes are found everywhere in the organizational communication literature. The case studies on employee involvement arrangements in worksites reveal tensions in communication and employee empowerment practices. The term 'paradox' comes from the Greek words *para* and *dokein*, and means to reconcile two apparently conflicting views.[61] Four main types of paradox are apparent in management practices to improve organizational performance: structure, agency, identity and power.[62]

Although teams are intended to enhance productivity by empowering workers to make decisions, senior management make the 'really important decisions', for example on investment in new technology. In other words, workers can participate in learning, innovating and voicing their opinions using only the channels established by the organization.

The idea of agency refers to an individual's sense of being, and a feeling that she or he can or does make a difference.[63] A conflict may arise if self-managed work teams rely on the active subordination of team members to the will of the team. Members must retain their creative individuality while accepting 'our way'. Consequently, workers may become ambivalent and hesitant about participating in such a regime.

The paradox of identity addresses issues of boundaries, space and the divide between the in-group and the out-group. The paradox involves commitment to the group, embracing learning, discussion, diversity and difference. However, 'commitment is expected to equal agreement' (ref. 62, p. 380). Voicing an alternative view is seen as lack of commitment. The workers must comply with organizational priorities.

The paradox of power centres on issues of leadership, access to resources, opportunities for voice and the shaping of employee behaviour. It is argued that managers must meet the challenge of nurturing creativity and innovation in an atmosphere of 'Be an independent thinker, just as I have commanded you.'

The area of organizational communications is part of the broader field of organizational behaviour studies. In this chapter, we have explored a body of literature that many standard organizational behaviour texts have previously neglected. The nature of communication and the links between communication, power and decision making suggest that metaphors, cultural diversity, gender and rhetorical adroitness deserve greater attention in management theory and practice.

Chapter summary

◻ We have explained that the nature of the communication process established in the organization reflects the management style, degree of employee participation, culture and efficiency of the workplace. A knowledge of theories clarifies our understanding of organizational communications and enables us to explain a variety of practical issues, such as where the idea of the organization originated and what motivates people to work.

◻ It is important not to give one theory prominence over another. The three major perspectives for understanding organizational communications – functionalist, interpretivist and critical – allow us to comprehend the central role that communications has in the management process. The metaphors used to describe the perspectives – for example, machine, organism and psychic prison – enhance our ability to view communications as being not just about the transmission and exchange of information in the context of organizational efficiency, but rather as being central to the other processes of power, leadership and decision making.

◻ We have emphasized that individuals engage with their world through specific codes and practices (verbal, non-verbal and written language). Language creates the organizational concepts that define the culture of an organization and give form to notions of control, delegation and rationality. Meetings are an example of the management of meaning. The choice of media, interaction and personal dynamics is part of the creation of texts within an organization, which in turn contributes to the establishment of its culture.

◻ We went on to explain how an understanding of the cultural and organizational dynamics of cross-cultural communications will enhance organizational effectiveness and business performance. E. T. Hall provides a useful system for understanding the communication implications of culture, both verbal and non-verbal.

◻ Research has revealed differences between the conversational styles of men and women. As managers, women try to develop *rapport* with colleagues, whereas men often *report* information or problems. It is important to embrace and welcome diversity in the organization to facilitate creativity and encourage the learning community. However, there are paradoxes tied up with the concepts of individual, micro- and macro-identities, and these might inhibit full participation in the organization. Although workers might apparently be encouraged to be creative, the organization typically places limitations on where, how and when they can speak.

◻ The material reviewed in this chapter illustrates that managers are aware of the importance of persuasive communication in their role as negotiators. The growth of teams, globalization and the need to retain employees require managers to acquire expertise as accomplished presenters of rational arguments. A knowledge of the rhetorical context of the communication process enables the manager to create a managerially biased social reality.

Key concepts

4 Ss model of speech making   398
Aristotle's model of rhetoric   397
channels of communication   391–393
exchange model of communication   387
Generation Y   394
non-verbal communication   392
social networking sites   392
transmission model of communication   386–387

Vocab checklist for ESL students

☐ Communications, communicate
☐ Culture, cultural
☐ Dialogue
☐ Discourse community
☐ Empirical approach
☐ Feedback
☐ Formal channels
☐ Functionalist perspective
☐ Genre
☐ Grapevine
☐ High-context culture
☐ Informal channels
☐ Language
☐ Low-context culture
☐ Interpretivism
☐ Media richness
☐ Negotiation, negotiate, negotiable
☐ Rhetoric, rhetorical
☐ Symbolic interactionism

Chapter review questions

1. Explain the difference between a transmission model of communication and an exchange model.
2. If communication is so central to the management process, why do managers often fail to communicate effectively to others in the organization?
3. To what extent does electronic transmission affect communications?
4. What kind of communication skills should managers concentrate on?
5. How important is the context in explaining the success or failure of particular forms and styles of communication?
6. How important is face-to-face communication in a modern organization and why?

Chapter research questions

1. Practise your communication skills by forming a diverse study group including if possible, an international student(s).

(a) Given your experience with Facebook and Twitter, discuss whether social networking sites and texting are threatening to turn face-to-face conversation into a lost art. If so, do you envisage any communication problems? (b) Is the use of text-speak and emoticons in workplace email unprofessional? What do you think of this trend? (c) Given the trend in electronic communications, is face-to-face communication appropriate/ essential at any time in the workplace? Why? Give examples.

2. Obtain a copy of *Inside the Workplace: Findings from the 2004 Workplace Employment Relations Survey* (2006). After reading pages 134–9, comment on the importance of the development of direct communication methods to employees' ratings of managers.

3. Read Leah Reynolds and others' (2008) article 'The Gen Y Imperative'.[44] If the proposals outlined in the article are put into practice, will the key insights of Generation Y bring about a fundamental shift in how leaders think strategically about organizational communications?

Further reading

Baier, K. (2008) 'Diversity dialogue', *Communication World*, September–October, pp. 40–1.

Coupland, C., Brown, A. D., Daniels, K. and Humphreys, M. (2008) 'Saying it with feeling: analysing speakable emotions', *Human Relations*, **61**(3), pp. 327–53.

Eisenberg, E. M. and Goodall, H. L. (2007) *Organizational Communication: Balancing Creativity and Constraint* (5th edn), New York: St Martin's Press.

Martin, J. and Nakayama, T. (2007) *Intercultural Communication in Contexts* (4th edn), Mountain View, CA: Mayfield.

Morgan, G. (1980) 'Paradigms, metaphors, and puzzle solving in organization theory', *Administrative Science Quarterly*, **25**, pp. 605–22.

Reynolds, L., Campbell Bush, E. and Geist, R. (2008) 'The Gen Y imperative', *Communication World*, March–April, pp. 19–22.

Chapter case study 1

Cancelling Casual Friday at Sydney's CLD Bank

Background

Banks are currently facing extremely difficult political and economic conditions. In 2009, David Viniar, Goldman Sachs's chief financial officer, said market conditions remained 'dangerous'. Most venerable banks have only survived by huge government bail-outs. Government interventions, however, draw criticism from politicians about how they do business. They question a business model that relies on rewarding top performers handsomely. Other criticisms focus on high-risk behaviour and on whether US and European banks should have so much invested in Asian banks. With so many people losing their life savings and pensions, bank executives have been the targets in the populist backlash too. Stones thrown through Sir Fred Goodwin's windows in Edinburgh, UK, are an example of public anger and vilification. Recent trends show, in the first quarter of 2010, improved revenue for banks, but the longer-term outlook remains sobering. In 2006,

banks made an average return on equity of 17 per cent. To return to double digits, banks will have to cut costs by well over $100 million for every $100 billion of assets they hold.

The company: CLD Bank

CLD Bank's head office is located in London, UK. CLD Bank is one of the largest banking and financial services organizations in the world. Its global network comprises around 8900 branches in 72 countries in Europe, the Asia-Pacific region, the Americas, the Middle East and Africa. The bank brands itself as 'the world's caring bank'. In Australia, the CLD Bank Group offers a full range of financial services through a network of 34 branches. CLD Bank's employee policies aim to attract and motivate talented people who have the drive and enthusiasm to find innovative ideas to fulfil the bank's customers' needs. CLD Bank's values include placing great importance on respecting each other and embracing ideas, cultures and abilities.

Ian Green is the branch manager at CLD Bank located on George Street, Sydney, Australia, having been transferred from a branch in London, UK. He came to the branch just 3 months ago with a dynamic reputation based on efficiency and 'getting things done'.

The team leaders' meeting, October

At the regular team leaders' meeting, chaired by Ian Green, Jenny Gibson mentioned the upcoming Halloween festivities and the recent tradition for bank employees to wear costumes and offer candies to customers. This practice, and what is known as 'Casual Fridays', when staff members are permitted to wear jeans and casual apparel, although not as widely celebrated in Australia as it is in North America, is popular among the largely young employees at the branch. Both practices were introduced by the previous manager, a Canadian, 5 years ago. Ian said both practices were inappropriate and unprofessional. Several team leaders spoke out in favour of the practice and said how popular the tradition had become. After a short discussion, Ian Green said he appreciated their input but, 'There is a widely held perception that banks have become too cavalier, and the wearing of casual clothes doesn't help to counter that view,' he said. Hence he would be sending out a memo cancelling the practice. Two days later, the following memo was sent to each team leader for comment before it was due to be distributed to every branch employee:

DRAFT

DATE: October 15, 2010

TO: All Staff Members

FROM: Ian Green, Branch Manager

SUBJECT: CANCEL CASUAL FRIDAY AND HALLOWEEN

I am sorry to inform you that CLD Bank can no longer condone the continuation of 'Casual Friday'. Beginning November 1, ALL staff will dress in a professional manner every working day.

Also it has been decided that the Halloween festivities, for example wearing costumes and eating candies, will no longer happen at the end of the month.

In these troubled times, it is important for us all to remember that we need to conduct ourselves in a professional manner at all times.

When Jenny Gibson received a copy of the memo, she discussed it with another team leader whom she could trust: 'I don't think Ian is aware how important Casual Friday and the "Mischief Night" office party are to team morale,' she said. 'Ian would certainly benefit if he developed his humour skills,' added her colleague. 'I'm going to see him tomorrow to try to persuade him to change his mind,' said Jenny Gibson.

Tasks

Read the OB in Focus on Humour in the Workplace, above. Working individually or in groups, prepare some notes Jenny Gibson could use for her meeting with Ian Green, and address the following questions.

1. What is the value of humour in the workplace?
2. Can you suggest any improvements to the memo that needs to be made before being distributed to staff if Jenny fails to convince Ian not to cancel Casual Friday?

Further information

Crawford, C. B. (1994) 'Theory and implications regarding the utilization of strategic humor by leaders', *Journal of Leadership Studies*, **1**, pp. 53–68.

Romero, E. and Pescosolido, A. (2008) 'Humor and group effectiveness', *Human Relations*, **61**(3), pp. 395–418.

www.halloween-australia.com for comments on Halloween in Australia.

Note

The case study is fictitious. It was written by Carolyn Forshaw, formerly of Thompson Rivers University, BC, Canada.

Chapter case study 2

Edenvale Hospital

 Visit www.palgrave.com/business/brattonob2e to view this case study

 ## Web-based assignment

We have explained that the nature of the communication process established in the organization reflects the management style, degree of employee participation, culture and efficiency of the workplace. Communication is essential for effective decision making. Ineffective communication is linked to a 'command and control' vision of management.

This web-based assignment requires you to investigate the extent of communication processes in workplaces in Britain. Visit the website for the Findings from the 2004 Workplace Survey – www.berr.gov.uk/whatwedo/employment/research%2Devaluation/wers%2D2004 – and review the survey findings. What arrangements for direct communications with employees are most popular in (a) the private sector, and (b) the public sector? Based on your understanding of this chapter, what 'downward' communications arrangements do you believe are most effective? Explain your answer.

 ## OB in Film

According to the Book of Genesis, humanity was united and all spoke the same language. However, the inhabitants of the city of Babel built an enormous tower with the intention of reaching heaven and for their own glory, rather than for the worship of God. This displeased God, who came down, gave them different languages and scattered them across the Earth. This is the biblical explanation of why people speak different languages.

Drawing from this biblical story, the title of the film *Babel* (2005) indicates that it is about language and miscommunication. Critically, it is about the crises caused by failures of communication. In this film, three stories are interwoven. The first revolves around the accidental shooting of an American woman on a tourist bus. The second focuses on a deaf-mute Japanese girl. The subject of the third story is the Mexican nanny of the shot American woman.

As you watch the film, try to identify the nature, causes and repercussions of miscommunication in each of the three stories.

Note: This feature was written by Professor Jon Billsberry, Senior Research Fellow, Open University Business School, UK.

 ### Bonus OB in Film feature

Visit www.palgrave.com/business/brattonob2e to see how *My Cousin Vinnie* (1992) can be considered in relation to the subject of communication.

 ## References

1 Tamburri, R. (2009) 'Communicating in bad times', *University Affairs*, May, pp. 18–20.
2 Bratton, J., Grint, K. and Nelson, D. (2005) *Organizational Leadership*, Mason, OH: Thomson-South-Western.
3 Dean, J. W. Jr. and Sharfman, M. P. (1996) 'Does decision process matter? A study of strategic decision making effectiveness', *Academy of Management Journal*, **39**(2), pp. 368–96.
4 Holmes, S. (2008) 'Obama: oratory and originality'. Available at http://news.bbc.co.uk/1/hi/world/americas/7735014.stm (accessed October 9, 2009).
5 Byers, P. Y. (ed.) (1997) *Organizational Communication: Theory and Behaviour*, Boston: Allyn & Bacon.
6 Stacks, D., Hickson, M. and Hill, S. (1991) *Introduction to Communication Theory*, Fort Worth, TX: Holt, Rinehart & Winston.
7 Guffey, M., Rhodes, K. and Rogin, P. (2005) *Business Communication: Process and Product* (4th edn), Scarborough, ON: Thomson Nelson.
8 Calas, M. B. and Smircich, L. (1996) 'From the woman's point of view: feminist approaches to organization studies', pp. 212–51 in S. Clegg and C. Hardy (eds), *Studying Organization: Theory and Method*, Thousand Oaks, CA: Sage.
9 Howells, C. A. (1987) *Private and Fictional Words*, London: Methuen.
10 Macionis, J. J., Jansson, S. M. and Benoit, C. M. (2005) *Society: The Basics* (3rd edn), Toronto: Pearson.
11 Hodson, R. and Sullivan, T. A. (2002) *The Social Organization of Work* (3rd edn), Belmont, CA: Wadsworth/Thomson Learning.
12 Goffman, E. (1967) *Interaction Ritual: Essays on Face to Face Behavior*, New York: Anchor.
13 Bilton, T., Bonnett, K., Jones, R. and Lawson, T. (2002) *Introductory Sociology*, London: Palgrave Macmillan.

14 Weick, K. (1979) *The Social Psychology of Organizing* (2nd edn), New York: McGraw-Hill.

15 Gray, R. and Robertson, L. (2005) 'Effective communication starts at the top', *Communication World*, **22**(July), p. 4.

16 Smith, R. C. (1993) 'Images of organizational communication: root metaphors of the organization–communication relation', paper presented at the International Communication Association Conference, Washington, DC.

17 Taylor, J. R. (1995) 'Shifting from a heteronomous to an autonomous world view of organizational communication: communication theory on the cusp', *Communication Theory*, **5**(1), pp. 1–35.

18 Putnam, L. L., Philips, N. and Chapman, P. (1999) 'Metaphors of communication and organization', pp. 125–47 in S. Clegg, C. Hardy and W. Nord (eds), *Managing Organizations. Current Issues*, Thousand Oaks, CA: Sage.

19 Townley, B. (1994) *Reframing Human Resource Management: Power, Ethics and the Subject of Work*, London: Sage.

20 Neher, W. W. (1997) *Organizational Communication*, Boston, MA: Allyn & Bacon.

21 Field, R. and House, R. (1995) *Human Behaviour in Organizations: A Canadian Perspective*, Ontario: Prentice Hall.

22 Robbins, S. P. (1990) *Organization Theory: Structure, Design, and Applications* (3rd edn), Englewood Cliffs, NJ: Prentice-Hall.

23 Scott, quoted in Eisenberg, E. M. and Goodall, H. L. (1997) *Organizational Communication: Balancing Creativity and Constraint*, New York: St. Martin's Press.

24 Robbins, S. P. and Langton, N. (2001) *Organizational Behaviour: Concepts, Controversies, Applications* (2nd edn), Toronto: Prentice-Hall.

25 McShane, S. L. (2006) *Canadian Organizational Behaviour* (6th edn), Boston, MA: McGraw-Hill.

26 Daft, R. L. and Huber, G. P. (1987) 'How organizations learn: a communication framework', *Research in the Sociology of Organizations*, **5**, pp. 1–36.

27 Grint, K. (2000) *The Arts of Leadership*, Oxford: Oxford University Press.

28 Neher, W. W. (1997) *Organizational Communication*, Boston, MA: Allyn & Bacon.

29 Morgan, G. (1980) 'Paradigms, metaphors, and puzzle solving in organization theory', *Administrative Science Quarterly*, **25**, pp. 605–22.

30 Yuval-Davis, N. (1997) *Cultural Reproductions and Gender Relations: Gender and Nation*, London: Sage.

31 Kellaway, L. (2009) Available at: www.ft.com/comment/columnist/lucykellaway (accessed May 5, 2009).

32 Ashcroft, B., Griffiths, G. and Tiffin, H. (1989) *The Empire Writes Back*, London: Routledge.

33 Riley, P. (1983) 'A structurationist account of political cultures', *Administrative Science Quarterly*, **28**, pp. 414–37.

34 Morgan, G. (1986) *Images of Organization*, London: Sage.

35 Alvesson, M. and Due Billing, Y. (1997) *Understanding Gender in Organizations*, London: Sage.

36 Filipczak, P. (1996) 'The soul of the hog', *Training*, **33**(February), pp. 38–42.

37 Eisenberg, E. M. and Goodall, H. L. (1997) *Organizational Communication: Balancing Creativity and Constraint*, New York: St Martin's Press.

38 Alvesson, M. (1996) *Communication, Power and Organization*, New York: Walter de Gruyter.

39 Mintzberg, H. (1973) *The Nature of Managerial Work*, New York: Harper & Row.

40 Freedman, A. and Medway, P. (eds) (1994) *Genre and the New Rhetoric*, London: Taylor & Francis.

41 Freedman, A. and Medway, P. (eds) (1994) *Learning and Teaching Genre*, Portsmouth, NH: Heinemamn.

42 Mengis, J. and Eppler, M. J. (2008) 'Understanding and managing conversations from knowledge perspective: an analysis of the roles and rules of face-to-face conversations in organizations', *Organizational Studies*, **29**(10), pp. 1287–13.

43 El Akkad, O. (2009) 'The medium is no longer the message', *Globe and Mail*, March 10, p. A3.

44 Reynolds, L., Campbell Bush, E. and Geist, R. (2008) 'The Gen Y imperative', *Communication World*, March–April, pp. 19–22.

45 Witherspoon, P. D. (1997) *Communicating Leadership: An Organizational Perspective*, Needham Heights, MA: Allyn & Bacon.

46 Grint, K. (2001) 'Martin Luther King's "Dream Speech": the rhetoric of social leadership', pp. 359–408 in *The Arts of Leadership*, New York: Oxford University Press.

47 Stewart, R. (1967) *Managers and their Jobs*, Basingstoke: Macmillan.

48 Goleman, D. (1998) 'What makes a leader?', *Harvard Business Review*, November–December, pp. 93–102.

49 Black, O (1996) 'Addressing the issue of good communication', People Management (online). Available at: http://proquest.umi.com

50 Coe, R. M. (1990) *Process, Form, and Substance: A Rhetoric for Advanced Writers* (2nd edn), Upper Saddle River, NJ: Prentice Hall.

51 Kidd, J., Xue, L. and Richter, F.-J. (2001) *Maximizing Human Intelligence Deployment in Asian Business*, Basingstoke: Palgrave Macmillan.

52 Nkomo, S. M. and Cox, T. Jr. (1999) 'Diverse identities in organizations', pp. 88–101 in S. Clegg, C. Hardy and W. Nord (eds), *Managing Organizations: Current Issues*, Thousand Oaks, CA: Sage.

53 Clegg, S., Hardy, C. and Nord, W. (eds) (1999) *Managing Organizations: Current Issues*, Thousand Oaks, CA: Sage.

54 Cited in Nkomo, S. M. and Cox, T. Jr. (1999) 'Diverse identities in organizations', pp. 88–101 in S. Clegg, C. Hardy and W. Nord (eds), *Managing Organizations: Current Issues*, Thousand Oaks, CA: Sage.

55 Tan, J.-S. (1998) 'Communication, cross cultural', in M. Poole and M. Warner (eds), *International Encyclopaedia of Business and Management*, London: Thomson.

56 Parker, I. (1992) *Discourse Dynamics: Critical Analysis for Social and Individual Psychology*, London: Routledge.

57 Hall, E. T. (1976) *Beyond Culture*, New York: Doubleday.

58 Byron, K. (2008) 'Differential effects of male and female managers' non-verbal emotional skills on employees' ratings', *Journal of Management Psychology*, **23**(2), pp. 118–34.

59 Bilton,T., Bonnett, K., Jones, R. and Lawson, T. (2002) *Introductory Sociology*, London: Palgrave Macmillan

60 Tannen, D. (1990) *You Just Don't Understand: Women and Men in Conversation*, New York: Ballantine Books.

61 Krippendorff, K. (1985) 'On the ethics of constructing communications', ICA presidential address, Honolulu, Hawaii, and quoted in E. M. Eisenberg and H. L. Goodall (2004) *Organizational Communication: Balancing Creativity and Constraint* (4th edn), New York: St Martin's Press, p. 26.

62 Stohl, C. and Cheney, G. (2001) 'Participatory processes/paradoxical practices', *Management Communication Quarterly*, **14**(3), pp. 349–407.

63 Giddens, A. (1984) *The Constitution of Society*, Cambridge: Polity Press.

64 Bratton, J. and Gold, J. (2007) *Human Resource Management: Theory and Practice* (4th edn), Basingstoke: Palgrave.

chapter 15
Decision making and ethics

chapter outline

- Introduction
- The nature of decision making
- The rhetorics of decision making
- The realities of decision making
- Employee involvement in decision making
- Ethics and corporate social responsibility
- Developing decision-making skills
- Summary and end-of-chapter features
- Chapter case study 1: Ethical decision making at Primark Apparel
- Chapter case study 2: A new venture for Echo Generation Publishing

chapter objectives

After completing this chapter, you should be able to:

- define organizational decision making
- explain the rational model of decision process
- compare and contrast the rational model with how managers actually make decisions
- describe the benefits of employee involvement in decision making
- explain the meaning of ethics, and business ethics
- discuss the nature of corporate social responsibility
- discuss structured group interventions to improve group process and the quality of group decisions

Introduction

In technical terms, it was a piece of foam about the size of a laptop computer that caused the disintegration on re-entry into Earth's atmosphere of the space shuttle *Columbia* in February 2003. However, a scathing US government report concluded that the root cause of the fatal crash was managerial myopia and the culture of the US National Aeronautics and Space Administration (NASA). Individuals in NASA made decisions affecting *Columbia*. Senior managers determined NASA's goals, mission schedules and budget. Middle-level managers also made decisions impacting on *Columbia*'s mission. They determined production schedules, space shuttle design and safety, and decided to reduce its workforce and rely increasingly on outside contractors. NASA's engineers 'found themselves in the unusual position of having to prove that the situation was *unsafe* – a reversal of the usual requirement to prove that a situation *is safe*,' the report states.[1]

Of course, making decisions is not the sole prerogative of managers. Non-managerial employees at NASA also made decisions that affected their work and *Columbia*. The more obvious of these decisions might include whether to comply with a request made by a manager, knowing that safety standards were being compromised. Individual decision making is therefore an important part of organizational behaviour.

The work conducted at NASA is frequently used to illustrate the highest levels of cognitive ability, reflected in the popular comment 'This isn't rocket science.' So how could so many smart people who *do* engage in rocket science make a series of such bad decisions? We shall find out in this chapter. First, however, we define decision making and present a model of decision making that characterizes the process as a rational act. As we work through this model, we will be especially concerned with exploring the neoclassical economic assumption that managers act rationally towards a common purpose, and the practical limitations of managerial rationality.

The limits of managerial rationality are perhaps best illustrated by recent decision making in the finance sector. Explaining why no one foresaw the timing, extent and severity of the global economic recession that began in 2008–09, a group of eminent economists tell of irrational factors such as the 'psychology of denial', of the 'feel-good factor' and 'wishful thinking combined with hubris'.[2] Unsurprisingly, from the G20 summit to the workplace, business ethics and corporate social responsibility (CSR) are now a priority. This chapter closes with a look at ethics in decision making and CSR before examining some techniques to improve decision making. The purpose of the chapter is to situate decision making in the context of managerial rationales, opportunities, constraints and power.

The nature of decision making

decision making: a conscious process of making choices between one or more alternatives with the intention of moving towards some desired state of affairs

Decision making is the conscious process of making choices from among several alternatives with the intention of moving towards some desired course of action.[3-6] Three things are noteworthy about this definition. First, decision making involves making a *choice* between several action alternatives: for instance, NASA's engineers can choose to have a spacecraft carry more or less inventory, and can decide to use different materials or rely on external contractors to make and assemble space components. Second, decision making is a *process* that involves more than simply the final choice among the alternatives – if a NASA manager decides to outsource work, we want to know how this decision was reached. Finally, the 'action' mentioned in the definition typically involves some commitment of *resources*, such as money, personnel or time. The *Columbia* shuttle project required a substantial resource commitment.

Decision making is possibly the most important management function. Ever since Fayol's seminal work,[7] which identified management as a series of rational activities related to planning, organizing, directing and controlling, it has been appreciated that managerial behaviour involves decision making. This perspective of management assumes that managers act rationally as they continually strive to enhance the efficiency and competitive position of the organization. The control perspective of management also proceeds from the general assumption that managers act rationally, which, according to this school, involves making decisions designed to maximize control of the labour process and the level of 'surplus' extracted from workers.

Table 15.1 shows that organizational decision making can be studied at different levels: the individual, group and organizational. Each level centres on its own set of assumptions and theoretical approach, and its own key issues. However, the levels are interconnected, each one influencing and being affected by the other two levels.

> Before reading on, think about your own work experience, or your knowledge of work organizations. Can you think of a group or an individual decision that has led to success or failure?
>
> **stop reflect**

table 15.1 Levels of organizational decision-making behaviour

Level of analysis	Theoretical approaches	Key issues
Organizational	Theories of organization power, politics, conflict and decision making	Effects of power, politics and conflict
Group	Group conformity, group dynamics, group size and networks	Effects of group dynamics, individuals' perceptions and behaviours
Individual	Information-processing theory Cognitive psychology	Information overload Personal biases

The rhetorics of decision making

The rhetoric and debate about organizational decision making draws heavily on what is referred to as the 'rational' economic model of decision making. The model has its roots in neoclassical economic theory. Managers continually strive to find the right mix of factor inputs (such as raw materials, machinery and labour) to enable them to minimize per unit production costs and maximize profits. The rational economic model underscores the importance of managerial decision making on the issues of resource allocation, efficiency and labour productivity. The model is primarily normative, providing a guide on how managerial decision making ought to be done. It is shown in Figure 15.1.

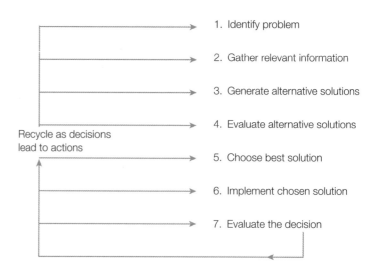

1. Identify problem

2. Gather relevant information

3. Generate alternative solutions

4. Evaluate alternative solutions

Recycle as decisions lead to actions

5. Choose best solution

6. Implement chosen solution

7. Evaluate the decision

figure 15.1 A rational decision-making model

The first step in the rational decision model is to identify a problem or recognize an opportunity. A *problem* is the deviation between the current and the desired situation – the gap between 'what is' and 'what ought to be'. An *opportunity* is a deviation between current expectations and a potentially better situation, which had not previously been expected. In other words, decision makers realize that alternative decisions may produce outcomes beyond current expectations or goals.

The second step is to gather all relevant information related to the problem or opportunity, and the third step is to generate a list of possible solutions. This typically involves searching for off-the-shelf or ready-made solutions, such as practices that have been effective elsewhere in similar situations. Step four is to evaluate each alternative solution. In a purely rational process, this involves decision makers identifying all factors against which the alternatives are judged, assigning weights reflecting the importance of those factors, rating each alternative on those factors, and then calculating each alternative's total value from the ratings and factor weights.

Step five involves choosing the best solution based on the systematic rating exercise, and in step six, the chosen solution is implemented. The final step in the rational decision-making model involves evaluating the decision to see whether the solution has narrowed the gap between 'what is' and 'what ought to be'. Ideally, these seven steps are informed by relevant and objective feedback in the form of a feedback loop.

Assumptions of the rational economic decision-making model

Assumptions inevitably enter analyses of decision making. Take, for example, problem identification: this first step in the decision-making process makes assumptions about rationality. In the case of NASA's managerial decisions, one might ask, why outsource work in the first place? Perhaps in order to ensure safety standards are not compromised, NASA engineers could manufacture and assemble the shuttle's components on site under rigorous supervision. Or why assume that outside contractors can meet safety standards and remain within budget? Perhaps the criterion for the decision is not simply to choose the low-cost option.

Multiple criteria might be to balance the cost of the component, the demonstrable safety results and the time taken to deliver the component. In order to be rational, NASA decision makers must assign weights to each of these three criteria. The weights indicate how important each is compared with the others. Given these weights, a new optimal production operation can be chosen. Although the decision to rely on outside contractors, for example, appears to fit the rational model, assumptions have been built into the solution.

Criterion weights are assumptions because they are based on the values and preferences of the decision maker. The point we are making here is that even decisions made with the rational model have assumptions built into them. These assumptions deal with the way the problem is identified and the way objectives are defined. The designers of the rational decision-making model hold a cluster of assumptions about human tendencies when it comes to decision making in the workplace. Let us briefly review some of those assumptions:

- *Problem clarity.* The problem is clear and unambiguous. The decision maker is assumed to have complete information regarding the decision situation.
- *Known options.* It is assumed that the decision maker can identify all the relevant criteria and can list all the viable alternatives. Additionally, the decision maker is aware of all the possible consequences of each alternative.
- *Clear preferences.* Rationality assumes that the criteria and alternatives can be ranked and weighted to reflect their importance.
- *Constant preferences.* It is assumed that the specific decision criteria are constant and that the weights assigned to them are stable over time.
- *Maximum pay-off.* The rational decision maker will choose the alternative that yields the highest efficiency or return on factor inputs.
- *No time or cost constraints.* The rational decision maker can obtain full information about criteria and alternatives because it is assumed that there are no time or cost constraints.

Examine your own choice of which college or university to attend. To what extent did your decision follow the rational decision-making approach?

stop reflect

The realities of decision making

The rational model is a rhetoric used by managers at the very top of an organizational bureaucracy, and it reinforces managers' claim to knowledge and competence. There is evidence, however, that this normative model of decision making is rarely realized either fully or extensively in practice. Over the last three decades, numerous organizational theories have attempted to explain why individuals, groups and organizations fail to follow the rational model. We shall discuss major impediments to rational decision making that operate at the individual, group and organizational levels.

At the individual level

Individual rationality is constrained by at least four factors: information-processing failure, perceptual biases, intuition and emotion, and escalation of commitment.

Information-processing failures

Individual managers do not make wholly rational decisions because they may not acquire sufficient information to make a 'perfect' decision, or they may have too much information, and this prevents them from making a good decision. Individuals may make bad or non-rational decisions because of incomplete information. Herbert Simon called this **bounded rationality**.[8] The bounds of rationality often force managers to make decisions based on **intuition**, or what is commonly called their 'gut feeling'. Although intuitive decisions may be seen as non-rational because they do not follow the model, it can be argued that hunches or guesses can be an effective way to decide as the subconscious brain may be providing the conscious brain with information.[9]

bounded rationality: processing limited and imperfect information and satisficing (see text) rather than maximizing when choosing between alternatives

intuition: the ability to know when a problem or opportunity exists and select the best course of action without conscious reasoning

information overload: a situation in which the receiver becomes overwhelmed by the information that needs to be processed. It may be caused by the *quantity* of the information to be processed, the *speed* at which the information presents itself or the *complexity* of the information to be processed

satisficing: selecting a solution that is satisfactory, or 'good enough', rather than optimal or 'the best'

Although incomplete or imperfect information can be a barrier to rational decision making, too much information can also prevent optimal decisions. **Information overload** is the reception of more information than is necessary to make effective decisions. Rather than improving decision making, information overload can lead to errors, omissions, delays and cutting corners. Managers facing information overload often attempt to use all the information at hand, and then get confused and permit irrelevant or low-quality information to influence their decisions.

For example, you may have experienced information overload when writing an essay. To impress your instructor, you attempt to incorporate too many viewpoints and too many references into the paper, and this results in a disjointed, confusing and low-quality essay. So the lesson here is that more information does not necessarily lead to optimal decisions.

Managers may also choose the first alternative that does the job, or meets the requirements of the problem to a satisfactory degree, rather than the 'best' alternative. Simon called this behaviour **satisficing** – selecting an alternative that is satisfactory rather than optimal. Satisficing occurs because of information overload. It is not possible to identify all the feasible alternatives, and information about the alternatives is imperfect.

Even if individuals have all the relevant information, they cannot possibly think through all the alternatives and the outcomes of those alternatives as prescribed by the rational model because they lack the cognitive capacity.[10] This is not because they are dim-witted, but rather because managers typically have limited time in which to make decisions, and some decisions simply do not lend themselves to purely rational 'scientific' calculation. Complex managerial decisions usually involve both measurable and non-measurable, or qualitative, considerations. Consequently, managers normally look at only a few alternatives, and only some of the main outcomes of those alternatives.

Students of decision process theory essentially argue that decisions are made and actions taken depending on the individuals who happen to be involved and the alternatives they happen to identify. For example, there are scores of MBA programmes to choose from and dozens of modules to consider, yet people typically evaluate only a few MBA offerings and the main features of each programme of studies. In summary, although relevant and timely information improves decisions, managers often obtain less or more information than is necessary for adequate decision making.

Perceptual biases

Along with processing information and evaluating quantitative and qualitative considerations, individuals make imperfect decisions because of flawed perceptions. As we learned in Chapter 5, selective interest mechanisms cause relevant information to be unconsciously filtered out. Moreover, managers, workers and others with vested interests try to influence people's perceptions so that it is more or less likely that a situation is perceived as an opportunity or challenge.

Another perceptual problem, also noted in Chapter 5, is that people see opportunities or challenges through their mental models. These working models of reality help individuals make sense of their world, but they also perpetuate assumptions that obscure new realities. Table 15.2 presents a list of these individual biases in decision making. For example, people judge actions that are more vivid in their memory, they fail to pay sufficient attention to the skewed effects of sample size when evaluating the importance of data, and they tend to be overconfident about the accuracy of their judgement when addressing moderately to extremely difficult problems.

table 15.2 Individual biases in decision making

Perceptual bias	Description
Ease of recall	Individuals judge events that are more easily recalled from memory to be more numerous than events of equal frequency whose instances are less easily recalled
Insensitivity to sample size	Individuals frequently fail to appreciate the role of sample size in evaluating the accuracy of sample information
Overconfidence	Individuals tend to be overconfident about the accuracy of their judgement when they answer moderately to extremely difficult questions
Method of memory search	Individuals are biased in their assessment of the frequency of events based upon the way their memory structure affects the search process
Illusory correlation	Individuals tend to overestimate the probability of two events co-occurring when their memory recall finds that the two events have occurred together in the past
Hindsight	After finding out whether or not an event has occurred, individuals tend to overestimate the degree to which they would have predicted the event without the benefit of hindsight
Regression to the mean	Individuals fail to note the statistical fact that extreme events tend to regress to the mean on subsequent trials

Intuition and emotion

Individuals can make decisions based on their intuition. This is usually called making a decision by 'gut instinct'. Many managers will tell you that they pay attention to their intuition or hunches when making decisions. Intuition is the ability to know when an opportunity or problem exists and to select the best course of action without conscious reasoning. These intuitions are, however, rarely the sole factor in the decision-making process. Individuals quite often analyse the available information, and then turn to their intuition to complete the process.

Intuitive decisions may be seen as non-rational because they do not follow the rational model, but research evidence suggests that intuition can play a role in strategic decision making.[11–13] More than 80 per cent of organizational knowledge – information that has been edited, put into context, and analysed in a way that makes it meaningful to decision makers – is implicit and is difficult to quantify or even describe accurately.[14] It is suggested that intuition is the channel through which individuals use their implicit or tacit knowledge. Tacit knowledge is the wisdom learned from life experience, observation and insight, which is not clearly understood and is therefore impossible to transfer to others.

To grasp the significance of tacit knowledge in decision making, try to describe the physical characteristics of a good friend who buys antiques for a living. Now try to describe the methods your friend would use to make purchase decisions at an auction. The former involves explicit knowledge, while the latter involves your tacit knowledge of your friend. At an auction, your friend's behaviour appears to be instinctual, but it is based on her or his past experience, what she or he has heard and read, and the state of the market for a particular antique. Thus, intuition allows individuals to draw on a vast reservoir of knowledge, experience and process discoveries.

The neoclassical rational model neglects to factor into the process the effects of emotions on individual decision making.[15] Emotions may shape decision making. Although we know that the rational dimension of the brain processes information about the various alternatives (imperfectly, because of cognitive capacity and time limits, as we have just learned), the emotional dimension more rapidly creates emotional markers that attract individuals to some alternatives and cause them to be repelled by others.

Work and Society: The decision maker's dilemma: where to go for advice

Although rational models of decision making still enjoy strong support among some scholars, they have been under attack for over a decade. Many critics suggest that models of rational decision making are misleading. A richer model of decision making must recognize the role in decision making of influences that are not fully present in the conscious experience of the decision maker. These influences will include such factors as emotions, tacit knowledge and personal values that the decision maker has failed to acknowledge or articulate.

To accept that decisions are influenced by factors that are not wholly accessible to a person's conscious experience is not necessarily to accept a model of decision making that portrays people as 'puppets' whose thought processes are driven by factors they cannot understand or control. It is merely to suggest that decision-making processes are not necessarily transparent to the decision maker, and that the quality of decision making is likely to improve as a person's self-awareness increases.

A fascinating account of how increased self-awareness might improve decision making was published recently in the journal *Small Group Research*. The author, Meikuan Huang (2009), offers readers a 'conceptual framework' to enable them to think about decision making in the context of group functioning. He argues that high-quality decision making depends on knowledge, and that knowledge is rarely controlled by one individual. More typically, knowledge is distributed across groups or among people who belong to a single group. A challenge for decision makers is to access reliable knowledge (expertise) from the people in an organization who possess that expertise.

What factors influence how decision makers perceive the distribution of expertise in an organization? Huang does not provide definitive answers to this question. Instead he offers a number of hypotheses that he believes should guide future research in this area. Huang starts by introducing readers to a thought-provoking research question that he encountered in an earlier study:

Are you more likely to turn to competent jerks or lovable fools when you need information at work? In other words would you seek information from a colleague best able to do the job or just from someone you like? (p. 324)

He then provides some background information that will enable readers to link questions about knowledge sharing to the larger topic of group functioning. Two key ideas help to establish this link: transactive memory system (TMS), which he defines as 'a shared system for encoding, sorting

and retrieving information' (p. 326); and positive affect (PA), which he defines as 'an individual's disposition to experience positive mood states' (p. 326). Huang hopes these two ideas will help readers to appreciate how emotional factors might influence knowledge sharing in ways that are not fully transparent to decision makers.

Having provided readers with this context, Huang introduces a number of hypotheses. Two of the most interesting are the following:

1. Group members with higher PA are more likely than those with lower PA to overestimate other members' expertise.
2. Group members with similar PA are more likely to retrieve information from each other than from members with dissimilar PA.

In the concluding section to his article, Huang offers a number of suggestions for managers. The following passage describes his notion of a 'group affect map':

> *Abundant research has shown the benefit of knowing who knows what in a group or organization and scholars and consultants have recommended the use of mapping who knows what in the format of a knowledge network ... mapping of the affective relationships ["who-likes-whom"] in a group network could meaningfully complement a group's knowledge maps. (p. 340)*

 stop!   Do you think that Huang's two hypotheses will be supported by the evidence and, if so, what are the lessons for decision makers?

Consider the idea of a group affect map that Huang mentions in his conclusion. This might help decision makers to become more aware of the emotional factors that influence their information-sharing practices. But such a map might prove controversial and divisive. Why might this be?

Sources and further information

Haidt, J. (2001) 'The emotional dog and its rational tail: a social intuitionist approach to moral judgement', *Psychological Review*, **108**(4), pp. 814–34.

Huang, M.(2009) 'A conceptual framework of the effects of positive affect and affective relationships on group knowledge networks', *Small Group Research*, **40**(3), pp. 323–46.

Note: This feature was written by David MacLennan, Assistant Professor at Thompson Rivers University, BC, Canada.

Take the three primary emotions of fear, hope and pleasure, for example. The first two are closely associated with the notion of confidence, which, it is argued, is the defining factor in how people address the challenges they face.[16] Fear is the absence of confidence. If our work life is dominated by fear, we are apprehensive about the present and expect the future to become more unstable. By contrast, hope is an expression of confidence. And pleasure is the feeling of satisfaction or gratification. We can summarise the potential effects of these three emotions on decision making with three formulas: Fear is 'Oh, my God, the economy is so bad, how can I safeguard my job?'; hope is 'I want to do it, I can do it, and I will do it'; and pleasure is 'Wow, it may be risky, but it's a great deal.' Extending the notion we discussed in Chapter 5, that the emotional bias in our schema to maximize pleasure feelings lies at the heart of irrational impulsive decision making, to the banking crisis that began in 2008–09, banking executives were driven by the pleasurable feelings of 'easy reward' and ignored the long-term risks.[17]

Some research suggests that people's general disposition or mood can support or obstruct the decision-making process. Specifically, individuals tend to evaluate alternatives more accurately when in a negative or neutral mood, whereas they tend to engage in more perceptual biases when they are in a positive mood. This suggests that we need to be aware that decision making and logical analysis are affected by human emotion.

The rational model disregards the effects of gender and ethnicity on the decision-making process, which suggests that its underlying character is a male-related phenomenon and not applicable to all employees. This is illustrated by Judge Sonia Sotomayor's candid acknowledgement that ethnicity and gender influence the decision-making process. Judge Sotomayor, President Barack Obama's nominee to the US Supreme Court, suggests that 'A judge may and will make a difference in our judging. I would hope that a wise Latina woman with the richness of her experiences would more often than not reach a better conclusion than a white man who hasn't lived that life'.[18] Clearly, social factors, such as how collective social norms and expectations frame 'sense making' or problem definition, tend to be neglected in orthodox treatments of decision making.[19] As we saw in Chapter 14, there are important differences between the conversational styles of men and women. It seems plausible that gender can create communication barriers in the decision-making process when, as some academics have argued, women have a 'different voice'.

plate 53 A wise Latina woman and a white man: how might their judgements differ?

Source: iStockphoto

The difference thesis contends that men see conversation as a tool – to exchange information, accomplish a task or preserve power – while women see conversation as a way to nurture, support and empathize, and that female managers use a more open communication style when dealing with people issues than typical male managers. Radical feminists might argue that the collective and systematic oppression of women by men results in different moral values. Women construct and value knowledge in ways that are relational, and oriented more towards sustaining relationships than achieving autonomy and power. Adopting this view of women – the notion that they have a different voice and a more holistic view of reality – suggests that the decision-making process will be strongly influenced by the gender balance of the decision makers.[20–23]

Escalation of commitment

escalation of commitment: the tendency to allocate more resources to a failing course of action or to repeat an apparently bad decision

The fourth factor that limits individual rationality in decision making is **escalation of commitment** to a losing course of action. Although it is clear why an individual would become more committed to a decision whose outcomes are positive, why does commitment sometimes increase when outcomes are negative? For example, a project manager reviewing lack of progress and a financial planner examining declining share prices might increase their commitment to their initial decision.

The objective characteristics of a project will be important in determining continued commitment to a decision.[24,25] For example, large early losses or major setbacks can cause a project to be abandoned, while small losses or minor setbacks can be tolerated. However, as small losses become larger, the total loss accumulates, until so much is committed that an individual will tolerate future risk to try to avoid the certain loss. If the individual decision maker determines that early losses are the result of a temporary problem and that further investment is likely to ensure a good return, project commitment is likely to increase.

Psychological and political factors can also cause an individual to escalate commitment to a decision. Despite large losses, individuals can tend to become more committed to a course of action when their decision is explicit and unambiguous, irrevocable, made publicly, made repeatedly and/or personally important.

> **Can you think of examples in which a CEO, politician or military commander showed escalated commitment to a bad decision?**
>
> **stop reflect**

plate 54 Group decision making might allow individual members to escape responsibility and to encourage 'groupthink'.

Source: Getty Images

At the group level

> **For more information on the experiments undertaken by Asch and Milgram visit: www2. qeliz.ac.uk/psychology/Asch.htm and www.stanleymilgram.com/ milgram.php**
>
> **weblink**

As we discussed in a preceding chapter, the phenomenon of group conformity or groupthink has the potential to undermine a group's ability to make effective decisions. Just how strongly do group norms influence individual behaviour and decision making when the situation is unmistakable? Research by Solomon Asch, Stanley Milgram and Irving Janis provided the answer to this question (see Chapter 9).[26,27] The research findings demonstrate 'groupthink' resulting in an illusion of the invulnerability of the group, a belief in the inherent morality of the group, and peer pressure to create group conformity.

At the organization level

Individuals and groups in work organizations do not make decisions in a vacuum. Individual and group decision making is polycontextual: that is, it involves multiple ongoing tasks, and changing interlocking constraints and opportunities. Each individual and group decision invokes its own microworld, informed by a stream of information and alternatives that shape perception and talk, the decision and ways of acting. The neoclassical rational model of decision making has been insightfully likened to a garbage can:

> To understand processes within organizations we view a choice opportunity as a garbage can into which various kinds of problems and solutions are dumped by participants as they are generated. The mix of garbage in a single can depends upon the mix of cans available, on the labels attached to alternative cans, on what garbage is currently being produced and on the speed with which garbage is collected and removed from the situation. (ref. 10, p. 2)

Rather than viewing managerial decision making as linear and mechanistic, 'decision process' theorists view decision making as a cyclical process of acting and reacting to various problems, necessities and opportunities. To better comprehend decision making in such a 'garbage can' organization, consider organizational decision making as a reflective learning process involving some thinking ahead, reflection on action, as well as some adjustment en route. Others have pointed out that strategic decisions, typically taught as an example of senior-level managerial rationality, are rarely 'purely deliberate, just as few are purely emergent. One means no learning, the other means no control' (ref. 28, p. 11).

The organization itself constrains decision makers. Historical precedents, the organization's human resource systems and imposed time constraints shape organizational decision making. Decisions on the future evolve from reflection on past experience, and decisions made in the past are ghosts that continually haunt current choices. For instance, past commitments may constrain current options. In the 1970s, for example, when consumers demanded more energy-efficient small cars because of soaring petrol prices, North American car manufacturers' choices were constrained by past decisions to invest in machinery to produce gas-inefficient large cars.

The organization's human resource management system influences decision makers. Managers are strongly influenced in their decision making by the criteria by which they are evaluated and rewarded. For example, if a manager believes that the section or division under her or his control is operating most efficiently when there are 'zero defects', we should not be surprised to find the manager avoiding risks and making decisions that discourage other workers from experimenting and trying new ways of doing their tasks.

Time not only disciplines workers, but also imposes deadlines on decision makers. A multitude of decisions must be made quickly to satisfy the requirements of production or customers. For example, managers need to complete budgets by an organizationally imposed deadline. These self-imposed time constraints put pressure on decision makers and often make it difficult, if not impossible, to gather all the information they might like to have before making a final choice. For example, a manager might need to purchase a piece of equipment before the end of the budget year, since the rule is 'spend it or lose it'. Thus, past decisions and established routines, as well as human resources assumptions and practices, become embedded in managerial practices over time and, together with time constraints, they influence how decision makers define and perceive problems, which shapes organizational decision making.

An alternative approach to explaining the nature of organizational decision making is the **political theory model**. The proponents of this model characterize the workplace as a purposive miniature society, with politics pervading all managerial decision making. By 'politics' we mean the power relationships between

political theory model: an approach to understanding decision making whose adherents assert that formal organizations comprise groups that have separate interests, goals and values, and in which power and influence are needed in order to reach decisions

managers and relevant others, and the capacity of an individual manager to influence in turn others who are in a state of dependence. This perspective to studying decision making offers an approach that examines individual managers as 'knowledgeable human agents' functioning within a dynamic arena where they compete for resources, power and status.

Thus, managers may attach great importance to forming alliances and building networks of cooperative relationships with other important decision makers in their organization. For example, a college president may decide to break up a department of continuing education and 'decentralize' the provision of life-long learning programmes to other divisions in the college, to sustain his or her power, and to warn other recalcitrant administrators to 'watch out'.

Organizations need a governance structure that encourages multiple voices and stimulates change. Such a political environment is often required because of the ambiguity and uncertainty identified under the decision process model, which compels decision makers to rely on more subjective criteria. Politics also encourages multiple voices to be heard on an issue. And political manoeuvring may dislodge the 'vested interest' of an organization and stimulate necessary change: 'It is politics that is able to work as a kind of "invisible hand" – "invisible underhand" would be a better term – to promote necessary change' (ref. 29, p. 250). The political perspective, however, has been criticized for failing to give sufficient attention to 'power struggles' in the workplace.[30,31]

The decision process and political theories offer alternative insights into the nature of managerial decision making on a day-to-day basis. Rather than viewing decisions as a series of linear and rational steps, these schools of thought see managerial decision making as a cycle involving enactment, reflection on experience, reframing of meaning and re-enactment under conditions of competition, ambiguity and uncertainty, often subject to the 'invisible hand' of internal politicking. Not surprisingly, organizational decision making may appear complex, variable, inconsistent and often contradictory. However, it would be a mistake to believe that managerial decision making really is chaotic and irrational. Underneath the surface, it might be more rational in substance than it is in form.[32] Senior managers are generally able to use their power to impose rationality. It is also true that the management process takes place in an environment of capitalist employment relations, where it is overarched by powerful organizational and market imperatives. These permit few substantial irrational decisions that would threaten the organization's standing or competitive position.

Employee involvement in decision making

employee involvement: the degree to which employees influence how their work is organized and carried out

Employee involvement (EI) is entrenched in contemporary management theory. It is most often associated with theories of post-bureaucratic organizational structures, work teams and 'diffuse' or 'empowered' styles of managerial leadership. EI refers to the degree to which subordinates influence how their work is organized and performed. Meaningful decision making requires that workers are able to exert some influence over their work and the conditions under which they work.

EI initiatives suggest a commonality of interest between workers and management. Managerially driven EI initiatives can only be understood in their historical and sociological context. Employers tend to pursue EI practices to improve employee cooperation and enhance productivity, and for their rhetorical appeal for change. The emergence and take-up of EI practices is clearly linked to changes in work organization, and tends to be faddish in character.[33,34]

There are two types of EI: direct and indirect. *Direct involvement* refers to those forms of participation where individual workers are involved in the decision-making processes that affect their everyday work routines, albeit often in a very limited way. Examples of direct EI include briefing groups, quality circles, problem-solving teams and self-managed teams (see Chapter 9 for a discussion on work groups). At the lowest level, involvement involves asking workers for information. They might not even know what the problem is about and do not make recommendations. At a moderate level of direct involvement, workers are told about the problem and asked to provide recommendations to the decision maker. At the highest level of direct involvement, the decision-making process is handed over to workers. They identify the problem, choose the best alternative and implement their choice.

Indirect involvement refers to those forms of worker participation where representatives or delegates of the main body of workers participate in the strategic decision-making process. Examples of indirect participation include joint consultation committees, European Works Councils and 'worker directors'. All these forms are associated with the broader notion of industrial democracy. Some European Union countries require worker involvement at both the worksite and corporate levels through a process of co-determination. In Sweden and Germany, for instance, employee representatives sit on supervisory boards, making decisions about executive salaries and recommendations about the company's strategic goals. At the same time, employers must consult with employee representation committees regarding matters of new technology, employment staffing, and work and human resource processes. Survey data indicates that indirect EI became less extensive in the period between 1980 and 2004.[35–37] Equally revealing about the era of globalization – the 1990s – is the growing proportion of workers who reported dissatisfaction with the amount of input they had over workplace decisions.[38]

industrial democracy: a broad term used to describe a range of programmes, processes and social institutions designed to provide greater employee involvement and influence in the decision-making process, and to exchange ideas on how to improve working conditions and product and service quality in the workplace

---

Critical insight

Ethics in decision making

Is 'business ethics' a contradiction in terms? Should ethics play a part in everyday managerial decision making in organizations? In an influential essay, the American economist Milton Friedman argued that the role of ethics in business management is rather limited: 'there is one and only one social responsibility of business – to use its resources and engage in activities designed to increase its profits'.[39] Others have countered that business managers can pursue a socially responsible course without the objectionable results claimed by Friedman.[40] Those who manage organizations have to work out their own code of conduct, but the ethical framework in which decision making takes place is embedded in society.[41]

Barring legal interventions, others have noted that the major incentive for organizations to engage in ethical activities is customer power. Shell's behaviour over the Brent Spar incident is an example of how customer boycotts can change corporate behaviour. There is evidence, however, that ethical human resources practices are more likely to be offered to permanent knowledge workers employed within an organization's legal boundaries, than to routine production or in-service workers on non-standard employment contracts.[42]

Read the chapter on 'The ethical context of HRM' by Karen Legge.[42] What business does ethics have in business organizations? In an era defined by increasing economic globalization and virtual organizations, can organizations manage people at work and engage in value-added activities in an ethical way?

Advantages of employee involvement

The support for EI needs to be viewed within the context of changing business and associated employment strategies, where the purpose of the latter is to secure employee support for high-performance work systems.[43] EI directly supports management's goals. In many respects, workers are the barometer of the organization. When operations or machines fail to meet performance standards, workers are usually the first to know. Thus, EI ensures that problems are quickly identified and corrected.

weblink

For general
information on EI schemes,
go to www.idea.gov.uk/idk/
core/page.do?pageId=8457481,
www.acas.org.uk and www.berr.
gov.uk (Britain); http://hrdc-drhc.
gc.ca and www.clc-ctc.ca
(Canada); www.hreonline.
com (USA)

EI also supports management's goals indirectly through commitment.[44] The general premise is that increasing workers' involvement in decision making will strengthen organizational citizenship. That is, involving people in decision making potentially increases their commitment to the organization's goals, and that in turn will result in enhanced performance. Surveys of managers have shown that EI is typically initiated by management, with the objective of enhancing worker commitment to organizational goals.[44–47] The involvement–commitment cycle is shown in Figure 15.2, and is the reverse of the vicious circle of control first discussed by Clegg and Dunkerley.[48]

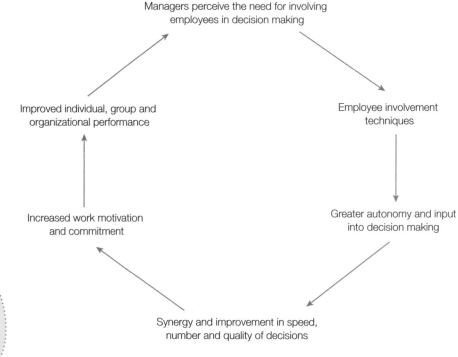

What
do you think of the
assumptions underpinning the
involvement–commitment cycle?
Can the growth of EI be explained
by employer 'needs', or are there
other forces determining
this employee relations
practice?

**stop
reflect**

figure 15.2 The involvement-commitment cycle

Management theorists have put forward three main reasons for senior management to introduce EI schemes: moral, economic and behavioural:[49]

- First, EI is derived from an ethical, political and moral base. The argument is that, in a democratic society, workers should be involved in the decision-making process when the outcomes of those decisions impact on their lives. EI presents a socially acceptable management style and projects 'a socially responsible stance' (ref. 50, p. 32).

weblink

For more
examples of companies
introducing EI practices, go to the
websites of the following companies:
General Electric (www.ge.com), Walmart
(www.walmart.com), IBM (www.ibm.com),
AkzoNobel (www.akzonobel.com), or another
company you are studying. Once there,
go to 'employee participation' or/and
'communications' and follow
the prompts

- Second, EI, according to the 'model of excellence' school in North America, improves the quality of decision making and productivity. Groups or communities of practice bring more input and diversity of views into the decision process. The evidence indicates that a group, team or community of practice will generally generate higher-quality decisions.
  - Decisions made collectively tend to lead to increased acceptance of a solution. Members who participated in making a decision are more likely to support the decision and encourage others to accept it. Research on the link between EI and a firm's performance suggests that giving employees a 'voice' on a range of organizational decisions yields benefits for both the organization and the workforce.[51–54]

● Furthermore, EI potentially reduces employee misbehaviour: by accepting EI interventions, 'Employers hope that participative mechanisms will create a greater coincidence of interests between employers and employees, thereby increasing trust, reducing the potential for conflict, and increasing the potential for an effective mutual influence process' (ref. 55, p. 53). As critics point out, EI practices can be used to 'educate' and 'reconstitute' the individual as a more malleable and productive employee.[33,56,57]

OB ▶ in focus   Teams make better decisions than individuals

Teams clearly outperform individuals in economic decision making. That is the key result of a recent laboratory study by Professor Kocher and Professor Sutter. The two researchers show that the type of the decision maker – an individual or a team – makes a significant difference in an interactive economic environment, whether it is the investment and marketing strategies of companies and fund managers, or the budget and monetary policy making of governments and central banks.

Small teams are smarter decision makers than individuals because they are better at processing information and better at predicting other decision makers' choices. The growing importance of teams in organizations and decision making in general renders these findings highly relevant. Decision-making teams are everywhere, including families, boards of directors, legislatures and committees. Households and firms, the main players in the economy, are typically not individuals but teams of people with a joint stake in their decisions. Similarly, political and military decisions as well as decisions on monetary policy are frequently taken by teams rather than by individuals.

In the laboratory setting that the researchers used to study the differences in decision making between small teams and individuals, there are four decision makers. Each of them can choose a number between (and including) zero and 100. The winner of the game is the decision maker with the number that is closest to two-thirds of the average of the four chosen numbers. The game is repeated four times. Despite its simplicity, this so-called 'beauty-contest' or 'guessing' game captures important features of investment decisions in financial markets. Kocher and Sutter find that teams (consisting of three people) are much better at guessing what other decision makers do in this game. In their experiment, teams win the game about 80 per cent more often than individuals in cases where small teams compete against individuals.

Source: M. Kocher and M. Sutter (2005) 'The decision maker matters: individual versus group behaviour in experimental beauty-contest games', *Economic Journal*, Wiley-Blackwell. For further information, visit www.res.org.uk/society/mediabriefings/pdfs/2005/jan05/kocher-sutter.pdf

---

Ethics and corporate social responsibility

So far, we have considered individual, group and organizational decision making, but have given little consideration to whether that decision making is ethical or unethical. Ethics and CSR are increasingly important due to high-profile cases of unethical managerial behaviour. Examples include Kenneth Lay and David Duncan of Enron, Bernard Ebbers and Scott Sullivan of WorldCom, Martha Stewart of Martha Stewart Inc., Fausto Tonna at Parmalat, Conrad Black of Hollinger International, and Bernard Madoff of Madoff Investment Securities and former chair of NASDAQ Stock Market.

Public criticism about white-collar crime caused a member of the Toronto Stock Exchange's Committee on Corporate Governance to state:

It is important, both to the corporate community and to society in general, that business achieve a higher degree of credibility. To do this, business must put its own house in order, starting with fundamental ethics and corporate governance issues and flowing on to responding more actively and publicly to the concerns of our society. (ref. 58, p. 34–5)

These white-collar crimes and the collective recognition that egregious and unethical behaviour has calamitous consequences, from loss of jobs (Royal Bank of Scotland, AIG) to loss of savings and retirement funds (Enron, Madoff), and government bail-outs (US and European banks), leads to an increasing public distrust of corporations. In 2009, collective anger over unethical and high-risk behaviour focused public attention on the need for business institutions to define their standards of ethical behaviour, and on the need for new CSR strategies and, moreover, greater government regulation. This section, therefore, follows naturally from the discussion of decision making. In it, we shall define business ethics and examine the nature of CSR.

Business ethics

ethics: the study of moral principles or values that determine whether actions are right or wrong, and outcomes are good or bad

Underscoring the notion of CSR and forging its implementation is the concept of ethics. Ethics is, according to the *Oxford Dictionary*, 'a set of moral principles'. In work organizations, ethics are a set of moral principles and values that govern the behaviour and decisions of individuals or groups. In essence, they involve values of about right and wrong. Any set of ethical principles does not emerge in a vacuum, but reflects the cultural values and norms of society. For example, bribing officials for contracts is regarded as bad in Western cultures. *Ethical dilemmas* arise when two or more values conflict, for example when a pharmaceutical company has to meet profit targets but the process involves the testing of a new drug on animals. In the past, business ethics consisted mainly of legally driven, compliance-based codes that guided workplace behaviour when making decisions on the improper use of the organization's resources or conflicts of interest. In an ever more globalized economy, an increasing number of companies are undergoing 'a program of moral reform' (ref. 59, p. 35) that involves crafting value-based ethical policies that are compatible with cross-global operations. The objective is to help employees make informed decisions when faced with new ethical situations.

The ethical dimension of *employment* policies and practices relates to the selection of employees (for example, the avoidance of discrimination), rewards (for example, the notion of fairness), training (for example, equal opportunities), health and safety (for example, a full disclosure of chemicals used in the workplace, including any harmful long-term effects) and the protection of whistleblowers.[60] The ethical issues affecting *consumers* relate to how the marketing mix is applied to consumers, including, for example, product safety and testing, price fixing, respect for privacy, false labelling of products and misleading advertising.[61] The ethical dimension of *environmental* issues, for instance carbon emissions, conservation and wasteful packaging, is a classic illustration of an ethical dilemma. For example, petroleum companies extracting 'dirty oil' from the oil sands in Alberta, Canada, satisfy shareholders' returns in preference to reducing carbon emissions and pollution.

Political issues refer to the lobbying of politicians to pass or not pass legislation that impacts adversely on business interests. They also relate to the politics of globalization. This includes the ability of global corporations to shape or circumvent national laws and local interests. Therefore, the ability of large multinational corporations to exert significant power in their host countries is an ethical concern. Multinational corporations face the twin pressures of cost reductions and differentiation to satisfy local markets — that is to say, there is on the one hand a pressure to cut costs by homogenizing goods and, on the other, a pressure to provide products that are uniquely tailored to

Do you believe organizations should act ethically or, in their search for 'competitive advantage', should they maximize shareholder return? Is it the competitive context or individual traits that cause unethical behaviour?

stop reflect

figure 15.3 Ethical issues in business

Source: iStockphoto

plate 55 The ethical dimension of environmental issues – for instance, carbon emissions, conservation, wasteful packaging – is a classic illustration of an ethical dilemma. For example, do these apples really need to be shrink-wrapped? What pressures on companies might have led to the over-packaging of foodstuffs? Do recent advertising campaigns such as 'A low carbon diet = locally produced' suggest that this trend might be changing?

For more information on CSR, visit the websites of UK-based Business in the Community at www.bitc.org.uk and US-based Business for Social Responsibility at www.bsr.org

weblink

suit specific markets.[62] Under such competitive conditions, the system of business regulations in host countries becomes an important factor in deciding where global corporations operate. Unsurprisingly, governments in developing countries increasingly face pressure to weaken their regulations for employment (for example, workplace safety), products (for example, automobile exhaust emissions and clinical trials) and ecological controls to attract overseas investment. In her book *No Logo*, Naomi Klein offers a scathing criticism of global companies that exploit the world's poor. In particular, she identifies two key ethical concerns: unfair trading practices and the lack of human rights.[63]

The ethical issues affecting corporate *governance* relate to issues associated with what some sociologists call *corporate crime*. Studies show that corporate crime is not confined to a few 'bad apples', but is pervasive and widespread. In addition to violations linked to employment, marketing and the environment, violations also occur in financial practices (for example, corporate tax avoidance or illegal bribes to secure contracts) and administrative practices (for example, non-compliance with national laws).[64]

Corporate social responsibility

Although The Body Shop, famous for its 'ethical' manufacturing and retailing operations, is a well-known contemporary company adopting an ethical approach to business, there is evidence – 20 years after the disastrous oil spillage by *Exxon Valdez* of March 24, 1989 – that CSR is now a priority: it is a concept whose time has come.[65,66] CSR involves the application of business ethics, and concerns the ethical principle that an organization should be accountable for how its behaviour might affect local communities, society and the planet.

CSR is not new. Since the British Industrial Revolution (around 1780–1830), companies such as Cadbury and Rowntree have adopted progressive employment standards and provided housing for their workers. Some employers established model villages to house their workforce. Cadbury established Bournville, Lever Brothers instituted Port Sunlight, and one of the earliest metropolis villages was at Saltaire, around the textile mills of Titus Salt near Bradford. These actions by early factory owners are often referred to as paternalistic management, as they are based on the premodern assumption that employers have a responsibility to look after the welfare of their employees.[32] Many of these early progressive employers were influenced by their Quaker beliefs.

CSR is based on the *stakeholder theory* of the firm, which contends that organizations should be managed not purely in the interests of maximizing shareholder return, but also in the interests of a range of groups or stakeholders that have a legitimate interest in the organization as well, such as employees, customers, the local community, suppliers and environment and society in general.[67] The core premise is that the organization has an obligation to other various groups in society to whom the company is responsible. The concept of CSR is problematic because, as we explained in Chapter 1, it is people, not organizations, who make decisions and engage in unethical behaviour. In the same vein, unarguably only *people*, and not inanimate objects such as organizations, can be responsible for human actions.

Some of the worst examples of corporate social *irresponsibility* have occurred in developing economies. In Bhopal, India, for example, a chemical plant owned by the US global company Union Carbide engaged in chemical production under conditions that would have been illegal in the USA. On December 3, 1984, the plant experienced a major leak. Within hours, 3000 people were dead, 15,000 more dying in the

Recently the Indian government deregulated the telecommunications industry, including changes to employment regulations, in order to increase foreign investment in call centres. Is it socially responsible when corporations encourage host countries to deregulate employment or health and safety standards? (See Maitra and Jasjit, 2005.[69])

stop reflect

aftermath, and 200,000 were seriously injured; half a million still carry special health cards. Eventually, the organization paid out just $470 million in compensation.[68]

CSR has been characterized as a multilayered concept with four interrelated responsibilities: economic, legal, ethical and philanthropic.[70] According to this model, the raison d'être of organizations is to produce goods and services for profit or within budget. Organizations must pursue their economic responsibilities within the legal and regulatory framework. Ethical responsibility means that organizations should operate in a manner consistent with the dominant values of society. Philanthropic responsibility extends CSR beyond legal compliance to actively promoting good in the community through collaborative projects in relation to education, employability and economic renewal, or being a good 'corporate citizen' (see the UK Business in the Community website, in the Web Link above). There is some evidence to suggest that an ethical approach to business will improve the financial performance of the organization and contribute towards the job satisfaction of employees.[71,72]

Research evidence suggests that ethical behaviour and CSR are a function of *both* the individual's values and the context in which the decision-making process occurs. Figure 15.4 offers a model to account for ethical or unethical decision-making behaviour, drawing on the work of Trevino,[73] Carroll,[59] and Bratton et al.[74]

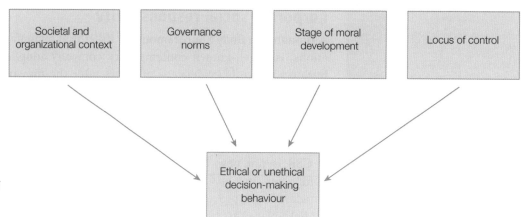

figure 15.4 Determinants of ethical behaviour in work organizations

The *societal and organizational context* refers to an individual's perception of societal and organizational expectations. Does society or the organization encourage and support ethical behaviour by rewarding it, or discourage unethical behaviour by punishing it? Public policy statements, codes of ethics, financial performance expectations, appraisal methods that evaluate means as well as ends, visible recognition and promotion for employees who display high ethical behaviour, and visible punishment for those who act unethically, are all examples of societal and organizational context that are likely to promote high ethical decision making.

Commenting on the public backlash against US corporate leaders accused and convicted of engaging in fraudulent accounting practices, one of us elsewhere noted:

> Simply focusing on [individual] traits such as honesty and integrity inappropriately separates the leader from the followers and the context. Those corporate leaders ... who engaged in criminal or highly unethical practices ... did so largely because of profound changes in the context. In the late 1990s, shareholder-value-driven capitalism emphasized stock appreciation, the use of stock options to compensate leaders, and the attainment of short-term financial targets, which produced a culture of avarice. (ref. 74, p. 323)

Governance norms focus on democratic decision making that is intended to encourage free and full discussion in order to stimulate the mutual informal

including allowing shy members to speak who would otherwise be reluctant to contribute in a full group situation, avoiding domination by an extrovert member and eliminating some social pressure from the majority to conform. Research has demonstrated that the stepladder technique is effective at improving group decision making, although Winquist and Franz's study had difficulty replicating the positive outcomes.[78]

Computer-mediated brainstorming

Computer-mediated brainstorming permits decision makers to share ideas while minimizing many of the problems in group dynamics described earlier. An online facilitator begins the process by posting a problem or question. Members then post their answers or ideas on their computer terminal. All the group's ideas are posted anonymously and randomly on the computer screens. Members individually rank or vote electronically on the ideas or solutions presented. Typically, face-to-face discussion follows the computer-mediated process.

Research suggests that computer-mediated brainstorming generates more ideas than traditional face-to-face brainstorming, and that participants are more confident and motivated to participate in the decision-making process than in other group structures.[79] Computer-mediated brainstorming groups tend to be more egalitarian than face-to-face groups: that is, gender and status barriers tend to be broken down, and participation is more evenly distributed among men and women members than in face-to-face meetings.

The Delphi technique

Delphi technique: a structured team decision-making process of systematically pooling the collective knowledge of experts on a particular subject to make decisions, predict the future or identify opposing views

The Delphi technique methodically collates the collective knowledge of experts on a particular subject to scan the environment, predict the future, make decisions or identify opposing views. Its name derives from the future-telling ability of the famous Greek Delphic oracle. Delphi participants do not meet face to face – they may be located in different parts of the country or world, and may not know each other's identity. As with the computer-mediated brainstorming process, decision makers do not know who 'owns' the ideas or possible solutions. The Delphi method relies solely on a nominal group, and participants – usually experts in a relevant field – do not engage in face-to-face interaction.

Typically, Delphi group members submit ideas or possible solutions to the facilitator in response to a series of questionnaires. The respondents' replies are compiled and returned to the group for a second round of comments. This process may be repeated a couple more times until consensus or dis-consensus emerges. It should be emphasized that the 'experts' taking part do not actually make a final decision: they provide expert advice and information for organizational decision makers.

The advantage of the Delphi technique is that the process pools a large number of expert judgements while avoiding the problems of conformity and polarization that can occur in interacting groups. A disadvantage of the method is the rather lengthy time-frame involved, and its effectiveness depends on the respondents' interest in the problem and commitment to the organization.

As we can see, decision making is a complex phenomenon because it involves dealing with technical matters and power struggles. The five processes reviewed can help employees deal with the technical challenges and minimize human biases and errors. But decision making is central to innovation and organizational change and relations in the workplace. In this sense, it is at the heart of relationships of class and gender domination. The neoclassical rational model of decision making is associated with bureaucratic managerial structures, as well as a vision of managers as omnipresent and omnipotent. The extent to which organizations can be designed with decentralized decision-making processes is examined in Chapter 10.

Chapter summary

□ When, in July 2006, the owners of the TV company CHUM Ltd decided to sell their company to Bell Globemedia of Canada, 281 people became redundant. Peter Murdoch, media vice-president of the Communications Energy and Paperworks Union, which represents employees in CHUM newsrooms, said 'It's absolutely a sense of betrayal. It's a sense of bewilderment.' From a different angle, CHUM chief executive Jay Switzer commenting on the sale said 'This is a challenged sector and we have some work to do'.[80] Such decisions by top managers impact on people on an almost daily basis in the corporate world.

□ Decision making, the conscious process of making choices from among several alternatives to achieve a desired course of action, is said to be perhaps the most important management function. We have explained that decision making is central to managers' ability to alter the activities of the organization and influence the behaviour of employees, and is at the heart of relationships of class and gender domination. Decision making is a complex phenomenon because it involves technical problems and power struggles.

□ We have explained that the dynamics of organizations create a need for decision making. Decisions can be viewed as being primarily concerned with the allocation of resources and exercise of power. The neoclassical rational model of decision making has eight steps: identify the problem, define the objectives to be met, make a decision of who to involve in the solution and how to make the decision, generate alternatives, evaluate those alternatives, make a choice from among the alternatives, implement the choice, and follow up on the results of the decision. As decisions lead to actions and the discovery of new problems, another cycle of the rational model is begun.

□ In reality, decision makers must suffer from bounded rationality. They do not have free and easy access to information, and the human mind has limited information-processing capacity and is susceptible to a variety of cognitive biases. In addition, time constraints and political considerations can outweigh anticipated economic gain.

□ We have addressed a number of structured group techniques designed to improve group processes and the quality of group decisions, including brainstorming, the nominal group technique, the stepladder technique, computer-mediated brainstorming and the Delphi technique.

□ The neoclassical rational model neglects to factor into the process the effects of gender on individual and group decision making. Nor does it consider social factors, such as how social norms and expectations frame sense making or problem definition and the decision-making process. We have reviewed some of the literature which suggests that women construct and value knowledge in ways that are relational and oriented more towards sustaining relationships than achieving autonomy and power. The notion that women have a different voice and take a more holistic view of reality suggests that decision-making processes are influenced by the gender balance of the decision makers.

□ Groups can make higher-quality decisions than individuals, but they might also experience groupthink and make decisions that are more risky or conservative than those of individuals. Research has demonstrated that groups do not necessarily make better-quality decisions.

□ Society, as well as organizations, is increasingly concerned about unethical behaviour and its consequences, from loss of jobs to loss of savings and retirement funds, and from to government bail-outs to an increasingly collective distrust of corporations. Business ethics is about conducting business in an ethical manner and generating revenue with integrity. One response to public concern about unethical behaviour has been to develop codes of conduct so that individual decision makers with different moral standards and bases of moral judgement will have a consistent basis for their decisions.

□ 'Corporate social responsibility' refers to the ethical principle that an organization should be accountable for how its behaviour affects local communities, society and the plant. Violations, for example, of health and safety regulations and environmental pollution affect large numbers of people in developed and developing economies; such managerial behaviour has been referred by some criminologists to as 'corporate crime'.

□ Finally, decision making traditionally remains associated with a 'command and control' vision of management, as well as a vision of managers as omnipresent and omnipotent. Decision making in the organization can be improved by using the four group processes described above.

Key concepts

bounded rationality	411
brainstorming	426
computer-mediated brainstorming	427
corporate crime	423
corporate social responsibility	423–424
Delphi technique	427
employee involvement	418–419
escalation of commitment	416
ethics in decision making	422
nominal group technique	426

Vocab checklist for ESL students

☐ Assumption, assume
☐ Bounded rationality
☐ Brainstorming
☐ Decision making
☐ Delphi technique
☐ Divergent thinking
☐ Employee involvement
☐ Escalation of commitment
☐ Ethics, ethical
☐ Industrial democracy

- ☐ Information overload
- ☐ Intuition, intuitive
- ☐ Nominal
- ☐ Political theory model
- ☐ Rationality, rationalize, rational
- ☐ Satisficing
- ☐ Socialization, socialize, social

⟨?⟩ Chapter review questions

1. 'For the most part, individual decision making in organizations is an irrational process.' Do you agree or disagree? Discuss.

2. What factors do you think differentiate good decision makers from poor ones? Relate your answer to the eight-step rational decision-making model.

3. If group decisions consistently achieve better-quality outcomes than those achieved by individuals, how did the phrase 'a camel is a horse designed by a committee' become so popular and ingrained in our culture?

4. Are unethical decisions more a function of the individual decision maker or the decision maker's work environment? Explain.

5. To what extent do you believe managerial practices to be unethical, and how might unethical behaviour be restricted?

6. What are the arguments for and against corporate social responsibility?

⟨?⟩ Chapter research questions

1. Many ethical dilemmas derive from the conflict between the desire to maximize shareholder return and the wish to make decisions that are ethically justified. Form a study group including, if possible, an international student(s). Give examples of companies facing an ethical dilemma in (a) marketing, (b) employee relations, and (c) carbon management and environmental issues. What would a CSR partnership programme for McDonald's look like? How might unethical behaviour be restricted?

2. Obtain a copy of Patrick Maclagan's book, *Management and Morality* (see Further Reading, below). After reading Chapter 2, 'Personal values and moral development', explain the author's statement that there is 'a logical relationship' between individual values and decision making and action in organizations.

3. Read Robert Giacalone et al.'s article, 'On ethics and social responsibility: the impact of materialism, postmaterialism, and hope' (listed in Further Reading, below). What does the study tell us about how individual values play a role in predicting ethical decision making?

⟨▤⟩ Further reading

Fulop, L., et al. (2009) 'Decision making in organizations', pp. 667–708 in S. Linstead, L. Fulop and S. Lilley (eds), *Management and Organization: A Critical Text*, 2nd edn, Basingstoke: Palgrave.

Dennis, A. R. and Valacich, J. S. (1999) 'Electronic brainstorming: illusions and patterns of productivity', *Information Systems Research*, **10**(2), pp. 375–7.

Derry, R. (1989) 'An empirical study of moral reasoning among managers', *Journal of Business Ethics*, **8**(11), pp. 855–62.

Donaldson, T. (1999) 'Making stakeholder theory whole', *Academy of Management Review*, **24**(2), pp. 237–41.

Forte, A. (2004) 'Antecedents of managers' moral reasoning', *Journal of Business Ethics*, **51**(4), pp. 315–47.

Giacalone, R. A., Jurkiewicz, C.L. and Deckop, J. R. (2008) 'On ethics and social responsibility: the impact of materialism, postmaterialism, and hope', *Human Relations*, **61**(4), pp. 483–514.

Harley, B., Hyman, J. and Thompson, P. (2005) *Participation and Democracy at Work*, Basingstoke: Palgrave.

Maclagan, P. (1998) *Management and Morality*, London: Sage.

Marx, R., Stubbart, C., Traub, V. and Cavanaugh, M. (1987) 'The NASA space shuttle disaster: a case study', *Journal of Management Case Studies*, **3**, pp. 300–18.

Miller, S. J., Hickson, D. and Wilson, S. D. (1999) 'Decision making in organizations', pp. 43–62 in S. R. Clegg, C. Hardy and W. Nord (eds), *Managing Organizations: Current Issues*, London: Sage.

Munby, D. K. and Putnam, L. L. (1992) 'The politics of emotion: a feminist reading of bounded rationality', *Academy of Management Review*, **17**, pp. 465–86.

Ryan, L. V. (1994) 'Ethics codes in British companies', *Business Ethics*, **3**(1), pp. 54–64.

Sagie, A. and Aycan, Z. (2003) 'A cross-cultural analysis of participative decision-making in organizations', *Human Relations*, **56**(4), pp. 453–73.

Winquist, J. and Franz, T. (2008) 'Does the stepladder technique improve group decision making? A series of failed replications', *Group Dynamics: Theory, Research and Practice*, **12**(4), pp. 255–67.

Winstanley, D. and Woodall, J. (eds) (2000) *Ethical Issues in Contemporary Human Resource Management*, Basingstoke: Palgrave.

Yakabuski, K. (2008) 'The kindness of corporations', *Report on Business*, July–August, pp. 66–71.

 Chapter case study 1

Ethical decision making at Primark Apparel

Background

Over the last 10 years, the competitive UK retail clothing industry has seen discount chains increase their share of the $51 billion market. Such chains as Matalan, Peacocks and Primark Stores offer brands demanded by an increasingly value-focused consumer. Although continued growth in the market will come from the success of these retailers, it is expected that depressed demand and the prevalence of discounters will result in only a modest expansion in the next few years.

As UK clothing suppliers have lower productivity than leading European competitors, the opportunities for low-cost foreign clothing suppliers to provide to these discount chains have increased. This has resulted in imports making up an estimated two-thirds of the value of the UK clothing market. Traditional sources, primarily Hong Kong and India, are now facing competition from countries such as Morocco and Romania.

The company

Primark is one of the largest discount chains, with 187 stores located in Ireland, Holland, Spain and the UK. It employs more than 27,000 people, and ranks as Great Britain's second largest clothing retailer by volume and the leading retailer in value clothing. It is expanding more rapidly than any other British retailer. Its primary customer base are those under 35 years old who are fashion-conscious and want high-quality clothing at reasonable prices.

Primark prides itself on being a member of the Ethical Trading Initiative, which is an alliance of companies, trade unions and non-profit organizations that aims to promote respect for the rights of people in factories and farms worldwide. Primark's commitment to monitoring and improving the working conditions of their 400 suppliers is reflected in their Code of Conduct, which stipulates, among other standards, that the suppliers must pay living wages and ensure that working hours are not excessive.

Using internal Ethical Trade Managers and third-party auditors, the company conducts over 300 audits of their suppliers every year. All potential new suppliers are audited prior to commencing work with Primark, and must meet the company's ethical standards in order to be added to their supply chain. Primark continually reviews its auditing methodologies to improve its ability to identify non-compliance with these standards by its suppliers. Training is offered to suppliers to help them deal with any issues that are found.

The problem

In early 2009, an undercover investigation by the BBC revealed that workers in a Manchester factory, owned by a supplier to Primark, were on duty for up to 12 hours a day, earning only £3.50 an hour. Some workers were employed illegally and were working in poor conditions.

As the BBC had previously revealed that Primark contractors in India had employed children in slum workshops, Primark took these new allegations seriously. It immediately commenced an investigation of the supplier that was conducted by auditors and senior Primark personnel. The results of the audit were not positive; some findings included inaccurate records of rates of pay, fabricated payslips understating the hours worked, excessive working hours and cash payments made to the employees. During the investigation, Primark agreed to remove all references to the Ethical Trade Initiative from 140 of its store fronts.

A Primark representative remarked: 'There are no excuses. We are absolutely committed to ensuring that the factories who sell to us treat their workers fairly and equitably.' On its website, Primark stated that the supplier had to improve if they were to remain in Primark's supply chain. Primark also made the commitment to help the supplier improve its employment and management practices.

Task

On your own, or in a small group, discuss the following:

1. Is it realistic for Primark to control the ethical practices of all its suppliers? If not, why?
2. How could Primark's management evaluation and reward systems be used as encouragement?
3. As a possible member of Primark's target customer base, what decision would you make about purchasing their products in light of the revelations by the BBC? What role, if any, do ethics play in that decision?

Essential reading

Ferrell, O.C, Fraedrich, J. and Ferrell, L. (2006) *Business Ethics: Ethical Decision Making and Cases*, Boston: Houghton Mifflin Company.

For more information on the UK retail clothing industry, visit www.infomat.com/research/infre0000282.html

To learn about the Ethical Trading Initiative, go to www. ethicaltrade.org

Note

This case study was written by Lori Rilkoff, MSc, CHRP, Senior Human Resources Manager at the City of Kamloops, and lecturer in HRM at Thompson Rivers University, BC, Canada.

 Chapter case study 2

A new venture for Echo Generation Publishing

 Visit www.palgrave.com/business/brattonob2e to view this case study

 ## Web-based assignment

Decision making has been acknowledged as the fundamental element in the manager's job. Yet it is a complex phenomenon because it involves not only technical considerations, but also power struggles. It remains associated to a 'command and control' vision of management, as well as to a vision of managers as omnipresent and omnipotent. Decision making can be improved by using group processes that help to minimize the biases and errors.

This web-based assignment requires you to investigate the extent of decentralized decision-making processes. We would like you visit the websites for the findings from the 2004 Workplace Survey: www.workteams.org; www.berr.gov.uk/whatwedo/employment/research%2Devaluation/wers%2D2004/

What type of manager–employee decision-making processes are you likely to find in the workplace? What issues are discussed at these decentralized committees? What appears to be excluded from discussion? Do committees make 'good' decisions? Explain your answer.

OB in film

Apollo 13 (1995) has some excellent scenes that show decision making. The film tells the story of the effort of US astronaut Jim Lovell, his crew and NASA to return their damaged spacecraft back to Earth. One scene shows NASA's mission control flight director Gene Kranz (played by Ed Harris) writing on a chalkboard and saying, 'So you are telling me you can only give our guys 45 hours.' The scene ends when he leaves the room insisting 'Failure is not an option.' What do the scenes tell us about the decision-making process? Are the decisions made primarily by an individual or by a group?

References

1   *Globe and Mail*, 'Managerial myopia attacked', August 27, 2003, p. A10.

2   Stewart, H. (2009) 'Economists tell Queen how they failed to see the recession coming', *Observer*, July 26, pp. 1, 5.

3   March, J. G. (1997) 'Understanding how decisions happen in organizations', pp. 9–32 in Z. Shapira (ed.), *Organizational Decision Making*, New York: Cambridge University Press.

4   Miller, S. J., Hickson, D. and Wilson, S. D. (1999) 'Decision-making in organizations', pp. 43–62 in S. R. Clegg, C. Hardy and W. Nord (eds), *Managing Organizations: Current Issues*, London: Sage.

5   Mintzberg, H. (1979) *The Structure of Organizations*, Englewood Cliffs, NJ: Prentice-Hall.

6   Shull, F. A., Delbecq, A. L. and Cummings, L. (1970) *Organizational Decision Making*, New York: McGraw-Hill.

7   Fayol, H. (1949) *General and Industrial Management*, London: Pitman.

8   Simon, H. A. (1957) *Administrative Behaviour*, New York: Macmillan.

9   Levine, S. B. (1990) 'Understanding industrial relations in modern Japan', *Industrial and Labor Relations Review*, **43**(2), pp. 326–7.

10 Cohen, M. D., March, J. G. and Olsen, P. (1972) 'A garage can model of organizational choice', *Administrative Science Quarterly*, **17**, pp. 1–25.

11 Brockmann, E. N. and Anthony, W. P. (1998) 'The influence of tacit knowledge and collective mind on strategic planning', *Journal of Managerial Issues*, **10**(Spring), pp. 204–22.

12 Leonard, D. and Sensiper, S. (1998) 'The role of tacit knowledge in group innovation', *California Management Review*, **40**(Spring), pp. 112–32.

13 Lieberman, M.D. (2000) 'Intuition: a social cognitive neuroscience approach', *Psychological Bulletin*, **126**, pp. 109–37.

14 Stamps, D. (1999) 'Is knowledge management a fad?', *Training*, **36**(3), pp. 36–42.

15 Ashkanasy, N. M., Zerbe, C. E. and Hartel, J. (2002) 'Introduction: managing emotions in a changing workplace', pp. 3–18 in N. Ashkanasy, C. Zerbe and J. Hartel (eds), *Managing Emotions in the Workplace*, New York: Sharpe.

16 Moisi, D. (2009) *The Geopolitics of Emotion*, New York: Doubleday.

17 House of Commons Treasury Committee (2009) *Banking Crisis: Dealing with the Failure of the UK Banks*. London: Stationery Office.

18 Verma, S. (2009) 'From the Bronx to the top court in the land: the American dream comes true', *Globe and Mail*, May 27, p. A11.

19 Martin, J. (2000) 'Hidden gendered assumptions in mainstream organizational theory and research', *Journal of Management Inquiry*, **9**(2), pp. 207–16.

20 Gilligan, C. (1982) *In a Different Voice*, Cambridge, MA: Harvard University Press.

21 Smith, D. (1987) *The Everyday World as Problematic: A Feminist Sociology*, Boston, MA: Northeastern University Press.

22 Wilson, F. M. (2003) *Organizational Behaviour and Gender*, Farnham: Ashgate.

23 Millett, K. (1985) *Sexual Politics*, London: Virago.

24 Staw, B. and Ross, J. (1989) 'Understanding behavior in escalation situations', *Science*, **246**, pp. 216–20.

25 Ross, J. and Staw, B (1993) 'Organization escalation and exit: lessons from the Shoreham nuclear power plant', *Academy of Management Journal*, **36**, pp. 701–32.

26 Asch, S. E. (1951) 'Effects of group pressure upon modification and distortion of judgements', in H. Guetzkow (ed.), *Groups, Leadership and Men*, New York: Carnegie Press.

27 Milgram, S. (1973) *Obedience and Authority*, London: Tavistock.

28 Mintzberg, H., Ahlstrand, B. and Lampel, J. (1998) *Strategy Safari: A Guided Tour Through the Wilds of Strategic Management*, New York: Free Press.

29 Mintzberg, H. (1989) *Mintzberg on Management*, New York: Free Press.

30 Salaman, G. (1979) *Work Organizations: Resistance and Control*, London: Longman.

31 Willmott, H. (1989) 'Images and ideals of managerial work', *Journal of Management Studies*, **21**(3), pp. 349–68.

32 Godard, J. (2005) *Industrial Relations: The Economy and Society* (3rd edn), Concord, ON: Captus Press.

33 Ramsay, H. (1991) 'Reinventing the wheel: a review of the development and performance of employee involvement', *Human Resource Management Journal*, **1**, pp. 1–22.

34 Harley, B., Hyman, J. and Thompson, P. (2005) *Participation and Democracy at Work*, Basingstoke: Palgrave.

35 Cully, M., Woodland, S., O'Reilly, A. and Dix, G. (1999) *Britain at Work*, London: Routledge.

36 Kersley, B., Alpin, C, Forth, J., Bryson, A., Bewley, H., Dix, G. and Oxenbridge, S. (2005) *Inside the Workplace: First Findings from the 2004 Workplace Employment Relations Survey (WERS 2004)*, London: Department of Trade and Industry.

37 Millward, N., Bryson, A. and Forth, J. (2000) *All Change at Work: British Employee Relations 1980–1998*, London: Routledge.

38 Kelly, J. (2006) 'Labor movements and mobilization', pp. 283–304 in S. Ackroyd, R. Batt, P. Thompson and P. S. Tolbert (eds), *The Oxford Handbook of Work and Organization*, New York: Oxford University Press.

39 Friedman, M. (1970) 'The social responsibility of business is to increase its profits', *New York Times Magazine*, September 13, p. 32.

40 Mulligan, T. (1986) 'A critique of Milton Friedman's essay "The social responsibility of business is to increase its profits"', *Journal of Business Ethics*, **16**(1), pp. 265–9.

41 Cadbury, A. (1987) 'Ethical managers make their own rules', *Harvard Business Review*, September/October, pp. 69–73.

42 Legge, K. (2000) 'The ethical context of HRM', pp. 23–40 in D. Winstanley and J. Woodall (eds), *Ethical Issues in Contemporary Human Resource Management*, Basingstoke: Palgrave.

43 Bratton, J. and Gold, J. (2007) *Human Resource Management: Theory and Practice* (4th edn), Basingstoke: Palgrave.

44 Marchington, M. (2001) 'Employee involvement', pp. 232–52 in J. Storey (ed.), *Human Resource Management: A Critical Text*, London: Thomson Learning.

45 Delbridge, R. and Whitfield, K. (2001) 'Employee perceptions of job influence and organizational participation', *Industrial Relations*, **40**(3), pp. 472–89.

46 Marchington, M., Goodman, J., Wilkinson, A. and Ackers, P. (1992) *Recent Developments in Employee Involvement*, Employment Department Research Series Number 1, London: HMSO.

47 Benders, J. (2005) 'Team working: a tale of partial participation', pp. 55–74 in D. Knights, P. Thompson, C. Smith and H. Willmott (eds), *Participation and Democracy at Work*, Basingstoke: Palgrave.

48 Clegg, S. and Dunkerley, D. (1980) *Organization, Class and Control*, London: Routledge & Kegan Paul.

49 Verma, A. and Taras, D. (2005) 'Managing the high-involvement workplace', pp. 134–73 in M. Gunderson, A. Ponak and D. Taras (eds), *Union-Management Relations in Canada* (5th edn), Toronto: Addison Wesley.

50 Marchington, M. and Wilding, P. (1983) 'Employee involvement inaction?', *Personnel Management*, pp. 73–83.

51 Mackie, K. S., Holahan, C. and Gottlieb, N. (2001) 'Employee involvement management practices, work stress, and depression in employees of a human services residential care facility', *Human Relations*, **54**(8), pp. 1065–92.

52 Mabey, C, Skinner, D. and Clark, D. (eds) (1998) *Experiencing Human Resource Management*, London: Sage.

53 Verma, A. and Taras, D. (2001) 'Employee involvement in the workplace', in M. Gunderson, A. Ponak and D. Taras (eds), *Union–Management Relations in Canada* (4th edn), Don Mills, ON: Addison-Wesley.

54 Heller, F., Pusic, E., Strauss, G. and Wilpert, B. (1998) *Organizational Participation: Myth and Reality*, Oxford: Oxford University Press.

55 Beer, M., Spector, B., Lawrence, P. R., Quin Mills, D. and Walton, R. E. (1984) *Managing Human Assets*, New York: Free Press.

56 Townley, B. (1994) *Reframing Human Resource Management: Power, Ethics and the Subject of Work*, London: Sage.

57 Legge, K. (2005) *Human Resource Management: Rhetorics and Realities* (2nd edn), Basingstoke: Palgrave.

58 Brown, quoted in W. K. Carroll (2004) *Corporate Power in a Globalizing World: A Study of Elite Social Organization*, Don Mills, ON: Oxford University Press.

59 Carroll, W. K. (2004) *Corporate Power in a Globalizing World: A Study of Elite Social Organization*, Don Mills, ON: Oxford University Press.

60 Winstanley, D. and Woodall, J. (2000) (eds) *Ethical Issues in Contemporary Human Resource Management*, Basingstoke: Palgrave.

61 Jobber, D. (2007) *Principles and Practice of Marketing* (5th edn), London: McGraw-Hill.

62 Bartlett, C. A. and Ghoshal, S. (1989) *Managing across Borders: The Transnational Solution*, London: Random House.

63 Klein, N. (2000) *No Logo*, London: Flamingo.

64 Slapper, G. and Tombs, S. (1999) *Corporate Crime*, Essex: Longman.

65 Yakabuski, K. (2008) 'The kindness of corporations', *Report on Business*, July–August, pp. 66–71.

66 Moon, J. (2002) 'Corporate social responsibility: an overview', in C. Hartley (ed.) *The International Directory of Corporate Philanthropy*, London: Europa Books.

67 Donaldson, T. and Preston, L. E. (1995) 'The stakeholder theory of the corporation: concepts, evidence and implications', *Academy of Management Review*, **20**(1), pp. 15–19.

68 Saul, J. R. (2005) *The Collapse of Globalism*, Toronto: Viking.

69 Maitra, M. and Jasjit, S. (2005) 'Corruption and corporate social responsibility', in *Proceedings of the 47th Meeting of International Business*, Quebec, July 9–12.

70 Carroll, A. B. and Buchholtz, A. K. (2000) *Business and Society: Ethics and Stakeholder Management*, Mason, OH: South-Western.

71 Wilson, A. (1997) 'Business and its social responsibility', in P. W. F. Davies (ed.), *Current Issues in Business Ethics*, London: Routledge.

72 Koh, H. C. and Boo, E. H. (2001) 'The link between organizational ethics and job satisfaction: a study of managers in Singapore', *Journal of Business Ethics*, **29**(4), pp. 309–24.

73 Trevino, L. K. (1986) 'Ethical decision making in organizations: a person-situation interactionist model', *Academy of Management Review*, July 11, pp. 601–17.

74 Bratton, J., Grint, K. and Nelson, D. (2005) *Organizational Leadership*, Mason, OH: Thomson-South-Western.

75 Burns, J. M. (1978) *Leadership*, New York: Harper & Row.

76 Gardner, J. W. (1990) *On Leadership*, New York: Free Press.

77 Madsen, D. B. and Finger, J. R. (1978) 'Comparison of a written feedback procedure, group brainstorming, and individual brainstorming', *Journal of Applied Psychology*, **63**(1), pp. 120–3.

78 Winquist, J. and Franz, T. (2008) 'Does the stepladder technique improve group decision making? A series of failed replications', *Group Dynamics: Theory, Research and Practice*, **12**(4), pp. 255–67.

79 Dennis, A. R. and Valacich, J. S. (1999) 'Electronic brainstorming: illusions and patterns of productivity', *Information Systems Research*, **10**(2), pp. 375–7.

80 Robertson, G. (2006) 'Layoffs come as a deal is unveiled', *Globe and Mail*, July 13, p. A6.

chapter 16
Power, politics and conflict

chapter outline

- Introduction
- Power: a matter of definitions
- Power: evidence from the workplace
- Summary and end-of-chapter features
- Chapter case study 1: Aiming for a paperless world
- Chapter case study 2: Las Vegas general strike

chapter objectives

After completing this chapter, you should be able to:

- recognize and explain key debates concerning the concept of power in the context of the organizational behaviour field
- understand and explain the following key concepts: systems of power, authority, influence and hegemony
- compare and contrast major macro-theoretical approaches to the concept of power in the writings of Mann, Foucault, Lukes, Weber and Gramsci
- discuss possible implications of theories and research for workplace practice

Introduction

In the field of physics, 'power' is defined as a quantity expressing the rate at which energy is transformed into work. In fact, thermodynamic laws see energy as flowing in one direction only. In addition, power is active. The concept that slows it down, 'resistance', is passive. We begin with these points for a reason. Simply put, some of these basic principles appear remarkably persistent in many common-sense views about the notion of 'power' in its more general forms, what it is and how it works.

This chapter takes up the issue of power and behaviour in work organizations. It provides an introduction to a range of thinking and research in order to help provide tools with which to expand your understanding. As some recent researchers have commented, 'Changes in power almost invariably lead to changes in behavior' (ref. 1, p. 135). (See also Ailon[2] for further commentary on the gaps in organizational theorists' thinking about power, and Crane et al.[3] for a discussion of this matter in relation to business studies, with a specific focus on the work of Michel Foucault.)

Throughout, however, we explicitly reject the common-sense view of power. We argue that power is not simply something the powerful have and the powerless lack. Power, to borrow from the late French philosopher Michel Foucault, is not possessed – it is exercised. In addition, power does not simply limit what people do (that is, as Foucault also says, it does not simply 'say no'), but rather it is productive too (it also says 'yes' to certain behaviours). Across the work of the many intellectuals we discuss in this chapter, some look at macro-phenomena such as politics, society and history, and some look at micro-phenomena such as everyday practice. Still others focus on the many elements in between and the connections between the two. What is clear is that the most astute understandings of power see it as being, at its heart, relational or interactive in nature.

Although it is most often a charge levelled at the work of others, it has been fairly common in recent organizational behaviour writing to note that power as a concept is underdeveloped in this literature. In fact, it has been noted in the editorial introduction to a special journal issue devoted to the concept of power that very little has been written by behavioural analysts on the topic.[4] There are some important indications that this trend may, however, be changing. Nevertheless, it runs like a thread throughout the chapter that, building on what has just been established, power is not an individual phenomenon. Despite the fact that the figure of the 'powerful person' appears in all our lives, there is in fact no individual who creates, constitutes or sustains 'power' as such.

Imagine, for example, the power of a police officer, a judge, a professor or a CEO. What are all the 'things' – the history, the traditions, the institutions, the distribution of resources, the socially granted authority and so on – that are necessarily in place to create this seemingly individual embodiment of 'power'? Take away the vastly networked, social, material, historical, cultural and ideological dimensions of the phenomenon, and what we find is that the person's 'power' virtually disappears. Imagine the power of a plumber (for example, when you have a flooded bathroom) or a secretary (for example, when their manager needs some important documents in an emergency). Here too, the power that these individuals may appear to embody, upon closer examination, rests on the particular situation as much as on any individual possession of power per se.

The point here is that while individuals may embody a variety of traits that seem to constitute and legitimize their 'power', we must not confuse individual traits with power as such, because where changes occur across the many dimensions of power – the cultural, the organizational, the political or the situational – the meaning of these traits can be radically transformed. Indeed, it is important to also remember that the exercise of power is often more contested, more conflictual, than is sometimes evident at first glance.

In this sense, we begin, as we usually must, with the matter of definitions and related but distinct terms. Indeed, a sizeable proportion of this chapter must grapple directly with these matters of definition.

> Before proceeding with your reading of the chapter, take a moment to think about your definition of the term 'power'. Do you hold any of the 'common-sense' views on power discussed above? As you make your way through your reading, be sure to keep in mind that a good definition of power should offer you the capacity to see the areas through which it might be questioned, challenged or altered where warranted

stop reflect

Power: a matter of definitions

power: a term defined in multiple ways, involving cultural values, authority, influence and coercion as well as control over the distribution of symbolic and material resources. At its broadest, power is defined as a social system that imparts patterned meaning

A reasonable starting point for many discussions of **power** is some version of the sociologist Robert Dahl's much-quoted phrase, 'A has power over B to the extent that he can get B to do something that B would not otherwise do' (ref. 5, p. 202–3). Closely related to this is a definition by French and Raven that likewise focuses on the potential ability of one individual to influence another within a certain social system.[6] In fact, French and Raven went on to develop five bases of power, the most important of which, first suggested by Warren,[7] are those related to systemic reward and coercion.

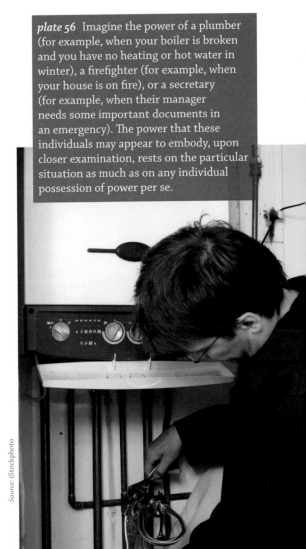

plate 56 Imagine the power of a plumber (for example, when your boiler is broken and you have no heating or hot water in winter), a firefighter (for example, when your house is on fire), or a secretary (for example, when their manager needs some important documents in an emergency). The power that these individuals may appear to embody, upon closer examination, rests on the particular situation as much as on any individual possession of power per se.

Source: iStockphoto

Our goal in this chapter is to incorporate such statements into a more comprehensive understanding of power, and then test the current analyses of power in work organizations in relation to this new understanding. In doing this, we might add to Dahl's basic definition to relate it directly to the paid workplace: power is the ability to say no to certain behaviours, yes to others, and to shape how something should be done. And, building further on this as Alion does, we can add that it is equally vital to know as much as possible about what 'B would otherwise do'.[2] Alion's article offers a summary of the six ways in which 'what B would otherwise do' are typically understood by organizational researchers, arguing that there is an important difference between what are referred to as 'political' versus 'Foucauldian' approaches to power in organizations

This, of course, is inseparable from many of the other issues addressed in the text, including equity and diversity, the organization of labour processes, the selection of technologies, the technical and social divisions of labour, and the accountability and reporting structures and pacing that shape, or rather influence, 'power' in organizations.

It is vital that we recognize that, to complicate matters further, the concept of 'power' is often confused with the relatively distinct questions of 'influence' and 'authority'. We see this, in fact, in the definitions of both Dahl and French and Raven. The goal of our definition here is to recognize that **authority** is closely related to, but analytically distinct from, the concept of power. Authority, as it is defined in the social science literature, also tends to have a complex relational dimension, but can be said to involve power granted by some form of active or passive consent – whether the consent is linked to specific individuals, groups or institutions – which bestows on it some level of legitimacy. (A fascinating treatment of this notion of coercion, consent and legitimacy can be read in the analysis of the American system of slavery as documented by Genovese.[8]) Some theorists use these words in ways that overlap a good deal. For example, the German sociologist Max Weber's work deals with issues of power but mostly elaborates on types of authority.

The issue of **legitimacy** opens up a range of important questions, which we discuss more directly below. Legitimacy depends on one's perspective in communities, organizations, institutions and the world (as a worldview). What is legitimate for some may not be legitimate for others, and this can and does change over time, and according to situations.

Even here, in these conceptually humble beginnings, we see that our rejection of individual models of power in favour of relational ones holds firm. In order to move further beyond conventional discussions of power, we can look beyond organization-based literature to some of the most general, macro approaches.

Traditionally, the field of social theory has understood the concept of power in broad macro terms. Indeed, there is a noticeable preoccupation with how the state, the Church, electoral politics, the military, and sometimes corporations and economic systems, may or may not be involved in systems of power. One of the key writers of this type is Michael Mann. His *Sources of Social Power* is considered a key text in these theoretical discussions, and builds from a detailed study of ancient Rome and world religions.[9] The 'sources of social power' are determined to be ideological, military, political and economic. Indeed, Mann goes on to say that the object of this type of social power approach should be the development of an analysis of 'multiple overlapping and intersecting socio-spatial networks of power' (ref. 9, p. 1).

Power, in this approach, is diffuse and what we might call 'infrastructural'. It can be understood, according to Mann, by taking into account a specific set of universal relations or dynamics: universalism–particularism, equality–hierarchy, cosmopolitanism–uniformity, decentralization–centralization and civilization–militarism. Each is concerned with the dynamic between control and diffuse freedoms and,

authority: the power granted by some form of either active or passive consent that bestows legitimacy

legitimacy: a term describing agreement with the rights and responsibilities associated with a position, social values, system and so on when applied to his four sources of social power, produces a way of thinking about power that has been influential in social theory as well as history.

Mann's type of approach more or less rejects the explanation of power as simply a form of 'institutionalization' (which we discuss in relation to Weber below), but another key example that is influential in the mainstream social theory tradition is the work of Anthony Giddens.[10] His work on the 'central problems of social theory' seeks to provide an overarching approach while avoiding what he sees as the pitfalls of many broad social theories of power (from schools of social theory such as Marxism, phenomenology and structural-functionalism). His theory of **structuration** is intended to demonstrate the complex interrelations of human freedom (or agency) and determination (or structure), and emphasizes that, in the modern world, there has been a fundamental shift based on the enormous growth in the resources (what he refers to as 'containers') of power. Central to Giddens' thesis are societal surveillance, capitalist enterprise, industrial production and centralized control over the 'means of violence' by the state (Figure 16.1).[10]

structuration: a concept focusing on balancing the dichotomies of agency, or human freedom, and social organization, or structures where individual choices are seen as partially constrained, but they remain choices nonetheless

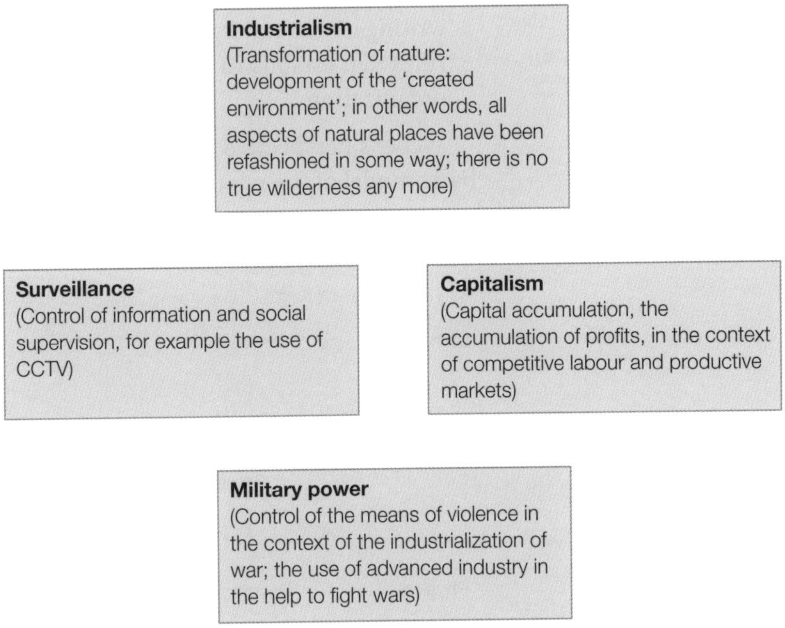

Industrialism
(Transformation of nature: development of the 'created environment'; in other words, all aspects of natural places have been refashioned in some way; there is no true wilderness any more)

Surveillance
(Control of information and social supervision, for example the use of CCTV)

Capitalism
(Capital accumulation, the accumulation of profits, in the context of competitive labour and productive markets)

Military power
(Control of the means of violence in the context of the industrialization of war; the use of advanced industry in the help to fight wars)

figure 16.1 Giddens' model of power

It is important to the theory of structuration that these sources of power are not 'out there', but are rather the result of specific forms of human interaction mixed with 'authority' and a distribution of 'resources', which together shape and control time and space. This is important, in part, because of its lack of what we would call 'closure'. That is, power is always an open, historical question: things can and do change.

Although we do not review it here, it is worth noting the meta-theory of German social theorist Jürgen Habermas. He describes **ideology** as structure of communication (in his theory of communicative action) that has been systematically distorted by power in such a way as to mostly exclude the realm of daily human activity (what Habermas calls the 'lifeworld') when its activity does not align with dominant institutions and their unique interests and needs. Such domination comes to penetrate individuals' lifeworld, personal identity and inner mental experience – on the same level of analysis dealt with by Giddens' approach to human interaction – leading to their further domination by social systems.

ideology: a term with multiple uses, but in particular referring to perceptions of reality as distorted by class interests, and the ideas, legal arrangements and culture that arise from class relations (a term taken from Marx)

Finally, we should note that, for Giddens, all individuals 'have power', but this power is influenced and constrained by the distribution of different types of resource. In this model, there are 'allocative resources', which refer to control over physical things such as money or property, and there are also 'authoritative resources', which involve control over people's practices. For example, a business owner has the allocative resources of her capital, as well as authoritative resources granted by our legal institutions to set her workplace up in the way she feels most appropriate.

This can lead us to a deeper discussion of the relations between power and authority. Having influenced researchers including Mann, Giddens and Habermas, Max Weber's work on the basic types of authority is closely linked to, although not the same as, the theories of power we have outlined. That is, Weber's theory of authority can be much more closely related to individuals, despite the fact that, ultimately, his approach too is a relational one. Authority necessarily involves others who grant this authority or legitimacy through complex systems of power.

Weber outlines three types of authority:

- *Charismatic authority* refers to leaders who are able to exercise power based on their personal traits.
- *Traditional authority* is dependent on a historical trajectory of past authority.
- *Rational authority*. Weber is most widely known for his analysis of this in his writing on bureaucracy. Here, authority rests on a specific system of laws or rules that establish a hierarchy in, for example, a public or private sector work organization.

Weber's perspective on authority is echoed in the work of Wrong, who lays out a basic model of the relations between influence and power (Figure 16.2).[11]

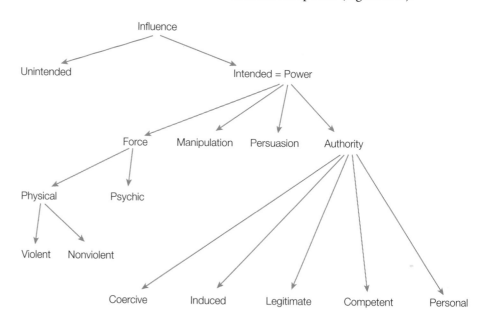

figure 16.2 Wrong on influence and power

Source: Wrong (1979),[11] p. 24

Another key body of writing on the concept of power is Steven Lukes' *Power: A Radical View*.[12] Lukes' theory is partially summarised in Figure 16.3. Lukes understands power and authority with the notion of 'bringing about consequences' not unlike, for instance, the way a teacher might seek to encourage students to complete their reading assignments prior to lectures. Part of this type of analysis is the recognition that obtaining compliance can require a multifaceted effort. It can be secured by the use of force or by people choosing to surrender to (or be led by) others. In fact, each is usually involved, as we shall see in our discussion of Gramsci later on. When people choose to accept the will of others as legitimate, we can, according to Lukes, describe the relationship as one of authority. Some of the studies of behaviour in organizations that we discuss in the following section of this chapter appear to draw on this type of approach.

Work and Society: Worker autonomy as a contentious issue: the many dimensions of power

In their major study of work in contemporary society, Tilly and Tilly (1998) identify a broad range of issues that may prove contentious for workers. This list includes employer coercion, compensation (wages), outsourcing, discrimination, qualifications, union rights and worker autonomy. How such contentious issues are resolved depends on the exercise of power.

But what do we mean by power in this context? Steven Lukes (2007, p. 59) offers the following definition:

In social and political contexts, we typically attribute power to agents when we hold them responsible for bringing about significant outcomes.

Power, Lukes continues, always involves 'a mechanism – a causal process that links the powerful with the outcomes they can bring about' (p. 59). He adds that 'power, in its most general sense, involves the capacity to advance one's interests and affect the interests of others, whether negatively or positively' (p. 60).

Much of this is quite straightforward. It would be possible to use Lukes' definition of power to analyse how any one of the contentious issues outlined above was resolved. For example, we could identify the agents who exercise power and investigate the mechanisms they employ to advance their interests with respect to any of these contentious issues.

However, the study of power becomes more complicated when two other aspects of power are considered. The first complication in the study of power concerns what some would call the structural dimensions of power. Examples of the structural dimensions of power are large-scale inequalities in resource allocation and the formal rules (for example, laws and regulations) present in the environments where power is exercised. A second complicating issue in the study of power concerns what some would call its symbolic dimension. The symbolic dimension of power is evident when the values and thought processes of the less powerful support the exercise of power by the powerful.

Lukes' approach to power will become clearer if we focus on one of the Tillys' contentious issues. The issue of autonomy includes both task complexity and worker discretion. Autonomy is widely recognized as a key aspect of job satisfaction. It has also been associated with creativity, quality and productivity at work. In what sense is autonomy a political issue?

Using Lukes' analysis as a guide, we could respond by asking 'Who has an interest in expanding or restricting worker autonomy, and what mechanisms do they employ to advance their interests?' When we look at general trends in the world of work, it would appear that there has been a tendency for employers to consider worker autonomy as somehow not in the interests of the employer. How else would one explain various initiatives to deskill workers throughout the industrialized world?

But Lukes' analysis of power would lead us to proceed carefully in exploring the question of interests. Lukes insists that it is a mistake to think that 'the power of the powerful [always] affects others' interests adversely' (p. 60). According to Lukes, 'power can be empowering, even transformative, increasing others' resources, capabilities and effectiveness' (p. 60). So the work of identifying different interest groups in the workplace does not provide us with an automatic answer to how power will be exercised in the area of worker autonomy. In some instances, powerful groups may believe that it is in their interest to increase the capabilities of the less powerful and therefore to encourage worker autonomy.

What about the structural and symbolic dimensions of power? With regard to the structural dimension, it is worth noting that there are significant cross-national variations in how powerful groups view the issue of worker autonomy. In some countries, governments have stepped in and made the defence of worker autonomy a focus of regulation and state action (Gallie, 2007). With regard to the symbolic dimensions of power, Lukes would ask us to consider the circumstances in which worker autonomy emerges as a contentious issue. Perhaps the culture of some work environments makes it almost unthinkable to raise the question of worker autonomy.

stop! Take a moment to reflect on some of the issues raised by Lukes' approach to power. Can you think of examples of situations where employer groups have sought to encourage worker autonomy?

Why have some governments made worker autonomy a focus of regulation and state action? In what work environments would the issue of worker autonomy fail to make the agenda of contentious issues?

Sources and further information

Gallie, D. (2007) 'Production regimes, employment regimes, and the quality of work', pp. 1–34 in D. Gallie (ed.), *Employment Regimes and the Quality of Work*, Oxford: Oxford University Press.
Lukes, S. (2007) 'Power', *Contexts*, **6**(3), pp. 59–61.
Tilly, C. and Tilly, C. (1998) *Work Under Capitalism*, Boulder, CO: Westview Press.

Note: This feature was written by David MacLennan, Assistant Professor at Thompson Rivers University, BC, Canada.

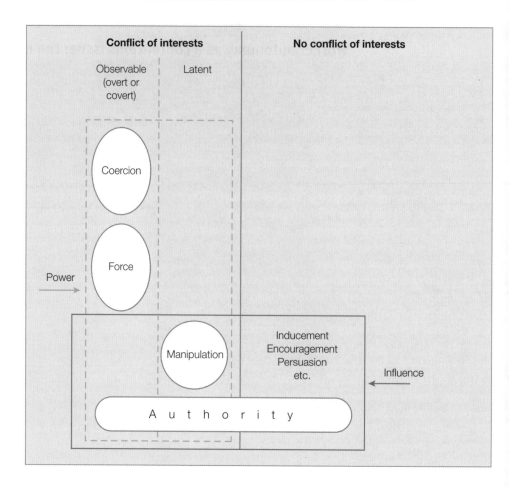

figure 16.3 Steven Luke's vision of power

conflict of interest: a condition in which the needs of one party (such as an individual or group) run counter to the needs of another

Take a moment to think back to your own employment experiences (or those of friends or family members, if you have none of your own as yet). How can you distinguish between Weber's concept of 'authority' and the broader systems of power as discussed in Lukes or Giddens? How has the social infrastructure of power systems supported the 'authority' of those in charge?

stop reflect

Equally important to Lukes' explanation are the conditions of a **conflict of interest**. The identification of structural and idiosyncratic conflicts of interest is a key challenge for organizational behaviour literature. Where, for example, is conflict just a matter of fine-tuning existing organizational structures and simply rooted in the contingencies and unpredictability of everyday life, and where might conflict be so deeply rooted in a structure that to challenge it is to simultaneously challenge the very nature of the organization itself? As Figure 16.3 shows, where such structural conflicts of interest do not exist, Lukes uses the word 'influence'. Where structural conflicts of interest exist, he uses the word 'power'. Both planned decision making (overt and covert varieties) and latent (or unintended) uses of power play a role in Lukes' model, while issues of authority, not unlike those outlined by Weber, operate in both non-conflict and conflict of interest contexts.

Additional definitions of power to consider

Up to this point, we have looked at what can be called traditional social theory approaches to power. They help us think outside common-sense views. There are, however, still other perspectives to consider. One of these is found in the work of Michel Foucault, another key thinker in the field of social theory. His work in, among many other texts, *Discipline and Punish* and *Power/Knowledge*,[13,14] although oriented by a stated interest in the 'micro-politics' of power and preoccupied with individual identity or 'subjectivity', is in the end a very broad macro theory as well. In this way, Foucault, like Giddens, is interested in breaking down the distinction between individuals and society, or 'agency' and 'structure'. Unlike Lukes, however, Foucault's definitions of power make it even clearer that there is a double edge to power. It prevents some behaviours while at the same time positively encouraging others, both at the broadest political and historical levels and at the deepest level of individual identity:

> it seems to me now that the notion of repression is quite inadequate for capturing what is precisely the productive aspect of power. In defining the effects of power as repression, one adopts a purely juridical conception of such power, one identifies power with a law which says no, power is taken above all as carrying the force of a prohibition. Now I believe that this is a wholly negative, narrow, skeletal conception of power, one which has been curiously widespread. If power were never anything but repressive, if it never did anything but to say no, do you really think one would be brought to obey it? What makes power hold good, what makes it accepted, is simply the fact that it doesn't only weigh on us as a force that says 'no', but that it traverses and produces things, it induces pleasure, forms knowledge, produces discourse. It needs to be considered as a productive network which runs through the whole social body, much more than a negative instance whose function is repression. (ref. 14, p. 119)

For Foucault, power is all-pervasive. Indeed, power constitutes what we know as a society, including, of course, how we think about work organizations. Power is everywhere: 'there are no "margins" for those who break with the system' (ref. 14, p. 141). Thus, in Foucault's analysis, power is discussed in terms of the many ways through which it is exercised – 'economies of power', 'regimes of power', 'networks of power', 'technologies of power'.[3]

An important distinction that some researchers make here, however, concerns the difference between Foucauldian approaches to power and what are often referred to as political theories of organizational power:

> Foucaultians claimed that the two are characterized by an all-encompassing inseparability. Political theorists claimed that *politics* are everywhere: people always seek ways to fulfill their parochial interests, always want to impose upon others that which they would otherwise do despite legitimate power structures and at times in contrast to them. Foucaultians claimed that *power* is everywhere: what people see as their interests as well as the strategies they devise for achieving these interests are determined by existing power structures or discursive practices and to a considerable extent serve to reinforce them. (ref. 2, p. 783)

For a key example of the political approach to power in organizations, see Astley and Sachdeva.[15]

Thus, although there are important overlaps between the Foucauldian and political approaches to power, an important distinction should be recognized. An important tool for this recognition is hegemony. **Hegemony** is an important term in critical political theory that involves the complexity and mixture of consensus and conflict, and hence power relations in a broad sense. It derives from the Greek, where it originally referred to a leader or ruler (*egemon*), but was taken up in the English language in the nineteenth century, and has come to describe a very nuanced form of sociopolitical predominance. It describes control that is both direct and indirect, and rests on the notion of a whole way of seeing the world, a 'normal reality' or 'common sense'.

Specifically, the term 'hegemony' can express two types of power relations. The first describes a group's *domination* over other groups, and the second describes a group's *leadership*. The concept represents a whole body of practices as well as expectations, assignment of energies, and ordinary understandings of the world in terms of meanings and values. In essence, the concept expresses the relationships

hegemony: a conception of power that includes both conflict as well as consent and leadership by generating a particular worldview or 'common sense' on relevant and appropriate action of leadership and domination that produce a general sense of coordinated reality for most people. However, it is a concept that lends itself to a wider discussion than Foucault's thesis encourages. Power is seen as all-pervasive in the sense that there can also be something called 'counter-hegemony'. Counter-hegemony is composed of and expresses competing ways of seeing the world and behaving, although this behaviour can at times be clandestine and underdeveloped.

The term 'hegemony' is now most closely associated with the writings of an early twentieth-century Italian Marxist, Antonio Gramsci. Gramsci used a historical analysis of specific periods of French and Italian society in order to refer to a system of alliances within a 'hegemonic bloc' of interests. A bloc necessarily contains significant competing interests, but it is unified on some core principles. This bloc was dependent on what Gramsci referred to as the 'powerful system of fortresses and earthworks' of civil society, including the multitude of social, economic, cultural organizational, group and corresponding ideologies among which there is significant room for compromise (although only on non-hegemonic terrain).[16] As the English cultural studies theorist Raymond Williams notes, however, much influential work on counter-hegemonic practices has ignored contemporary scenes of consensus and conflict, including work organization. This is not without its problems.[17]

Critical insight

Based on your own current or past employment experiences, try to apply Gramsci's notion of a 'hegemonic bloc' by tracing the key groups that hold sway in an organization. Look at how they differ and what principles they share a commitment to. Finally, consider any 'counter-hegemonic' groups in the organization. How unified are they? How is their degree of unity related to how they challenge the hegemonic bloc?

An important contribution to our general understanding of power, and in turn of power as it relates to work organizations and behaviour, comes from the notion of emergent forms of practice that lie in some form of opposition to a dominant or hegemonic bloc in the sense that Gramsci and Williams described. First, the notion provides a basic framework for understanding the character of alternative (resistant) practices in opposition to a complex of dominant presumptions. An entire subschool of industrial sociology/organizational studies literature has specifically addressed the issue of resistance.[18] Building from this notion, we can see that organizational behaviour emerging from non-dominant (that is, workers' rather than managers') standpoints need not strictly reproduce a particular hegemonic order. It can at times run tangentially to it, and possibly even in direct opposition to it. In both cases, it represents an active, living process in which alternatives struggle against incorporation.

In less abstract terms, we are talking about people's behaviour that is rooted in processes that align with the basic assumptions and structures of the organization, have little to do with these dominant assumptions, or in some cases actively resist the major premises upon which the organization is based. This type of resistance can be ongoing and persistent, or more likely it is to be seen in certain conflictual situations such as during collective bargaining, or within a specific department of an organization that is having difficulties for one reason or another. To put this in the language of social class, we are talking about organizational behaviour that can be easily incorporated into capitalism, is somehow outside this logic, or opposes capitalism in some way either persistently or idiosyncratically (and everything in between).

These macro theories of power in studies of society set the context. We can now turn to a consideration of theories of power in local, everyday interaction or behaviour. Analyses of micro-interaction form another distinct set of theories on power. For example, we can ask what Nietzsche's '**will to power**' (a term that defines social interaction as an ongoing contest between people constantly striving to exercise power over others) might mean in terms of behaviour in organizations. Is the 'will to power' a generalized (overt or covert) phenomenon, as Nietzsche's work suggests, or are there other central motivations in people's lives?

The work of another famous micro-sociologist, Erving Goffman, is also relevant in this context. His analysis of 'contests' as a major frame of social interaction offers a fascinating exploration of how people think and negotiate order in their daily interactions. Another concept that has similarities, although it is not the same as Goffman's notion of 'contests', comes from the school of sociology called **game theory**. This is a subset of the rational choice tradition,[19] and is popular among economists and economic sociologists for its apparent pragmatism.

This school of thought, which focuses on the notion of contests or games, invites us to understand individual actors as acting in a way in which they believe will provide the best outcome for them, given their objectives, resources and circumstances as they see them. Its focus is on voluntary actions and inter-actor exchange, and it encompasses both conflictual contests and cooperative games. In relation to game theory and the rational choice tradition, it begins from the rather traditional economic assumption that individuals act to maximize their utility (that is, to do as well as is possible in the circumstances).

We can also consider micro-interactions through the work of discourse analyst Robin Tolmach Lakoff, which is discussed by Krippendorff.[20] How might 'power' be evident in this simple, everyday exchange?:

Man: Wanna go to the movies?
Woman: Oh, I don't know. Do you?

Krippendorf correctly points out that this is one example of a very common, gendered 'language game' that allows us to explore a host of possibilities. The male makes a proposal. The female has several options in response, including ignoring, accepting, counter-proposing and clarifying (and in fact a vast array of others).

Her different options (including the response she gives above) allow us to consider the system of power in operation at the micro level. For example, a counter-proposal might signal some sort of equal power relation; a stern rejection might signal an unequal power relation; a deferral (as in her response above) might signal another form of unequal power relation; and of course any and all of the possibilities might be part of a clever, expanded set of negotiations that defy simplistic categorization.

Ailon's work can, in turn, be used to understand the option potentially open to this woman in terms of Dahl's traditional definition of power, which we used to begin this chapter.[2] In this exchange, of course, the word 'power' is never used. The point here is that we can quite easily, even in this smallest of examples, draw into our analysis the concept of power. We can also see how it can include a whole infrastructure of, for example, gender relations.

Finally, returning to the work of Erving Goffman for a moment, micro-power can also be understood as part of people's 'presentation of self in everyday life'.[21] It is echoed in the work of a range of others such as Finkelstein,[22] who writes extensively on how people's physical appearance or self-presentation involves a whole range of broader

will to power: the notion that people are inherently driven to develop and expand power and control in their environments

game theory: a social theory premised on the notion that people do what is best for themselves given their resources and circumstances, as in some form of a competitive game

stop reflect

The example of going to the movies can readily be extended to a work context. How might you go about a micro-analysis of the following exchange?
Woman: Tell me how to fix this Xerox machine.
Man: Oh, don't you worry about this, honey. Leave it to me.
Now take a next step and continue the exchange, taking account of the distinct backdrops of power and/or gender relations

plate 57 The micro-management of appearances has been understood for some time to be a vital component of how 'power' operates. The distinctive wig and black robe give barristers an air of distance and authority.

Source: Cheryl Dainty and Ben Harding

'macro-forces' or systems of power. (See also the work of Marks that we reviewed in our case study at the end of Chapter 8.[23])

In a particularly striking section of her book, Finkelstein gives an example of a Jewish prisoner in a Nazi concentration camp. His memoirs show him taking incredible pains to keep himself 'respectable' in appearance. As the prisoner notes, his captors' general beliefs about his 'respectability' could in fact hold the balance between life and death: 'He needed no more than his spruce suit and his emaciated and shaven face in the midst of the flock of his sordid and slovenly colleagues to stand out and thereby receive benefits from his captors' (ref. 22, p. 136). This is an extreme example, but the point is that the micro-management of appearances has been understood for some time to be a vital component of how 'power' operates. It provides a mechanism of sorting, in Finkelstein's terms of 'social passport and credential', for how people can participate in the systems of power they are presented with.

> **stop reflect**
>
> Can the management of appearances hold the balance between success and failure in organizations? What instances of this have you seen in your own experiences? How are appearances given meanings in relation to broader 'systems of power' within and beyond a specific work organization? Explore company dress codes as best you can over the Internet. Although some dress code demands are related to health and safety, others are not. How does power in organizations work in terms of a dress code? What ideological values are represented in such codes? A recent book by Ruth Rubenstein discusses *Dress Codes: Meaning and Messages in American Culture*.[24] What further details does it give you about the relationship between appearance and power?

Power: evidence from the workplace

Through the 1990s and into the new millennium, the number of strikes by employees in industrialized countries around the world has tended to decline.[25] What are we to make of this? Should we conclude that the power struggles in organizations have been reduced, giving way to greater consensus? Not according to some researchers.[26,27] Collinson's work is worth looking at in detail for its discussion of power in organizations. It represents an important type of research that has linked past discussions from industrial sociology and labour process theory (a stream in the field of sociology of work) to more contemporary concerns about individuals, identity and meaning under what are sometimes referred to as 'postmodern' conditions of globalization and the (apparently) 'new' knowledge or information economy.

Collinson argues that despite the decline of formal workplace disputes, the power struggle continues to rage on in diffuse and pervasive forms. Power is exemplified not simply by either domination *or* resistance in organizations, but rather domination *and* resistance. In this context, power is to be found in situations of apparent consent and domination as well as where there is resistance. Collinson maintains that labour process theory has made a distinctive contribution to the analysis of work by highlighting the 'irreducible interrelationship between employee resistance and managerial control ... Emphasizing the extensive power asymmetries in contemporary organizations' (ref. 26, p. 25). He goes on to claim that the founding preoccupations of traditional labour process theory with scientific management and Taylorism are still relevant, as is the classic critique offered in the work of Harry Braverman (also see the discussion of Braverman's work in Chapter 2).[28]

Collinson's specific contribution, however, emerges from his assessment that knowledge and information are key aspects of power. He draws on the work of Foucault, on writers who make use of Mann's work on power[29] and on the 'game metaphor',[30] but goes on to say that, despite the seemingly uneven distribution of access to organizational knowledge and information, other forms of knowledge are available to workers (that is, technical and production-based knowledge). These alternative resources can be mobilized through a wide variety of strategies, and this variety in turn accounts for the very uneven and variegated results of power struggles in organizations.

The first of the two main strategies he outlines is 'resistance by distance', in which workers restrict information from management. This is referred to as a type of 'escape attempt', and a denial of involvement or interest in work processes. The second strategy, 'resistance through persistence', involves efforts to extract information from management. In a sense, this involves voluntarily increasing involvement and interest in work processes. Of course, management in this framework tries to use the opposite strategies of extracting and restricting information respectively, and this results in a complex spiral of control resistance, greater efforts at control and so on, or rather a series of strategies and counter-strategies.

Finally, Collinson emphasizes the role played by both management and workers' personal identities, or we might say social background, which significantly shapes which strategy is used. He qualifies his conclusions, which depend heavily on the exact context, but in general concludes that 'resistance through persistence' turns out to be a more effective strategy. However, as he notes, neither strategy constitutes a deep challenge to the structure of power (that is, management rights) in organizations.

The key point for this chapter is that, although power is often revealed in overt forms of conflict and resistance (such as strikes, sabotage or simply a lack of cooperation), both subtle and alternative forms of resistance can also be identified. You should be able to understand that better in the light of the various conceptual frameworks we explored earlier in the chapter.

Even the existence of consensus can be used to support the claim that work organizations are in many ways constituted by power relations. Drawing on Collinson as well as Kondo,[31] we can note that effective resistance requires elements of conformity to a rival power source. Collinson sees this as discursive and knowledge based, but we would suggest that this concept can easily be extended to include well-functioning communities of workers: bargaining units, neighbourhoods, social movements or occupational groupings. This brings us back in a sense to Giddens' claim that 'everyone has power', but that it is expressed in different ways depending on the (allocative and authoritative) resources. There is the power of enforcing democracies, forcing people to learn, and ultimately the power to remake existing power relations into something better.

Although there is not exactly a flood of interest in power issues in most of the recent empirical research outlined in the main organizational behaviour journals, these nevertheless reveal a significant consideration of issues of power. Studies in this area deal with a variety of topics, such as practical governance and managerial practices in work organizations. Often, although not exclusively, there is a particular interest in organizational change initiatives. Below we explore some key findings of the most recent studies that touch on important issues in the field. The aim is to balance our earlier conceptual discussion with some more concrete findings.

In a provocative study of relations between supervisors and their subordinates, Elangovan and Xie[32] explore the results and perceptions of supervisory 'power'. Even this brief introductory line reveals that they conceive power in a way that is partially, not absolutely, at odds with the relational perspective we have developed here. The focus is on employees and supervisors, which is obviously a relational issue, but Elangovan and Xie tend to see power largely as something a supervisor has, rather than as a dimension of the social system (on the macro or micro level). A relational perspective, on the other hand, would highlight how power is systemic, put into effect or reproduced by all individuals subjected to the system, and not, for example, simply traceable to the characteristics of a particular supervisor. Nevertheless, they offer some important findings on how power is *experienced* by the individuals subject to it.

Among the important issues in workplaces today are motivation, on the one hand, and stress and people's individual and collective responses to it, on the other. These authors find that people's backgrounds play an important role in their behaviour. For example, they focus on the issue of 'self-esteem'. This is seen as a product of nurture as opposed to nature: that is, it is inextricably linked to people's lives inside the workplace, as well as to their lives outside work, and indeed developmentally before they ever began to work. Broader theories of power also see these expansive connections as important. Elangovan and Xie conclude that those with low self-esteem show signs of higher motivation and lower stress as their perceptions of supervisory power increase. Importantly, those with high self-esteem actually show lower motivation and increased stress when they give a higher score to the perceived power of their supervisor.

This has important implications for the types of worker that the typical work organization appears to favour. Elangovan and Xie go on to explore the concept of 'locus of control', which we discussed earlier, looking at workers with internal or external orientations (see also the discussion of this issue in Chapter 4). Those with an internal orientation were seen to respond to different types of power, authority and influence (the authors tending to see these as equivalent). Their motivation levels drop in relation to the perceived rewards and the levels of coercive power that they associate with supervisors. Those with a predominantly external locus of control had lower stress levels when they gave higher assessments of expert power to their supervisors.

Broadly similar dynamics to those analysed by Elangovan and Xie are seen in two other important recent studies. Overbeck and Park,[33] and Raghubir and Valenzuela,[34] explore the relationship between positional power and the strategic use of 'social in/attention' in different work team contexts. Like Elangovan and Xie, these researchers make some important observations, particularly about how managerial decision making takes place, but the way in which they frame 'power' in organizational behaviour as involving an individual/positional use of resources tends to downplay the broader systemic nature of power as something that is exercised.

Collinson's approach to resistance can be applied to these findings. For example, the changing levels of motivation and stress can be interpreted as representing a form of resistance. This might be turned inwards in the form of stress or loss of psychological commitment to the organization, but it is still apparent. Both motivation and stress are, of course, also the roots of more outward resistance, which could lead to expression in the form of political action (say, becoming more active in an employee association or union), industrial action or, at its most individualist level, sabotage or simply resigning from the organization.

Self-esteem is seen to be an important variable, but how does it come to be established? Mann's goal of identifying 'overlapping socio-spatial networks of power' might offer us some help in this context. Likewise, the work of Richard Sennett provides an accessible exploration of how deep wounds to self-esteem are inflicted in the form of 'hidden injuries'[35] and a 'corrosion of character'.[36] These writers help to show how visible symptoms have ideological, social and even political roots. To what degree could Giddens' interest in exploring the power of 'surveillance' be brought to play in looking at how stress develops in relation to perceived power issues? Might increased surveillance in the workplace actually force conflict inward to produce these effects?

If surveillance and control are more often something that the powerful do to the less powerful, it makes some sense to highlight briefly the study of the choice, contingencies and organizational politics involved when those with less power respond. The last of these is particular difficult to study, albeit widely recognized. As Morgan and Kristensen note, organizations can be seen as highly complex configurations of ongoing micro-political power conflicts at different levels, in which strategizing social actors/groups inside and outside the firm interact with each other and create temporary balances of power that shape how formal organizational relationships and processes actually work in practice.[37]

In such complex organizational settings, what does the research tell us about how low-power actors, groups or units respond? According to a recent study by Bouquet and Birkinshaw,[38] 'low-power actors' gain influence in either or both of two ways:

- by adopting creative strategies to effectively challenge the status quo in an organization (or one's position within the status quo of an organization)
- by engaging in **political gaming** within their organization to push their agendas through existing circuits of power.

The first method refers to strategies such as attempting to build one's profile in a company, building relationships with supervisors or managers within the existing power structure of an organization, taking the initiative or, more radically, challenging the way in which business is done and breaking with established norms by working around the standard practices. The second method, political gaming, refers to recognizing and acting on and through existing

plate 58 Surveillance and control is more often something that the powerful do to the less powerful. Might increased surveillance in the workplace actually force conflict?

Source: iStockphoto

political gaming: a common practice in organizations, which has proven challenging to research, that involves recognition and organizational action based on existing factions, coalitions and cliques that make up any organization in order to engage in intentional acts of influence to enhance or protect oneself or one's group or department

exit and voice: a concept referring to the basic choice that defines an important part of employees' experience at work: they can either exit (leave) or exercise their 'voice' (have a say) in how the workplace is run

factions, coalitions and cliques that make up any organization – in other words, engaging in intentional acts of influence to enhance or protect oneself, one's group or one's department.

Ultimately, however, there are a limited set of options for employees to exercise in organizations. One way of understanding these choices is through what has been referred to as the issue of **exit and voice**. Research exploring these types of choice has long been a subject of debate in industrial sociology, and it may be useful here to read the work of Ailon[2] in relation to the classic 'exit or voice' choice since these are only two of the options available to employees when conflict arises. We touch on it above, and it is dealt with in the organizational behaviour tradition by the researchers Mayes and Ganster.[39] In a rich and detailed look at the responses of public service workers to questions posed in questionnaires and interviews, these authors detail the relationship between 'voice' (or 'political action') and 'exit' behaviours on the one hand, and job stress on the other. Importantly, this analysis builds from observations that can be roughly aligned with Collinson's model of alternative, countervailing sources of power.

In Mayes and Ganster's terms, the countervailing source lies outside the bounds of the employee's formal, legitimate role in the organization. For these authors, what is at the heart of the matter is the fit between the employee and the environment. They note that when employees sense 'ambiguity' in their role in the organization, this is an immobilizing factor: it prevents their achieving 'voice' via political action in the workplace. This sense of ambiguity is found, Mayes and Ganster add, despite high levels of organizational commitment.

How can we understand variables such as worker–organization 'fit' and 'commitment' in relation to our opening set of theoretical discussions? Certainly, Foucault's and Gramsci's discussion of domination and consent as two sides of the same 'power coin' is useful here. Commitment, for example, is the side of power that Foucault speaks of when he describes 'induce[ing] pleasure, form[ing] knowledge, produce[ing] discourse. It needs to be considered as a productive network' (ref. 14, p. 119). That is, commitment is what comes out when power works in a positive and productive way.

We could also tentatively link this to Lukes' distinction between power in the context of 'conflicts of interest', which may or may not be apparent. When conflicts of interest are evident, power is reflected as coercion, force and manipulation, whereas when they are not, it is expressed as inducement and encouragement. It is not hard to see that stress, resistance, exit and voice flow from the former a good deal more often than from the latter.

One of the most fascinating and recent sets of exchanges on the matter of 'power' in the organizational behaviour tradition is to be found in a special issue of the *Journal of Organizational Behavior Management*.[40] At the centre of the debate is the work of Sonia Goltz and Amy Hietapelto, and the question of resistance to organizational change.[41] Goltz and Hietapelto's operant and strategic contingency models of power are based on the behavioural approach, as the concept of 'operant' might suggest. They are linked to the founder of this psychological tradition (B. F. Skinner), to the management of stimulus response, and in some sense to punishment and reward. Despite its classical behaviourialist stance, this model includes some form of relational analysis. To extend this, we might say that it focuses on the relations of the distribution of authority over the application of consequences. Built on well-established operant principles, Goltz and Hietapelto's model states that 'the power an individual has' is based on:

- how many reinforcing and aversive stimuli the power holder controls

- which important dimensions of these stimuli, such as magnitude, delay and frequency, the power holder controls
- which particular combinations and dimensions of the reinforcing and aversive stimuli the power holder controls
- for how many people the power holder controls these stimuli.

If we set aside the obvious major shortcoming of this model (the suggestion that people 'have' power – see our discussion of Foucault above), we can see that it marshals a range of valuable evidence, including that power is subject to both intentional and unintentional results. We might compare this with, for example, Wrong's model outlined above. One very interesting component of the model, which fits into the broad perspective on power introduced here, is that both those who lead and those who follow are subject to this leadership experience, and behave in ways consistent with notions of 'resistance' in organizations. The authors also insist that a central unit of analysis for power and resistance is the change to pre-existing relationships of action and consequence.

The special issue of the *Journal of Organizational Behavior* also includes a range of articles that provide critiques of Goltz and Hietapelto, and constructively extend or challenge their thinking. Quite separate from each author's critique of Goltz and Hietapelto, we can also apply many of the basic conceptual observations we have developed over the course of this chapter. In Boyce's contribution, for example, we might note that there is a need for conceptual clarity.[42] Boyce's work raises some questions when seen in the light of Collinson's observations, for example how is 'resistance' related to power, and from whose perspective is power and resistance defined?

Another contributor, Malott, takes Goltz and Hietapelto to task for their presumptuous leaps from laboratory findings to real-world applications,[43] while Geller extends the discussions further.[44] The consequences someone controls and/or is subject to in any organizational structure are shown to be an expression of organizational power. In support of the Goltz and Hietapelto model, Geller goes on to show that power can, in fact, be measured in terms of quality and quantity of control over consequences.

To conclude this section, we can briefly look back at the work of Mann and others in posing the question, 'How on earth can students of organizational behaviour see the linkages between practice in workplaces and such broad ideological, military and political-economic sources?' To accomplish this intellectual jump, you first need, as we have seen, to move from individual to relational perspectives on power.

It is not difficult to understand how broader national ideologies or local ideological cultures surrounding particular workplaces are implicated in 'power'. Of course, it should be obvious that political economic factors, such as market dynamics, industrial relations and employment law, and trade policy, all deeply affect the phenomenon of power. However, even in highly developed capitalist countries, the military (including the police) provide an important foundation to the industrial relations legal regime. In many cases in history in North America and Europe, the police and even the army have been called out to intervene in workplace-based conflicts. They do this whenever worker–managerial conflict reaches levels, or is concerned with issues, that those in power judge to be unacceptable to the principles of the economic system. These principles include challenges to the private ownership of economic resources (such as factories or even forests).

Visit the following interactive website for additional perspectives on power that will further enhance your understanding of ideas in this area: www.educationforum.co.uk/sociology_2/power2.htm

weblink

OB and globalization

Under pressure: the rise of workplace bullying in trying economic times

In an increasingly globalized world, an economic downturn can have far-reaching effects. Compounding regional and national impacts of recession are the impacts associated with global forces, such as the outsourcing of manufacturing and information technology jobs, which can put additional stresses on workers by further limiting job openings. In such an economic climate, workers can find themselves competing against dozens of equally qualified applicants for a single position. Those who are employed may worry about job security.

One manifestation of these economic pressures is the rise of bullying, also called mobbing or psychological harassment, within the workplace. Workplace bullies target fellow workers and use tactics such as verbal abuse, intimidation, rumour, belittlement and embarrassment to force their colleagues out of a job or to prevent them from advancing within the organization. Often, the victims do not report this abuse out of fear of losing their jobs. Recent studies of workplace bullying have found that it is a phenomenon that happens in many countries around the world, and within many different types of organizations. Espinosa (2009) describes how workplace bullying has become more common in Chilean organizations, mirroring the recent rise in unemployment and shrinking job market in that country:

> *The lack of job security and stability has forced workers to tolerate increasingly poor working conditions and even outright mistreatment and abuse. While some of these abuses are tangibly evident, there are also more subtle forms of emotional or psychological harassment which are equally damaging.*

Espinosa also notes that workplace bullies disproportionately target workers they deem to be most vulnerable, including 'women, sexual and ethnic minorities and people with HIV/AIDS'.

According to lawyer Adriana Muñoz, who advocates for organizational policies and legal penalties against workplace bullies, this behaviour is 'largely intangible' and often 'hidden in the subtleties of daily interactions between people. It can take the form of words, gestures, actions or attitudes that do not constitute physical abuse and are therefore extremely difficult to quantify' (Espinosa, 2009). The results of workplace bullying can include lowered morale, decreased productivity, a decline in workplace attendance and even an increase in on-the-job accidents. In short, the economic stresses that can precipitate psychological harassment in the workplace can, in turn, create additional economic and social troubles for organizations.

Economist and organizational management specialist Denise Salin has written about management techniques to address and quell workplace bullying. She explains that organizations at the greatest risk of harbouring and enabling workplace bullies are most often those with a laissez-faire approach management where expectations about work roles and appropriate behaviours are undefined, where bullies do not expect to face consequences for their actions, and where they are successful in achieving their desired ends. Salin (2008, p. 223) asserts, 'If bullying is to be prevented, it is thus important both to raise the cost, i.e. the risk of being discovered and reprimanded, and to reduce the incentives.'

In a study of how a number of human resources managers addressed workplace bullying in Finland, Salin (2008, p. 228) found that the most effective antibullying measures included widely publicized workplace policies against bullying and the institution of 'sophisticated' human resource management techniques such as performance-based pay, regular performance appraisals and frequent employee 'attitude surveys'. In an economic climate where instability – real or perceived – can give rise to workplace bullying, managers who can recognize and put a stop to these destructive behaviours are well positioned to help their employees and organizations weather tough times in the shifting global economy.

stop!   Imagine that you are a manager of an organization and a worker comes to you claiming that he or she is being bullied by some co-workers. What approaches would you take to address the situation?

Espinosa links workplace bullying to economic uncertainty. Can you think of other cultural, social or structural attributes of organizations that might also enable bullying in the workplace (for example, an organizational culture that condones sexist or racist jokes)?

Sources and further information

Espinosa, M. C. (2009) 'Chile: working with the enemy', Inter Press Service News Agency. Available at: http://ipsnews.net/news.asp?idnews=29934.

Rayner, C., Hoel, H. and Cooper, C. L. (2002) *Workplace Bullying: What We Know, Who Is To Blame, and What Can We Do?* London: Taylor & Francis.

Salin, D (2003) 'Ways of explaining workplace bullying: a review of enabling, motivating and precipitating structures and processes in the work environment', *Human Relations*, **56**(10), pp. 1213–32.

Salin, D. (2008) 'The prevention of workplace bullying as a question of human resource management: measures adopted and underlying organizational factors', *Scandinavian Journal of Management*, **24**, pp. 221–31.

The Devil Wears Prada (2006): This film pays particular attention to how bullying workplace relationships affect the characters' work and personal lives.

www.workplacebullying.org provides more information and resources on workplace bullying.

Note: This feature was written by Gretchen Fox, PhD, Anthropologist, Timberline Natural Resource Group, Canada.

Chapter summary

- In this chapter, we began with broad theory, to provide a basis for a better appreciation of grounded research at the work organization level. Common-sense views of power were outlined to explore the half-truths in them. Power appears to us to be 'embodied' in individuals, as something they possess and exert. However, macro theories of power show that there are many deep social roots or 'sources' of power systems, including the influences of ideology, military, politics and economics. Gramsci and Foucault outlined perhaps the most extensive theories of power, noting that it is anywhere and everywhere, because it constitutes the very way we talk and think about ourselves, let alone our organizational surroundings. Importantly, these two authors argue that power is a coin with two sides: on the one, consent, accommodation and domination; on the other, lack of commitment, stress, resistance, political action and 'voice'.

- This knowledge was then applied to a critical look at key examples of work organization research. Collinson is a representative example of the new social analysis of organization, which links old industrial sociology with labour process theory and the contemporary analysis of meaning and identity in the workplace. We then explored some key examples of organizational behaviour research that deal directly with the concept of 'power'. The organizational behaviour field has hardly seen a flood of research on the topic of 'power', and when it does consider this, it usually adds the prefix 'perceived', further limiting the strength of its analysis. Nevertheless, some fascinating and provocative findings and debates were detailed.

- Clearly, not all power, authority and influence is bad. Good parenting, teaching, policing, political advocacy and, in a certain sense management, can be understood as positive influences. The question of legitimacy, which in turn evokes questions of larger political and economic systems, comes into play as we recognize that there are two main justifications for disobedience to authority. One is when a subject is commanded to do something outside the legitimate range of the commanding authority, and the other is when the history of acquiring the commanding authority is no longer considered to be legitimate or acceptable (which includes being an unjust burden).

- These types of challenge to authority, building from the Gramscian and possibly the Foucauldian models above, start with recognizing people's complicity in the taken-for-granted nature of systems of power, or rather hegemonic blocs of assumptions. Challengers dare to articulate these taken-for-granted assumptions in order to engage in a rational analysis of legitimacy. What some refer to as a crisis in organizational commitment or loyalty may be the thin edge of this kind of wedge. Underlying it are frequently the types of challenge to the status quo or political gaming, for example. That is, it represents the removal of blind obedience, an erosion of the 'other side' of the power coin, consent and complicity. Managers as well as workers (and students of organizational behaviour!) have a right to think through and question the sources of legitimacy. Mahatma Gandhi, Martin Luther King

and others operated on the principle of removal of consent, which for our purposes relates directly to a broad, social perspective on power.

Key concepts

authority 436	
hegemony 441	
influence 438	
micropolitics of power 443	
power/motivation/stress relations 446	
relational perspective on power 443	
sources of countervailing power 442	
sources of social power 436	

Vocab checklist for ESL students

- ☐ Authority, authorize
- ☐ Conflict of interest
- ☐ Exit and voice
- ☐ Game theory
- ☐ Hegemony
- ☐ Ideology, idealize, ideological
- ☐ Influence, influential
- ☐ Legitimacy, legitimize, legitimate
- ☐ Micropolitics
- ☐ Power
- ☐ Structuration
- ☐ Will to power

Chapter review questions

1. What is the substance of the different social theoretic models of Mann, Giddens, Foucault, Weber, Lukes and Gramsci?
2. What is the difference between power and authority?
3. What is the relationship between power and resistance?
4. What is meant by the phrases 'power is relational' and 'power is not possessed, it is exercised'?
5. What are the strengths and weaknesses in current conceptualizations of 'power' in organizational behaviour research?

Chapter research questions

1. Early in the chapter, you will remember a basic definition of power provided by Robert Dahl ('A has power over B to the extent that he can get B to do something that B would not otherwise do'). You will have also seen that another definition of power (from Michel Foucault) suggested that it is not enough to simply understand power's ability to 'say no' (as it also 'says yes'). Now take a moment to discuss some examples of 'power' in your organizational life (whether this is in terms of past work experiences, or even in your school life) in both of these terms. Which are easiest to identify? Why might this be? And what is the significance of forms of power that are

particularly difficult to identify? Might there be a special role for such forms of hidden power in the establishment of instances described in this chapter as 'hegemony'?

2. A valuable addition to how one can begin looking into power in organizational behaviour relates to what some researchers have called 'organizational misbehaviour'. A book by Stephen Ackroyd and Paul Thompson entitled *Organizational Misbehaviour* (published by Sage in 1999) summarises this notion very well. Review the introductory descriptions of organizational misbehaviour in this book with special attention to the summary diagram on page 25. Now use these ideas to speak to family or friends about their work experiences (or think of some examples from your own work life) in order to generate a list of at least three examples of organizational misbehaviour. If you choose to read further in the book, you will find more specific discussions of the role of absenteeism, sexual harassment, 'soldiering' and humour that may provide further help. Once compiled, share these examples in discussion with your fellow students, and then discuss how these examples speak to the concepts of power, politics and conflict presented in this chapter.

3. As a final research question for this chapter, we take its ideas a step further by looking at the role of something so fundamental to our work lives that it is virtually always taken for granted, and as such is both invisible and extremely 'powerful' in its invisibility: this is the question of the relationship between power, organizations and *space*. How does space – this most basic element of our behaviour – relate to power, politics and conflict in organizational life? Take a moment to consider this on your own, and then discuss it with a fellow student. Do you find it difficult to imagine that 'space' can play a role in creating and recreating forms of power? If you do, you are not alone. Luckily for us, a recent book by Dale and Burrell called *The Spaces of Organization and the Organization of Space: Power, Identity and Materiality at Work* (published by Palgrave, 2008) provides us with important resources for thinking in this area. Review the introduction of the book (and other chapters if you like) and see if their discussion provides you with some new ways of thinking about these relationships. For example, do things like the architecture of workplaces have a relationship to how we think about ourselves (i.e. our identity) and others, or the corporate culture of a workplace – and if so how may these teach us something about power, politics and conflict?

Further reading

Clegg, S. (1989) *Frameworks of Power*, London: Sage.

Foucault, M. (1980) *Power/Knowledge*, edited by C. Gordon, New York: Pantheon.

Lukes, S. (1974) *Power: A Radical View*, Basingstoke: Macmillan.

French, J. R. P. and Raven, B. H. (1959) 'The bases of social power', pp. 150–67 in D. Cartwright (ed.), *Studies of Social Power*, AnnArbor, MI: Institute for Social Research.

Sennett, R. (1980) *Authority*, London: Faber & Faber.

 Chapter case study 1

Aiming for a paperless world

Setting

In their book, *The Myth of the Paperless Office*, authors Abigail Sellen and Richard Harper note that office paper use makes up 30–40 per cent of total paper consumption in the USA and Britain, with the average American worker using an estimated 10,000 sheets of paper every year. Although it was originally believed that the use of computers would decrease the reliance on paper, the implementation of networked access to the Internet and company intranets typically results in more documents being printed. The introduction of an e-mail system alone can cause a 40 per cent increase in paper use.

Despite this, organizations have increasingly striven to become 'paperless' in the hope of not only reducing the costs directly associated with paper, but also achieving greater efficiency, 'moving forward' and motivating change. However, Sellen and Harper caution that concentrating on a goal to eliminate paper can prevent organizations from identifying organizational work practices and value systems that really should be the focus of change.

The problem

FACTS Inc., a medium-sized accounting firm located in Basingstoke in south-east England, had gone through tremendous changes in the past year: a merger with another company, a new CEO and lay-offs caused by a decline in the local economy. Many of those affected by the lay-offs had been with FACTS for most of their career, and their abrupt departure caused fear and distrust among the employees who had remained. Absenteeism due to stress leaves suddenly became commonplace. Staff morale was only worsened by the announcement at a recent shareholder meeting that several senior executives would be receiving large bonuses at the end of that fiscal year.

At that same meeting, the company's new CEO, Frank Webster, introduced himself to the audience as an 'environmental champion'. Downplaying the bonuses, he instead focused the meeting on the 'green' strategies he intended to implement during his first year with the company, proclaiming that 'accounting firms are the "watchdog" of the business world and we need to set an example by demonstrating environmentally friendly practices'. He laid out a corporate programme targeted at saving energy and conserving resources, with an initial focus on eliminating paper use. FACTS, he said, would be a paperless organization within 2 years.

The first step was to establish a paperless task force, which would identify key areas of the business and key processes involving the most paper use. When a call to the workforce failed to recruit volunteers, the CEO simply assigned management employees to the task force. Foremost on the task force's agenda was the implementation of an electronic records retention system to reduce paper usage, followed by the roll-out of a new corporate policy allowing only double-sided printing for company documents. Photocopiers and printers were adjusted to default to this setting.

Such policies and attempts to implement the new 'green' initiatives were quickly met with cynicism and scepticism on the part of the workers. Jokes about the next policy mandating 'paperless toilets' began to circulate throughout the offices. Returning to work after a holiday weekend, several managers found their office floors covered in hundreds of documents, with single-sided printing, produced by photocopiers that had been left to run continuously until depleted of paper.

Frank Webster, shocked at the workplace response, quickly assembled his management team for an urgent meeting to review why the new corporate programme had failed to gain acceptance by the employees.

Tasks

Reflect on Collinson's research regarding power in the workplace. As a manager at the review meeting, consider how you would answer the following questions:

1. How might the rise in staff absenteeism have been an indication of how the workers would react to the new 'green' strategies?

2. How did the workers' technical knowledge assist them in using a 'resistance by distance' strategy in dealing with the 'paperless policy'?

Essential reading

Ackroyd, S. and Thompson, P. (1999) *Organizational Misbehaviour*, London: Sage.

Sellen, A. and Harper, R. (2002) *The Myth of the Paperless Office*, Massachusetts: Massachusetts Institute of Technology.

Thompson, P. and McHugh, D. (2002) 'Power, conflict and resistance', Chapter 9 in *Work Organizations*, New York: Palgrave.

Note

This case study was written by Lori Rilkoff, MSc, CHRP, Senior Human Resources Manager at the City of Kamloops, and lecturer in HRM at Thompson Rivers University, BC, Canada.

 Chapter case study 2

Las Vegas general strike

 Visit www.palgrave.com/business/brattonob2e to view this case study

 Web-based assignment

The discussion in this chapter provided the basis for a comparison of different theories of power. Take some time to obtain (either online or in your library) and read the discussion of power in the special 2002 issue of *Journal of Organizational Behavior Management*.[40] Further background reading on the concept of power can be found at: www.experiencefestival.com/power_sociology/articleindex.

After reviewing the material, do as we began to do in the last section of this chapter: test the assumptions of the conceptualizations of power in this issue against the broader social theories of power we outlined in the first half of the chapter.

 OB in film

One of the best environments for looking at power, influence, authority and conflict is in the political environment. A particularly good example of this is the film, *Milk* (2008), which tracks the rise of gay rights campaigner Harvey Milk to political power in San Francisco. He was the first openly gay person to achieve public office in the USA.

The film is very good in capturing different ways in which Milk is effective in working for the rights of his community. In addition, the film depicts how those opposing his movement use power and influence against him. As you watch the film, try to map the changes in Milk's power, influence and authority. In doing so, assess how effective each is. To what extent is Milk more effective when holding an elected post, that is, in power, compared with his campaigning prior to being elected?

Note: This feature was written by Professor Jon Billsberry, Senior Research Fellow, Open University Business School, UK.

 Bonus OB in Film feature

Visit www.palgrave.com/business/brattonob2e to see how *Oleanna* (1994) can be considered in relation to the subject of leadership.

References

1 Sivanathan, N., Pillutla, M. and Murnighan, J. K. (2008) 'Power gained, power lost', *Organizational Behavior and Human Decision Processes*, **105**, pp. 135–46.

2 Ailon, G. (2006) 'What B would otherwise do: a critique of conceptualizations of "power" in organizational theory', *Organization*, **13**(6), pp. 771–800.

3 Crane, A., Knights, D. and Starkey, K. (2008) 'The conditions of our freedom: Foucault, organization, and ethics', *Business Ethics Quarterly*, **18**(3), pp. 299–320.

4 Austin, J. (2002) 'Editorial', *Journal of Organizational Behavior Management*, **22**(3), pp. 1–2.

5 Dahl, R. A. (1957) 'On the concept of power', *Behavioral Science*, **2**, pp. 201–15.

6 French, J. P. R. Jr. and Raven, B. (1960) 'The bases of social power', pp. 607–23 in D. Cartwright and A. Zander (eds), *Group Dynamics*, New York: Harper & Row.

7 Warren, D. I. (1968) 'Power, visibility, and conformity in formal organizations', *American Sociological Review*, **6**, pp. 951–70.

8 Genovese, E. (1972) *Roll Jordan Roll: The World the Slaves Made*, New York: Vintage Books.

9 Mann, M. (1986) *Sources of Social Power*, Cambridge: Cambridge University Press.

10 Giddens, A. (1985) *A Contemporary Critique of Historical Materialism*, Volume 2: *The Nation State and Violence*, Cambridge: Polity Press.

11 Wrong, D. H. (1979) *Power: Its Forms, Bases, and Uses*, Oxford: Wiley-Blackwell.

12 Lukes, S. (1974) *Power: A Radical View*, Basingstoke: Macmillan.

13 Foucault, M. (1977) *Discipline and Punish: The Birth of the Prison*, New York: Pantheon.

14 Foucault, M. (1980) *Power/Knowledge*, ed. C. Gordon, New York: Pantheon.

15 Astley, W. and Sachdeva, P. (1984) 'Structural sources of intraorganizational power: a theoretical synthesis', *Academy of Management Review*, **9**(1), pp. 104–13.

16 Gramsci, A. (1971) *Selections from the Prison Notebooks*, London: Lawrence & Wishart.

17 Williams, R. (1977) *Marxism and Literature*, Oxford: Oxford University Press.

18 Roscigno, V. and Hodson, R. (2004) 'The organizational and social foundations of worker resistance', *American Sociological Review*, **69**(1), pp. 14–39.

19 Coleman, A. and Fararo, T. (eds) (1991) *Rational Choice Theory*, Berkeley, CA: University of California Press.

20 Krippendorff, K. (1995) 'Undoing power', *Critical Studies in Mass Communication*, **12**(2), pp. 101–32.

21 Goffman, E. (1959) *The Presentation of Self in Everyday Life*, New York: Anchor.

22 Finkelstein, J. (1995) *The Fashioned Self*, Cambridge: Polity Press.

23 Marks, M. (2008) 'Looking different, acting different: struggles for equality within the South African Police Service', *Public Administration*, **86**(3), pp. 643–58.

24 Rubenstein, R. (2001) *Dress Codes: Meaning and Messages in American Culture*, Boulder, CO: Westview Press.

25 Krahn, H. and Lowe, G. (2002) *Work, Industry and Canadian Society* (4th edn), Toronto: Thomson Nelson.

26 Collinson, D. (1994) 'Strategies of resistance: power, knowledge and subjectivity in the workplace', pp. 25–68 in J. Jermier, D. Knights and W. Nord (eds), *Resistance and Power in Organizations*, New York: Routledge.

27 Aligisakis, M. (1997) 'Labour disputes in Western Europe: typology and tendencies', *International Labour Review*, **136**(1), pp. 73–94.

28 Braverman, H. (1974) *Labor and Monopoly Capitalism: The Degradation of Work in the Twentieth Century*, New York: Monthly Review Press.

29 Clegg, S. (1989) *Frameworks of Power*, London: Sage.

30 Burawoy, M. (1979) *Manufacturing Consent*, Chicago: University of Chicago Press.

31 Kondo, D. (1990) *Crafting Selves: Power, Discourse and Identity in a Japanese Factory*, Chicago: University of Chicago Press.

32 Elangovan, A. R. and Xie, J. L. (1999) 'Effects of perceived power of supervisor on subordinate stress and motivation: the moderating role of subordinate characteristics', *Journal of Organizational Behavior*, **20**(3), pp. 359–74.

33 Overbeck, J. and Park, B. (2006) 'Powerful perceivers, powerless objects: flexibility of powerholders' social attention', *Organizational Behaviour and Human Decision Processes*, **99**(2), pp. 227–44.

34 Raghubir, P. and Valenzuela, A. (2006) 'Centers-of-inattention: position biases in decision-making', *Organizational Behaviour and Human Decision Processes*, **99**(1), pp. 66–80.

35 Sennett, R. and Cobb, J. (1972) *Hidden Injuries of Class*, New York: Anchor.

36 Sennett, R. (1998) *The Corrosion of Character*, New York: Norton.

37 Morgan, G. and Kristensen, P. (2006) 'The contested space of multinationals: varieties of institutionalism, varieties of capitalism', *Human Relations*, **59**(11), pp. 1467–90.

38 Bouquet, C. and Birkinshaw, J. (2008) 'Managing power in the multinational corporation: how low-power actors gain influence', *Journal of Management*, **34**(3), pp. 477–508.

39 Mayes, B. and Ganster, D. (1988) 'Exit and voice: a test of hypotheses based on the fight/flight response to job stress', *Journal of Organizational Behavior*, **9**(3), pp. 99–117.

40 *Journal of Organizational Behaviour* (1982) Volume 22, Number 3.

41 Goltz, S. and Hietapelto, A. (2002) 'Using the operant and strategic contingencies models of power to understand resistance to change', *Journal of Organizational Behavior Management*, **22**(3), pp. 3–22.

42 Boyce, T. (2002) 'The power is in parsimony: commentary on Goltz's operant analysis of power interpretation of resistance to change', *Journal of Organizational Behavior Management*, **22**(3), pp. 23–7.

43 Malott, R. (2002) 'Power in organizations', *Journal of Organizational Behavior Management*, **22**(3), pp. 51–60.

44 Geller, E. S. (2002) 'Leadership to overcome resistance to change: it takes more than consequence control', *Journal of Organizational Behavior Management*, **22**(3), pp. 29–49.

chapter 17
Human resource management

chapter objectives

After studying this chapter, you should be able to:

- explain the nature of human resource management
- summarise the key human resource management functions
- explain the theoretical issues surrounding the human resource management debate
- explain the meaning of strategic human resource management and give an overview of its conceptual framework
- explain how developments in global capitalism affect corporate and human resource strategies in multinational corporations

Introduction

This book has covered a wide range of theories and research on individual employees, work groups, organizational design and processes to provide an understanding of work and behaviour in workplaces. We have highlighted how organizational behaviour is a result of complex processes involving how work and organization are designed and redesigned, how technology is introduced and used in the labour process, and how employees perceive, act in and respond to the external environment, the distribution of power, technological change and other interventions by management. However, although we have made direct reference to employment relations, there has been little discussion on employment relations practices developed by management.

human resource management: an approach to managing employment relations which emphasizes that leveraging people's capabilities is important to achieving competitive advantage

In recent years, the practices used to manage people in the workplace have assumed new prominence as concerns persist about global competition. It is argued that market imperatives require managers to change the way they manage the employment relationship to allow for the most effective utilization of people in the organization.

The 1990s were characterized by the increasing ascendancy and influence of the human resources (HR) function. During this period, a debate emerged on the concept of **human resource management** (HRM) that had its theoretical roots in US business schools. A seminal book edited by John Storey in 1989, *New Perspectives on Human Resource Management?*,[1] generated the 'first wave' of debate on the nature and ideological significance of 'progressive' HRM. A 'second wave' of debate emerged with four distinct themes: the significance of the economic and social context in shaping and reshaping the HRM arena, the links between HRM and performance, new organizational forms and relationships, and the importance of workplace learning.[2] This debate, mostly among academics, produced normative models, provided evidence of a direct connection between 'bundles' of best HRM practices and organizational performance, and exposed familiar conflicts in the social world of work.

strategic human resource management: the process of linking the human resource function with the strategic objectives of the organization in order to improve performance

A 'third wave' of HRM debate explored an approach to HRM labelled **strategic human resource management** (SHRM). Both terms – human resource management and strategic human resource management – have, however, been contested. For some, HRM is simply a grander term for 'personnel management', representing 'old wine in new bottles'. Others argue that HRM is quite distinct in theory and practice, and reflects something like a paradigm shift in the management of the employment relationship.

a meshing of both 'product market' and sociocultural logics.[22] Analytically, both HRM scholars and practitioners are more comfortable with the contextual variables included in the model because it conforms to the reality of the employment relationship: an amalgamation of business and societal expectations.[23] The stakeholder interests recognize the importance of 'trade-offs', either explicitly or implicitly, between the interests of owners and those of employees and their organizations, the unions. Although the model is still vulnerable to the charge of 'unitarism', it is a much more pluralist frame of reference than is found in some other models.

HRM policy choices emphasize that management's decisions and actions in HR management can be fully appreciated only if it is recognized that they result from an interaction between constraints and choices. The model sees management as a real actor, capable of making at least some degree of unique contribution within environmental and organizational parameters, and of influencing those parameters themselves over time.[5] The HR outcomes are high employee commitment to organizational goals and high individual performance, leading to cost-effective products or services. The underlying assumptions here are that employees have talents that are rarely fully utilized at work, and that they show a desire to experience growth through work. Thus, the Harvard HRM model takes the view that employment relations should be managed on the basis of the assumptions inherent in McGregor's approach to people-related issues, which he labelled 'Theory Y' (see Chapter 7) – the theory that people work because they want to and not because they have to. Thus, the Theory Y view assumes that when workers are given challenging assignments and autonomy over work assignments, they will respond with high motivation, high commitment and high performance.[24]

The long-term outcomes distinguish between three levels: individual, organizational and societal. At the individual employee level, the long-term outputs comprise the psychological rewards that workers receive in exchange for effort. At the organizational level, increased effectiveness ensures the survival of the organization. In turn, at the societal level, some of society's goals (for example, employment and growth) are attained as a result of fully utilizing people at work.

A feedback loop is the sixth component of the Harvard model. As we have discussed, the situational factors influence HRM policy and choices. Conversely, however, long-term outcomes might influence the situational factors, stakeholder interests and HR policies. The feedback loop in Figure 17.2 reflects this two-way relationship.

An advantage of the Harvard model is that it serves as a heuristic device for explaining the nature and significance of key HR practices. The model was developed as a teaching aid for the university's MBA syllabus in HRM in the early 1980s.[25] It also contains elements that are analytical (that is, situational factors, stakeholders and strategic choice levels) and prescriptive (that is, notions of commitment, competence and so on).[23] Another advantage of the Harvard model is the classification of inputs and outcomes at both organizational and societal level, creating the basis for a critique of comparative HRM.[23] One weakness is the absence of a coherent theoretical basis for measuring the relationship between HR inputs, outcomes and performance.

The Warwick model of HRM

This model comes from the Centre for Corporate Strategy and Change at the University of Warwick, UK, where it was developed by two researchers, Hendry and Pettigrew.[8] The Warwick model extends the Harvard framework by drawing on its analytical aspects. The model takes account of business strategy and HR practices, the external and internal context in which these activities take place, and the processes by which change takes place, including interactions between changes in both context and content.

The strength of the model is that it identifies and classifies important environmental influences on HRM. It maps the connections between the outer (wider environment) and inner (organizational) contexts, and explores how HRM adapts to changes in the context. The implication is that those organizations achieving an alignment between the external and internal contexts will experience superior performance. A weakness of the model is that the process whereby internal HR practices are linked to business output or performance is not developed.

The five elements of the model are:

- outer context
- inner context
- business strategy content
- HRM context
- HRM content.

These are shown in Figure 17.3.

> **Reviewing the three models, what beliefs and assumptions do you find implied in them? For example, look at the direction of the arrows in the Fombrun et al. model (see Figure 17.1, above). What is the message for managers? What organizational behaviour theories do you see in each model? What is missing?**
>
> **stop reflect**

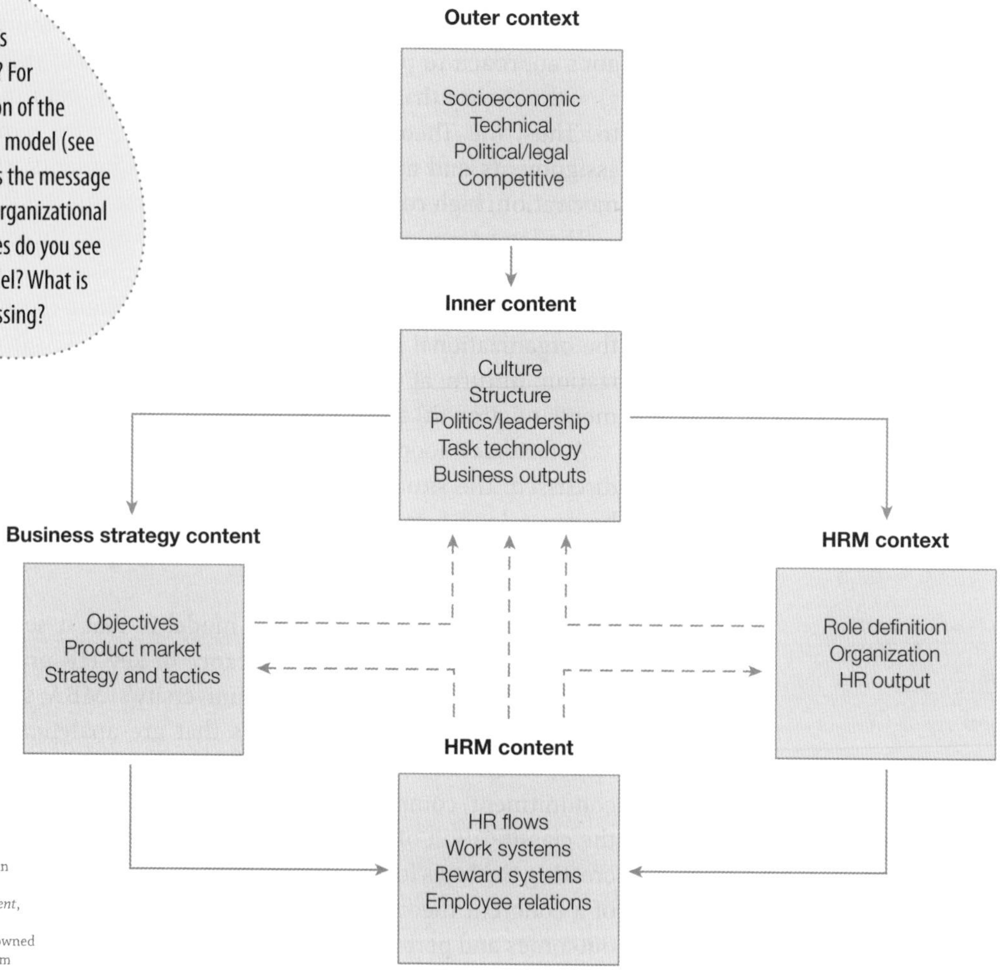

figure 17.3 The Warwick model of HRM

Source: Hendry, C. and Pettigrew, A. (1990) 'Human resource management: an agenda for the 1990s', *International Journal of Human Resource Management*, 1(1), Routledge/Taylor & Francis Ltd, pp. 17–44. Originally published by Routledge, which is now owned by Taylor & Francis. http://www.informaworld.com

Strategic human resource management

By the mid-1980s, an increasing number of HRM academics were emphasizing the need for HRM to focus on aligning the organization's HR function with its competitive strategy: in other words for HRM to have a 'strategic' role.[26] This approach, not surprisingly, saw a new labelling: 'strategic human resource management'. Just as the term 'human resource management' has been contested, so too has the notion of SHRM.

The SHRM literature is rooted in 'manpower' [sic] planning. But it is the work of influential management gurus, affirming the importance of the effective management of people as a source of competitive advantage, that encouraged academics to develop frameworks emphasizing the strategic role of the HR function.

The precise meaning of SHRM is problematic. It is unclear, for example, whether the term refers to an outcome or a process.[27] For some, SHRM is an outcome: 'as organizational systems designed to achieve sustainable competitive advantage through people'.[28] For others, it is viewed as a process: 'the process by which organizations seek to link the human, social, and intellectual capital of their members to the strategic needs of the firm' (ref. 27, p. 6).

John Purcell made a significant contribution to research on business HRM strategy by identifying what he labelled 'upstream' and 'downstream' types of strategic decisions.[29] The upstream or 'first-order' strategic decisions are concerned with the long-term direction of the corporation. If a first-order decision is made to take over another company, for example, a Germany company acquiring a software company in Ireland, a second set of considerations apply concerning the extent to which the new operation is to be integrated with or separate from existing operations. These are classified as downstream or 'second-order' strategic decisions. Different strategies, for example HRM, are called 'third-order' strategic decisions because they establish the basic parameters for managing people in the workplace. In theory at least, 'strategy in human resources management is determined in the context of first-order, long-run decisions on the direction and scope of the firm's activities and purpose ... and second-order decisions on the structure of the firm,' wrote Purcell (ref. 29, p. 71).

Another part of the SHRM debate has focused on the integration or 'fit' of business strategy with the HR strategy. This shift in managerial thought calls for the HR function to be 'strategically integrated', and is shown in Beer and colleagues' model of HRM. The authors saw a need to establish a close two-way relationship or 'fit' between the external business strategy and the elements of the internal HR strategy: 'An organization's HRM policies and practices must fit with its strategy in its competitive environment and with the immediate business conditions that it faces' (ref. 5, p. 25).

The concept of integration has three aspects:

1. the linking of HR policies and practices with the strategic management process of the organization
2. the internalization of the importance of HR on the part of line managers
3. the integration of the workforce into the organization to foster commitment to or an 'identity of interest' with the strategic goals.

'matching' model: a human resources strategy that seeks to 'fit' or align the organization's internal human resources strategy with its external competitive strategy

resource-based model: a human resources strategy that views employees as an asset as opposed to a cost, and assumes that the sum of people's knowledge and distinctive competencies has the potential to serve as a source of competitive advantage

Not surprisingly, this approach to SHRM has been referred to as the 'matching' model. Early interest in the 'matching' model is evident in a model by Devanna and associates. HRM and strategy structure follow and feed upon one another and are influenced by environmental forces (Figure 17.4).

An alternative formulation of SHRM is grounded in the belief that each employee is an asset as opposed to a variable cost. This approach to SHRM is called the resource-based model. The essence of the argument is that superior organizational performance through exploiting unique skills and human intellectual capital is underscored when advanced technology and other inanimate resources are readily available to competing organizations. The sum of people's knowledge and intellectual capital, and social relationships, has the potential to provide non-substitutable capabilities that serve as a source of competitive advantage.[30]

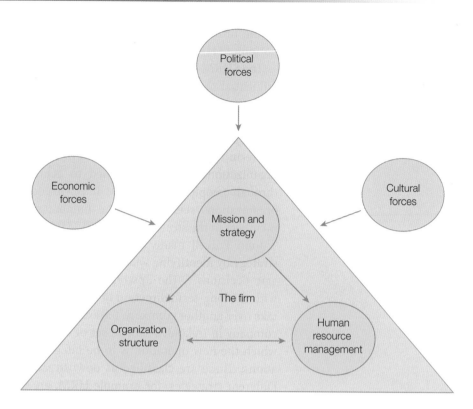

figure 17.4 A matching model of strategic HRM

Source: Fombrun, Tichy and Devanna (1984)[4]

This approach has raised questions about the inextricable connection between work-related learning, the mobilization of employee consent through learning strategies, and competitive advantage. Given the upsurge of interest in resource-based models, and in particular the new 'workplace learning' discourse, we need to take a closer look at this conceptual model.

The origins of the resource-based model can be traced back to Selznick,[31] who suggested that work organizations each possess a 'distinctive competence' that enables them to outperform their competitors, and to Penrose,[32] who challenged the view (which had largely been taken for granted by economists) that a firm's resources are homogeneous, and instead conceptualized the firm as a collection of 'heterogeneous' resources. Over three decades later, organizational theorists argued that *sustained* competitive advantage is not achieved through an analysis of an organization's external market position, but through a careful analysis of the skills and capabilities possessed by people in the organization, characteristics that competitors find themselves unable to imitate. Putting it in terms of a simple strengths–weaknesses–opportunities–threats analysis, the resource-based perspective emphasizes the strategic importance of exploiting internal 'strengths' and neutralizing internal 'weaknesses'.[33]

Figure 17.5 summarizes the relationships between resources and capabilities, strategies and sustained competitive advantage. Four characteristics are important in sustaining competitive advantage: value, rarity, inimitability and non-substitutability. From this perspective, the collective learning in the workplace on the part of managers and non-managers, especially on how to coordinate workers' diverse knowledge and skills and integrate diverse information technology, is a strategic asset that rivals find difficult to replicate. In other words, management capabilities are critical to harnessing the organization's human assets.

Others emphasize the strategic importance of managers identifying (or at least predicting) and marshalling 'a set of complementary and specialized resources and capabilities which are scarce, durable, not easily traded, and difficult to imitate' to enable the company to earn 'economic rent' (that is, profits) (ref. 34, p. 37).

International HRM and strategic international HRM

Academics have debated the difference between international HRM (IHRM) and strategic international HRM (SIHRM). For example, IHRM has been defined as 'HRM issues and problems arising from the internationalization of business, and the HRM strategies, policies and practices which firms pursue in response to the internationalization process' (ref. 53, p. 288). It has been argued that IHRM tends to celebrate a dominant Western type of culture, one that emphasizes the subordination of domestic culture and domestic employment practices to corporate culture and corporate HRM practices.[54] As a result, many contemporary IHRM studies tend to be seen as a managerial tool unashamedly connected to the neo-liberal corporate agenda.

As we discussed above, SHRM is the process of explicitly linking the HRM function with the strategic management goals of the organization. Thus, SIHRM is described in terms of connecting IHRM with the business strategy of a global organization: a multinational or transnational company (MNC or TNC). In defining SIHRM, we follow others and define it here as the HR policies and processes that result from the global competitive activities of MNCs, and that explicitly connect international HR practices and processes with the worldwide strategic goals of those companies.

The SIHRM literature acknowledges the need to address the tension between the global and local. This tension concerns balancing global competitiveness strategies (rationalization and integration) and local responsiveness (flexibility) strategies pursued by MNCs alongside leveraging global learning within and across the MNC. Thus, SIHRM links 'IHRM explicitly with the strategy and with the MNC' (ref. 51, p. 23).

Critics have, not surprisingly, questioned both the effects and the wisdom of transplanting Western HR policies and practices into culturally diverse domestic environments. Global companies share with their domestic counterparts the intractable problem of managing the employment relationship to reduce the indeterminacy resulting from the unspecified nature of the employment contract. To apply this perspective to IHRM, it would seem that the role of knowledge to make people in the workplace more manageable is further problematized by the intertwining of highly complex local, regional, national and global cultures.[55]

> For further information on cultural diversity go to http://global.broad.msu.edu/ibc; www.shrm.org/diversity; www.shrm.org/Research/FutureWorkplaceTrends
>
> **weblink**

The internationalization of the HRM cycle

The global business strategies examined above, and in particular the supposed ascendancy of TNCs with global communication networks, have far-reaching implications for IHRM function and practices. In leveraging the core HR activities, MNCs must achieve a dynamic balance between the pressures for central control and the pressures for local responsiveness across diverse national locations and intercultural contexts.[56] Here, we extend the HRM cycle (see Figure 17.1, above) to briefly explore the international aspects of recruitment and selection, rewards, training and development, and performance appraisal. Each part of the IHRM 'cycle' contributes to the international job performance of individual employees and the strategic goals of the global organization.

This conceptual framework (Figure 17.7) adds the dimensions of cultural diversity and national employment regimes. Others have noted that cultural diversity poses a number of new challenges for managing these four HR practices. The MNC typically has a multicultural workforce made up of employees from a variety of ethnic, racial and religious backgrounds, with very different cultural values and customs.

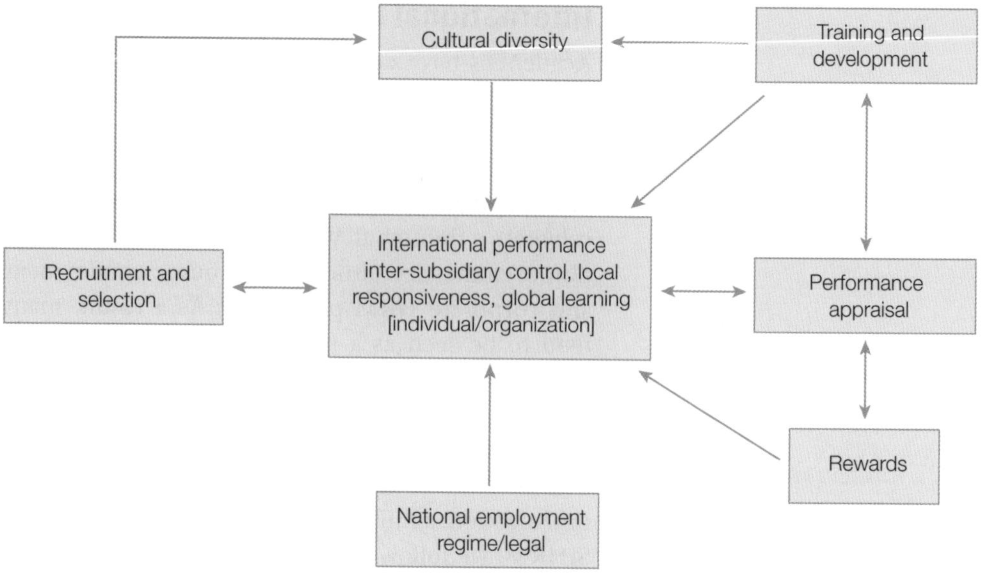

figure 17.7 The international HRM cycle

Source: Adapted from Mabey et al. (1998, p. 210)[87]

Indeed, it has been suggested that the central operating method for the global company is the creation and effective management of multicultural work teams that represent diversity in competencies, levels of experience, cultural and language backgrounds.[57]

International recruitment and selection

A TNC transmits management 'know-how', and in most IHRM publications, recruitment and selection are seen primarily as an issue of expatriate selection. Problems seem to occur because the focus of decision making is embedded in the local culture and norms where the MNC's corporate office is located, and therefore expatriate staff at the company's head office may have little idea what culturally derived expectations would be needed to 'fit' the local context where the person recruited is to work.[58] Informal selection decisions are also often affected by illogical elements such **ethnocentrism**, ignorance, stereotyping and sometimes discrimination.[59,60]

ethnocentrism: the tendency to regard one's own culture and group as the standard, and thus superior, whereas all other groups are seen as inferior

International rewards

Managing international rewards requires that managers responsible for implementing HR policies and practices are familiar with a range of other issues, including the foreign country's employment law, national labour relations, the availability of particular allowances or benefits, and currency fluctuations in particular host countries. Studies suggest that effective performance management requires that expatriates should know whether and how their performance in their overseas assignment is linked to pay and the next step in their career.[61]

International training and development

The notion of strategic alignment suggests that MNCs will tend to provide managers, knowledge workers and key technical personnel with the competencies for the successful transfer of the distinctive competencies and culture of the organization from the parent headquarters to the subsidiaries.

The term 'glass border' describes the irrational assumption held by some parent country top managers that female managers are less suitable than men for overseas appointments. What can be done to promote equal opportunities for female managers to undertake international assignments?

stop reflect

International performance appraisal

The desire to control and predict an employee's current and potential job performance has resulted in both national and global firms developing integrated performance appraisal systems. Studies show that performance appraisal is the favoured way to ensure that strategic employee competencies, employee behaviour and motivation are enacted effectively in the host country.[62]

The convergence/divergence debate

A common question in the IHRM literature is whether there is a trend towards a **convergence** of HR practices resulting from globalization, reflecting the dominant influence of US capitalism. So does globalization bring into being a convergence of HR practices? To address this conundrum, we have drawn on various studies to examine the convergence/divergence debate, which is expressed diagrammatically in Figure 17.8.[63,64]

Of course, this is an extreme simplification, but the general understanding in the diagram is that Western capitalism works on a left-to-right order of domination, with line A representing various theories of how Western capitalist globalization exploits resources and markets through direct economic and political control. Lines BD and CE represent differing concepts of the ideological regulation of people employed in organizations – of different kinds, such as state-owned enterprises (SOEs), joint ventures (JVs) and foreign-invested enterprises (FIEs) – in developing (globalized) countries. This regulation includes subordination through legal and trade institutions (such as the World Trade Organization (WTO), the World Bank, the International Monetary Fund (IMF), the International Labour Organization (ILO) and the European Union) and the manufacture of consent (for instance, through the spread of Western popular culture in films and literature).

For further information on comparative HRM, go to http://findarticles.com for 'comparative HRM'; www.hreonline.com (USA); www.clc-ctc.ca (Canada)

weblink

Theories that recognize a tendency to converge that proceeds only along line A are in essence rationale theories of management: that is, they reject the basic thesis that national employment regimes, cultural diversity, norms and social contradictions are countervailing forces against the convergence of HR practices. However, theories that explore the path of capitalist global economic power primarily along line BD focus on the effects of national government employment laws, local business systems and the influence of professional fields of knowledge in different countries on shaping 'Western' HR practices. Theories that focus primarily on line CE in this diagram examine the ways in which a standard global culture tends to develop through the strategic use and spread of Western consumerism, advertising, popular culture and literature and so on.

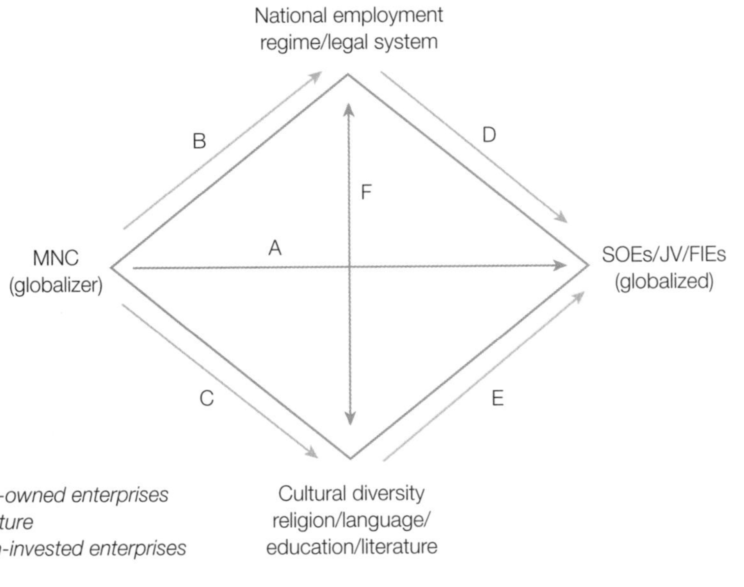

If we combine these forces, and look at the totality of the interplay stemming from a different national institutional set-up and different ethnic or national cultures (that is, lines BD and CE), we see a tendency to challenge the dominance of Anglo-Saxon HR practices. This would undermine the HR–performance linkage and force a divergence of HR practices worldwide.

This pattern of globalized relations is further complicated through the complex intertwining relationships between national institutional and legal regimes – at the top of line F – and cultural and political backgrounds – at the bottom of line F. These, it is argued, help to regulate globalized capitalist relations.[65]

SOEs: state-owned enterprises
JV: joint venture
FIEs: foreign-invested enterprises

figure 17.8 Diagram representing the convergence/divergence debate on IHRM

Source: Adapted from Tiffin and Lawson (1994, p. 18)[64]

Although global and national relations are complex, Figure 17.8 clearly suggests a plausible challenge to a universal vision of order and convergence on Western HR practices. These countervailing forces stem from local rationalities, local realities, local political ideologies and local culture.[66,67] Evidence of continued diversity in local or national patterns of economic activity and employment relations has contributed to the notion of 'varieties of capitalism'. Although the global economy continues to be more interconnected, 'societies with different institutional arrangements will continue to develop and reproduce varied systems of economic organization with different economic and social capabilities in particular industries and sectors' (ref. 67, p. 3).

Others have persuasively argued that with the existence of distinct national contexts and cross-cultural differences, the notion of a 'European' or 'Asian' HRM model is problematic, and the 'universalist' assumption that Protestant Anglo-Saxon HRM philosophy and HR individual-oriented practices are directly transferable is wrong.[68] To illustrate the point, any comparative analysis of European HR practices begs the question, 'What really constitutes Europe?' The whole of Europe, excluding Russia and Turkey, comprises a landmass not much more than half the size of China or the USA. However, in the intensity of its internal differences and contrasts, Europe is said to be unique.[69] At the last count, it comprised 46 countries: 27 of these were members of the European Union in 2009. All have their distinct and overlapping histories, politics, cultures and memories, and many languages – the European Union has 23 official languages and more than 60 indigenous regional or minority language communities.[70]

Similarly, any grand claim of an 'Asian' HRM model is even more problematic. Asia comprises a wide range of countries, national institutional systems and complex diverse cultures. As we discussed in an earlier chapter, competitive advantage in most Asian countries is based on cheap manual and intellectual labour, yet some Asian countries use highly skilled paid workers. Some Asian countries are marked by cultural homogeneity, while others are marked by cultural diversity. Within the Asian-Pacific region, 2200 languages are spoken (Professor W. Foley, personal communication),[43] and people believe in widely different religions and philosophies, ranging from Buddhism, Confucianism and Hinduism to Islam and Christianity.

Despite economic pressures towards convergence, strikingly resilient differences in cultural and institutional contexts produce divergent employment relationships.[71] Following on from the notion of diversity in national business systems, more reflective observers are increasingly acknowledging that the issue of convergence and divergence in European HRM 'needs more careful nuance than has been the case hitherto', and European national institutional patterns are so variable that 'no common model is likely to emerge in the foreseeable future' (ref. 72, p. 268). Thus, cross-national research suggests that national conceptions of better HR practices remain dominant.[73]

In a similar way, studies suggest that there is a considerable divergence of HR practices in Asian economies. Contrary to the convergence hypothesis underpinning globalization, the idea that 'best' HR practices have 'universal' application does not hold water when they have to be applied in the context of a different national institutional profile, culture and variety of capitalism. In Japan, for example, employment practices are embedded in national social relations and shared social values, rather than modelled on those in the USA.[21] In the Republic of China, there have been noteworthy shifts away from the 'iron rice bowl' system to a more 'market-responsive' system of employment relations, but this is still some way from the HRM ideal-type Western model.[74]

Contemporary HR practices in Asia partially reflect identifiable enduring continuities that stretch back to either a colonial or a post-revolutionary era. A central aspect of practice in former colonies is 'patriarchal authoritarianism' rather than the rational-bureaucratic style dominant in North America.

The persistence of national HR practices will endure because managers know how these work in practice and the likely outcomes.[75] At best, it is argued,

As you read this section, consider to what extent Western 'best HR practices' can be applied to the Asian business environment, culture and values

stop reflect

For further information on HRM in Asia–Pacific countries, go to www.wfpma.com (APFHRM being the Asia Pacific Federation of Human Resource Management). The site includes newsletters, publications and contact information for HR professionals

weblink

globalization may be causing an increasing degree of 'relative convergence' across 'regional clusters' such as China, South Korea and Japan, resulting from globally driven market forces.[76] Thus, the theory of a universal model of HRM (which often is interpreted to mean a Protestant Anglo-American model of HRM) is challenged by national rationalities, national institutional settings, and national, regional and local cultures. We would therefore expect to find that HR practices differ between countries, by sector, by size and by ownership of the work organization.

Critical insight

HRM best practices: chimera or cul-de-sac?

HRM theorists have cautioned against an overemphasis on a model of 'best' practice in HRM and on the notion of 'best fit' between HRM strategy and business strategy. John Purcell, for example, argues that a body of US and UK HRM literature has led to extravagant claims for the universal applicability of the best practice model, which suggests that 'one hat fits all' for successful HR activity.

Obtain a copy of Purcell's article, 'Best practice and best fit: chimera or cul-de-sac?'[77] Why is the notion that a bundle of best HR practices is universally applicable problematic for (1) UK-based organizations, and (2) MNCs operating outside the European Union?

Paradoxes in human resource management

The more critical evaluations of HRM models expose internal paradoxes. Paradox involves ambiguity and inconsistency, two or more positions that each sound reasonable, yet conflict or even contradict each other. Paradox is inherent in HRM. It results when, in pursuit of a specific organizational goal or goals, managers call for or carry out actions that are in opposition to the very goal(s) the organization is attempting to accomplish.

Critics of the HRM model have drawn upon the Weberian notion of a 'paradox of consequences' arising from HRM policies and practices.[78] For example, new organizational designs have been introduced to improve productivity and employee autonomy. On the other hand, the productivity benefits arising from the new organizational forms are accompanied by a number of negative effects on the 'psychological contract', which have the effect of undermining other goals such as retaining employee loyalty and commitment. More broadly, there is ambiguity over whether the main role of the HRM function is a 'caring' or a 'controlling' or 'manipulative' one.

An incisive critique of the HRM phenomenon identifies further ambiguities in the 'soft' and 'hard' schools of HRM.[49] There is a huge difference between the 'rhetoric' and 'reality' of HRM. Whereas, for example, the rhetoric asserts that 'we are all managers now' as a result of 'empowerment', it conceals the legitimate question of whether a social group holding privileges (senior management) and material returns can hold on to power. Similarly, the inclusion of the HR director in the strategic management team, the act of 'giving away HR management' to line managers, and the outsourcing of more specialized HR activities might ultimately lead to the end of the HR professional: the 'big hat, no cattle' syndrome.[79,80] The tendency in UK companies to be ruled by short-term accounting controls might well undermine the long-term HR employee-development-oriented goals.[81]

One notable feature of much of the HRM literature is the tendency for the research and debate on the HRM model to be gender blind. More recently, however, there has been more interest in the gender implications of HRM models.[82–84] The HRM model might be at odds with the promotion of equal opportunities, and pronouncements on the value of diversity and individual learning are part of the rhetoric rather than the reality.

Chapter summary

- In this chapter, we examined the development of HRM, and emphasized that it is a product of its times, linked to the ascendancy of a new political and economic ideology, and to the changed conditions of national and global capitalism.

- We examined three widely cited HRM models. The US models include Fombrun et al. and Beer et al. One European HRM model developed by British academics Hendry and Pettigrew extends Beer's Harvard framework by drawing on its analytical aspects, connecting the outer (wider environment) and inner (organizational) contexts, and exploring how HRM adapts to changes in the context.

- We discussed a core assumption underlying much of the SHRM research and literature, that each of the main types of generic competitive strategy used by organizations (such as a cost leadership or differentiation strategy) is associated with a different approach to managing people, that is, with a different HR strategy.

- We examined the so-called 'matching model' and the 'resource-based' SHRM model. The former focuses on the notion of 'fit', while the latter places emphasis on an organization's human endowments as a strategy for sustained competitive advantage. Paradox is an ongoing part of the employment relationship. The more critical evaluations of HRM expose internal paradoxes.

- The driving force behind the growth of interest in SIHRM and IHRM is the resurgence of neo-liberalism and the unprecedented growth in global markets. Critics argue that unfettered markets have created a new international division of labour, causing the transfer of manufacturing jobs from high-wage old industrialized regions to low-wage developing economies. They also argue that IHRM tends to emphasize the subordination of national culture and national employment practices to corporate culture and HR practices.

- The cross-national transfer of Anglo-Saxon HR practices for recruitment and selection, rewards, training and development, and performance appraisal will require some degree of cultural sensitivity, as well as consultation with host country nationals about local suitability.

- Despite the economic and political pressures from globalization, a divergence of HR practices continues to remain. This is influenced and shaped by national and organizational cultures in the developed and the developing world. Variations in national regulatory systems, labour markets, business-related institutions, and cultural and polyethnic contexts are likely to constrain or shape any tendency towards 'convergence' or a 'universal' model of 'better' HR practice. The sheer variation of economies, national institutional profiles and cultures makes claims for convergence simplistic and problematic.

Key concepts

collective bargaining	461
human resource management	456
international human resource management	471
resource-based model	467
strategic human resource management	466
trade unions	457

Vocab checklist for ESL students

- ☐ Change agent
- ☐ Convergence thesis
- ☐ Ethnocentrism, ethnocentric
- ☐ High-performance working environment
- ☐ Human capital
- ☐ Human resource management
- ☐ Human resource management cycle
- ☐ International human resource management
- ☐ Leverage
- ☐ Matching model
- ☐ Resource-based model
- ☐ Stakeholder
- ☐ Strategic human resource management
- ☐ Strategy, strategize, strategic
- ☐ Workplace wellness

Chapter review questions

1. What role does HRM play in organizations?
2. Is it possible to adopt a Theory Y philosophy in SHRM?
3. What does a 'resource-based' SHRM model of competitive advantage mean? What are the implications for HRM of this competitive strategy?
4. How can HRM practices generate superior organizational performance?
5. What are meant by strategic international HRM and international HRM?
6. Discuss how differences in national institutional systems influence a corporation's decision to locate its profit-making operations.

Chapter research questions

1. Form a study group of three to five people. Each group member should go to the website of an HR-related organization (for example, www.hrhq.com) or an HR-related magazine (for example, www.peoplemanagement.co.uk or www.hrreporter.com). Reviewing the current articles and news, what are the key people-related issues facing managers and HR specialists? Do the issues correspond to the HR areas identified in the theoretical models reviewed in this chapter?
2. Obtain a copy of *Searching for the Human in Human Resource Management* by Bolton and Houlihan (2007; see Further

structure that best fits a strategy, technology and environment. Several theoretical frameworks were examined around the notion of bureaucratic and post-bureaucratic. We explained the contingency view of formal organizational design, which suggests that a change in business strategy may require a change in organizational design, for example moving from a functional to a team-based organizational structure. It was explained how the external domain influences the formal structure and functioning of a work organization, and how, in turn, the organization's leaders influence the wider society.

In Chapter 11, we emphasized how comparative, international analyses of concepts, theoretical debates and policies and programmes provide an important basis for understanding how technology is related to work and organizational behaviour. We suggested a broad, multilevelled approach which advocates that organizational behaviour students need to think of technology as a social phenomenon by recognizing both consent and conflict within processes of adoption. Through our review of the literature, we hoped to stimulate a variety of questions, but perhaps more importantly, students should be in a better position to understand, evaluate and perhaps even affect the current landscape and trajectory of new technology, work and related issues in our society today.

In Chapter 12, we explored also the nature of organizational culture, which we defined as a pattern of shared basic assumptions, beliefs, values, artefacts, stories and behaviours, and discussed how the concept has become closely associated with the notion of postmodern organizations and management theory around strategic human resource management. Two approaches to the study of culture were examined. First is the managerialist-oriented approach, which treats organizational culture as a *variable*: it is something that an organization *has* and can be managed. Second is the critical-oriented approach, which conceptualizes culture as something that an organization '*is*', a metaphor that emphasizes the symbolic, consciousness and subjective aspects of the formal workplace. Advocates of the '*is*' approach to understanding organizational culture tend to be more interested in interpreting organizations than in providing prescriptive 'how to' remedies to increase performance variables.

Chapter 13 explained that leadership is a dialectical process wherein an individual persuades others to do something they would not otherwise do; it is a result of the interaction between the leader and followers within some context and is equated with power. It was explained that leadership is not the same as management. Management is associated with functions such as planning, organizing, controlling and efficiency, whereas leadership is associated with vision making and significant change. Management processes produce a degree of order and consistency in work behaviour. Leadership processes produce significant change or movement. We reviewed the major perspectives of leadership, including trait, behaviour, contingency, transformational, power and gender-influence and substitutes for leadership. In this, we noted that the systematic research on leadership has evolved from a narrow focus on the leader's traits to a multidimensional model of leadership that looks at the exercise of leadership as a complex reciprocal process affected by the interaction between the leader, the followers and the opportunities and constraints afforded by the external and internal contexts in which they find themselves. Finally, we looked at John Kotter's leadership model for organizational change, noting its strengths and limitations.

Chapter 14 explained how the communication process established in the workplace reflects management style, the degree of employee involvement in decision making and organizational culture. Three major perspectives for understanding organizational communications were presented – functionalist, interpretivist and critical – to allow us to comprehend the central role that communications has in the management process. The metaphors used to describe the perspectives were said to enhance our ability to view communications as not just the transmission and exchange of information in the context of organizational efficiency, but rather as central to the other processes of power, leadership and decision making. We emphasized that through symbols (verbal, non-verbal and written language) human beings engage their world. Language creates the organizational concepts that define the culture of an organization and give form to notions of control, delegation and rationality. Finally, we provided evidence that revealed the differences between the conversational styles of men and women. As managers, women try to develop a 'rapport' with their colleagues, whereas men often 'report' information or problems. Although individuals are encouraged to be creative, the organization places limitations on them in the form of where, how and when they can speak.

Chapter 15 examined different models of decision making and introduced issues of ethics and corporate social responsibility. We were careful to explain that, in reality, decision makers must suffer from bounded rationality. They do not have free and easy access to information, and the human mind has limited information-processing capacity, and is susceptible to a variety of cognitive biases. Furthermore, time constraints and political considerations can outweigh anticipated economic gain. It was noted that organizations are increasingly concerned about their members making ethical decisions and, given the nefarious behaviour of some corporate executives, their interest in corporate social responsibility. We explained that decision making in the organization can be improved by using four techniques: brainstorming, the nominal group technique, the stepladder, computer-mediated brainstorming and the Delphi technique.

Chapter 16 explored the abstract concept of power. Power appears to be 'embodied' in individuals, something they possess and exert. In reviewing the macro theories of power, we explored the many deep social roots or 'sources' of power systems, including, along the way, the influences of ideology, military, politics and economics. We said that Gramsci and Foucault outlined perhaps the most extensive theories of power, noting that it is ubiquitous because it constitutes the very way we talk and think about ourselves, let alone our organizational surroundings. Importantly, these two authors were clear in their argument that power is indeed composed of a coin with two sides: on the one, consent, accommodation and domination; on the other, lack of commitment, stress, resistance, political action and 'voice'. We then moved on to explore some key examples of organizational behaviour research that deal directly with the concept of 'power'. We argued that managers as well as workers (and students of organizational behaviour!) have a right to think through and question our current arrangements for their legitimacy. Mahatma Ghandi, Martin Luther King and others operated on the principle of removal of consent, which, for our purposes, speaks directly to a broad, social perspective on power.

The future of work and organizational behaviour

The scale of the global economic recession that started in 2008–09, the interdependencies and particularities of organizational needs and the multidimensional nature of workplace change or even transformation have made the task of predicting the trajectory of work and organizational behaviour a heroic, some may say foolhardy, challenge. Without wishing to privilege any particular theme, this section considers several organizational behaviour themes that we have addressed in this book. Using the integrated model (see Figure 1.2) used in the preceding chapters and drawing heavily from Kersley et al.'s survey findings,[2] we will indicate possible future directions of matters and discourse related to organizational behaviour.

In the early twenty-first century, much of the debate in organizational behaviour has been about the growth of non-standard or precarious employment, the quality of work, balancing responsibilities inside and outside work, the search for performance-enhancing employment practices, the process of organizational transformation and the alleged shift to post-bureaucratic organizations. The decline in trade union power has excluded alternative employee 'voices' and freed up the scope for unilateral management decision making. Union decline has left workers increasingly vulnerable to deregulation, flexible labour practices and work intensification, and consequentially to work-related stress and psychological meltdown.

The research evidence affirms that the employer is an 'active agent'[3] in transforming work patterns in terms of redrawing the boundaries between standard 'core' and non-standard 'precarious' employment. Evidence points to the continuing growth of precarious employment arrangements in Canada, the European Union, the USA and many parts of Asia.[4] The new employment relationships have profound implications for organizational behaviour theorists and practitioners. Most of existing organizational behaviour theories and frameworks are implicitly grounded in the dominant paradigm of standard employment,[5] and therefore more inclusive models of precarious employment need to be developed. One basic question to be addressed concerns how workers' motivation and commitment are mediated by factors associated with non-standard employment contracts in the new organizational context. As precarious/low-security employment policies and practices become increasingly prevalent, the 'standard employment' paradigm is fast becoming an anachronism to future organizational behaviour researchers. Between 1998 and 2004, survey data also affirm that new forms of work have resulted in an intensification of work: 'Employees' perceptions of work intensity have not changed … their jobs required them to work very hard and … they never seemed to have enough time to get their work done' (ref. 5, p. 317).

In the UK, the findings of the 2004 Workplace Employment Relations Survey[2] did not reveal, for the most part, a demonstrable connection between 'better' work and employment practices and organizational performance. Neither did the influential study find evidence that human resource management has become more 'strategic' in UK workplaces. The pursuit of a competitive strategy of low costs and developing human capital may well therefore be confined to 'leading-edge' organizations in which competitive advantage depends more on leveraging the skills of knowledge workers.

New work configuration and employment arrangements cannot be uncoupled from their organizational and national contexts.[6–8] As we explained in an earlier chapter, the notion of post-bureaucratic organizations, often characterized as 'lean' or 'networks' or 'virtual', has in recent years become an important theme in organizational behaviour studies. It has been notably associated with the accelerating growth of global capitalism and information technology, and concomitantly with corporate governance and new flexible employment practices. At the heart of notions of post-bureaucratic organizations is the idea of a more flexible, empowered and cooperative workforce, together with a strategically integrated set of employment relations. A central aspect of work in post-bureaucratic organizations involves individuals being rewarded on the basis of individual or/and organizational performance. As others have persuasively argued, the new employment arrangements have, paradoxically, revitalized Weber's typology of bureaucracy. Analysing primarily qualitative data from global automotive companies between 2000 and 2001, it is reported that new performance-related incentives have generated behavioural rules that reinforce bureaucratic control in the workplace: 'Bureaucratic forms of control have been refined rather than supplanted', they state.[9] Arguably, the binary bureaucratic/post-bureaucratic view of organizational design may be a somewhat misleading analytical device.

OB in focus   A culture of overwork exacts an extreme price

'BEIJING – At China's biggest telecoms maker, every new employee is issued with a mattress. The reason? So they can grab a nap beneath their desks, day or night, when they succumb to exhaustion from their endless working hours.

The frenetic work habits of the 40,000 employees of Huawei Technologies have become known as the 'mattress culture' – and it's a prime example of the intense pressures that kill up to one million Chinese workers every year.

Until recently, China was proud of its mattress culture. The employees of Huawei were icons of the tireless zeal that transformed China into the 'workshop of the world.'

Many worked for months without a day off, sleeping in their offices at night so they could keep working as soon as they awoke.

But there is mounting concern about the toll of death and illness from overwork. Experts estimate that 600,000 to one million Chinese workers are dying from it every year.

Huawei, previously seen as a model company, is now a symbol of the overwork phenomenon. One of its star employees, 25-year-old software engineer Hu Xinyu, died suddenly May 28 after nearly a month of overtime work.

He was a former athlete and sports enthusiast, yet he became so exhausted at the company that he often slept at his office instead of going home.

His death has helped ignite a national debate about the culture of excessive work. The Chinese media have documented a growing number of deaths caused by overwork, and Chinese websites and Internet forums have questioned the national economic model.

'Working is important, but it can't be more important than life,' one young office worker said in a website debate about Mr. Hu's death.

Almost all sectors of Chinese society, from manual labourers to intellectuals, are prone to overwork. In the past five years, for example, 135 professors and other scholars in Beijing have died prematurely as a result of overwork, according to media reports. Their average age was just 53.

Another report concluded that the life expectancy of intellectuals in Shanghai has dropped by five years in the past decade. And a survey of 2,600 high-tech workers in Beijing found that 84 per cent were unhappy with their excessive workload and nearly 90 per cent were worried about the impact on their health.

'People are starting to look at the human cost of China's phenomenal growth rate,' said Robin Munro, research director at China Labour Bulletin, a labour-rights organization based in Hong Kong.

'Many Chinese people are beginning to question whether their society is benefiting from this relentless drive for great-power status. When you have up to a million people dropping dead from overwork, it's a calamitous situation.

'These are the kinds of shocking numbers you might expect from a disease epidemic. It's an awful indictment of the work culture in China and the pressures on ordinary people.'

Under Chinese law, he noted, workers are prohibited from working more than 36 hours of overtime a month. Yet this limit is routinely exceeded in most export-oriented manufacturing industries.

'It's the mentality of a slave-labour camp,' Mr. Munro said. 'The entire work culture is distorted. There's so much emphasis on making money in China, and working extraordinary hours is seen as the way to do it.'

Even the state-owned propaganda newspaper, People's Daily, has criticized the amount of overwork, which it blames partly on the rising unemployment rate and the 14 million jobless people in the country.

'With the growing numbers of people ready to take their places, few workers are willing to turn down overtime,' the newspaper said in an editorial last month.

One of the most poignant cases was the story of Gan Hongying, a 35-year-old worker in a garment factory in southern China.

Desperate to raise money for her husband and two young children, she worked 22 hours of overtime in a four-day period this spring. She began to complain of dizziness and headaches, and she talked constantly of how she needed to sleep.

On May 30, after more than 54 hours of work over four days, she died suddenly. Her last words to her sister were: 'I am so tired. Give me the key to your home, I want to have a rest.'

After her death, a local newspaper investigated and found that the garment factory had routinely forced its employees to work overtime.

If the workers failed to finish their orders, the factory gate was sometimes locked to keep them inside, and they were threatened with a loss of pay.

The investigation found that 70 per cent of factories in the Pearl River delta of southern China, where Ms. Gan worked, had required its employees to work more than the legal maximum of overtime every week.

Source: Geoffrey York (2006), 'A culture of overwork exacts an extreme price: thousands of Chinese are literally being worked to death,' *Globe and Mail*, August 21, p. A2.

plate 61 At the heart of notions of post-bureaucratic organizations is a flexible, empowered and cooperative workforce. The Internet adds a 'space dimension' to organizational culture, and research suggests that it might require us to re-evaluate existing conceptions of organizational culture.

Both mainstream and critical organizational behaviour literature bears witness to an increasing and accelerating interest in understanding the importance of analysing organizational behaviour within its societal fabric. We have departed from most standard organizational behaviour texts by recognizing the need for an analytical readjustment in organizational behaviour analysis that values insights from sociological, feminist and anthropological theories. The uneven effects of global capitalism have created disparities both between and within organizations. Not only this, but dominant organizational behaviour ideology and research have ignored one of the central insights of classical sociological theory, namely that the behaviours of people in organizations and management practices are embedded in wider institutional, cultural and social relations.[10] As such, any management intervention is demonstrably diffused, enacted, adapted and applied in ways that simultaneously change or transform existing employment relations, yet are necessarily collectively internalized into existing interdependencies in society.[7] This makes the 'effects' of any management intervention in the workplace unpredictable if it is analysed only within a sanitized organizational, rather than a societal, context.

The importance of embeddedness can also be illustrated at a macro level. At the time of completing the second edition of this book, the synchronized global financial and economic crisis that began in 2008–09 was still reverberating through advanced and developing countries. And in spite of the focus on economic matters, the problem of global warming remained a part of mainstream popular culture and discourse. There appeared to be a seismic shift in public opinion recognizing that governments do, indeed, have a role to play in regulating business activities, and that organizations must invest and engage in activities that provide for a sustainable lifestyle. Another example of the importance of embeddedness relates to organizational governance. As some iconic US corporate executives completed their term of imprisonment, and while others were publicly reviled for their arrogance, incompetence and greed, the global recession caused a growing backlash against corporate CEOs receiving huge bonuses and, in some cases, against fraudulent accounting practices.

President George W. Bush's rhetoric in 2002 promised harsh punishment for corporate executives who 'cooked the books' and violated public trust. The implication here is that removing a few 'bad apples' could solve corporate white-collar

Source: Nick Tutton

plate 62 In spite of the current focus on economic matters, the problem of global warming remains a part of mainstream popular culture and discourse. There appears to be a seismic shift in public opinion that recognizes that governments do, indeed, have a role to play in regulating business activities, and organizations must invest and engage in activities that provide for a sustainable lifestyle.

crime. However, the notion of the embedded organization suggests that simply focusing on traits – for instance, honesty and integrity – separates top organizational leaders from the context. Those corporate leaders who engaged in criminal or highly unethical practices did so largely because of profound ideological changes in society. From the early 1990s, shareholder-value-driven capitalism emphasized stock appreciation, the use of stock options to compensate senior executives and the attainment of short-term financial targets, which produced a culture of avarice. According to the US Federal Reserve Board chairman, Alan Greenspan, the late 1990s produced 'an outsized increase in opportunities for avarice. [And] an infectious greed seemed to grip much of our business community' (ref. 11, p. 323). In addition, in 2009, an investigation by the House of Commons Treasury Committee into the conditions causing the UK banking crisis partly blamed the crisis on monumental 'mismanagement' coupled with 'a culture of easy reward'.

Thus, we are reminded that managers operate within a wider institutional, cultural and social context, and changing the way managers behave requires a fundamental change in organizational context and culture. When we wrote in 2006 in the first edition of this book that reports of nefarious corporate behaviour require 'changing the way organizations are regulated by government, changing the way managers are compensated, and changing the values that ultimately prevail in society', we never expected an endorsement for such actions from leading politicians such as French President Nicolas Sarkozy or US President Barack Obama. In 2009, the London G20 summit on the world financial and economic crisis increased pressure on national governments and global institutions to create systems of regulations and corporate governance to curb organizations' managers from conducting either illegal or highly unethical behaviour, or to bring in less risky behaviour, in order to make Western capitalism more efficient, accountable and socially acceptable. Intellectually and politically, the ideology of Anglo-American market fundamentalism has been found deficient. Consequent changes to national and international regulations and policies may change the nature of capitalism. Such an outcome may be profound for the way in which work and people are organized and managed in the workplace.

The notion of embeddedness is also relevant when studying organizational behaviour. With a few notable exceptions (e.g. Mills et al.,[12] and Wilson[13]), most organizational behaviour textbooks and research is embedded within a dominant managerialist perspective, which serves the interests of big business, as well as being largely race, ethnicity and gender blind. The vast majority of organizational behaviour textbooks present the managerialist approach, with its primary focus on organizational efficiency, effectiveness and performance, as the *logical* approach. Workers are typically represented as a 'problem' in need of being 'controlled' or 'motivated'. Managers, however, are portrayed as being primarily engaged in *rational* activities designed to increase profits for shareholders, for the most part without exercising wider social responsibilities. Within the dominant managerialist paradigm, there is generally a malign neglect of the interests and ideas of women workers, of racial minorities, of non-Christians and of those who are disabled. Yet women's work experiences, for example, may be quite different from those of white, male workers. Similarly, black women's work experiences may be quite different from those of their white sisters.

The powerful arguments presented by feminist writers to redefine employment relations can be equally applied to the interdisciplinary field of organizational behaviour.[14-16] We would suggest that the conventional treatment of organizational behaviour has presented an undertheorized and sanitized analysis of the workplace. Most mainstream organizational behaviour theories are implicitly grounded in the dominant Protestant Anglo-Saxon paradigm of 'individualism', 'managerialism', 'standard work' and male hegemony. Similar to research in other areas of social studies, more inclusive frameworks of organizational behaviour must be developed. The literature pertaining to workplace diversity/equity issues has shown that it represents important dynamics in the early twenty-first century, with globalization and immigration creating ever more diverse societies and organizational settings. As such, diversity/equity analyses will continue to be one of the core research issues in the foreseeable future. Finally, for us, the dominant perspective of organizational behaviour, which mainly eschews the importance of class, gender, race, ethnicity, disability and the wider social fabric in which waged work is embedded, helps to preserve the status quo. In our view, organizational behaviour will be more relevant to students if cognisance is given to the notion of social embeddedness and the interests and ideas of women, racial minorities, non-Christians and those who are disabled. This book has tried to address this imbalance. We hope it stimulates a variety of serious work-related questions, and perhaps even helps to forge a more equitable workplace in the future.

Reflecting on the journey

Your sojourn into the field of organizational behaviour is now drawing to a close, and the time has come for you to reflect on what you have learned from this journey. Adult education scholars emphasize the need for critical reflection as an essential component of the learning process. Critical reflection is like using a mirror to help us to look back and evaluate past experiences and thought processes. Reflective learning occurs when we examine past experiences, question old assumptions and attach new meanings to old experiences. There are several ways of engaging in the process of critical reflection. One approach is to read your learning journal, which we set as a web-based assignment in Chapter 1. Questions you may ask are: How well did the organizational behaviour material connect to your other management courses? What taken-for-granted assumptions were made by your professors? What new meanings have you attached to old experiences? Were the examples that are supposed to be common to all students consistent with your own life or work experience?

Alternatively, go back systematically through the additional reading listed at the end of each chapter in this book. Other sources of information, particularly material that tends to differ from the approach in this book, provide a mirror for us and allow us to look at topics from another perspective. Furthermore, other people – friends, relatives and co-workers – also provide mirrors for us, allowing us to understand organizational behaviour from another perspective. Talk to other people about the topics covered in this book. Your own past experience of the workplace is also excellent material for critical reflection, and can provide an insight into many of the topics explored in this book. To help you start the reflection process, go back to the beginning of each chapter and consider whether you have personally achieved the major learning objectives. Finally, we hope our guided tour through the field of organizational behaviour has proved worthwhile, and we hope you remain positive yet sceptical, rather than negative and cynical.

References

1   Bratton, J., Denham, D. and Deutschmann, L. (2009) *Capitalism and Classical Sociological Theory*, Toronto: UTP.

2   Kersley, B., Alpin, C., Forth, J. et al. (2005) *Inside the Workplace: First Findings from the 2004 Workplace Employment Relations Survey (WERS 2004)*, London: Department of Trade and Industry.

3   Rubery, J. (1998) 'Employers and the labour market', pp. 251–80 in D. Gallie (ed.), *Employment in Britain*, Oxford: Blackwell.

4   Connelly, C. and Gallagher, D. (2004) 'Emerging trends in contingent work research', *Journal of Management*, **30**(6), pp. 959–83.

5   Pfeffer, J. and Baron, N. (1988) 'Taking the workers back out: recent trends in the structures of employment', *Research in Organizational Behaviour*, **10**, 257–303.

6   Morris, J. (2004) 'The future of work: organizational and international perspectives', *International Journal of Human Resource Management*, **15**(2), pp. 263–75.

7   Maurice, M. and Sorge, A. (2000) *Embedding Organizations*, Amsterdam: John Benjamins.

8   Jacoby, S. M. (2005) *The Embedded Corporation: Corporate Governance and Employment Relations in Japan and the United States*, Princeton, NJ: Princeton University Press.

9   Pulignano, V. and Stewart, P. (2006) 'Bureaucracy transcended? New patterns of employment regulation and labour control in the international automotive industry', *New Technology, Work and Employment*, **21**(2), pp. 90–106.

10   Smart, B. (2003) *Economy, Culture and Society*, Buckingham: Oxford University Press.

11   Quoted in Bratton, J., Grint, K. and Nelson, D. (2005) *Organizational Leadership*, Mason, OH: Thomson-South-Western, p. 232.

12   Mills, A., Simmons, A. and Helms Mills, J. (2005) *Reading Organizational Theory* (3rd edn), Toronto: Garamond.

13   Wilson, F. M. (2003) *Organizational Behaviour and Gender*, Farnham: Ashgate.

14   Wajcman, J. (2000) 'Feminism facing industrial relations in Britain', *British Journal of Industrial Relations*, **38**(2), pp. 183–201.

15   Hansen, L. L. (2002) 'Rethinking the industrial relations tradition', *Employee Relations*, **24**(2), pp. 190–210.

16   Healy, G., Hansen, L. L. and Ledwith, S. (2006) 'Editorial: still uncovering gender in industrial relations', *Industrial Relations Journal*, **37**(4), pp. 290–8.

Glossary

A

activity theory a view of adult learning that envisions learning as a social process whereby individual and group agency and learning occurs through interlocking human activity systems shaped by social norms and a community of practice

alienation a feeling of powerlessness and estrangement from other people and from oneself

andragogy the processes associated with the organization and practice of teaching adults; more specifically, various kinds of interaction in facilitating learning situations

anomie a state condition in which social control becomes ineffective as a result of the loss of shared values and a sense of purpose in society

appropriation the process through which, in capitalist workplaces, a proportion of the value produced in work activities – above investment in raw materials, equipment, health benefits, facilities and so on – is retained under the private control of owners, ownership groups and/or investors. A more critical perception of this process sees it as 'exploitation' of collective activities of the organization for private use

artefacts the observable symbols and signs of an organization's culture

authority the power granted by some form of either active or passive consent that bestows legitimacy

B

bottom-up processing perception led predominantly by gathering external sensory data and then working out what they mean

bounded rationality processing limited and imperfect information and satisficing rather than maximizing when choosing between alternatives

bourgeoisie (or capitalist class) Karl Marx's term for the class comprising those who own and control the means of production

brainstorming a freewheeling, face-to-face meeting where team members generate as many ideas as possible, piggy-back on the ideas of others, and avoid evaluating anyone's ideas during the idea-generation stage

bureaucracy an organizational model characterized by a hierarchy of authority, a clear division of labour, explicit rules and procedures, and impersonality in personnel matters

bureaucratization a tendency towards a formal organization with a hierarchy of authority, a clear division of labour and an emphasis on written rules

business process re-engineering a radical change of business processes by applying information technology to integrate operations, and maximizing their value-added content

C

capitalism an economic system characterized by private ownership of the means of production, from which personal profits can be derived through market competition and without government intervention

capitalist modernity a term used to characterize the stages in the history of social relations dating roughly from the 1780s that is characterized by the constant revolutionizing of production and culture

causal attribution the explanations an individual chooses to use, either internal (about the person) or external (about the situation), and either stable or transitory

centralization the degree to which formal decision authority is held by a small group of people, typically those at the top of the organizational hierarchy

ceremonies planned events that represent more formal social artefacts than rituals

change agent a generic term for an individual championing or facilitating change in the organization

class the relative location of a person or group within a larger society, based on wealth, power, prestige or other valued resources

class conflict a term for the struggle between the capitalist class and the working class

class consciousness Karl Marx's term for awareness of a common identity based on a person's position in the means of production

classical conditioning a view of 'instrumental' learning whose adherents assert that the reinforcement is non-contingent on the animal's behaviour, that is, it is delivered without regard to the animal's behaviour. By contrast, in instrumental conditioning, the delivery of the reinforcement is contingent – dependent – on what the animal does

cohesiveness refers to all the positive and negative forces or social pressures that cause individuals to maintain their membership in specific groups

commodification in Marxist theory, the production of goods and services (commodities) for exchange in the marketplace, as opposed to the direct consumption of commodities

communication the process by which information is transmitted and understood between two or more people

communities of practice informal groups bound together by shared expertise and a passion for a particular activity or interest

competencies the abilities, values, personality traits and other characteristics of people that lead to a superior performance

competitive advantage the ability of a work organization to add more value for its customers and shareholders than its rivals, and thus gain a position of advantage in the marketplace

complexity the intricate departmental and interpersonal relationships that exist within a work organization

configurations defining technology as the combination of social and technical factors. Configurations are a complex mix of standardized and locally customized elements that are highly specific to an organization.

conflict the process in which one party perceives that its interests are being opposed or negatively affected by another party

conflict of interest a condition in which the needs of one party (such as an individual or group) run counter to the needs of another

conflict perspective the sociological approach that views groups in society as engaged in a continuous power struggle for the control of scarce resources

consideration the extent to which a leader is likely to nurture job relationships, and encourage mutual trust and respect between the leader and his or her subordinates

constructionism the view that researchers actively construct reality on the basis of their understandings, which are mainly culturally fashioned and shared. It contrasts with realism

constructivist approach an approach to technology that tends not to focus on social or political influences but instead sees technologies as defined strictly in how they are put to use

contingency approach the idea that a particular action may have different consequences in different situations

contradictions contradictions are said to occur within social systems when the various principles that underlie these social arrangements conflict with each other

control the collection and analysis of information about all aspect of the work organization and the use of comparisons that are either historical and/or based on benchmarking against another business unit

convergence thesis the hypothesis that industrialized societies become increasingly alike in their political, social, cultural and employment characteristics

core competency the underlying core characteristics of an organization's workforce that result in effective performance and give a competitive advantage to the firm

corporate social responsibility an organization's moral obligation to its stakeholders

corporation a large-scale organization that has legal powers (such as the ability to enter into contracts and buy and sell property) separate from its individual owner or owners

co-variation model Kelley's model that uses information about the co-occurrence of a person, behaviour and potential causes to work out an explanation

creativity the capacity to develop an original product, service or idea that makes a socially recognized contribution

critical approach an approach to technology that tends to focus on how the social and political effects are produced through contestation and negotiation

critical realism a realist epistemology which asserts that the study of human behaviour should be concerned with the identification of the structures that generate that behaviour in order to change it

cultural relativism the appreciation that all cultures have intrinsic worth and should be judged and understood on their own terms

culture the knowledge, language, values, customs and material objects that are passed from person to person and from one generation to the next in a human group or society

D

decision making a conscious process of making choices between one or more alternatives with the intention of moving toward some desired state of affairs

deductive approach research in which the investigator begins with a theory and then collects information and data to test the theory

deindustrialization a term to describe the decline of the manufacturing sector of the economy

Delphi technique a structured team decision-making process of systematically pooling the collective knowledge of experts on a particular subject to make decisions, predict the future or identify opposing views

deskilling a reduction in the proficiency needed to perform a specific job, which leads to a corresponding reduction in the wages paid for that job

dialectic refers to the movement of history through the transcendence of internal contradictions that in turn produce new contradictions, themselves requiring solutions

dialogue a process of conversation among team members in which they learn about each other's mental models and assumptions, and eventually form a common model for thinking within the team

discourse a way of talking about and conceptualizing an issue, presented through concepts, ideas and vocabulary that recur in texts

discourse community a way of talking about and conceptualizing an issue, presented through ideas and concepts, spoken or written, within a social group or community (such as lawyers or physicians)

discrimination the actions or practices of dominant group members (or their representatives) that have a harmful impact on the members of a subordinate group

distributive justice justice based on the principle of fairness of outcomes

divergent thinking involves reframing a problem in a unique way and generating different approaches to the issue

divisional structure an organizational structure that groups employees around geographical areas, clients or outputs

division of labour the allocation of work tasks to various groups or categories of employee

dyad a group consisting of two members

E

the economy the social institution that ensures the maintenance of society through the production, distribution and consumption of goods and services

effort-to-performance (E→P) expectancy the individual's perceived probability that his or her effort will result in a particular level of performance

ego according to Sigmund Freud, the rational, reality-oriented component of personality that imposes restrictions on the innate pleasure-seeking drives of the id

emotional labour the effort, planning and control needed to express organizationally desired emotions during interpersonal transactions

empathy a person's ability to understand and be sensitive to the feelings, thoughts and situations of others

empirical approach research that attempts to answer questions through a systematic collection and analysis of data

empiricism an approach to the study of social reality that suggests that only knowledge gained through experience and the senses is acceptable

employee involvement the degree to which employees influence how their work is organized and carried out

employment equity a strategy to eliminate the effects of discrimination and to make employment opportunities available to groups who have been excluded

empowerment a psychological concept in which people experience more self-determination, meaning, competence and impact regarding their role in the organization

enskilling changes in work, often involving technology, that result in an increase in the skill level of workers. The issue of control is often implicated

environment refers to the broad economic, political, legal and social forces that are present in the minds of the organization's members and may influence their decision making and constrain their strategic choices, such as the national business system

epistemology a theory of knowledge particularly used to refer to a standpoint on what should pass as acceptable knowledge

equity theory the theory that explains how people develop perceptions of fairness in the distribution and exchange of resources

ERG theory Alderfer's motivation theory of three instructive needs arranged in a hierarchy, in which people progress to the next higher need when a lower one is fulfilled, and regress to a lower need if unable to fulfil a higher one

escalation of commitment the tendency to allocate more resources to a failing course of action or to repeat an apparently bad decision

ethics the study of moral principles or values that determine whether actions are right or wrong, and outcomes are good or bad

ethnocentrism the tendency to regard one's own culture and group as the standard, and thus superior, whereas all other groups are seen as inferior

exchange value the price at which commodities (including labour) trade on the market

exit and voice a concept referring to the basic choice that defines an important part of employees' experience at work they can either exit (leave) or exercise their 'voice' (have a say) in how the workplace is run

expectancy theory a motivation theory based on the idea that work effort is directed toward behaviours that people believe will lead to desired outcomes

explicit knowledge knowledge that is ordered and can be communicated between people

extrinsic motivator a wide range of external outcomes or rewards to motivate employees, including bonuses or increases in pay

extrinsic reward a wide range of external outcomes or rewards to motivate employees

extroversion a personality dimension that characterizes people who are outgoing, talkative, sociable and assertive

F

factor analysis a statistical technique used for a large number of variables to explain the pattern of relationships in the data

factory system a relatively large work unit that concentrated people and machines in one building, enabling the specialization of productive functions and, at the same time, a closer supervision of employees than did the pre-industrial putting-out system. Importantly, the factory system gave rise to the need for a new conception of time and organizational behaviour

false consensus effect the tendency to over-estimate the degree to which other people will think and behave in the same way as we do

feedback any information that people receive about the consequences of their behaviour

feminism the belief that all people – both women and men – are equal and that they should be valued equally and have equal rights

feminist perspective the sociological approach that focuses on the significance of gender in understanding and explaining the inequalities that exist between men and women in the household, in the paid labour force and in the realms of politics, law and culture

Fiedler's contingency model suggests that leader effectiveness depends on whether the person's natural leadership style is appropriately matched to the situation

flexibility action in response to global competition, including employees performing a number of tasks (functional flexibility), the employment of part-time and contract workers (numerical flexibility), and performance-related pay (reward flexibility)

Fordism a term used to describe mass production using assembly-line technology that allowed for greater division of labour and time and motion management, techniques pioneered by the American car manufacturer Henry Ford in the early twentieth century

formal channels a communication process that follows an organization's chain of command

formalization the degree to which organizations standardize behaviour through rules, procedures, formal training and related mechanisms

formal organization a highly structured group formed for the purpose of completing certain tasks or achieving specific goals

'free-rider' problem the fear firms have that if they invest in training for workers, these workers might eventually leave the firm for one offering higher wages/benefits, thus losing the firm its investment

functional configuration an organizational structure that organizes employees around specific knowledge or other resources

functionalist perspective the sociological approach that views society as a stable, orderly system

functional theory a sociological perspective emphasizing that human action is governed by relatively stable structures

fundamental attribution error the tendency to favour internal attributions for the behaviour of others but external ones to explain our own behaviour

G

game theory a social theory premised on the notion that people do what is best for themselves given their resources and circumstances, as in some form of a competitive game

gender the culturally and socially constructed differences between females and males found in the meanings, beliefs and practices associated with 'femininity' and 'masculinity'

gender bias behaviour that shows favouritism towards one gender over the other

gender identity a person's perception of the self as female or male

gender role attitudes, behaviour and activities that are socially defined as appropriate for each sex and are learned through the socialization process

gender socialization the aspect of socialization that contains specific messages and practices concerning the nature of being female or male in a specific group or society

genre a term to describe the different kinds of writing and reading in the workplace, including, reports, letters and memoranda

Gestalt a German word that means form or organization; Gestalt psychology emphasizes organizational processes in learning. The Gestalt slogan, 'The whole is greater than the sum of the parts,' draws attention to relationships between the parts

glass ceiling the pattern of employment opportunities that disproportionately limits the achievement of top administrative posts by certain social groups

globalization when an organization extends its activities to other parts of the world, actively participates in other markets, and competes against organizations located in other countries

goals the immediate or ultimate objectives that employees are trying to accomplish from their work effort

goal setting the process of motivating employees and clarifying their role perceptions by establishing performance objectives

grapevine an unstructured and informal communication network founded on social relationships rather than organizational charts or job descriptions

group context refers to anything from the specific task a work group is engaged in to the broad environmental forces that are present in the minds of group members and may influence them

group dynamics the systematic study of human behaviour in groups, including the nature of groups, group development, and the interrelations between individuals and groups, other groups and other elements of formal organizations

group norms the unwritten rules and expectations that specify or shape appropriate human behaviour in a work group or team

group processes refers to group member actions, communications and decision making

group structure a stable pattern of social interaction among work group members created by a role structure and group norms

groupthink the tendency of highly cohesive groups to value consensus at the price of decision quality

growth needs a person's needs for self-esteem through personal achievement, as well as for self-actualization

H

halo and horns effect a perceptual error whereby our general impression of a person, usually based on one prominent characteristic, colours the perception of other characteristics of that person

hegemony a conception of power that includes both conflict as well as consent and leadership by generating a particular worldview or 'common sense' on relevant and appropriate action

high-context culture a culturally sanctioned style of communication that assumes high levels of shared knowledge and so uses very concise, sometimes obscure, speech

high-performance working environment describes efforts to manage employment relations and work operations using a set of distinctive 'better' human resource practices. These are intended to improve outcomes such as employee commitment, flexibility and cooperation, which in turn enhance the organization's competitive advantage

horizontal or 'lean' structure an integrated system of manufacturing, originally developed by Toyota in Japan. The emphasis is on flexibility and team work

horizontal tension tensions and contradictions that emerge in terms of people's participation in group endeavours irrespective of hierarchical institutional relationships

HRM cycle an analytical framework that diagrammatically connects human resource selection, appraisal, development and rewards to organizational performance

human capital the view that people are worth investing in as a form of capital, that people's performance and the results achieved can be considered as a return on investment and assessed in terms of cost and benefits

human relations a school of management thought that emphasizes the importance of social processes in the organization

human resource management an approach to managing employment relations which emphasizes that leveraging people's capabilities is important to achieving competitive advantage

human rights the conditions and treatment expected for all human beings

hypotheses statements making empirically testable declarations that certain variables and their corresponding measure are related in a specific way proposed by theory

hypothesis in search studies, a tentative statement of the relationship between two or more concepts or variables

I

id Sigmund Freud's term for the component of personality that includes all of the individual's basic biological drives and needs that demand immediate gratification

ideal type an abstract model that describes the recurring characteristics of some phenomenon

ideology a term with multiple uses, but in particular referring to perceptions of reality as distorted by class interests, and the ideas, legal arrangements and culture that arise from class relations (a term taken from Marx)

idiographic approach an approach to explanation in which we seek to explain the relationships among variables within a particular case or event; it contrasts with nomothetic analysis

impression management the process of trying to control or influence the impressions of oneself that other people form

individualism the extent to which a person values independence and personal uniqueness

industrial democracy a broad term used to describe a range of programmes, processes and social institutions designed to provide greater employee involvement and influence in the decision-making process, and to exchange ideas on how to improve working conditions and product and service quality in the workplace

Industrial Revolution the relatively rapid economic transformation that began in Britain in the 1780s. It involved a factory- and technology-driven shift from agriculture and small cottage-based manufacturing to manufacturing industries, and the consequences of that shift for virtually all human activities

informal channels a communication process that follows unofficial means of communication, sometimes called 'the grapevine', usually based on social relations in which employees talk about work

informal group two or more people who form a unifying relationship around personal rather than organizational goals

informal structure a term used to describe the aspect of organizational life in which participants' day-to-day activities and interactions ignore, bypass or do not correspond with the official rules and procedures of the bureaucracy

information overload a situation in which the receiver becomes overwhelmed by the information that needs to be processed. It may be caused by the quantity of the information to be processed, the speed at which the information presents itself or the complexity of the information to be processed

in-groups groups to which someone perceives he or she belongs, which he or she accordingly evaluates favourably

initiating part of a behavioural theory of leadership that describes the degree to which a leader defines and structures her or his own role and the roles of followers towards attainment of the group's assigned goals

instrumentalist or technocratic approach approaches to technology that are uncritical of its broader social, political and economic significance, viewing technologies as autonomous and positive

instrumentality a term associated with process theories of motivation, referring to an individual's perceived probability that good performance will result in valued outcomes or rewards, measured on a scale from 0 (no chance) to 1 (certainty)

integrative approach explains the effectiveness of a leader in terms of influence on the way the followers view themselves and interpret the context and events around them

intellectual capital the sum of an organization's human capital, structural capital and relationship capital

interactionism what people do when they are in one another's presence, for example in a work group or team

international human resource management refers to all the human resource management policies and practices used to manage people in companies operating in more than one country

interpretivism the view held in many qualitative studies that reality comes from shared meaning among people in that environment

intrinsic motivator a wide range of motivation interventions in the workplace, from inner satisfaction from following some action (such as recognition by an employer or co-workers) to intrinsic pleasures derived from an activity (such as playing a musical instrument for pleasure)

intrinsic reward inner satisfaction following some action (such as recognition by an employer or co-workers) or intrinsic pleasures derived from an activity (such as playing a musical instrument for pleasure)

introversion a personality dimension that characterizes people who are territorial and solitary

intuition the ability to know when a problem or opportunity exists and select the best course of action without conscious reasoning

J

job characteristics model a job design model that relates the motivational properties of jobs to specific personal and organizational consequences of those properties

job design the process of assigning tasks to a job, including the interdependency of those tasks with other jobs

job enlargement increasing the number of tasks employees perform in their jobs

job enrichment employees are given more responsibility for scheduling, coordinating and planning their own work

job rotation the practice of moving employees from one job to another

job satisfaction a person's attitude regarding his or her job and work content

K

knowledge work paid work that is of an intellectual nature, non-repetitive and result-oriented, engages scientific and/or artistic knowledge, and demands continuous learning and creativity

knowledge worker a worker who depends on her or his skills, knowledge and judgement established through additional training and/or schooling

L

labour power the potential gap between a worker's capacity or potential to work and its exercise

labour process the process whereby labour is applied to materials and technology to produce goods and services that can be sold in the market as commodities. The term is typically applied to the distinctive labour processes of capitalism in which owners/managers design, control and monitor work tasks so as to maximize the extraction of surplus value from the labour activity of workers

language a system of symbols that express ideas and enable people to think and communicate with one another

leadership influencing, motivating and enabling others to contribute towards the effectiveness and success of the organizations of which they are members

learning the processes of constructing new knowledge and its ongoing reinforcement

learning contract a learning plan that links an organization's competitive strategy with an individual's key learning objectives. It enumerates the learning and/or competencies that are expected to be demonstrated at some point in the future

learning cycle a view of adult learning that emphasizes learning as a continuous process

legitimacy a term describing agreement with the rights and responsibilities associated with a position, social values, system and so on

leverage the use and exploitation by an employer of his or her resources, particularly human resources, to their full extent. The term is often linked to the resource-based human resource management model

life chances Weber's term for the extent to which persons have access to important scarce resources such as food, clothing, shelter, education and employment

life-long learning the belief that adults should be encouraged, and given the opportunity, to learn either formally in education institutions or informally on or off the job

linguistic relativity the theory that the language we speak has such a fundamental influence on the way we interpret the world that we think differently from those who speak a different language

locus of control a personality trait referring to the extent to which people believe events are within their control

looking-glass self Cooley's term for the way in which a person's sense of self is derived from the perceptions of others

low-context culture a culturally sanctioned style of communication that assumes low levels of shared knowledge and so uses verbally explicit speech

Luddites a group of textile workers, led by General Ned Ludd in early nineteenth-century England, who systematically smashed new workplace technologies because they directly undermined their working knowledge and economic interests as workers

M

macrostructures overarching patterns of social relations that lie outside and above a person's circle of intimates and acquaintances

management by objectives a participative goal-setting process in which organizational objectives are cascaded down to work units and individual employees

'matching' model a human resources strategy that seeks to 'fit' or align the organization's internal human resources strategy with its external competitive strategy

matrix structure a type of departmentalization that overlays a divisionalized structure (typically a project team) with a functional structure

McDonaldization (also known as 'McWork' or 'McJobs') a term used to symbolize the new realities of corporate-driven globalization that engulf young people in the twenty-first century, including simple work patterns, electronic controls, low pay and part-time and temporary employment

means of production an analytical construct that contains the forces of production and the relations of production, which, when combined, define the socioeconomic character of a society

mechanical solidarity a term to describe the social cohesion that exists in pre-industrial societies, in which there is a minimal division of labour and people feel united by shared values and common social bonds

mechanistic organization an organizational structure with a narrow span of control and high degrees of formalization and centralization

media richness refers to the number of channels of contact afforded by a communication medium, so, for example, face-to-face interaction would be at the high end of media richness, and a memorandum would fall at the low end of media richness

microstructures the patterns of relatively intimate social relations formed during face-to-face interaction

mores norms that are widely observed and have great moral significance

motivation the forces within a person that affect his or her direction, intensity and persistence of voluntary behaviour

Myers–Briggs Type Indicator (MBTI) a personality test that measures personality traits

N

needs deficiencies that energize or trigger behaviours to satisfy those needs

needs hierarchy theory Maslow's motivation theory of five instinctive needs arranged in a hierarchy, whereby people are motivated to fulfil a higher need as a lower one becomes gratified

negative reinforcement occurs when the removal or avoidance of a consequence increases or maintains the frequency or future probability of a behaviour

negotiation occurs whenever two or more conflicting parties attempt to resolve their divergent goals by redefining the terms of their interdependence

neo-Fordism/post-Fordism the development from mass production assembly lines to more flexible manufacturing processes

networking cultivating social relationships with others to accomplish one's goals

network structure a set of strategic alliances that an organization creates with suppliers, distributors and manufacturers to produce and market a product. Members of the network work together on a long-term basis to find new ways to improve efficiency and increase the quality of their products

nomothetic approach an approach to explanation in which we seek to identify relationships between variables across many cases

norms the informal rules and expectations that groups establish to regulate the behaviour of their members

O

objectification Karl Marx's term to describe the action of human labour on resources to produce a commodity, which under the control of the capitalist remains divorced from and opposed to the direct producer

objectivism an ontological position which asserts that the meaning of social phenomena has an existence independent of individuals; compare this with constructionism

occupation a category of jobs that involve similar activities at different work sites

ontology a theory of whether social entities such as organizations can and should be considered as objective entities with a reality external to the specific social actors, or as social constructions built up from the perceptions and behaviour of these actors

open systems organizations that take their sustenance from the environment, and in turn affect that environment through their output

operant conditioning a technique for associating a response or behaviour with a consequence

organic organization an organizational structure with a wide span of control, little formalization and decentralized decision making

organic solidarity a term for the social cohesion that exists in industrial (and perhaps post-industrial) societies, in which people perform very specialized tasks and feel united by their mutual dependence

organizational behaviour the systematic study of formal organizations and of what people think, feel and do in and around organizations

organizational commitment the employee's emotional attachment to, identification with and involvement in a particular organization

organizational culture the basic pattern of shared assumptions, values and beliefs governing the way employees in an organization think about and act on problems and opportunities

organizational design the process of creating and modifying organizational structures

organizational justice in organizational behaviour literature, the perceived fairness of outcomes, procedures and the treatment of individuals

organizational learning the knowledge management process in which organizations acquire, share and use knowledge to succeed

organizational politics behaviours that others perceive as self-serving tactics for personal gain at the expense of other people and possibly the organization

organizational structure the formal reporting relationships, groups, departments and systems of the organization

organization chart a diagram showing the grouping of activities and people within a formal organization to achieve the goals of the organization efficiently

out-groups groups to which someone perceives he or she does not belong, which he or she accordingly evaluates unfavourably

P

paradigm a term used to describe a cluster of beliefs that dictates for researchers in a particular discipline what should be studied, how research should be conducted and how the results should be interpreted

participatory design an approach to design and implementation of technologies that is premised on user participation

path–goal leadership theory a contingency theory of leadership based on the expectancy theory of motivation, which relates several leadership styles to specific employee and situational contingencies

patriarchy a hierarchical system of social organization in which cultural, political and economic structures are controlled by men

peer group a group of people who are linked by common interests, equal social position and (usually) similar age

perceived self-efficacy a person's belief in his or her capacity to achieve something

perception the process of selecting, organizing and interpreting information in order to make sense of the world around us

perceptual bias an automatic tendency to attend to certain cues that do not necessarily support good judgements

perceptual set describes what happens when we get stuck in a particular mode of perceiving and responding to things based on what has gone before

performance-to-outcome (P→O) expectancy the perceived probability that a specific behaviour or performance level will lead to specific outcomes

personal identity the ongoing process of self-development through which we construct a unique sense of ourselves and our relationship to the world around us

personality the relatively stable pattern of behaviours and consistent internal states that explain a person's behavioural tendencies

perspective an overall approach to or viewpoint on some subject

phenomenological approach a philosophy concerned with how researchers make sense of the world around them, and whose adherents believe that the social researcher must 'get inside people's heads' to understand how they perceive and interpret the world

political gaming a common practice in organizations, which has proven challenging to research, that involves recognition and organizational action based on existing factions, coalitions and cliques that make up any organization in order to engage in intentional acts of influence to enhance or protect oneself or one's group or department

political theory model an approach to understanding decision making whose adherents assert that formal organizations comprise groups that have separate interests, goals and values, and in which power and influence are needed in order to reach decisions

positive reinforcement occurs when the introduction of a consequence increases or maintains the frequency or future probability of a behaviour

positivism a view held in quantitative research in which reality exists independently of the perceptions and interpretations of people; a belief that the world can best be understood through scientific inquiry

post-industrial economy an economy that is based on the provision of services rather than goods

postmodernism the sociological approach that attempts to explain social life in modern societies that are characterized by post-industrialization, consumerism and global communications

power a term defined in multiple ways, involving cultural values, authority, influence and coercion as well as control over the distribution of

symbolic and material resources. At its broadest, power is defined as a social system that imparts patterned meaning

power–influence approach an approach that examines processes of influence between leaders and followers, and explains leadership effectiveness in terms of the amount and type of power possessed by an organizational leader and how that power is exercised

primacy effect a perceptual error in which we quickly form an opinion of people based on the first information we receive about them

procedural justice justice based on the principle of fairness of the procedures employed to achieve outcomes

proletariat (or working class) Karl Marx's term for those who must sell their labour because they have no other means of earning a livelihood

psychological climate the psychological well-being of individuals, organizations and communities and how this may fluctuate over time

psychological contract an individual's beliefs about the terms and conditions of a reciprocal exchange agreement between that person and another party

putting-out system a pre-industrial, home-based form of production in which the dispersed productive functions were coordinated by an entrepreneur

Q

qualitative research refers to the gathering and sorting of information through a variety of techniques, including interviews, focus groups and observations, and inductive theorizing

quantitative research refers to research methods that emphasize numerical precision and deductive theorizing

R

rationality the process by which traditional methods of social organization, characterized by informality and spontaneity, are gradually replaced by efficiently administered formal rules and procedures – bureaucracy

realism the idea that a reality exists out there independently of what and how researchers think about it. It contrasts with constructionism

recency effect a perceptual error in which the most recent information dominates our perception of others

reflexive learning a view of adult learning that emphasizes learning through self-reflection

relationship behaviour focuses on manager's activities that show concern for followers, look after subordinates' welfare and nurture supportive relationships with followers, as opposed to behaviours that concentrate on completing tasks

reliability in sociological research, the extent to which a study or research instrument yields consistent results

resource-based model a human resources strategy that views employees as an asset as opposed to a cost, and assumes that the sum of people's knowledge and distinctive competencies has the potential to serve as a source of competitive advantage

rhetoric the management of symbols (such as a language) in order to encourage and coordinate social action. 'Rhetorical sensitivity' is the tendency for a speaker to adapt her or his messages to audiences to allow for the level knowledge, ability level, mood or beliefs of the listener

rituals the programmed routines of daily organizational life that dramatize the organization's culture

role a set of behaviours that people are expected to perform because they hold certain positions in a team and organization

role ambiguity uncertainty about job duties, performance expectations, level of authority and other job conditions

role conflict conflict that occurs when people face competing demands

role perceptions a person's beliefs about what behaviours are appropriate or necessary in a particular situation, including the specific tasks that make up the job, their relative importance, and the preferred behaviours to accomplish those tasks

S

satisficing selecting a solution that is satisfactory, or 'good enough', rather than optimal or 'the best' schema a set of interrelated mental processes that enable us to make sense of something on the basis of limited information

scientific management this involves systematically partitioning work into its smallest elements and standardizing tasks to achieve maximum efficiency

selective attention the ability of someone to focus on only some of the sensory stimuli that reach them

self-actualization a term associated with Maslow's theory of motivation, referring to the desire for personal fulfilment, to become everything that one is capable of becoming

self-efficacy the beliefs people have about their ability to perform specific situational task(s) successfully

self-fulfilling prophecy an expectation about a situation that of itself causes what is anticipated to actually happen

self-managed work teams cross-functional work groups organized around work processes that complete an entire piece of work requiring several interdependent tasks, and that have substantial autonomy over the execution of those tasks

semiotics the systematic study of the signs and symbols used in communications

sex a term used to describe the biological and anatomical differences between females and males

sexual harassment the unwelcome conduct of a sexual nature that detrimentally affects the work environment or leads to adverse job-related consequences for its victims

situated learning an approach that views adult learning as a process of enculturation, where people consciously and subconsciously construct new knowledge from the actions, processes, behaviour and context in which they find themselves

skill variety the extent to which employees must use different skills and talents to perform tasks in their job

social capital the value of relationships between people, embedded in network links that facilitate trust and communication vital to overall organizational performance

social identity the perception of a 'sameness' or 'belongingness' to a human collective with common values, goals or experiences

social identity theory the theory concerned with how we categorize and understand the kind of person we are in relation to others

social interaction the process by which people act toward or respond to other people

socialization the life-long process of social interaction through which individuals acquire a self-identity and the physical, mental and social skills needed for survival in society

social-learning theory a theory stating that much learning occurs by observing others and then modelling the behaviours that lead to favourable outcomes and avoiding the behaviours that lead to punishing consequences

social solidarity the state of having shared beliefs and values among members of a social group, along with intense and frequent interaction among group members

social structure the stable pattern of social relationships that exist within a particular group or society

society a large social grouping that shares the same geographical territory and is subject to the same political authority and dominant cultural expectations

sociology the systematic study of human society and social interaction

span of control the number of people directly reporting to the next level in the organizational hierarchy

specialization the allocation of work tasks to categories of employee or groups. Also known as division of labour

status the social ranking of people; the position an individual occupies in society or in a social group or work organization

stereotyping the process of assigning traits to people based on their membership of a social category

sticky floor the pattern of employment opportunities that disproportionately concentrates certain social groups at lower-level jobs

strategic business unit a term to describe corporate development that divides the corporation's operations into strategic business units, which allows comparisons between each strategic business unit. According to advocates, corporate managers are better able to determine whether they need to change the mix of businesses in their portfolio

strategic choice the idea that an organization interacts with its environment rather being totally determined by it

strategic human resource management the process of linking the human resource function with the strategic objectives of the organization in order to improve performance

strategy the long-term planning and decision-making activities undertaken by managers that are related to meeting organizational goals

structuration a concept focusing on balancing the dichotomies of agency, or human freedom, and social organization, or structures where individual choices are seen as partially constrained, but they remain choices nonetheless

substantive approach an approach that tends to see technologies as producing negative social and political effects

superego Sigmund Freud's term for the human conscience, consisting of the moral and ethical aspects of personality

surplus value the portion of the working day during which workers produce value that is appropriated by the capitalist

survey a research method in which a number of respondents are asked identical questions through a systematic questionnaire or interview

symbolic interactionism the sociological approach that views society as the sum of the interactions of individuals and groups

systems theory a set of theories based on the assumption that social entities, such as work organizations, can be viewed as if they were self-regulating bodies exploiting resources from their environment (inputs) and transforming the resources (exchanging and processing) to provide goods and services (outputs) in order to survive

T

taboos mores so strong their violation is considered to be extremely offensive, unmentionable and even criminal

tacit knowledge knowledge embedded in our actions and ways of thinking, and transmitted only through observation and experience

task behaviour focuses on the degree to which a leader emphasizes the importance of assigning followers to tasks, and maintaining standards – in other words, 'getting things done', as opposed to behaviours that nurture supportive relationships

task identity the degree to which a job requires the completion of a whole or an identifiable piece of work

task significance the degree to which the job has a substantial impact on the organization and/or larger society

Taylorism a process of determining the division of work into its smallest possible skill elements, and how the process of completing each task can be standardized to achieve maximum efficiency. Also referred to as scientific management

teams groups of two or more people who interact and influence each other, are mutually accountable for achieving common objectives, and perceive themselves as a social entity within an organization

technology the means by which organizations transform inputs into outputs, or rather the mediation of human action. This includes mediation by tools and machines as well as rules, social convention, ideologies and discourses

technology agreements agreements with legal standing that set in place rules for negotiation over technological selection, adoption and implementation

theory a set of logically interrelated statements that attempts to describe, explain and (occasionally) predict social events. A general set of propositions that describes interrelationships among several concepts

top-down processing perception led predominantly by existing knowledge and expectations rather than by external sensory data

trade union an organization whose purpose is to represent the collective interest of workers

transformational learning a view that adult learning involving self-reflection can lead to a transformation of consciousness, new visions and new courses of action

U

urbanization the process by which an increasing proportion of a population lives in cities rather than in rural areas

V

valence the anticipated satisfaction or dissatisfaction that an individual feels toward an outcome

validity in sociological research, the extent to which a study or research instrument accurately measures what it is supposed to measure

value a collective idea about what is right or wrong, good or bad, and desirable or undesirable in a particular culture

values stable, long-lasting beliefs about what is important in a variety of situations

Verstehen a method of understanding human behaviour by situating it in the context of an individual's or actor's meaning

vertical tension tensions and contradictions that emerge in terms of hierarchical institutional relationships

'virtual' organization an organization composed of people who are connected by video-teleconferences, the Internet and computer-aided design systems, and who may rarely, if ever, meet face to face

W

will to power the notion that people are inherently driven to develop and expand power and control in their environments

work ethic a set of values that stresses the importance of work to the identity and sense of worth of the individual and encourages an attitude of diligence in the mind of the people

work group two or more employees in face-to-face interaction, each aware of their positive interdependence as they endeavour to achieve mutual work-related goals

work–life balance the interplay between working life, the family and the community, in terms of both time and space

work organization a deliberately formed social group in which people, technology and resources are deliberately co-coordinated through formalized roles and relationships to achieve a division of labour designed to attain a specific set of objectives efficiently. It is also known as formal organization

work orientation an attitude towards work that constitutes a broad disposition towards certain kinds of paid work

workplace wellness all human resource and health and safety programmes, and interventions that can assist an employee to live at her or his highest possible level as a whole person, including the physical, social, emotional and spiritual, and expand an employee's potential to live and work more effectively

Index of personal names

Subject index

Index of film titles